Reformed Confessions
Harmonized

Joel R. Beeke (Ph.D., Westminster Theological Seminary, Philadelphia) is pastor of Heritage Netherlands Reformed Congregation in Grand Rapids, Michigan, professor of systematic theology and homiletics at Puritan Reformed Theological Seminary, editor of *Banner of Sovereign Grace Truth,* and president of Reformation Heritage Books and Inheritance Publishers. He is author of several books, including *The Quest for Full Assurance: The Legacy of Calvin and His Successors.*

Sinclair B. Ferguson (Ph.D., University of Aberdeen) is pastor of St. George's Tron Parish Church, Glasgow, Scotland, and assistant editor of the *Banner of Truth.* He served as professor of systematic theology at Westminster Theological Seminary (Philadelphia) for many years. He is author of numerous books, including *John Owen on the Christian Life.*

Reformed Confessions Harmonized

Joel R. Beeke
Sinclair B. Ferguson
Editors

Baker Books

A Division of Baker Book House Co
Grand Rapids, Michigan 49516

Published by Baker Books
a division of Baker Book House Company
P.O. Box 6287, Grand Rapids, MI 49516-6287

Fourth printing, September 2002

Printed in the United States of America

Library of Congress Cataloging-in-Publication Data

Reformed confessions harmonized / Joel R. Beeke, Sinclair B. Ferguson,
    editors.
       p.   cm.
    Includes bibliographical references.
    ISBN 0-8010-5222-X (pbk.)
    1. Reformed Church—Creeds.   I. Beeke, Joel R., 1952–
II. Ferguson, Sinclair B.
BX9428.A1R44   1999
238′.42—dc21   98-50178

For current information about all releases from Baker Book
House, visit our web site:
        http://www.bakerbooks.com

Contents

Foreword

The sixteenth- and seventeenth-century Reformed churches produced several families of orthodox Reformed confessions that differentiated the Reformed faith from both Roman Catholicism and other groups of Protestant churches. The most well-known of these groups of confessions include the *Swiss* family, represented by the First and Second Helvetic Confessions (1536; 1566) and the Helvetic Consensus Formula (1675); the *Scottish-English* family, represented by the Scots Confession (1560), the Thirty-Nine Articles (1563), the Westminster Confession of Faith (1646–1647), and the Shorter and Larger Catechisms (1647) of the Westminster Assembly; and the *Dutch-German* family, represented by the Three Forms of Unity: the Belgic Confession of Faith (1561), the Heidelberg Catechism (1563), and the Canons of Dort (1618–1619).

Of those Reformed confessions, the seven most diligently adhered to by various Reformed denominations today are the Three Forms of Unity, the Second Helvetic Confession, and the Westminster Confession and Catechisms. I prepared this harmony of these seven confessions at the request of a group of editors of Reformed periodicals. The harmony follows a subject format and uses the most standard English translations or versions of the confessions. Minimal updating of spelling and punctuation has been made for consistency. The editors believe this harmony will promote easy access to the content of great Reformed confessions and will also help Dutch Reformed, Hungarian Reformed, English Presbyterian, and other Reformed Christians gain a deeper appreciation for one another's confessions.

The harmony includes an annotated Reformed bibliography designed to help beginners and advanced students of the Reformed faith. I have structured the subject divisions and the bibliography in accord with the articles of the Belgic Confession of Faith, the oldest Reformed confession in the harmony. I would welcome suggestions for additions to this bibliography for future printings. Forward suggestions to me at 2919 Leonard NE, Grand Rapids, MI 49525 (fax 616-977-0889; e-mail jrbeeke@aol.com).

I thank my gracious friend, Sinclair B. Ferguson, for assisting me with writing the historical introduction to the seven Reformed confessions contained in this harmony. I also thank my typesetters, Gary and Linda den Hollander, who have meticulously typeset and proofread the document. May God graciously use this volume to arouse a deeper appreciation for our Reformed confessions and to stimulate more communion among Reformed believers throughout the English-speaking world, regardless of which Reformed family they belong to. The beauty of this book is that it underscores the harmony among Reformed confessions, despite the diversity of various historical traditions.

Joel R. Beeke

Historical Introduction to the Reformed Confessions

Belgic Confession of Faith (1561)

The oldest of the seven confessions in this harmony is the Belgic Confession of Faith, taken from the seventeenth-century Latin designation *Confessio Belgica*. *Belgica* referred to the whole of the Low Countries, both north and south, today divided into the Netherlands and Belgium. Other names for the Belgic Confession include the Walloon Confession and the Netherlands Confession.

The Belgic Confession's chief author was Guido de Brès (1522–1567), a Reformed itinerant pastor. During the sixteenth century, the Reformed churches in the Netherlands experienced severe persecution at the hands of Philip II of Spain, an ally of the Roman Catholic Church. In 1561, de Brès prepared this confession in French as an apology for the persecuted band of Reformed believers in the Lowlands who formed the so-called churches under the cross. De Brès was most likely assisted by fellow pastors, who wanted to prove to their persecutors that the adherents of the Reformed faith were not rebels, but law-abiding citizens who professed biblical doctrines. The confession was modeled after the Gallic Confession, a 1559 French Reformed confession, which, in turn, modeled Calvin's design.

Basically, the Belgic Confession follows what has become the traditional doctrinal order of Reformed systematic theology: the doctrines concerning God (theology proper, articles 1–11), man (anthropology, articles 12–15), Christ (Christology, articles 16–21), salvation (soteriology, articles 22–26), the church (ecclesiology, articles 27–35), and the last things (eschatology, article 37). Article 36 addresses the theocratic nature of civil government. Though it follows an objective doctrinal order, the confession has a warm, experiential, personal spirit, helped by its repeated use of the pronoun *we*.

The year after it was written, a copy of the confession was sent to King Philip II, along with a statement that the petitioners were ready to obey the government in all things lawful, but would "offer their backs to stripes, their tongues to knives, their mouths to gags, and their whole bodies to the fire, well knowing that those who follow Christ must take His cross and deny themselves," rather than deny the truth expressed in the confession. Neither the confession nor the petition persuaded Spanish authorities to be more tolerant of the Protestants, however. In 1567, de Brès became one martyr among thousands who sealed their faith with blood. Nevertheless, his work has endured as a convincing statement of Reformed doctrine.

The Belgic Confession was readily received by Reformed churches in the Netherlands after its translation into Dutch in 1562. In 1566, it was revised by the Synod of Antwerp. Subsequently, it was regularly adopted by national Dutch synods held during the last three decades of the sixteenth century. After a further revision, the Synod of Dort (1618–1619) adopted the confession as a doctrinal standard to which all office-bearers in the Reformed churches had to subscribe.

Heidelberg Catechism (1563)

The Heidelberg Catechism was written in Heidelberg, Germany, at the request of Elector Frederick III (1516–1576), ruler of the Palatinate, an influential German province. The pious prince commissioned Zacharius Ursinus (1534–1583), a twenty-eight-year-old professor of theology at Heidelberg University, and Caspar Olevianus (1536–1587), Frederick's twenty-six-year-old court preacher, to prepare a Reformed catechism for instructing young people and guiding pastors and teachers. Ursinus was primarily responsible for the content of the catechism, while Olevianus was probably more involved with final composition and editing. The learning of Ursinus and the eloquence of Olevianus are evident in the final product, which has been called "a catechism of unusual power and beauty, an acknowledged masterpiece." Frederick indicates that many others, including the theological faculty and chief officers of the Palatinate church, contributed to the finished document.

After the catechism was approved by a Heidelberg synod in January 1563, three more German editions, each including small additions, as well as a Latin translation were published the same year in Heidelberg. The fourth edition has long been regarded as the official text of the catechism. The Dutch translation sanctioned by the Synod of Dort, from which our English text is rendered, was made from that edition.

When the first edition of the Heidelberg Catechism appeared, the German Bible had not yet been divided into verses. Consequently, the Scripture passages listed in the margin included only book and chapter. Moreover, the catechism's questions were not numbered. A Latin translation soon rectified these problems by including verse references and numbered questions. The catechism was also divided into fifty-two sections so that one section—referred to as a "Lord's Day"—could be preached on each Sunday of the year.

The catechism contains more proof texts than most catechisms because its authors wanted it to be "an echo of the Bible." The proof texts were to be regarded as an important part of the catechism, as Frederick notes in the original preface: "The Scripture proof by which the faith of the children is confirmed, are such [texts] only as have been selected with great pains from the divinely inspired Scriptures."

The Heidelberg Catechism's 129 questions and answers are divided into three parts, patterned after the book of Romans. After a moving introduction about the true believer's comfort, questions 3–11 cover the experience of sin and misery (Rom. 1–3:20); questions 12–85 cover redemption in Christ and faith (Rom. 3:21–11:36), along with a lengthy exposition of the Apostles' Creed and the sacraments; questions 86–129 cover true gratitude for God's deliverance (Rom. 12–16), primarily through a study of the Ten Commandments and the Lord's Prayer. The catechism presents doctrines with clarity and warmth. Its content is more subjective than objective, more spiritual than dogmatic. Not surprisingly, this personal, devotional catechism, as exemplified by its use of singular pronouns, has been called "the book of comfort" for Christians.

Already in 1563 the catechism was translated into Dutch by Petrus Dathenus and published in his metrical Psalter in 1566. Its experiential and practical content won the love of God's people in the Netherlands. Within months after the catechism was published in Dutch, Peter Gabriel set a precedent for Dutch ministers by preaching from the catechism every Sunday afternoon. The catechism was approved by the synods of Wesel (1568), Emden (1571), Dort (1578), the Hague (1586), and Dort (1618–1619), which officially adopted it as the second of the Three Forms of Unity. The Synod of Dort also made weekly preaching of the catechism mandatory.

The Heidelberg Catechism has since been translated into all European and dozens of Asiatic and African languages. It has circulated more widely than any other book except the Bible, Thomas à Kempis's *The Imitation of Christ,* and John Bunyan's *Pilgrim's Progress.* Soundly Calvinistic, yet moderate in tone and irenic in spirit, this "book of comfort" remains the most widely used and warmly praised catechism of the Reformation.

Second Helvetic Confession (1566)

The First Helvetic Confession had its origins in 1536 in a concern to harmonize and solidify Reformation teaching by providing a common Swiss confession (*Helvetii* being the Latin designation for the people of East Gaul, now Switzerland). Although appreciated by Luther himself, it foundered because of disagreement over the "real presence" of Christ at the Lord's Supper, an issue later resolved—at least for Calvinists and Zwinglians—in the Zurich Consensus (*Consensus Tigurinus*) of 1549.

The Second Helvetic Confession is of greater significance, but had more personal origins. It began life in the form of a personal confession and testimony written by Heinrich Bullinger in 1562. In 1564, during the plague which Bullinger contracted when it ravaged Zurich, he revised his earlier work in anticipation of his death. Although his wife and three daughters died, Bullinger survived. Asked by Frederick III, Elector of the Palatinate, to provide an exposition of the Reformed faith, Bullinger provided him with a copy of his work. Frederick had it translated into German before his appearance to defend himself against Lutheran criticism at the Imperial Diet of 1566. Following some revision at a conference in Zurich that same year, the confession was agreed to by Berne, Biel, Geneva, the Grisons, Mühlhausen, Schaffhausen, and St. Gall. It was thereafter widely approved in Scotland, Hungary, Poland, and elsewhere.

The Second Helvetic Confession is in fact a compact manual of Reformed theology, containing thirty chapters and extending to some twenty thousand words. Written against the background of the definitive edition of Calvin's *Institutes* (1559) as well as the Counter-Reformation assembly at Trent (1545–1563), it formulates Reformed theology in a comprehensive summary. Beginning with Scripture it moves through the loci of systematic theology, striking characteristic Reformed and Calvinian notes: the preaching of the Word of God is the Word of God (ch. 1); Christ is the mirror in which we are to contemplate our election (ch. 10); providence and predestination are given separate treatments; the body and blood of Christ are received not carnally but spiritually, that is, by the Holy Spirit. But practical religious issues are also of major concern: prayer and singing, the question of holy days, catechizing, visitation of the sick, and burial of the dead are discussed (chs. 23–26) as well as issues surrounding marriage and celibacy and the role of the magistrate (chs. 29–30).

The Second Helvetic Confession was thus a mature statement of Reformed theology for the second half of the sixteenth century. Well-received internationally, it was translated into Dutch, English, Polish, Italian, Magyar, Turkish, and Arabic. It stands as a worthy testimony to the labors and faith of Heinrich Bullinger.

Canons of Dort (1618–1619)

The Judgment of the Synod of Dort on the Five Main Points of Doctrine in Dispute in the Netherlands is popularly known as the Canons of Dort or the Five Articles Against the Remonstrants. It consists of doctrinal statements adopted by the Synod of Dort, which met in the city of Dordrecht in 1618–1619. Although this was a national synod of the Reformed Churches of the Netherlands, it had an international character. It was comprised of twenty-seven foreign delegates representing eight countries in addition to its sixty-two Dutch delegates.

The Synod of Dort was held to settle a serious controversy in the Dutch churches initiated by the rise of Arminianism. Jacob Arminius (1560–1609), a theological professor at Leiden University, differed from the Reformed faith on a number of important points. After Arminius's death, forty-three of his followers presented their heretical views to the States General of the Netherlands. In this document, called the Remonstrance of 1610, and even more explicitly in later writings, the Arminians taught (1) election based on foreseen faith, (2) the universality of Christ's atonement, (3) the free will and partial depravity of man, (4) the resistibility of grace, and (5) the possibility of a lapse from grace. They asked for the revision of the Reformed churches' doctrinal standards and for government protection of Arminian views. The Arminian-Calvinism conflict became so severe that it led the Netherlands to the brink of civil war. Finally in 1617, the States General voted 4–3 to call a national synod to address the problem of Arminianism.

The synod held 154 formal sessions over a period of seven months (November 1618 to May 1619). Thirteen Arminian theologians, led by Simon Episcopius, tried to delay the work of the synod and divide the delegates. Their efforts proved unsuccessful. Under the leadership of Johannes Bogerman, the Arminians were dismissed.

The synod then developed the canons, which thoroughly rejected the Remonstrance of 1610 and scripturally set forth the Reformed doctrine on the debated points. These points, known as the five points of Calvinism, are: unconditional election, limited atonement, total depravity, irresistible grace, and the perseverance of saints. Though these points do not represent all of Calvinism and are better regarded as Calvinism's five answers to the five errors of Arminianism, they certainly lie at the heart of the Reformed faith, particularly of Reformed soteriology, for they flow out of the principle of absolute divine sovereignty in saving sinners. They may be summarized as follows: (1) Unconditional election and saving faith are sovereign gifts of God. (2) While the death of Christ is sufficient to expiate the sins of the whole world, its saving efficacy is limited to the elect. (3, 4) All people are so totally depraved and corrupted by sin that they cannot exercise free will toward, nor effect any part of, their salvation. In sovereign grace God irresistibly calls and regenerates the elect to newness of life. (5) God graciously preserves the redeemed so that they persevere until the end, even though they may be troubled by many infirmities as they seek to make their calling and election sure. Simply stated, the subject matter of the canons is sovereign grace conceived, sovereign grace merited, sovereign grace needed and applied, and sovereign grace preserved.

Although the canons have only four sections, we speak of five points or heads of doctrine because the canons were structured to correspond with the five articles of the 1610 Remonstrance. The third and fourth sections were combined into one because the Dortian divines considered them to be inseparable, and hence designated them as "Head of Doctrine III/IV."

The canons are unique because of their role as a judicial decision in the Arminian controversy. The original preface called the canons a "judgment, in which both the true view, agreeing with God's Word, concerning the aforesaid five points of doctrine is explained, and the false view, disagreeing with God's Word, is rejected." The canons are limited, however. They focus only on the five points of disputed doctrine. Each section of the document includes a positive and a negative part; the former, an exposition of Reformed doctrine on the subject, the latter, a rejection of corresponding Arminian errors. In all, the canons contain fifty-nine articles of exposition and thirty-four rejections of error.

The canons form a scriptural, balanced document on specific doctrines. They are the only Form of Unity that was written by an ecclesiastical assembly and that represented the view of all the Reformed churches of their day. All Dutch and foreign delegates, whether of supralapsarian or infralapsarian persuasion, without exception affixed their signatures to the canons. Then they joined in a service of thanksgiving to praise God for preserving the doctrine of sovereign grace among the Reformed churches.

Westminster Confession of Faith (1647)

The Confession of Faith produced by the Westminster divines has undoubtedly been one of the most influential documents of the post-Reformation period of the Christian church. A carefully worded exposition of seventeenth-century Reformed theology, the calmness of its sentences largely hides the tempestuousness of the political backcloth against which it was written.

The Westminster Assembly was convened in 1643 after years of tension between Charles I and his increasingly Puritan Parliament. Meeting under the chairmanship of the learned William Twisse against the king's express wishes, its original vision was to effect closer uniformity of faith and practice throughout his realm. The original task of the delegates was to revise the Thirty-Nine Articles of the Church of England, but following the signing of the Solemn League and Covenant, this developed into the more specific and exacting task of framing theological and ecclesiastical formulas that would bring the Church of England into conformity with the doctrine and practice of the Presbyterian Church of Scotland.

Ministerial delegates from the Kirk (who declined to become members of the Assembly) were the great ecclesiastical statesman Alexander Henderson, the high Calvinistic theologian and exponent of Reformed piety Samuel Rutherford, the extraordinarily gifted young George Gillespie, and the fascinating Robert Baillie (in whose *Letters and Journals* we find snapshots of the Assembly's activities and personalities). The Scots insisted on also sending ruling elders as representatives, thus illustrating their commitment to the government of the church by both teaching and ruling elders.

For all practical purposes these Scottish delegates constituted the most powerful group among those who gathered in the Chapel of Henry VII and later in the Jerusalem Chamber at Westminster Abbey, London, during the years of discussion and debate. While the majority of the delegates seem to have been of varying degrees of Presbyterian persuasion, Episcopalians and Independents were also represented, the latter group (which included Thomas Goodwin and Jeremiah Burroughs) at times exasperating the Scots.

The various documents composed by the Assembly proceeded through a process of committee work in the afternoons, followed by plenary discussion on the floor of the Assembly in the mornings, with regular additional gatherings for worship, fast days, and the like. Despite disagreements, the divines produced one of the truly monumental documents of church history, which has instructed, directed, and profoundly influenced Presbyterian churches worldwide ever since. The Confession of Faith, alongside the Shorter Catechism, has influenced Presbyterianism even more profoundly than Calvin's *Institutes*.

The Westminster Confession of Faith represents a high point in the development of federal theology, and its inner dynamic is powerfully covenantal. Divided into thirty-three chapters, it carefully covers the whole range of Christian doctrine, beginning with Scripture as the source of knowledge of divine things (following the First and Second Helvetic Confessions, the Formula of Concord, and the Irish Articles). It continues with an exposition of God and His decrees, creation, providence, and the fall (II–VI) before turning to expound the covenant of grace, the work of Christ, and, at length, the application of redemption (X–XVIII). While criticism is sometimes voiced that the confession is a deeply scholastic document (e.g., it has no separate chapter on the Holy Spirit), it is now increasingly noted that it is the first confession in the history of Christianity to have a separate chapter on adoption (XII)—perhaps the least scholastic of all doctrines. Careful attention is given under various chapter headings to questions of law and liberty, as well as to the doctrine of the church and sacraments (XXV–XXIX) and the last things (XXXII–XXXIII).

While the confession was composed by disciplined theological minds, it also displays the influence of men with deep pastoral and preaching experience. It is an outstanding expression of classical Reformed theology framed for the needs of the people of God.

Westminster Shorter Catechism (1647)

The Westminster Assembly produced two catechisms. The shorter of these contains 107 questions to which, generally speaking, single-sentence answers are formulated, although occasionally a more detailed response is given. The pattern followed is broadly that of the Confession of Faith, but here the theological definitions given are compact and concise.

The most notable and famous feature of the Catechism is the brilliance of its first question and answer:

"What is the chief end of man? Man's chief end is to glorify God, and to enjoy him for ever." But equally important, if less often recognized, is its stress that this is to be accomplished by conformity to the Word and will of God. Hence careful attention is given to the exposition of the Decalogue (questions 41–81). Far from being an indication of actual or incipient legalism, the Westminster divines themselves regarded this as an essential lesson in Christian living. For them the knowledge of God's will lay largely in living for Christ in the power of the Spirit in order to fulfill the will of the heavenly Father revealed in Scripture.

Westminster Larger Catechism (1648)

The Larger Catechism shares the theology and many of the characteristics of its better known companion, but covers more ground in greater detail. It contains 196 questions and answers, many of the latter extending to over one-hundred-word compound complex sentences.

Demanding greater powers of memorization, the usefulness of the Larger Catechism lies less in its memorizability than in its value as a teaching aid framed in the catechetical form. Philip Schaff expressed the opinion that its intended function might have been to promote the kind of catechetical preaching common in the continental Reformed tradition. While that is unsubstantiated and quite unlikely, it is true that the Larger Catechism serves well as a useful guidebook for preaching on doctrinal themes. In this sense it identifies the key elements and issues that ought to be addressed in such preaching.

Following five opening questions indicating that it is from Scripture that we learn who God is, how we may know Him and what He requires, questions 6–90 teach us what we are to believe about Him. Questions 91–196 spell out the duties of the Christian life.

As is the case with the Shorter Catechism, this emphasis on the obedience of the Christian is set within a strong and full grasp of God's grace in Christ. The divines set out to provide a well-structured guide to applying the Word of God in the practical context of everyday life. While few may have the mental energy to memorize the Larger Catechism, it continues to provide a valuable guidebook to Christian thinking and living.

Joel R. Beeke
Puritan Reformed Theological Seminary
Grand Rapids, Michigan

Sinclair B. Ferguson
St. George's Tron Parish Church
Glasgow, Scotland

Belgic Confession (1561)	Heidelberg Catechism (1563)	Second Helvetic Confession (1566)	Canons of Dort (1619)
	Q. 1: What is thy only comfort in life and death? A.: That I with body and soul, both in life and death,[1] am not my own,[2] but belong unto my faithful Savior Jesus Christ;[3] who, with His precious blood,[4] hath fully satisfied for all my sins,[5] and delivered me from all the power of the devil;[6] and so preserves me[7] that without the will of my heavenly Father, not a hair can fall from my head;[8] yea, that all things must be subservient to my salvation,[9] and therefore, by His Holy Spirit, He also assures me of eternal life,[10] and makes me sincerely willing and ready, henceforth, to live unto Him.[11]		

[1] 1 Cor. 6:19-20
[2] Rom. 14:7-9
[3] 1 Cor. 3:23
[4] 1 Pet. 1:18-19
[5] John 1:17
[6] 1 John 3:8; Heb. 2:14-15
[7] John 6:39; John 10:28-29
[8] Luke 21:18; Matt. 10:30
[9] Rom. 8:28
[10] 2 Cor. 1:22; 2 Cor. 5:5
[11] Rom. 8:14; Rom. 7:22

Westminster Confession of Faith (1647)	Westminster Shorter Catechism (1647)	Westminster Larger Catechism (1648)
	Q. 1: What is the chief end of man? A.: Man's chief end is to glorify God,[1] and to enjoy Him for ever.[2] [1] 1 Cor. 10:31; Rom. 11:36 [2] Ps. 73:25-28	*Q. 1: What is the chief and highest end of man?* A.: Man's chief and highest end is to glorify God,[1] and fully to enjoy Him for ever.[2] [1] Rom. 11:36; 1 Cor. 10:31 [2] Ps. 73:24-28; John 17:21-23

Theology:
The Doctrine of God

Belgic Confession (1561)	Heidelberg Catechism (1563)	Second Helvetic Confession (1566)	Canons of Dort (1619)

The Being and Attributes of God

Article 1

There Is One Only God

We all believe with the heart, and confess with the mouth, that there is one only simple[1] and spiritual[2] Being, which we call God; and that He is eternal,[3] incomprehensible,[4] invisible,[5] immutable,[6] infinite,[7] almighty, perfectly wise,[8] just,[9] good,[10] and the overflowing fountain of all good.[11]

---

[1] Eph. 4:6; Deut. 6:4; 1 Tim. 2:5; 1 Cor. 8:6
[2] John 4:24
[3] Isa. 40:28
[4] Rom. 11:33
[5] Rom. 1:20
[6] Mal. 3:6
[7] Isa. 44:6
[8] 1 Tim. 1:17
[9] Jer. 12:1
[10] Matt. 19:17
[11] James 1:17; 1 Chron. 29:10-12

Q. 94: What doth God enjoin in the first commandment?

A.: That I, as sincerely as I desire the salvation of my own soul, avoid and flee from all idolatry,[1] sorcery, soothsaying, superstition,[2] invocation of saints, or any other creatures;[3] and learn rightly to know the only true God;[4] trust in Him alone;[5] with humility and patience[6] submit to Him;[7] expect all good things from Him only;[8] love,[9] fear,[10] and glorify[11] Him with my whole heart; so that I renounce and forsake all creatures,[12] rather than commit even the least thing contrary to His will.[13]

---

[1] 1 Cor. 6:9-10; 1 Cor. 10:7, 14
[2] Lev. 18:21; Deut. 18:10-12
[3] Matt. 4:10; Rev. 19:10
[4] John 17:3
[5] Jer. 17:5, 7
[6] Heb. 10:36; Col. 1:11; Rom. 5:3-4; Phil. 2:14
[7] 1 Pet. 5:5-6
[8] Ps. 104:27; Isa. 45:7; James 1:17
[9] Deut. 6:5; Matt. 22:37
[10] Deut. 6:5; Matt. 10:28
[11] Matt. 4:10
[12] Matt. 5:29-30; Acts 5:29; Matt. 10:37
[13] Matt. 5:19

Q. 95: What is idolatry?

A.: Idolatry is, instead of, or besides that one true God who has manifested Himself in His Word, to contrive, or have any other object, in which men place their trust.[1]

---

[1] 2 Chron. 16:12; Phil. 3:18-19; Gal. 4:8; Eph. 2:12

III. Of God; the Unity and the Trinity

1. We believe and teach that God is one in essence or nature, subsisting by Himself, allsufficient in Himself, invisible, without a body, infinite, eternal, the Creator of all things both visible and invisible, the chief good, living, quickening and preserving all things, almighty and supremely wise, gentle or merciful, just and true.

2. And we detest the multitude of gods, because it is expressly written, "The LORD our God is one LORD" (Deut. 6:4). "I am the LORD thy God,.... thou shalt have no other gods before Me" (Exod. 20:2-3). "I am the LORD, and there is none else, there is no God beside Me.... I am the LORD, and there is none else.... a just God and a Saviour; there is none beside Me" (Isa. 45:6, 21). "The LORD God, merciful and gracious, longsuffering, and abundant in goodness and truth" (Exod. 34:6).

Westminster Confession of Faith (1647)	Westminster Shorter Catechism (1647)	Westminster Larger Catechism (1648)

II. Of God, and of the Holy Trinity

1. There is but one only,[1] living, and true God,[2] who is infinite in being and perfection,[3] a most pure spirit,[4] invisible,[5] without body, parts,[6] or passions;[7] immutable,[8] immense,[9] eternal,[10] incomprehensible,[11] almighty,[12] most wise,[13] most holy,[14] most free,[15] most absolute;[16] working all things according to the counsel of His own immutable and most righteous will,[17] for His own glory;[18] most loving,[19] gracious, merciful, long-suffering, abundant in goodness and truth, forgiving iniquity, transgression, and sin;[20] the rewarder of them that diligently seek Him;[21] and withal, most just, and terrible in His judgments,[22] hating all sin,[23] and who will by no means clear the guilty.[24]

[1] Deut. 6:4; 1 Cor. 8:4, 6
[2] 1 Thes. 1:9; Jer. 10:10
[3] Job 11:7-9; 26:14
[4] John 4:24
[5] 1 Tim. 1:17
[6] Deut. 4:15-16; John 4:24; Luke 24:39
[7] Acts 14:11, 15
[8] James 1:17; Mal. 3:6
[9] 1 Ki. 8:27; Jer. 23:23-24
[10] Ps. 90:2; 1 Tim. 1:17
[11] Ps. 145:3
[12] Gen. 17:1; Rev. 4:8
[13] Rom. 16:27
[14] Isa. 6:3; Rev. 4:8
[15] Ps. 115:3
[16] Exod. 3:14
[17] Eph. 1:11
[18] Prov. 16:4; Rom. 11:36
[19] 1 John 4:8, 16
[20] Exod. 34:6-7
[21] Heb. 11:6
[22] Neh. 9:32-33
[23] Ps. 5:5-6
[24] Nah. 1:2-3; Exod. 34:7

2. God hath all life,[1] glory,[2] goodness,[3] blessedness,[4] in and of Himself; and is alone in and unto Himself all-sufficient, not standing in need of any creatures which He hath made,[5] nor deriving any glory from them,[6] but only manifesting His own glory in, by, unto, and upon them. He is the alone fountain of all being, of whom, through whom, and to whom are all things;[7] and hath most sovereign dominion over them, to do by them, for them, or upon them whatsoever Himself pleaseth.[8] In His sight all things are open and manifest,[9] His knowledge is infinite, infallible, and independent upon the creature,[10] so as nothing is to Him contingent, or uncertain.[11] He is most holy in all His counsels, in all His works, and in all His commands.[12]

Q. 4: What is God?

A.: God is a Spirit,[1] infinite,[2] eternal,[3] and unchangeable,[4] in His being,[5] wisdom,[6] power,[7] holiness,[8] justice, goodness, and truth.[9]

[1] John 4:24
[2] Job 11:7-9
[3] Ps. 90:2
[4] James 1:17
[5] Exod. 3:14
[6] Ps. 147:5
[7] Rev. 4:8
[8] Rev. 15:4
[9] Exod. 34:6-7

Q. 5: Are there more Gods than one?

A.: There is but One only, the living and true God.[1]

[1] Deut. 6:4; Jer. 10:10

Q. 6: What do the Scriptures make known of God?

A.: The Scriptures make known what God is,[1] the persons in the Godhead,[2] His decrees,[3] and the execution of His decrees.[4]

[1] Heb. 11:6
[2] 1 John 5:17
[3] Acts 15:14-15, 18
[4] Acts 4:27-28

Q. 7: What is God?

A.: God is a Spirit,[1] in and of Himself infinite in being,[2] glory,[3] blessedness,[4] and perfection;[5] all-sufficient,[6] eternal,[7] unchangeable,[8] incomprehensible,[9] everywhere present,[10] almighty,[11] knowing all things,[12] most wise,[13] most holy,[14] most just,[15] most merciful and gracious, long-suffering, and abundant in goodness and truth.[16]

[1] John 4:24
[2] Exod. 3:14; Job 11:7-9
[3] Acts 7:2
[4] 1 Tim. 6:15
[5] Matt. 5:48
[6] Gen. 17:1
[7] Ps. 90:2
[8] Mal. 3:6; James 1:17
[9] 1 Ki. 8:27
[10] Ps. 139:1-13
[11] Rev. 4:8
[12] Heb. 4:13; Ps. 147:5
[13] Rom. 16:27
[14] Isa. 6:3; Rev. 15:4
[15] Deut. 32:4
[16] Exod. 34:6

Q. 8: Are there more Gods than one?

A.: There is but One only, the living and true God.[1]

[1] Deut. 6:4; 1 Cor. 8:4, 6; Jer. 10:10

Belgic Confession (1561)	Heidelberg Catechism (1563)	Second Helvetic Confession (1566)	Canons of Dort (1619)

Revelation

Article 2

By What Means God is Made Known Unto Us

We know Him by two means: first, by the creation, preservation, and government of the universe;[1] which is before our eyes as a most elegant book, wherein all creatures, great and small, are as so many characters leading us to contemplate *the invisible things of God*, namely, *His eternal power and divinity*, as the apostle Paul saith (Rom. 1:20). All which things are sufficient to convince men, and leave them without excuse.

Secondly, He makes Himself more clearly and fully known to us by His holy and divine Word;[2] that is to say, as far as is necessary for us to know in this life, to His glory and our salvation.

[1] Ps. 19:2; Eph. 4:6
[2] Ps. 19:8; 1 Cor. 12:6

Q. 122: Which is the first petition?

A.: "Hallowed be Thy name";[1] that is, grant us, first, rightly to know Thee,[2] and to sanctify, glorify and praise Thee in all Thy works, in which Thy power, wisdom, goodness, justice, mercy and truth, are clearly displayed.[3]

[1] Matt. 6:9
[2] John 17:3; Jer. 9:23-24; Matt. 16:17; James 1:5
[3] Ps. 119:137-138; Luke 1:46; Ps. 145:8-9

Head III and IV

Article 6

What therefore neither the light of nature, nor the law could do, that God performs by the operation of the Holy Spirit through the Word or ministry of reconciliation, which is the glad tidings concerning the Messiah, by means whereof it hath pleased God to save such as believe, as well under the Old, as under the New Testament.

Article 7

This mystery of His will God discovered to but a small number under the Old Testament; under the New (the distinction between various peoples having been removed), He reveals Himself to many without any distinction of people. The cause of this dispensation is not to be ascribed to the superior worth of one nation above another,

Westminster Confession of Faith (1647)	Westminster Shorter Catechism (1647)	Westminster Larger Catechism (1648)
To Him is due from angels and men, and every other creature, whatsoever worship, service, or obedience He is pleased to require of them.[13]		

[1] John 5:26
[2] Acts 7:2
[3] Ps. 119:68
[4] 1 Tim. 6:15; Rom. 9:5
[5] Acts 17:24-25
[6] Job 22:2-3
[7] Rom. 11:36
[8] Rev. 4:11; 1 Tim. 6:15; Dan. 4:25, 35
[9] Heb. 4:13
[10] Rom. 11:33-34; Ps. 147:5
[11] Acts 15:18; Ezek. 11:5
[12] Ps. 145:17; Rom. 7:12
[13] Rev. 5:12-14

I. Of the Holy Scriptures

1. Although the light of nature, and the works of creation and providence do so far manifest the goodness, wisdom, and power of God, as to leave men inexcusable;[1] yet they are not sufficient to give that knowledge of God, and of His will, which is necessary unto salvation.[2] Therefore it pleased the Lord, at sundry times, and in divers manners, to reveal Himself, and to declare that His will unto His Church;[3] and afterwards, for the better preserving and propagating of the truth, and for the more sure establishment and comfort of the Church against the corruption of the flesh, and the malice of Satan and of the world, to commit the same wholly unto writing:[4] which maketh the Holy Scripture to be most necessary;[5] those former ways of God's revealing His will unto His people being now ceased.[6]

[1] Rom. 2:14-15; 1:19-20; Ps. 19:1-3; Rom. 1:32; 2:1
[2] 1 Cor. 1:21; 2:13-14
[3] Heb. 1:1
[4] Prov. 22:19-21; Luke 1:3-4; Rom. 15:4; Matt. 4:4, 7, 10; Isa. 8:19-20
[5] 2 Tim. 3:15; 2 Pet. 1:19
[6] Heb. 1:1-2

Q. 2: How doth it appear that there is a God?

A. The very light of nature in man, and the works of God, declare plainly that there is a God;[1] but His Word and Spirit only do sufficiently and effectually reveal Him unto men for their salvation.[2]

[1] Rom. 1:19-20; Ps. 19:1-3; Acts 17:28
[2] 1 Cor. 2:9-10; 2 Tim. 3:15-17; Isa. 59:21

Belgic Confession (1561)	Heidelberg Catechism (1563)	Second Helvetic Confession (1566)	Canons of Dort (1619)
			nor to their making a better use of the light of nature, but results wholly from the sovereign good pleasure and unmerited love of God. Hence they, to whom so great and so gracious a blessing is communicated above their desert, or rather notwithstanding their demerits, are bound to acknowledge it with humble and grateful hearts, and with the apostle to adore, not curiously to pry into the severity and justice of God's judgments displayed to others, to whom this grace is not given.

The Holy Scriptures

Article 3

The Written Word of God

We confess that this Word of God was not sent nor delivered by the will of man, but that *holy men of God spake as they were moved by the Holy Ghost*, as the apostle Peter saith.[1] And that afterwards God, from a special care which He has for us and our salvation, commanded His servants, the prophets[2] and apostles,[3] to commit His revealed Word to writing; and He Himself wrote with His own finger the two tables of the law.[4] Therefore we

Q. 19: *Whence knowest thou this?*

A.: From the holy gospel, which God Himself first revealed in Paradise;[1] and afterwards published by the patriarchs and prophets,[2] and represented by the sacrifices and other ceremonies of the law;[3] and lastly, has fulfilled it by His only begotten Son.[4]

[1] Gen. 3:15
[2] Gen. 22:17-18; Gen. 28:14; Rom. 1:2; Heb. 1:1; John 5:46
[3] Heb. 10:7-8
[4] Rom. 10:4; Heb. 13:8

Q. 22: *What is then necessary for a Christian to believe?*

I. Of the Holy Scripture Being the True Word of God

1. We believe and confess the Canonical Scriptures of the holy prophets and apostles of both Testaments to be the true Word of God, and to have sufficient authority of themselves, not of men. For God Himself spake to the fathers, prophets, apostles, and still speaks to us through the Holy Scriptures.

2. And in this Holy Scripture, the universal Church of Christ has all things fully expounded which belong to a saving faith, and also to the framing of a life acceptable to God; and in this respect it is expressly commanded of God that nothing be either put to or taken from the same (Deut. 4:2; Rev. 22:18-19).

3. We judge, therefore, that from these Scriptures are to be taken true wisdom and godliness, the reformation and government of churches; as also instruction in all duties of piety; and, to be short, the confirmation of doctrines, and the confutation

Head I

Article 3

And that men may be brought to believe, God mercifully sends the messengers of these most joyful tidings to whom He will and at what time He pleaseth; by whose ministry men are called to repentance and faith in Christ crucified. "How then shall they call on Him in whom they have not believed? and how shall they believe in Him of whom they have not heard? and how shall they hear without a preacher? And how shall they preach, except

Westminster Confession of Faith (1647)	Westminster Shorter Catechism (1647)	Westminster Larger Catechism (1648)

I. Of the Holy Scripture

2. Under the name of Holy Scripture, or the Word of God written, are now contained all the books of the Old and New Testament, which are these:

Of the Old Testament:

Genesis	Ecclesiastes
Exodus	The Song of Songs
Leviticus	Isaiah
Numbers	Jeremiah
Deuteronomy	Lamentations
Joshua	Ezekiel
Judges	Daniel
Ruth	Hosea
I Samuel	Joel
II Samuel	Amos
I Kings	Obadiah
II Kings	Jonah
I Chronicles	Micah
II Chronicles	Nahum
Ezra	Habakkuk
Nehemiah	Zephaniah
Esther	Haggai
Job	Zechariah
Psalms	Malachi;
Proverbs	

Q. 2: What rule hath God given to direct us how we may glorify and enjoy Him?

A.: The Word of God, which is contained in the Scriptures of the Old and New Testaments,[1] is the only rule to direct us how we may glorify and enjoy Him.[2]

[1] 2 Tim. 3:16; Eph. 2:20
[2] 1 John 1:3-4

Q. 3: What do the Scriptures principally teach?

A.: The Scriptures principally teach what man is to believe concerning God, and what duty God requires of man.[1]

[1] 2 Tim. 1:13; 3:16

Q. 3: What is the Word of God?

A.: The Holy Scriptures of the Old and New Testament are the Word of God,[1] the only rule of faith and obedience.[2]

[1] 2 Tim. 3:16; 2 Pet. 1:19-21
[2] Eph. 2:20; Rev. 22:18-19; Isa. 8:20; Luke 16:29, 31; Gal. 1:8-9; 2 Tim. 3:15-16

Q. 4: How doth it appear that the Scriptures are the Word of God?

A.: The Scriptures manifest themselves to be the Word of God, by their majesty[1] and purity;[2] by the consent of all the parts,[3] and the scope of the whole, which is to give all glory to God;[4] by their light and power to convince and convert sinners, to comfort and build up believers unto salvation:[5] but the Spirit of God bearing witness by and with the Scriptures in the heart of man, is alone able fully to persuade it that they are the very Word of God.[6]

[1] Hos. 8:12; 1 Cor. 2:6-7, 13; Ps. 119:18, 129
[2] Ps. 12:6; 119:140

Belgic Confession (1561)	Heidelberg Catechism (1563)	Second Helvetic Confession (1566)	Canons of Dort (1619)

Belgic Confession (1561)

call such writings holy and divine Scriptures.

[1] 2 Pet. 1:21
[2] Exod. 24:4; Ps. 102:19; Hab. 2:2
[3] 2 Tim. 3:16; Rev. 1:11
[4] Exod. 31:18

Article 4
Canonical Books of the Holy Scriptures

We believe that the Holy Scriptures are contained in two books, namely, the Old and New Testaments, which are canonical, against which nothing can be alleged. These are thus named in the Church of God.

The books of the Old Testament are: the five books of Moses, namely, Genesis, Exodus, Leviticus, Numbers, Deuteronomy; the books of Joshua, Judges, Ruth, the two books of Samuel, the two of the Kings, two books of the Chronicles, commonly called Paralipomenon, the first of Ezra, Nehemiah, Esther, Job, the Psalms of David, the three books of Solomon, namely, the Proverbs, Ecclesiastes, and the Song of Songs; the four great prophets, Isaiah, Jeremiah, Ezekiel, and Daniel; and the twelve lesser prophets, namely, Hosea, Joel, Amos, Obadiah, Jonah, Micah, Nahum, Habakkuk, Zephaniah, Haggai, Zechariah, and Malachi.

Those of the New Testament are: the four evangelists, namely, Matthew, Mark, Luke, and John; the Acts of the Apostles; the fourteen epistles of the apostle Paul, namely, one to the Romans, two to the Corinthians, one to the

Heidelberg Catechism (1563)

A.: All things promised us in the gospel,[1] which the articles of our catholic undoubted Christian faith briefly teach us.

[1] John 20:31; Matt. 28:19-20

Q. 98: *But may not images be tolerated in the churches as books to the laity?*

A.: No, for we must not pretend to be wiser than God, who will have His people taught, not by dumb images,[1] but by the lively preaching of His Word.[2]

[1] 2 Tim. 3:16; 2 Pet. 1:19
[2] Jer. 10:1; Hab. 2:18-19

Second Helvetic Confession (1566)

of all errors, with all exhortations; according to that word of the apostle, "All scripture is given by inspiration of God, and is profitable for doctrine, for reproof," etc. (2 Tim. 3:16-17). Again, "These things write I unto thee," says the apostle to Timothy, "...that thou mayest know how thou oughtest to behave thyself in the house of God," etc. (1 Tim. 3:14-15). Again, the selfsame apostle to the Thessalonians: "When," says he, "ye received the word of God which ye heard of us, ye received it not as the word of men, but as it is in truth, the word of God," etc. (1 Thes. 2:13). For the Lord Himself has said in the gospel, "It is not ye that speak, but the Spirit of your Father which speaketh in you"; therefore "he that heareth you heareth Me; and he that despiseth you despiseth Me" (Matt. 10:20; Luke 10:16; John 13:20).

4. Wherefore when this Word of God is now preached in the church by preachers lawfully called, we believe that the very Word of God is preached, and received of the faithful; and that neither any other Word of God is to be feigned, nor to be expected from heaven: and that now the Word itself which is preached is to be regarded, not the minister that preaches; who, although he be evil and a sinner, nevertheless the Word of God abides true and good.

5. Neither do we think that therefore the outward preaching is to be thought as fruitless because the instruction in true religion depends on the inward illumination of the Spirit, or because it is written "they shall teach no more every man his neighbour...for they shall all know Me" (Jer. 31:34), and "neither is he that planteth any thing, neither he that watereth; but God that giveth the increase" (1 Cor. 3:7). For albeit "No man can come to Me, except the Father which hath sent Me draw him" (John 6:44), and be inwardly lightened by the Holy Spirit, yet we know undoubtedly that it is the will of God that His Word should be preached even outwardly. God could indeed, by His Holy Spirit, or by the ministry of an angel, without the ministry of St. Peter, have taught Cornelius in the Acts; but, nevertheless, He refers him to Peter, of whom the angel speaking says, "He shall tell thee what thou oughtest to do" (Acts 10:6).

6. For He that illuminates inwardly by giving men the Holy Spirit, the self-same, by way of commandment, said unto His disciples, "Go ye into all the world, and preach the gospel to every creature" (Mark 16:15). And so Paul preached the Word outwardly to Lydia, a purple-seller among the Philippians; but the Lord inwardly opened the woman's heart (Acts 16:14).

Canons of Dort (1619)

they be sent?" (Rom. 10:14-15).

Head II
Article 5
Moreover, the promise of the gospel is, that whosoever believeth in Christ crucified, shall not perish, but have everlasting life. This promise, together with the command to repent and believe, ought to be declared and published to all nations, and to all persons promiscuously and without distinction, to whom God out of His good pleasure sends the gospel.

Head III and IV
Article 8
As many as are called by the gospel are unfeignedly called. For God hath most earnestly and truly declared in His Word what will be acceptable to Him; namely, that all who are called, should comply with the invitation. He, moreover, seriously promises eternal life and rest to as many as shall come to Him and believe on Him.

Article 17
As the almighty operation of God, whereby He prolongs and supports this our natural life, does not exclude, but requires the use of means, by which God of His infinite mercy and goodness hath chosen to exert His influence, so also the before-mentioned supernatural operation of God, by which we are regenerated, in no wise excludes or subverts

Westminster Confession of Faith (1647)	Westminster Shorter Catechism (1647)	Westminster Larger Catechism (1648)

Westminster Confession of Faith (1647)

Of the New Testament:

The Gospels according to
Matthew
Mark
Luke
John
The Acts of the
Apostles
Paul's Epistles to
the Romans
Corinthians I
Corinthians II
Galatians
Ephesians
Philippians
Colossians
Thessalonians I

Thessalonians II
To Timothy I
To Timothy II
To Titus
To Philemon
The Epistle to the
Hebrews
The Epistle of James
The first and second
Epistles of Peter
The first, second, and third
Epistles of John
The Epistle of Jude
The Revelation of John.

All which are given by inspiration of God to be the rule of faith and life.[1]

[1] Luke 16:29, 31; Eph. 2:20; Rev. 22:18-19; 2 Tim. 3:16

4. The authority of the Holy Scripture, for which it ought to be believed, and obeyed, dependeth not upon the testimony of any man, or Church; but wholly upon God (who is truth itself) the author thereof: and therefore it is to be received, because it is the Word of God.[1]

[1] 2 Pet. 1:19, 21; 2 Tim. 3:16; 1 John 5:9; 1 Thes. 2:13

5. We may be moved and induced by the testimony of the Church to an high and reverend esteem of the Holy Scripture.[1] And the heavenliness of the matter, the efficacy of the doctrine, the majesty of the style, the consent of all the parts, the scope of the whole (which is, to give all glory to God), the full discovery it makes of the only way of man's salvation, the many other incomparable excellencies, and the entire perfection thereof, are arguments whereby it doth abundantly evidence itself to be the Word of God: yet notwithstanding, our full persuasion and assurance of the infallible truth and divine authority thereof, is from the inward work of the Holy Spirit bearing witness by and with the Word in our hearts.[2]

[1] 1 Tim. 3:15
[2] 1 John 2:20, 27; John 16:13-14; 1 Cor. 2:10-12; Isa. 59:21

6. The whole counsel of God concerning all things necessary for His own glory, man's salvation, faith and life, is either expressly set down in Scripture, or by good and necessary consequence may be deduced from Scripture: unto which nothing at any time is to be added, whether by new revelations of the Spirit, or traditions of men.[1] Nevertheless, we acknowledge the inward illumination of the Spirit of God to be necessary for the saving understanding of such

Westminster Larger Catechism (1648)

[3] Acts 10:43; 26:22
[4] Rom. 3:19, 27
[5] Acts 18:28; Heb. 4:12; James 1:18; Ps. 19:7-9; Rom. 15:4; Acts 20:32
[6] John 16:13-14; 1 John 2:20, 27; John 20:31

Q. 5: *What do the Scriptures principally teach?*

A.: The Scriptures principally teach, what man is to believe concerning God, and what duty God requires of man.[1]

[1] 2 Tim. 1:13

Belgic Confession (1561)	Heidelberg Catechism (1563)	Second Helvetic Confession (1566)	Canons of Dort (1619)

Galatians, one to the Ephesians, one to the Philippians, one to the Colossians, two to the Thessalonians, two to Timothy, one to Titus, one to Philemon, and one to the Hebrews; the seven epistles of the other apostles, namely, one of James, two of Peter, three of John, one of Jude; and the Revelation of the apostle John.

Article 5

From Whence the Holy Scriptures Derive Their Dignity and Authority

We receive all these books, and these only, as holy and canonical, for the regulation, foundation, and confirmation of our faith; believing, without any doubt, all things contained in them, not so much because the Church receives and approves them as such, but more especially because the Holy Ghost witnesseth in our hearts that they are from God, whereof they carry the evidence in themselves. For the very blind are able to perceive that the things foretold in them are fulfilling.

Article 7

The Sufficiency of the Holy Scriptures to be the Only Rule of Faith

We believe that those Holy Scriptures fully contain the will of God, and that whatsoever man ought to believe unto salvation is sufficiently taught therein.[1] For since the whole manner of worship which God requires of us is written

And the same Paul, upon an elegant gradation fitly placed in the tenth chapter to the Romans, at last infers, "So then faith cometh by hearing, and hearing by the word of God" (Rom. 10:17).

7. We know, in the meantime, that God can illuminate whom and when He will, even without the external ministry, which is a thing appertaining to His power; but we speak of the usual way of instructing men, delivered unto us from God, both by commandment and examples.

8. We therefore detest all the heresies of Artemon, the Manichaeans, the Valentinians, of Cerdon, and the Marcionites, who denied that the Scriptures proceeded from the Holy Spirit; or else received not, or interpolated and corrupted, some of them.

II. Of Interpreting the Holy Scriptures; and of Fathers, Councils, and Traditions

1. The apostle Peter has said that "no prophecy of the scripture is of any private interpretation" (2 Pet. 1:20). Therefore we do not allow all kinds of exposition. Whereupon we do not acknowledge that which they call the meaning of the Church of Rome for the true and natural interpretation of the Scriptures; which, forsooth, the defenders of the Romish Church do strive to force all men simply to receive; but we acknowledge only that interpretation of Scriptures for orthodox and genuine which, being taken from the Scriptures themselves (that is, from the spirit of that tongue in which they were written, they being also weighed according to the circumstances and expounded according to the proportion of places, either of like or of unlike, also of more and plainer), accords with the rule of faith and charity, and makes notably for God's glory and man's salvation.

2. Wherefore we do not despise the interpretations of the holy Greek and Latin fathers, nor reject their disputations and treatises as far as they agree with the Scriptures; but we do modestly dissent from them when they are found to set down things differing from, or altogether contrary to, the Scriptures. Neither do we think that we do them any wrong in this matter; seeing that they all, with one consent, will not have their writings matched with the Canonical Scriptures, but bid us allow of them so far forth as they either agree with them or disagree.

3. And in the same order we also place the decrees and canons of councils.

4. Wherefore we suffer not ourselves, in controversies about religion or matters of faith, to be

the use of the gospel, which the most wise God has ordained to be the seed of regeneration and food of the soul. Wherefore, as the apostles, and teachers who succeeded them, piously instructed the people concerning this grace of God, to His glory, and the abasement of all pride, and in the meantime, however, neglected not to keep them by the sacred precepts of the gospel in the exercise of the Word, sacraments and discipline; so even to this day, be it far from either instructors or instructed to presume to tempt God in the Church by separating what He of His good pleasure hath most intimately joined together. For grace is conferred by means of admonitions; and the more readily we perform our duty, the more eminent usually is this blessing of God working in us, and the more directly is His work advanced; to whom alone all the glory both of means, and of their saving fruit and efficacy is forever due. Amen.

Head V

Article 14

And as it hath pleased God, by the preaching of the gospel, to begin this work of grace in us, so He preserves, continues, and perfects it by the hearing and reading of His Word, by meditation thereon, and by the exhortations, threatenings, and promises thereof, as well as by the use of the sacraments.

Westminster Confession of Faith (1647)	Westminster Shorter Catechism (1647)	Westminster Larger Catechism (1648)

things as are revealed in the Word:[2] and that there are some circumstances concerning the worship of God, and government of the Church, common to human actions and societies, which are to be ordered by the light of nature, and Christian prudence, according to the general rules of the Word, which are always to be observed.[3]

[1] 2 Tim. 3:15-17; Gal. 1:8-9; 2 Thes. 2:2
[2] John 6:45; 1 Cor. 2:9-12
[3] 1 Cor. 11:13-14; 14:26, 40

7. All things in Scripture are not alike plain in themselves, nor alike clear unto all:[1] yet those things which are necessary to be known, believed, and observed for salvation, are so clearly propounded, and opened in some place of Scripture or other, that not only the learned, but the unlearned, in a due use of the ordinary means, may attain unto a sufficient understanding of them.[2]

[1] 2 Pet. 3:16
[2] Ps. 119:105, 130

8. The Old Testament in Hebrew (which was the native language of the people of God of old), and the New Testament in Greek (which, at the time of the writing of it, was most generally known to the nations), being immediately inspired by God, and, by His singular care and providence, kept pure in all ages, are therefore authentical;[1] so as, in all controversies of religion, the Church is finally to appeal unto them.[2] But, because these original tongues are not known to all the people of God, who have right unto, and interest in the Scriptures, and are commanded, in the fear of God, to read and search them,[3] therefore they are to be translated into the vulgar language of every nation unto which they come,[4] that, the Word of God dwelling plentifully in all, they may worship Him in an acceptable manner;[5] and, through patience and comfort of the Scriptures, may have hope.[6]

[1] Matt. 5:18
[2] Isa. 8:20; Acts 15:15; John 5:39, 46
[3] John 5:39
[4] 1 Cor. 14:6, 9, 11-12, 24, 27-28
[5] Col. 3:16
[6] Rom. 15:4

9. The infallible rule of interpretation of Scripture is the Scripture itself: and therefore, when there is a question about the true and full sense of any Scripture (which is not manifold, but one), it must be searched and known by other places that speak more clearly.[1]

[1] 2 Pet. 1:20-21; Acts 15:15-16

Belgic Confession (1561)	Heidelberg Catechism (1563)	Second Helvetic Confession (1566)	Canons of Dort (1619)

Belgic Confession (1561)

in them at large, it is unlawful for any one, though an apostle, to teach otherwise[2] than we are now taught in the Holy Scriptures: *nay, though it were an angel from heaven*, as the apostle Paul saith.[3] For since it is forbidden *to add unto or take away any thing from the Word of God*,[4] it doth thereby evidently appear that the doctrine thereof is most perfect and complete in all respects. Neither do we con- sider of equal value any writing of men, however holy these men may have been, with those divine Scriptures;[5] nor ought we to consider custom, or the great multitude, or antiquity, or succession of times and persons, or councils, decrees, or statutes, as of equal value with the truth of God,[6] for the truth is above all; for all men are of themselves liars,[7] and more vain than vanity itself. Therefore we reject with all our hearts whatsoever doth not agree with this infallible rule[8] which the apostles have taught us, saying, *Try the spirits whether they are of God.*[9] Likewise, *If there come any unto you, and bring not this doctrine, receive him not into your house.*[10]

---

[1] Rom. 15:4; John 4:25; 2 Tim. 3:15-17; 1 Pet. 1:1; Prov. 30:5; Rev. 22:18; John 15:15; Acts 2:27
[2] 1 Pet. 4:11; 1 Cor. 15:2-3; 2 Tim. 3:14; 1 Tim. 1:3; 2 John 10
[3] Gal. 1:8-9; 1 Cor. 15:2; Acts 26:22; Rom. 15:4; 1 Pet. 4:11; 2 Tim. 3:14
[4] Deut. 12:32; Prov. 30:6; Rev. 22:18; John 4:25
[5] Matt. 15:3; 17:5; Mark 7:7; Isa. 1:12; 1 Cor. 2:4

Second Helvetic Confession (1566)

pressed with the bare testimonies of fathers or decrees of councils; much less with received customs, or with the multitude of men being of one judgment, or with prescription of long time. Therefore, in controversies of religion or matters of faith, we can not admit any other judge than God Himself, pronouncing by the Holy Scriptures what is true, what is false, what is to be followed, or what is to be avoided. So we do not rest but in the judgment of spiritual men, drawn from the Word of God. Certainly Jeremiah and other prophets did vehemently condemn the assemblies of priests gathered against the law of God; and diligently forewarned us that we should not hear the fathers, or tread in their path who, walking in their own inventions, swerved from the law of God (Ezek. 20:18).

5. We do likewise reject human traditions, which, although they be set out with goodly titles, as though they were divine and apostolical, delivered to the Church by the lively voice of the apostles, and, as it were, by the hands of apostolical men, by means of bishops succeeding in their room, yet, being compared with the Scriptures, disagree with them; and that by their disagreement bewray themselves in no wise to be apostolical. For as the apostles did not disagree among themselves in doctrine, so the apostles' scholars did not set forth things contrary to the apostles. Nay, it were blasphemous to avouch that the apostles, by lively voice, delivered things contrary to their writings. Paul affirms expressly that he taught the same things in all churches (1 Cor. 4:17). And, again, "We," says he, "write none other things unto you, than what ye read or acknowledge" (2 Cor. 1:13). Also, in another place, he witnesses that he and his disciples — to wit, apostolic men — walked in the same way, and jointly by the same Spirit did all things (2 Cor. 12:18). The Jews also, in time past, had their traditions of elders; but these traditions were severely confuted by the Lord, showing that the keeping of them hinders God's law, and that God is in vain worshiped of such (Matt. 15:8-9; Mark 7:6-7).

Westminster Confession of Faith (1647)	Westminster Shorter Catechism (1647)	Westminster Larger Catechism (1648)
10. The supreme judge by which all controversies of religion are to be determined, and all decrees of councils, opinions of ancient writers, doctrines of men, and private spirits, are to be examined, and in whose sentence we are to rest, can be no other but the Holy Spirit speaking in the Scripture.[1] [1] Matt. 22:29, 31; Eph. 2:20; Acts 28:25		

Belgic Confession (1561)	Heidelberg Catechism (1563)	Second Helvetic Confession (1566)	Canons of Dort (1619)
[6] Isa. 1:12; Rom. 3:4; 2 Tim. 4:3-4 [7] Ps. 62:10 [8] Gal. 6:16; 1 Cor. 3:11; 2 Thes. 2:2 [9] 1 John 4:1 [10] 2 John 10			

The Apocrypha

Article 6

The Difference Between the Canonical and Apocryphal Books

We distinguish these sacred books from the apocryphal, viz., the third and fourth book of Esdras, the books of Tobias, Judith, Wisdom, Jesus Syrach, Baruch, the appendix to the book of Esther, the Song of the Three Children in the Furnace, the History of Susannah, of Bell and the Dragon, the Prayer of Manasses, and the two books of the Maccabees. All of which the Church may read and take instruction from, so far as they agree with the canonical books; but they are far from having such power and efficacy as that we may from their testimony confirm any point of faith or of the Christian religion; much less to detract from the authority of the other sacred books.

I. Of the Holy Scripture Being the True Word of God

9. And yet we do not deny that certain books of the Old Testament were by the ancient authors called *Apocryphal,* and by others *Ecclesiastical;* to wit, such as they would have to be read in the churches, but not alleged to avouch or confirm the authority of faith by them. As also Augustine, in his *De Civitate Dei,* book 18, chapter 38, makes mention that "in the books of the Kings, the names and books of certain prophets are reckoned"; but he adds that "they are not in the canon," and that "those books which we have suffice unto godliness."

Westminster Confession of Faith (1647)	Westminster Shorter Catechism (1647)	Westminster Larger Catechism (1648)

I. Of the Holy Scriptures

3. The books commonly called Apocrypha, not being of divine inspiration, are no part of the canon of the Scripture, and therefore are of no authority in the Church of God, nor to be any otherwise approved, or made use of, than other human writings.[1]

[1] Luke 24:27, 44; Rom. 3:2; 2 Pet. 1:21

Belgic Confession (1561)	Heidelberg Catechism (1563)	Second Helvetic Confession (1566)	Canons of Dort (1619)

The Holy Trinity

Article 8

God is One in Essence, Yet Distinguished in Three Persons

According to this truth and this Word of God, we believe in one only God, who is one single essence,[1] in which are three persons,[2] really, truly, and eternally distinct, according to their incommunicable properties; namely, the Father, and the Son, and the Holy Ghost.[3] The Father is the cause, origin, and beginning of all things, visible and invisible;[4] the Son is the word,[5] wisdom,[6] and image of the Father;[7] the Holy Ghost is the eternal power and might,[8] proceeding from the Father and the Son.[9] Nevertheless God is not by this distinction divided into three, since the Holy Scriptures teach us that the Father, and the Son, and the Holy Ghost have each His personality, distinguished by their properties; but in such wise that these three persons are but one only God. Hence then, it is evident that the Father is not the Son, nor the Son the Father, and likewise the Holy Ghost is neither the Father nor the Son. Nevertheless these persons thus distinguished are not divided nor intermixed; for the Father hath not assumed the flesh, nor hath the Holy Ghost, but the Son

Q. 24: How are these articles divided?

A.: Into three parts; the first is of God the Father and our creation;[1] the second, of God the Son and our redemption;[2] the third, of God the Holy Ghost and our sanctification.[3]

---

[1] Gen. 1
[2] 1 Pet. 1:18-19
[3] 1 Pet. 1:21-22

Q. 25: Since there is but one only divine essence,[1] why speakest thou of Father, Son, and Holy Ghost?

A.: Because God hath so revealed Himself in His Word,[2] that these three distinct persons are the one only true and eternal God.

---

[1] Deut. 6:4
[2] Gen. 1:26; Isa. 61:1; John 14:16-17; 1 John 5:7; John 1:13; Matt. 28:19; 2 Cor. 13:14

III. Of God; the Unity and the Trinity

3. We nevertheless believe and teach that the same infinite, one, and indivisible God is in person inseparably and without confusion distinguished into the Father, the Son, and the Holy Spirit: so, as the Father has begotten the Son from eternity, the Son is begotten in an unspeakable manner; and the Holy Spirit proceeds from them both, and that from eternity, and is to be worshiped with them both. So that there are not three Gods, but three persons, consubstantial, coeternal, and coequal; distinct, as touching their persons; and, in order, one going before another, yet without any inequality. For, as touching their nature or essence, they are so joined together that they are but one God; and the divine essence is common to the Father, the Son, and the Holy Spirit.[1]

4. For the Scripture has delivered unto us a manifest distinction of persons; the angel, among other things, saying thus to the Blessed Virgin, "The Holy Ghost shall come upon thee, and the power of the Highest shall overshadow thee: therefore also that holy thing which shall be born of thee shall be called the Son of God" (Luke 1:35). Also, in the baptism of Christ, a voice was heard from heaven, saying, "This is My beloved Son" (Matt. 3:17). The Holy Spirit also appeared in the likeness of a dove (John 1:32). And when the Lord Himself commanded to baptize, He commanded to baptize "in the name of the Father, and of the Son, and of the Holy Ghost" (Matt. 28:19). In like manner, elsewhere in the gospel He said, "the Comforter, which is the Holy Ghost, whom the Father will send in My name, He shall teach you all things" (John 14:26). Again He says, "when the Comforter is come, whom I will send unto you from the Father, even the Spirit of truth, which proceedeth from the Father, He shall testify of Me," etc. (John 15:26). In short, we receive the Apostles' Creed, because it delivers unto us the true faith.

5. We therefore condemn the Jews and the Mohammedans, and all those who blaspheme that sacred and adorable Trinity. We also condemn all heresies and heretics who teach that the Son and the Holy Spirit are God only in name; also, that there is in the Trinity something created, and that serves and ministers unto another; finally, that there is in it something unequal, greater or less, corporeal or corporeally fashioned, in manners or in will diverse, either confounded or

Westminster Confession of Faith (1647)	Westminster Shorter Catechism (1647)	Westminster Larger Catechism (1648)

II. Of God, and of the Holy Trinity

3. In the unity of the Godhead there be three persons, of one substance, power, and eternity: God the Father, God the Son, and God the Holy Ghost:[1] the Father is of none, neither begotten, nor proceeding; the Son is eternally begotten of the Father;[2] the Holy Ghost eternally proceeding from the Father and the Son.[3]

[1] 1 John 5:7; Matt. 3:16-17; 28:19; 2 Cor. 13:14
[2] John 1:14, 18
[3] John 15:26; Gal. 4:6

Q. 6: How many persons are there in the Godhead?

A.: There are three persons in the Godhead: the Father, the Son, and the Holy Ghost; and these three are one God, the same in substance, equal in power and glory.[1]

[1] 1 John 5:7; Matt. 28:19

Q. 9: How many persons are there in the Godhead?

A.: There be three persons in the Godhead, the Father, the Son, and the Holy Ghost; and these three are one true, eternal God, the same in substance, equal in power and glory; although distinguished by their personal properties.[1]

[1] 1 John 5:7; Matt. 3:16-17; 28:19; 2 Cor. 13:14; John 10:30

Q. 10: What are the personal properties of the three persons in the Godhead?

A.: It is proper to the Father to beget the Son,[1] and to the Son to be begotten of the Father,[2] and to the Holy Ghost to proceed from the Father and the Son from all eternity.[3]

[1] Heb. 1:5-6, 8
[2] John 1:14, 18
[3] John 15:26; Gal. 4:6

Belgic Confession (1561)	Heidelberg Catechism (1563)	Second Helvetic Confession (1566)	Canons of Dort (1619)

Belgic Confession (col. 1):

only.[10] The Father hath never been without His Son, or without His Holy Ghost. For they are all three coeternal and coessential. There is neither first nor last; for they are all three one, in truth, in power, in goodness, and in mercy.

[1] Isa. 43:10
[2] 1 John 5:7; Heb. 1:3
[3] Matt. 28:19
[4] 1 Cor. 8:6; Col. 1:16
[5] John 1:1-2; Rev. 19:13; Prov. 8:12
[6] Prov. 8:12,22
[7] Col. 1:15; Heb. 1:3
[8] Matt. 12:28
[9] John 15:26; Gal. 4:6
[10] Phil. 2:6-7; Gal. 4:4; John 1:14

Second Helvetic Confession (col. 3):

sole by itself: as if the Son and Holy Spirit were the affections and proprieties of one God the Father — as the Monarchists, the Novatians, Praxeas, the Patripassians, Sabellius, Samosatenus, Aëtius, Macedonius, the Anthropomorphites, Arius, and such like, have thought.

[1] Lest any man should slander us, as though we did make the persons all existing together, but not all of the same essence, or else did make a God of divers natures joined together in one, you must understand this joining together so as that all the persons (though distinct one from the other in properties) be yet but one and the same whole Godhead, or so that all and every of the persons have the whole and absolute Godhead.

Belgic Confession (cont.)

Article 9

The Proof of the Foregoing Article of the Trinity of Persons in One God

All this we know, as well from the testimonies of Holy Writ as from their operations, and chiefly by those we feel in ourselves. The testimonies of the Holy Scriptures, that teach us to believe this Holy Trinity, are written in many places of the Old Testament, which are not so necessary to enumerate as to choose them out with discretion and judgment. In Genesis 1:26, 27, God saith: *Let us make man in our image, after our likeness, etc.*[1] *So God created man in His own image, male and female created He them.* And Genesis 3:22: *Behold, the man is become as one of us.*[2] From this saying, *Let us make man in our image,* it appears that there are more persons than one in the Godhead; and when He saith *God created,* He signifies the unity. It is true He doth not say how many persons there are, but that which appears to us somewhat obscure in the Old Testament is very plain in the New.

For when our Lord was baptized in Jordan,[3] the voice of the Father was heard, saying, *This is My beloved Son:* the Son was seen in the water, and the Holy Ghost appeared in the shape of a dove. This form is also instituted by Christ in the baptism of all believers. *Baptize all nations, in the name of the Father and of the Son, and of the Holy Ghost.*[4] In the gospel of Luke the angel Gabriel thus addressed Mary, the mother of our Lord: *The Holy Ghost shall come upon thee, and the power of the Highest shall overshadow thee, therefore also that holy thing which shall be born of thee shall be called the Son of God.*[5] Likewise, *The grace of our Lord Jesus Christ, and the love of God, and the communion of the Holy Ghost be with you.*[6] And, *There are three that bear record in heaven, the Father, the Word, and the Holy Ghost, and these three are one.*[7] In all which places we are fully taught that there are three persons in one only divine essence. And although this doctrine far surpasses all human understanding, nevertheless we now believe it by means of the Word of God, but expect hereafter to enjoy the perfect knowledge and benefit thereof in heaven.[8]

Moreover we must observe the particular offices and operations of these three persons towards us. The Father is called our Creator by His power;[9] the Son is our Savior and Redeemer by His blood;[10] the Holy Ghost is our Sanctifier by His dwelling in our hearts.[11]

This doctrine of the Holy Trinity hath always been defended and maintained by the true Church, since the times of the apostles to this very day, against the Jews, Mohammedans, and some false Christians and heretics, as Marcion, Manes, Praxeas, Sabellius, Samosatenus, Arius, and such like, who have been justly condemned by the orthodox fathers.

Therefore, in this point, we do willingly receive the three creeds, namely, that of the Apostles, of Nice, and of Athanasius; likewise that which, conformable thereunto, is agreed upon by the ancient fathers.

[1] Gen. 1:26-27
[2] Gen. 3:22
[3] Matt. 3:16-17
[4] Matt. 28:19
[5] Luke 1:35
[6] 2 Cor. 13:13
[7] 1 John 5:7
[8] Ps. 45:8; Isa. 61:1
[9] Eccl. 12:3; Mal. 2:10; 1 Pet. 1:2
[10] 1 Pet. 1:2; 1 John 1:7; 4:14
[11] 1 Cor. 6:11; 1 Pet. 1:2; Gal. 4:6; Titus 3:5; Rom. 8:9; John 14:16

Westminster Confession of Faith (1647)	Westminster Shorter Catechism (1647)	Westminster Larger Catechism (1648)

Belgic Confession (1561)	Heidelberg Catechism (1563)	Second Helvetic Confession (1566)	Canons of Dort (1619)

The Godhead of the Son

Article 10

Jesus Christ is True and Eternal God

We believe that Jesus Christ, according to His divine nature, is the only begotten Son of God,[1] begotten from eternity,[2] not made nor created (for then He would be a creature), but coessential[3] and coeternal[4] with the Father, *the express image of His person, and the brightness of His glory,*[5] equal unto Him in all things.[6] He is the Son of God, not only from the time that He assumed our nature, but from all eternity,[7] as these testimonies, when compared together, teach us. Moses saith that *God created the world;*[8] and John saith that *all things were made by that Word,* which he calleth God.[9] And the apostle saith that *God made the worlds by His Son;*[10] likewise, that *God created all things by Jesus Christ.*[11] Therefore it must needs follow that He who is called God, the Word, the Son, and Jesus Christ did exist at that time when all things were created by Him.[12] Therefore the prophet Micah saith: *His goings forth have been from of old, from everlasting.*[13] And the apostle: *He hath neither beginning of days nor end of life.*[14] He therefore is that true, eternal, and almighty God, whom we invoke, worship, and serve.

[1] John 1:18, 49

Q. 17: Why must He in one person be also very God?

A.: That He might by the power of His Godhead sustain in His human nature the burden of God's wrath;[1] and might obtain for, and restore to us, righteousness and life.[2]

[1] 1 Pet. 3:18; Acts 2:24; Isa. 53:8
[2] 1 John 1:2; Jer. 23:6; 2 Tim. 1:10; John 6:51

Q. 18: Who then is that Mediator, who is in one person both very God, and a real righteous man?

A.: Our Lord Jesus Christ,[1] "who of God is made unto us wisdom, and righteousness, and sanctification, and redemption."[2]

[1] Matt. 1:23; 1 Tim. 3:16; Luke 2:11
[2] 1 Cor. 1:30

Q. 33: Why is Christ called the only begotten Son of God, since we are also the children of God?

A.: Because Christ alone is the eternal and natural Son of God;[1] but we are children adopted of God, by grace, for His sake.[2]

[1] John 1:1; Heb. 1:2
[2] Rom. 8:15-17; Eph. 1:5-6

XI. Of Jesus Christ, Being True God and Man, and the Only Savior of the World

1. Moreover, we believe and teach that the Son of God, our Lord Jesus Christ, was from all eternity predestinated and foreordained of the Father to be the Savior of the world. And we believe that He was begotten, not only then, when He took flesh of the Virgin Mary, nor yet a little before the foundations of the world were laid; but before all eternity, and that of the Father after an unspeakable manner. For Isaiah says (53:8), "who shall declare His generation?" And Micah says (5:2), "whose goings forth have been from of old, from everlasting." And John says (1:1), "In the beginning was the Word, and the Word was with God, and the Word was God," etc.

2. Therefore the Son is coequal and consubstantial with the Father, as touching His divinity: true God, not by name only, or by adoption, or by special favor, but in substance and nature (Phil. 2:6). Even as the apostle says elsewhere, "This is the true God, and eternal life" (1 John 5:20). Paul also says, "whom He hath appointed heir of all things, by whom also He made the worlds; who being the brightness of His glory, and the express image of His person, and upholding all things by the word of His power" (Heb. 1:2-3). Likewise, in the gospel, the Lord Himself says, "And now, O Father, glorify Thou Me with Thine own self with the glory which I had with Thee before the world was" (John 17:5). Also elsewhere it is written in the gospel, "Therefore the Jews sought the more to kill Him, because He not only had broken the sabbath, but said also that God was His Father, making Himself equal with God" (John 5:18).

3. We therefore do abhor the blasphemous doctrine of Arius, and all the Arians, uttered against the Son of God; and especially the blasphemies of Michael Servetus, the Spaniard, and of his complices, which Satan through them has, as it were, drawn out of hell, and most boldly and impiously spread abroad throughout the world against the Son of God.

Head II

Article 4

This death derives its infinite value and dignity from these considerations because the person who submitted to it was not only really man and perfectly holy, but also the only begotten Son of God, of the same eternal and infinite essence with the Father and the Holy Spirit, which qualifications were necessary to constitute Him a Savior for us; and because it was attended with a sense of the wrath and curse of God due to us for sin.

Westminster Confession of Faith (1647)	Westminster Shorter Catechism (1647)	Westminster Larger Catechism (1648)

VIII. Of Christ the Mediator

2. The Son of God, the second person of the Trinity, being very and eternal God, of one substance and equal with the Father, did, when the fullness of time was come, take upon Him man's nature,[1] with all the essential properties, and common infirmities thereof, yet without sin;[2] being conceived by the power of the Holy Ghost, in the womb of the Virgin Mary, of her substance.[3] So that two whole, perfect, and distinct natures, the Godhead and the manhood, were inseparably joined together in one person, without conversion, composition, or confusion.[4] Which person is very God, and very man, yet one Christ, the only Mediator between God and man.[5]

[1] John 1:1, 14; 1 John 5:20; Phil. 2:6; Gal. 4:4
[2] Heb. 2:14, 16-17; Heb. 4:15
[3] Luke 1:27, 31, 35; Gal. 4:4
[4] Luke 1:35; Col. 2:9; Rom 9:5; 1 Pet. 3:18; 1 Tim. 3:16
[5] Rom. 1:3-4; 1 Tim. 2:5

Q. 21: Who is the Redeemer of God's elect?
A.: The only Redeemer of God's elect is the Lord Jesus Christ,[1] who, being the eternal Son of God, became man,[2] and so was, and continueth to be, God and man in two distinct natures, and one person, for ever.[3]

[1] 1 Tim. 2:5-6
[2] John 1:14; Gal. 4:4
[3] Rom. 9:5; Luke 1:35; Col. 2:9; Heb. 7:24-25

Q. 11: How doth it appear that the Son and the Holy Ghost are God equal with the Father?
A.: The Scriptures manifest that the Son and the Holy Ghost are God equal with the Father, ascribing unto them such names,[1] attributes,[2] works,[3] and worship,[4] as are proper to God only.

[1] Isa. 6:3, 5, 8 compared with John 12:41; Acts 28:25; 1 John 5:20; Acts 5:3-4
[2] John 1:1; Isa. 9:6; John 2:24-25; 1 Cor. 2:10-11
[3] Col. 1:16; Gen. 1:2
[4] Matt. 28:19; 2 Cor. 13:14

Q. 36: Who is the Mediator of the covenant of grace?
A.: The only Mediator of the covenant of grace is the Lord Jesus Christ,[1] who, being the eternal Son of God, of one substance and equal with the Father,[2] in the fulness of time became man,[3] and so was and continues to be God and man, in two entire distinct natures, and one person, for ever.[4]

[1] 1 Tim. 2:5
[2] John 1:1, 14; 10:30; Phil. 2:6
[3] Gal. 4:4
[4] Luke 1:35; Rom. 9:5; Col. 2:9; Heb. 7:24-25

Q. 38: Why was it requisite that the Mediator should be God?
A.: It was requisite that the Mediator should be God, that He might sustain and keep the human nature from sinking under the infinite wrath of God, and the power of death;[1] give worth and efficacy to His sufferings, obedience, and intercession;[2] and to satisfy God's justice,[3] procure His favor,[4] purchase a peculiar people,[5] give His Spirit to them,[6] conquer all their enemies,[7] and bring them to everlasting salvation.[8]

[1] Acts 2:24-25; Rom. 1:4; 4:25; Heb. 9:14
[2] Acts 20:28; Heb. 9:14; 7:25-28
[3] Rom. 3:24-26
[4] Eph. 1:6; Matt. 3:17
[5] Titus 2:13-14
[6] Gal. 4:6
[7] Luke 1:68-69, 71, 74
[8] Heb. 5:8-9; 9:11-15

Q. 40: Why was it requisite that the Mediator should be God and man in one person?
A: It was requisite that the Mediator, who was to reconcile God and man, should Himself be both God and man, and this in one person, that the proper works of each nature might be

Belgic Confession (1561)	Heidelberg Catechism (1563)	Second Helvetic Confession (1566)	Canons of Dort (1619)
[2] John 1:14; Col. 1:15 [3] John 10:30; Phil. 2:6 [4] John 1:2; 17:5; Rev. 1:8 [5] Heb. 1:3 [6] Phil. 2:6 [7] John 8:23, 58; 9:35-37; Acts 8:37; Rom. 9:5 [8] Gen. 1:1 [9] John 1:3 [10] Heb. 1:2 [11] Col. 1:16 [12] Col. 1:16 [13] Micah 5:2 [14] Heb. 7:3			

The Godhead of the Holy Spirit

Belgic Confession (1561)	Heidelberg Catechism (1563)	Second Helvetic Confession (1566)	Canons of Dort (1619)
Article 11 **The Holy Ghost is True and Eternal God** We believe and confess also that the Holy Ghost from eternity proceeds from the Father[1] and Son;[2] and therefore is neither made, created, nor begotten, but only proceedeth from both; who in order is the third person of the Holy Trinity; of one and the same essence, majesty, and glory with the Father and the Son; and therefore is the true and eternal God, as the Holy Scriptures teach us.[3] --- [1] Ps. 33:6,17; John 14:16 [2] Gal. 4:6; Rom. 8:9; John 15:26 [3] Gen. 1:2; Isa. 48:16; 61:1; Acts 5:3-4; 28:25; 1 Cor. 3:16; 6:19; Ps. 139:7	*Q. 53: What dost thou believe concerning the Holy Ghost?* A.: First, that He is true and coeternal God with the Father and the Son;[1] secondly, that He is also given me,[2] to make me by a true faith, partaker of Christ and all His benefits,[3] that He may comfort me[4] and abide with me for ever.[5] --- [1] Gen. 1:2; Isa. 48:16; 1 Cor. 3:16 [2] Matt. 28:19; 2 Cor. 1:22 [3] Gal. 3:14; 1 Pet. 1:2 [4] Acts 9:31 [5] John 14:16; 1 Pet. 4:14		

Westminster Confession of Faith (1647)	Westminster Shorter Catechism (1647)	Westminster Larger Catechism (1648)
		accepted of God for us,[1] and relied on by us, as the works of the whole person.[2] [1] Matt. 1:21, 23; 3:17; Heb. 9:14 [2] 1 Pet. 2:6
		Q. 11: How doth it appear that the Son and the Holy Ghost are God equal with the Father? A.: The Scriptures manifest that the Son and the Holy Ghost are God equal with the Father, ascribing unto them such names,[1] attributes,[2] works,[3] and worship,[4] as are proper to God only. [1] Isa. 6:3, 5, 8 compared with John 12:41; Acts 28:25; 1 John 5:20; Acts 5:3-4 [2] John 1:1; Isa. 9:6; John 2:24-25; 1 Cor. 2:10:11 [3] Col. 1:16; Gen. 1:2 [4] Matt. 28:19; 2 Cor. 13:14

Belgic Confession (1561)	Heidelberg Catechism (1563)	Second Helvetic Confession (1566)	Canons of Dort (1619)

God's Decrees and Predestination

Belgic Confession (1561)

Article 16

Eternal Election

We believe that all the posterity of Adam, being thus fallen into perdition and ruin by the sin of our first parents, God then did manifest Himself such as He is; that is to say, merciful and just:[1] merciful, since He delivers and preserves from this perdition all whom He, in His eternal and unchangeable counsel, of mere goodness hath elected in Christ Jesus our Lord, without any respect to their works;[2] just, in leaving others in the fall and perdition wherein they have involved themselves.[3]

[1] Rom. 9:18, 22-23; 3:12
[2] Rom. 9:15-16; 11:32; Eph. 2:8-10; Ps. 100:3; 1 John 4:10; Deut. 32:8; 1 Sam. 12:22; Ps. 115:5; Mal. 1:2; 2 Tim. 1:9; Rom. 8:29; 9:11, 21; 11:5-6; Eph. 1:4; Titus 3:4-5; Acts 2:47; 13:48; 2 Tim. 2:19-20; 1 Pet. 1:2; John 6:27; 15:16; 17:9
[3] Rom. 9:17-18; 2 Tim. 2:20

Heidelberg Catechism (1563)

Q. 54: What believest thou concerning the "holy catholic Church" of Christ?

A.: That the Son of God[1] from the beginning to the end of the world,[2] gathers,[3] defends, and preserves to Himself[4] by His Spirit and Word,[5] out of the whole human race,[6] a Church chosen to everlasting life,[7] agreeing in true faith; and that I am and for ever shall remain, a living member thereof.[8]

[1] John 10:11
[2] Gen. 26:4
[3] Rom. 9:24; Eph. 1:10
[4] John 10:16
[5] Isa. 59:21
[6] Deut. 10:14-15
[7] Acts 13:48
[8] 1 Cor. 1:8-9; Rom. 8:35

Second Helvetic Confession (1566)

X. Of the Predestination of God and the Election of the Saints

1. God has from the beginning freely, and of His mere grace, without any respect of men, predestinated or elected the saints, whom He will save in Christ, according to the saying of the apostle, "According as He hath chosen us in Him before the foundation of the world" (Eph. 1:4); and again, "Who hath saved us, and called us with an holy calling, not according to our works, but according to His own purpose and grace, which was given us in Christ Jesus, before the world began, but is now made manifest by the appearing of our Saviour Jesus Christ" (2 Tim 1:9-10).

2. Therefore, though not for any merit of ours, yet not without a means, but in Christ, and for Christ, did God choose us; and they who are now ingrafted into Christ by faith, the same also were elected. But such as are without Christ were rejected, according to the saying of the apostle, "Examine yourselves, whether ye be in the faith; prove your own selves. Know ye not your own selves, how that Jesus Christ is in you, except ye be reprobates?" (2 Cor. 13:5).

3. To conclude, the saints are chosen in Christ by God unto a sure end, which end the apostle declares when he says, "According as He hath chosen us in Him before the foundation of the world, that we should be holy and without blame before Him in love: having predestinated us unto the adoption of children by Jesus Christ to Himself, according to the good pleasure of His will" (Eph. 1:4-5).

4. And although God knows who are His, and now and then mention is made of the small number of the elect, yet we must hope well of all, and not rashly judge any man to be a reprobate: for Paul says to the Philippians, "I thank my God upon every remembrance of you," (now he speaks of the whole Church of the Philippians), "always in every prayer of mine for you all making request with joy, for your fellowship in the gospel from the first day until now; being confident of this very thing, that He which hath begun a good work in you will perform it until the day of Jesus Christ: even as it is meet for me to think this of you all" (Phil. 1:3-7).

5. And when the Lord was asked whether there were few that should be saved, He does not an-

Canons of Dort (1619)

Head I

Article 6

That some receive the gift of faith from God and others do not receive it proceeds from God's eternal decree, for "known unto God are all His works from the beginning of the world" (Acts 15:18). "Who worketh all things after the counsel of His own will" (Eph. 1:11). According to which decree, He graciously softens the hearts of the elect, however obstinate, and inclines them to believe, while He leaves the non-elect in His just judgment to their own wickedness and obduracy. And herein is especially displayed the profound, the merciful, and at the same time the righteous discrimination between men, equally involved in ruin; or that decree of election and reprobation revealed in the Word of God, which though men of perverse, impure and unstable minds wrest to their own destruction, yet to holy and pious souls affords unspeakable consolation.

Article 7

Election is the unchangeable purpose of God, whereby, before the foundation of the world, He hath out of mere grace, according to the sovereign good pleasure of His own will, chosen, from the whole human race,

Westminster Confession of Faith (1647)	Westminster Shorter Catechism (1647)	Westminster Larger Catechism (1648)

III. Of God's Eternal Decree

1. God from all eternity, did, by the most wise and holy counsel of His own will, freely, and unchangeably ordain whatsoever comes to pass:[1] yet so, as thereby neither is God the author of sin,[2] nor is violence offered to the will of the creatures; nor is the liberty or contingency of second causes taken away, but rather established.[3]

[1] Eph. 1:11; Rom. 11:33; Heb. 6:17; Rom. 9:15, 18
[2] James 1:13, 17; 1 John 1:5
[3] Acts 2:23; Matt. 17:12; Acts 4:27-28; John 19:11; Prov. 16:33

2. Although God knows whatsoever may or can come to pass upon all supposed conditions,[1] yet hath He not decreed any thing because He foresaw it as future, or as that which would come to pass upon such conditions.[2]

[1] Acts 15:18; 1 Sam. 23:11-12; Matt. 11:21, 23
[2] Rom. 9:11, 13, 16, 18

3. By the decree of God, for the manifestation of His glory, some men and angels are predestinated unto everlasting life;[1] and others foreordained to everlasting death.[2]

[1] 1 Tim. 5:21; Matt. 25:41
[2] Rom. 9:22-23; Eph. 1:5-6; Prov. 16:4

4. These angels and men, thus predestinated, and foreordained, are particularly and unchangeably designed, and their number so certain and definite, that it cannot be either increased or diminished.[1]

[1] 2 Tim. 2:19; John 13:18

5. Those of mankind that are predestinated unto life, God, before the foundation of the world was laid, according to His eternal and immutable purpose, and the secret counsel and good pleasure of His will, hath chosen, in Christ, unto everlasting glory,[1] out of His mere free grace and love, without any foresight of faith, or good works, or perseverance in either of them, or any other thing in the creature, as conditions, or causes moving Him thereunto:[2] and all to the praise of His glorious grace.[3]

[1] Eph. 1:4, 9, 11; Rom. 8:30; 2 Tim. 1:9; 1 Thes. 5:9
[2] Rom. 9:11, 13, 16; Eph. 1:4, 9
[3] Eph. 1:6, 12

6. As God hath appointed the elect unto glory,

Q. 7: What are the decrees of God?

A.: The decrees of God are, His eternal purpose, according to the counsel of His will, whereby, for His own glory, He hath foreordained whatsoever comes to pass.[1]

[1] Eph. 1:4, 11; Rom. 9:22-23

Q. 8: How doth God execute His decrees?

A.: God executeth His decrees in the works of creation and providence.

Q. 12: What are the decrees of God?

A.: God's decrees are the wise, free, and holy acts of the counsel of His will,[1] whereby, from all eternity, He hath, for His own glory, unchangeably foreordained whatsoever comes to pass in time,[2] especially concerning angels and men.

[1] Eph. 1:11; Rom. 11:33; 9:14-15, 18
[2] Eph. 1:4, 11; Rom. 9:22-23; Ps. 33:11

Q. 13: What hath God especially decreed concerning angels and men?

A.: God, by an eternal and immutable decree, out of His mere love, for the praise of His glorious grace, to be manifested in due time, hath elected some angels to glory;[1] and in Christ hath chosen some men to eternal life, and the means thereof:[2] and also, according to His sovereign power, and the unsearchable counsel of His own will, (whereby He extendeth or withholdeth favour as He pleaseth,) hath passed by and foreordained the rest to dishonour and wrath, to be for their sin inflicted, to the praise of the glory of His justice.[3]

[1] 1 Tim. 5:21
[2] Eph. 1:4-6; 2 Thes. 2:13-14
[3] Rom. 9:17-18, 21-22; Matt. 11:25-26; 2 Tim. 2:20; Jude 4; 1 Pet. 2:8

Q. 14: How doth God execute His decrees?

A.: God executeth His decrees in the works of creation and providence, according to His infallible foreknowledge, and the free and immutable counsel of His own will.[1]

[1] Eph. 1:11

Belgic Confession (1561)	Heidelberg Catechism (1563)	Second Helvetic Confession (1566)	Canons of Dort (1619)
		swer and tell them that few or many should be saved or damned, but rather He exhorts every man to "strive to enter in at the strait gate" (Luke 13:24): as if He should say, It is not for you rashly to inquire of these matters, but rather to endeavor that you may enter into heaven by the strait way. 6. Wherefore we do not allow of the wicked speeches of some who say, Few are chosen, and seeing I know not whether I am in the number of these few, I will not defraud my nature of her desires. Others there are who say, If I be predestinated and chosen of God, nothing can hinder me from salvation, which is already certainly appointed for me, whatsoever I do at any time; but if I be in the number of the reprobate, no faith or repentance will help me, seeing the decree of God can not be changed: therefore all teachings and admonitions are to no purpose. Now, against these men the saying of the apostle makes much, "And the servant of the Lord must not strive; but be gentle unto all men, apt to teach, patient, in meekness instructing those that oppose themselves; if God peradventure will give them repentance to the acknowledging of the truth; and that they may recover themselves out of the snare of the devil, who are taken captive by him at his will" (2 Tim. 2:24-26). 7. Besides, Augustine also teaches, that both the grace of free election and predestination, and also wholesome admonitions and doctrines, are to be preached (*Lib. de Bono Perseverantiae*, chap. 14). 8. We therefore condemn those who seek otherwhere than in Christ whether they be chosen from all eternity, and what God has decreed of them before all beginning. For men must hear the gospel preached, and believe it. If thou believest, and art in Christ, thou mayest undoubtedly hold that thou art elected. For the Father has revealed unto us in Christ His eternal sentence of predestination, as we even now showed out of the apostle, in 2 Tim. 1:9-10. This is therefore above all to be taught and well weighed, what great love of the Father toward us in Christ is revealed. We must hear what the Lord does daily preach unto us in His gospel: how He calls and says, "Come unto Me all ye that labor and are heavy laden, and I will give you rest" (Matt. 11:28); and, "God so loved the world, that He gave His only begotten Son, that whosoever believeth in Him should not perish, but have everlasting life" (John 3:16); also, "It is not the will of your Father in heaven, that one of these little ones should perish" (Matt. 18:14). 9. Let Christ, therefore, be our looking glass, in	which had fallen through their own fault from their primitive state of rectitude into sin and destruction, a certain number of persons to redemption in Christ, whom He from eternity appointed the Mediator and Head of the elect, and the foundation of salvation. This elect number, though by nature neither better nor more deserving than others, but with them involved in one common misery, God hath decreed to give to Christ, to be saved by Him, and effectually to call and draw them to His communion by His Word and Spirit, to bestow upon them true faith, justification and sanctification; and having powerfully preserved them in the fellowship of His Son, finally, to glorify them for the demonstration of His mercy and for the praise of His glorious grace, as it is written: "According as He hath chosen us in Him before the foundation of the world, that we should be holy and without blame before Him in love: having predestinated us unto the adoption of children by Jesus Christ to Himself, according to the good pleasure of His will, to the praise of the glory of His grace, wherein He hath made us accepted in the beloved" (Eph. 1:4-6). And elsewhere: "Whom He did predestinate, them He also called: and whom He called, them He also justified: and whom He justi-

Westminster Confession of Faith (1647)	Westminster Shorter Catechism (1647)	Westminster Larger Catechism (1648)

so hath He, by the eternal and most free purpose of His will, foreordained all the means thereunto.[1] Wherefore, they who are elected, being fallen in Adam, are redeemed by Christ,[2] are effectually called unto faith in Christ by His Spirit working in due season, are justified, adopted, sanctified,[3] and kept by His power, through faith, unto salvation.[4] Neither are any other redeemed by Christ, effectually called, justified, adopted, sanctified, and saved, but the elect only.[5]

[1] 1 Pet. 1:2; Eph. 1:4-5; 2:10; 2 Thes. 2:13
[2] 1 Thes. 5:9-10; Titus 2:14
[3] Rom. 8:30; Eph. 1:5; 2 Thes. 2:13
[4] 1 Pet. 1:5
[5] John 17:9; Rom. 8:28-39; John 6:64-65; 10:26; 8:47; 1 John 2:19

7. The rest of mankind God was pleased, according to the unsearchable counsel of His own will, whereby He extendeth or withholdeth mercy, as He pleaseth, for the glory of His sovereign power over His creatures, to pass by; and to ordain them to dishonour and wrath for their sin, to the praise of His glorious justice.[1]

[1] Matt. 11:25-26; Rom. 9:17-18, 21-22; 2 Tim. 2:19-20; Jude 4; 1 Pet. 2:8

8. The doctrine of this high mystery of predestination is to be handled with special prudence and care,[1] that men, attending the will of God revealed in His Word, and yielding obedience thereunto, may, from the certainty of their effectual vocation, be assured of their eternal election.[2] So shall this doctrine afford matter of praise, reverence, and admiration of God;[3] and of humility, diligence, and abundant consolation to all that sincerely obey the gospel.[4]

[1] Rom. 9:20; 11:33; Deut. 29:29
[2] 2 Pet. 1:10
[3] Eph. 1:6; Rom. 11:32
[4] Rom. 11:5-6, 20; 2 Pet. 1:10; Rom. 8:33; Luke 10:20

Belgic Confession (1561)	Heidelberg Catechism (1563)	Second Helvetic Confession (1566)	Canons of Dort (1619)
		whom we may behold our predestination. We shall have a most evident and sure testimony that we are written in the Book of Life if we communicate with Christ, and He be ours, and we be His, by a true faith. Let this comfort us in the temptation touching predestination, than which there is none more dangerous: that the promises of God are general to the faithful; in that he says, "Ask, and it shall be given you;... every one that asketh receiveth" (Luke 11:9-10). And, to conclude, we pray, with the whole Church of God, "Our Father which art in heaven" (Matt. 6:9); and in baptism, we are ingrafted into the body of Christ, and we are fed in His Church, oftentimes, with His flesh and blood, unto everlasting life. Thereby, being strengthened, we are commanded to "work out your own salvation with fear and trembling," according to that precept of Paul, in Philippians 2:12.	fied, them He also glorified" (Rom. 8:30). *Article 8* There are not various decrees of election, but one and the same decree respecting all those who shall be saved, both under the Old and New Testament; since the Scripture declares the good pleasure, purpose and counsel of the divine will to be one, according to which He hath chosen us from eternity, both to grace and glory, to salvation and the way of salvation, which He hath ordained that we should walk therein.

Canons of Dort (cont.)

Article 9

This election was not founded upon foreseen faith, and the obedience of faith, holiness, or any other good quality or disposition in man, as the prerequisite, cause or condition on which it depended; but men are chosen to faith and to the obedience of faith, holiness, etc.; therefore election is the fountain of every saving good, from which proceeds faith, holiness, and the other gifts of salvation, and finally eternal life itself, as its fruits and effects, according to that of the apostle: "He hath chosen us [not because we were but] that we should be holy, and without blame, before Him in love" (Eph. 1:4).

Article 10

The good pleasure of God is the sole cause of this gracious election, which doth not consist herein, that out of all possible qualities and actions of men God has chosen some as a condition of salvation; but that He was pleased out of the common mass of sinners to adopt some certain persons as a peculiar people to Himself, as it is written, "For the children being not yet born, neither having done any good or evil," etc., it was said (namely to Rebecca): "The elder shall serve the younger. As it is written, Jacob have I loved, but Esau have I hated" (Rom. 9:11-13). "And as many as were ordained to eternal life believed" (Acts 13:48).

Article 11

And as God Himself is most wise, unchangeable, omniscient and omnipotent, so the election made by Him can neither be interrupted nor changed, recalled or annulled; neither can the elect be cast away, nor their number diminished.

Article 12

The elect in due time, though in various degrees and in dif-

ferent measures, attain the assurance of this their eternal and unchangeable election, not by inquisitively prying into the secret and deep things of God, but by observing in themselves, with a spiritual joy and holy pleasure, the infallible fruits of election pointed out in the Word of God — such as a true faith in Christ, filial fear, a godly sorrow for sin, a hungering and thirsting after righteousness, etc.

Article 13

The sense and certainty of this election afford to the children of God additional matter for daily humiliation before Him, for adoring the depth of His mercies, for cleansing themselves, and rendering grateful returns of ardent love to Him, who first manifested so great love towards them. The consideration of this doctrine of election is so far from encouraging remissness in the observance of the divine commands or from sinking men in carnal security, that these, in the just judgment of God, are the usual effects of rash presumption or of idle and wanton trifling with the grace of election in those who refuse to walk in the ways of the elect.

Article 14

As the doctrine of divine election by the most wise counsel of God was declared by the prophets, by Christ Himself, and by the apostles, and is clearly revealed in the Scriptures, both of the Old and New Testament, so it is still to be published in due time and place in the Church of God, for which it was peculiarly designed, provided it be done with reverence, in the spirit of discretion and piety, for the glory of God's most holy Name, and for enlivening and comforting His people, without vainly attempting to investigate the secret ways of the Most High. "For I have not shunned to declare unto you all the counsel of God" (Acts 20:27); "O the depth of the riches both of the wis-

Westminster Confession of Faith (1647)	Westminster Shorter Catechism (1647)	Westminster Larger Catechism (1648)

dom and knowledge of God! how unsearchable are His judgments, and His ways past finding out! For who hath known the mind of the Lord? or who hath been His counsellor?" (Rom. 11:33-34); "For I say, through the grace given unto me, to every man that is among you, not to think of himself more highly than he ought to think; but to think soberly, according as God hath dealt to every man the measure of faith" (Rom. 12:3); "Wherein God, willing more abundantly to shew unto the heirs of promise the immutability of His counsel, confirmed it by an oath: that by two immutable things, in which it was impossible for God to lie, we might have a strong consolation, who have fled for refuge to lay hold upon the hope set before us" (Heb. 6:17-18).

Article 15

What peculiarly tends to illustrate and recommend to us the eternal and unmerited grace of election, is the express testimony of sacred Scripture that not all, but some only are elected, while others are passed by in the eternal decree; whom God, out of His sovereign, most just, irreprehensible and unchangeable good pleasure, hath decreed to leave in the common misery into which they have wilfully plunged themselves, and not to bestow upon them saving faith and the grace of conversion; but permitting them in His just judgment to follow their own ways, at last for the declaration of His justice, to condemn and perish them forever, not only on account of their unbelief, but also for all their other sins. And this is the decree of reprobation which by no means makes God the author of sin (the very thought of which is blasphemy), but declares Him to be an awful, irreprehensible, and righteous Judge and avenger thereof.

Article 16

Those who do not yet experience a lively faith in Christ, an assured confidence of soul, peace of conscience, an earnest endeavor after filial obedience, and glorying in God through Christ, efficaciously wrought in them, and do nevertheless persist in the use of the means which God hath appointed for working these graces in us, ought not to be alarmed at the mention of reprobation, nor to rank themselves among the reprobate, but diligently to persevere in the use of means, and with ardent desires devoutly and humbly to wait for a season of richer grace. Much less cause have they to be terrified by the doctrine of reprobation, who, though they seriously desire to be turned to God, to please Him only, and to be delivered from the body of death, cannot yet reach that measure of holiness and faith to which they aspire; since a merciful God has promised that He will not quench the smoking flax nor break the bruised reed. But this doctrine is justly terrible to those, who, regardless of God and of the Savior Jesus Christ, have wholly given themselves up to the cares of the world and the pleasures of the flesh, so long as they are not seriously converted to God.

Article 17

Since we are to judge of the will of God from His Word which testifies that the children of believers are holy, not by nature, but in virtue of the covenant of grace, in which they, together with the parents, are comprehended, godly parents have no reason to doubt of the election and salvation of their children whom it pleaseth God to call out of this life in their infancy.

Article 18

To those who murmur at the free grace of election and just severity of reprobation, we answer with the apostle: "Nay but, O man, who art thou that repliest against God?" (Rom. 9:20), and quote the language of our Savior: "Is it not lawful for Me to do what I will with Mine own?" (Matt. 20:15). And therefore with holy adoration of these mysteries, we exclaim in the words of the apostle: "O the depth of the riches both of the wisdom and knowledge of God! how unsearchable are His judgments, and His ways past finding out! For who hath known the mind of the Lord? or who hath been His counsellor? Or who hath first given to Him, and it shall be recompensed unto him again? For of Him, and through Him, and to Him, are all things: to whom be glory for ever. Amen" (Rom. 11:33-36).

Head II

Article 8

For this was the sovereign counsel, and most gracious will and purpose of God the Father, that the quickening and saving efficacy of the most precious death of His Son should extend to all the elect, for bestowing upon them alone the gift of justifying faith, thereby to bring them infallibly to salvation: that is, it was the will of God, that Christ by the blood of the cross, whereby He confirmed the new covenant, should effectually redeem out of every people, tribe, nation, and language, all those, and those only, who were from eternity chosen to salvation and given to Him by the Father; that He should confer upon them faith, which together with all the other saving gifts of the Holy Spirit, He purchased for them by His death; should purge them from all sin, both original and actual, whether committed before or after believing; and having faithfully preserved them even to the end, should at last bring them free from every spot and blemish to the enjoyment of glory in His own presence forever.

Article 9

This purpose proceeding from everlasting love towards the elect has from the beginning of the world to this day been powerfully accomplished, and will henceforward still continue to be accomplished, notwithstanding all the ineffectual opposition of the gates of hell, so that the elect in due time may be gathered together into one, and that there never may be wanting a Church composed of believers, the foundation of which is laid in the blood of Christ, which may steadfastly love and faithfully serve Him as their Savior, who as a bridegroom for his bride, laid down His life for them upon the cross, and which may celebrate His praises here and through all eternity.

Belgic Confession (1561)	Heidelberg Catechism (1563)	Second Helvetic Confession (1566)	Canons of Dort (1619)

Canons of Dort (cont.)

The true doctrine concerning election and rejection having been explained, the Synod **rejects** the errors of those who teach:

Rejection 1

That the will of God to save those who would believe and would persevere in faith and in the obedience of faith, is the whole and entire decree of election unto salvation, and that nothing else concerning this decree has been revealed in God's Word.

For these deceive the simple and plainly contradict the Scriptures which declare that God will not only save those who will believe, but that He has also from eternity chosen certain particular persons to whom above others He in time will grant both faith in Christ and perseverance, as it is written: "I have manifested Thy Name unto the men which Thou gavest Me out of the world" (John 17:6). "And as many as were ordained to eternal life believed" (Acts 13:48). And: "According as He hath chosen us in Him before the foundation of the world, that we should be holy and without blame before Him in love" (Eph. 1:4).

Rejection 2

That there are various kinds of election of God unto eternal life: the one general and indefinite, the other particular and definite; and that the latter in turn is either incomplete, revocable, nondecisive and conditional, or complete, irrevocable, decisive and absolute. Likewise: that there is one election unto faith and another unto salvation, so that election can be unto justifying faith without being a decisive election unto salvation. For this is a fancy of men's minds, invented regardless of the Scriptures, whereby the doctrine of election is corrupted, and this golden chain of our salvation is broken: "Moreover whom He did predestinate, them He also called: and whom He called, them He also justified: and whom He justified, them He also glorified" (Rom. 8:30).

Rejection 3

That the good pleasure and purpose of God, of which Scripture makes mention in the doctrine of election, does not consist in this, that God chose certain persons rather than others, but in this, that He chose out of all possible conditions (among which are also the works of the law), or out of the whole order of things, the act of faith which from its very nature is undeserving, as well as its incomplete obedience, as a condition of salvation, and that He would graciously consider this in itself as a complete obedience and count it worthy of the reward of eternal life. For by this injurious error the pleasure of God and the merits of Christ are made of none effect, and men are drawn away by useless questions from the truth of gracious justification and from the simplicity of Scripture, and this declaration of the apostle is charged as untrue: "Who hath saved us, and called us with an holy calling, not according to our works, but according to His own purpose and grace, which was given us in Christ Jesus before the world began" (2 Tim. 1:9).

Rejection 4

That in the election unto faith this condition is beforehand demanded, namely, that man should use the light of nature aright, be pious, humble, meek, and fit for eternal life, as if on these things election were in any way dependent. For this savors of the teaching of Pelagius, and is opposed to the doctrine of the apostle, when he writes: "Among whom also we all had our conversation in times past in the lusts of our flesh, fulfilling the desires of the flesh and of the mind; and were by nature the children of wrath, even as others. But God, who is rich in mercy, for His great love wherewith He loved us, even when we were dead in sins, hath quickened us together with Christ, (by grace ye are saved;) and hath raised us up together, and made us sit together in heavenly places in Christ Jesus: that in the ages to come He might show the exceeding riches of His grace in His kindness toward us through Christ Jesus. For by grace are ye saved through faith; and that not of yourselves: it is the gift of God: not of works, lest any man should boast" (Eph. 2:3-9).

Rejection 5

That the incomplete and nondecisive election of particular persons to salvation occurred because of a foreseen faith, conversion, holiness, godliness, which either began or continued for some time; but that the complete and decisive election occurred because of foreseen perseverance unto the end in faith, conversion, holiness and godliness; and that this is the gracious and evangelical worthiness for the sake of which he who is chosen is more worthy than he who is not chosen; and that therefore faith, the obedience of faith, holiness, godliness and perseverance are not fruits of the unchangeable election unto glory, but are conditions, which, being required beforehand, were foreseen as being met by those who will be fully elected, and are causes without which the unchangeable election to glory does not occur.

This is repugnant to the entire Scripture which constantly inculcates this and similar declarations: Election is not out of works, but of Him that calleth. "That the purpose of God according to election might stand, not of works, but of Him that calleth" (Rom. 9:11). "And as many as were ordained to eternal life believed" (Acts 13:48). "He hath chosen us in Him before the foundation of the world, that we should be holy" (Eph. 1:4). "Ye have not chosen Me, but I have chosen you" (John 15:16). "But if it be of works, then is it no more grace" (Rom. 11:6). "Herein is love, not that we loved God, but that He loved us, and sent His Son" (1 John 4:10).

Rejection 6

That not every election unto salvation is unchangeable, but that some of the elect, any decree of God notwithstanding, can yet perish and do indeed perish. By which gross error they make God to be changeable, and destroy the comfort which the godly obtain out of the firmness of their election, and contradict the Holy Scripture which teaches that the elect cannot be led astray: "Insomuch that, if it were possible, they shall deceive the very elect" (Matt. 24:24); that Christ

Westminster Confession of Faith (1647)	Westminster Shorter Catechism (1647)	Westminster Larger Catechism (1648)

does not lose those whom the Father gave Him: "And this is the Father's will which hath sent Me, that of all which He hath given Me I should lose nothing" (John 6:39); and that God hath also glorified those whom He foreordained, called and justified: "Moreover whom He did predestinate, them He also called: and whom He called, them He also justified: and whom He justified, them He also glorified" (Rom. 8:30).

Rejection 7

That there is in this life no fruit and no consciousness of the unchangeable election to glory, nor any certainty, except that which depends on a changeable and uncertain condition. For not only is it absurd to speak of an uncertain certainty, but also contrary to the experience of the saints, who by virtue of the consciousness of their election rejoice with the apostle and praise this favor of God, Ephesians 1; who according to Christ's admonition rejoice with His disciples that their names are written in heaven, "but rather rejoice, because your names are written in heaven" (Luke 10:20); who also place the consciousness of their election over against the fiery darts of the devil, asking: "Who shall lay any thing to the charge of God's elect?" (Rom. 8:33).

Rejection 8

That God, simply by virtue of His righteous will, did not decide either to leave anyone in the fall of Adam and in the common state of sin and condemnation, or to pass anyone by in the communication of grace which is necessary for faith and conversion. For this is firmly decreed: "Therefore hath He mercy on whom He will have mercy, and whom He will He hardeneth" (Rom. 9:18). And also this: "It is given unto you to know the mysteries of the kingdom of heaven, but to them it is not given" (Matt. 13:11). Likewise: "I thank Thee, O Father, Lord of heaven and earth, because Thou hast hid these things from the wise and prudent, and hast revealed them unto babes. Even so, Father: for so it seemed good in Thy sight" (Matt. 11:25-26).

Rejection 9

That the reason why God sends the gospel to one people rather than to another is not merely and solely the good pleasure of God, but rather the fact that one people is better and worthier than another to whom the gospel is not communicated. For this Moses denies, addressing the people of Israel as follows: "Behold, the heaven and the heaven of heavens is the LORD's thy God, the earth also, with all that therein is. Only the LORD had a delight in thy fathers to love them, and He chose their seed after them, even you above all people, as it is this day" (Deut. 10:14-15). And Christ said: "Woe unto thee, Chorazin! woe unto thee, Bethsaida! for if the mighty works, which were done in you, had been done in Tyre and Sidon, they would have repented long ago in sackcloth and ashes" (Matt. 11:21).

The true doctrine (concerning redemption) having been explained, the Synod **rejects** the errors of those who teach:

Rejection 1

That God the Father has ordained His Son to the death of the cross without a certain and definite decree to save any, so that the necessity, profitableness and worth of what Christ merited by His death might have existed, and might remain in all its parts complete, perfect and intact, even if the merited redemption had never in fact been applied to any person. For this doctrine tends to the despising of the wisdom of the Father and of the merits of Jesus Christ, and is contrary to Scripture. For thus saith our Savior: "I lay down My life for the sheep, and I know them" (John 10:15, 27). And the prophet Isaiah saith concerning the Savior: "When thou shalt make His soul an offering for sin, He shall see His seed, He shall prolong his days, and the pleasure of the LORD shall prosper in his hand" (Isa. 53:10). Finally, this contradicts the article of faith according to which we believe the catholic Christian Church.

Rejection 7

That Christ neither could die, needed to die, nor did die for those whom God loved in the highest degree and elected to eternal life, and did not die for these, since these do not need the death of Christ. For they contradict the apostle, who declares: "the Son of God, who loved me, and gave Himself for me" (Gal. 2:20). Likewise: "Who shall lay any thing to the charge of God's elect? It is God that justifieth. Who is he that condemneth? It is Christ that died" (Rom. 8:33-34), namely, for them; and the Savior who says: "I lay down My life for the sheep" (John 10:15). And: "This is My commandment, That ye love one another, as I have loved you. Greater love hath no man than this, that a man lay down his life for his friends" (John 15:12-13).

The true doctrine (concerning perseverance) having been explained, the Synod **rejects** the errors of those who teach:

Rejection 1

That the perseverance of the true believers is not a fruit of election or a gift of God gained by the death of Christ, but a condition of the new covenant, which (as they declare) man before his decisive election and justification must fulfill through his free will. For the Holy Scripture testifies that this follows out of election, and is given the elect in virtue of the death, the resurrection and intercession of Christ: "but the election hath obtained it, and the rest were blinded" (Rom. 11:7). Likewise: "He that spared not His own Son, but delivered Him up for us all, how shall He not with Him also freely give us all things? Who shall lay any thing to the charge of God's elect? It is God that justifieth. Who is he that condemneth? It is Christ that died, yea rather, that is risen again, who is even at the right hand of God, who also maketh intercession for us. Who shall separate us from the love of Christ?" (Rom. 8:32-35).

Conclusion

And this is the perspicuous, simple, and ingenuous declara-

Belgic Confession (1561)	Heidelberg Catechism (1563)	Second Helvetic Confession (1566)	Canons of Dort (1619)

Canons of Dort (cont.)

tion of the orthodox doctrine respecting the five articles which have been controverted in the Belgic churches, and the rejection of the errors with which they have for some time been troubled. This doctrine the Synod judges to be drawn from the Word of God and to be agreeable to the confessions of the Reformed churches. Whence it clearly appears that some whom such conduct by no means became, have violated all truth, equity, and charity, in wishing to persuade the public: "That the doctrine of the Reformed churches concerning predestination, and the points annexed to it, by its own genius and necessary tendency, leads off the minds of men from all piety and religion; that it is an opiate administered by the flesh and the devil, and the stronghold of Satan, where he lies in wait for all; and from which he wounds multitudes, and mortally strikes through many with the darts both of despair and security; that it makes God the author of sin, unjust, tyrannical, hypocritical; that it is nothing more than interpolated Stoicism, Manicheism, Libertinism, Turcism; that it renders men carnally secure, since they are persuaded by it that nothing can hinder the salvation of the elect, let them live as they please; and therefore, that they may safely perpetrate every species of the most atrocious crimes; and that if the reprobate should even perform truly all the works of the saints, their obedience would not in the least contribute to their salvation; that the same doctrine teaches that God, by a mere arbitrary act of His will, without the least respect or view to any sin, has predestinated the greatest part of the world to eternal damnation; and has created them for this very purpose; that in the same manner in which the election is the fountain and the cause of faith and good works, reprobation is the cause of unbelief and impiety; that many children of the faithful are torn guiltless from their mothers' breasts and tyrannically plunged into hell; so that neither baptism nor the prayers of the Church at their baptism, can at all profit by them"; and many other things of the same kind which the Reformed

Churches not only do not acknowledge, but even detest with their whole soul. Wherefore, this Synod of Dort, in the name of the Lord, conjures as many as piously call upon the name of our Savior Jesus Christ, to judge of the faith of the Reformed churches not from the calumnies, which on every side are heaped upon it; nor from the private expressions of a few among ancient and modern teachers, often dishonestly quoted or corrupted and wrested to a meaning quite foreign to their intention; but from the public confessions of the churches themselves and from the declaration of the orthodox doctrine, confirmed by the unanimous consent of all and each of the members of the whole Synod. Moreover, the Synod warns calumniators themselves to consider the terrible judgment of God which awaits them for bearing false witness against the confessions of so many churches, for distressing the consciences of the weak, and for laboring to render suspect the society of the truly faithful. Finally, this Synod exhorts all their brethren in the gospel of Christ to conduct themselves piously and religiously in handling this doctrine, both in the universities and churches; to direct it, as well in discourse as in writing, to the glory of the divine Name, to holiness of life, and to the consolation of afflicted souls; to regulate, by the Scripture, according to the analogy of faith, not only their sentiments, but also their language; and to abstain from all those phrases which exceed the limits necessary to be observed in ascertaining the genuine sense of the holy Scriptures, and may furnish insolent sophists with a just pretext for violently assailing or even vilifying the doctrine of the Reformed churches.

May Jesus Christ, the Son of God, who, seated at the Father's right hand, gives gifts to men, sanctify us in the truth, bring to the truth those who err, shut the mouths of the calumniators of sound doctrine, and endue the faithful minister of His Word with the spirit of wisdom and discretion, that all their discourses may tend to the glory of God and the edification of those who hear them. Amen.

Creation

Article 12

The Creation

We believe that the Father, by the Word, that is, by His Son,[1] created of nothing the heaven, the earth, and all creatures, as it seemed good unto Him, giving unto every creature its being, shape, form, and several offices to serve its Creator; that

Q. 6: Did God then create man so wicked and perverse?

A.: By no means; but God created man good,[1] and after His own image, in true righteousness and holiness,[2] that he might rightly know God his Creator, heartily love Him and live with Him in eternal

VII. Of the Creation of all Things; of Angels, the Devil, and Man

1. This good and almighty God created all things, both visible and invisible, by His eternal Word, and preserves the same also by His eternal Spirit: as David witnesses, saying, "By the word of the LORD were the heavens made; and all the host of them by the breath of His mouth" (Ps. 33:6); and, as the Scripture says, "And God saw every thing that He had made, and behold, it was very good" (Gen. 1:31), and made for the use and profit of man.

Westminster Confession of Faith (1647)	Westminster Shorter Catechism (1647)	Westminster Larger Catechism (1648)

IV. Of Creation

1. It pleased God the Father, Son, and Holy Ghost,[1] for the manifestation of the glory of His eternal power, wisdom, and goodness,[2] in the beginning, to create, or make of nothing, the world, and all things therein whether visible or invisible, in the space of six days; and all very good.[3]

[1] Heb. 1:2; John 1:2-3; Gen. 1:2; Job 26:13; 33:4
[2] Rom. 1:20; Jer. 10:12; Ps. 104:24; 33:5-6
[3] Gen. 1; Heb. 11:3; Col. 1:16; Acts 17:24

Q. 9: What is the work of creation?

A.: The work of creation is, God's making all things of nothing, by the word of His power, in the space of six days, and all very good.[1]

[1] Gen. 1; Heb. 11:3

Q. 10: How did God create man?

A.: God created man male

Q. 15: What is the work of creation?

A.: The work of creation is that wherein God did in the beginning, by the word of His power, make of nothing the world, and all things therein, for Himself, within the space of six days, and all very good.[1]

[1] Gen. 1; Heb. 11:3; Prov. 16:4

Q. 16: How did God create angels?

A.: God created all the angels[1] spirits,[2] immortal,[3] holy,[4] excelling in knowledge,[5] mighty in

Belgic Confession (1561)	Heidelberg Catechism (1563)	Second Helvetic Confession (1566)	Canons of Dort (1619)

He doth also still uphold and govern them by His eternal providence and infinite power[2] for the service of mankind,[3] to the end that man may serve his God.[4]

He also created the angels good,[5] to be His messengers[6] and to serve His elect;[7] some of whom are fallen from that excellency, in which God created them, into everlasting perdition;[8] and the others have, by the grace of God,[9] remained steadfast and continued in their primitive state. The devils and evil spirits are so depraved that they are enemies of God and every good thing, to the utmost of their power,[10] as murderers watching to ruin the Church and every member thereof, and by their wicked stratagems to destroy all;[11] and are therefore, by their own wickedness, adjudged to eternal damnation, daily expecting their horrible torments.[12] Therefore we reject and abhor the error of the Sadducees, who deny the existence of spirits and angels;[13] and also that of the Manichees, who assert that the devils have their origin of themselves, and that they are wicked of their own nature, without having been corrupted.

[1] Gen. 1:1; Isa. 40:26; Heb. 3:4; Rev. 4:11; 1 Cor. 8:6; John 1:3; Col. 1:16
[2] Heb. 1:3; Ps. 104:10; Acts 17:25
[3] 1 Tim. 4:3-4; Gen. 1:29-30; 9:2-3; Ps. 104:14-15
[4] 1 Cor. 3:22; 6:20; Matt. 4:10
[5] Col. 1:16
[6] Ps. 103:20; 34:8; 148:2

happiness to glorify and praise Him.[3]

[1] Gen. 1:31
[2] Gen. 1:26-27; Col. 3:10
[3] Eph. 1:6; 1 Cor. 6:20

2. Now, we say, that all those things do proceed from one beginning: and therefore we detest the Manichees and the Marcionites, who did wickedly imagine two substances and natures, the one of good, the other of evil; and also two beginnings and two gods, one contrary to the other — a good and an evil.

3. Among all the creatures, the angels and men are most excellent. Touching angels, the Holy Scripture says, "who maketh His angels spirits, His ministers a flaming fire" (Ps. 104:4); also, "Are they not all ministering spirits, sent forth to minister for them who shall be heirs of salvation?" (Heb. 1:14).

4. And the Lord Jesus Himself testifies of the devil, saying, "He was a murderer from the beginning, and abode not in the truth, because there is no truth in him. When he speaketh a lie, he speaketh of his own: for he is a liar, and the father of lies" (John 8:44).

5. We teach, therefore, that some angels persisted in obedience, and were appointed unto the faithful service of God and men; and that others fell of their own accord, and ran headlong into destruction, and so became enemies to all good, and to all the faithful, etc.

6. Now, touching man, the Spirit says that in the beginning he was created according to the image and likeness of God (Gen. 1:27); that God placed him in Paradise, and made all things subject unto him; which David doth most nobly set forth in the 8th Psalm. Moreover, God gave unto him a wife, and blessed them.

7. We say, also, that man doth consist of two, and those divers substances in one person; of a soul immortal (as that which being separated from his body doth neither sleep nor die), and a body mortal, which, notwithstanding, at the last judgment shall be raised again from the dead, that from henceforth the whole man may continue forever in life or in death.

8. We condemn all those who mock at, or by subtle disputations call into doubt, the immortality of the soul, or say that the soul sleeps, or that it is a part of God. To be short, we condemn all opinions of all men whatsoever who think otherwise of the creation of angels, devils, and men than is delivered unto us by the Scriptures in the Apostolic Church of Christ.

Westminster Confession of Faith (1647)	Westminster Shorter Catechism (1647)	Westminster Larger Catechism (1648)
2. After God had made all other creatures, He created man, male and female,[1] with reasonable and immortal souls,[2] endued with knowledge, righteousness, and true holiness, after His own image;[3] having the law of God written in their hearts,[4] and power to fulfil it:[5] and yet under a possibility of transgressing, being left to the liberty of their own will, which was subject unto change.[6] Beside this law written in their hearts, they received a command, not to eat of the tree of the knowledge of good and evil;[7] which while they kept, they were happy in their communion with God, and had dominion over the creatures.[8]	and female, after His own image, in knowledge, righteousness, and holiness, with dominion over the creatures.[1]	power,[6] to execute His commandments, and to praise His name,[7] yet subject to change.[8]
[1] Gen. 1:27	[1] Gen. 1:26-28; Col. 3:10; Eph. 4:24	[1] Col. 1:16
[2] Gen. 2:7; Eccl. 12:7; Lk. 23:43; Matt. 10:28		[2] Ps. 104:4
[3] Gen. 1:26; Col. 3:10; Eph. 4:24		[3] Matt. 22:30
[4] Rom. 2:14-15		[4] Matt. 25:31
[5] Eccl. 7:29		[5] 2 Sam. 14:17; Matt. 24:36
[6] Gen. 3:6; Eccl. 7:29		[6] 2 Thes. 1:7
[7] Gen. 2:17; 3:8-11, 23		[7] Ps. 103:20-21
[8] Gen. 1:26, 28		[8] 2 Pet. 2:4

Q. 17: How did God create man?

A.: After God had made all other creatures, He created man male and female;[1] formed the body of the man of the dust of the ground,[2] and the woman of the rib of the man,[3] endued them with living, reasonable, and immortal souls;[4] made them after His own image,[5] in knowledge,[6] righteousness, and holiness;[7] having the law of God written in their hearts,[8] and power to fulfil it,[9] and dominion over the creatures;[10] yet subject to fall.[11]

[1] Gen. 1:27
[2] Gen. 2:7
[3] Gen. 2:22
[4] Gen. 2:7; Job 35:11; Eccl. 12:7; Matt. 10:28; Lk. 23:43
[5] Gen. 1:27
[6] Col. 3:10
[7] Eph. 4:24
[8] Rom. 2:14-15
[9] Eccl. 7:29
[10] Gen. 1:28
[11] Gen. 3:6; Eccl. 7:29

Belgic Confession (1561)	Heidelberg Catechism (1563)	Second Helvetic Confession (1566)	Canons of Dort (1619)
[7] Heb. 1:14; Ps. 34:8 [8] John 8:44; 2 Pet. 2:4; Luke 8:31; Jude 6 [9] Matt. 25:31 [10] 1 Pet. 5:8; Job 1:7 [11] Gen. 3:1; Matt. 13:25; 2 Cor. 2:11; 11:3,14 [12] Matt. 25:41; Luke 8:30-31 [13] Acts 23:8			

Providence

Article 13

Divine Providence

We believe that the same God, after He had created all things, did not forsake them, or give them up to fortune or chance, but that He rules and governs them according to His holy will,[1] so that nothing happens in this world without His appointment;[2] nevertheless, God neither is the author of, nor can be charged with, the sins which are committed. For His power and goodness are so great and incomprehensible, that He orders and executes His work in the most excellent and just manner, even then when devils and wicked men act unjustly.[3] And as to what He doth surpassing human understanding, we will not curiously inquire into it further than our capacity will admit of; but with the greatest humility and reverence adore the righteous judgments of God which are hid from us,[4] contenting ourselves that we are disciples of Christ, to learn only those things

Q. 26: What believest thou when thou sayest, "I believe in God the Father, Almighty, Maker of heaven and earth?"

A.: That the eternal Father of our Lord Jesus Christ (who of nothing made heaven and earth, with all that is in them;[1] who likewise upholds and governs the same by His eternal counsel and providence)[2] is for the sake of Christ His Son, my God and my Father; on whom I rely so entirely, that I have no doubt but He will provide me with all things necessary for soul and body;[3] and further, that He will make whatever evils He sends upon me, in this valley of tears, turn out to my advantage;[4] for He is able to do it, being Almighty God,[5] and willing, being a faithful Father.[6]

[1] Gen. 1 and 2; Ps. 33:6
[2] Ps. 115:3; Matt. 10:29; Heb. 1:3; John 5:17
[3] John 1:12, 16; Rom. 8:15-16; Gal. 4:5-6; Eph. 1:5; 1 John 3:1
[4] Ps. 55:22; Matt. 6:26
[5] Rom. 8:28; Rom. 4:21
[6] Rom. 10:12; Matt. 6:26; Matt. 7:9-11

VI. Of the Providence of God

1. We believe that all things, both in heaven and in earth and in all creatures, are sustained and governed by the providence of this wise, eternal, and omnipotent God. For David witnesses and says, "The LORD is high above all nations, and His glory above the heavens. Who is like unto the LORD our God, who dwelleth on high, who humbleth Himself to behold the things that are in heaven, and in the earth!" (Ps. 113:4-6). Again, he says, "Thou compassest my path and my lying down, and art acquainted with all my ways. For there is not a word in my tongue, but, lo, O LORD, Thou knowest it altogether," etc. (Ps. 139:3-4). Paul also witnesses and says, "In Him we live, and move, and have our being" (Acts 17:28); and "of Him, and through Him, and to Him, are all things" (Rom. 11:36).

2. Therefore Augustine both truly and according to the Scripture said, in his book *De Agone Christi,* chap. 8, "The Lord said, 'Are not two sparrows sold for a farthing? and one of them shall not fall to the ground without the will of your Father.' By speaking thus He would give us to understand whatsoever men count most vile, that also is governed by the almighty power of God. For the truth, which said that all the hairs of our head are numbered, says also that the birds of the air are fed by Him, and the lilies of the field are clothed by Him."

3. We therefore condemn the Epicureans, who deny the providence of God, and all those who blasphemously affirm that God is occupied about the poles of heaven, and that He neither sees nor regards us or our affairs. The princely prophet David also condemned these men when he said, "LORD, how long shall the wicked, how long shall the wicked triumph?... they say, The LORD shall not see, neither shall the God of Jacob regard it. Understand, ye brutish

Westminster Confession of Faith (1647)	Westminster Shorter Catechism (1647)	Westminster Larger Catechism (1648)

V. Of Providence

1. God the great Creator of all things doth uphold,[1] direct, dispose, and govern all creatures, actions, and things,[2] from the greatest even to the least,[3] by His most wise and holy providence,[4] according to His infallible foreknowledge,[5] and the free and immutable counsel of His own will,[6] to the praise of the glory of His wisdom, power, justice, goodness, and mercy.[7]

[1] Heb. 1:3
[2] Dan. 4:34-35; Ps. 135:6; Acts 17:25-26, 28; Job 38; 39; 40; 41
[3] Matt. 10:29-31
[4] Prov. 15:3; Ps. 104:24; 145:17
[5] Acts 15:18; Ps. 94:8-11
[6] Eph. 1:11; Ps. 33:10-11
[7] Isa. 63:14; Eph. 3:10; Rom. 9:17; Gen. 45:7; Ps. 145:7

2. Although, in relation to the foreknowledge and decree of God, the first cause, all things come to pass immutably, and infallibly;[1] yet, by the same providence, He ordereth them to fall out, according to the nature of second causes, either necessarily, freely, or contingently.[2]

[1] Acts 2:23
[2] Gen. 8:22; Jer. 31:35; Exod. 21:13; Deut. 19:5; 1 Ki. 22:28, 34; Isa. 10:6-7

3. God, in His ordinary providence, maketh use of means,[1] yet is free to work without,[2] above,[3] and against them,[4] at His pleasure.

[1] Acts 27:31, 44; Isa. 55:10-11; Hos. 2:21-22
[2] Hos. 1:7; Matt. 4:4; Job 34:10
[3] Rom. 4:19-21
[4] 2 Ki. 6:6; Dan. 3:27

4. The almighty power, unsearchable wisdom, and infinite goodness of God so far manifest themselves in His providence, that it extendeth itself even to the first fall, and all other sins of angels and men;[1] and that not by a bare permission,[2] but such as hath joined with it a most

---

Q. 11: What are God's works of providence?

A.: God's works of providence are, His most holy,[1] wise,[2] and powerful preserving[3] and governing all His creatures, and all their actions.[4]

[1] Ps. 145:17
[2] Ps. 104:24; Isa. 28:29
[3] Heb. 1:3
[4] Ps. 103:19; Matt. 10:29-31

Q. 18: What are God's works of providence?

A.: God's works of providence are His most holy,[1] wise,[2] and powerful preserving[3] and governing[4] all His creatures; ordering them, and all their actions,[5] to His own glory.[6]

[1] Ps. 145:17
[2] Ps. 104:24; Isa. 28:29
[3] Heb. 1:3
[4] Ps. 103:19
[5] Matt. 10:29-31; Gen. 45:7
[6] Rom. 11:36; Isa. 63:14

Q. 19: What is God's providence towards the angels?

A.: God by His providence permitted some of the angels, wilfully and irrecoverably, to fall into sin and damnation,[1] limiting and ordering that, and all their sins, to His own glory;[2] and established the rest in holiness and happiness;[3] employing them all,[4] at His pleasure, in the administrations of His power, mercy, and justice.[5]

[1] Jude 6; 2 Pet. 2:4; Heb. 2:16; John 8:44
[2] Job 1:12; Matt. 8:31
[3] 1 Tim. 5:21; Mark 8:38; Heb. 12:22
[4] Ps. 104:4
[5] 2 Ki. 19:35; Heb. 1:14

Q. 20: What was the providence of God toward man in the estate in which he was created?

A.: The providence of God toward man in the estate in which he was created, was the placing him in Paradise, appointing him to dress it, giving him liberty to eat of the fruit of the earth;[1] putting the creatures under his dominion,[2] and ordaining marriage for his help;[3] affording him communion with Himself;[4] instituting the Sabbath;[5] entering into a covenant of life with him, upon condition of personal, perfect, and perpetual obedience,[6] of which the tree of life was a pledge;[7] and forbidding to eat of the tree of the knowledge of good and evil, upon the pain of death.[8]

Belgic Confession (1561)	Heidelberg Catechism (1563)	Second Helvetic Confession (1566)	Canons of Dort (1619)

which He has revealed to us in His Word without transgressing these limits.

This doctrine affords us unspeakable consolation, since we are taught thereby that nothing can befall us by chance, but by the direction of our most gracious and heavenly Father, who watches over us with a paternal care, keeping all creatures so under His power[5] that not a hair of our head (for they are all numbered), nor a sparrow, can fall to the ground, without the will of our Father,[6] in whom we do entirely trust; being persuaded that He so restrains the devil and all our enemies that, without His will and permission, they cannot hurt us. And therefore we reject that damnable error of the Epicureans, who say that God regards nothing, but leaves all things to chance.

[1] John 5:17; Heb. 1:3; Prov. 16:4; Ps. 104:9, etc.; Ps. 139:2, etc.
[2] James 4:15; Job 1:21; 1 Ki. 22:20; Acts 4:28; 1 Sam. 2:25; Ps. 115:3; 45:7; Amos 3:6; Deut. 19:5; Prov. 21:1; Ps. 105:25; Isa. 10:5-7; 2 Thes. 2:11; Ezek. 14:9; Rom. 1:28; Gen. 45:8; 1:20; 2 Sam. 16:10; Gen. 27:20; Ps. 75:7-8; Isa. 45:7; Prov. 16:4; Lam. 3:37-38; 1 Ki. 22:34,38; Exod. 21:13
[3] Matt. 8:31-32; John 3:8
[4] Rom. 11:33-34
[5] Matt. 8:31; Job 1:12; 2:6
[6] Matt. 10:29-30

Q. 27: What dost thou mean by the providence of God?

A.: The almighty and everywhere present power of God;[1] whereby, as it were by His hand, He upholds and governs heaven, earth, and all creatures;[2] so that herbs and grass, rain and drought,[3] fruitful and barren years, meat and drink,[4] health and sickness,[5] riches and poverty,[6] yea, and all things come, not by chance, but by His fatherly hand.[7]

[1] Acts 17:25-28
[2] Heb. 1:3
[3] Jer. 5:24
[4] Acts 14:17
[5] John 9:3
[6] Prov. 22:2; Job 1:21
[7] Matt. 10:29-30; Eph. 1:11

Q. 28: What advantage is it to us to know that God has created, and by His providence doth still uphold all things?

A.: That we may be patient in adversity;[1] thankful in prosperity;[2] and that in all things, which may hereafter befall us, we place our firm trust in our faithful God and Father,[3] that nothing shall separate us from His love;[4] since all creatures are so in His hand, that without His will they cannot so much as move.[5]

[1] Rom. 5:3; Ps. 39:10
[2] Deut. 8:10; 1 Thes. 5:18
[3] Rom. 5:3-6
[4] Rom. 8:38-39
[5] Job 1:12; Job 2:6; Matt. 8:31; Isa. 10:15

Q. 125: Which is the fourth petition?

A.: "Give us this day our daily bread";[1] that

---

among the people: and ye fools, when will ye be wise? He that planted the ear, shall He not hear? and He that hath formed the eye, shall He not see?" (Ps. 94:3, 7-9).

4. Notwithstanding, we do not condemn the means whereby the providence of God works as though they were unprofitable; but we teach that we must apply ourselves unto them, so far as they are commended unto us in the Word of God. Wherefore we dislike the rash speeches of such as say that if all things are governed by the providence of God, then all our studies and endeavors are unprofitable; it shall be sufficient if we leave or permit all things to be governed by the providence of God; and we shall not need hereafter to behave or act with carefulness in any matter. For though Paul did confess that he did sail by the providence of God, who had said to him, "as thou has testified of Me in Jerusalem, so must thou bear witness also at Rome" (Acts 23:11); who, moreover, promised and said, "There shall be no loss of any man's life among you,...there shall not an hair fall from the head of any of you" (Acts 27:22, 34); yet, the mariners devising how they might find a way to escape, the same Paul says to the centurion and to the soldiers, "Except these abide in the ship, ye cannot be saved" (Acts 27:31). For God, who has appointed every thing his end, He also has ordained the beginning and the means by which we must attain unto the end. The heathens ascribe things to blind fortune and uncertain chance; but St. James would not have us say, "Today or to morrow we will go into such a city, and continue there a year, and buy and sell"; but he adds, "For that ye ought to say, If the Lord will, we shall live, and do this, or that" (James 4:13, 15). And Augustine says, "All those things which seem to vain men to be done advisedly in the world, they do but accomplish His word because they are not done by His commandment." And, in his exposition of the 148th Psalm, "It seemed to be done by chance that Saul, seeking his father's asses, should light on the prophet Samuel"; but the Lord had before said to the prophet, "To morrow about this time I will send thee a man out of the land of Benjamin," etc. (1 Sam. 9:16).

Westminster Confession of Faith (1647)	Westminster Shorter Catechism (1647)	Westminster Larger Catechism (1648)

<table>
<tr><td>

wise and powerful bounding,[3] and otherwise ordering, and governing of them, in a manifold dispensation, to His own holy ends;[4] yet so, as the sinfulness thereof proceedeth only from the creature, and not from God, who, being most holy and righteous, neither is nor can be the author or approver of sin.[5]

---

[1] Rom. 11:32-34; 2 Sam. 24:1; 1 Chron. 21:1; 1 Ki. 22:22-23; 1 Chron. 10:4, 13-14; 2 Sam. 16:10; Acts 2:23; 4:27-28
[2] Acts 14:16
[3] Ps. 76:10; 2 Ki. 19:28
[4] Gen. 50:20; Isa. 10:6-7, 12
[5] James 1:13-14, 17; 1 John 2:16; Ps. 50:21

5. The most wise, righteous, and gracious God doth oftentimes leave, for a season, His own children to manifold temptations, and the corruption of their own hearts, to chastise them for their former sins, or to discover unto them the hidden strength of corruption and deceitfulness of their hearts, that they may be humbled;[1] and, to raise them to a more close and constant dependence for their support upon Himself, and to make them more watchful against all future occasions of sin, and for sundry other just and holy ends.[2]

---

[1] 2 Chron. 32:25-26, 31; 2 Sam. 24:1
[2] 2 Cor. 12:7-9; Ps. 73; 77:1, 10, 12; Mark 14:66f.; John 21:15-17

6. As for those wicked and ungodly men whom God, as a righteous Judge, for former sins, doth blind and harden, from them He not only withholdeth His grace whereby they might have been enlightened in their understandings, and wrought upon in their hearts;[1] but sometimes also withdraweth the gifts which they had,[2] and exposes them to such objects as their corruption makes occasion of sin;[3] and, withal, gives them over to their own lusts, the temptations of the world, and the power of Satan,[4] whereby it comes to pass that they harden themselves, even under those means which God useth for the softening of others.[5]

---

[1] Rom. 1:24, 26, 28; 11:7-8
[2] Deut. 29:4
[3] Matt. 13:12; 25:29
[4] Deut. 2:30; 2 Ki. 8:12-13
[5] Ps. 81:11-12; 2 Thes. 2:10-12; Exod. 7:3; 8:15, 32; 2 Cor. 2:15-16; Isa. 8:14; 1 Pet. 2:7-8; Isa. 6:9-10; Acts 28:26-27

7. As the providence of God doth, in general, reach to all creatures; so, after a most special manner, it taketh care of His Church, and disposeth all things to the good thereof.[1]

---

[1] 1 Tim. 4:10; Amos 9:8-9; Rom. 8:28; Isa. 43:3-5, 14

</td><td>

</td><td>

---

[1] Gen. 2:8, 15-16
[2] Gen. 1:28
[3] Gen. 2:18
[4] Gen. 1:26-29; Gen. 3:8
[5] Gen. 2:3
[6] Gal. 3:12; Rom. 10:5
[7] Gen. 2:9
[8] Gen. 2:17

</td></tr>
</table>

Belgic Confession (1561)	Heidelberg Catechism (1563)	Second Helvetic Confession (1566)	Canons of Dort (1619)
	is, be pleased to provide us with all things necessary for the body,[2] that we may thereby acknowledge Thee to be the only fountain of all good,[3] and that neither our care nor industry, nor even Thy gifts, can profit us without Thy blessing;[4] and therefore that we may withdraw our trust from all creatures and place it alone in Thee.[5]		

[1] Matt. 6:11
[2] Ps. 145:15; Matt. 6:25
[3] Acts 17:25; Acts 14:17
[4] 1 Cor. 15:58; Deut. 8:3; Ps. 127:1-2
[5] Ps. 62:11; Ps. 55:22

Anthropology:
The Doctrine of Man

Belgic Confession (1561)	Heidelberg Catechism (1563)	Second Helvetic Confession (1566)	Canons of Dort (1619)

The Fall of Man, Original Sin, and Punishment

Article 14 (part I)

The Creation and Fall of Man, and His Incapacity to Perform What is Truly Good

We believe that God created man out of the dust of the earth, and made and formed him after His own image and likeness,[1] good, righteous, and holy, capable in all things to will agreeably to the will of God.[2] But being in honor, he understood it not, neither knew his excellency,[3] but willfully subjected himself to sin, and consequently to death and the curse, giving ear to the words of the devil.[4] For the commandment of life, which he had received,[5] he transgressed; and by sin separated himself from God[6] who was his true life, having corrupted his whole nature,[7] whereby he made himself liable to corporal and spiritual death.[8] And being thus become wicked, perverse, and corrupt in all his ways, he hath lost all his excellent gifts which he had received from God,[9] and only retained a few remains thereof,[10] which, however, are sufficient to leave man without excuse;[11] for all the light which is in us is changed into darkness,[12] as the Scriptures teach us, saying: *The light shineth in darkness, and the darkness comprehendeth*[13] *it not*; where St.

Q. 5: Canst thou keep all these things perfectly?

A.: In no wise;[1] for I am prone by nature to hate God and my neighbor.[2]

[1] Rom. 3:10; John 1:8
[2] Rom. 8:7; Titus 3:3

Q. 7: Whence then proceeds this depravity of human nature?

A.: From the fall and disobedience of our first parents, Adam and Eve, in Paradise;[1] hence our nature is become so corrupt that we are all conceived and born in sin.[2]

[1] Gen. 3:6; Rom. 5:12, 18-19
[2] Ps. 5:15; Gen. 5:3

Q. 8: Are we then so corrupt that we are wholly incapable of doing any good, and inclined to all wickedness?

A.: Indeed we are,[1] except we are regenerated by the Spirit of God.[2]

[1] Gen. 6:5; Job 14:4; Job 15:14, 16
[2] John 3:5; Eph. 2:5

Q. 9: Doth not God then do injustice to man, by requiring from him in His law that which he cannot perform?

A.: Not at all;[1] for God made man capable of performing it;[2] but man, by the instigation of the devil,[3] and his own wilful disobedience, deprived himself and all his posterity of those divine gifts.[4]

[1] Eccl. 7:29
[2] John 8:44; 2 Cor. 11:3
[3] Gen. 3:4, 7
[4] Rom. 5:12

VIII. Of Man's Fall; Sin, and the Cause of Sin

1. Man was from the beginning created of God after the image of God, in righteousness and true holiness, good and upright; but by the instigation of the serpent and his own fault, falling from the goodness and uprightness, he became subject to sin, death, and divers calamities; and such a one as he became by his fall, such are all his offspring, even subject to sin, death, and sundry calamities.

2. And we take sin to be that natural corruption of man, derived or spread from our first parents unto us all, through which we, being drowned in evil concupiscence, and clean turned away from God, but prone to all evil, full of all wickedness, distrust, contempt, and hatred of God, can do no good of ourselves — no, not so much as think any (Matt. 12:34-35).

3. And, what is more, even as we do grow in years, so by wicked thoughts, words, and deeds, committed against the law of God, we bring forth corrupt fruits, worthy of an evil tree: in which respect we through our own desert, being subject to the wrath of God, are in danger of just punishment; so that we had all been cast away from God, had not Christ, the Deliverer, brought us back again.

4. By death, therefore, we understand not only bodily death, which is once to be suffered of us all for our sins, but also everlasting punishments due to our corruption and to our sins. For the apostle says, "We who were dead in trespasses and sins;...and were by nature the children of wrath, even as others. But God, who is rich in mercy,...even when we were dead in sins, quickened us together with Christ" (Eph. 2:1-5). Again, "As by one man sin entered into the world, and death by sin; and so death passed upon all men, for that all have sinned," etc. (Rom. 5:12).

5. We therefore acknowledge that original sin is in all men; we acknowledge that all other sins which spring therefrom are both called and are indeed sins, by what name soever they may be termed, whether mortal or venial, or also that which is called sin against the Holy Spirit, which is never forgiven.

6. We also confess that sins are not equal (John 5:16-17), although they spring from the same fountain of corruption and unbelief, but that some are more grievous than others (Mark 3:28-

Head I

Article 1

As all men have sinned in Adam, lie under the curse, and are deserving of eternal death, God would have done no injustice by leaving them all to perish, and delivering them over to condemnation on account of sin, according to the words of the apostle, "that every mouth may be stopped, and all the world may become guilty before God" (Rom. 3:19). And verse 23: "For all have sinned, and come short of the glory of God." And Romans 6:23: "For the wages of sin is death."

Head II

Article 1

God is not only supremely merciful, but also supremely just. And His justice requires (as He hath revealed Himself in His Word), that our sins committed against His infinite majesty should be punished, not only with temporal, but with eternal punishment, both in body and soul; which we cannot escape unless satisfaction be made to the justice of God.

Article 2

Since therefore we are unable to make that satisfaction in our own persons or to deliver ourselves from the wrath of God, He hath been pleased in His in-

Westminster Confession of Faith (1647)	Westminster Shorter Catechism (1647)	Westminster Larger Catechism (1648)

VI. Of the Fall of Man, of Sin and of the Punishment Thereof

1. Our first parents, being seduced by the subtilty and temptation of Satan, sinned, in eating the forbidden fruit.[1] This their sin, God was pleased, according to His wise and holy counsel, to permit, having purposed to order it to His own glory.[2]

[1] Gen. 3:13; 2 Cor. 11:3
[2] Rom. 11:32

2. By this sin they fell from their original righteousness and communion, with God,[1] and so became dead in sin,[2] and wholly defiled in all the parts and faculties of soul and body.[3]

[1] Gen. 3:6-8; Eccl. 7:29; Rom. 3:23
[2] Gen. 2:17; Eph. 2:1
[3] Titus 1:15; Gen. 6:5; Jer. 17:9; Rom. 3:10-18

3. They being the root of all mankind, the guilt of this sin was imputed;[1] and the same death in sin, and corrupted nature, conveyed to all their posterity descending from them by ordinary generation.[2]

[1] Gen. 1:27-28; 2:16-17; Acts 17:26; Rom. 5:12, 15-19; 1 Cor. 15:21-22, 45, 49
[2] Ps. 51:5; Gen. 5:3; Job 14:4; 15:14

4. From this original corruption, whereby we are utterly indisposed, disabled, and made opposite to all good,[1] and wholly inclined to all evil,[2] do proceed all actual transgressions.[3]

[1] Rom. 5:6; 8:7; 7:18; Col 1:21
[2] Gen. 6:5; 8:21; Rom. 3:10-12
[3] James 1:14-15; Eph. 2:2-3; Matt. 15:19

5. This corruption of nature, during this life, doth remain in those that are regenerated;[1] and although it be, through Christ, pardoned, and mortified; yet both itself, and all the motions thereof, are truly and properly sin.[2]

[1] 1 John 1:8, 10; Rom. 7:14, 17-18, 23; James 3:2; Prov. 20:9; Eccl. 7:20
[2] Rom. 7:5, 7-8, 25; Gal. 5:17

6. Every sin, both original and actual, being a transgression of the righteous law of God, and contrary thereunto,[1] doth, in its own nature, bring guilt upon the sinner,[2] whereby he is bound over to the wrath of God,[3] and curse of the law,[4] and so made subject to death,[5] with all miseries spiritual,[6] temporal,[7] and eternal.[8]

Q. 13: Did our first parents continue in the estate wherein they were created?

A.: Our first parents, being left to the freedom of their own will, fell from the estate wherein they were created, by sinning against God.[1]

[1] Gen. 3:6-8, 13; Eccl. 7:29

Q. 14: What is sin?

A.: Sin is any want of conformity unto, or transgression of, the law of God.[1]

[1] 1 John 3:4

Q. 15: What was the sin whereby our first parents fell from the estate wherein they were created?

A.: The sin whereby our first parents fell from the estate wherein they were created, was their eating the forbidden fruit.[1]

[1] Gen. 3:6, 12

Q. 16: Did all mankind fall in Adam's first transgression?

A.: The covenant being made with Adam, not only for himself, but for his posterity; all mankind, descending from him by ordinary generation, sinned in him, and fell with him, in his first transgression.[1]

[1] Gen. 2:16-17; Rom. 5:12; 1 Cor. 15:21-22

Q. 17: Into what estate did the fall bring mankind?

A.: The fall brought mankind into an estate of sin and misery.[1]

[1] Rom. 5:12

Q. 18: Wherein consists the

Q. 21: Did man continue in that estate wherein God at first created him?

A.: Our first parents being left to the freedom of their own will, through the temptation of Satan, transgressed the commandment of God in eating the forbidden fruit; and thereby fell from the estate of innocency wherein they were created.[1]

[1] Gen. 3:6-8, 13; Eccl. 7:29; 2 Cor. 11:3

Q. 22: Did all mankind fall in that first transgression?

A.: The covenant being made with Adam as a public person, not for himself only, but for his posterity, all mankind descending from him by ordinary generation,[1] sinned in him, and fell with him in that first transgression.[2]

[1] Acts 17:26
[2] Gen. 2:16-17; Rom. 5:12-20; 1 Cor. 15:21-22

Q. 23: Into what estate did the fall bring mankind?

A.: The fall brought mankind into an estate of sin and misery.[1]

[1] Rom. 5:12; 3:23

Q. 24: What is sin?

A.: Sin is any want of conformity unto, or transgression of, any law of God, given as a rule to the reasonable creature.[1]

[1] 1 John 3:4; Gal. 3:10, 12

Q. 25: Wherein consisteth the sinfulness of that estate whereinto man fell?

A.: The sinfulness of that estate whereinto man fell, consisteth in the guilt of Adam's first sin,[1] the want of that righteousness wherein he was created, and the corruption of his nature, whereby he is utterly indisposed, disabled, and made opposite unto all that is spiritually good, and wholly inclined to all evil, and that continually;[2] which is commonly called original sin, and from which do proceed all actual transgressions.[3]

[1] Rom. 5:12, 19
[2] Rom. 3:10-19; Eph. 21:-3; Rom. 5:6; 8:7-8; Gen. 6:5
[3] James 1:14-15; Matt. 15:19

Q. 26: How is original sin conveyed from our first parents unto their posterity?

A.: Original sin is conveyed from our first parents unto their posterity by natural generation, so as all that proceed from them in that way are conceived and born in sin.[1]

Belgic Confession (1561)	Heidelberg Catechism (1563)	Second Helvetic Confession (1566)	Canons of Dort (1619)

Belgic Confession (1561)

John calleth men darkness.

[1] Gen. 1:26; Eccl. 7:29; Eph. 4:24
[2] Gen. 1:31; Eph. 4:24
[3] Ps. 49:21; Isa. 59:2
[4] Gen. 3:6, 17
[5] Gen. 1:3, 7
[6] Isa. 59:2
[7] Eph. 4:18
[8] Rom. 5:12; Gen. 2:17; 3:19
[9] Rom. 3:10
[10] Acts 14:16-17; 17:27
[11] Rom. 1:20-21; Acts 17:27
[12] Eph. 5:8; Matt. 6:23
[13] John 1:5

Article 15

Original Sin

We believe that, through the disobedience of Adam, original sin is extended to all mankind;[1] which is a corruption of the whole nature, and a hereditary disease, wherewith infants themselves are infected even in their mother's womb,[2] and which produceth in man all sorts of sin, being in him as a root thereof;[3] and therefore is so vile and abominable in the sight of God that it is sufficient to condemn all mankind.[4] Nor is it by any means abolished or done away by baptism; since sin always issues forth from this woeful source, as water from a fountain: notwithstanding it is not imputed to the children of God unto condemnation, but by His grace and mercy is forgiven them. Not that they should rest securely in sin, but that a sense of this corruption should make believers often to sigh, desiring to be delivered from this body of death.[5] Wherefore we reject the error of the Pelagians, who assert

Heidelberg Catechism (1563)

Q. 10: Will God suffer such disobedience and rebellion to go unpunished?

A.: By no means; but is terribly displeased[1] with our original as well as actual sins; and will punish them in His just judgment temporally and eternally,[2] as He hath declared, "Cursed is every one that continueth not in all things, which are written in the book of the law, to do them."[3]

[1] Ps. 5:5
[2] Rom. 1:18; Deut. 28:15; Heb. 9:27
[3] Deut. 27:26; Gal. 3:10

Q. 11: Is not God then also merciful?

A.: God is indeed merciful,[1] but also just; therefore His justice requires[2] that sin which is committed against the most high majesty of God be also punished with extreme,[3] that is, with everlasting punishment of body and soul.[4]

[1] Exod. 34:6
[2] Exod. 20:5; Job 34:10-11
[3] Ps. 5:5-6
[4] Gen. 2:17; Rom. 6:23

Q. 12: Since then, by the righteous judgment of God, we deserve temporal and eternal punishment, is there no way by which we may escape that punishment, and be again received into favor?

A.: God will have His justice satisfied,[1] and therefore we must make this full satisfaction, either by ourselves or by another.[2]

[1] Exod. 20:5
[2] Deut. 24:16; 2 Cor. 5:14-15

Q. 13: Can we ourselves then make this satisfaction?

A.: By no means;[1] but

Second Helvetic Confession (1566)

29); even as the Lord has said, "It shall be more tolerable for the land of Sodom" than for the city that despises the word of the gospel (Matt. 10:15). We therefore condemn all those that have taught things contrary to these; but especially Pelagius, and all the Pelagians, together with the Jovinianists, who, with the Stoics, count all sins equal. We in this matter agree fully with St. Augustine, who produced and maintained his sayings out of the Holy Scriptures. Moreover, we condemn Florinus and Blastus (against whom also Irenaeus wrote), and all those who make God the author of sin; seeing it is expressly written, "Thou art not a God that hath pleasure in wickedness. Thou hatest all workers of iniquity. Thou shalt destroy them that speak leasing" (Ps. 5:4, 6). And, again, "When he (the devil) speaketh a lie, he speaketh of his own: because he is a liar, and the father of it" (John 8:44). Yea, there are even in ourselves sin and corruption enough, so that there is no need that God should infuse into us either a new or greater measure of wickedness.

7. Therefore, when God is said in the Scripture to harden (Exod. 7:13), to blind (John 12:40), and to deliver us up into a reprobate sense (Rom. 1:28), it is to be understood that God does it by just judgment, as a just judge and revenger. To conclude, as often as God in the Scripture is said and seems to do some evil, it is not thereby meant that man does not commit evil, but that God does suffer it to be done, and does not hinder it; and that by His just judgment, who could hinder it if He would: or because He makes good use of the evil of men, as He did in the sin of Joseph's brethren; or because Himself rules sins, that they break not out and rage more violently than is meet. St. Augustine, in his *Enchiridion*, says, "After a wonderful and unspeakable manner, that is not done beside His will which is done contrary to His will; because it could not be done if He should not suffer it to be done; and yet He doth not suffer it to be done unwillingly; neither would He, being God, suffer any evil to be done, unless, being also almighty, He could make good of evil." Thus far Augustine.

8. Other questions, as whether God would have Adam fall, or whether He forced him to fall, or why He did not hinder his fall, and such like, we account among curious questions (unless perchance the frowardness of heretics, or of men otherwise importunate, do compel us to open these points also out of the Word of God, as the godly doctors of the Church have oftentimes done); knowing that the Lord did forbid that man should eat of the forbidden fruit. and punished his transgression; and also that the

Canons of Dort (1619)

finite mercy to give His only begotten Son, for our surety, who was made sin, and became a curse for us and in our stead, that He might make satisfaction to divine justice on our behalf.

Head III and IV

Article 1

Man was originally formed after the image of God. His understanding was adorned with a true and saving knowledge of his Creator and of spiritual things; his heart and will were upright; all his affections pure; and the whole man was holy; but revolting from God by the instigation of the devil, and abusing the freedom of his own will, he forfeited these excellent gifts; and on the contrary entailed on himself blindness of mind, horrible darkness, vanity and perverseness of judgment, became wicked, rebellious, and obdurate in heart and will, and impure in his affections.

Article 2

Man after the fall begat children in his own likeness. A corrupt stock produced a corrupt offspring. Hence all the posterity of Adam, Christ only excepted, have derived corruption from their original parent, not by imitation, as the Pelagians of old asserted, but by the propagation of a vicious nature.

Article 3

Therefore all men are

Westminster Confession of Faith (1647)	Westminster Shorter Catechism (1647)	Westminster Larger Catechism (1648)

Westminster Confession of Faith (1647)

[1] 1 John 3:4
[2] Rom. 2:15; 3:9, 19
[3] Eph. 2:3
[4] Gal. 3:10
[5] Rom. 6:23
[6] Eph. 4:18
[7] Rom. 8:20; Lam. 3:39
[8] Matt. 25:41; 2 Thes. 1:9

Westminster Shorter Catechism (1647)

sinfulness of that estate where-into man fell?

A.: The sinfulness of that estate whereinto man fell, consists in the guilt of Adam's first sin, the want of original righteousness, and the corruption of his whole nature, which is commonly called original sin; together with all actual transgressions which proceed from it.[1]

[1] Rom. 5:12,19; 5:10-20; Eph. 2:1-3; James 1:14-15; Matt. 15:19

Q. 19: What is the misery of that estate whereinto man fell?

A.: All mankind by their fall lost communion with God,[1] are under His wrath and curse,[2] and so made liable to all miseries in this life, to death itself, and to the pains of hell forever.[3]

[1] Gen. 3:8, 10, 24
[2] Eph. 2:2-3; Gal. 3:10
[3] Lam. 3:39; Rom. 6:23; Matt. 25:41, 46

Westminster Larger Catechism (1648)

[1] Ps. 51:5; Job 14:4; 15:14; John 3:6

Q. 27: What misery did the fall bring upon mankind?

A.: The fall brought upon mankind the loss of communion with God,[1] His displeasure and curse; so as we are by nature children of wrath,[2] bond slaves to Satan,[3] and justly liable to all punishments in this world, and that which is to come.[4]

[1] Gen. 3:8, 10, 24
[2] Eph. 2:2-3
[3] 2 Tim. 2:26
[4] Gen. 2:17; Lam. 3:39; Rom. 6:23; Matt. 25:41, 46; Jude 7

Q. 28: What are the punishments of sin in this world?

A.: The punishments of sin in this world are either inward, as blindness of mind,[1] a reprobate sense,[2] strong delusions,[3] hardness of heart,[4] horror of conscience,[5] and vile affections;[6] or outward, as the curse of God upon the creatures for our sakes,[7] and all other evils that befall us in our bodies, names, estates, relations, and employments;[8] together with death itself.[9]

[1] Eph. 4:18
[2] Rom. 1:28
[3] 2 Thes. 2:11
[4] Rom. 2:5
[5] Isa. 33:14; Gen. 4:13; Matt. 27:4
[6] Rom. 1:26
[7] Gen. 3:17
[8] Deut. 28:15-18
[9] Rom. 6:21, 23

Q. 29: What are the punishments of sin in the world to come?

A.: The punishments of sin in the world to come, are everlasting separation from the comfortable presence of God, and most grievous torments in soul and body, without intermission, in hell-fire for ever.[1]

[1] 2 Thes. 1:9; Mark 9:43-44, 46, 48; Luke 16:24

Belgic Confession (1561)	Heidelberg Catechism (1563)	Second Helvetic Confession (1566)	Canons of Dort (1619)
that sin proceeds only from imitation. [1] Rom. 5:12-13; Ps. 51:7; Rom. 3:10; Gen. 6:3; John 3:6; Job 14:4 [2] Isa. 48:8; Rom. 5:14 [3] Gal. 5:19; Rom. 7:8, 10, 13, 17-18, 20, 23 [4] Eph. 2:3, 5 [5] Rom. 7:18, 24	on the contrary we daily increase our debt.[2] [1] Job 9:2-3; Job 15:14-16 [2] Matt. 6:12; Isa. 64:6 *Q. 14: Can there be found anywhere one, who is a mere creature, able to satisfy for us?* A.: None; for, first, God will not punish any other creature for the sin which man hath committed;[1] and further, no mere creature can sustain the burden of God's eternal wrath against sin, so as to deliver others from it.[2] [1] Ezek. 18:20 [2] Rev. 5:3; Ps. 49:8-9	things done are not evil in respect of the providence, will, and power of God, but in respect of Satan, and our will resisting the will of God.	conceived in sin, and by nature children of wrath, incapable of saving good, prone to evil, dead in sin, and in bondage thereto, and without the regenerating grace of the Holy Spirit, they are neither able nor willing to return to God, to reform the depravity of their nature, or to dispose themselves to reformation. *Article 4* There remain, however, in man since the fall, the glimmerings of natural light, whereby he retains some knowledge of God, of natural

Canons of Dort (cont.)

things, and of the differences between good and evil, and discovers some regard for virtue, good order in society, and for maintaining an orderly external deportment. But so far is this light of nature from being sufficient to bring him to a saving knowledge of God and to true conversion, that he is incapable of using it aright even in things natural and civil. Nay, further, this light, such as it is, man in various ways renders wholly polluted and holds it in unrighteousness, by doing which he becomes inexcusable before God.

The true doctrine (concerning redemption) having been explained, the Synod **rejects** the errors of those who teach:

Rejection 5
That all men have been accepted unto the state of reconciliation and unto the grace of the covenant, so that no one is worthy of condemnation on account of original sin, and that no one shall be condemned because of it, but that all are free from the guilt of original sin. For this opinion is repugnant to Scripture which teaches that we are by nature children of wrath (Eph. 2:3).

The true doctrine (concerning corruption and conversion) having been explained, the Synod **rejects** the errors of those who teach:

Rejection 1
That it cannot properly be said that original sin in itself suffices to condemn the whole human race or to deserve temporal and eternal punishment. For these contradict the apostle, who declares: "Wherefore, as by one man sin entered into the world, and death by sin; and so death passed upon all men,

for that all have sinned" (Rom. 5:12). And: "The judgment was by one to condemnation" (Rom. 5:16). And: "The wages of sin is death" (Rom. 6:23).

Rejection 2
That the spiritual gifts or the good qualities and virtues, such as goodness, holiness, righteousness, could not belong to the will of man when he was first created, and that these, therefore, could not have been separated therefrom in the fall. For such is contrary to the description of the image of God which the apostle gives in Ephesians 4:24, where he declares that it consists in righteousness and holiness, which undoubtedly belong to the will.

Rejection 3
That in spiritual death the spiritual gifts are not separate from the will of man, since the will in itself has never been corrupted, but only hindered through the darkness of the understanding and the irregularity of the affections; and that, these hindrances having been removed, the will can then bring into operation its native powers, that is, that the will of itself is able to will and to choose, or not to will and not to choose, all manner of good which may be presented to it. This is an innovation and an error, and tends to elevate the powers of the free will, contrary to the declaration of the prophet: "The heart is deceitful above all things, and desperately wicked" (Jer. 17:9); and of the apostle: "Among whom (sons of disobedience) also we all had our conversation in times past in the lusts of our flesh, fulfilling the desires of the flesh and of the mind" (Eph. 2:3).

Westminster Confession of Faith (1647)	Westminster Shorter Catechism (1647)	Westminster Larger Catechism (1648)

Canons of Dort (cont.)

Rejection 4

That the unregenerate man is not really nor utterly dead in sin, nor destitute of all powers unto spiritual good, but that he can yet hunger and thirst after righteousness and life, and offer the sacrifice of a contrite and broken spirit, which is pleasing to God. For these are contrary to the express testimony of Scripture. "Who were dead in trespasses and sins"; "Even when we were dead in sins" (Eph. 2:1, 5); and: "every imagination of the thoughts of his heart was only evil continually" (Gen. 6:5); "for the imagination of man's heart is evil from his youth" (Gen. 8:21).

Moreover, to hunger and thirst after deliverance from misery, and after life, and to offer unto God the sacrifice of a broken spirit, is peculiar to the regenerate and those that are called blessed. "Create in me a clean heart, O God; and renew a right spirit within me"; "Then shalt Thou be pleased with the sacrifices of righteousness, with burnt offering and whole burnt offering: then shall they offer bullocks upon Thine altar" (Ps. 51:10, 19); "Blessed are they which do hunger and thirst after righteousness: for they shall be filled" (Matt. 5:6).

Belgic Confession (1561)	Heidelberg Catechism (1563)	Second Helvetic Confession (1566)	Canons of Dort (1619)

God's Covenant with Man

Article 17

The Recovery of Fallen Man

We believe that our most gracious God, in His admirable wisdom and goodness, seeing that man had thus thrown himself into temporal and spiritual death, and made himself wholly miserable, was pleased to seek and comfort him when he trembling[1] fled from His presence, promising him that He would give His Son, who should *be made of a woman, to bruise the head of the serpent,* and would make him happy.[2]

[1] Gen. 3:8-9,19; Isa. 65:1-2
[2] Heb. 2:14; Gen. 22:18; Isa. 7:14; John 7:42; 2 Tim. 2:8; Heb. 7:14; Gen. 3:15; Gal. 4:4

Head II

The true doctrine (concerning redemption) having been explained, the Synod **rejects** the errors of those who teach:

Rejection 2

That it was not the purpose of the death of Christ that He should confirm the new covenant of grace through His blood, but only that He should acquire for the Father the mere right to establish with man such a covenant as He might please, whether of grace or of works. For this is repugnant to Scripture which teaches that Christ has become the Surety and Mediator of a better, that is, the new covenant, and that a testament is of force where death has occurred. "By so much was Jesus made a surety of a better testament" (Heb. 7:22); "And for this cause He is the Mediator of the new testament, that by means of death, for the redemption of the transgressions that were under the first testament, they which are called might receive the promise of eternal inheritance"; "For a testament is of force after men are dead: otherwise it is of no strength at all while the testator liveth" (Heb. 9:15, 17).

Westminster Confession of Faith (1647)	Westminster Shorter Catechism (1647)	Westminster Larger Catechism (1648)

VII. Of God's Covenant with Man

1. The distance between God and the creature is so great, that although reasonable creatures do owe obedience unto Him as their Creator, yet they could never have any fruition of Him as their blessedness and reward, but by some voluntary condescension on God's part, which He hath been pleased to express by way of covenant.[1]

---
[1] Isa. 40:13-17; Job 9:32-33; 1 Sam. 2:25; Ps. 113:5-6; 100:2-3; Job 22:2-3; 35:7-8; Luke 17:10; Acts 17:24-25

2. The first covenant made with man was a covenant of works,[1] wherein life was promised to Adam; and in him to his posterity,[2] upon condition of perfect and personal obedience.[3]

---
[1] Gal. 3:12
[2] Rom. 10:5; 5:12-20
[3] Gen. 2:17; Gal. 3:10

3. Man, by his fall, having made himself incapable of life by that covenant, the Lord was pleased to make a second,[1] commonly called the covenant of grace; wherein He freely offereth unto sinners life and salvation by Jesus Christ; requiring of them faith in Him, that they may be saved,[2] and promising to give unto all those that are ordained unto eternal life His Holy Spirit, to make them willing, and able to believe.[3]

---
[1] Gal. 3:21; Rom. 8:3; 3:20-21; Gen. 3:15; Isa. 42:6
[2] Mark 16:15, 16; John 3:16; Rom. 10:6, 9; Gal. 3:11
[3] Ezek. 36:26-27; John 6:44-45

4. This covenant of grace is frequently set forth in Scripture by the name of a testament, in reference to the death of Jesus Christ the Testator, and to the everlasting inheritance, with all things belonging to it, therein bequeathed.[1]

---
[1] Heb. 9:15, 16-17; 7:22; Luke 22:20; 1 Cor. 11:25

5. This covenant was differently administered in the time of the law, and in the time of the gospel:[1] under the law it was administered by promises, prophecies, sacrifices, circumcision, the paschal lamb, and other types and ordinances delivered to the people of the Jews, all foresignifying Christ to come;[2] which were, for that time, sufficient and efficacious, through the operation of the Spirit, to instruct and build up the elect in faith in the promised Messiah,[3] by whom they had full remission of sins,

Q. 12: What special act of providence did God exercise toward man in the estate wherein he was created?

A.: When God had created man, He entered into a covenant of life with him, upon condition of perfect obedience; forbidding him to eat of the tree of the knowledge of good and evil, upon the pain of death.[1]

---
[1] Gal. 3:12; Gen. 2:17

Q. 20: Did God leave all mankind to perish in the estate of sin and misery?

A.: God having, out of His mere good pleasure, from all eternity, elected some to everlasting life,[1] did enter into a covenant of grace, to deliver them out of the estate of sin and misery, and to bring them into an estate of salvation by a Redeemer.[2]

---
[1] Eph. 1:4
[2] Rom. 3:20-22; Gal. 3:21-22

Q. 20: What was the providence of God toward man in the estate in which he was created?

A.: The providence of God toward man in the estate in which he was created, was the placing him in Paradise, appointing him to dress it, giving him liberty to eat of the fruit of the earth;[1] putting the creatures under his dominion,[2] and ordaining marriage for his help;[3] affording him communion with himself;[4] instituting the Sabbath;[5] entering into a covenant of life with him, upon condition of personal, perfect, and perpetual obedience,[6] of which the tree of life was a pledge;[7] and forbidding to eat of the tree of the knowledge of good and evil, upon the pain of death.[8]

---
[1] Gen. 2:8, 15-16
[2] Gen. 1:28
[3] Gen. 2:18
[4] Gen. 1:26-29; Gen. 3:8
[5] Gen. 2:3
[6] Gal. 3:12; Rom. 10:5
[7] Gen. 2:9
[8] Gen. 2:17

Q. 30: Doth God leave all mankind to perish in the estate of sin and misery?

A.: God doth not leave all men to perish in the estate of sin and misery,[1] into which they fell by the breach of the first covenant, commonly called the covenant of works;[2] but of His mere love and mercy delivereth His elect out of it, and bringeth them into an estate of salvation by the second covenant, commonly called the covenant of grace.[3]

---
[1] 1 Thes. 5:9
[2] Gal. 3:10, 12
[3] Titus 3:4-7; Gal. 3:21; Rom. 3:20-22

Q. 31: With whom was the covenant of grace made?

A.: The covenant of grace was made with Christ as the second Adam, and in Him with all the elect as His seed.[1]

---
[1] Gal. 3:16; Rom. 5:15ff.; Isa. 53:10-11

Q. 32: How is the grace of God manifested in the second covenant?

A.: The grace of God is manifested in the second covenant, in that he freely provideth and offereth to sinners a Mediator,[1] and life and salvation by Him;[2] and requiring faith as the condition to interest them in Him,[3] promiseth and giveth His Holy Spirit[4] to all His elect, to work in them that faith,[5] with all other saving

Belgic Confession (1561)	Heidelberg Catechism (1563)	Second Helvetic Confession (1566)	Canons of Dort (1619)

Westminster Confession of Faith (1647)	Westminster Shorter Catechism (1647)	Westminster Larger Catechism (1648)

Westminster Confession of Faith (1647)

and eternal salvation; and is called the Old Testament.[4]

---

[1] 2 Cor. 3:6-9
[2] Heb. 8, 9, 10; Rom. 4:11; Col. 2:11-12; 1 Cor. 5:7
[3] 1 Cor. 10:1-4; Heb. 11:13; John 8:56
[4] Gal. 3:7-9, 14

6. Under the gospel, when Christ, the substance,[1] was exhibited, the ordinances in which this covenant is dispensed are the preaching of the Word, and the administration of the sacraments of baptism and the Lord's Supper:[2] which, though fewer in number, and administered with more simplicity, and less outward glory, yet, in them, it is held forth in more fullness, evidence, and spiritual efficacy,[3] to all nations, both Jews and Gentiles;[4] and is called the New Testament.[5] There are not therefore two covenants of grace, differing in substance, but one and the same, under various dispensations.[6]

---

[1] Col. 2:17
[2] Matt. 28:19-20; 1 Cor. 11:23-25
[3] Heb. 12:22-27; Jer. 31:33-34
[4] Matt. 28:19; Eph. 2:15-19
[5] Luke 22:20
[6] Gal. 3:14, 16; Acts 15:11; Rom. 3:21-23, 30; Ps. 32:1; Rom. 4:3, 6, 16-17, 23-24; Heb. 13:8

Westminster Larger Catechism (1648)

graces;[6] and to enable them unto all holy obedience,[7] as the evidence of the truth of their faith[8] and thankfulness to God,[9] and as the way which He hath appointed them to salvation.[10]

---

[1] Gen. 3:15; Isa. 42:6; John 6:27
[2] 1 John 5:11-12
[3] John 3:16; 1:12
[4] Prov. 1:23
[5] 2 Cor. 4:13
[6] Gal. 5:22-23
[7] Ezek. 36:27
[8] James 2:18, 22
[9] 2 Cor. 5:14-15
[10] Eph. 2:18

Q. 33: Was the covenant of grace always administered after one and the same manner?

A.: The covenant of grace was not always administered after the same manner, but the administrations of it under the Old Testament were different from those under the New.[1]

---

[1] 2 Cor. 3:6-9

Q. 34: How was the covenant of grace administered under the Old Testament?

A.: The covenant of grace was administered under the Old Testament, by promises,[1] prophecies,[2] sacrifices,[3] circumcision,[4] the passover,[5] and other types and ordinances, which did all fore-signify Christ then to come, and were for that time sufficient to build up the elect in faith in the promised Messiah,[6] by whom they then had full remission of sin, and eternal salvation.[7]

---

[1] Rom. 15:8
[2] Acts 3:20, 24
[3] Heb. 10:1
[4] Rom. 4:11
[5] 1 Cor. 5:7
[6] Heb. 8, 9, 10; 11:13
[7] Gal. 3:7-9, 14

Q. 35: How is the covenant of grace administered under the New Testament?

A.: Under the New Testament, when Christ the substance was exhibited, the same covenant of grace was and still is to be administered in the preaching of the Word,[1] and the administration of the sacraments of baptism[2] and the Lord's Supper;[3] in which grace and salvation are held forth in more fulness, evidence, and efficacy, to all nations.[4]

---

[1] Mark 16:15
[2] Matt. 28:19-20
[3] 1 Cor. 11:23-25
[4] 2 Cor. 3:6-9; Heb. 8:6, 10-11; Matt. 28:19

Belgic Confession (1561)	Heidelberg Catechism (1563)	Second Helvetic Confession (1566)	Canons of Dort (1619)

Free Will and Inability

Article 14 (part II)
Therefore we reject all that is taught repugnant to this concerning the free will of man, since man is but a slave to sin,[1] and has nothing of himself unless it is given him from heaven.[2] For who may presume to boast that he of himself can do any good, since Christ saith, *No man can come to Me, except the Father which hath sent Me draw him?*[3] Who will glory in his own will, who understands that to be carnally minded is enmity against God?[4] Who can speak of his knowledge, since *the natural man receiveth not the things of the Spirit of God?*[5] In short, who dare suggest any thought, since he knows that *we are not sufficient of ourselves to think any thing as of ourselves, but that our sufficiency is of God?*[6] And therefore what the apostle saith ought justly to be held sure and firm, that *God worketh in us both to will and to do of His good pleasure.*[7] For there is no will nor understanding, conformable to the divine will and understanding, but what Christ hath wrought in man; which He teaches us when He saith, *Without Me ye can do nothing.*[8]

[1] Isa. 26:12; Ps. 94:11; John 8:34; Rom. 6:17; 7:5, 17
[2] John 3:27; Isa. 26:12
[3] John 3:27; 6:44, 65
[4] Rom. 8:7
[5] 1 Cor. 2:14; Ps. 94:11
[6] 2 Cor. 3:5
[7] Phil. 2:13
[8] John 15:5

Q. 8: Are we then so corrupt that we are wholly incapable of doing any good, and inclined to all wickedness?
A.: Indeed we are,[1] except we are regenerated by the Spirit of God.[2]

[1] Gen. 6:5; Job 14:4; Job 15:14, 16
[2] John 3:5; Eph. 2:5

IX. Of Free-Will, and so of Man's Power and Ability

1. We teach in this matter, which at all times has been the cause of many conflicts in the Church, that there is a triple condition or estate of man to be considered. First, what man was before his fall — to wit, upright and free, who might both continue in goodness and decline to evil; but he declined to evil, and has wrapped both himself and all mankind in sin and death, as has been shown before.

2. Secondly, we are to consider what man was after his fall. His understanding, indeed, was not taken from him, neither was he deprived of his will, and altogether changed into a stone or stock. Nevertheless, these things are so altered in man that they are not able to do that now which they could do before his fall. For his understanding is darkened, and his will, which before was free, is now become a servile will; for it serveth sin, not nilling, but willing — for it is called a will, and not a nill. Therefore, as touching evil or sin, man does evil, not compelled either by God or the devil, but of his own accord; and in this respect he has a most free will. But whereas we see that oftentimes the most evil deeds and counsels of man are hindered by God, that they can not attain their end, this does not take from man liberty in evil, but God by His power does prevent that which man otherwise purposed freely: as Joseph's brethren did freely purpose to slay Joseph; but they were not able to do it, because it seemed otherwise good to God in His secret counsel.

3. But, as touching goodness and virtues, man's understanding does not of itself judge aright of heavenly things. For the evangelical and apostolical Scripture requires regeneration of every one of us that will be saved. Wherefore our first birth by Adam does nothing profit us to salvation. Paul says, "The natural man receiveth not the things of the Spirit," etc. (1 Cor. 2:14). The same Paul elsewhere denies that we are "sufficient of ourselves to think any thing as of ourselves" (2 Cor. 3:5).

4. Now, it is evident that the mind or understanding is the guide of the will; and, seeing the guide is blind, it is easy to be seen how far the will can reach. Therefore man, not as yet regenerate, has no free will to good, no strength to perform that which is good. The Lord says in

Head II

The true doctrine (concerning redemption) having been explained, the Synod **rejects** the errors of those who teach:

Rejection 3
That Christ by His satisfaction merited neither salvation itself for anyone, nor faith, whereby this satisfaction of Christ unto salvation is effectually appropriated; but that He merited for the Father only the authority or the perfect will to deal again with man, and to prescribe new conditions as He might desire, obedience to which, however, depended on the free will of man, so that it therefore might have come to pass that either none or all should fulfill these conditions. For these adjudge too contemptuously of the death of Christ, do in no wise acknowledge the most important fruit or benefit thereby gained, and bring again out of hell the Pelagian error.

Rejection 6
The use of the difference between meriting and appropriating, to the end that they may instill into the minds of the imprudent and inexperienced this teaching that God, as far as He is concerned, has been minded of applying to all equally the benefits

Westminster Confession of Faith (1647)	Westminster Shorter Catechism (1647)	Westminster Larger Catechism (1648)
IX. Of Free Will 1. God hath endued the will of man with that natural liberty, that it is neither forced, nor, by any absolute necessity of nature, determined to good, or evil.[1] [1] Matt. 17:12; James 1:14; Deut. 30:19 2. Man, in his state of innocency, had freedom, and power to will and to do that which was good and well pleasing to God;[1] but yet, mutably, so that he might fall from it.[2] [1] Eccl. 7:29; Gen. 1:26 [2] Gen. 2:16-17; 3:6 3. Man, by his fall into a state of sin, hath wholly lost all ability of will to any spiritual good accompanying salvation:[1] so as, a natural man, being altogether averse from that good,[2] and dead in sin,[3] is not able, by his own strength, to convert himself, or to prepare himself thereunto.[4] [1] Rom. 5:6; 8:7; John 15:5 [2] Rom. 3:10, 12 [3] Eph. 2:1, 5. Col. 2:13 [4] John 6:44, 65; Eph. 2:2-5; 1 Cor. 2:14; Titus 3:13, 4-5 4. When God converts a sinner, and translates him into the state of grace, He freeth him from his natural bondage under sin;[1] and, by His grace alone, enables him freely to will and to do that which is spiritually good;[2] yet so, as that by reason of his remaining corruption, he doth not perfectly, nor only, will that which is good, but doth also will that which is evil.[3] [1] Col. 1:13; John 8:34, 36 [2] Phil. 2:13; Rom 6:18, 22 [3] Gal. 5:17; Rom. 7:15, 18-19, 21, 23 5. The will of man is made perfectly and immutably free to do good alone in the state of glory only.[1] [1] Eph. 4:13; Heb. 12:23; 1 John 3:2; Jude 24	*Q. 82: Is any man able perfectly to keep the commandments of God?* A.: No mere man since the fall is able in this life perfectly to keep the commandments of God,[1] but doth daily break them in thought, word, and deed.[2] [1] Eccl. 7:20; 1 John 1:8, 10; Gal. 5:17 [2] Gen. 6:5; 8:21; Rom. 3:9-21; James 3:2-13	*Q. 149: Is any man able perfectly to keep the commandments of God?* A.: No man is able, either of himself,[1] or by any grace received in this life, perfectly to keep the commandments of God;[2] but doth daily break them in thought,[3] word, and deed.[4] [1] James 3:2; John 15:5; Rom. 8:3 [2] Eccl. 7:20; 1 John 1:8, 10; Gal. 5:17; Rom. 7:18-19 [3] Gen. 6:5; 8:21 [4] Rom. 3:9-19; James 3:2-13

Belgic Confession (1561)	Heidelberg Catechism (1563)	Second Helvetic Confession (1566)	Canons of Dort (1619)
		the gospel, "Verily, verily, I say unto you, whosoever committeth sin is the servant of sin" (John 8:34). And Paul the apostle says, "The carnal mind is enmity against God; for it is not subject to the law of God, neither indeed can be" (Rom. 8:7). 5. Furthermore, there is some understanding of earthly things remaining in man after his fall. For God has of mercy left him wit, though much differing from that which was in him before his fall. God commands us to garnish our wit, and therewithal He gives gifts and also the increase thereof. And it is a clear case that we can profit very little in all arts without the blessing of God. The Scripture, no doubt, refers all arts to God; yea, and the Gentiles also ascribe the beginnings of arts to the gods, as the authors thereof. 6. Lastly, we are to consider whether the regenerate have free will, and how far they have it. In regeneration the understanding is illuminated by the Holy Spirit, that it may understand both the mysteries and will of God. And the will itself is not only changed by the Spirit, but it is also endued with faculties, that, of its own accord, it may both will and do good (Rom. 8:4).	gained by the death of Christ; but that, while some obtain the pardon of sin and eternal life, and others do not, this difference depends on their own free will, which joins itself to the grace that is offered without exception, and that it is not dependent on the special gift of mercy, which powerfully works in them, that they rather than others should appropriate unto themselves this grace. For these, while they feign that they present this distinction in a sound sense, seek to instill into the people the destructive poison of the Pelagian errors.

Second Helvetic Confession (cont.)

Unless we grant this, we shall deny Christian liberty, and bring in the bondage of the law. Besides, the prophet brings in God speaking thus: "I will put my law in their inward parts, and write it in their hearts" (Jer. 31:33; Ezek. 36:27). The Lord also says in the gospel, "If the Son...make you free, ye shall be free indeed" (John 8:36). Paul also to the Philippians, "For unto you it is given in the behalf of Christ, not only to believe on Him, but also to suffer for His sake" (Phil. 1:29). And, again, "Being confident of this very thing, that He which hath begun a good work in you will perform it until the day of Jesus Christ" (ver. 6). Also, "For it is God which worketh in you both to will and to do of His good pleasure" (Phil. 2:13).

7. Where, nevertheless, we teach that there are two things to be observed — first, that the regenerate, in the choice and working of that which is good, do not only work passively, but actively; for they are moved of God that themselves may do that which they do. And Augustine does truly allege that saying that "God is said to be our helper; but no man can be helped but he that does somewhat." The Manichaeans did bereave man of all action, and made him like a stone and a block.

8. Secondly, that in the regenerate there remains infirmity. For, seeing that sin dwells in us, and that the flesh in the regenerate strives against the Spirit, even to our lives' end, they do not readily perform in every point that which they had purposed. These things are confirmed by the apostle (Rom. 7:13-26; Gal. 5:17).

9. Therefore, all free will is weak by reason of the relics of the old Adam remaining in us so long as we live, and of the human corruption which so nearly cleaves to us. In the meanwhile, because the strength of the flesh and the relics of the old man are not of such great force that they can wholly quench the work of the Spirit, therefore the faithful are called free, yet so that they do acknowledge their infirmity, and glory no whit at all of their free will. For that which St. Augustine does repeat so often out of the apostle ought always to be kept in mind by the faithful: "What hast thou that thou didst not receive? now if thou didst receive it, why dost thou glory, as if thou hadst not received it?" (1 Cor. 4:7). Hitherto may be added that that comes not straightway to pass which we have purposed, for the events of things are in the hand of God. For which cause Paul besought the Lord that He would prosper his journey (Rom. 1:10). Wherefore, in this respect also, free will is very weak.

10. But in outward things no man denies but that both the regenerate and the unregenerate have their free will; for man hath this constitution common with other creatures (to whom he is not inferior) to will some things and to nill other things. So he may speak or keep silence, go out of his house

Westminster Confession of Faith (1647)	Westminster Shorter Catechism (1647)	Westminster Larger Catechism (1648)

Second Helvetic Confession (cont.)

or abide within. Although herein also God's power is evermore to be marked, which brought to pass that Balaam could not go so far as he would (Numb. 24:13), and that Zacharias, coming out of the temple, could not speak as he would have done (Luke 1:22).

11. In this matter we condemn the Manichaeans, who deny that the beginning of evil unto man, being good, came from his free will. We condemn, also, the Pelagians, who affirm that an evil man has free will sufficiently to perform a good precept. Both these are confuted by the Scripture, which says to the former, "God hath made man upright" (Eccl. 7:29); and to the latter, "If the Son therefore shall make you free, ye shall be free indeed" (John 8:36).

Christology:
The Doctrine of Christ

Belgic Confession (1561)	Heidelberg Catechism (1563)	Second Helvetic Confession (1566)	Canons of Dort (1619)

Christ the Mediator

Article 17

The Recovery of Fallen Man

We believe that our most gracious God, in His admirable wisdom and goodness, seeing that man had thus thrown himself into temporal and spiritual death, and made himself wholly miserable, was pleased to seek and comfort him when he trembling[1] fled from His presence, promising him that He would give His Son, who should *be made of a woman, to bruise the head of the serpent,* and would make him happy.[2]

[1] Gen. 3:8-9,19; Isa. 65:1-2
[2] Heb. 2:14; Gen. 22:18; Isa. 7:14; John 7:42; 2 Tim. 2:8; Heb. 7:14; Gen. 3:15; Gal. 4:4

Q. 12: Since then, by the righteous judgment of God, we deserve temporal and eternal punishment, is there no way by which we may escape that punishment, and be again received into favor?

A.: God will have His justice satisfied,[1] and therefore we must make this full satisfaction, either by ourselves or by another.[2]

[1] Exod. 20:5
[2] Deut. 24:16; 2 Cor. 5:14-15

Q. 18: Who then is that Mediator, who is in one person both very God, and a real righteous man?

A.: Our Lord Jesus Christ,[1] "who of God is made unto us wisdom, and righteousness, and sanctification, and redemption."[2]

[1] Matt. 1:23; 1 Tim. 3:16; Luke 2:11
[2] 1 Cor. 1:30

V. Of the Adoration, Worship, and Invocation of God Through the Only Mediator Jesus Christ

2. But we teach that "God is to be adored and worshiped," as Himself has taught us to worship Him — to wit, "in spirit and in truth" (John 4:24); not with any superstition, but with sincerity, according to His Word, lest at any time He also say unto us, "Who hath required these things at your hand?" (Isa. 1:12; Jer. 6:20). For Paul also says, God "Neither is worshipped with men's hands, as though He needed any thing," etc. (Acts 17:25).

3. We, in all dangers and casualties of life, call on Him alone, and that by the mediation of the only Mediator, and our intercessor, Jesus Christ. For it is expressly commanded us, "Call upon Me in the day of trouble: I will deliver thee, and thou shalt glorify Me" (Ps. 50:15). Moreover, the Lord has made a most large promise, saying, "Whatsoever ye shall ask the Father,... He shall give it you" (John 16:23); and again, "Come unto Me, all ye that labour and are heavy laden, and I will give you rest" (Matt. 11:28). And seeing it is written, "How then shall they call on Him in whom they have not believed?" (Rom. 10:14), and we do believe in God alone; therefore we call upon Him only, and that through Christ. "For there is one God," says the apostle, "and one mediator between God and men, Christ Jesus" (1 Tim. 2:5). Again, "If any man sin, we have an advocate with the Father, Jesus Christ the righteous," etc. (1 John 2:1).

The Names of Christ

*Q. 29: Why is the Son of God called **Jesus,** that is a Savior?*

A.: Because He saveth us, and delivereth us from our sins;[1] and likewise, because we ought not to seek, neither can find salvation in any other.[2]

Westminster Confession of Faith (1647)	Westminster Shorter Catechism (1647)	Westminster Larger Catechism (1648)

VIII. Of Christ the Mediator

1. It pleased God, in His eternal purpose, to choose and ordain the Lord Jesus, His only begotten Son, to be the Mediator between God and man,[1] the Prophet,[2] Priest,[3] and King,[4] the Head and Savior of His Church,[5] the Heir of all things,[6] and Judge of the world:[7] unto whom He did from all eternity give a people, to be His seed,[8] and to be by Him in time redeemed, called, justified, sanctified, and glorified.[9]

[1] Isa. 42:1; 1 Pet. 1:19-20; John 3:16; 1 Tim. 2:5
[2] Acts 3:22
[3] Heb. 5:5-6
[4] Ps. 2:6. Luke 1:33
[5] Eph. 5:23
[6] Heb. 1:2
[7] Acts 17:31
[8] John 17:6; Ps. 22:30; Isa. 53:10
[9] 1 Tim. 2:6; Isa. 55:4-5; 1 Cor. 1:30

Q. 41: Why was our Mediator called Jesus?

A.: Our Mediator was called Jesus, because He saveth His people from their sins.[1]

[1] Matt. 1:21

Q. 42: Why was our Mediator called Christ?

A.: Our Mediator was called Christ, because He was anointed with the Holy Ghost above measure;[1] and so set apart, and fully furnished with all authority and ability,[2] to execute the

Belgic Confession (1561)	Heidelberg Catechism (1563)	Second Helvetic Confession (1566)	Canons of Dort (1619)
	[1] Matt. 1:21 [2] Acts 4:12 *Q. 30: Do such then believe in Jesus the only Savior, who seek their salvation and welfare of saints, of themselves, or anywhere else?* A.: They do not; for though they boast of Him in words, yet in deeds they deny Jesus the only deliverer and Savior;[1] for one of these two things must be true, that either Jesus is not a complete Savior or that they, who by a true faith receive this Savior, must find all things in Him necessary to their salvation.[2] [1] 1 Cor. 1:13,31; Gal. 5:4 [2] Col. 2:20; Isa. 9:6-7; Col. 1:19-20		

Heidelberg Catechism (cont.)

*Q. 31: Why is He called **Christ**, that is, anointed?*

A.: Because He is ordained of God the Father, and anointed with the Holy Ghost,[1] to be our chief Prophet and Teacher,[2] who has fully revealed to us the secret counsel and will of God concerning our redemption; and to be our only High Priest, who by the one sacrifice of His body, has redeemed us,[3] and makes continual intercession with the Father for us;[4] and also to be our eternal King,[5] who governs us by His word and Spirit, and who defends and preserves us[6] in (the enjoyment of) that salvation, He has purchased for us.

[1] Heb. 1:9
[2] Deut. 18:18; Acts 3:22; John 1:18; John 15:15; Matt. 11:27
[3] Ps. 110:4; Heb. 7:21; Heb. 10:14
[4] Rom. 8:34
[5] Ps. 2:6; Luke 1:33
[6] Matt. 28:18; John 10:28

Q. 32: But why art thou called a Christian?

A.: Because I am a member of Christ by faith,[1] and thus am partaker of His anointing;[2] that so I may confess His name,[3] and present myself a living sacrifice of thankfulness to Him;[4] and also that with a free and good conscience I may fight against sin and Satan in this life,[5] and afterwards reign with Him eternally, over all creatures.[6]

[1] 1 Cor. 6:15
[2] 1 John 2:27; Joel 2:28
[3] Matt. 10:32
[4] Rom. 12:1
[5] Eph. 6:11-12; 1 Tim. 1:18-19
[6] 2 Tim. 2:12

Q. 33: Why is Christ called the only begotten Son of God, since we are also the children of God?

A.: Because Christ alone is the eternal and natural Son of God;[1] but we are children adopted of God, by grace, for His sake.[2]

[1] John 1:1; Heb. 1:2
[2] Rom. 8:15-17; Eph. 1:5-6

Q. 34: Wherefore callest thou Him our Lord?

A.: Because He hath redeemed us, both soul and body, from all our sins, not with gold or silver, but with His precious blood, and hath delivered us from all the power of the devil; and thus hath made us His own property.[1]

[1] 1 Pet. 1:18-19; 1 Cor. 6:20

Westminster Confession of Faith (1647)	Westminster Shorter Catechism (1647)	Westminster Larger Catechism (1648)
		offices of prophet,[3] priest,[4] and king[5] of His Church,[6] in the estate both of His humiliation and exaltation. [1] John 3:34; Ps. 45:7 [2] John 6:27; Matt. 28:18-20 [3] Acts 3:21-22; Luke 4:18, 21 [4] Heb. 5:5-7; 4:14-15 [5] Ps. 2:6; Matt. 21:5; Isa. 9:6-7 [6] Phil. 2:6-11

Belgic Confession (1561)	Heidelberg Catechism (1563)	Second Helvetic Confession (1566)	Canons of Dort (1619)

The Natures of Jesus Christ

Article 19

The Union and Distinction of the Two Natures in the Person of Christ

We believe that by this conception the person of the Son is inseparably united and connected with the human nature; so that there are not two Sons of God, nor two persons, but two natures united in one single person; yet that each nature retains its own distinct properties. As then the divine nature hath always remained uncreated, without beginning of days or end of life,[1] filling heaven and earth, so also hath the human nature not lost its properties, but remained a creature, having beginning of days, being a finite nature, and retaining all the properties of a real body.[2] And though He hath by His resurrection given immortality to the same, nevertheless He hath not changed the reality of His human nature; forasmuch as our salvation and resurrection also depend on the reality of His body.

But these two natures are so closely united in one person, that they were not separated even by His death. Therefore that which He, when dying, commended into the hands of His Father, was a real human spirit, departing from His

Q. 15: What sort of a mediator and deliverer then must we seek for?

A.: For one who is very man,[1] and perfectly righteous; and yet more powerful than all creatures; that is, one who is also very God.[2]

[1] 1 Cor. 15:21; Rom. 8:3
[2] Rom. 9:5; Isa. 7:14

Q. 16: Why must He be very man, and also perfectly righteous?

A.: Because the justice of God requires that the same human nature which hath sinned, should likewise make satisfaction for sin;[1] and one, who is himself a sinner, cannot satisfy for others.[2]

[1] Rom. 5:12, 15
[2] 1 Pet. 3:18; Isa. 53:11

Q. 17: Why must He in one person be also very God?

A.: That He might by the power of His Godhead sustain in His human nature the burden of God's wrath;[1] and might obtain for, and restore to us, righteousness and life.[2]

[1] 1 Pet. 3:18; Acts 2:24; Isa. 53:8
[2] 1 John 1:2; Jer. 23:6; 2 Tim. 1:10; John 6:51

XI. Of Jesus Christ, Being True God and Man, and the Only Savior of the World

6. We acknowledge, therefore, that there be in one and the same Jesus Christ our Lord two natures — the divine and the human nature; and we say that these two are so conjoined or united that they are not swallowed up, confounded, or mingled together; but rather united or joined together in one person (the properties of each nature being safe and remaining still), so that we do worship one Christ our Lord, and not two. I say one, true God and man, as touching His divine nature, of the same substance with us, and "in all points tempted like as we are, yet without sin" (Heb. 4:15).

7. As, therefore, we detest the heresy of Nestorius, which makes two Christs of one and dissolves the union of the person, so do we abominate the madness of Eutyches and of the Monothelites and Monophysites, who overthrow the propriety of the human nature.

8. Therefore we do not teach that the divine nature in Christ did suffer, or that Christ, according to His human nature, is yet in the world, and so in every place. For we do neither think nor teach that the body of Christ ceased to be a true body after His glorifying, or that it was deified and so deified that it put off its properties, as touching body and soul, and became altogether a divine nature and began to be one substance alone; therefore we do not allow or receive the unwitty subtleties, and the intricate, obscure, and inconstant disputations of Schwenkfeldt, and such other vain janglers, about this matter; neither are we Schwenkfeldians.

Westminster Confession of Faith (1647)	Westminster Shorter Catechism (1647)	Westminster Larger Catechism (1648)

VIII. Of Christ the Mediator

2. The Son of God, the second person of the Trinity, being very and eternal God, of one substance and equal with the Father, did, when the fullness of time was come, take upon Him man's nature,[1] with all the essential properties, and common infirmities thereof, yet without sin;[2] being conceived by the power of the Holy Ghost, in the womb of the Virgin Mary, of her substance.[3] So that two whole, perfect, and distinct natures, the Godhead and the manhood, were inseparably joined together in one person, without conversion, composition, or confusion.[4] Which person is very God, and very man, yet one Christ, the only Mediator between God and man.[5]

[1] John 1:1, 14; 1 John 5:20; Phil. 2:6; Gal. 4:4
[2] Heb. 2:14, 16-17; Heb. 4:15
[3] Luke 1:27, 31, 35; Gal. 4:4
[4] Luke 1:35; Col. 2:9; Rom. 9:5; 1 Pet. 3:18; 1 Tim. 3:16
[5] Rom. 1:3-4; 1 Tim. 2:5

3. The Lord Jesus, in His human nature thus united to the divine, was sanctified, and anointed with the Holy Spirit, above measure,[1] having in Him all the treasures of wisdom and knowledge;[2] in whom it pleased the Father that all fullness should dwell;[3] to the end that, being holy, harmless, undefiled, and full of grace and truth,[4] He might be thoroughly furnished to execute the office of a Mediator and Surety.[5] Which office He took not unto Himself, but was thereunto called by His Father,[6] who put all power and judgment into His hand, and gave Him commandment to execute the same.[7]

[1] Ps. 45:7; John 3:34
[2] Col. 2:3
[3] Col. 1:19
[4] Heb. 7:26; John 1:14
[5] Acts 10:38; Heb. 12:28; 7:22
[6] Heb. 5:4-5
[7] John 5:22, 27; Matt. 28:18; Acts 2:36

7. Christ, in the work of mediation, acts according to both natures, by each nature doing that which is proper to itself;[1] yet, by reason of the unity of the person, that which is proper to one nature is sometimes in Scripture attributed to the person denominated by the other nature.[2]

[1] Heb. 9:14; 1 Pet. 3:18
[2] Acts 20:28; John 3:13; 1 John 3:16

Q. 21: Who is the Redeemer of God's elect?
A.: The only Redeemer of God's elect is the Lord Jesus Christ,[1] who, being the eternal Son of God, became man,[2] and so was, and continueth to be, God and man in two distinct natures, and one person, for ever.[3]

[1] 1 Tim. 2:5-6
[2] John 1:14; Gal. 4:4
[3] Rom. 9:5; Luke 1:35; Col. 2:9; Heb. 7:24-25

Q. 36: Who is the Mediator of the covenant of grace?
A.: The only Mediator of the covenant of grace is the Lord Jesus Christ,[1] who, being the eternal Son of God, of one substance and equal with the Father,[2] in the fulness of time became man,[3] and so was and continues to be God and man, in two entire distinct natures, and one person, for ever.[4]

[1] 1 Tim. 2:5
[2] John 1:1, 14; 10:30; Phil. 2:6
[3] Gal. 4:4
[4] Luke 1:35; Rom. 9:5; Col. 2:9; Heb. 7:24-25

Q. 38: Why was it requisite that the Mediator should be God?
A.: It was requisite that the Mediator should be God, that He might sustain and keep the human nature from sinking under the infinite wrath of God, and the power of death;[1] give worth and efficacy to His sufferings, obedience, and intercession;[2] and to satisfy God's justice,[3] procure His favor,[4] purchase a peculiar people,[5] give His Spirit to them,[6] conquer all their enemies,[7] and bring them to everlasting salvation.[8]

[1] Acts 2:24-25; Rom. 1:4; 4:25; Heb. 9:14
[2] Acts 20:28; Heb. 9:14; 7:25-28
[3] Rom. 3:24-26
[4] Eph. 1:6; Matt. 3:17
[5] Titus 2:13-14
[6] Gal. 4:6
[7] Luke 1:68-69, 71, 74
[8] Heb. 5:8-9; 9:11-15

Q. 39: Why was it requisite that the Mediator should be man?
A.: It was requisite that the Mediator should be man, that He might advance our nature,[1] perform obedience to the law,[2] suffer and make intercession for us in our nature,[3] have a fellow feeling of our infirmities;[4] that we might receive the adoption of sons,[5] and have comfort and access with boldness unto the throne of grace.[6]

[1] Heb. 2:16
[2] Gal. 4:4
[3] Heb. 2:14; 7:24-25
[4] Heb. 4:15
[5] Gal. 4:5
[6] Heb. 4:16

Belgic Confession (1561)	Heidelberg Catechism (1563)	Second Helvetic Confession (1566)	Canons of Dort (1619)
body.[3] But in the meantime the divine nature always remained united with the human, even when He lay in the grave; and the Godhead did not cease to be in Him, any more than it did when He was an infant, though it did not so clearly manifest itself for a while. Wherefore we confess that He is *very God* and *very man*: very God by His power to conquer death, and very man that He might die for us according to the infirmity of His flesh.			

[1] Heb. 7:3
[2] 1 Cor. 15:13, 21; Phil. 3:21; Matt. 26:11; Acts 1:2,11; 3:21; Luke 24:39; John 20:25, 27
[3] Luke 23:46; Matt. 27:50

The Offices of Christ

Article 21 **The Satisfaction of Christ, Our Only High Priest, For Us** We believe that Jesus Christ is ordained with an oath to be an everlasting High Priest, after the order of Melchizedek;[1] and that He hath presented Himself in our behalf before the Father, to appease His wrath by His full satisfaction,[2] by offering Himself on the tree of the cross, and pouring out His precious blood to purge away our sins; as the prophets had foretold. For it is written, *He was wounded for our transgressions, He was*	*Q. 31: Why is He called Christ, that is, anointed?* A.: Because He is ordained of God the Father, and anointed with the Holy Ghost,[1] to be our chief Prophet and Teacher,[2] who has fully revealed to us the secret counsel and will of God concerning our redemption; and to be our only High Priest, who by the one sacrifice of His body, has redeemed us,[3] and makes continual intercession with the Father for us;[4] and also to be our eternal King,[5] who governs us by His word and Spirit, and who defends and preserves us[6] in	**XI. Of Jesus Christ, Being True God and Man, and the Only Savior of the World** 16. For we teach and believe that this Jesus Christ our Lord is the only and eternal Savior of mankind, yea, and of the whole world, in whom all are saved before the law, under the law, and in the time of the gospel, and so many as shall yet be saved to the end of the world. For the Lord Himself, in the gospel, says, "He that entereth not by the door into the sheepfold, but climbeth up some other way, the same is a thief and a robber" (John 10:1). "I am the door of the sheep" (ver. 7). And also in another place of the same gospel He says, "Abraham rejoiced to see My day: and he saw it, and was glad" (John 8:56). And the apostle Peter says, "Neither is there salvation in any other: for there is none other name under heaven given among men, whereby we must be saved" (Acts 4:12). We believe, therefore, that through the grace of our Lord Jesus Christ we shall be saved, even as our fathers were. For Paul says, that our fathers "did all eat the same spiritual meat; and did all	

Westminster Confession of Faith (1647)	Westminster Shorter Catechism (1647)	Westminster Larger Catechism (1648)

VIII. Of Christ the Mediator

1. It pleased God, in His eternal purpose, to choose and ordain the Lord Jesus, His only begotten Son, to be the Mediator between God and man,[1] the Prophet,[2] Priest,[3] and King,[4] the Head and Savior of His Church,[5] the Heir of all things,[6] and Judge of the world:[7] unto whom He did from all eternity give a people, to be His seed,[8] and to be by Him in time redeemed, called, justified, sanctified, and glorified.[9]

[1] Isa. 42:1; 1 Pet. 1:19-20; John 3:16; 1 Tim. 2:5
[2] Acts 3:22
[3] Heb. 5:5-6
[4] Ps. 2:6. Luke 1:33
[5] Eph. 5:23
[6] Heb. 1:2
[7] Acts 17:31
[8] John 17:6; Ps. 22:30; Isa. 53:10
[9] 1 Tim. 2:6; Isa. 55:4-5; 1 Cor. 1:30

8. To all those for whom Christ has purchased redemption, He does certainly and effectually apply and communicate the same;[1] making intercession for them,[2] and revealing unto them,

Q. 23: What offices doth Christ execute as our Redeemer?
A.: Christ, as our Redeemer, executeth the offices of a prophet, of a priest, and of a king, both in His estate of humiliation and exaltation.[1]

[1] Acts 3:21-22; Heb. 12:25; 2 Cor. 13:3; Heb. 5:5-7; 7:25; Ps. 2:6; Isa. 9:6-7; Matt. 21:5; Ps. 2:8-11

Q. 24: How doth Christ execute the office of a prophet?
A.: Christ executeth the office of a prophet, in revealing to us, by His Word and Spirit, the will of God for our salvation.[1]

[1] John 1:18; 1 Pet. 1:10-12; John 15:15; 20:31

Q. 43: How doth Christ execute the office of a prophet?
A.: Christ executeth the office of a prophet, in His revealing to the Church,[1] in all ages, by His Spirit and Word,[2] in divers ways of administration,[3] the whole will of God,[4] in all things concerning their edification and salvation.[5]

[1] John 1:18
[2] 1 Pet. 1:10-12
[3] Heb. 1:1-2
[4] John 15:15
[5] Acts 20:32; Eph. 4:11-13; John 20:31

Q. 44: How doth Christ execute the office of a priest?
A.: Christ executeth the office of a priest, in His once offering Himself a sacrifice without spot to God,[1] to be a reconciliation for the sins of His people;[2] and in making continual intercession for them.[3]

[1] Heb. 9:14, 28
[2] Heb. 2:17
[3] Heb. 7:25

Belgic Confession (1561)	Heidelberg Catechism (1563)	Second Helvetic Confession (1566)	Canons of Dort (1619)
bruised for our iniquities: the chastisement of our peace was upon Him, and with His stripes we are healed. He was brought as a lamb to the slaughter, and numbered with the transgressors;[3] and condemned by Pontius Pilate as a malefactor, though he had first declared Him innocent.[4] Therefore, *He restored that which He took not away,*[5] and *suffered the just for the unjust,*[6] as well in His body as in His soul, feeling the terrible punishment which our sins had merited; insomuch that *His sweat became like unto drops of blood falling on the ground.*[7] He called out, *My God, My God, why hast Thou forsaken Me?*[8] and hath suffered all this for the remission of our sins. Wherefore we justly say with the apostle Paul, *that we know nothing but Jesus Christ, and Him crucified;*[9] *we count all things but loss and dung for the excellency of the knowledge of Christ Jesus our Lord,*[10] in whose wounds we find all manner of consolation. Neither is it necessary to seek or invent any other means of being reconciled to God, than this only sacrifice, once offered, by which believers are made perfect forever.[11] This is also the reason why He was called by the angel of God, *Jesus,* that is to say, *Savior,* because He should save His people from their sins.[12] ―――― [1] Ps.110:4; Heb. 5:10	(the enjoyment of) that salvation, He has purchased for us. ―――― [1] Heb. 1:9 [2] Deut. 18:18; Acts 3:22; John 1:18; John 15:15; Matt. 11:27 [3] Ps. 110:4; Heb. 7:21; Heb. 10:14 [4] Rom. 8:34 [5] Ps. 2:6; Luke 1:33 [6] Matt. 28:18; John 10:28	drink the same spiritual drink: for they drank of that spiritual Rock that followed them: and that Rock was Christ" (1 Cor. 10:3-4). And therefore we read that John said, that Christ was that "Lamb slain from the foundation of the world" (Rev. 13:8); and that John the Baptist witnesseth, that Christ is that "Lamb of God, which taketh away the sin of the world" (John 1:29). 17. Wherefore we do plainly and openly profess and preach, that Jesus Christ is the only Redeemer and Savior of the world, the King and High Priest, the true and looked-for Messiah, that holy and blessed one (I say) whom all the shadows of the law, and the prophecies of the prophets, did prefigure and promise; and that God did supply and send Him unto us, so that now we are not to look for any other. And now there remains nothing, but that we all should give all glory to Him, believe in Him, and rest in Him only, contemning and rejecting all other aids of our life. For they are fallen from the grace of God, and make Christ of no value unto themselves, whosoever they be that seek salvation in any other things besides Christ alone (Gal. 5:4).	

Westminster Confession of Faith (1647)	Westminster Shorter Catechism (1647)	Westminster Larger Catechism (1648)

Westminster Confession of Faith (1647)

in and by the Word, the mysteries of salvation;[3] effectually persuading them by His Spirit to believe and obey, and governing their hearts by His Word and Spirit;[4] overcoming all their enemies by His almighty power and wisdom, in such manner, and ways, as are most consonant to His wonderful and unsearchable dispensation.[5]

[1] John 6:37, 39; 10:15-16
[2] 1 John 2:1-2; Rom. 8:34
[3] John 15:13, 15; Eph. 1:7-9; John 17:6
[4] John 14:16; Heb. 12:2; 2 Cor. 4:13; Rom. 8:9, 14; 15:18-19; John 17:17
[5] Ps. 110:1; 1 Cor. 15:25-26; Mal. 4:2-3; Col. 2:15

Westminster Shorter Catechism (1647)

Q. 25: How doth Christ execute the office of a priest?

A.: Christ executeth the office of a priest, in His once offering up of Himself a sacrifice to satisfy divine justice,[1] and reconcile us to God;[2] and in making continual intercession for us.[3]

[1] Heb. 9:14, 28
[2] Heb. 2:17
[3] Heb. 7:24-25

Q. 26: How doth Christ execute the office of a king?

A.: Christ executeth the office of a king, in subduing us to Himself,[1] in ruling[2] and defending us,[3] and in restraining and conquering all His and our enemies.[4]

[1] Acts 15:14-16
[2] Isa. 33:22
[3] Isa. 32:1-2
[4] 1 Cor. 15:25; Ps. 110

Westminster Larger Catechism (1648)

Q. 45: How doth Christ execute the office of a king?

A.: Christ executeth the office of a king, in calling out of the world a people to Himself,[1] and giving them officers,[2] laws,[3] and censures, by which He visibly governs them;[4] in bestowing saving grace upon His elect,[5] rewarding their obedience,[6] and correcting them for their sins,[7] preserving and supporting them under all their temptations and sufferings,[8] restraining and overcoming all their enemies,[9] and powerfully ordering all things for His own glory,[10] and their good;[11] and also in taking vengeance on the rest, who know not God, and obey not the gospel.[12]

[1] Acts 15:14-16; Isa. 55:4-5; Gen. 49:10; Ps. 110:3
[2] Eph. 4:11-12; 1 Cor. 12:28
[3] Isa. 33:22
[4] Matt. 18:17-18; 1 Cor. 5:4-5
[5] Acts 5:31
[6] Rev. 22:12; 2:10
[7] Rev. 3:19
[8] Isa. 63:9
[9] 1 Cor. 15:25; Ps. 110:1-2
[10] Rom. 14:10-11
[11] Rom. 8:28
[12] 2 Thes. 1:8-9; Ps. 2:8-9

Belgic Confession (1561)	Heidelberg Catechism (1563)	Second Helvetic Confession (1566)	Canons of Dort (1619)

Belgic Confession (cont.)

2 Col. 1:14; Rom. 5:8-9; Col. 2:14; Heb. 2:17; 9:14; Rom. 3:24; 8:2; John 15:3; Acts 2:24; 13:28; John 3:16; 1 Tim. 2:6
3 Isa. 53:5, 7, 12
4 Luke 23:22, 24; Acts 13:28; Ps. 22:16; John 18:38; Ps. 69:5; 1 Pet. 3:18
5 Ps. 69:5
6 1 Pet. 3:18
7 Luke 22:44
8 Ps. 22:2; Matt. 27:46
9 1 Cor. 2:2
10 Phil. 3:8
11 Heb. 9:25-26; 10:14
12 Matt. 1:21; Acts 4:12

Article 26

Christ's Intercession

We believe that we have no access unto God but alone through the only Mediator and Advocate, Jesus Christ the righteous,[1] who therefore became man, having united in one person the divine and human natures, that we men might have access to the divine Majesty, which access would otherwise be barred against us. But this Mediator, whom the Father hath appointed between Him and us, ought in no wise affright us by His majesty, or cause us to seek another according to our fancy.[2] For there is no creature, either in heaven or on earth, who loveth us more than Jesus Christ;[3] *who, though He was in the form of God, yet made Himself of no reputation, and took upon Him the form of a man and of a servant for us,*[4] *and was made like unto His brethren in all things.* If, then, we should seek for another mediator, who would be well affected towards us, whom could we find who loved us more than He who laid down His life for us, even when we were His enemies?[5] And if we seek for one who hath power and majesty, who is there that hath so much of both as *He who sits at the right hand of His Father,* and who hath *all power in heaven and on earth?*[6] And who will sooner be heard than the own well-beloved Son of God?

Therefore it was only through distrust that this practice of dishonoring instead of honoring the saints was introduced, doing that which they never have done nor required, but have, on the contrary, steadfastly rejected, according to their bounden duty, as appears by their writings.[7] Neither must we plead here our unworthiness; for the meaning is not that we should offer our prayers to God on account of our own worthiness, but only on account of the excellency and worthiness of the Lord Jesus Christ,[8] whose righteousness is become ours by faith.

Therefore the apostle, to remove this foolish fear or, rather, distrust from us, justly saith that *Jesus Christ was made like unto His brethren in all things, that He might be a merciful and faithful High Priest, to make reconciliation for the sins of the people. For in that He Himself hath suffered, being tempted, He is able to succor them that are tempted.*[9] And further to encourage us, he adds: *Seeing, then, that we have a great High Priest that is passed into the heavens, Jesus the Son of God, let us hold fast our profession. For we have not an High Priest which cannot be touched with the feeling of our infirmities; but was in all points tempted like as we are, yet without sin. Let us therefore come boldly unto the throne of grace, that we may obtain mercy, and find grace to help in time of need.*[10] The same apostle saith: *Having boldness to enter into the holiest by the blood of Jesus, let us draw near with a true heart in full assurance of faith,* etc.[11] Likewise, *Christ hath an unchangeable priesthood, wherefore He is able also to save them to the uttermost that come unto God by Him, seeing He ever liveth to make intercession for them.*[12]

What more can be required? since Christ Himself saith: *I am the way, and the truth, and the life; no man cometh unto the Father but by Me.*[13] To what purpose should we then seek another advocate,[14] since it hath pleased God to give us His own Son as our Advocate?[15] Let us not forsake Him to take another, or rather to seek after another, without ever being able to find Him; for God well knew, when He gave Him to us, that we were sinners.

Therefore, according to the command of Christ, we call upon the heavenly Father through Jesus Christ our only Mediator, as we are taught in the Lord's Prayer;[16] being assured that whatever we ask of the Father in His Name will be granted us.[17]

1 1 Tim. 2:5; 1 John 2:1; Rom. 8:33
2 Hos. 13:9; Jer. 2:13, 33
3 John 10:11; 1 John 4:10; Rom. 5:8; Eph. 3:19; John 15:13
4 Phil. 2:7
5 Rom. 5:8
6 Mark 16:19; Col. 3:1; Rom. 8:33; Matt. 11:27; 28:18
7 Acts 10:26; 14:15
8 Dan. 9:17-18; John 16:23; Eph. 3:12; Acts 4:12; 1 Cor. 1:31; Eph. 2:18
9 Heb. 2:17-18
10 Heb. 4:14-16
11 Heb. 10:19, 22
12 Heb. 7:24, 25
13 John 14:6
14 Ps. 44:21
15 1 Tim. 2:5; 1 John 2:1; Rom. 8:33
16 Luke 11:2
17 John 4:17; 16:23; 14:13

Westminster Confession of Faith (1647)	Westminster Shorter Catechism (1647)	Westminster Larger Catechism (1648)

Belgic Confession (1561)	Heidelberg Catechism (1563)	Second Helvetic Confession (1566)	Canons of Dort (1619)

The States of Christ

Article 18

Of the Incarnation of Jesus Christ

We confess, therefore, that God did fulfull the promise which He made to the fathers by the mouth of His holy prophets[1] when He sent into the world, at the time appointed by Him, His own only-begotten and eternal Son, *who took upon Him the form of a servant, and became like unto man,*[2] really assuming the true human nature, with all its infirmities, sin excepted,[3] being conceived in the womb of the blessed Virgin Mary, by the power of the Holy Ghost, without the means of man;[4] and did not only assume human nature as to the body, but also a true human soul,[5] that he might be a real man. For since the soul was lost as well as the body, it was necessary that He should take both upon Him, to save both. Therefore we confess (in opposition to the heresy of the Anabaptists, who deny that Christ assumed human flesh of His mother) that Christ is become *a partaker of the flesh and blood of the children;*[6] that He is a *fruit of the loins of David* after the flesh;[7] *made of the seed of David according to the flesh;*[8] a *fruit of the womb* of the Virgin Mary;[9] *made of a woman;*[10] a *branch* of David;[11] a shoot of *the root of Jesse;*[12] *sprung from*

Q. 35: What is the meaning of these words —*"He was conceived by the Holy Ghost, born of the Virgin Mary"?*

A.: That God's eternal Son, who is,[1] and continueth true and eternal God,[2] took upon Him the very nature of man, of the flesh and blood of the Virgin Mary,[3] by the operation of the Holy Ghost;[4] that He might also be the true seed of David,[5] like unto His brethren in all things, sin excepted.[6]

[1] John 1:1; Col. 1:15; Ps. 2:7
[2] Rom. 9:5; 1 John 5:20
[3] John 1:14; Gal. 4:4
[4] Matt. 1:18; Luke 1:35
[5] Ps. 132:2; Acts 2:30; Rom. 1:3
[6] Phil. 2:7; Heb. 4:15

Q. 36: What profit dost thou receive by Christ's holy conception and nativity?

A.: That He is our Mediator,[1] and with His innocence and perfect holiness, covers in the sight of God, my sins,[2] wherein I was conceived and brought forth.

[1] Heb. 2:16-17
[2] Ps. 32:1; 1 Cor. 1:30; Rom. 8:34

Q. 37: What dost thou understand by the words, "He suffered"?

A.: That He, all the time that He lived on earth, but especially at the end of His life, sustained in body and soul[1] the wrath of God against

XI. Of Jesus Christ, Being True God and Man, and the Only Savior of the World

4. We also teach and believe that the eternal Son of the eternal God was made the Son of man, of the seed of Abraham and David (Matt. 1:25); not by the means of any man, as Ebion affirmed, but that He was most purely conceived by the Holy Spirit, and born of Mary, who was always a virgin, even as the history of the gospel does declare. And Paul says, "He took not on Him the nature of angels; but He took on Him the seed of Abraham" (Heb. 2:16). And John the apostle says, "every spirit that confesseth not that Jesus Christ is come in the flesh is not of God" (1 John 4:3). The flesh of Christ, therefore, was neither flesh in show only, nor yet flesh brought from heaven, as Valentinus and Marcion dreamed.

5. Moreover, our Lord Jesus Christ had not a soul without sense and reason, as Apollinaris thought; nor flesh without a soul, as Eunomius did teach; but a soul with its reason, and flesh with its senses, by which senses He felt true griefs in the time of His passion, even as He himself witnessed when He said, "My soul is exceeding sorrowful, even unto death" (Matt. 26:38); and, "Now is My soul troubled," etc. (John 12:27).

9. Moreover, we believe that our Lord Jesus Christ did truly suffer and die for us in the flesh, as Peter says (1 Pet. 4:1). We abhor the most impious madness of the Jacobites, and all the Turks, who execrate the passion of our Lord. Yet we deny not but that "the Lord of glory," according to the saying of Paul, was crucified for us (1 Cor. 2:8); for we do reverently and religiously receive and use the communication of properties drawn from the Scripture, and used of all antiquity in expounding and reconciling places of Scripture which at first sight seem to disagree one from another.

10. We believe and teach that the same Lord Jesus Christ, in that true flesh in which He was crucified and died, rose again from the dead; and that He did not rise up another flesh, but retained a true body. Therefore, while His disciples thought that they did see the spirit of their Lord Christ, He showed them His hands and feet, which were marked with the prints of the nails and wounds, saying, "Behold My hands and My feet, that it is I Myself: handle Me, and

Westminster Confession of Faith (1647)	Westminster Shorter Catechism (1647)	Westminster Larger Catechism (1648)

VIII. Of Christ the Mediator

4. This office the Lord Jesus did most willingly undertake;[1] which that He might discharge, He was made under the law,[2] and did perfectly fulfil it;[3] endured most grievous torments immediately in His soul,[4] and most painful sufferings in His body;[5] was crucified, and died,[6] was buried, and remained under the power of death, yet saw no corruption.[7] On the third day He arose from the dead,[8] with the same body in which He suffered,[9] with which also He ascended into heaven, and there sitteth at the right hand of His Father,[10] making intercession,[11] and shall return, to judge men and angels, at the end of the world.[12]

[1] Ps. 40:7-8; Heb. 10:5-10; John 10:18; Phil. 2:8
[2] Gal. 4:4
[3] Matt. 3:15; 5:17
[4] Matt. 26:37-38; Luke 22:44; Matt. 27:46
[5] Matt. 26; 27
[6] Phil. 2:8
[7] Acts 2:23-24, 27; 13:37; Rom. 6:9
[8] 1 Cor. 15:3-5
[9] John 20:25, 27
[10] Mark 16:19
[11] Rom. 8:34; Heb. 9:24; 7:25
[12] Rom. 14:9-10; Acts 1:11; 10:42; Matt. 13:40-42; Jude 6; 2 Pet. 2:4

Q. 22: How did Christ, being the Son of God, become man?

A.: Christ, the Son of God, became man, by taking to Himself a true body,[1] and a reasonable soul,[2] being conceived by the power of the Holy Ghost, in the womb of the Virgin Mary, and born of her,[3] yet without sin.[4]

[1] Heb. 2:14, 16; 10:5
[2] Matt. 26:38
[3] Luke 1:27, 31, 35, 42; Gal. 4:4
[4] Heb. 4:15; 7:26

Q. 27: Wherein did Christ's humiliation consist?

A.: Christ's humiliation consisted in His being born, and that in a low condition,[1] made under the law,[2] undergoing the miseries of this life,[3] the wrath of God,[4] and the cursed death of the cross;[5] in being buried,[6] and continuing under the power of death for a time.[7]

[1] Luke 2:7
[2] Gal. 4:4
[3] Heb. 12:2-3; Isa. 53:2-3
[4] Luke 22:44; Matt. 27:46
[5] Phil. 2:8
[6] 1 Cor. 15:3-4
[7] Acts 2:24-27, 31

Q. 28: Wherein consisteth Christ's exaltation?

A.: Christ's exaltation consisteth in His rising again from the dead on the third day,[1] in ascending up into heaven,[2] in sitting at the right hand of God the Father,[3] and in coming to judge the world at the last day.[4]

[1] 1 Cor. 15:4
[2] Mark 16:19
[3] Eph. 1:20
[4] Acts 1:11; 17:31

Q. 37: How did Christ, being the Son of God, become man?

A.: Christ the Son of God became man, by taking to Himself a true body, and a reasonable soul,[1] being conceived by the power of the Holy Ghost in the womb of the Virgin Mary, of her substance, and born of her,[2] yet without sin.[3]

[1] John 1:14; Matt. 26:38
[2] Luke 1:27, 31, 35, 42; Gal. 4:4
[3] Heb. 4:15; 7:26

Q. 46: What was the estate of Christ's humiliation?

A.: The estate of Christ's humiliation was that low condition, wherein He for our sakes, emptying Himself of His glory, took upon Him the form of a servant, in His conception and birth, life, death, and after His death, until His resurrection.[1]

[1] Phil. 2:6-8; Luke 1:31; 2 Cor. 8:9; Acts 2:24

Q. 47: How did Christ humble Himself in His conception and birth?

A.: Christ humbled Himself in His conception and birth, in that, being from all eternity the Son of God, in the bosom of the Father, He was pleased in the fulness of time to become the Son of man, made of a woman of low estate, and to be born of her; with divers circumstances of more than ordinary abasement.[1]

[1] John 1:14, 18; Gal. 4:4; Luke 2:7

Q. 48: How did Christ humble Himself in His life?

A.: Christ humbled Himself in His life, by subjecting Himself to the law,[1] which He perfectly fulfilled;[2] and by conflicting with the indignities of the world,[3] temptations of Satan,[4] and infirmities in His flesh, whether common to the nature of man, or particularly accompanying that His low condition.[5]

[1] Gal. 4:4
[2] Matt. 5:17; Rom. 5:19
[3] Ps. 22:6; Heb. 12:2-3
[4] Matt. 4:1-12; Luke 4:13
[5] Heb. 2:17-18; 4:15; Isa. 52:13-14

Q. 49: How did Christ humble Himself in His death?

A.: Christ humbled Himself in His death, in that having been betrayed by Judas,[1] forsaken by His disciples,[2] scorned and rejected by the world,[3] condemned by Pilate, and tormented by His persecutors;[4] having also conflicted with

Belgic Confession (1561)	Heidelberg Catechism (1563)	Second Helvetic Confession (1566)	Canons of Dort (1619)
the tribe of Judah;[13] descended from the Jews according to the flesh:[14] of the seed of Abraham, since He took on Him the seed of Abraham,[15] and became like unto His brethren in all things, sin excepted;[16] so that in truth He is our Immanuel, that is to say, God with us.[17]	the sins of all mankind; that so by His passion, as the only propitiatory sacrifice,[2] He might redeem our body and soul from everlasting damnation, and obtain for us the favor of God, righteousness and eternal life.	see; for a spirit hath not flesh and bones, as ye see Me have" (Luke 24:39).	

[1] Isa. 11:1; Luke 1:55; Gen. 26:4; 2 Sam. 7:12; Ps. 132:11; Acts 13:23
[2] 1 Tim. 2:5; 3:16; Phil. 2:7
[3] Heb. 2:14-15; 4:15
[4] Luke 1:31, 34-35
[5] Matt. 26:38; John 12:27
[6] Heb. 2:14
[7] Acts 2:30
[8] Ps. 132:11; Rom. 1:3
[9] Luke 1:42
[10] Gal. 4:4
[11] Jer. 33:15
[12] Isa. 11:1
[13] Heb. 7:14
[14] Rom. 9:5
[15] Gen. 22:18; 2 Sam. 7:12; Matt. 1:1; Gal. 3:16
[16] Heb. 2:15-17
[17] Isa. 7:14; Matt. 1:23

[1] 1 Pet. 2:24; Isa. 53:12
[2] 1 John 2:2; Rom. 3:25

Q. 38: Why did He suffer under Pontius Pilate as judge?

A.: That He, being innocent, and yet condemned by a temporal judge,[1] might thereby free us from the severe judgment of God to which we were exposed.[2]

[1] Luke 23:14; John 19:4; Ps. 69:4
[2] Gal. 3:13-14

Q. 39: Is there anything more in His being crucified than if He had died some other death?

A.: Yes, there is; for thereby I am assured, that He took on Him the curse which lay upon me; for the death of the cross was accursed of God.[1]

[1] Deut. 21:23; Gal. 3:13

Q. 40: Why was it necessary for Christ to humble Himself even unto death?

A.: Because with respect to the justice and truth of God, satisfaction for our sins could be made no otherwise[1] than by the death of the Son of God.[2]

[1] Gen. 2:17
[2] Heb. 2:9-10; Phil. 2:8

11. We believe that our Lord Jesus Christ, in the same flesh, did ascend above all the visible heavens into the very highest heaven, that is to say, the seat of God and of the blessed spirits, unto the right hand of God the Father. Although it does signify an equal participation of glory and majesty, yet it is also taken for a certain place; of which the Lord, speaking in the gospel, says, that He will "go to prepare a place" for us (John 14:2). Also the apostle Peter says, "Whom the heaven must receive until the times of restitution of all things" (Acts 3:21).

12. And out of heaven the same Christ will return unto judgment, even then when wickedness shall chiefly reign in the world, and when Antichrist, having corrupted true religion, shall fill all things with superstition and impiety, and shall most cruelly waste the Church with fire and bloodshed. Now Christ shall return to redeem His, and to abolish Antichrist by His coming, and to judge the quick and the dead (Acts 17:31). For the dead shall arise, and those that shall be found alive in that day (which is unknown unto all creatures) shall be changed in the twinkling of an eye (1 Cor. 15:51-52). And all the faithful shall be taken up to meet Christ in the air (1 Thes. 4:17); that thenceforth they may enter with Him into heaven, there to live forever (2 Tim. 2:11); but the unbelievers, or ungodly, shall descend with the devils into hell, there to burn forever, and never to be delivered out of torments (Matt. 25:41).

13. We therefore condemn all those who deny the true resurrection of the flesh, and those who think amiss of the glorified bodies, as did Joannes Hierosolymitanus, against whom Jerome wrote. We also condemn those who have thought that both the devils and all the wicked shall at length be saved and have an end of their torments; for the Lord Himself has absolutely set it down that "their worm dieth not, and the fire is not quenched" (Mark 9:44).

14. Moreover, we condemn the Jewish dreams, that before the day of judgment there shall be a golden age in the earth, and that the godly shall possess the kingdoms of the world, their wicked enemies being trodden under foot; for the evangelical truth (Matt. 24 and 25, Luke 21), and the apostolic doctrine (in the second epistle to the Thessalonians 2, and in the second epistle to Timothy 3 and 4) is found to teach far otherwise.

15. Furthermore, by His passion or death, and by all those things which He did and suffered

Westminster Confession of Faith (1647)	Westminster Shorter Catechism (1647)	Westminster Larger Catechism (1648)
		the terrors of death, and the powers of darkness, felt and borne the weight of God's wrath,[5] He laid down His life an offering for sin,[6] enduring the painful, shameful, and cursed death of the cross.[7]

[1] Matt. 27:4
[2] Matt. 26:56
[3] Isa. 53:2-3
[4] Matt. 27:26-50; John 19:34
[5] Luke 22:44; Matt. 27:46
[6] Isa. 53:10
[7] Phil. 2:8; Heb. 12:2; Gal. 3:13

Q. 50: Wherein consisted Christ's humiliation after His death?

A.: Christ's humiliation after His death consisted in His being buried,[1] and continuing in the state of the dead, and under the power of death till the third day;[2] which hath been otherwise expressed in these words, He descended into hell.

[1] 1 Cor. 15:3-4
[2] Ps. 16:10; Acts 2:24-27, 31; Rom. 6:9; Matt. 12:40

Q. 51: What was the estate of Christ's exaltation?

A.: The estate of Christ's exaltation comprehendeth His resurrection,[1] ascension,[2] sitting at the right hand of the Father,[3] and His coming again to judge the world.[4]

[1] 1 Cor. 15:4
[2] Mark 16:19
[3] Eph. 1:20
[4] Acts 1:11; 17:31

Q. 52: How was Christ exalted in His resurrection?

A.: Christ was exalted in His resurrection, in that, not having seen corruption in death, (of which it was not possible for Him to be held,[1]) and having the very same body in which He suffered, with the essential properties thereof,[2] (but without mortality, and other infirmities belonging to this life,) really united to His soul,[3] He rose again from the dead the third day by His own power;[4] whereby He declared Himself to be the Son of God,[5] to have satisfied divine justice,[6] to have vanquished death, and him that had the power of it,[7] and to be Lord of quick and dead:[8] all which He did as a public person,[9] the head of His Church,[10] for their justification,[11] quickening in grace,[12] support against enemies,[13] and to assure them of their resurrection from the dead at the last day.[14]

[1] Acts 2:24, 27
[2] Luke 24:39
[3] Rom. 6:9; Rev. 1:18
[4] John 10:18
[5] Rom. 1:4
[6] Rom. 8:34

Belgic Confession (1561)	Heidelberg Catechism (1563)	Second Helvetic Confession (1566)	Canons of Dort (1619)

Heidelberg Catechism (1563)

Q. 41: Why was He also "buried"?

A.: Thereby to prove that He was really dead.[1]

---
[1] Acts 13:29; Mark 15:43, 46

Q. 42: Since then Christ died for us, why must we also die?

A.: Our death is not a satisfaction for our sins, but only an abolishing of sin, and a passage into eternal life.[1]

---
[1] John 5:24; Phil. 1:23

Q. 43: What further benefit do we receive from the sacrifice and death of Christ on the cross?

A.: That by virtue thereof our old man is crucified, dead and buried with Him;[1] that so the corrupt inclinations of the flesh may no more reign in us,[2] but that we may offer ourselves unto Him a sacrifice of thanksgiving.[3]

---
[1] Rom. 6:6-7
[2] Rom. 6:12
[3] Rom. 12:1

Q. 44: Why is there added, "He descended into hell"?

A.: That in my greatest temptations, I may be assured, and wholly comfort myself in this, that my Lord Jesus Christ, by His inexpressible anguish, pains, terrors, and hellish agonies, in which He was plunged during all His sufferings, but especially on the cross, hath delivered me from the anguish and torments of hell.[1]

---
[1] Isa. 53:10; Matt. 27:46

Second Helvetic Confession (1566)

for our sakes from the time of His coming in the flesh, our Lord reconciled His heavenly Father unto all the faithful (Rom. 5:10); purged their sin (Heb. 1:3); spoiled death, broke in sunder condemnation and hell; and by His resurrection from the dead brought again and restored life and immortality (Rom. 4:25; 1 Cor. 15:17; 2 Tim. 1:10). For He is our righteousness, life, and resurrection (John 6:44); and, to be short, He is the fullness and perfection, the salvation and most abundant sufficiency, of all the faithful. For the apostle says, "For it pleased the Father that in Him should all fullness dwell" (Col. 1:19), "And ye are complete in Him" (Col. 2:10).

18. And, to speak many things in a few words, with a sincere heart we believe, and with liberty of speech we freely profess, whatsoever things are defined out of the Holy Scriptures, and comprehended in the creeds, and in the decrees of those four first and most excellent councils — held at Nicaea, Constantinople, Ephesus, and Chalcedon — together with blessed Athanasius's creed and all other creeds like to these, touching the mystery of the incarnation of our Lord Jesus Christ; and we condemn all things contrary to the same.

Westminster Confession of Faith (1647)	Westminster Shorter Catechism (1647)	Westminster Larger Catechism (1648)
		[7] Heb. 2:14 [8] Rom. 14:9 [9] 1 Cor. 15:21-22 [10] Eph. 1:20, 22-23; Col. 1:18 [11] Rom. 4:25 [12] Eph. 2:1, 5-6; Col. 2:12 [13] 1 Cor. 15:25-27 [14] 1 Cor. 15:20

Q. 53: How was Christ exalted in His ascension?

A.: Christ was exalted in His ascension, in that having after His resurrection often appeared unto and conversed with His apostles, speaking to them of the things pertaining to the kingdom of God,[1] and giving them commission to preach the gospel to all nations,[2] forty days after His resurrection, He, in our nature, and as our head,[3] triumphing over enemies,[4] visibly went up into the highest heavens, there to receive gifts for men,[5] to raise up our affections thither,[6] and to prepare a place for us,[7] where Himself is, and shall continue till His second coming at the end of the world.[8]

[1] Acts 1:2-3
[2] Matt. 28:19-20
[3] Heb. 6:20
[4] Eph. 4:8
[5] Acts 1:9-11; Eph. 4:10; Ps. 68:18
[6] Col. 3:1-2
[7] John 14:3
[8] Acts 3:21

Q. 54: How is Christ exalted in His sitting at the right hand of God?

A.: Christ is exalted in His sitting at the right hand of God, in that as God-man He is advanced to the highest favor with God the Father,[1] with all fulness of joy,[2] glory,[3] and power over all things in heaven and earth;[4] and doth gather and defend His Church, and subdue their enemies; furnisheth His ministers and people with gifts and graces,[5] and maketh intercession for them.[6]

[1] Phil. 2:9
[2] Acts 2:28; Ps. 16:11
[3] John 17:5
[4] Eph. 1:22; 1 Pet. 3:22
[5] Eph. 4:10-12; Ps. 110:1
[6] Rom. 8:34

Q. 55: How doth Christ make intercession?

A.: Christ maketh intercession, by His appearing in our nature continually before the Father in heaven,[1] in the merit of His obedience and sacrifice on earth,[2] declaring His will to have it applied to all believers;[3] answering all accusations against them,[4] and procuring for them quiet of conscience, notwithstanding daily failings,[5] access with boldness to the throne of grace,[6] and acceptance of their persons[7] and services.[8]

Belgic Confession (1561)	Heidelberg Catechism (1563)	Second Helvetic Confession (1566)	Canons of Dort (1619)

Heidelberg Catechism (cont.)

Q. 45: What doth the resurrection of Christ profit us?

A.: First, by His resurrection He has overcome death, that He might make us partakers of that righteousness which He had purchased for us by His death;[1] secondly, we are also by His power raised up to a new life;[2] and lastly, the resurrection of Christ is a sure pledge of our blessed resurrection.[3]

---
[1] 1 Cor. 15:16
[2] Rom. 6:4; Col. 3:1
[3] 1 Cor. 15; Rom. 8:11

Q. 46: How dost thou understand these words, "He ascended into heaven"?

A.: That Christ, in sight of His disciples, was taken up from earth into heaven;[1] and that He continues there for our interest[2] until He comes again to judge the quick and the dead.

---
[1] Acts 1:9; Mark 16:19
[2] Heb. 4:14; Rom. 8:34; Eph. 4:10

Q. 47: Is not Christ then with us even to the end of the world, as He hath promised?

A.: Christ is very man and very God; with respect to His human nature, He is no more on earth;[1] but with respect to His Godhead, majesty, grace and spirit, He is at no time absent from us.

---
[1] Acts 3:21; John 3:13; John 16:28; Matt. 28:20

Q. 48: But if His human nature is not present, wherever His Godhead is, are not then these two natures in Christ separated from one another?

A.: Not at all, for since the Godhead is illimitable and omnipresent,[1] it must necessarily follow that the same is beyond the limits of the human nature He assumed,[2] and yet is nevertheless in this human nature, and remains personally united to it.

---
[1] Acts 7:49; Matt. 24:30
[2] Matt. 28:20; John 16:28; John 17:11; John 3:13

Q. 49: Of what advantage to us is Christ's ascension into heaven?

A.: First, that He is our Advocate in the presence of His Father in heaven;[1] secondly, that we have our flesh in heaven as a sure pledge that He, as the head, will also take up to Himself, us, His members;[2] thirdly, that He sends us His Spirit as an earnest,[3] by whose power we "seek the things which are above, where Christ sitteth on the right hand of God, and not things on earth."[4]

---
[1] Heb. 9:24; 1 John 2:2; Rom. 8:34
[2] John 14:2; Eph. 2:6
[3] John 14:16; 2 Cor. 1:22; 2 Cor. 5:5
[4] Col. 3:1; Phil. 3:20

Q. 50: Why is it added, "and sitteth at the right hand of God"?

A.: Because Christ is ascended into heaven for this end, that He might appear as head of His Church,[1] by whom the Father governs all things.[2]

---
[1] Eph. 1:20-22; Col. 1:18
[2] Matt. 28:18; John 5:22

Q. 51: What profit is this glory of Christ, our Head, unto us?

A.: First, that by His Holy Spirit He pours out heavenly graces upon us His members;[1] and then that by His power He defends and preserves us against all enemies.[2]

---
[1] Eph. 4:8
[2] Ps. 2:9; John 10:28

Q. 52: What comfort is it to thee that "Christ shall come again to judge the quick and the dead"?

A.: That in all my sorrows and persecutions, with uplifted head I look for the very same person, who before offered Himself for my sake to the tribunal of God, and has removed all curse from me, to come as judge from heaven;[1] who shall cast all His and my enemies into everlasting condemnation,[2] but shall translate me with all His chosen ones to Himself, into heavenly joys and glory.[3]

---
[1] Luke 21:28; Rom. 8:23-24; 1 Thes. 4:16
[2] 2 Thes. 1:6-9; Matt. 25:41
[3] Matt. 25:34

Westminster Confession of Faith (1647)	Westminster Shorter Catechism (1647)	Westminster Larger Catechism (1648)
		[1] Heb. 9:12, 24 [2] Heb. 1:3 [3] John 3:16; 17:9, 20, 24 [4] Rom. 8:33-34 [5] Rom. 5:1-2; 1 John 2:1-2 [6] Heb. 4:16 [7] Eph. 1:6 [8] 1 Pet. 2:5 *Q. 56: How is Christ to be exalted in His coming again to judge the world?* A.: Christ is to be exalted in His coming again to judge the world, in that He, who was unjustly judged and condemned by wicked men,[1] shall come again at the last day in great power,[2] and in the full manifestation of His own glory, and of His Father's, with all His holy angels,[3] with a shout, with the voice of the archangel, and with the trumpet of God,[4] to judge the world in righteousness.[5] [1] Acts 3:14-15 [2] Matt. 24:30 [3] Luke 9:26; Matt. 25:31 [4] 1 Thes. 4:16 [5] Acts 17:31 *Q. 57: What benefits hath Christ procured by His mediation?* A.: Christ, by His mediation, hath procured redemption,[1] with all other benefits of the covenant of grace.[2] [1] Heb. 9:12 [2] 2 Cor. 1:20

Belgic Confession (1561)	Heidelberg Catechism (1563)	Second Helvetic Confession (1566)	Canons of Dort (1619)

God's Just Mercy in Christ

Article 20 **God Hath Manifested His Justice and Mercy in Christ** We believe that God, who is perfectly merciful and just, sent His Son to assume that nature in which the disobedience was committed, to make satisfaction in the same, and to bear the punishment of sin by His most bitter passion and death.[1] God therefore manifested His justice against His Son when He laid our iniquities[2] upon Him, and poured forth His mercy and goodness on us, who were guilty and worthy of damnation, out of mere and perfect love, giving His Son unto death for us, and raising Him for our justification,[3] that through Him we might obtain immortality and life eternal. ――――――― [1] Heb. 2:14; Rom. 8:3, 32-33 [2] Isa. 53:6; John 1:29; 1 John 4:9 [3] Rom. 4:25	*Q. 11: Is not God then also merciful?* A.: God is indeed merciful,[1] but also just; therefore His justice requires[2] that sin which is committed against the most high majesty of God be also punished with extreme,[3] that is, with everlasting punishment of body and soul.[4] ――――――― [1] Exod. 34:6 [2] Exod. 20:5; Job 34:10-11 [3] Ps. 5:5-6 [4] Gen. 2:17; Rom. 6:23		**Head II** *Article 2* Since therefore we are unable to make that satisfaction in our own persons or to deliver ourselves from the wrath of God, He hath been pleased in His infinite mercy to give His only begotten Son, for our surety, who was made sin, and became a curse for us and in our stead, that He might make satisfaction to divine justice on our behalf.

The Promises of the Gospel

	Q. 19: Whence knowest thou this? A.: From the holy gospel, which God Himself first revealed in Paradise;[1] and afterwards published by the patriarchs and prophets,[2] and represented by the sacrifices and	***XIII. Of the Gospel of Jesus Christ: also of Promises; of the Spirit and of the Letter*** 1. The gospel, indeed, is opposed to the law: for the law works wrath, and does announce a curse; but the gospel does preach grace and blessing. John also says, "The law was given by Moses, but grace and truth came by Jesus Christ" (John 1:17). Yet, notwithstanding, it is most certain that they who were before the law, and under the law, were not altogether destitute of the gospel. For	**Head II** *Article 5* Moreover, the promise of the gospel is, that whosoever believeth in Christ crucified, shall not perish, but have everlasting life. This promise, together with

Westminster Confession of Faith (1647)	Westminster Shorter Catechism (1647)	Westminster Larger Catechism (1648)
VIII. Of Christ the Mediator 5. The Lord Jesus, by His perfect obedience, and sacrifice of Himself, which He through the eternal Spirit, once offered up unto God, has fully satisfied the justice of His Father;[1] and purchased, not only reconciliation, but an everlasting inheritance in the kingdom of heaven, for all those whom the Father has given unto Him.[2]		

[1] Rom. 5:19; Heb. 9:14, 16; 10:14; Eph. 5:2; Rom. 3:25-26
[2] Dan. 9:24, 26; Col. 1:19-20; Eph. 1:11, 14; John 17:2; Heb. 9:12, 15

VIII. Of Christ the Mediator

6. Although the work of redemption was not actually wrought by Christ till after His incarnation, yet the virtue, efficacy, and benefits thereof were communicated unto the elect, in all ages successively from the beginning of the world, in and by those promises, types, and sacrifices, wherein He was revealed, and signified to be the seed of the woman which should bruise the serpent's head; and the Lamb slain from

Belgic Confession (1561)	Heidelberg Catechism (1563)	Second Helvetic Confession (1566)	Canons of Dort (1619)
	other ceremonies of the law;[3] and lastly, has fulfilled it by His only begotten Son.[4] [1] Gen. 3:15 [2] Gen. 22:17-18; Gen. 28:14; Rom. 1:2; Heb. 1:1; John 5:46 [3] Heb. 10:7-8 [4] Rom. 10:4; Heb. 13:8	they had notable evangelical promises, such as these: "And I will put enmity between thee and the woman, and between thy seed and her seed; it shall bruise thy head, and thou shalt bruise His heel" (Gen. 3:15). "In thy seed shall all the nations of the earth be blessed" (Gen. 22:18). The Lord thy God will raise up unto thee a Prophet from the midst of thee, of thy brethren, like unto me; etc. (Deut. 18:15; Acts 3:22, and 7:37). 2. And we do acknowledge that the fathers had two kinds of promises revealed unto them, even as we have. For some of them were of present and transitory things: such as were the promises of the land of Canaan, and of victories; and such as are nowadays concerning our daily bread. Other promises there were then, and are now, of heavenly and everlasting things; as of God's favor, remission of sins, and life everlasting, through faith in Jesus Christ. Now, the fathers had not only outward or earthly, but spiritual and heavenly promises in Christ. For the apostle Peter says, "Of which salvation the prophets have enquired and searched diligently, who prophesied of the grace that should come unto you" (1 Pet. 1:10). Whereupon the apostle Paul also says, that the gospel of God was "promised afore by His prophets in the holy scriptures" (Rom. 1:2). Hereby, then, it appears evident that the fathers were not altogether destitute of all the gospel.	the command to repent and believe, ought to be declared and published to all nations, and to all persons promiscuously and without distinction, to whom God out of His good pleasure sends the gospel.

Westminster Confession of Faith (1647)	Westminster Shorter Catechism (1647)	Westminster Larger Catechism (1648)
the beginning of the world; being yesterday and today the same, and forever.[1] [1] Gal. 4:4-5; Gen. 3:15; Rev. 13:8; Heb. 13:8		

Soteriology:
The Doctrine of Salvation

Belgic Confession (1561)	Heidelberg Catechism (1563)	Second Helvetic Confession (1566)	Canons of Dort (1619)

Common Grace and External Calling

Belgic Confession (1561)	Heidelberg Catechism (1563)	Second Helvetic Confession (1566)	Canons of Dort (1619)
Article 14 **The Creation and Fall of Man, and His Incapacity to Perform What is Truly Good** And being thus become wicked, perverse, and corrupt in all his ways, he hath lost all his excellent gifts which he had received from God,[1] and only retained a few remains thereof,[2] which, however, are sufficient to leave man without excuse. ―――――― [1] Rom. 3:10 [2] Acts 14:16-17; 17:27			**Head III & IV** *Article 8* As many as are called by the gospel are unfeignedly called. For God hath most earnestly and truly declared in His Word what will be acceptable to Him; namely, that all who are called, should comply with the invitation. He, moreover, seriously promises eternal life and rest to as many as shall come to Him and believe on Him. *Article 9* It is not the fault of the gospel nor of Christ, offered therein, nor of God, who calls men by the gospel and confers upon them various gifts, that those who are called by the ministry of the Word refuse to come and be converted. The fault lies in themselves, some of whom when called, regardless of their danger, reject the word of life; others, though they receive it, suffer it not to make a lasting impression on their heart; therefore, their joy, arising only from a temporary faith, soon vanishes and they fall away; while others choke the seed of the Word by perplexing cares and the pleasures of this world, and produce no fruit. This our Savior teaches in the parable of the sower (Matt. 13).

Westminster Confession of Faith (1647)	Westminster Shorter Catechism (1647)	Westminster Larger Catechism (1648)

X. Of Effectual Calling

4. Others, not elected, although they may be called by the ministry of the Word,[1] and may have some common operations of the Spirit,[2] yet they never truly come unto Christ, and therefore cannot be saved:[3] much less can men, not professing the Christian religion, be saved in any other way whatsoever, be they never so diligent to frame their lives according to the light of nature, and the laws of that religion they do profess.[4] And to assert and maintain that they may, is very pernicious, and to be detested.[5]

[1] Matt. 22:14
[2] Matt. 7:22; 13:20-21; Heb. 6:4-5
[3] John 6:64-66; 8:24
[4] Acts 4:12; John 14:6; Eph. 2:12; John 4:22; 17:3
[5] 2 John 9-11; 1 Cor. 16:22; Gal. 1:6-8

XVI. Of Good Works

7. Works done by unregenerate men, although for the matter of them they may be things which God commands; and of good use both to themselves and others:[1] yet, because they proceed not from a heart purified by faith;[2] nor are done in a right manner, according to the Word;[3] nor to a right end, the glory of God,[4] they are therefore sinful, and cannot please God, or make a man meet to receive grace from God:[5] and yet, their neglect of them is more sinful and displeasing unto God.[6]

[1] 2 Ki. 10:30-31; 1 Ki. 21:27, 29; Phil. 1:15-16, 18
[2] Gen. 4:5; Heb. 11:4, 6
[3] 1 Cor. 13:3; Isa. 1:12
[4] Matt. 6:2, 5, 16
[5] Hag. 2:14; Titus 1:15; Amos 5:21-22; Hosea 1:4; Rom. 9:16; Titus 3:15
[6] Ps. 14:4; 36:3; Job 21:14-15; Matt. 25:41-43, 45; 23:3

Q. 60: Can they who have never heard the gospel, and so know not Jesus Christ, nor believe in Him, be saved by their living according to the light of nature?

A.: They who, having never heard the gospel,[1] know not Jesus Christ,[2] and believe not in him, cannot be saved,[3] be they never so diligent to frame their lives according to the light of nature,[4] or the laws of that religion which they profess;[5] neither is there salvation in any other, but in Christ alone,[6] who is the Saviour only of His body the church.[7]

[1] Rom. 10:14
[2] 2 Thes. 1:8-9; Eph. 2:12; John 1:10-12
[3] John 8:24; Mark 16:16
[4] 1 Cor. 1:20-24
[5] John 4:22; Rom. 9:31-32; Phil. 3:4-9
[6] Acts 4:12
[7] Eph. 5:23

Q. 68: Are the elect only effectually called?

A.: All the elect, and they only, are effectually called;[1] although others may be, and often are, outwardly called by the ministry of the Word,[2] and have some common operations of the Spirit;[3] who, for their wilful neglect and contempt of the grace offered to them, being justly left in their unbelief, do never truly come to Jesus Christ.[4]

[1] Acts 13:48
[2] Matt. 22:14
[3] Matt. 7:22; 13:20-21; Heb. 6:4-6
[4] John 12:38-40; Acts 28:25-27; John 6:64-65; Ps. 81:11-12

Belgic Confession (1561)	Heidelberg Catechism (1563)	Second Helvetic Confession (1566)	Canons of Dort (1619)

Canons of Dort (cont.)

The true doctrine (concerning corruption and conversion) having been explained, the Synod **rejects** the errors of those who teach:

Rejection 5

That the corrupt and natural man can so well use the common grace (by which they understand the light of nature), or the gifts still left him after the fall, that he can gradually gain by their good use a greater, namely, the evangelical or saving grace and salvation itself. And that in this way God on His part shows Himself ready to reveal Christ unto all men, since He applies to all sufficiently and efficiently the means necessary to conversion. For the experience of all ages and the Scriptures do

both testify that this is untrue. "He sheweth His word unto Jacob, His statutes and His judgments unto Israel. He hath not dealt so with any nation: and as for His judgments, they have not known them" (Ps. 147:19-20). "Who in times past suffered all nations to walk in their own ways" (Acts 14:16). And: "Now when they (Paul and his companions) had gone throughout Phrygia and the region of Galatia, and were forbidden of the Holy Ghost to preach the word in Asia, after they were come to Mysia, they assayed to go into Bithynia: but the Spirit suffered them not" (Acts 16:6-7).

Effectual Calling and Regeneration

			Heads III & IV *Article 6* What therefore neither the light of nature, nor the law could do, that God performs by the operation of the Holy Spirit through the Word or ministry of reconciliation, which is the glad tidings concerning the Messiah, by means whereof it hath pleased God to save such as believe, as well under the Old, as under the New Testament. *Article 10* But that others who are called by the gospel obey the call and are converted is not to be ascribed to the proper exercise of free will, whereby one distinguishes himself above others, equally furnished with grace sufficient for faith and conversions as the proud heresy of Pelagius maintains; but it must be wholly ascribed to God, who as

Westminster Confession of Faith (1647)	Westminster Shorter Catechism (1647)	Westminster Larger Catechism (1648)

X. Of Effectual Calling

1. All those whom God hath predestinated unto life, and those only, He is pleased, in His appointed and accepted time, effectually to call,[1] by His Word and Spirit,[2] out of that state of sin and death, in which they are by nature to grace and salvation, by Jesus Christ;[3] enlightening their minds spiritually and savingly to understand the things of God,[4] taking away their heart of stone, and giving unto them an heart of flesh;[5] renewing their wills, and, by His almighty power, determining them to that which is good,[6] and effectually drawing them to Jesus Christ:[7] yet so, as they come most freely, being made willing by His grace.[8]

[1] Rom. 8:30, 11:7; Eph. 1:10-11
[2] 2 Thes. 2:13-14; 2 Cor. 3:3, 6
[3] Rom. 8:2; Eph. 2:1-5; 2 Tim. 1:9-10
[4] Acts 26:18; 1 Cor. 2:10, 12; Eph. 1:17-18
[5] Ezek. 36:26
[6] Ezek. 11:19; Phil. 2:13; Deut. 30:6; Ezek. 36:27
[7] Eph. 1:19; John 6:44-45
[8] Songs 1:4; Ps. 110:3; John 6:37; Rom. 6:16-18

2. This effectual call is of God's free and special grace alone, not from anything at all foreseen in man,[1] who is altogether passive therein, until, being quickened and renewed by the Holy Spirit,[2] he is thereby enabled to answer this call, and to embrace the grace offered and conveyed in it.[3]

[1] 2 Tim. 1:9; Titus 3:4-5; Eph. 2:4-5, 8-9; Rom. 9:11
[2] 1 Cor. 2:14; Rom. 8:7; Eph. 2:5
[3] John 6:37; Ezek. 36:27; John 5:25

Q. 29: How are we made partakers of the redemption purchased by Christ?

A.: We are made partakers of the redemption purchased by Christ, by the effectual application of it to us[1] by His Holy Spirit.[2]

[1] John 1:11-12
[2] Titus 3:5-6

Q. 30: How doth the Spirit apply to us the redemption purchased by Christ?

A.: The Spirit applieth to us the redemption purchased by Christ, by working faith in us,[1] and thereby uniting us to Christ in our effectual calling.[2]

[1] Eph. 1:13-14; John 6:37, 39; Eph. 2:8
[2] Eph. 3:17; 1 Cor. 1:9

Q. 31: What is effectual calling?

A.: Effectual calling is the work of God's Spirit,[1] whereby, convincing us of our sin and misery,[2] enlightening our minds in the knowledge of Christ,[3] and renewing our wills,[4] He doth persuade and enable us to embrace Jesus

Q. 58: How do we come to be made partakers of the benefits which Christ hath procured?

A.: We are made partakers of the benefits which Christ hath procured, by the application of them unto us,[1] which is the work especially of God the Holy Ghost.[2]

[1] John 1:11-12
[2] Titus 3:5-6

Q. 59: Who are made partakers of redemption through Christ?

A.: Redemption is cetainly applied, and effectually communicated, to all those for whom Christ hath purchased it;[1] who are in time by the Holy Ghost enabled to believe in Christ according to the gospel.[2]

[1] Eph. 1:13-14; John 6:37, 39; 10:15-16
[2] Eph. 2:8; 2 Cor. 4:13

Q. 66: What is that union which the elect have with Christ?

A.: The union which the elect have with Christ is the work of God's grace,[1] whereby they are spiritually and mystically, yet really and inseparably, joined to Christ as their head and husband;[2] which is done in their effectual calling.[3]

[1] Eph. 1:22, 2:6-8
[2] 1 Cor. 6:17; John 10:28; Eph. 5:23, 30
[3] 1 Pet. 5:10; 1 Cor. 1:9

Q. 67: What is effectual calling?

A.: Effectual calling is the work of God's almighty power and grace,[1] whereby (out of His

Belgic Confession (1561)	Heidelberg Catechism (1563)	Second Helvetic Confession (1566)	Canons of Dort (1619)

Canons of Dort (cont.)

He has chosen His own from eternity in Christ, so He confers upon them faith and repentance, rescues them from the power of darkness, and translates them into the kingdom of His own Son, that they may show forth the praises of Him who hath called them out of darkness into His marvelous light; and may glory not in themselves, but in the Lord according to the testimony of the apostles in various places.

Article 11

But when God accomplishes His good pleasure in the elect or works in them true conversion, He not only causes the gospel to be externally preached to them and powerfully illuminates their mind by His Holy Spirit, that they may rightly understand and discern the things of the Spirit of God; but by the efficacy of the same regenerating Spirit, pervades the inmost recesses of the man; He opens the closed, and softens the hardened heart, and circumcises that which was uncircumcised, infuses new qualities into the will, which though heretofore dead, He quickens; from being evil, disobedient, and refractory, He renders it good, obedient, and pliable; actuates and strengthens it, that like a good tree, it may bring forth the fruits of good actions.

Article 12

And this is the regeneration so highly celebrated in Scripture and denominated a new creation: a resurrection from the dead, a making alive, which God works in us without our aid. But this is in no wise effected merely by the external preaching of the gospel, by moral suasion, or such a mode of operation, that after God has performed His part, it still remains in the power of man to be regenerated or not, to be converted or to continue unconverted; but it is evidently a supernatural work, most powerful, and at the same time most delightful, astonishing, mysterious, and ineffable; not inferior in efficacy to creation or the resurrection from the dead, as the Scripture inspired by the author of this work declares; so that all in whose heart God works in this marvelous manner are certainly, infallibly, and effectually regenerated, and do actually believe. Whereupon the will thus renewed is not only actuated and influenced by God, but in consequence of this influence, becomes itself active. Wherefore also, man is himself rightly said to believe and repent, by virtue of that grace received.

Article 13

The manner of this operation cannot be fully comprehended by believers in this life. Notwithstanding which, they rest satisfied with knowing and experiencing that by this grace of God they are enabled to believe with the heart, and love their Savior.

Article 15

God is under no obligation to confer this grace upon any; for how can He be indebted to man, who had no previous gifts to bestow, as a foundation for such recompense? Nay, who has nothing of his own but sin and falsehood? He therefore who becomes the subject of this grace, owes eternal gratitude to God, and gives Him thanks forever. Whoever is not made partaker thereof, is either altogether regardless of these spiritual gifts and satisfied with his own condition, or is in no apprehension of danger and vainly boasts the possession of that which he has not. With respect to those who make an external profession of faith and live regular lives, we are bound, after the example of the apostle, to judge and speak of them in the most favorable manner. For the secret recesses of the heart are unknown to us. And as to others, who have not yet been called, it is our duty to pray for them to God, who calls the things that are not, as if they were. But we are in no wise to conduct ourselves towards them with haughtiness, as if we had made ourselves to differ.

Article 16

But as man by the fall did not cease to be a creature endowed with understanding and will, nor did sin which pervaded the whole race of mankind deprive him of the human nature, but brought upon him depravity and spiritual death; so also this grace of regeneration does not treat men as senseless stocks and blocks, nor takes away their will and its properties, neither does violence thereto; but spiritually quickens, heals, corrects, and at the same time sweetly and powerfully bends it; that where carnal rebellion and resistance formerly prevailed, a ready and sincere spiritual obedience begins to reign, in which the true and spiritual restoration and freedom of our will consist. Wherefore unless the admirable Author of every good work wrought in us, man could have no hope of recovering from his fall by his own free will, by the abuse of which, in a state of innocence, he plunged himself into ruin.

The true doctrine (concerning corruption and conversion) having been explained, the Synod **rejects** the errors of those who teach:

Rejection 6

That in the true conversion of man no new qualities, powers or gifts can be infused by God into the will, and that therefore faith through which we are first converted, and because of which we are called believers, is not a quality or gift infused by God, but only an act of man, and that it cannot be said to be a gift, except in respect of the power to attain to this faith. For thereby they contradict the Holy Scriptures which declare that God infuses new qualities of faith, of obedience, and of the consciousness of His love into our hearts: "I will put My law in their inward parts, and write it in their hearts" (Jer. 31:33). And: "I will pour water upon him that is thirsty, and floods upon the dry ground: I will pour My Spirit upon thy seed" (Isa. 44:3). And: "the love of God is shed abroad in our hearts by the Holy Ghost which is given unto us" (Rom. 5:5). This is also repugnant to the continuous practice of the Church, which prays by the mouth of the prophet thus: "turn Thou me, and I shall be turned" (Jer. 31:18).

Westminster Confession of Faith (1647)	Westminster Shorter Catechism (1647)	Westminster Larger Catechism (1648)
3. Elect infants, dying in infancy, are regenerated, and saved by Christ, through the Spirit,[1] who worketh when, and where, and how He pleaseth:[2] so also are all other elect persons who are incapable of being outwardly called by the ministry of the Word.[3] --- [1] Luke 18:15-16; Acts 2:38-39; John 3:3, 5; 1 John 5:12; Rom. 8:9 [2] John 3:8 [3] 1 John 5:12; Acts 4:12	Christ, freely offered to us in the gospel.[5] --- [1] 2 Tim. 1:9; 2 Thes. 2:13-14 [2] Acts 2:37 [3] Acts 26:18 [4] Ezek. 36:26-27 [5] John 6:44-45; Phil. 2:13 *Q. 32: What benefits do they that are effectually called partake of in this life?* A.: They that are effectually called do in this life partake of justification,[1] adoption,[2] and sanctification, and the several benefits which in this life do either accompany or flow from them.[3] --- [1] Rom. 8:30 [2] Eph. 1:5 [3] 1 Cor. 1:26, 30	free and special love to His elect, and from nothing in them moving Him thereunto[2]) He doth, in His accepted time, invite and draw them to Jesus Christ, by His Word and Spirit;[3] savingly enlightening their minds,[4] renewing and powerfully determining their wills,[5] so as they (although in themselves dead in sin) are hereby made willing and able freely to answer His call, and to accept and embrace the grace offered and conveyed therein.[6] --- [1] John 5:25; Eph. 1:18-20; 2 Tim. 1:8-9 [2] Titus 3:4-5; Eph. 2:4-5, 7-9; Rom. 9:11 [3] 2 Cor. 5:20; 6:1-2; John 6:44; 2 Thes. 2:13-14 [4] Acts 26:18; 1 Cor. 2:10, 12 [5] Ezek. 11:19; 36:26-27; John 6:45 [6] Eph. 2:5; Phil. 2:13; Deut. 30:6 *Q. 68: Are the elect only effectually called?* A.: All the elect, and they only, are effectually called.[1] --- [1] Acts 13:48

Canons of Dort (cont.)

Rejection 7

That the grace whereby we are converted to God is only a gentle advising, or (as others explain it), that this is the noblest manner of working in the conversion of man, and that this manner of working, which consists in advising, is most in harmony with man's nature; and that there is no reason why this advising grace alone should not be sufficient to make the natural man spiritual, indeed, that God does not produce the consent of the will except through this manner of advising; and that the power of the divine working, whereby it surpasses the working of Satan, consists in this, that God promises eternal, while Satan promises only temporal goods. But this is altogether Pelagian and contrary to the whole Scripture which, besides this, teaches yet another and far more powerful and divine manner of the Holy Spirit's working in the conversion of man, as in Ezekiel: "A new heart also will I give you, and a new spirit will I put within you: and I will take away the stony heart out of your flesh, and I will give you an heart of flesh" (Ezek. 36:26).

Rejection 8

That God in the regeneration of man does not use such powers of His omnipotence as potently and infallibly bend man's will to faith and conversion; but that all the works of grace having been accomplished, which God employs to convert man, man may yet so resist God and the Holy Spirit when God intends man's regeneration and wills to regenerate him, and indeed that man often does so resist that he prevents entirely his regeneration, and that it therefore remains in man's power to be

regenerated or not. For this is nothing less than the denial of all the efficiency of God's grace in our conversion, and the subjecting of the working of the Almighty God to the will of man, which is contrary to the apostles, who teach: "who believe, according to the working of His mighty power" (Eph. 1:19). And: "That our God would…fulfil all the good pleasure of His goodness, and the work of faith with power" (2 Thes. 1:11). And: "According as His divine power hath given unto us all things that pertain unto life and godliness" (2 Pet. 1:3).

Rejection 9

That grace and free will are partial causes, which together work the beginning of conversion, and that grace, in order of working, does not precede the working of the will; that is, that God does not efficiently help the will of man unto conversion until the will of man moves and determines to do this. For the ancient Church has long ago condemned this doctrine of the Pelagians according to the words of the apostle: "So then it is not of him that willeth, nor of him that runneth, but of God that sheweth mercy" (Rom. 9:16). Likewise: "For who maketh thee to differ from another? and what hast thou that thou didst not receive?" (1 Cor. 4:7). And: "For it is God which worketh in you both to will and to do of His good pleasure" (Phil. 2:13).

Belgic Confession (1561)	Heidelberg Catechism (1563)	Second Helvetic Confession (1566)	Canons of Dort (1619)

Saving Faith

Article 22
Our Justification Through Faith in Jesus Christ

We believe that, to attain the true knowledge of this great mystery, the Holy Ghost kindleth in our hearts an upright faith, which embraces Jesus Christ with all His merits, appropriates Him,[1] and seeks nothing more besides Him.[2] For it must needs follow, either that all things which are requisite to our salvation are not in Jesus Christ, or if all things are in Him, that then those who possess Jesus Christ through faith have complete salvation in Him.[3] Therefore, for any to assert that Christ is not sufficient, but that something more is required besides Him, would be too gross a blasphemy; for hence it would follow that Christ was but half a Savior.

Therefore we justly say with Paul, *that we are justified by faith alone*, or *by faith without works*.[4] However, to speak more clearly, we do not mean that faith itself justifies us, for it is only an instrument with which we embrace Christ our Righteousness. But Jesus Christ, imputing to us all His merits, and so many holy works which He hath done for us and in our stead, is our Righteousness.[5] And faith is an instrument that keeps us in communion with Him in all His benefits,

---

Q. 20: Are all men then, as they perished in Adam, saved by Christ?

A.: No; only those who are ingrafted into Him,[1] and receive all His benefits, by a true faith.[2]

[1] Matt. 1:21; Isa. 53:11
[2] John 1:12-13; Rom. 11:20; Heb. 10:39

Q. 21: What is true faith?

A.: True faith is not only a certain knowledge, whereby I hold for truth all that God has revealed to us in His Word,[1] but also an assured confidence,[2] which the Holy Ghost[3] works by the gospel in my heart,[4] that not only to others, but to me also, remission of sin,[5] everlasting righteousness and salvation[6] are freely given by God, merely of grace, only for the sake of Christ's merits.[7]

[1] John 6:69; John 17:3; Heb. 11:3, 6
[2] Eph. 3:12
[3] Rom. 4:16, 20-21; Heb. 11:1; Eph. 3:12; Rom. 1:16; 1 Cor. 1:21; Acts 16:14; Matt. 16:17; John 3:5
[4] Rom. 10:14, 17; Matt. 9:2
[5] Rom. 5:1
[6] Gal. 2:20
[7] Rom. 3:24-26

Q. 22: What is then necessary for a Christian to believe?

A.: All things promised us in the gospel,[1] which the articles of our catholic undoubted Christian faith briefly teach us.

[1] John 20:31; Matt. 28:19-20

XVI. Of Faith and Good Works; of Their Reward, and of Man's Merit

1. Christian faith is not an opinion or human persuasion, but a sure trust, and an evident and steadfast assent of the mind; it is a most sure comprehension of the truth of God, set forth in the Scriptures and in the Apostles' Creed; yea, and of God Himself, the chief blessedness; and especially of God's promise, and of Christ, who is the consummation of all the promises. And this faith is the mere gift of God, because God alone of His power does give it to His elect, according to measure; and that when, to whom, and how much He will; and that by His Holy Spirit, through the means of preaching the gospel and of faithful prayer. This faith has also its measures of increase, which, unless they were likewise given of God, the apostles would never have said, "Lord, increase our faith" (Luke 17:5).

2. Now, all these things which we have hitherto said of faith, the apostles taught them before us, even as we set them down. For Paul says, "Faith is the substance," or sure subsistence, "of things hoped for, the evidence," or clear and certain comprehension, "of things not seen" (Heb. 11:1). And again he says that "all the promises of God in Him are yea, and in Him Amen" (2 Cor. 1:20). And the same apostle says to the Philippians that "unto you it is given in the behalf of Christ, not only to believe on Him, but also to suffer for His sake" (Phil. 1:29). And also, "according as God hath dealt to every man the measure of faith" (Rom. 12:3). And again, "All men have not faith" (2 Thes. 3:2); and, "them . . . that obey not the gospel" (2 Thes. 1:8). Besides, Luke witnesses and says, "As many as were ordained to eternal life believed" (Acts 13:48). And therefore Paul also calls faith "the faith of God's elect" (Titus 1:1). And, again, "Faith cometh by hearing, and hearing by the word of God" (Rom. 10:17). And in other places he oftentimes wills men to pray for faith. And the same also called faith powerful, and that showeth itself by love (Gal. 5:6). This faith, pacifies the conscience, and opens to us a free access unto God; that with confidence we may come unto Him, and may obtain at His hands whatsoever is profitable and necessary. The same faith keeps us in our duty which we owe to God and to our neighbor, and fortifies our patience in adversity; it frames and makes a true confession, and (in a word) it brings forth good fruit of all sorts.

Head I
Article 2

But in this the love of God was manifested, that He sent His only begotten Son into the world, that whosoever believeth on Him should not perish, but have everlasting life. "In this was manifested the love of God toward us, because that God sent His only begotten Son into the world, that we might live through Him" (1 John 4:9). "For God so loved the world, that He gave His only begotten Son, that whosoever believeth in Him should not perish, but have everlasting life" (John 3:16).

Article 3

And that men may be brought to believe, God mercifully sends the messengers of these most joyful tidings to whom He will and at what time He pleaseth; by whose ministry men are called to repentance and faith in Christ crucified. "How then shall they call on Him in whom they have not believed? and how shall they believe in Him of whom they have not heard? and how shall they hear without a preacher? And how shall they preach, except they be sent?" (Rom. 10:14-15).

Article 4

The wrath of God abideth upon those who believe

Westminster Confession of Faith (1647)	Westminster Shorter Catechism (1647)	Westminster Larger Catechism (1648)

XI. Of Justification

2. Faith, thus receiving and resting on Christ and His righteousness, is the alone instrument of justification:[1] yet is it not alone in the person justified, but is ever accompanied with all other saving graces, and is no dead faith, but worketh by love.[2]

[1] John 1:12; Rom. 3:28; 5:1
[2] James 2:17, 22, 26; Gal. 5:6

XIV. Of Saving Faith

1. The grace of faith, whereby the elect are enabled to believe to the saving of their souls,[1] is the work of the Spirit of Christ in their hearts,[2] and is ordinarily wrought by the ministry of the Word,[3] by which also, and by the administration of the sacraments, and prayer, it is increased and strengthened.[4]

[1] Heb. 10:39
[2] 2 Cor. 4:13; Eph. 1:17-19; 2:8
[3] Rom. 10:14, 17
[4] 1 Pet. 2:2; Acts 20:32; Rom. 4:11; Luke 17:5; Rom. 1:16-17

2. By this faith, a Christian believeth to be true whatsoever is revealed in the Word, for the authority of God Himself speaking therein;[1] and acteth differently upon that which each particular passage thereof containeth; yielding obedience to the commands,[2] trembling at the threatenings,[3] and embracing the promises of God for this life, and that which is to come.[4] But the principal acts of saving faith are accepting, receiving, and resting upon Christ alone for justification, sanctification, and eternal life, by virtue of the covenant of grace.[5]

[1] John 4:42; 1 Thes. 2:13; 1 John 5:10; Acts 24:14
[2] Rom. 16:26
[3] Isa. 66:2
[4] Heb. 11:13; 1 Tim. 4:8
[5] John 1:12; Acts 16:31; Gal. 2:20; Acts 15:11

3. This faith is different in degrees, weak or strong;[1] may be often and many ways assailed, and weakened, but gets the victory:[2] growing up in many to the attainment of a full assurance, through Christ,[3] who is both the author and finisher of our faith.[4]

[1] Heb. 5:13-14; Rom. 4:19-20; Matt. 6:30; 8:10
[2] Luke 22:31-32; Eph. 6:16; 1 John 5:4-5
[3] Heb. 6:11-12; 10:22; Col. 2:2
[4] Heb. 12:2

Q. 85: What doth God require of us, that we may escape his wrath and curse, due to us for sin?

A.: To escape the wrath and curse of God, due to us for sin, God requireth of us faith in Jesus Christ, repentance unto life,[1] with diligent use of all the outward means whereby Christ communicateth to us the benefits of redemption.[2]

[1] Acts 20:21
[2] Prov. 2:1-5; 8:33-36; Isa. 55:3

Q. 86: What is faith in Jesus Christ?

A.: Faith in Jesus Christ is a saving grace,[1] whereby we receive and rest upon Him alone for salvation, as He is offered to us in the gospel.[2]

[1] Heb. 10:39
[2] John 1:12; Isa. 26:3-4; Phil. 3:9; Gal. 2:16

Q. 72: What is justifying faith?

A.: Justifying faith is a saving grace,[1] wrought in the heart of a sinner by the Spirit[2] and Word of God,[3] whereby he, being convinced of his sin and misery, and of the disability in himself and all other creatures to recover him out of his lost condition,[4] not only assenteth to the truth of the promise of the gospel,[5] but receiveth and resteth upon Christ and His righteousness, therein held forth, for pardon of sin,[6] and for the accepting and accounting of his person righteous in the sight of God for salvation.[7]

[1] Heb. 10:39
[2] 2 Cor. 4:13; Eph. 1:17-19
[3] Rom. 10:14, 17
[4] Acts 2:37; Acts 16:30; John 16:8-9; Rom. 5:6; Eph. 2:1; Acts 4:12
[5] Eph. 1:13
[6] John 1:12; Acts 16:31, 10:43
[7] Phil. 3:9; Acts 15:11

Q. 73: How doth faith justify a sinner in the sight of God?

A.: Faith justifies a sinner in the sight of God, not because of those other graces which do always accompany it, or of good works that are the fruits of it,[1] nor as if the grace of faith, or any act thereof, were imputed to him for his justification;[2] but only as it is an instrument by which he receiveth and applieth Christ and His righteousness.[3]

[1] Gal. 3:11; Rom. 3:28
[2] Rom. 4:5; 10:10
[3] John 1:12; Phil 3:9; Gal. 2:16

Q. 153: What doth God require of us, that we may escape His wrath and curse due to us by reason of the transgression of the law?

A.: That we may escape the wrath and curse of God due to us by reason of the transgression of the law, He requireth of us repentance toward God, and faith toward our Lord Jesus Christ,[1] and the diligent use of the outward means whereby Christ communicates to us the benefits of His mediation.[2]

[1] Acts 20:21; Matt. 3:7-8; Luke 13:3, 5; Acts 16:30-31; John 3:16, 18
[2] Prov. 2:1-5; 8:33-36

Belgic Confession (1561)	Heidelberg Catechism (1563)	Second Helvetic Confession (1566)	Canons of Dort (1619)
which, when they become ours, are more than sufficient to acquit us of our sins. --- [1] Eph. 3:16-17; Ps. 51:13; Eph. 1:17-18; 1 Cor. 2:12 [2] 1 Cor. 2:2; Acts 4:12; Gal. 2:21; Jer. 23:6; 1 Cor. 1:30; Jer. 31:10 [3] Matt. 1:21; Rom. 3:27; 8:1, 33 [4] Rom. 3:27; Gal. 2:6; 1 Pet. 1:4-5; Rom. 10:4 [5] Jer. 23:6; 1 Cor. 1:30; 2 Tim. 1:2; Luke 1:77; Rom. 3:24-25; 4:5; Ps. 32:1-2; Phil. 3:9; Titus 3:5; 2 Tim. 1:9	*Q. 23: What are these articles?* A.: I. I believe in God the Father, Almighty, Maker of heaven and earth; II. And in Jesus Christ, His only begotten Son, our Lord; III. Who was conceived by the Holy Ghost, born of the Virgin Mary; IV. Suffered under Pontius Pilate; was crucified, dead, and buried; He descended into hell; V. The third day He arose again from the dead; VI. He ascended into heaven, and sitteth at the right hand of God the Father Almighty; VII. From thence He shall come to judge the quick and the dead; VIII. I believe in the Holy Ghost; IX. I believe an holy catholic church; the communion of saints; X. The forgiveness of sins; XI. The resurrection of the body; XII. And the life everlasting. Amen. *Q. 53: What dost thou believe concerning the Holy Ghost?* A.: First, that He is true and coeternal God with the Father and the Son;[1] secondly, that He is also given me,[2] to make me by a true faith, partaker of Christ and all His benefits,[3] that He may comfort me[4] and abide with me for ever.[5] --- [1] Gen. 1:2; Isa. 48:16; 1 Cor. 3:16 [2] Matt. 28:19; 2 Cor. 1:22 [3] Gal. 3:14; 1 Pet. 1:2 [4] Acts 9:31 [5] John 14:16; 1 Pet. 4:14 *Q. 61: Why sayest thou that thou art righteous by faith only?* A: Not that I am acceptable to God, on account of the worthiness		not this gospel. But such as receive it, and embrace Jesus the Savior by a true and living faith, are by Him delivered from the wrath of God and from destruction, and have the gift of eternal life conferred upon them. *Article 5* The cause or guilt of this unbelief, as well as of all other sins, is no wise in God, but in man himself; whereas faith in Jesus Christ and salvation through Him is the free gift of God, as it is written: "For by grace are ye saved through faith; and that not of yourselves: it is the gift of God" (Eph. 2:8). "For unto you it is given in the behalf of Christ, not only to believe on Him," etc. (Phil. 1:29). *Article 6* That some receive the gift of faith from God and others do not receive it proceeds from God's eternal decree, for "known unto God are all His works from the beginning of the world" (Acts 15:18). "Who worketh all things after the counsel of His own will" (Eph. 1:11). According to which decree, He graciously softens the hearts of the elect, however obstinate, and inclines them to believe, while He leaves the non-elect in His just judgment to their own wickedness and obduracy. And herein is especially displayed the profound, the merciful, and at the same

Westminster Confession of Faith (1647)	Westminster Shorter Catechism (1647)	Westminster Larger Catechism (1648)

Heidelberg Catechism (cont.)

of my faith,[1] but because only the satisfaction, righteousness, and holiness of Christ, is my righteousness before God;[2] and that I cannot receive and apply the same to myself any other way than by faith only.[3]

---

[1] Ps. 16:2; Eph. 2:8-9
[2] 1 Cor. 1:30; 1 Cor. 2:2
[3] 1 John 5:10

Canons of Dort (cont.)

time the righteous discrimination between men, equally involved in ruin; or that decree of election and reprobation revealed in the Word of God, which though men of perverse, impure and unstable minds wrest to their own destruction, yet to holy and pious souls affords unspeakable consolation.

Head II

Article 6

And whereas many who are called by the gospel do not repent nor believe in Christ, but perish in unbelief, this is not owing to any defect or insufficiency in the sacrifice offered by Christ upon the cross, but is wholly to be imputed to themselves.

Article 7

But as many as truly believe, and are delivered and saved from sin and destruction through the death of Christ, are indebted for this benefit solely to the grace of God, given them in Christ from everlasting, and not to any merit of their own.

Heads III and IV

Article 13

The manner of this operation cannot be fully comprehended by believers in this life. Notwithstanding which, they rest satisfied with knowing and experiencing that by this grace of God they are enabled to believe with the heart, and love their Savior.

Article 14

Faith is therefore to be considered as the gift of God, not on account of its being offered by God to man, to be accepted or rejected at his pleasure; but because it is in reality conferred, breathed, and infused into him; or even because God bestows the power or ability to believe, and then expects that man should by the exercise of his own free will, consent to the terms of salvation and actually believe in Christ; but because He who works in man both to will and to do, and indeed all things in all, produces both the will to believe and the act of believing also.

Belgic Confession (1561)	Heidelberg Catechism (1563)	Second Helvetic Confession (1566)	Canons of Dort (1619)

Justification

Article 23
Wherein Our Justification Before God Consists

We believe that our salvation consists in the remission of our sins for Jesus Christ's sake, and that therein our righteousness before God is implied; as David and Paul teach us, declaring this to be the happiness of man, that God imputes righteousness to him without works.[1] And the same apostle saith, *that we are justified freely by His grace, through the redemption which is in Jesus Christ.*[2]

And therefore we always hold fast this foundation, ascribing all the glory to God,[3] humbling ourselves before Him, and acknowledging ourselves to be such as we really are, without presuming to trust in any thing in ourselves, or in any merit of ours,[4] relying and resting upon the obedience of Christ crucified alone,[5] which becomes ours when we believe in Him.[6] This is sufficient to cover all our iniquities, and to give us confidence in approaching to God;[7] freeing the conscience of fear, terror, and dread, without following the example of our first father, Adam, who, trembling, attempted to cover himself with fig-leaves.[8] And, verily, if we should appear before God, relying on ourselves or on any

Q. 1: What is thy only comfort in life and death?
A.: That I with body and soul, both in life and death,[1] am not my own,[2] but belong unto my faithful Savior Jesus Christ;[3] who, with His precious blood,[4] hath fully satisfied for all my sins,[5] and delivered me from all the power of the devil.[6]

---
[1] 1 Cor. 6:19-20
[2] Rom. 14:7-9
[3] 1 Cor. 3:23
[4] 1 Pet. 1:18-19
[5] John 1:7
[6] 1 John 3:8; Heb. 2:14-15

Q. 37: What dost thou understand by the words, "He suffered"?
A.: That He, all the time that He lived on earth, but especially at the end of His life, sustained in body and soul[1] the wrath of God against the sins of all mankind; that so by His passion, as the only propitiatory sacrifice,[2] He might redeem our body and soul from everlasting damnation, and obtain for us the favor of God, righteousness and eternal life.

---
[1] 1 Pet. 2:24; Isa. 53:12
[2] 1 John 2:2; Rom. 3:25

Q. 38: Why did He suffer under Pontius Pilate as judge?
A.: That He, being innocent, and yet condemned by a temporal judge,[1] might thereby free us from the severe judgment of God to which we were exposed.[2]

XV. Of the True Justification of the Faithful
1. To justify, in the apostle's disputation touching justification, does signify to remit sins, to absolve from the fault and the punishment thereof, to receive into favor, to pronounce a man just. For the apostle says to the Romans, "It is God that justifieth. Who is he that condemneth?" (Rom. 8:33-34). Here, to justify and to condemn are opposed. And in the Acts of the Apostles the apostle says, "Through this man is preached unto you the forgiveness of sins: and by Him all that believe are justified from all things, from which ye could not be justified by the law of Moses" (Acts 13:38-39). For in the law, also, and in the prophets, we read, "If there be a controversy between men, and they come unto judgment, that the judges may judge them; then they shall justify the righteous, and condemn the wicked" (Deut. 25:1). And in Isaiah 5:22-23, "Woe unto them . . . which justify the wicked for reward."

2. Now, it is most certain that we are all by nature sinners, and before the judgment-seat of God convicted of ungodliness, and guilty of death. But we are justified — that is, acquitted from sin and death — by God the Judge, through the grace of Christ alone, and not by any respect or merit of ours. For what is more plain than that which Paul says? — "For all have sinned, and come short of the glory of God; being justified freely by His grace through the redemption that is in Christ Jesus" (Rom. 3:23-24).

3. For Christ took upon Himself and bare the sins of the world, and did satisfy the justice of God. God, therefore, is merciful unto our sins for Christ alone, that suffered and rose again, and does not impute them unto us. But He imputes the justice of Christ unto us for our own; so that now we are not only cleansed from sin, and purged, and holy, but also endued with the righteousness of Christ; yea, and acquitted from sin, death, and condemnation (2 Cor. 5:19-21); finally, we are righteous, and heirs of eternal life. To speak properly, then, it is God alone that justifieth us, and that only for Christ, by not imputing unto us our sins, but imputing Christ's righteousness unto us (Rom. 4:23-25).

4. But because we do receive this justification, not by any works, but by faith in the mercy of God and in Christ; therefore, we teach and believe, with the apostle, that sinful man is justified only

Head II
Article 3
The death of the Son of God is the only and most perfect sacrifice and satisfaction for sin, and is of infinite worth and value, abundantly sufficient to expiate the sins of the whole world.

The true doctrine (concerning redemption) having been explained, the Synod **rejects** the errors of those who teach:

Rejection 4
That the new covenant of grace, which God the Father, through the mediation of the death of Christ, made with man, does not herein consist that we by faith, inasmuch as it accepts the merits of Christ, are justified before God and saved, but in the fact that God having revoked the demand of perfect obedience of faith, regards faith itself and the obedience of faith, although imperfect, as the perfect obedience of the law, and does esteem it worthy of the reward of eternal life through grace. For these contradict the Scriptures: "Being justified freely by His grace through the redemption that is in Christ Jesus: whom God hath set forth to be a propitiation through faith in His blood" (Rom. 3:24-25). And these proclaim, as did the wicked Socinus, a new and strange justification

Westminster Confession of Faith (1647)	Westminster Shorter Catechism (1647)	Westminster Larger Catechism (1648)

XI. Of Justification

1. Those whom God effectually calls, He also freely justifieth;[1] not by infusing righteousness into them, but by pardoning their sins, and by accounting and accepting their persons as righteous; not for any thing wrought in them, or done by them, but for Christ's sake alone; nor by imputing faith itself, the act of believing, or any other evangelical obedience to them, as their righteousness; but by imputing the obedience and satisfaction of Christ unto them,[2] they receiving and resting on Him and His righteousness by faith; which faith they have not of themselves, it is the gift of God.[3]

[1] Rom. 8:30; 3:24
[2] Rom. 4:5-8; 2 Cor. 5:19, 21; Rom. 3:22, 24-25, 27-28; Titus 3:5, 7; Eph. 1:7; Jer. 23:6; 1 Cor. 1:30-31; Rom. 5:17-19
[3] Acts 10:44; Gal. 2:16; Phil. 3:9; Acts 13:38-39; Eph. 2:7-8

2. Faith, thus receiving and resting on Christ and His righteousness, is the alone instrument of justification:[1] yet is it not alone in the person justified, but is ever accompanied with all other saving graces, and is no dead faith, but worketh by love.[2]

[1] John 1:12; Rom. 3:28; 5:1
[2] James 2:17, 22, 26: Gal. 5:6

3. Christ, by His obedience and death, did fully discharge the debt of all those that are thus justified, and did make a proper, real, and full satisfaction to His Father's justice in their behalf.[1] Yet, in as much as He was given by the Father for them;[2] and His obedience and satisfaction accepted in their stead;[3] and both, freely, not for any thing in them; their justification is only of free grace;[4] that both the exact justice, and rich grace of God might be glorified in the justification of sinners.[5]

[1] Rom. 5:8-10, 19; 1 Tim. 2:5-6; Heb. 10:10, 14; Dan. 9:24, 26; Isa. 53:4-6, 10-12
[2] Rom. 8:32
[3] 2 Cor. 5:21; Matt. 3:17; Eph. 5:2
[4] Rom. 3:24; Eph. 1:7
[5] Rom. 3:26; Eph. 2:7

4. God did, from all eternity, decree to justify all the elect,[1] and Christ did, in the fullness of time, die for their sins, and rise again for their justification:[2] nevertheless, they are not justified,

---

Q. 33: What is justification?

A.: Justification is an act of God's free grace, wherein He pardoneth all our sins,[1] and accepteth us as righteous in His sight,[2] only for the righteousness of Christ imputed to us,[3] and received by faith alone.[4]

[1] Rom. 3:24-25; 4:6-8
[2] 2 Cor. 5:19, 21
[3] Rom. 5:17-19
[4] Gal. 2:16; Phil. 3:9

Q. 69: What is the communion in grace, which the members of the invisible church have with Christ?

A.: The communion in grace, which the members of the invisible church have with Christ, is their partaking of the virtue of His mediation, in their justification,[1] adoption,[2] sanctification, and whatever else in this life manifests their union with Him.[3]

[1] Rom. 8:30
[2] Eph. 1:5
[3] 1 Cor. 1:30

Q. 70: What is justification?

A.: Justification is an act of God's free grace unto sinners,[1] in which He pardoneth all their sins, accepteth and accounteth their persons righteous in His sight;[2] not for any thing wrought in them, or done by them,[3] but only for the perfect obedience and full satisfaction of Christ, by God imputed to them,[4] and received by faith alone.[5]

[1] Rom. 3:22, 24-25; 4:5
[2] 2 Cor. 5:19, 21; Rom. 3:22, 24-25, 27-28
[3] Titus 3:5, 7; Eph. 1:7
[4] Rom. 5:17-19; Rom. 4:6-8
[5] Acts 10:43; Gal. 2:16; Phil. 3:9

Q. 71: How is justification an act of God's free grace?

A.: Although Christ, by His obedience and death, did make a proper, real, and full satisfaction to God's justice in the behalf of them that are justified;[1] yet inasmuch as God accepteth the satisfaction from a Surety, which He might have demanded of them, and did provide this surety, His own only Son,[2] imputing His righteousness to them,[3] and requiring nothing of them for their justification but faith,[4] which also is His gift,[5] their justification is to them of free grace.[6]

[1] Rom. 5:8-10, 19
[2] 1 Tim. 2:5-6; Heb. 10:10; Matt. 20:28; Dan. 9:24, 26; Isa. 53:4-6, 10-12; Heb. 7:22; Rom. 8:32; 1 Pet. 1:18-19
[3] 2 Cor. 5:21
[4] Rom. 3:24-25
[5] Eph. 2:8
[6] Eph. 1:7

Belgic Confession (1561)	Heidelberg Catechism (1563)	Second Helvetic Confession (1566)	Canons of Dort (1619)

Belgic Confession (1561)

other creature, though ever so little, we should, alas! be consumed.[9] And therefore every one must pray with David: *O Lord, enter not into judgment with Thy servant: for in Thy sight shall no man living be justified.*[10]

[1] Luke 1:77; Col. 1:14; Ps. 32:1-2; Rom. 4:6-7
[2] Rom. 3:23-24; Acts 4:12
[3] Ps. 115:1; 1 Cor. 4:7; Rom. 4:2
[4] 1 Cor. 4:7; Rom. 4:2; 1 Cor. 1:29, 31
[5] Rom. 5:19
[6] Heb. 11:6-7; Eph. 2:8; 2 Cor. 5:19; 1 Tim. 2:6
[7] Rom. 5:1; Eph. 3:12; 1 John 2:1
[8] Gen. 3:7
[9] Isa. 33:14; Deut. 27:26; James 2:10
[10] Ps. 130:3; Matt. 18:23-26; Ps. 143:2; Luke 16:15

Heidelberg Catechism (1563)

[1] Luke 23:14; John 19:4; Ps. 69:4
[2] Gal. 3:13-14

Q. 39: Is there anything more in His being crucified than if He had died some other death?

A.: Yes, there is; for thereby I am assured, that He took on Him the curse which lay upon me; for the death of the cross was accursed of God.[1]

[1] Deut. 21:23; Gal. 3:13

Q. 45: What doth the resurrection of Christ profit us?

A.: First, by His resurrection He has overcome death, that He might make us partakers of that righteousness which He had purchased for us by His death;[1] secondly, we are also by His power raised up to a new life;[2] and lastly, the resurrection of Christ is a sure pledge of our blessed resurrection.[3]

[1] 1 Cor. 15:16
[2] Rom. 6:4; Col. 3:1
[3] 1 Cor. 15; Rom. 8:11

Q. 56: What believest thou concerning "the forgiveness of sins"?

A.: That God, for the sake of Christ's satisfaction,[1] will no more remember my sins, neither my corrupt nature, against which I have to struggle all my life long; but will graciously impute to me the righteousness of Christ,[2] that I may never be condemned before the tribunal of God.[3]

[1] 1 John 2:2; 2 Cor. 5:19, 21
[2] Jer. 31:34; Ps. 103:3-4, 10-11; Rom. 8:1-3
[3] John 3:18

Second Helvetic Confession (1566)

by faith in Christ, not by the law or by any works. For the apostle says, "We conclude that a man is justified by faith without the deeds of the law" (Rom. 3:28). "If Abraham were justified by works, he hath whereof to glory; but not before God. For what saith the scripture? Abraham believed God, and it was counted unto him for righteousness. But to him that worketh not, but believeth on Him that justifieth the ungodly, his faith is counted for righteousness" (Rom. 4:2-3, 5; Gen. 15:6). And again, "For by grace are ye saved through faith; and that not of yourselves: it is the gift of God: not of works, lest any man should boast," etc. (Eph. 2:8-9). Therefore, because faith does apprehend Christ our righteousness, and does attribute all the praise of God in Christ; in this respect justification is attributed to faith, chiefly because of Christ, whom it receives, and not because it is a work of ours; for it is the gift of God. Now, that we do receive Christ by faith the Lord shows at large (John 6:27, 33, 35, 48-58), where He puts eating for believing, and believing for eating. For as by eating we receive meat, so by believing we are made partakers of Christ.

5. Therefore, we do not divide the benefit of justification, giving part to the grace of God or to Christ, and part to ourselves, our charity, works, or merit; but we do attribute it wholly to the praise of God in Christ, and that through faith. Moreover, our charity and our works can not please God if they be done of such as are not just; wherefore, we must first be just before we can love or do any just works. We are made just (as we have said) through faith in Christ, by the mere grace of God, who does not impute unto us our sins, but imputes unto us the righteousness of Christ; yea, and our faith in Christ He imputes for righteousness unto us. Moreover, the apostle does plainly derive love from faith, saying, "Now the end of the commandment is charity out of a pure heart, and of a good conscience, and of faith unfeigned" (1 Tim. 1:5).

6. Wherefore, in this matter we speak not of a feigned, vain, or dead faith, but of a lively and quickening faith; which, for Christ (who is life, and gives life), whom it apprehends, both is indeed, and is so called, a lively faith, and does prove itself to be lively by lively works. And, therefore, James does speak nothing contrary to this doctrine; for he speaks of a vain and dead faith, which certain bragged of, but had not Christ living within them by faith. And also James says that works do justify (chap. 2:14-26), yet he is not contrary to Paul (for then he were to be rejected); but he shows that Abraham did

Canons of Dort (1619)

of man before God against the consensus of the whole church.

Westminster Confession of Faith (1647)	Westminster Shorter Catechism (1647)	Westminster Larger Catechism (1648)

until the Holy Spirit doth, in due time, actually apply Christ unto them.[3]

[1] Gal. 3:8; 1 Pet. 1:2, 19-20; Rom. 8:30
[2] Gal. 4:4; 1 Tim. 2:6; Rom. 4:25
[3] Col. 1:21-22; Gal. 2:16; Titus 3:4-7

5. God doth continue to forgive the sins of those that are justified;[1] and, although they can never fall from the state of justification,[2] yet they may, by their sins, fall under God's fatherly displeasure, and not have the light of His countenance restored unto them, until they humble themselves, confess their sins, beg pardon, and renew their faith and repentance.[3]

[1] Matt. 6:12; 1 John 1:7, 9; 2:1-2
[2] Luke 22:32; John 10:28; Heb. 10:14
[3] Ps. 89:31-33; 51:7-12; 32:5; Matt. 26:75; 1 Cor. 11:30, 32; Luke 1:20

6. The justification of believers under the Old Testament was, in all these respects, one and the same with the justification of believers under the New Testament.[1]

[1] Gal. 3:9, 13-14; Rom. 4:22-24; Heb. 13:8

Belgic Confession (1561)	Heidelberg Catechism (1563)	Second Helvetic Confession (1566)	Canons of Dort (1619)
	Q. 59: But what doth it profit thee now that thou believest all this? A.: That I am righteous in Christ, before God, and an heir of eternal life.[1] ―――― [1] Rom. 5:1; Rom. 1:17; John 3:36 *Q. 60: How art thou righteous before God?* A.: Only by a true faith in Jesus Christ;[1] so that, though my conscience	declare his lively and justifying faith by works. And so do all the godly, who yet trust in Christ alone, not to their own works. For the apostle said again, "Nevertheless I live; yet not I, but Christ liveth in me: and the life which I now live in the flesh, I live by the faith of the Son of God, who loved me, and gave Himself for me. I do not frustrate the grace of God; for if righteousness come by the law, then Christ is dead in vain" (Gal. 2:20-21).	

Heidelberg Catechism (cont.)

accuse me, that I have grossly transgressed all the commandments of God, and kept none of them,[2] and am still inclined to all evil;[3] notwithstanding, God, without any merit of mine,[4] but only of mere grace,[5] grants[6] and imputes to me[7] the perfect satisfaction, righteousness and holiness of Christ;[8] even so, as if I never had had, nor committed any sin; yea, as if I had fully accomplished all that obedience which Christ has accomplished for me,[9] inasmuch as I embrace such benefit with a believing heart.[10]

――――
[1] Rom. 3:22; Gal. 2:16; Eph. 2:8-9
[2] Rom. 3:9
[3] Rom. 7:23
[4] Rom. 3:24
[5] Titus 3:5; Eph. 2:8-9
[6] Rom. 4:4-5; 2 Cor. 5:19
[7] 1 John 2:1
[8] Rom. 3:24-25
[9] 2 Cor. 5:21
[10] Rom. 3:28; John 3:18

Q. 61: Why sayest thou that thou art righteous by faith only?
A.: Not that I am acceptable to God, on account of the worthiness of my faith,[1] but because only the satisfaction, righteousness, and holiness of Christ, is my righteousness before God;[2] and that I cannot receive and apply the same to myself any other way than by faith only.[3]

――――
[1] Ps. 16:2; Eph. 2:8-9
[2] 1 Cor. 1:30; 1 Cor. 2:2
[3] 1 John 5:10

Q. 84: How is the kingdom of heaven opened and shut by the preaching of the holy gospel?
A.: Thus: when according to the command of Christ[1] it is declared and publicly testified to all and every believer, that, whenever they receive the promise of the gospel by a true faith,[2] all their sins are really forgiven them of God for the sake of Christ's merits.

――――
[1] Matt. 28:19
[2] John 3:18, 36; Mark 16:16

Q. 126: Which is the fifth petition?
A.: "And forgive us our debts as we forgive our debtors";[1] that is, be pleased for the sake of Christ's blood, not to impute to us poor sinners our transgressions, nor that depravity which always cleaves to us;[2] even as we feel this evidence of Thy grace in us, that it is our firm resolution from the heart to forgive our neighbor.[3]

――――
[1] Matt. 6:12
[2] Ps. 51:1; 1 John 2:1-2
[3] Matt. 6:14-15

Westminster Confession of Faith (1647)	Westminster Shorter Catechism (1647)	Westminster Larger Catechism (1648)

Belgic Confession (1561)	Heidelberg Catechism (1563)	Second Helvetic Confession (1566)	Canons of Dort (1619)

Sanctification

Article 24

Man's Sanctification and Good Works

We believe that this true faith, being wrought in man by the hearing of the Word of God and the operation of the Holy Ghost,[1] doth regenerate and make him a new man, causing him to live a new life,[2] and freeing him from the bondage of sin.[3] Therefore it is so far from being true, that this justifying faith makes men remiss in a pious and holy life,[4] that on the contrary without it they would never do anything out of love to God, but only out of self-love or fear of damnation.

---
[1] 1 Pet. 1:23; Rom. 10:17; John 5:24
[2] 1 Thes. 1:5; Rom. 8:15; John 6:29; Col. 2:12; Phil. 1:1, 29; Eph. 2:8
[3] Acts 15:9; Rom. 6:4, 22; Titus 2:12; John 8:36
[4] Titus 2:12

Q. 32: But why art thou called a Christian?

A.: Because I am a member of Christ by faith,[1] and thus am partaker of His anointing;[2] that so I may confess His name,[3] and present myself a living sacrifice of thankfulness to Him;[4] and also that with a free and good conscience I may fight against sin and Satan in this life,[5] and afterwards reign with Him eternally, over all creatures.[6]

---
[1] 1 Cor. 6:15
[2] 1 John 2:27; Joel 2:28
[3] Matt. 10:32
[4] Rom. 12:1
[5] Eph. 6:11-12; 1 Tim. 1:18-19
[6] 2 Tim. 2:12

Q. 43: What further benefit do we receive from the sacrifice and death of Christ on the cross?

A.: That by virtue thereof our old man is crucified, dead and buried with Him;[1] that so the corrupt inclinations of the flesh may no more reign in us,[2] but that we may offer ourselves unto Him a sacrifice of thanksgiving.[3]

---
[1] Rom. 6:6-7, etc.
[2] Rom. 6:12
[3] Rom. 12:1

Q. 76: What is it then to eat the crucified body, and drink the shed blood of Christ?

A.: It is not only to embrace with a believing heart all the sufferings and death of Christ, and thereby to obtain the pardon of sin and

Head I
Article 13
The sense and certainty of this election afford to the children of God additional matter for daily humiliation before Him, for adoring the depth of His mercies, for cleansing themselves, and rendering grateful returns of ardent love to Him, who first manifested so great love towards them.

Head V
Article 13
Neither does renewed confidence of persevering produce licentiousness or a disregard to piety in those who are recovering from backsliding; but it renders them much more careful and solicitous to continue in the ways of the Lord, which He hath ordained, that they who walk therein may maintain an assurance of persevering, lest by abusing His fatherly kindness, God should turn away His gracious countenance from them, to behold which is to the godly dearer than life, the withdrawing whereof is more bitter than death, and they in consequence hereof should fall into more grievous torments of conscience.

Westminster Confession of Faith (1647)	Westminster Shorter Catechism (1647)	Westminster Larger Catechism (1648)

XIII. Of Sanctification

1. They, who are once effectually called, and regenerated, having a new heart, and a new spirit created in them, are further sanctified, really and personally, through the virtue of Christ's death and resurrection,[1] by His Word and Spirit dwelling in them:[2] the dominion of the whole body of sin is destroyed,[3] and the several lusts thereof are more and more weakened and mortified;[4] and they more and more quickened and strengthened in all saving graces,[5] to the practice of true holiness, without which no man shall see the Lord.[6]

[1] 1 Cor. 6:11; Acts 20:32; Phil. 3:10; Rom. 6:5-6
[2] John 17:17; Eph. 5:26; 2 Thes. 2:13
[3] Rom. 6:6, 14
[4] Gal. 5:24; Rom. 8:13
[5] Col. 1:11; Eph. 3:16-19
[6] 2 Cor. 7:1; Heb. 12:14

2. This sanctification is throughout, in the whole man;[1] yet imperfect in this life, there abiding still some remnants of corruption in every part;[2] whence ariseth a continual and irreconcilable war, the flesh lusting against the Spirit, and the Spirit against the flesh.[3]

[1] 1 Thes. 5:23
[2] 1 John 1:10; Rom. 7:18, 23; Phil. 3:12
[3] Gal. 5:17; 1 Pet. 2:11

3. In which war, although the remaining corruption, for a time, may much prevail;[1] yet, through the continual supply of strength from the sanctifying Spirit of Christ, the regenerate part doth overcome;[2] and so, the saints grow in grace,[3] perfecting holiness in the fear of God.[4]

[1] Rom. 7:23
[2] Rom. 6:14; 1 John 5:4; Eph. 4:15-16
[3] 2 Pet. 3:18; 2 Cor. 3:18
[4] 2 Cor. 7:1

Q. 35: What is sanctification?

A.: Sanctification is the work of God's free grace,[1] whereby we are renewed in the whole man after the image of God,[2] and are enabled more and more to die unto sin, and live unto righteousness.[3]

[1] 2 Thes. 2:13
[2] Eph. 4:23-24
[3] Rom. 6:4, 6; Rom. 8:1

Q. 75: What is sanctification?

A.: Sanctification is a work of God's grace, whereby they whom God hath, before the foundation of the world, chosen to be holy, are in time, through the powerful operation of His Spirit[1] applying the death and resurrection of Christ unto them,[2] renewed in their whole man after the image of God;[3] having the seeds of repentance unto life, and all other saving graces, put into their hearts,[4] and those graces so stirred up, increased, and strengthened,[5] as that they more and more die unto sin, and rise unto newness of life.[6]

[1] Eph. 1:4; 1 Cor. 6:11; 2 Thes. 2:13
[2] Rom. 6:4-6
[3] Eph. 4:23-24
[4] Acts 11:18; 1 John 3:9
[5] Jude 20; Heb. 6:11-12; Eph. 3:16-19; Col. 1:10-11
[6] Rom. 6:4, 6, 14; Gal. 5:24

Q. 77: Wherein do justification and sanctification differ?

A.: Although sanctification be inseparably joined with justification,[1] yet they differ, in that God in justification imputeth the righteousness of Christ;[2] in sanctification His Spirit infuseth grace, and enableth to the exercise thereof;[3] in the former, sin is pardoned;[4] in the other, it is subdued:[5] the one doth equally free all believers from the revenging wrath of God, and that perfectly in this life, that they never fall into condemnation;[6] the other is neither equal in all,[7] nor in this life perfect in any,[8] but growing up to perfection.[9]

[1] 1 Cor. 6:11; 1:30
[2] Rom. 4:6, 8
[3] Ezek. 36:7
[4] Rom. 3:24-25
[5] Rom. 6:6, 14
[6] Rom. 8:33-34
[7] 1 John 2:12-14; Heb. 5:12-14
[8] 1 John 1:8, 10
[9] 2 Cor. 7:1; Phil. 3:12-14

Q. 78: Whence ariseth the imperfection of sanctification in believers?

A.: The imperfection of sanctification in believers ariseth from the remnants of sin abiding in every part of them, and the perpetual lustings of the flesh against the spirit; whereby they are often foiled with temptations, and fall into many sins,[1] are hindered in all their spiritual services,[2] and their best works are imperfect and defiled in the sight of God.[3]

Belgic Confession (1561)	Heidelberg Catechism (1563)	Second Helvetic Confession (1566)	Canons of Dort (1619)

Heidelberg Catechism (cont.)

life eternal;[1] but also, besides that, to become more and more united to His sacred body, by the Holy Ghost, who dwells both in Christ and in us;[2] so that we, though Christ is in heaven[3] and we on earth, are notwithstanding "flesh of His flesh, and bone of His bone";[4] and that we live, and are governed forever by one spirit, as members of the same body are by one soul.[5]

[1] John 6:35, 40, 47-48, 50-51, 53-54
[2] John 6:55-56
[3] Acts 3:21; Acts 1:9-11; 1 Cor. 11:26
[4] Eph. 5:29-32; 1 Cor. 6:15, 17, 19; 1 John 3:24
[5] John 6:56-58; Eph. 4:15-16

Q. 86: Since then we are delivered from our misery, merely of grace, through Christ, without any merit of ours, why must we still do good works?

A.: Because Christ, having redeemed and delivered us by His blood, also renews us by His Holy Spirit after His own image; that so we may testify, by the whole of our conduct, our gratitude to God for His blessings,[1] and that He may be praised by us;[2] also, that every one may be assured in himself of his faith by the fruits thereof;[3] and that by our godly conversation others may be gained to Christ.[4]

[1] 1 Cor. 6:19-20; Rom. 6:13; Rom. 12:1-2; 1 Pet. 2:5, 9-10
[2] Matt. 5:16; 1 Pet. 2:12
[3] 2 Pet. 1:10; Gal. 5:6, 24
[4] 1 Pet. 3:1-2; Matt. 5:16; Rom. 14:19

Q. 115: Why will God then have the ten commandments so strictly preached, since no man in this life can keep them?

A.: First, that all our lifetime we may learn more and more to know our sinful nature,[1] and thus become the more earnest in seeking the remission of sin and righteousness in Christ;[2] likewise, that we constantly endeavor and pray to God for the grace of the Holy Spirit, that we may become more and more

conformable to the image of God, till we arrive at the perfection proposed to us in a life to come.[3]

[1] John 1:9; Rom. 3:20; Rom. 5:13; Rom. 7:7
[2] Rom. 7:24
[3] 1 Cor. 9:24; Phil. 3:12-14

Q. 122: Which is the first petition?

A.: **"Hallowed be Thy name"**;[1] that is, grant us, first, rightly to know Thee,[2] and to sanctify, glorify and praise Thee in all Thy works, in which Thy power, wisdom, goodness, justice, mercy and truth are clearly displayed;[3] and further also, that we may so order and direct our whole lives, our thoughts, words and actions, that Thy Name may never be blasphemed, but rather honored and praised on our account.[4]

[1] Matt. 6:9
[2] John 17:3; Jer. 9:23-24; Matt. 16:17; James 1:5
[3] Ps. 119:137-138; Luke 1:46; Ps. 145:8-9
[4] Ps. 115:1; Ps. 71:8

Q. 124: Which is the third petition?

A.: **"Thy will be done on earth as it is in heaven"**;[1] that is, grant that we and all men may renounce our own will,[2] and without murmuring obey Thy will,[3] which is only good; that so every one may attend to and perform the duties of his station and calling[4] as willingly and faithfully as the angels do in heaven.[5]

[1] Matt. 6:10
[2] Matt. 16:24; Titus 2:12
[3] Luke 22:42
[4] 1 Cor. 7:24; Eph. 4:1
[5] Ps. 103:20

Adoption

Q. 33: Why is Christ called the only begotten Son of God, since we are also the children of God?

A.: Because Christ alone is the eternal and natural Son of God;[1] but we are children adopted of God, by grace, for His sake.[2]

[1] John 1:1; Heb. 1:2
[2] Rom. 8:15-17; Eph. 1:5-6

Head V

Article 6

But God, who is rich in mercy, according to His unchangeable purpose of election, does not wholly withdraw the Holy Spirit from His own people, even in their melancholy falls; nor suffers them to proceed so far as to lose the grace of adop-

Westminster Confession of Faith (1647)	Westminster Shorter Catechism (1647)	Westminster Larger Catechism (1648)
		[1] Rom. 7:18, 23; Mark 14:66ff. Gal. 2:11-12 [2] Heb. 12:1 [3] Isa. 64:6; Exod. 28:38

XII. Of Adoption

All those that are justified, God vouchsafeth, in and for His only Son Jesus Christ, to make partakers of the grace of adoption,[1] by which they are taken into the number, and enjoy the liberties and privileges of the children of God,[2] have His name put upon them,[3] receive the spirit of adoption,[4] have access to the throne of grace with boldness,[5] are enabled to cry, Abba, Father,[6] are pitied,[7] protected,[8] provided for,[9] and chastened by Him as by a Father:[10] yet never cast off,[11] but sealed to the day of redemption;[12] and inherit the promises,[13] as heirs of everlasting salvation.[14]

Q. 34: What is adoption?

A.: Adoption is an act of God's free grace,[1] whereby we are received into the number, and have a right to all the privileges, of the sons of God.[2]

---

[1] 1 John 3:1
[2] John 1:12; Rom. 8:17

Q. 74: What is adoption?

A.: Adoption is an act of the free grace of God,[1] in and for His only Son Jesus Christ,[2] whereby all those that are justified are received into the number of His children,[3] have His name put upon them,[4] the Spirit of His Son given to them,[5] are under His fatherly care and dispensations,[6] admitted to all the liberties and privileges of the sons of God, made heirs of all the promises, and fellow heirs with Christ in glory.[7]

---

[1] 1 John 3:1
[2] Eph. 1:5; Gal. 4:4-5
[3] John 1:12
[4] 2 Cor. 6:18; Rev. 3:12

Belgic Confession (1561)	Heidelberg Catechism (1563)	Second Helvetic Confession (1566)	Canons of Dort (1619)
			tion, and forfeit the state of justification, or to commit the sin unto death; nor does He permit them to be totally deserted, and to plunge themselves into everlasting destruction.

Repentance and Conversion

Belgic Confession (1561)	Heidelberg Catechism (1563)	Second Helvetic Confession (1566)	Canons of Dort (1619)
	Q. 2: How many things are necessary for thee to know, that thou, enjoying this comfort, mayest live and die happily? A.: Three,[1] the first, how great my sins and miseries are;[2] the second, how I may be delivered from all my sins and miseries;[3] the third, how I shall express my gratitude to God for such deliverance.[4] [1] Luke 24:47 [2] 1 Cor. 6:10-11; John 9:41; Rom. 3:10, 19 [3] John 17:3 [4] Eph. 5:8-10 *Q. 81: For whom is the Lord's Supper instituted?* A.: For those who are truly sorrowful for their sins,[1] and yet trust that these are forgiven them for the sake of Christ; and that their remaining infirmities are covered by His passion and death;[2] and who also earnestly desire to have their faith more and more strengthened, and their lives more	*XIV. Of Repentance, and the Conversion of Man* 1. The gospel has the doctrine of repentance joined with it; for so said the Lord in the gospel, "And that repentance and remission of sins should be preached in His name among all nations" (Luke 24:47). 2. By repentance we understand the change of the mind in a sinful man stirred up by the preaching of the gospel through the Holy Spirit, and received by a true faith: by which a sinful man does acknowledge his natural corruption, and all his sins, seeing them convinced by the Word of God, and is heartily grieved for them; and does not only bewail and freely confess them before God with shame, but also does loathe and abhor them with indignation, thinking seriously of present amendment, and of a continual care of innocency and virtue, wherein to exercise himself holily all the rest of his life. 3. And surely this is true repentance — namely, an unfeigned turning unto God and to all goodness, and a serious return from the devil and from all evil. Now we do expressly say, that this repentance is the mere gift of God, and not the work of our own strength. For the apostle directs the faithful minister diligently to instruct "those that oppose themselves; if God peradventure will give them repentance to the acknowledging of the truth" (2 Tim. 2:25). Also the sinful woman in the gospel, who washed Christ's feet with her tears; and Peter, who bitterly wept and bewailed his denial of his Master — do manifestly show what mind the penitent man should have, to wit, very earnestly lamenting his sins	**Head V** *Article 7* For in the first place, in these falls He preserves in them the incorruptible seed of regeneration from perishing or being totally lost; and again, by His Word and Spirit, certainly and effectually renews them to repentance, to a sincere and godly sorrow for their sins, that they may seek and obtain remission in the blood of the Mediator, may again experience the favor of a reconciled God, through faith adore His mercies, and henceforward more diligently work out their own salvation with fear and trembling.

Westminster Confession of Faith (1647)	Westminster Shorter Catechism (1647)	Westminster Larger Catechism (1648)
[1] Eph. 1:5; Gal. 4:4-5 [2] Rom. 8:17; John 1:12 [3] Jer. 14:9; 2 Cor. 6:18; Rev. 3:12 [4] Rom. 8:15 [5] Eph. 3:12; Rom. 5:2 [6] Gal. 4:6 [7] Ps. 103:13 [8] Prov. 14:26 [9] Matt. 6:30, 32; 1 Pet. 5:7 [10] Heb. 12:6 [11] Lam. 3:31 [12] Eph. 4:30 [13] Heb. 6:12 [14] 1 Pet. 1:3-4; Heb. 1:14		[5] Gal. 4:6 [6] Ps. 103:13; Prov. 14:26; Matt. 6:32 [7] Heb. 6:12; Rom. 8:17

XV. Of Repentance Unto Life

1. Repentance unto life is an evangelical grace,[1] the doctrine whereof is to be preached by every minister of the gospel, as well as that of faith in Christ.[2]

[1] Zech. 12:10; Acts 11:18
[2] Luke 24:47; Mark 1:15; Acts 20:21

2. By it, a sinner, out of the sight and sense not only of the danger, but also of the filthiness and odiousness of his sins, as contrary to the holy nature, and righteous law of God; and upon the apprehension of His mercy in Christ to such as are penitent, so grieves for, and hates his sins, as to turn from them all unto God,[1] purposing and endeavouring to walk with Him in all the ways of His commandments.[2]

[1] Ezek. 18:30-31; 36:31; Isa. 30:22; Ps. 51:4; Jer. 31:18-19; Joel 2:12-13; Amos 5:15; Ps. 119:128; 2 Cor. 7:11
[2] Ps. 119:6, 59, 106; Luke 1:6; 2 Ki. 23:25

3. Although repentance be not to be rested in, as any satisfaction for sin, or any cause of the pardon thereof,[1] which is the act of God's free grace in Christ;[2] yet it is of such necessity to all sinners, that none may expect pardon without it.[3]

[1] Ezek. 36:31-32; 16:61-63
[2] Hos. 14:2, 4; Rom. 3:24; Eph. 1:7
[3] Luke 13:3, 5; Acts 17:30-31

4. As there is no sin so small, but it deserves damnation;[1] so there is no sin so great, that it can bring damnation upon those who truly repent.[2]

Q. 87: What is repentance unto life?

A.: Repentance unto life is a saving grace,[1] whereby a sinner, out of a true sense of his sin,[2] and apprehension of the mercy of God in Christ,[3] doth, with grief and hatred of his sin, turn from it unto God,[4] with full purpose of, and endeavour after, new obedience.[5]

[1] Acts 11:18
[2] Acts 2:37-38
[3] Joel 2:12; Jer. 3:22
[4] Jer. 31:18-19; Ezek. 36:31
[5] 2 Cor. 7:11; Isa. 1:16-17

Q. 76: What is repentance unto life?

A.: Repentance unto life is a saving grace,[1] wrought in the heart of a sinner by the Spirit[2] and Word of God,[3] whereby, out of the sight and sense, not only of the danger,[4] but also of the filthiness and odiousness of his sins,[5] and upon the apprehension of God's mercy in Christ to such as are penitent,[6] he so grieves for[7] and hates his sins,[8] as that he turns from them all to God,[9] purposing and endeavouring constantly to walk with Him in all the ways of new obedience.[10]

[1] 2 Tim. 2:25
[2] Zech. 12:10
[3] Acts 11:18, 20-21
[4] Ezek. 18:28, 30, 32; Luke 15:17-18; Hos. 2:6-7
[5] Ezek. 36:31; Isa. 30:22
[6] Joel 2:12-13
[7] Jer. 31:18-19
[8] 2 Cor. 7:11
[9] Acts 26:18; Ezek. 14:6; 1 Ki. 8:47-48
[10] Ps. 119:6, 59, 128; Luke 1:6; 2 Ki. 23:25

Belgic Confession (1561)	Heidelberg Catechism (1563)	Second Helvetic Confession (1566)	Canons of Dort (1619)

Heidelberg Catechism (1563)

holy;[3] but hypocrites, and such as turn not to God with sincere hearts, eat and drink judgment to themselves.[4]

[1] Matt. 5:3, 6; Luke 7:37-38; Luke 15:18-19
[2] Ps. 103:3
[3] Ps. 116:12-14; 1 Pet. 2:11-12
[4] 1 Cor. 10:20, etc.; 1 Cor. 11:28, etc.; Titus 1:16; Ps. 50:15-16

Q. 87: *Cannot they then be saved, who, continuing in their wicked and ungrateful lives, are not converted to God?*

A.: By no means; for the Holy Scripture declares that no unchaste person, idolator, adulterer, thief, covetous man, drunkard, slanderer, robber, or any such like, shall inherit the kingdom of God.[1]

[1] 1 Cor. 6:9-10; Eph. 5:5-6; 1 John 3:14-15; Gal. 5:21

Q. 88: *Of how many parts doth the true conversion of man consist?*

A.: Of two parts: of the mortification of the old, and the quickening of the new man.[1]

[1] Rom. 6:4-6; Eph. 4:22-23; Col. 3:5; 1 Cor. 5:7

Q. 89: *What is the mortification of the old man?*

A.: It is a sincere sorrow of heart that we have provoked God by our sins, and more and more to hate and flee from them.[1]

[1] Ps. 51:3, 8, 17; Luke 15:18; Rom. 8:13; Joel 1:12-13

Q. 90: *What is the quickening of the new man?*

A.: It is a sincere joy of heart in God, through

Second Helvetic Confession (1566)

committed. Moreover, the prodigal son, and the publican in the gospel, that is compared with the Pharisee, do set forth unto us a most fit pattern of confessing our sins to God. The prodigal son said, "Father, I have sinned against heaven, and before thee, and am no more worthy to be called thy son; make me as one of thy hired servants" (Luke 15:18-19). The publican, also, not daring to lift up his eyes to heaven, but smiting his breast, cried, "God be merciful to me a sinner" (Luke 18:13). And we doubt not but the Lord received them to mercy. For John the apostle says, "If we confess our sins, He is faithful and just to forgive us our sins, and cleanse us from all unrighteousness. If we say that we have not sinned, we make Him a liar, and His word is not in us" (1 John 1:9-10).

4. We believe that this sincere confession, which is made to God alone, either privately between God and the sinner, or openly in the church, where that general confession of sins is rehearsed, is sufficient; and that it is not necessary for the obtaining of remission of sins that any man should confess his sins unto the priest, whispering them into his ears, that, the priest laying his hands on his head, he might receive absolution: because we find no commandment nor example thereof in the Holy Scripture. David protests and says, "I acknowledge my sin unto Thee, and mine iniquity have I not hid. I said, I will confess my transgressions unto the LORD; and Thou forgavest the iniquity of my sin" (Ps. 32:5). Yea, and the Lord, teaching us to pray, and also to confess our sins, said, "After this manner therefore pray ye: Our Father which art in heaven… forgive us our debts, as we forgive our debtors" (Matt. 6:9, 12). It is requisite, therefore, that we should confess our sins unto God, and be reconciled with our neighbor, if we have offended him. And the apostle James, speaking generally of confession, says, "Confess your faults one to another" (James 5:16). If so be that any man, being overwhelmed with the burden of his sins, and troublesome temptations, will privately ask counsel, instruction, or comfort, either of a minister of the Church, or of any other brother that is learned in the law of God, we do not mislike it. Like as also we do fully allow that general and public confession which is wont to be rehearsed in the church, and in holy meetings (whereof we spake before), being, as it is, agreeable with the Scripture.

7. But how diligent and careful every penitent man ought to be in the endeavor of a new life, and in slaying the old man and raising up the new man, the examples in the gospel do teach us. For the Lord said to him whom He had

Westminster Confession of Faith (1647)	Westminster Shorter Catechism (1647)	Westminster Larger Catechism (1648)

[1] Rom. 6:23; 5:12; Matt. 12:36
[2] Isa. 55:7; Rom. 8:1; Isa. 1:16, 18

5. Men ought not to content themselves with a general repentance, but it is every man's duty to endeavour to repent of his particular sins, particularly.[1]

[1] Ps. 19:13; Luke 19:8; 1 Tim. 1:13, 15

6. As every man is bound to make private confession of his sins to God, praying for the pardon thereof;[1] upon which, and the forsaking of them, he shall find mercy;[2] so, he that scandalizeth his brother, or the Church of Christ, ought to be willing, by a private or public confession, and sorrow for his sin, to declare his repentance to those that are offended,[3] who are thereupon to be reconciled to him, and in love to receive him.[4]

[1] Ps. 51:4-5, 7, 9, 14; Ps. 32:5-6
[2] Prov. 28:13; 1 John 1:9
[3] James 5:16; Luke 17:3-4; Josh. 7:19; Ps. 51
[4] 2 Cor. 2:8

Belgic Confession (1561)	Heidelberg Catechism (1563)	Second Helvetic Confession (1566)	Canons of Dort (1619)
	Christ,[1] and with love and delight to live according to the will of God in all good works.[2] [1] Rom. 5:1-2; Rom. 14:17; Isa. 57:15 [2] Rom. 6:10-11; 1 Pet. 4:2; Gal. 2:20 *Q. 114: But can those who are converted to God perfectly keep these commandments?* A.: No, but even the holiest men, while in this life, have only a small beginning of this obedience;[1] yet so, that with a sincere resolution they begin to live, not only according to some, but all the commandments of God.[2] [1] Rom. 7:14 [2] Rom. 7:22, 15, etc.; James 3:2	healed of the palsy, "Behold, thou art made whole: sin no more, lest a worse thing come unto thee" (John 5:14). Likewise to the woman taken in adultery He said, "Go and sin no more" (John 8:11). By which words He did not mean that any man could be free from sin while he lived in this flesh; but He does commend unto us diligence and an earnest care, that we (I say) should endeavor by all means, and beg of God by prayer, that we fall not again into sins, out of which we are risen after the manner, and that we may not be overcome of the flesh, the world, or the devil. Zacchaeus, the publican, being received into favor by the Lord, cried out, in the gospel, "Behold, Lord, the half of my goods I give to the poor; and if I have taken any thing from any man by false accusation, I restore him fourfold" (Luke 19:8). After the same manner we preach that restitution and mercy, yea, and giving of alms, are necessary for them who truly repent. And, generally, out of the apostle's words we exhort men, saying, "Let not sin therefore reign in your mortal body, that ye should obey it in the lusts thereof. Neither yield ye your members as instruments of unrighteousness unto sin: but yield yourselves unto God" (Rom. 6:12-13).	

Second Helvetic Confession (cont.)

8. Wherefore we condemn all the ungodly speeches of those who abuse the preaching of the gospel, and say, To return unto God is very easy, for Christ has purged all our sins. Forgiveness of sins is easily obtained; what, therefore, will it hurt to sin? And, We need not take any great care for repentance, etc. Notwithstanding, we always teach that an entrance unto God is open for all sinners, and that this God does forgive all the sins of the faithful, only that one sin excepted which is committed against the Holy Ghost (Mark 3:28-29).

9. And, therefore, we condemn the old and new Novatians and Catharists; and especially we condemn the pope's painful doctrine of penance. And against his simony and simoniacal indulgences we use that sentence of Simon Peter, "Thy money perish with thee, because thou hast thought that the gift of God may be purchased with money. Thou hast neither part nor lot in this matter: for thy heart is not right in the sight of God" (Acts 8:20-21).

10. We also disallow those who think that themselves, by their own satisfactions, can make recompense for their sins committed. For we teach that Christ alone, by His death and passion, is the satisfaction, propitiation, and purging of all sins (Isa. 53:4). Nevertheless, we cease not to urge, as was before said, the mortification of the flesh; and yet we add further, that it must not be proudly thrust upon God for a satisfaction of our sins (1 Cor. 8:8); but must humbly, as it becomes the sons of God, be performed, as a new obedience, to show thankful minds for the deliverance and full satisfaction obtained by the death and satisfaction of the Son of God.

Westminster Confession of Faith (1647)	Westminster Shorter Catechism (1647)	Westminster Larger Catechism (1648)

Belgic Confession (1561)	Heidelberg Catechism (1563)	Second Helvetic Confession (1566)	Canons of Dort (1619)

Good Works

Article 24

Man's Sanctification and Good Works

Therefore it is impossible that this holy faith can be unfruitful in man; for we do not speak of a vain faith,[1] but of such a faith as is called in Scripture *a faith that worketh by love,*[2] which excites man to the practice of those works which God has commanded in His Word. Which works, as they proceed from the good root of faith, are good and acceptable in the sight of God, forasmuch as they are all sanctified by His grace; howbeit they are of no account towards our justification.[3] For it is by faith in Christ that we are justified, even before we do good works;[4] otherwise they could not be good works, any more than the fruit of a tree can be good before the tree itself is good.[5]

Therefore we do good works, but not to merit by them (for what can we merit?) nay, we are beholden to God for the good works we do, and not He to us,[6] since it is He that worketh in us both to will and to do of His good pleasure.[7] Let us therefore attend to what is written: *When ye shall have done all those things which are commanded you, say we are unprofitable servants: we have done that which was our duty to do.*[8]

Q. 62: But why cannot our good works be the whole or part of our righteousness before God?

A.: Because that the righteousness, which can be approved of before the tribunal of God, must be absolutely perfect, and in all respects conformable to the divine law;[1] and also, that our best works in this life are all imperfect and defiled with sin.[2]

[1] Gal. 3:10; Deut. 27:26
[2] Isa. 64:6

Q. 63: What! Do not our good works merit, which yet God will reward in this and in a future life?

A.: This reward is not of merit, but grace.[1]

[1] Luke 17:10

Q. 64: But doth not this doctrine make men careless and profane?

A.: By no means: for it is impossible that those, who are implanted into Christ by a true faith, should not bring forth fruits of thankfulness.[1]

[1] Matt. 7:17-18; John 15:5

Q. 86: Since then we are delivered from our misery, merely of grace, through Christ, without any merit of ours, why must we still do good works?

A.: Because Christ, having redeemed and delivered us by His blood, also renews us by His Holy Spirit after His own image; that so we may testify,

XVI. Of Faith and Good Works; of Their Reward, and of Man's Merit

2. And good works (which are good indeed) proceed from a lively faith by the Holy Spirit, and are done of the faithful according to the will or rule of God's Word. For Peter the apostle says, "And beside this, giving all diligence, add to your faith virtue; and to virtue knowledge; and to knowledge, temperance" etc. (2 Pet. 1:5-6).

3. It was said before that the law of God, which is the will of God, did prescribe unto us the pattern of good works. And the apostle says, "This is the will of God, even your sanctification, that ye abstain from fornication: that no man go beyond and defraud his brother in any matter" (1 Thes. 4:3, 6). But as for such works and worships of God as are taken up upon our own liking, which St. Paul calls "will worship" (Col. 2:23), they are not allowed nor liked of God. Of such the Lord says in the gospel, "In vain do they worship Me, teaching for doctrines the commandments of men" (Matt. 15:9).

4. We therefore disallow all such manner of works, and we approve and urge men unto such as are according to the will and commandment of God. Yea, and these same works that are agreeable to God's will must be done, not to the end to merit eternal life by them; for "eternal life," as the apostle says, is "the gift of God" (Rom. 6:23), nor for ostentation's sake, which the Lord does reject (Matt. 6:1, 5, 16), nor for lucer, which also He dislikes (Matt. 23:23), but to the glory of God, to commend and set forth our calling, and to yield thankfulness unto God, and also for the profit of our neighbors. For the Lord says again in the gospel, "Let your light so shine before men, that they may see your good works, and glorify your Father which is in heaven" (Matt. 5:16). Likewise the apostle Paul says, "Walk worthy of the vocation wherewith ye are called" (Eph. 4:1). Also, "Whatsoever ye do," says he, "in word or deed, do all in the name of the Lord Jesus, giving thanks to God and the Father by Him" (Col. 3:17). "Look not every man on his own things, but every man also on the things of others" (Phil. 2:4). And, "let ours also learn to maintain good works for necessary uses, that they be not unfruitful" (Titus 3:14)

5. Notwithstanding, therefore, that we teach with the apostle that a man is justified by faith in Christ, and not by any good works (Rom.

Head V

Article 12

This certainty of perseverance, however, is so far from exciting in believers a spirit of pride or of rendering them carnally secure, that on the contrary, it is the real source of humility, filial reverence, true piety, patience in every tribulation, fervent prayers, constancy in suffering, and in confessing the truth, and of solid rejoicing in God; so that the consideration of this benefit should serve as an incentive to the serious and constant practice of gratitude and good works, as appears from the testimonies of Scripture and the examples of the saints.

Westminster Confession of Faith (1647)	Westminster Shorter Catechism (1647)	Westminster Larger Catechism (1648)

XVI. Of Good Works

1. Good works are only such as God hath commanded in His holy Word,[1] and not such as, without the warrant thereof, are devised by men, out of blind zeal, or upon any pretence of good intention.[2]

[1] Micah 6:8; Rom. 12:2; Heb. 13:21
[2] Matt. 15:9; Isa. 29:13; 1 Pet. 1:18; Rom. 10:2; John 16:2; 1 Sam. 15:21-23

2. These good works, done in obedience to God's commandments, are the fruits and evidences of a true and lively faith:[1] and by them believers manifest their thankfulness,[2] strengthen their assurance,[3] edify their brethren,[4] adorn the profession of the gospel,[5] stop the mouths of the adversaries,[6] and glorify God,[7] whose workmanship they are, created in Christ Jesus thereunto,[8] that, having their fruit unto holiness, they may have the end, eternal life.[9]

[1] James 2:18, 22
[2] Ps. 116:12-13; 1 Pet. 2:9
[3] 1 John 2:3, 5; 2 Pet. 1:5-10
[4] 2 Cor. 9:2; Matt. 5:16
[5] Titus 2:5, 9-12; 1 Tim. 6:1
[6] 1 Pet. 2:15
[7] 1 Pet. 2:12; Phil. 1:11; John 15:8
[8] Eph. 2:10
[9] Rom. 6:22

3. Their ability to do good works is not at all of themselves, but wholly from the Spirit of Christ.[1] And that they may be enabled thereunto, beside the graces they have already received, there is required an actual influence of the same Holy Spirit, to work in them to will, and to do, of His good pleasure:[2] yet are they not hereupon to grow negligent, as if they were not bound to perform any duty unless upon a special motion of the Spirit; but they ought to be diligent in stirring up the grace of God that is in them.[3]

[1] John 15:4-6; Ezek. 36:26-27
[2] Phil. 2:13; 4:13; 2 Cor. 3:5
[3] Phil. 2:12; Heb. 6:11-12; 2 Pet. 1:3, 5, 10-11; Isa. 64:7; 2 Tim. 1:6; Acts 26:6-7; Jude 20-21

4. They who, in their obedience, attain to the greatest height which is possible in this life, are so far from being able to supererogate, and to do more than God requires, as that they fall short of much which in duty they are bound to do.[1]

[1] Luke 17:10; Neh. 13:22; Job 9:2-3; Gal. 5:17

Q. 78: Whence ariseth the imperfection of sanctification in believers?

A.: The imperfection of sanctification in believers ariseth from the remnants of sin abiding in every part of them, and the perpetual lustings of the flesh against the spirit; whereby they are often foiled with temptations, and fall into many sins,[1] are hindered in all their spiritual services,[2] and their best works are imperfect and defiled in the sight of God.[3]

[1] Rom. 7:18, 23; Mark 14:66ff.; Gal. 2:11-12
[2] Heb. 12:1
[3] Isa. 64:6; Exod. 28:38

Belgic Confession (1561)	Heidelberg Catechism (1563)	Second Helvetic Confession (1566)	Canons of Dort (1619)

Belgic Confession (1561)

In the meantime we do not deny that God rewards our good works, but it is through His grace that He crowns His gifts.[9] Moreover, though we do good works, we do not found our salvation upon them;[10] for we can do no work but what is polluted by our flesh, and also punishable;[11] and although we could perform such works, still the remembrance of one sin is sufficient to make God reject them. Thus, then, we would always be in doubt, tossed to and fro without any certainty, and our poor consciences would be continually vexed if they relied not on the merits of the suffering and death of our Savior.[12]

[1] Titus 3:8; John 15:5; Heb. 11:6; 1 Tim. 1:5
[2] 1 Tim. 1:5; Gal. 5:6; Titus 3:8
[3] 2 Tim. 1:9; Rom. 9:32; Titus 3:5
[4] Rom. 4:4; Gen. 4:4
[5] Heb. 11:6; Rom. 14:23; Gen. 4:4; Matt. 7:17
[6] 1 Cor. 4:7; Isa. 26:12; Gal. 3:5; 1 Thes. 2:13
[7] Phil. 2:13
[8] Luke 17:10
[9] Matt. 10:42; 25:34-35; Rev. 3:12,21; Rom. 2:6; Rev. 2:11; 2 John 8; Rom. 11:6
[10] Eph. 2:9-10
[11] Isa. 64:6
[12] Isa. 28:16; Rom. 10:11; Hab. 2:4

Heidelberg Catechism (1563)

by the whole of our conduct, our gratitude to God for His blessings,[1] and that He may be praised by us;[2] also, that every one may be assured in himself of his faith by the fruits thereof,[3] and that by our godly conversation others may be gained to Christ.[4]

[1] 1 Cor. 6:19-20; Rom. 6:13; Rom. 12:1-2; 1 Pet. 2:5, 9-10
[2] Matt. 5:16; 1 Pet. 2:12
[3] 2 Pet. 1:10; Gal. 5:6, 24
[4] 1 Pet. 3:1-2; Matt. 5:16; Rom. 14:19

Q. 91: But what are good works?

A.: Only those which proceed from a true faith,[1] are performed according to the law of God,[2] and to His glory;[3] and not such as are founded on our imaginations or the institutions of men.[4]

[1] Rom. 14:23
[2] 1 Sam. 15:22; Eph. 2:2, 10
[3] 1 Cor. 10:31
[4] Deut. 12:32; Ezek. 20:18; Matt. 15:9

Second Helvetic Confession (1566)

3:28), yet we do not lightly esteem or condemn good works; because we know that a man is not created or regenerated through faith that he should be idle, but rather that without ceasing he should do those things which are good and profitable. For in the gospel the Lord says, "Every good tree bringeth forth good fruit" (Matt. 7:17); and, again, "He that abideth in Me, and I in him, the same bringeth forth much fruit" (John 15:5). And, lastly, the apostle says, "For we are His workmanship, created in Christ Jesus unto good works, which God hath before ordained that we should walk in them (Eph. 2:10). And again, "Who gave Himself for us, that He might redeem us from all iniquity, aud purify unto Himself a peculiar people, zealous of good works" (Titus 2:14). We therefore condemn all those who do contemn good works, and do babble that they are needless and not to be regarded. Nevertheless, as was said before, we do not think that we are saved by good works, or that they are so necessary to salvation that no man was ever saved without them. For we are saved by grace and by the benefit of Christ alone. Works do necessarily proceed from faith; but salvation is improperly attributed to them, which is most properly ascribed to grace. That sentence of the apostle is very notable: "If by grace, then not of works; otherwise grace is no more grace. But if it be of works, then is it not of grace: otherwise works were no more work" (Rom. 11:6).

6. Now the works which we do are accepted and allowed of God through faith; because they who do them please God by faith in Christ, and also the works themselves are done by the grace of God through His Holy Spirit. For St. Peter says that "in every nation he that feareth Him, and worketh righteousness, is accepted with Him" (Acts 10:35). And Paul also, we "do not cease to pray for you, ... that ye might walk worthy of the Lord unto all pleasing, being fruitful in every good work" (Col. 1:9-10). Here, therefore, we diligently teach, not false and philosophical, but true virtues, true good works, and the true duties of a Christian man. And this we do with all the diligence and earnestness that we can inculcate and beat into men's minds; sharply reproving the slothfulness and hypocrisy of all those who with their mouths praise and profess the gospel, and yet with their shameful life do dishonor the same; setting before their eyes, in this case, God's horrible threatenings, large promises, and bountiful rewards, and that by exhorting, comforting, and rebuking.

7. For we teach that God does bestow great rewards on them that do good, according to that saying of the prophet, "Refrain thy voice from

Westminster Confession of Faith (1647)	Westminster Shorter Catechism (1647)	Westminster Larger Catechism (1648)

5. We cannot by our best works merit pardon of sin, or eternal life at the hand of God, by reason of the great disproportion that is between them and the glory to come; and the infinite distance that is between us and God, whom, by them, we can neither profit, nor satisfy for the debt of our former sins,[1] but when we have done all we can, we have done but our duty, and are unprofitable servants:[2] and because, as they are good, they proceed from His Spirit;[3] and as they are wrought by us, they are defiled, and mixed with so much weakness and imperfection, that they cannot endure the severity of God's judgment.[4]

[1] Rom. 3:20; 4:2, 4, 6; Eph. 2:8-9; Titus 3:5-7; Rom. 8:18; Ps. 16:2; Job 22:2-3; 35:7-8
[2] Luke 17:10
[3] Gal. 5:22-23
[4] Isa. 64:6; Gal. 5:17; Rom. 7:15, 18; Ps. 143:2; 130:3

6. Notwithstanding, the persons of believers being accepted through Christ, their good works also are accepted in Him;[1] not as though they were in this life wholly unblamable and unreprovable in God's sight;[2] but that He, looking upon them in His Son, is pleased to accept and reward that which is sincere, although accompanied with many weaknesses and imperfections.[3]

[1] Eph. 1:6; 1 Pet. 2:5; Exod. 28:38; Gen. 4:4; Heb. 11:4
[2] Job. 9:20; Ps. 143:2
[3] Heb. 13:20-21; 2 Cor. 8:12; Heb. 6:10; Matt. 25:21, 23

7. Works done by unregenerate men, although for the matter of them they may be things which God commands; and of good use both to themselves and others:[1] yet, because they proceed not from a heart purified by faith;[2] nor are done in a right manner, according to the Word;[3] nor to a right end, the glory of God,[4] they are therefore sinful, and cannot please God, or make a man meet to receive grace from God:[5] and yet, their neglect of them is more sinful and displeasing unto God.[6]

[1] 2 Ki. 10:30-31; 1 Ki. 21:27, 29; Phil. 1:15-16, 18
[2] Gen. 4:5; Heb. 11:4, 6
[3] 1 Cor. 13:3; Isa. 1:12
[4] Matt. 6:2, 5, 16
[5] Hag. 2:14; Titus 1:15; Amos 5:21-22; Hosea 1:4; Rom. 9:16; Titus 3:15
[6] Ps. 14:4; 36:3; Job 21:14-15; Matt. 25:41-43, 45; 23:3

Belgic Confession (1561)	Heidelberg Catechism (1563)	Second Helvetic Confession (1566)	Canons of Dort (1619)

Second Helvetic Confession (cont.)

weeping,...for thy work shall be rewarded" (Jer. 31:16). In the gospel also the Lord said, "Rejoice, and be exceeding glad: for great is your reward in heaven" (Matt. 5:12). And, "whosoever shall give to drink unto one of these little ones a cup of cold water only in the name of a disciple, verily I say unto you, he shall in no wise lose his reward" (Matt. 10:42). Yet we do not attribute this reward, which God gives, to the merit of the man that receives it, but to the goodness, or liberality, and truth of God, which promises and gives it; who, although He owe nothing to any, yet He has promised to give a reward to those that faithfully worship Him, notwithstanding that He do also give them grace to worship Him. Besides, there are many things unworthy the majesty of God, and many imperfect things are found in the works even of the saints; and yet because God does receive into favor and embrace those who work them for Christ's sake, therefore He performs unto them the promised reward. For otherwise our righteousness is compared to a menstruous cloth (Isa. 64:6); yea, and the Lord in the gospel says, "So likewise ye, when ye shall have done all those things which are commanded you, say, We are unprofitable servants: we have done that which was our duty to do" (Luke 17:10). So that though we teach that God does give a reward to our good deeds, yet withal we teach, with Augustine, that "God doth crown in us, not our deserts, but His own gifts." And, therefore, whatsoever reward we receive, we say that it is a grace, and rather a grace than a reward: because those good things which we do, we do them rather by God than by ourselves; and because Paul says, "What hast thou that thou didst not receive? now if thou didst receive it, why dost thou glory, as if thou hadst not received it?" (1 Cor. 4:7). Which thing also the blessed martyr Cyprian does gather out of this place, that "we must not boast of anything, seeing nothing is our own." We therefore condemn those who defend the merits of men, that they may make frustrate the grace of God.

Perseverance

Q. 1: What is thy only comfort in life and death?

A.: ...and so preserves me[1] that without the will of my heavenly Father, not a hair can fall from my head;[2] yea, that all things must be subservient to my salvation.[3]

---

[1] John 6:39; John 10:28-29
[2] Luke 21:18; Matt. 10:30
[3] Rom. 8:28

Q. 46: How dost thou understand these words, "He ascended into heaven"?

A.: That Christ, in sight of His disciples, was taken up from earth into heaven;[1] and that He continues there for our interest[2] until He comes again to judge the quick and the dead.

---

[1] Acts 1:9; Mark 16:19
[2] Heb. 4:14; Rom. 8:34; Eph. 4:10

Head I

Article 11

And as God Himself is most wise, unchangeable, omniscient and omnipotent, so the election made by Him can neither be interrupted nor changed, recalled or annulled; neither can the elect be cast away, nor their number diminished.

The true doctrine concerning election and rejection having been explained, the Synod **rejects** the errors of those who teach:

Rejection 6

That not every election unto salvation is unchangeable, but that some of the elect, any decree of God notwith-

Westminster Confession of Faith (1647)	Westminster Shorter Catechism (1647)	Westminster Larger Catechism (1648)

XI. Of Justification

5. God doth continue to forgive the sins of those that are justified;[1] and, although they can never fall from the state of justification,[2] yet they may, by their sins, fall under God's fatherly displeasure, and not have the light of His countenance restored unto them, until they humble themselves, confess their sins, beg pardon, and renew their faith and repentance.[3]

[1] Matt. 6:12; 1 John 1:7, 9; 2:1-2
[2] Luke 22:32; John 10:28; Heb. 10:14
[3] Ps. 89:31-33; 51:7-12; 32:5; Matt. 26:75; 1 Cor. 11:30, 32; Luke 1:20

XVII. Of Perseverance of the Saints

1. They, whom God hath accepted in His Beloved, effectually called, and sanctified by His Spirit, can neither totally nor finally fall away from the state of grace, but shall certainly persevere therein to the end, and be eternally saved.[1]

[1] Phil. 1:6; 2 Pet. 1:10; John 10:28-29; 1 John 3:9; 1 Pet. 1:5, 9

2. This perseverance of the saints depends not upon their own free will, but upon the immu-

Q. 36: What are the benefits which in this life do accompany or flow from justification, adoption, and sanctification?

A.: The benefits which in this life do accompany or flow from justification, adoption, and sanctification, are, assurance of God's love, peace of conscience,[1] joy in the Holy Ghost,[2] increase of grace,[3] and perseverance therein to the end.[4]

[1] Rom. 5:1-2, 5
[2] Rom. 14:17
[3] Prov. 4:18
[4] 1 John 5:13; 1 Pet. 1:5

Q. 79: May not true believers, by reason of their imperfections, and the many temptations and sins they are overtaken with, fall away from the state of grace?

A.: True believers, by reason of the unchangeable love of God,[1] and His decree and covenant to give them perseverance,[2] their inseparable union with Christ,[3] His continual intercession for them,[4] and the Spirit and seed of God abiding in them,[5] can neither totally nor finally fall away from the state of grace,[6] but are kept by the power of God through faith unto salvation.[7]

[1] Jer. 31:3
[2] 2 Tim. 2:19; Heb. 13:20-21; 2 Sam. 23:5
[3] 1 Cor. 1:8-9
[4] Heb. 7:25; Luke 22:32
[5] 1 John 3:9; 2:27
[6] Jer. 32:40; John 10:28
[7] 1 Pet. 1:5

Belgic Confession (1561)	Heidelberg Catechism (1563)	Second Helvetic Confession (1566)	Canons of Dort (1619)
	Q. 47: Is not Christ then with us even to the end of the world, as He hath promised? A.: Christ is very man and very God; with respect to His human nature, He is no more on earth;[1] but with respect to His Godhead, majesty, grace and spirit, He is at no time absent from us. --- [1] Acts 3:21; John 3:13; John 16:28; Matt. 28:20 *Q. 49: Of what advantage to us is Christ's ascension into heaven?* A.: First, that He is our Advocate in the presence of His Father in heaven;[1] secondly, that we have our flesh in heaven as a sure pledge that He, as the head, will also take up to Himself, us, His members;[2] thirdly, that He sends us His Spirit as an earnest,[3] by whose power we "seek the things which are above, where Christ sitteth on the right hand of God, and not things on earth."[4] --- [1] Heb. 9:24; 1 John 2:2; Rom. 8:34 [2] John 14:2; Eph. 2:6 [3] John 14:16; 2 Cor. 1:22; 2 Cor. 5:5 [4] Col. 3:1; Phil. 3:20 *Q. 51: What profit is this glory of Christ, our Head, unto us?* A.: First, that by His Holy Spirit He pours out heavenly graces upon us His members;[1] and then that by His power He defends and preserves us against all enemies.[2] --- [1] Eph. 4:8 [2] Ps. 2:9; John 10:28		standing, can yet perish and do indeed perish. By which gross error they make God to be changeable, and destroy the comfort which the godly obtain out of the firmness of their election, and contradict the Holy Scripture which teaches that the elect cannot be led astray: "Insomuch that, if it were possible, they shall deceive the very elect" (Matt. 24:24); that Christ does not lose those whom the Father gave Him: "And this is the Father's will which hath sent Me, that of all which He hath given Me I should lose nothing" (John 6:39); and that God hath also glorified those whom He foreordained, called and justified: "Moreover whom He did predestinate, them He also called: and whom He called, them He also justified: and whom He justified, them He also glorified" (Rom. 8:30). **Head II** *Article 9* This purpose proceeding from everlasting love towards the elect has from the beginning of the world to this day been powerfully accomplished, and will henceforward still continue to be accomplished, notwithstanding all the ineffectual opposition of the gates of hell, so that the elect in due time may be gathered together into one, and that there never may be wanting a church composed of believers, the foundation of

Westminster Confession of Faith (1647)	Westminster Shorter Catechism (1647)	Westminster Larger Catechism (1648)
tability of the decree of election, flowing from the free and unchangeable love of God the Father;[1] upon the efficacy of the merit and intercession of Jesus Christ,[2] the abiding of the Spirit, and of the seed of God within them,[3] and the nature of the covenant of grace:[4] from all which ariseth also the certainty and infallibility thereof.[5]		

[1] 2 Tim. 2:18-19; Jer. 31:3
[2] Heb. 10:10, 14; 13:20-21; 9:12-15; Rom. 8:33-39; John 17:11, 24; Luke 22:32; Heb. 7:25
[3] John 14:16-17; 1 John 2:27; 3:9
[4] Jer. 32:40
[5] John 10:28; 2 Thes. 3:3; 1 John 2:19

3. Nevertheless, they may, through the temptations of Satan and of the world, the prevalency of corruption remaining in them, and the neglect of the means of their preservation, fall into grievous sins;[1] and, for a time, continue therein:[2] whereby they incur God's displeasure,[3] and grieve His Holy Spirit,[4] come to be deprived of some measure of their graces and comforts,[5] have their hearts hardened,[6] and their consciences wounded;[7] hurt and scandalize others,[8] and bring temporal judgments upon themselves.[9]

[1] Matt. 26:70, 72, 74
[2] Ps. 51:title, 14
[3] Isa. 64:5, 7,9; 2 Sam. 11:27
[4] Eph. 4:30
[5] Ps. 51:8, 10, 12; Rev. 2:4; Songs 5:2-4, 6
[6] Isa. 63:17; Mark 6:52; 16:14
[7] Ps. 32:3-4; 51:8
[8] 2 Sam. 12:14
[9] Ps. 89:31-32; 1 Cor. 11:32

Belgic Confession (1561)	Heidelberg Catechism (1563)	Second Helvetic Confession (1566)	Canons of Dort (1619)

Heidelberg Catechism (cont.)

Q. 53: What dost thou believe concerning the Holy Ghost?

A.: First, that He is true and coeternal God with the Father and the Son;[1] secondly, that He is also given me,[2] to make me by a true faith, partaker of Christ and all His benefits,[3] that He may comfort me[4] and abide with me for ever.[5]

---
[1] Gen. 1:2; Isa. 48:16; 1 Cor. 3:16
[2] Matt. 28:19; 2 Cor. 1:22
[3] Gal. 3:14; 1 Pet. 1:2
[4] Acts 9:31
[5] John 14:16; 1 Pet. 4:14

Q. 54: What believest thou concerning the "holy catholic church" of Christ?

A.: That the Son of God[1] from the beginning to the end of the world,[2] gathers,[3] defends, and preserves to Himself[4] by His Spirit and Word,[5] out of the whole human race,[6] a Church chosen to everlasting life,[7] agreeing in true faith; and that I am and for ever shall remain, a living member thereof.[8]

---
[1] John 10:11
[2] Gen. 26:4
[3] Rom. 9:24; Eph. 1:10
[4] John 10:16
[5] Isa. 59:21
[6] Deut. 10:14-15
[7] Acts 13:48
[8] 1 Cor. 1:8-9; Rom. 8:35, etc.

Q. 127: Which is the sixth petition?

A.: "And lead us not into temptation, but deliver us from evil";[1] that is, since we are so weak in ourselves that we cannot stand a moment;[2] and besides this, since our mortal enemies, the devil,[3] the world,[4] and our own flesh,[5] cease not to assault us, do Thou therefore preserve and strengthen us by the power of Thy Holy Spirit, that we may not be overcome in this spiritual warfare, but constantly and strenuously may resist our foes[6] till at last we obtain a complete victory.[7]

---
[1] Matt. 6:13
[2] Rom. 8:26; Ps. 103:14
[3] 1 Pet. 5:8
[4] Eph. 6:12; John 15:19
[5] Rom. 7:23; Gal. 5:17
[6] Matt. 26:41; Mark 13:33
[7] 1 Thes. 3:13; 1 Thes. 5:23

Canons of Dort (cont.)

which is laid in the blood of Christ, which may steadfastly love and faithfully serve Him as their Savior, who as a bridegroom for his bride, laid down His life for them upon the cross, and which may celebrate His praises here and through all eternity.

Head V

Article 1

Whom God calls, according to His purpose, to the communion of His Son, our Lord Jesus Christ, and regenerates by the Holy Spirit, He delivers also from the dominion and slavery of sin in this life; though not altogether from the body of sin and from the infirmities of the flesh, so long as they continue in this world.

Article 2

Hence spring daily sins of infirmity, and hence spots adhere to the best works of the saints, which furnish them with constant matter for humiliation before God, and flying for refuge to Christ crucified; for mortifying the flesh more and more by the spirit of prayer, and by holy exercises of piety; and for pressing forward to the goal of perfection, till being at length delivered from this body of death, they are brought to reign with the Lamb of God in heaven.

Article 3

By reason of these remains of indwelling sin, and the temptations of sin and of the world, those who are converted could not persevere in a state of grace if left to their own strength. But God is faithful, who having conferred grace, mercifully confirms and powerfully preserves them therein, even to the end.

Article 4

Although the weakness of the flesh cannot prevail against the power of God, who confirms and preserves true believers in a state of grace, yet converts are not always so influenced and actuated by the Spirit of God, as not in some particular instances sinfully to deviate from the guidance of divine grace, so as to be seduced by, and comply with the lusts of the flesh; they must, therefore, be constant in watching and prayer that they be not led into temptation. When these are neglected, they are not only liable to be drawn into great and heinous sins by Satan, the world and the flesh, but sometimes by the righteous permission of God actually fall into these evils. This the lamentable fall of David, Peter, and other saints described in Holy Scripture demonstrates.

Article 5

By such enormous sins, however, they very highly offend God, incur a deadly guilt, grieve the Holy Spirit, interrupt the exercise of faith, very grievously wound their consciences, and sometimes lose the sense of God's favor for a time, until on their returning into the right way of serious repentance, the light of God's fatherly countenance again shines upon them.

Article 6

But God, who is rich in mercy, according to His unchangeable purpose of election, does not wholly withdraw the Holy Spirit from His own people, even in their melancholy falls; nor suffers them to proceed so far as to lose the grace of adoption, and forfeit the state of justification, or to commit the

Westminster Confession of Faith (1647)	Westminster Shorter Catechism (1647)	Westminster Larger Catechism (1648)

Canons of Dort (cont.)

sin unto death; nor does He permit them to be totally deserted, and to plunge themselves into everlasting destruction.

Article 7

For in the first place, in these falls He preserves in them the incorruptible seed of regeneration from perishing or being totally lost; and again, by His Word and Spirit, certainly and effectually renews them to repentance, to a sincere and godly sorrow for their sins, that they may seek and obtain remission in the blood of the Mediator, may again experience the favor of a reconciled God, through faith adore His mercies, and henceforward more diligently work out their own salvation with fear and trembling.

Article 8

Thus, it is not in consequence of their own merits or strength, but of God's free mercy, that they do not totally fall from faith and grace, nor continue and perish finally in their backslidings; which, with respect to themselves, is not only possible, but would undoubtedly happen; but with respect to God, it is utterly impossible, since His counsel cannot be changed nor His promise fail, neither can the call according to His purpose be revoked, nor the merit, intercession and preservation of Christ be rendered ineffectual, nor the sealing of the Holy Spirit be frustrated or obliterated.

Article 9

Of this preservation of the elect to salvation and of their perseverance in the faith, true believers for themselves may and do obtain assurance according to the measure of their faith, whereby they arrive at the certain persuasion that they ever will continue true and living members of the church; and that they experience forgiveness of sins, and will at last inherit eternal life.

Article 10

This assurance, however, is not produced by any peculiar revelation contrary to, or independent of the Word of God; but springs from faith in God's promises, which He has most abundantly revealed in His Word for our comfort; from the testimony of the Holy Spirit witnessing with our spirit that we are children and heirs of God (Rom. 8:16); and lastly, from a serious and holy desire to preserve a good conscience and to perform good works. And if the elect of God were deprived of this solid comfort that they shall finally obtain the victory and of this infallible pledge or earnest of eternal glory, they would be of all men the most miserable.

Article 11

The Scripture moreover testifies that believers in this life have to struggle with various carnal doubts and that under grievous temptations they are not always sensible of this full assurance of faith and certainty of persevering. But God, who is the Father of all consolation, does not suffer them to be tempted above that they are able, but will with the temptation also make a way to escape that they may be able to bear it (1 Cor. 10:13), and by the Holy Spirit again inspires them with the comfortable assurance of persevering.

Article 12

This certainty of perseverance, however, is so far from exciting in believers a spirit of pride or of rendering them carnally secure, that on the contrary, it is the real source of humility, filial reverence, true piety, patience in every tribulation, fervent prayers, constancy in suffering, and in confessing the truth, and of solid rejoicing in God; so that the consideration of this benefit should serve as an incentive to the serious and constant practice of gratitude and good works, as appears from the testimonies of Scripture and the examples of the saints.

Article 13

Neither does renewed confidence of persevering produce licentiousness or a disregard to piety in those who are recovering from backsliding; but it renders them much more careful and solicitous to continue in the ways of the Lord, which He hath ordained, that they who walk therein may maintain an assurance of persevering, lest by abusing His fatherly kindness, God should turn away His gracious countenance from them, to behold which is to the godly dearer than life, the withdrawing whereof is more bitter than death, and they in consequence hereof should fall into more grievous torments of conscience.

Article 14

And as it hath pleased God, by the preaching of the gospel, to begin this work of grace in us, so He preserves, continues, and perfects it by the hearing and reading of His Word, by meditation thereon, and by the exhortations, threatenings, and promises thereof, as well as by the use of the sacraments.

Article 15

The carnal mind is unable to comprehend this doctrine of the perseverance of the saints and the certainty thereof, which God hath most abundantly revealed in His Word, for the glory of His Name, and the consolation of pious souls, and which He impresses upon the hearts of the faithful. Satan abhors it; the world ridicules it; the ignorant and hypocrite abuse, and heretics oppose it; but the spouse of Christ hath always most tenderly loved and constantly defended it as an inestimable treasure; and God, against whom neither counsel nor strength can prevail, will dispose her to continue this conduct to the end. Now, to this one God, Father, Son, and Holy Spirit, be honor and glory forever. Amen.

The true doctrine (concerning perseverance) having been explained, the Synod **rejects** the errors of those who teach:

Rejection 1

That the perseverance of the true believers is not a fruit of election or a gift of God gained by the death of Christ, but a condi-

Belgic Confession (1561)	Heidelberg Catechism (1563)	Second Helvetic Confession (1566)	Canons of Dort (1619)

Canons of Dort (cont.)

tion of the new covenant, which (as they declare) man before his decisive election and justification must fulfill through his free will. For the Holy Scripture testifies that this follows out of election, and is given the elect in virtue of the death, the resurrection and intercession of Christ: "but the election hath obtained it, and the rest were blinded" (Rom. 11:7). Likewise: "He that spared not His own Son, but delivered Him up for us all, how shall He not with Him also freely give us all things? Who shall lay any thing to the charge of God's elect? It is God that justifieth. Who is he that condemneth? It is Christ that died, yea rather, that is risen again, who is even at the right hand of God, who also maketh intercession for us. Who shall separate us from the love of Christ?" (Rom. 8:32-35).

Rejection 2

That God does indeed provide the believer with sufficient powers to persevere and is ever ready to preserve these in him, if he will do his duty; but that though all things which are necessary to persevere in faith and which God will use to preserve faith are made use of, it even then ever depends on the pleasure of the will whether it will persevere or not. For this idea contains an outspoken Pelagianism, and while it would make men free, it makes them robbers of God's honor, contrary to the prevailing agreement of the evangelical doctrine, which takes from man all cause of boasting and ascribes all the praise for this favor to the grace of God alone; and contrary to the apostle, who declares that it is God "Who shall also confirm you unto the end, that ye may be blameless in the day of our Lord Jesus Christ" (1 Cor. 1:8).

Rejection 3

That the true believers and regenerate not only can fall from justifying faith and likewise from grace and salvation wholly and to the end, but indeed often do fall from this and are lost forever. For this conception makes powerless the grace, justification, regeneration, and continued keeping by Christ, contrary to the expressed words of the apostle Paul: "That, while we were yet sinners, Christ died for us. Much more then, being now justified by His blood, we shall be saved from wrath through Him" (Rom. 5:8-9). And contrary to the apostle John: "Whosoever is born of God doth not commit sin; for His seed remaineth in him: and he cannot sin, because he is born of God" (1 John 3:9). And also contrary to the words of Jesus Christ: "I give unto them eternal life; and they shall never perish, neither shall any man pluck them out of My hand. My Father, which gave them Me, is greater than all; and no man is able to pluck them out of My Father's hand" (John 10:28-29).

Rejection 4

That true believers and regenerate can sin the sin unto death or against the Holy Spirit. Since the same apostle John, after having spoken in the fifth chapter of his first epistle, verses 16 and 17, of those who sin unto death and having forbidden to pray for them, immediately adds to this in verse 18: "We know that whosoever is born of God sinneth not (meaning a sin of that character); but he that is begotten of God keepeth himself, and that wicked one toucheth him not" (1 John 5:18).

Rejection 5

That without a special revelation we can have no certainty of future perseverance in this life. For by this doctrine the sure comfort of the true believers is taken away in this life and the doubts of the papist are again introduced into the Church, while the Holy Scriptures constantly deduce this assurance, not from a special and extraordinary revelation, but from the marks proper to the children of God and from the constant promises of God. So especially the apostle Paul: "Nor any other creature, shall be able to separate us from the love of God, which is in Christ Jesus our Lord" (Rom. 8:39). And John declares: "And he that keepeth His commandments dwelleth in Him, and He in him. And hereby we know that He abideth in us, by the Spirit which He hath given us" (1 John 3:24).

Rejection 6

That the doctrine of the certainty of perseverance and of salvation from its own character and nature is a cause of indolence and is injurious to godliness, good morals, prayers and other holy exercises, but that on the contrary it is praiseworthy to doubt. For these show that they do not know the power of divine grace and the working of the indwelling Holy Spirit. And they contradict the apostle John, who teaches the opposite with express words in his first epistle: "Beloved, now are we the sons of God, and it doth not yet appear what we shall be: but we know that, when He shall appear, we shall be like Him; for we shall see Him as He is. And every man that hath this hope in Him purifieth himself, even as He is pure" (1 John 3:2-3). Furthermore, these are contradicted by the example of the saints, both of the Old and the New Testament, who though they were assured of their perseverance and salvation, were nevertheless constant in prayers and other exercises of godliness.

Rejection 7

That the faith of those who believe for a time does not differ from justifying and saving faith except only in duration. For Christ Himself, in Matthew 13:20, Luke 8:13, and in other places, evidently notes, besides this duration, a threefold difference between those who believe only for a time and true believers, when He declares that the former receive the seed in stony ground, but the latter in the good ground or heart; that the former are without root, but the latter have a firm root; that the former are without fruit, but that the latter bring forth their fruit in various measure with constancy and steadfastness.

Rejection 8

That it is not absurd that one having lost his first regeneration, is again and even often born anew. For these deny by this doctrine the incorruptibleness of the seed of God, whereby

Westminster Confession of Faith (1647)	Westminster Shorter Catechism (1647)	Westminster Larger Catechism (1648)

Canons of Dort (cont.)

we are born again, contrary to the testimony of the apostle Peter: "Being born again, not of corruptible seed, but of incorruptible" (1 Peter 1:23).

Rejection 9
That Christ has in no place prayed that believers should infallibly continue in faith. For they contradict Christ Himself, who says: "I have prayed for thee (Simon), that thy faith fail not" (Luke 22:32); and the evangelist John, who declares that

Christ has not prayed for the apostles only, but also for those who through their word would believe: "Holy Father, keep through Thine own name those whom Thou hast given Me," and: "I pray not that Thou shouldest take them out of the world, but that Thou shouldest keep them from the evil"; "Neither pray I for these alone, but for them also which shall believe on Me through their word" (John 17:11, 15, 20).

Belgic Confession (1561)	Heidelberg Catechism (1563)	Second Helvetic Confession (1566)	Canons of Dort (1619)

Assurance

	Heidelberg Catechism		**Canons of Dort**

Q. 1: What is thy only comfort in life and death?

A.: . . . by His Holy Spirit, He also assures me of eternal life,[1] and makes me sincerely willing and ready, henceforth, to live unto Him.[2]

---
[1] 2 Cor. 1:22; 2 Cor. 5:5
[2] Rom. 8:14; Rom. 7:22

Q. 79: Why then doth Christ call the bread His body, and the cup His blood, or the new covenant in His blood; and Paul, the "communion of the body and blood of Christ"?

A.: Christ speaks thus not without great reason, namely, not only thereby to teach us that as bread and wine support this temporal life, so His crucified body and shed blood are the true meat and drink whereby our souls are fed to eternal life;[1] but more especially by these visible signs and pledges to assure us that we are as really partakers of His true body and blood (by the operation of the Holy Ghost) as we receive by the mouths of our bodies these holy signs in remembrance of Him;[2] and that all His sufferings and obedience are as certainly ours, as if we had in our own persons suffered and made satisfaction for our sins to God.[3]

---
[1] John 6:51, 55-56
[2] 1 Cor. 10:16-17; 1 Cor. 11:26-28; Eph. 5:30
[3] Rom. 5:9, 18-19; Rom. 8:4

Head I

Article 12

The elect in due time, though in various degrees and in different measures, attain the assurance of this their eternal and unchangeable election, not by inquisitively prying into the secret and deep things of God, but by observing in themselves, with a spiritual joy and holy pleasure, the infallible fruits of election pointed out in the Word of God — such as a true faith in Christ, filial fear, a godly sorrow for sin, a hungering and thirsting after righteousness, etc.

The true doctrine concerning election and rejection having been explained, the Synod **rejects** the errors of those who teach:

Rejection 8

That God, simply by virtue of His righteous will, did not decide either to leave anyone in the fall of Adam and in the common state of sin and condemnation, or to pass anyone by in the communication of grace which is necessary for faith and conversion. For this is firmly decreed: "Therefore hath He mercy on whom He will have mercy, and whom He will He hardeneth" (Rom. 9:18). And also this: "It is given unto you to know the mysteries of the kingdom of heaven, but

Westminster Confession of Faith (1647)	Westminster Shorter Catechism (1647)	Westminster Larger Catechism (1648)

XIV. Of Saving Faith

3. This faith is different in degrees, weak or strong;[1] may be often and many ways assailed, and weakened, but gets the victory:[2] growing up in many to the attainment of a full assurance, through Christ,[3] who is both the author and finisher of our faith.[4]

---
[1] Heb. 5:13-14; Rom. 4:19-20; Matt. 6:30; 8:10
[2] Luke 22:31-32; Eph. 6:16; 1 John 5:4-5
[3] Heb. 6:11-12; 10:22; Col. 2:2
[4] Heb. 12:2

XVIII. Of Assurance of Grace and Salvation

1. Although hypocrites and other unregenerate men may vainly deceive themselves with false hopes and carnal presumptions of being in the favor of God, and estate of salvation[1] (which hope of theirs shall perish):[2] yet such as truly believe in the Lord Jesus, and love Him in sincerity, endeavouring to walk in all good conscience before Him, may, in this life, be certainly assured that they are in the state of grace,[3] and may rejoice in the hope of the glory of God, which hope shall never make them ashamed.[4]

---
[1] Job 8:13-14; Micah 3:11; Deut. 29:19; John 8:41
[2] Matt. 7:22-23
[3] 1 John 2:3; 3:14, 18-19, 21, 24; 5:13
[4] Rom. 5:2, 5

2. This certainty is not a bare conjectural and probable persuasion grounded upon a fallible hope;[1] but an infallible assurance of faith founded upon the divine truth of the promises of salvation,[2] the inward evidence of those graces unto which these promises are made,[3] the testimony of the Spirit of adoption witnessing with our spirits that we are the children of God,[4] which Spirit is the earnest of our inheritance, whereby we are sealed to the day of redemption.[5]

---
[1] Heb. 6:11, 19
[2] Heb. 6:17-18
[3] 2 Pet. 1:4-5, 10-11; 1 John 2:3; 3:14; 2 Cor. 1:12
[4] Rom. 8:15-16
[5] Eph. 1:13-14; 4:30; 2 Cor. 1:21-22

3. This infallible assurance does not so belong to the essence of faith, but that a true believer may wait long, and conflict with many difficulties, before he be partaker of it:[1] yet, being enabled by the Spirit to know the things which are freely given him of God, he may, without extraordinary revelation, in the right use of

---

Q. 36: What are the benefits which in this life do accompany or flow from justification, adoption, and sanctification?

A.: The benefits which in this life do accompany or flow from justification, adoption, and sanctification, are, assurance of God's love, peace of conscience,[1] joy in the Holy Ghost,[2] increase of grace,[3] and perseverance therein to the end.[4]

---
[1] Rom. 5:1-2, 5
[2] Rom. 14:17
[3] Prov. 4:18
[4] 1 John 5:13; 1 Pet. 1:5

Q. 80: Can true believers be infallibly assured that they are in the estate of grace, and that they shall persevere therein unto salvation?

A.: Such as truly believe in Christ, and endeavor to walk in all good conscience before Him,[1] may, without extraordinary revelation, by faith grounded upon the truth of God's promises, and by the Spirit enabling them to discern in themselves those graces to which the promises of life are made,[2] and bearing witness with their spirits that they are the children of God,[3] be infallibly assured that they are in the estate of grace, and shall persevere therein unto salvation.[4]

---
[1] 1 John 2:3
[2] 1 Cor. 2:12; 1 John 3:14, 18-19, 21, 24; 4:13, 16; Heb. 6:11-12
[3] Rom. 8:16
[4] 1 John 5:13

Q. 81: Are all true believers at all times assured of their present being in the estate of grace, and that they shall be saved?

A.: Assurance of grace and salvation not being of the essence of faith,[1] true believers may wait long before they obtain it;[2] and, after the enjoyment thereof, may have it weakened and intermitted, through manifold distempers, sins, temptations, and desertions;[3] yet are they never left without such a presence and support of the Spirit of God as keeps them from sinking into utter despair.[4]

---
[1] Eph. 1:13
[2] Isa. 50:10; Ps. 88
[3] Ps. 77:1-12; 51:8, 12; 31:22; 22:1
[4] 1 John 3:9; Job 13:15; Ps. 73:15, 23; Isa. 54:7-10

Belgic Confession (1561)	Heidelberg Catechism (1563)	Second Helvetic Confession (1566)	Canons of Dort (1619)

Canons of Dort (cont.)

Q. 86: Since then we are delivered from our misery, merely of grace, through Christ, without any merit of ours, why must we still do good works?

A.: . . . also, that every one may be assured in himself of his faith by the fruits thereof.[1]

[1] 2 Pet. 1:10; Gal. 5:6, 24

Q. 129: What doth the word "Amen" signify?

A.: "Amen" signifies it shall truly and certainly be, for my prayer is more assuredly heard of God than I feel in my heart that I desire these things of Him.[1]

[1] 2 Cor. 1:20; 2 Tim. 2:13

to them it is not given" (Matt. 13:11). Likewise: "I thank Thee, O Father, Lord of heaven and earth, because Thou hast hid these things from the wise and prudent, and hast revealed them unto babes. Even so, Father: for so it seemed good in Thy sight" (Matt. 11:25-26).

Head V

Article 9

Of this preservation of the elect to salvation and of their perseverance in the faith, true believers for themselves may and do obtain assurance according to the measure of their faith, whereby they arrive at the certain persuasion that they ever will continue true and living members of the church; and that they experience forgiveness of sins, and will at last inherit eternal life.

Article 10

This assurance, however, is not produced by any peculiar revelation contrary to, or independent of the Word of God; but springs from faith in God's promises, which He has most abundantly revealed in His Word for our comfort; from the testimony of the Holy Spirit witnessing with our spirit that we are children and heirs of God (Rom. 8:16); and lastly, from a serious and holy desire to preserve a good conscience and to perform good works. And if the elect of God were deprived of this solid comfort that they shall finally obtain the victory and of this infallible pledge or earnest of eternal glory, they would be of all men the most miserable.

Article 11

The Scripture moreover testifies that believers in this life have to struggle with various carnal doubts and that under grievous temptations they are not always sensible of this full assurance of faith and certainty of persevering. But God, who is the Father of all consolation, does not suffer them to be tempted above that they are able, but will with the temptation also make a way to escape that they may be able to bear it (1 Cor. 10:13), and by the Holy Spirit again inspires them with the comfortable assurance of persevering.

Article 13

Neither does renewed confidence of persevering produce licentiousness or a disregard to piety in those who are recovering from backsliding; but it renders them much more careful and solicitous to continue in the ways of the Lord, which He hath ordained, that they who walk therein may maintain an assurance of persevering, lest by abusing His fatherly kindness, God should turn away His gracious countenance from them, to behold which is to the godly dearer than life, the withdrawing whereof is more bitter than death, and they in consequence hereof should fall into more grievous torments of conscience.

The true doctrine (concerning perseverance) having been explained, the Synod **rejects** the errors of those who teach:

Rejection 5

That without a special revelation we can have no certainty of future perseverance in this life. For by this doctrine the sure comfort of the true believers is taken away in this life and the doubts of the papist are again introduced into the church, while the Holy Scriptures constantly deduce this assurance, not from a special and extraordinary revelation, but from the marks proper to the children of God and from the constant promises

Westminster Confession of Faith (1647)	Westminster Shorter Catechism (1647)	Westminster Larger Catechism (1648)

ordinary means, attain thereunto.[2] And therefore it is the duty of every one to give all diligence to make his calling and election sure,[3] that thereby his heart may be enlarged in peace and joy in the Holy Ghost, in love and thankfulness to God, and in strength and cheerfulness in the duties of obedience,[4] the proper fruits of this assurance; so far is it from inclining men to looseness.[5]

---

[1] 1 John 5:13; Isa. 1:10; Mark 9:24; Ps. 88; 77:1-12
[2] 1 Cor. 2:12; 1 John 4:13; Heb. 6:11-12; Eph. 3:17-19
[3] 2 Pet. 1:10
[4] Rom. 5:1-2, 5; 14:17; 15:13; Eph. 1:3-4; Ps. 4:6-7; Ps. 119:32
[5] 1 John 2:1-2; Rom. 6:1-2; Titus 2:11-12, 14; 2 Cor. 7:1; Rom. 8:1, 12; 1 John 3:2-3; Ps. 130:4; 1 John 1:6-7

4. True believers may have the assurance of their salvation in divers ways shaken, diminished, and intermitted; as, by negligence in preserving of it, by falling into some special sin which woundeth the conscience and grieveth the Spirit; by some sudden or vehement temptation, by God's withdrawing the light of His countenance, and suffering even such as fear Him to walk in darkness and to have no light:[1] yet are they never utterly destitute of that seed of God, and life of faith, that love of Christ and the brethren, that sincerity of heart, and conscience of duty, out of which, by the operation of the Spirit, this assurance may, in due time, be revived;[2] and by the which, in the mean time, they are supported from utter despair.[3]

---

[1] Songs 5:2-3, 6; Ps. 51:8, 12, 14; Eph. 4:30-31; Ps. 77:1-10; Matt. 26:69-72; Ps. 31:22; Ps. 88; Isa. 1:10
[2] 1 John 3:9; Luke 22:32; Job 13:15; Ps. 73:15; 51:8, 12; Isa. 1:10
[3] Micah 7:7-9; Jer. 32:40; Isa. 54:7-10; Ps. 22:1; Ps. 88

Canons of Dort (cont.)

of God. So especially the apostle Paul: "Nor any other creature, shall be able to separate us from the love of God, which is in Christ Jesus our Lord" (Rom. 8:39). And John declares: "And he that keepeth His commandments dwelleth in Him, and He in him. And hereby we know that He abideth in us, by the Spirit which He hath given us" (1 John 3:24).

Rejection 6
That the doctrine of the certainty of perseverance and of salvation from its own character and nature is a cause of indolence and is injurious to godliness, good morals, prayers and other holy exercises, but that on the contrary it is praiseworthy to doubt. For these show that they do not know the power of divine grace and the working of the indwelling Holy Spirit. And they contradict the apostle John, who teaches the oppo-

site with express words in his first epistle: "Beloved, now are we the sons of God, and it doth not yet appear what we shall be: but we know that, when He shall appear, we shall be like Him; for we shall see Him as He is. And every man that hath this hope in Him purifieth himself, even as He is pure" (1 John 3:2-3). Furthermore, these are contradicted by the example of the saints, both of the Old and the New Testament, who though they were assured of their perseverance and salvation, were nevertheless constant in prayers and other exercises of godliness.

Belgic Confession (1561)	Heidelberg Catechism (1563)	Second Helvetic Confession (1566)	Canons of Dort (1619)

The Law of God

Article 25

The Abolishing of the Ceremonial Law

We believe that the ceremonies and figures of the law ceased at the coming of Christ,[1] and that all the shadows are accomplished; so that the use of them must be abolished among Christians;[2] yet the truth and substance of them remain with us in Jesus Christ, in whom they have their completion. In the meantime we still use the testimonies taken out of the law and the prophets, to confirm us in the doctrine of the gospel,[3] and to regulate our life in all honesty to the glory of God, according to His will.

[1] Rom. 10:4
[2] Gal. 5:2-4; 3:1; 4:10-11; Col. 2:16-17
[3] 2 Pet. 1:19

Q. 3: Whence knowest thou thy misery?

A.: Out of the law of God.[1]

[1] Rom. 3:20

Q. 4: What doth the law of God require of us?

A.: Christ teaches us that briefly, Matthew 22:37-40, "Thou shalt love the Lord thy God with all thy heart, with all thy soul, and with all thy mind, and with all thy strength. This is the first and the great commandment; and the second is like unto it, Thou shalt love thy neighbor as thyself. On these two commandments hang all the law and the prophets."[1]

[1] Luke 10:27

Q. 92: What is the law of God?

A.: God spake all these words, Exodus 20, Deuteronomy 5, saying, I am the LORD thy God, which have brought thee out of the land of Egypt, out of the house of bondage.
I. Thou shalt have no other gods before Me.
II. Thou shalt not make unto thee any graven image, or any likeness of any thing that is in heaven above, or that is in the earth beneath, or that is in the water under the earth: thou shalt not bow down thyself to them, nor serve them; for I the LORD thy God am a jealous God, visiting the iniquity of the fathers upon the children unto the third and fourth generation of them that hate Me; and

XII. Of the Law of God

1. We teach that the will of God is set down unto us in the law of God; to wit, what He would have us to do, or not to do, what is good and just, or what is evil and unjust. We therefore confess that "the law is holy, ... and good" (Rom. 7:12); and that this law is, by the finger of God, either written in the hearts of men (Rom. 2:15), and so is called the law of nature, or engraven in the two tables of stone, and more largely expounded in the books of Moses (Exod. 20:1-17; Deut. 5:22). For plainness' sake we divide it into the moral law, which is contained in the commandments, or the two tables expounded in the books of Moses; into the ceremonial, which does appoint ceremonies and the worship of God; and into the judicial law, which is occupied about political and domestic affairs.

2. We believe that the whole will of God,[1] and all necessary precepts, for every part of this life, are fully delivered in this law. For otherwise the Lord would not have forbidden that any thing should be either added to or taken away from this law (Deut. 4:2, 12:32); neither would He have commanded us to go straight forward in this, and not to decline out of the way, either "to the right hand or to the left" (Josh. 1:7).

3. We teach that this law was not given to men, that we should be justified by keeping it; but that, by the knowledge thereof, we might rather acknowledge our infirmity, sin, and condemnation; and so, despairing of our strength, might turn unto Christ by faith. For the apostle says plainly, "The law worketh wrath" (Rom. 4:15); and "by the law is the knowledge of sin" (Rom. 3:20); and, "If there had been a law given which could have given life, verily righteousness should have been by the law. But the scripture (to wit, of the law) hath concluded all under sin, that the promise by faith of Jesus Christ might be given to them that believe" (Gal. 3:21-22). "Wherefore, the law was our schoolmaster to bring us unto Christ, that we might be justified by faith" (ver. 24). For neither could there ever, neither at this day can any flesh satisfy the law of God, and fulfill it, by reason of the weakness in our flesh,[2] which remains and sticks fast in us, even to our last breath. For the apostle says again, "For what the law could not do, in that it was weak through the flesh, God sending His own Son in the likeness of sinful flesh, and for

Heads III and IV
Article 5

In the same light are we to consider the law of the decalogue, delivered by God to His peculiar people the Jews by the hands of Moses. For though it discovers the greatness of sin, and more and more convinces man thereof, yet as it neither points out a remedy nor imparts strength to extricate him from misery, and thus being weak through the flesh leaves the transgressor under the curse, man cannot by this law obtain saving grace.

Westminster Confession of Faith (1647)	Westminster Shorter Catechism (1647)	Westminster Larger Catechism (1648)

XIX. Of the Law of God

1. God gave to Adam a law, as a covenant of works, by which He bound him and all his posterity, to personal, entire, exact, and perpetual obedience, promised life upon the fulfilling, and threatened death upon the breach of it, and endued him with power and ability to keep it.[1]

[1] Gen. 1:26-27; 2:17; Rom. 2:14-15; 10:5; 5:12, 19; Gal. 3:10, 12; Eccl. 7:29; Job 28:28

2. This law, after his fall, continued to be a perfect rule of righteousness; and, as such, was delivered by God upon Mount Sinai, in ten commandments, and written in two tables:[1] the first four commandments containing our duty towards God; and the other six, our duty to man.[2]

[1] James 1:25; 2:8, 10-12; Rom. 13:8-9; Deut. 5:32; 10:4; Exod. 24:1
[2] Matt. 22:37-40

3. Besides this law, commonly called moral, God was pleased to give to the people of Israel, as a Church under age, ceremonial laws, containing several typical ordinances, partly of worship, prefiguring Christ, His graces, actions, sufferings, and benefits;[1] and partly, holding forth divers instructions of moral duties.[2] All which ceremonial laws are now abrogated, under the New Testament.[3]

[1] Heb. 9; 10:1; Gal. 4:1-3; Col. 2:17
[2] 1 Cor. 5:7; 2 Cor. 6:17; Jude 23
[3] Col. 2:14, 16-17; Dan. 9:27; Eph. 2:15-16

Q. 39: What is the duty which God requireth of man?

A.: The duty which God requireth of man, is obedience to His revealed will.[1]

[1] Micah 6:8; 1 Sam. 15:22

Q. 40: What did God at first reveal to man for the rule of his obedience?

A.: The rule which God at first revealed to man for his obedience, was the moral law.[1]

[1] Rom. 2:14-15; 10:5

Q. 41: Where is the moral law summarily comprehended?

A.: The moral law is summarily comprehended in the ten commandments.[1]

[1] Deut. 10:4; Matt. 19:17

Q. 42: What is the sum of the ten commandments?

A.: The sum of the ten commandments is, To love the Lord our God with all our heart, with all our soul, with all our strength, and with all our mind; and our neighbor as ourselves.[1]

[1] Matt. 22:37-40

Q. 43: What is the preface to the ten commandments?

A.: The preface to the ten commandments is in these words, "I am the Lord thy God, which have brought thee out of the land of Egypt, out of the house of bondage."[1]

[1] Exod. 20:2

Q. 44: What doth the preface to the ten commandments teach us?

A.: The preface to the ten

Q. 91: What is the duty which God requireth of man?

A.: The duty which God requireth of man, is obedience to His revealed will.[1]

[1] Rom. 12:1-2; Micah 6:8; 1 Sam. 15:22

Q. 92: What did God at first reveal unto man as the rule of his obedience?

A.: The rule of obedience revealed to Adam in the estate of innocence, and to all mankind in him, besides a special command not to eat of the fruit of the tree of the knowledge of good and evil, was the moral law.[1]

[1] Gen. 1:26-27; Rom. 2:14-15; 10:5; Gen. 2:17

Q. 93: What is the moral law?

A.: The moral law is the declaration of the will of God to mankind, directing and binding everyone to personal, perfect, and perpetual conformity and obedience thereunto, in the frame and disposition of the whole man, soul and body,[1] and in performance of all those duties of holiness and righteousness which he oweth to God and man:[2] promising life upon the fulfilling, and threatening death upon the breach of it.[3]

[1] Deut. 5:1-3, 31, 33; Luke 10:26-27; Gal. 3:10; 1 Thes. 5:23
[2] Luke 1:75; Acts 24:16
[3] Rom. 10:5; Gal. 3:10, 12

Q. 94: Is there any use of the moral law to man since the fall?

A.: Although no man, since the fall, can attain to righteousness and life by the moral law;[1] yet there is great use thereof, as well common to all men, as peculiar either to the unregenerate, or the regenerate.[2]

[1] Rom. 8:3; Gal. 2:16
[2] 1 Tim. 1:8

Q. 95: Of what use is the moral law to all men?

A.: The moral law is of use to all men, to inform them of the holy nature and will of God,[1] and of their duty, binding them to walk accordingly;[2] to convince them of their disability to keep it, and of the sinful pollution of their nature, hearts, and lives:[3] to humble them in the sense of their sin and misery,[4] and thereby help them to a clearer sight of the need they have of Christ,[5] and of the perfection of His obedience.[6]

[1] Lev. 11:44-45; Lev. 20:7-8; Rom. 7:12
[2] Micah 6:8; James 2:10-11
[3] Ps. 19:11-12; Rom. 3:20; 7:7
[4] Rom. 3:9, 23
[5] Gal. 3:21-22
[6] Rom. 10:4

Q. 96: What particular use is there of the moral law to unregenerate men?

A.: The moral law is of use to unregenerate men, to awaken their consciences to flee from wrath to come,[1] and to drive them to

Belgic Confession (1561)	Heidelberg Catechism (1563)	Second Helvetic Confession (1566)	Canons of Dort (1619)
	shewing mercy unto thousands of them that love Me, and keep My commandments. III. Thou shalt not take the name of the LORD thy God in vain; for the LORD will not hold him guiltless that taketh His name in vain. IV. Remember the Sabbath day, to keep it holy. Six days shalt thou labour and do all thy work: but the seventh day is the Sabbath of the LORD thy God: in it thou shalt not do any work, thou, nor thy son, nor thy daughter, nor thy manservant, nor thy maidservant, nor thy cattle, nor thy stranger that is within thy gates: for in six days the LORD made heaven and earth, the sea, and all that in them is, and rested the seventh day: wherefore the LORD blessed the Sabbath day, and hallowed it. V. Honour thy father and thy mother: that thy days may be long upon the land which the LORD thy God giveth thee. VI. Thou shalt not kill. VII. Thou shalt not commit adultery. VIII. Thou shalt not steal. IX. Thou shalt not bear false witness against thy neighbour. X. Thou shalt not covet thy neighbour's house, thou shalt not covet thy neighbour's wife, nor his manservant, nor his maidservant, nor his ox, nor his ass, nor any thing that is thy neighbour's. *Q. 93: How are these commandments divided?* A.: Into two tables;[1] the first of which teaches us how we must behave towards God; the second, what duties we owe to our neighbor.[2] [1] Exod. 34:28-29 [2] Deut. 4:13	sin, condemned sin in the flesh" (Rom. 8:3). Therefore, Christ is the perfecting of the law, and our fulfilling of it; who, as He took away the curse of the law, when He was made a curse for us (Gal. 3:13), so does He communicate unto us by faith His fulfilling thereof, and His righteousness and obedience are imputed unto us. 4. The law of God,[3] therefore, is thus far abrogated; that is, it does not henceforth condemn us, neither work wrath in us; "for ye are not under the law, but under grace" (Rom. 6:14). Moreover, Christ did fulfill all the figures of the law; wherefore the shadow ceased when the body came, so that, in Christ, we have now all truth and fullness. Yet we do not therefore disdain or reject the law. We remember the words of the Lord, saying, "Think not that I am come to destroy the law, or the prophets: I am not come to destroy, but to fulfil" (Matt. 5:17). We know that in the law[4] are described unto us the kinds of virtues and vices. We know that the Scripture of the law,[5] if it be expounded by the gospel, is very profitable to the Church, and that therefore the reading of it is not to be banished out of the Church. For although the countenance of Moses was covered with a veil, yet the apostle affirms that the "veil is done away in Christ" (2 Cor. 3:14). We condemn all things which the old or new heretics have taught against the law of God. [1] Understand, as concerning those things which men are bound to perform to God, and also to their neighbors. [2] That is, any man, although he be regenerate. [3] To wit, the moral law, comprehended in the ten commandments. [4] To wit, in the moral law. [5] To wit, the ceremonial law.	

Westminster Confession of Faith (1647)	Westminster Shorter Catechism (1647)	Westminster Larger Catechism (1648)

Westminster Confession of Faith (1647)

4. To them also, as a body politic, He gave sundry judicial laws, which expired together with the state of that people; not obliging any other now, further than the general equity thereof may require.[1]

[1] Exod. 21; 22:1-29; Gen. 49:10; 1 Pet. 2:13-14; Matt. 5:17, 38-39; 1 Cor. 9:8-10

5. The moral law doth for ever bind all, as well justified persons as others, to the obedience thereof;[1] and that, not only in regard of the matter contained in it, but also in respect of the authority of God the Creator, who gave it.[2] Neither doth Christ, in the gospel, any way dissolve, but much strengthen this obligation.[3]

[1] Rom. 13:8-10; Eph. 6:2; 1 John 2:3-4, 7-8
[2] James 2:10-11
[3] Matt. 5:17-19; James 2:8; Rom. 3:31

6. Although true believers be not under the law, as a covenant of works, to be thereby justified, or condemned;[1] yet is it of great use to them, as well as to others; in that, as a rule of life informing them of the will of God, and their duty, it directs and binds them to walk accordingly;[2] discovering also the sinful pollutions of their nature, hearts, and lives;[3] so as, examining themselves thereby, they may come to further conviction of, humiliation for, and hatred against sin,[4] together with a clearer sight of the need they have of Christ, and the perfection of His obedience.[5] It is likewise of use to the regenerate, to restrain their corruptions, in that it forbids sin:[6] and the threatenings of it serve to show what even their sins

Westminster Shorter Catechism (1647)

commandments teacheth us, That because God is the Lord, and our God, and Redeemer, therefore we are bound to keep all His commandments.[1]

[1] Luke 1:74-75; 1 Pet. 1:15-19

Westminster Larger Catechism (1648)

Christ;[2] or, upon their continuance in the estate and way of sin, to leave them inexcusable,[3] and under the curse thereof.[4]

[1] 1 Tim. 1:9-10
[2] Gal. 3:24
[3] Rom. 1:20; 2:15
[4] Gal. 3:10

Q. 97: *What special use is there of the moral law to the regenerate?*
A.: Although they that are regenerate, and believe in Christ, be delivered from the moral law as a covenant of works,[1] so as thereby they are neither justified[2] nor condemned;[3] yet, besides the general uses thereof common to them with all men, it is of special use, to shew them how much they are bound to Christ for his fulfilling it, and enduring the curse thereof in their stead, and for their good;[4] and thereby to provoke them to more thankfulness, and to express the same in their greater care to conform themselves thereunto as the rule of their obedience.[5]

[1] Rom. 6:14; Rom. 7:4, 6; Gal. 4:4-5
[2] Rom. 3:20
[3] Gal. 5:23; Rom. 8:1
[4] Rom. 7:24-25; Gal. 3:13-14; Rom. 8:3-4
[5] Luke 1:68-69, 74-75; Col. 1:12-14; Rom. 7:22; Titus 2:11-14

Q. 98: *Where is the moral law summarily comprehended?*
A.: The moral law is summarily comprehended in the ten commandments, which were delivered by the voice of God upon Mount Sinai, and written by Him in two tables of stone;[1] and are recorded in the twentieth chapter of Exodus. The first four commandments containing our duty to God, and the other six our duty to man.[2]

[1] Deut. 10:4; Exod. 34:1-4
[2] Matt. 22:37-40

Q. 99: *What rules are to be observed for the right understanding of the ten commandments?*
A.: For the right understanding of the ten commandments, these rules are to be observed:

1. That the law is perfect, and bindeth everyone to full conformity in the whole man unto the righteousness thereof, and unto entire obedience for ever; so as to require the utmost perfection of every duty, and to forbid the least degree of every sin.[1]

[1] Ps. 19:7; James 2:10; Matt. 5:21-22

2. That it is spiritual, and so reacheth the understanding, will, affections, and all other powers of the soul; as well as words, works, and gestures.[2]

[2] Rom. 7:14; Deut. 6:5; Matt. 22:37-39; 5:21-22, 27-28, 33-34, 37-39, 43-44

3. That one and the same thing, in divers respects, is required or forbidden in several commandments.[3]

[3] Col. 3:5; Amos 8:5; Prov. 1:19; 1 Tim. 6:10

4. That as, where a duty is commanded, the contrary sin is forbidden;[4] and, where a sin is forbidden, the contrary duty is commanded:[5] so, where a promise is annexed, the contrary threatening is included;[6] and, where a threatening is annexed, the contrary promise is included.[7]

[4] Isa. 58:13; Deut. 6:13; Matt. 4:9-10; 15:4-6

Belgic Confession (1561)	Heidelberg Catechism (1563)	Second Helvetic Confession (1566)	Canons of Dort (1619)

Westminster Confession of Faith (1647)	Westminster Shorter Catechism (1647)	Westminster Larger Catechism (1648)
deserve; and what afflictions, in this life, they may expect for them, although freed from the curse thereof threatened in the law.[7] The promises of it, in like manner, shew them God's approbation of obedience, and what blessings they may expect upon the performance thereof:[8] although not as due to them by the law as a covenant of works.[9] So as, a man's doing good, and refraining from evil, because the law encourageth to the one and detereth from the other, is no evidence of his being under the law; and not under grace.[10]		[5] Matt. 5:21-25; Eph. 4:28 [6] Exod. 20:12; Prov. 30:17 [7] Jer. 18:7-8; Exod. 20:7; Ps. 15:1, 4-5; Ps. 24:4-5 5. That what God forbids, is at no time to be done;[8] what He commands, is always our duty;[9] and yet every particular duty is not to be done at all times.[10] [8] Job 13:7-8; Rom. 3:8; Job 36:21; Heb. 11:25 [9] Deut. 4:8-9 [10] Matt. 12:7 6. That under one sin or duty, all of the same kind are forbidden or commanded; together with all the causes, means, occasions, and appearances thereof, and provocations thereunto.[11] [11] Matt. 5:21-22, 27-28; 15:4-6; Heb. 10:24-25; 1 Thes. 5:22; Jude 23; Gal. 5:26; Col. 3:21 7. That what is forbidden or commanded to ourselves, we are bound, according to our places, to endeavour that it may be avoided or performed by others, according to the duty of their places.[12] [12] Exod. 20:10; Lev. 19:17; Gen. 18:19; Josh. 24:15; Deut. 6:6-7 8. That in what is commanded to others, we are bound, according to our places and callings, to be helpful to them;[13] and to take heed of partaking with others in what is forbidden them.[14] [13] 2 Cor. 1:24 [14] 1 Tim. 5:22; Eph. 5:11
[1] Rom. 6:14; Gal. 2:16; 3:13; 4:4-5; Acts 13:39; Rom. 8:1 [2] Rom. 7:12, 22, 25; Ps. 119:4-6; 1 Cor. 7:19; Gal. 5:14, 16, 18-23 [3] Rom. 7:7; 3:20 [4] James 1:23-25; Rom. 7:9, 14, 24 [5] Gal. 3:24; Rom. 7:24-25; 8:3-4 [6] James 2:11; Ps. 119:101, 104, 128 [7] Ezra 9:13-14; Ps. 89:30-34 [8] Lev. 26:1-14; 2 Cor. 6:16; Eph. 6:2-3; Ps. 37:11; Matt. 5:5; Ps. 19:11 [9] Gal. 2:16; Luke 17:10 [10] Rom. 6:12, 14; 1 Pet. 3:8-12; Ps. 34:12-16; Heb. 12:28-29		*Q. 100: What special things are we to consider in the ten commandments?* A.: We are to consider, in the ten commandments, the preface, the substance of the commandments themselves, and several reasons annexed to some of them, the more to enforce them.
7. Neither are the forementioned uses of the law contrary to the grace of the gospel, but do sweetly comply with it;[1] the Spirit of Christ subduing and enabling the will of man to do that freely, and cheerfully, which the will of God, revealed in the law, requireth to be done.[2]		*Q. 101: What is the preface to the ten commandments?* A.: The preface to the ten commandments is contained in these words, *I am the Lord thy God, which have brought thee out of the land of Egypt, out of the house of bondage.*[1] Wherein God manifesteth His sovereignty, as being JEHOVAH, the eternal, immutable, and almighty God;[2] having His being in and of Himself,[3] and giving being to all His words[4] and works:[5] and that He is a God in covenant, as with Israel of old, so with all His people;[6] who, as He brought them out of their bondage in Egypt, so He delivereth us from our spiritual thraldom;[7] and that therefore we are bound to take Him for our God alone, and to keep all His commandments.[8]
[1] Gal. 3:21 [2] Ezek. 36:27; Heb. 8:10; Jer. 31:33		[1] Exod. 20:2 [2] Isa. 44:6 [3] Exod. 3:14 [4] Exod. 6:3 [5] Acts 17:24, 28 [6] Gen. 17:7; Rom. 3:29 [7] Luke 1:74-75 [8] 1 Pet. 1:15-18; Lev. 18:30; 19:37 *Q. 102: What is the sum of the four commandments which contain our duty to God?* A.: The sum of the four commandments containing our duty to God is, to love the Lord our God with all our heart, and with all our soul, and with all our strength, and with all our mind.[1] [1] Luke 10:27

Belgic Confession (1561)	Heidelberg Catechism (1563)	Second Helvetic Confession (1566)	Canons of Dort (1619)

The First Commandment

Belgic Confession (1561)	Heidelberg Catechism (1563)	Second Helvetic Confession (1566)	Canons of Dort (1619)
	Q. 94: What doth God enjoin in the first commandment? A.: That I, as sincerely as I desire the salvation of my own soul, avoid and flee from all idolatry,[1] sorcery, soothsaying, superstition,[2] invocation of saints, or any other creatures;[3] and learn rightly to know the only true God;[4] trust in Him alone;[5] with humility and patience[6] submit to Him;[7] expect all good things from Him only;[8] love,[9] fear,[10] and glorify[11] Him with my whole heart; so that I renounce and forsake all creatures,[12] rather than commit even the least thing contrary to His will.[13] [1] 1 Cor. 6:9-10; 1 Cor. 10:7, 14 [2] Lev. 18:21; Deut. 18:10-12 [3] Matt. 4:10; Rev. 19:10 [4] John 17:3 [5] Jer. 17:5, 7 [6] Heb. 10:36; Col. 1:11; Rom. 5:3-4; Phil. 2:14 [7] 1 Pet. 5:5-6 [8] Ps. 104:27; Isa. 45:7; James 1:17 [9] Deut. 6:5; Matt. 22:37 [10] Deut. 6:5; Matt. 10:28 [11] Matt. 4:10 [12] Matt. 5:29-30; Acts 5:29; Matt. 10:37 [13] Matt. 5:19		

Westminster Confession of Faith (1647)	Westminster Shorter Catechism (1647)	Westminster Larger Catechism (1648)
		Q. 122: What is the sum of the six commandments which contain our duty to man? A.: The sum of the six commandments which contain our duty to man, is, to love our neighbor as ourselves,[1] and to do to others what we would have them to do to us.[2] --- [1] Matt. 22:39 [2] Matt. 7:12

Q. 45: Which is the first commandment?

A.: The first commandment is, "Thou shalt have no other gods before me."[1]

---
[1] Exod. 20:3

Q. 46: What is required in the first commandment?

A.: The first commandment requireth us to know and acknowledge God to be the only true God, and our God;[1] and to worship and glorify Him accordingly.[2]

---
[1] 1 Chron. 28:9; Deut. 26:17
[2] Matt. 4:10; Ps. 29:2

Q. 47: What is forbidden in the first commandment?

A.: The first commandment forbiddeth the denying,[1] or not worshipping and glorifying, the true God as God,[2] and our God;[3] and the giving of that worship and glory to any other, which is due to Him alone.[4]

---
[1] Ps. 14:1
[2] Rom. 1:21
[3] Ps. 81:10-11
[4] Rom. 1:25-26

Q. 48: What are we specially taught by these words [before Me] in the first commandment?

A.: These words [before Me] in the first command-

Q. 103: Which is the first commandment?

A.: The first commandment is, *Thou shall have no other gods before Me.*[1]

---
[1] Exod. 20:3

Q. 104: What are the duties required in the first commandment?

A.: The duties required in the first commandment are, the knowing and acknowledging of God to be the only true God, and our God;[1] and to worship and glorify Him accordingly,[2] by thinking,[3] meditating,[4] remembering,[5] highly esteeming,[6] honouring,[7] adoring,[8] choosing,[9] loving,[10] desiring,[11] fearing of Him;[12] believing Him;[13] trusting,[14] hoping,[15] delighting,[16] rejoicing in Him;[17] being zealous for Him;[18] calling upon Him, giving all praise and thanks,[19] and yielding all obedience and submission to Him with the whole man;[20] being careful in all things to please Him,[21] and sorrowful when in any thing He is offended;[22] and walking humbly with Him.[23]

---
[1] 1 Chron. 28:9; Deut. 26:17; Isa. 43:10; Jer. 14:22
[2] Ps. 95:6-7; Matt. 4:10; Ps. 29:2
[3] Mal. 3:16
[4] Ps. 63:6
[5] Eccl. 12:1
[6] Ps. 71:19
[7] Mal. 1:6
[8] Isa. 45:23
[9] Josh. 24:15, 22
[10] Deut. 6:5
[11] Ps. 73:25
[12] Isa. 8:13
[13] Exod. 14:31
[14] Isa. 26:4
[15] Ps. 130:7
[16] Ps. 37:4
[17] Ps. 32:11
[18] Rom. 12:11; Num. 25:11
[19] Phil. 4:6
[20] Jer. 7:23; James 4:7
[21] 1 John 3:22
[22] Jer. 31:18; Ps. 119:136
[23] Micah 6:8

Q. 105: What are the sins forbidden in the first commandment?

A.: The sins forbidden in the first commandment, are, atheism, in denying or not having a God;[1] idolatry, in having or worshipping more gods than one, or any with or instead of the true God;[2] the not having and avouching Him for God, and our God;[3] the omission or neglect of any thing due to Him, required in this commandment;[4] ignorance,[5] forgetfulness,[6] misapprehensions,[7] false opinions,[8] unworthy and wicked thoughts of Him;[9] bold and curious searching into His secrets;[10] all profaneness,[11] hatred of God;[12] self-love,[13] self-seeking,[14] and all other inordinate and immoderate setting of our mind, will, or affections upon other things, and taking them off from Him in whole or in part;[15] vain credulity,[16] unbelief,[17] heresy,[18] misbelief,[19] distrust,[20] despair,[21] incorrigibleness,[22] and insensibleness under judgments,[23] hardness of heart,[24] pride,[25] presumption,[26] car-

Belgic Confession (1561)	Heidelberg Catechism (1563)	Second Helvetic Confession (1566)	Canons of Dort (1619)
	Q. 95: What is idolatry? A.: Idolatry is, instead of, or besides that one true God who has manifested Himself in His word, to contrive, or have any other object, in which men place their trust.[1] ___ [1] 2 Chron. 16:12; Phil. 3:18-19; Gal. 4:8; Eph. 2:12		

Westminster Confession of Faith (1647)	Westminster Shorter Catechism (1647)	Westminster Larger Catechism (1648)
	ment teach us, That God, who seeth all things, taketh notice of, and is much displeased with, the sin of having any other god.[1] [1] Ezek. 8:5-6; Ps. 46:20-21	nal security,[27] tempting of God;[28] using unlawful means,[29] and trusting in unlawful means;[30] carnal delights and joys;[31] corrupt, blind, and indiscreet zeal;[32] lukewarmness,[33] and deadness in the things of God;[34] estranging ourselves, and apostatizing from God;[35] praying, or giving any religious worship, to saints, angels, or any other creatures;[36] all compacts and consulting with the devil,[37] and hearkening to his suggestions;[38] making men the lords of our faith and conscience;[39] slighting and despising God and His commands;[40] resisting and grieving of His Spirit,[41] discontent and impatience at His dispensations, charging Him foolishly for the evils He inflicts on us;[42] and ascribing the praise of any good we either are, have, or can do, to fortune,[43] idols,[44] ourselves,[45] or any other creature.[46]

Reference notes (Larger Catechism):

[1] Ps. 14:1; Eph. 2:12
[2] Jer. 2:27-28; 1 Thes. 1:9
[3] Ps. 81:11
[4] Isa. 43:22-24
[5] Jer. 4:22; Hos. 4:1, 6
[6] Jer. 2:32
[7] Acts 17:23, 29
[8] Isa. 40:18
[9] Ps. 50:21
[10] Deut. 29:29
[11] Titus 1:16; Heb. 12:16
[12] Rom. 1:30
[13] 2 Tim. 3:2
[14] Phil. 2:21
[15] 1 John 2:15-16; 1 Sam. 2:29; Col. 3:2, 5
[16] 1 John 4:1
[17] Heb. 3:12
[18] Gal. 5:20; Tit. 3:10
[19] Acts 26:9
[20] Ps. 78:22
[21] Gen. 4:13
[22] Jer. 5:3
[23] Isa. 42:25
[24] Rom. 2:5
[25] Jer. 13:15
[26] Ps. 19:13
[27] Zeph. 1:12
[28] Matt. 4:7
[29] Rom. 3:8
[30] Jer. 17:5
[31] 2 Tim. 3:4
[32] Gal. 4:17; John 16:2; Rom. 10:2; Luke 9:54-55
[33] Rev. 3:16
[34] Rev. 3:1
[35] Ezek. 14:5; Isa. 1:4-5
[36] Rom. 10:13-14; Hos. 4:12; Acts 10:25-26; Rev. 19:10; Matt. 4:10; Col. 2:18; Rom. 1:25
[37] Lev. 20:6; 1 Sam. 28:7, 11; 1 Chron. 10:13-14
[38] Acts 5:3
[39] 2 Cor. 1:24; Matt. 23:9
[40] Deut. 32:15; 2 Sam. 12:9; Prov. 13:13
[41] Acts 7:51; Eph. 4:30
[42] Ps. 73:2-3, 13-15, 22; Job 1:22
[43] 1 Sam. 6:7-9
[44] Dan. 5:23
[45] Deut. 8:17; Dan. 4:30
[46] Hab. 1:16

Q. 106: What are we specially taught by these words [before Me] in the first commandment?

A.: These words *[before Me]* or before My face, in the first commandmentment, teach us, that God, who seeth all things, taketh special notice of, and is much displeased with, the sin of having any other God: that so it may be an argument to dissuade from it, and to aggravate it as a most impudent provocation:[1] as also to persuade us to do as in His sight, whatever we do in His service.[2]

[1] Ezek. 8:5-6; Ps. 44:20-21
[2] 1 Chron. 28:9

Belgic Confession (1561)	Heidelberg Catechism (1563)	Second Helvetic Confession (1566)	Canons of Dort (1619)

The Second Commandment

Q. 96: What doth God require in the second commandment?

A.: That we in no wise represent God by images,[1] nor worship Him in any other way than He has commanded in His Word.[2]

---

[1] Deut. 4:15; Isa. 40:18; Rom. 1:23, etc.; Acts 17:29
[2] 1 Sam. 15:23; Deut. 12:30

Q. 97: Are images then not at all to be made?

A.: God neither can, nor may be represented by any means.[1] But as to creatures, though they may be represented, yet God forbids to make, or have any resemblance of them, either in order to worship them or to serve God by them.[2]

---

[1] Deut. 4:15-16; Isa. 46:5; Rom. 1:23
[2] Exod. 23:24; Exod. 34:13-14; Num. 33:52; Deut. 7:5

Q. 98: But may not images be tolerated in the churches, as books to the laity?

A.: No, for we must not pretend to be wiser than God, who will have His people taught, not by dumb images,[1] but by the lively preaching of His Word.[2]

---

[1] 2 Tim. 3:16; 2 Pet. 1:19
[2] Jer. 10:1, etc.; Hab. 2:18-19

IV. Of Idols; or of Images of God, of Christ, and of Saints

1. And because God is an invisible Spirit, and an incomprehensible essence, He cannot, therefore, by any art or image be expressed. For which cause we fear not, with the Scripture, to term the images of God mere lies.

2. We do therefore reject not only the idols of the Gentiles, but also the images of Christians. For although Christ took upon Him man's nature, yet He did not therefore take it that He might set forth a pattern for carvers and painters. He denied that He came "to destroy the law, or the prophets" (Matt. 5:17), but images are forbidden in the law and the prophets (Deut. 4:15; Isa. 44:9). He denied that His bodily presence would profit the Church, but promised that He would by His Spirit be present with us forever (John 16:7; 2 Cor. 5:5).

3. Who would, then, believe that the shadow or picture of His body doth any whit benefit the godly? And seeing that He abideth in us by the Spirit, we are therefore the temples of God (1 Cor. 3:16); but "what agreement hath the temple of God with idols?" (2 Cor. 6:16). And seeing that the blessed spirits and saints in heaven, while they lived here, abhorred all worship done unto themselves (Acts 3:12; 14:15; Rev. 19:10; 22:9), and spake against images, who can think it likely that the saints in heaven, and the angels, are delighted with their own images, whereunto men do bow their knees, uncover their heads, and give such other like honor?

4. But that men might be instructed in religion, and put in mind of heavenly things and of their own salvation, the Lord commanded to preach the gospel (Mark 16:15) — not to paint and instruct the laity by pictures; He also instituted sacraments, but He nowhere appointed images.

5. Furthermore, in every place which way soever we turn our eyes, we may see the lively and true creatures of God, which if they be marked, as is meet, they do much more effectually move the beholder than all the images or vain, unmovable, rotten, and dead pictures of all men whatsoever; of which the prophet spake truly, "...eyes have they, but they see not," etc. (Ps. 115:5).

6. Therefore we approve the judgment of Lactantius, an ancient writer, who says, "Undoubtedly there is no religion where there is a picture."

Westminster Confession of Faith (1647)	Westminster Shorter Catechism (1647)	Westminster Larger Catechism (1648)

XXI. Of Religious Worship, and the Sabbath Day

1. The light of nature sheweth that there is a God, who hath lordship and sovereignty over all, is good, and doth good unto all, and is therefore to be feared, loved, praised, called upon, trusted in, and served, with all the heart, and with all the soul, and with all the might.[1] But the acceptable way of worshipping the true God is instituted by Himself, and so limited by His own revealed will, that He may not be worshipped according to the imaginations and devices of men, or the suggestions of Satan, under any visible representation, or any other way not prescribed in the holy Scripture.[2]

[1] Rom. 1:20; Acts 17:24; Ps. 119:68; Jer. 10:7; Ps. 31:23; 18:3; Rom. 10:12; Ps. 62:8; Josh. 24:14; Mark 12:33
[2] Deut. 12:32; Matt. 15:9; Acts 17:25; Matt. 4:9-10; Deut. 15:1-20; Exod. 20:4-6; Col. 2:23

2. Religious worship is to be given to God, the Father, Son, and Holy Ghost; and to Him alone;[1] not to angels, saints, or any other creature:[2] and, since the fall, not without a Mediator; nor in the mediation of any other but of Christ alone.[3]

[1] Matt. 4:10; John 5:23; 2 Cor. 13:14
[2] Col. 2:18; Rev. 19:10; Rom. 1:25
[3] John 14:6; 1 Tim. 2:5; Eph. 2:18; Col. 3:17

3. Prayer, with thanksgiving, being one special part of religious worship,[1] is by God required of all men:[2] and, that it may be accepted,

Q. 49: Which is the second commandment?

A.: The second commandment is, "Thou shalt not make unto thee any graven image, or any likeness of anything that is in heaven above, or that is in the earth beneath, or that is in the water under the earth: thou shalt not bow down thyself to them, nor serve them: for I the LORD thy God am a jealous God, visiting the iniquity of the fathers upon the children unto the third and fourth generation of them that hate Me; and shewing mercy unto thousands of them that love Me, and keep My commandments."[1]

[1] Exod. 20:4-6

Q. 50: What is required in the second commandment?

A.: The second commandment requireth the receiving, observing, and keeping pure and entire, all such religious worship and ordinances as God hath appointed in His Word.[1]

[1] Deut. 32:46; Matt. 28:20; Acts 2:42

Q. 51: What is forbidden in the second commandment?

A.: The second commandment forbiddeth the worshipping of God by images,[1] or any other way not appointed in His Word.[2]

[1] Deut. 4:15-19; Exod. 32:5, 8
[2] Deut. 12:31-32

Q. 52: What are the reasons annexed to the second commandment?

A.: The reasons annexed to the second commandment are, God's sovereignty over us,[1] His

Q. 107: Which is the second commandment?

A.: The second commandment is, *Thou shalt not make unto thee any graven image, or any likeness of any thing that is in heaven above, or that is in the earth beneath, or that is in the water under the earth: thou shalt not bow down thyself to them, nor serve them: for I the LORD thy God am a jealous God, visiting the iniquity of the fathers upon the children unto the third and fourth generation of them that hate Me; and shewing mercy unto thousands of them that love Me, and keep My commandments.*[1]

[1] Exod. 20:4-6

Q. 108: What are the duties required in the second commandment?

A.: The duties required in the second commandment are, the receiving, observing, and keeping pure and entire, all such religious worship and ordinances as God hath instituted in His Word;[1] particularly prayer and thanksgiving in the name of Christ;[2] the reading, preaching, and hearing of the Word;[3] the administration and receiving of the sacraments;[4] Church government and discipline;[5] the ministry and maintenance thereof;[6] religious fasting;[7] swearing by the name of God,[8] and vowing unto Him:[9] as also the disapproving, detesting, opposing, all false worship;[10] and, according to each one's place and calling, removing it, and all monuments of idolatry.[11]

[1] Deut. 32:46-47; Matt. 28:20; Acts 2:42; 1 Tim. 6:13-14
[2] Phil. 4:6; Eph. 5:20
[3] Deut. 17:18-19; Acts 15:21; 2 Tim. 4:2; James 1:21-22; Acts 10:33
[4] Matt. 28:19; 1 Cor. 11:23-30
[5] Matt. 18:15-17; 16:19; 1 Cor. 5; 12:28
[6] Eph. 4:11-12; 1 Tim. 5:17-18; 1 Cor. 9:7-15
[7] Joel 2:12-13; 1 Cor. 7:5
[8] Deut. 6:13
[9] Isa. 19:21; Ps. 76:11
[10] Acts 17:16-17; Ps. 16:4
[11] Deut. 7:5; Isa. 30:22

Q. 109: What are the sins forbidden in the second commandment?

A.: The sins forbidden in the second commandment are, all devising,[1] counselling,[2] commanding,[3] using,[4] and any wise approving, any religious worship not instituted by God Himself;[5] tolerating a false religion;[6] the making any representation of God, of all or of any of the three persons, either inwardly in our mind, or outwardly in any kind of image or likeness of any creature whatsoever;[7] all worshipping of it,[8] or God in it or by it;[9] the making of any representation of feigned deities,[10] and all worship of them, or service belonging to them;[11] all superstitious devices,[12] corrupting the worship of God,[13] adding to it, or taking from it,[14] whether invented and taken up of ourselves,[15] or received by tradition from others,[16] though under the title of antiquity,[17] custom,[18] devotion,[19] good intent, or any other pretence whatsoever;[20] simony;[21] sacrilege;[22] all neglect,[23] contempt,[24] hindering,[25] and opposing the worship and ordinances which God hath appointed.[26]

[1] Numb. 15:39
[2] Deut. 13:6-8
[3] Hosea 5:11; Micah 6:16
[4] 1 Ki. 11:33; 12:33
[5] Deut. 12:30-32
[6] Deut. 13:6-12; Zech. 13:2-3; Rev. 2:2, 14-15, 20; 17:12, 16-17
[7] Deut. 4:15-19; Acts 17:29; Rom. 1:21-23, 25

Belgic Confession (1561)	Heidelberg Catechism (1563)	Second Helvetic Confession (1566)	Canons of Dort (1619)
		And we affirm that the blessed bishop Epiphanius did well, who, finding on the church-doors a veil, that had painted on it the picture, as it might be, of Christ or some saint or other, he cut and took it away; for that, contrary to the authority of the Scriptures, he had seen the picture of a man to hang in the Church of Christ: and therefore he charged that from henceforth no such veils, which were contrary to religion, should be hung up in the Church of Christ, but that rather such scruple should be taken away which was unworthy of the Church of Christ and all faithful people. Moreover, we approve this sentence of St. Augustine, "Let not the worship of men's works be a religion unto us; for the workmen themselves that make such things are better, whom yet we ought not to worship" (*De Vera Religione*, cap. 55). *V. Of the Adoration, Worship, and Invocation of God Through the Only Mediator Jesus Christ* 1. We teach to adore and worship the true God alone. This honor we impart to none, according to the commandment of the Lord, "Thou shalt worship the Lord thy God, and Him alone shalt thou worship," or "Him only shalt thou serve" (Matt. 4:10). Surely all the prophets inveighed earnestly against the people of Israel whensoever they did adore and worship strange gods, and not the only true God. 2. But we teach that God is to be adored and worshiped, as Himself has taught us to worship Him — to wit, "in spirit and in truth" (John 4:24); not with any superstition, but with sincerity, according to His Word, lest at any time He also say unto us, "Who hath required this at your hand?" (Isa. 1:12; Jer. 6:20). For Paul also says, "Neither is (God) worshipped with men's hands, as though He needed any thing," etc. (Acts 17:25). 4. Therefore we do neither adore, worship, nor pray unto the saints in heaven, or to other gods; neither do we acknowledge them for our intercessors or mediators before the Father in heaven. For God and the Mediator Christ do suffice us; neither do we impart unto others the honor due to God alone and to His Son, because He has plainly said, "My glory will I not give to another" (Isa. 42:8); and because Peter has said, "There is no other name under heaven given among men, whereby we must be saved," but the name of Christ (Acts 4:12). Those, doubtless, who rest in Him by faith do not seek any thing without Christ. 5. Yet, for all that, we do neither despise the	

Westminster Confession of Faith (1647)	Westminster Shorter Catechism (1647)	Westminster Larger Catechism (1648)

it is to be made in the name of the Son,[3] by the help of His Spirit,[4] according to His will,[5] with understanding, reverence, humility, fervency, faith, love and perseverance;[6] and, if vocal, in a known tongue.[7]

[1] Phil. 4:6
[2] Ps. 65:2
[3] John 14:13-14; 1 Pet. 2:5
[4] Rom. 8:26
[5] 1 John 5:14
[6] Ps. 47:7; Eccl. 5:1-2; Heb. 12:28; Gen. 18:27; James 5:16; 1:6-7; Mark 11:24; Matt. 6:12, 14-15; Col. 4:2; Eph. 6:18
[7] 1 Cor. 14:14

4. Prayer is to be made for things lawful;[1] and for all sorts of men living, or that shall live hereafter:[2] but not for the dead,[3] nor for those of whom it may be known that they have sinned the sin unto death.[4]

[1] 1 John 5:14
[2] 1 Tim. 2:1-2; John 17:20; 2 Sam. 7:29; Ruth 4:12
[3] 2 Sam. 12:21-23; Luke 16:25-26; Rev. 14:13
[4] 1 John 5:16

5. The reading of the Scriptures with godly fear,[1] the sound preaching[2] and conscionable hearing of the Word, in obedience unto God, with understanding, faith and reverence,[3] singing of psalms with grace in the heart;[4] as also, the due administration and worthy receiving of the sacraments instituted by Christ, are all parts of the ordinary religious worship of God:[5] beside religious oaths,[6] vows,[7] solemn fastings,[8] and thanksgivings upon special occasions,[9] which are, in their several times and seasons, to be used in an holy and religious manner.[10]

[1] Acts 15:21; Rev. 1:3
[2] 2 Tim. 4:2
[3] James 1:22; Acts 10:33; Matt. 13:19; Heb. 4:2; Isa. 66:2

propriety in us,[2] and the zeal He hath to His own worship.[3]

[1] Ps. 95:2-3, 6
[2] Ps. 45:11
[3] Exod. 34:13-14

[8] Dan. 3:18; Gal. 4:8
[9] Exod. 32:5
[10] Exod. 32:8
[11] 1 Ki. 18:26, 28; Isa. 65:11
[12] Acts 17:22; Col. 2:21-23
[13] Mal. 1:7-8, 14
[14] Deut. 4:2
[15] Ps. 106:39
[16] Matt. 15:9
[17] 1 Pet. 1:18
[18] Jer. 44:17
[19] Isa. 65:3-5; Gal. 1:13-14
[20] 1 Sam. 13:11-12; 15:21
[21] Acts 8:18
[22] Rom. 2:22; Mal. 3:8
[23] Exod. 4:24-26
[24] Matt. 22:5; Mal. 1:7, 13
[25] Matt. 23:13
[26] Acts 13:44-45; 1 Thes. 2:15-16

Q. 110: What are the reasons annexed to the second commandment, the more to enforce it?

A.: The reasons annexed to the second commandment, the more to enforce it, contained in these words, *For I the LORD thy God am a jealous God, visiting the iniquity of the fathers upon the children unto the third and fourth generation of them that hate Me; and shewing mercy unto thousands of them that love Me, and keep My commandments,*[1] are, besides God's sovereignty over us, and propriety in us,[2] His fervent zeal for His own worship,[3] and His revengeful indignation against all false worship, as being a spiritual whoredom;[4] accounting the breakers of this commandment such as hate Him, and threatening to punish them unto divers generations;[5] and esteeming the observers of it such as love Him and keep His commandments, and promising mercy to them unto many generations.[6]

[1] Exod. 20:5-6
[2] Ps. 45:11; Rev. 15:3-4
[3] Exod. 34:13-14
[4] 1 Cor. 10:20-22; Jer. 7:18-20; Ezek. 16:26-27; Deut. 32:16-20
[5] Hosea 2:2-4
[6] Deut. 5:29

Belgic Confession (1561)	Heidelberg Catechism (1563)	Second Helvetic Confession (1566)	Canons of Dort (1619)

Second Helvetic Confession (cont.)

saints nor think basely of them; for we acknowledge them to be the lively members of Christ, the friends of God, who have gloriously overcome the flesh and the world. We therefore love them as brethren, and honor them also; yet not with any worship, but with an honorable opinion of them, and with just praises of them. We also do imitate the saints, for we desire, with the most earnest affections and prayers, to be followers of their faith and virtues; to be partakers, also, with them of everlasting salvation; to dwell together with them everlastingly with God, and to rejoice with them in Christ. And in this point we approve that saying of St. Augustine, in his book, *De Vera Religione*, "Let not the worship of men departed be any religion unto us; for, if they have lived holily, they are not so to be esteemed as that they seek such honors, but they will have us to worship Him by whose illumination they rejoice that we are fellow-servants as touching the reward. They are therefore to be honored for imitation, not to be worshiped for religion's sake," etc.

6. And we much less believe that the relics of saints are to be adored and worshiped. Those ancient holy men seemed sufficiently to have honored their dead if they had honestly committed their bodies to the earth after the soul was gone up into heaven; and they thought that the most noble relics of their ancestors were their virtues, doctrine, and faith; which as they commended with the praise of the dead, so they did endeavor to express the same so long as they lived upon earth.

The Third Commandment

Q. 99: What is required in the third commandment?

A.: That we, not only by cursing[1] or perjury, but also by rash swearing,[2] must not profane or abuse the name of God; nor by silence or connivance be partakers of these horrible sins in others; and, briefly, that we use the holy name of God[3] no otherwise than with fear and reverence, so that He may be rightly confessed[4] and worshipped by us,[5] and be glorified in all our words and works.

---

[1] Lev. 24:11; Lev. 19:12; Matt. 5:37; Lev. 5:4
[2] Isa. 45:23-24
[3] Matt. 10:32
[4] 1 Tim. 2:8
[5] 1 Cor. 3:16-17

Q. 100: Is then the profaning of God's Name by swearing and cursing so heinous a sin that His wrath is kindled against those who do not endeavor, as much as in them lies, to

V. Of the Adoration, Worship, and Invocation of God Through the Only Mediator Jesus Christ

7. Those ancient men did not swear but by the name of the only Jehovah, as it is commanded by the law of God. Therefore, as we are forbidden to swear by the name of strange gods (Exod. 23:13; Josh. 23:7), so we do not swear by saints, although we be requested thereunto. We therefore in all these things do reject that doctrine which gives too much honor unto the saints in heaven.

Westminster Confession of Faith (1647)	Westminster Shorter Catechism (1647)	Westminster Larger Catechism (1648)

Westminster Confession of Faith (cont.)

[4] Col. 3:16; Eph. 5:19; James 5:13
[5] Matt. 28:19; 1 Cor. 11:23-29; Acts 2:42
[6] Deut. 6:13; Neh. 10:29
[7] Isa. 19:21; Eccl. 5:4-5
[8] Joel 2:12; Esth. 4:16; Matt. 9:15; 1 Cor. 7:5
[9] Ps. 107; Esth. 9:22
[10] Heb. 12:28

6. Neither prayer, nor any other part of religious worship, is now, under the gospel, either tied unto, or made more acceptable by any place in which it is performed, or towards which it is directed:[1] but God is to be worshipped everywhere,[2] in spirit and truth;[3] as, in private families[4] daily,[5] and in secret, each one by himself;[6] so, more solemnly in the public assemblies, which are not carelessly or wilfully to be neglected, or

forsaken, when God, by His Word or providence, calleth thereunto.[7]

[1] John 4:21
[2] Mal. 1:11; 1 Tim. 2:8
[3] John 4:23-24
[4] Jer. 10:25; Deut. 6:6-7; Job 1:5; 2 Sam. 6:18, 20; 1 Pet. 3:7; Acts 10:2
[5] Matt. 6:11
[6] Matt. 6:6; Eph. 6:18
[7] Isa. 56:6-7; Heb. 10:25; Prov. 1:20-21, 24; 8:34; Acts 13:42; Luke 4:16; Acts 2:42

XXII. Of Lawful Oaths and Vows

1. A lawful oath is part of religious worship,[1] wherein, upon just occasion, the person swearing solemnly calleth God to witness what he asserteth, or promiseth, and to judge him according to the truth or falsehood of what he sweareth.[2]

[1] Deut. 10:20
[2] Exod. 20:7; Lev. 19:12; 2 Cor. 1:23; 2 Chron. 6:22-23

2. The name of God only is that by which men ought to swear, and therein it is to be used with all holy fear and reverence.[1] Therefore, to swear vainly, or rashly, by that glorious and dreadful Name; or, to swear at all by any other thing, is sinful, and to be abhorred.[2] Yet, as in matters of weight and moment, an oath is warranted by the Word of God, under the new testament as well as under the old;[3] so a lawful oath, being imposed by law-

Q. 53: Which is the third commandment?

A.: The third commandment is, "Thou shalt not take the name of the LORD thy God in vain: for the LORD will not hold him guiltless that taketh His name in vain."[1]

[1] Exod. 20:7

Q. 54: What is required in the third commandment?

A.: The third commandment requireth the holy and reverent use of God's names,[1] titles,[2] attributes,[3] ordinances,[4] word,[5] and works.[6]

[1] Matt. 6:9; Deut. 28:58
[2] Ps. 68:4
[3] Rev. 15:3-4
[4] Mal. 1:11, 14
[5] Ps. 138:1-2
[6] Job 36:24

Q. 55: What is forbidden in the third commandment?

A.: The third commandment forbiddeth all profaning or abusing of any thing whereby God maketh Himself known.[1]

Q. 111: Which is the third commandment?

A.: The third commandment is, *Thou shalt not take the name of the LORD thy God in vain: for the LORD will not hold him guiltless that taketh His name in vain.*[1]

[1] Exod. 20:7

Q. 112: What is required in the third commandment?

A.: The third commandment requires, That the name of God, His titles, attributes,[1] ordinances,[2] the word,[3] sacraments,[4] prayer,[5] oaths,[6] vows,[7] lots,[8] His works,[9] and whatsoever else there is whereby He makes Himself known, be holily and reverently used in thought,[10] meditation,[11] word,[12] and writing;[13] by a holy profession,[14] and answerable conversation,[15] to the glory of God,[16] and the good of ourselves,[17] and others.[18]

[1] Matt. 6:9; Deut. 28:58; Ps. 29:2; 68:4; Rev. 15:3-4
[2] Mal. 1:14; Eccl. 5:1
[3] Ps. 138:2
[4] 1 Cor. 11:24-25, 28-29
[5] 1 Tim. 2:8
[6] Jer. 4:2
[7] Eccl. 5:2, 4-6
[8] Acts 1:24, 26
[9] Job 36:24
[10] Mal. 3:16
[11] Ps. 8:1, 3-4, 9
[12] Col. 3:17; Ps. 105:2, 5
[13] Ps. 102:18
[14] 1 Pet. 3:15; Micah 4:5
[15] Phil. 1:27
[16] 1 Cor. 10:31
[17] Jer. 32:39
[18] 1 Pet. 2:12

Q. 113: What are the sins forbidden in the third commandment?

A. The sins forbidden in the third commandment are, the not using of God's name as is required;[1] and the abuse of it in an ignorant,[2]

Belgic Confession (1561)	Heidelberg Catechism (1563)	Second Helvetic Confession (1566)	Canons of Dort (1619)
	prevent and forbid such cursing and swearing? A.: It undoubtedly is, for there is no sin greater or more provoking to God than the profaning of His Name;[1] and therefore He has commanded this sin to be punished with death.[2] [1] Lev. 5:1 [2] Lev. 24:15 Q. 101: *May we then swear religiously by the name of God?* A.: Yes, either when the magistrates demand it of the subjects or when necessity requires us thereby to confirm fidelity and truth to the glory of God and the safety of our neighbor;[1] for such an oath is founded on God's Word,[2] and therefore was justly used by the saints, both in the Old and New Testament.[3] [1] Exod. 22:11; Neh. 13:25 [2] Deut. 6:13; Heb. 6:16 [3] Gen. 21:24; Josh. 9:15, 19; 1 Sam. 24:22; 2 Cor. 1:23; Rom. 1:9 Q. 102: *May we also swear by saints or any other creatures?* A.: No; for a lawful oath is calling upon God as the only one who knows the heart, that He will bear witness to the truth and punish me if I swear falsely;[1] which honor is due to no creature.[2] [1] 2 Cor. 1:23 [2] Matt. 5:34-35		

Westminster Confession of Faith (1647)	Westminster Shorter Catechism (1647)	Westminster Larger Catechism (1648)

ful authority, in such matters, ought to be taken.[4]

[1] Deut. 6:13
[2] Exod. 20:7; Jer. 5:7; Matt. 5:34, 37; James 5:12
[3] Heb. 6:16; 2 Cor. 1:23; Isa. 65:16
[4] 1 Ki. 8:31; Neh. 13:25; Ezra 10:5

3. Whosoever taketh an oath ought duly to consider the weightiness of so solemn an act, and therein to avouch nothing but what he is fully persuaded is the truth:[1] neither may any man bind himself by oath to any thing but what is good and just, and what he believeth so to be, and what he is able and resolved to perform.[2] Yet it is a sin to refuse an oath touching any thing that is good and just, being imposed by lawful authority.[3]

[1] Exod. 20:7; Jer. 4:2
[2] Gen. 24:2-3, 5-6, 8-9
[3] Num. 5:19, 21; Neh. 5:12; Exod. 22:7-11

4. An oath is to be taken in the plain and common sense of the words, without equivocation, or mental reservation.[1] It cannot oblige to sin; but in any thing not sinful, being taken, it binds to performance, although to a man's own hurt.[2] Nor is it to be violated, although made to heretics, or infidels.[3]

[1] Jer. 4:2; Ps. 24:4
[2] 1 Sam. 25:22, 32-34; Ps. 15:4
[3] Ezek. 17:16, 18-19; Josh. 9:18-19; 2 Sam. 21:1

5. A vow is of the like nature with a promissory oath, and ought to be made with the like religious care, and to be performed with the like faithfulness.[1]

[1] Isa. 19:21; Eccl. 5:4-6; Ps. 61:8; 66:13-14

6. It is not to be made to any creature, but to God alone:[1] and that it may be accepted,

---

[1] Mal. 1:6-7, 12; 2:2; 3:14

Q. 56: What is the reason annexed to the third commandment?
A.: The reason annexed to the third commandment is, that however the breakers of this commandment may escape punishment from men, yet the Lord our God will not suffer them to escape His righteous judgment.[1]

[1] 1 Sam. 2:12, 17, 22, 29; 3:13; Deut. 28:58-59

---

vain,[3] irreverent, profane,[4] superstitious,[5] or wicked mentioning, or otherwise using His titles, attributes,[6] ordinances,[7] or works,[8] by blasphemy,[9] perjury;[10] all sinful cursings,[11] oaths,[12] vows,[13] and lots;[14] violating of our oaths and vows, if lawful;[15] and fulfilling them, if of things unlawful;[16] murmuring and quarreling at,[17] curious prying into,[18] and misapplying of God's decrees[19] and providences;[20] misinterpreting,[21] misapplying,[22] or any way perverting the Word, or any part of it,[23] to profane jests,[24] curious or unprofitable questions, vain janglings, or the maintaining of false doctrines;[25] abusing it, the creatures, or any thing contained under the name of God, to charms,[26] or sinful lusts and practices;[27] the maligning,[28] scorning,[29] reviling,[30] or any wise opposing of God's truth, grace, and ways;[31] making profession of religion in hypocrisy, or for sinister ends;[32] being ashamed of it,[33] or a shame to it, by unconformable,[34] unwise,[35] unfruitful,[36] and offensive walking,[37] or backsliding from it.[38]

[1] Mal. 2:2
[2] Acts 17:23
[3] Prov. 30:9
[4] Mal. 1:6-7, 12; Mal. 3:14
[5] 1 Sam. 4:3-5; Jer. 7:4, 9-10, 14, 31; Col. 2:20-22
[6] 2 Ki. 18:30, 35; Exod. 5:2; Ps. 139:20
[7] Ps. 50:16-17
[8] Isa. 5:12
[9] 2 Ki. 19:22; Lev. 24:11
[10] Zech. 5:4; 8:17
[11] 1 Sam. 17:43; 2 Sam. 16:5
[12] Jer. 5:7; 23:10
[13] Deut. 23:18; Acts 23:12, 14
[14] Esth. 3:7; 9:24; Ps. 22:18
[15] Ps. 24:4; Ezek. 17:16, 18-19
[16] Mark 6:26; 1 Sam. 25:22, 32-34
[17] Rom. 9:14, 19-20
[18] Deut. 29:29
[19] Rom. 3:5, 7; 6:1-2
[20] Eccl. 8:11; 9:3; Ps. 39
[21] Matt. 5:21
[22] Ezek. 13:22
[23] 2 Pet. 3:16; Matt. 22:24-31
[24] Isa. 22:13; Jer. 23:34, 36, 38
[25] 1 Tim. 1:4, 6-7; 6:4-5, 20; 2 Tim. 2:14; Titus 3:9
[26] Deut. 18:10-14; Acts 19:13
[27] 2 Tim. 4:3-4; Rom. 13:13-14; 1 Ki. 21:9-10; Jude 4
[28] Acts 13:45; 1 John 3:12
[29] Ps. 1:1; 2 Pet. 3:3
[30] 1 Pet. 4:4
[31] Acts 13:45-46, 50; Acts 4:18; 19:9; 1 Thes. 2:16; Heb. 10:29
[32] 2 Tim. 3:5; Matt. 23:14; 6:1-2,5, 16
[33] Mark 8:38
[34] Ps. 73:14-15
[35] 1 Cor. 6:5-6; Eph. 5:15-17
[36] Isa. 5:4; 2 Pet. 1:8-9
[37] Rom. 2:23-24
[38] Gal. 3:1, 3; Heb. 6:6

Q. 114: What reasons are annexed to the third commandment?
A.: The reasons annexed to the third commandment, in these words, [The LORD thy God,] and, [For the LORD will not hold him guiltless that taketh His name in vain,[1]] are, because He is the Lord and our God, therefore His Name is not to be profaned, or any way abused by us;[2] especially because He will be so far from acquitting and sparing the transgressors of this commandment, as that He will not suffer them to escape His righteous judgment,[3] albeit many such escape the censures and punishments of men.[4]

[1] Exod. 20:7
[2] Lev. 19:12
[3] Ezek. 36:21-23; Deut. 28:58-59; Zech. 5:2-4
[4] 1 Sam. 2:12, 17, 22, 24; 1 Sam. 3:13

Belgic Confession (1561)	Heidelberg Catechism (1563)	Second Helvetic Confession (1566)	Canons of Dort (1619)

The Fourth Commandment

Belgic Confession (1561)	Heidelberg Catechism (1563)	Second Helvetic Confession (1566)	Canons of Dort (1619)
	Q. 103: What doth God require in the fourth commandment? A.: First, that the ministry of the gospel and the schools be maintained;[1] and that I, especially on the Sabbath, that is, on the day of rest,[2] diligently frequent the Church of God[3] to hear His word, to use the sacraments,[4] publicly to call upon the Lord,[5] and contribute to the relief of the poor,[6] as becomes a Christian. Secondly, that all the days of my life I cease from my evil works, and yield myself to the Lord, to work by His Holy Spirit in me; and thus begin in this life the eternal Sabbath.[7] [1] Deut. 12:19; Titus 1:5; 1 Tim. 3:14-15; 1 Cor. 9:11; 2 Tim. 2:2; 1 Tim. 3:15 [2] Lev. 23:3 [3] Acts 2:42, 46; 1 Cor. 14:19, 29, 31 [4] 1 Cor. 11:33 [5] 1 Tim. 2:1 [6] 1 Cor. 16:2 [7] Isa. 66:23		

Westminster Confession of Faith (1647)	Westminster Shorter Catechism (1647)	Westminster Larger Catechism (1648)

Westminster Confession of Faith (cont.)

it is to be made voluntarily, out of faith, and conscience of duty, in way of thankfulness for mercy received, or for the obtaining of what we want, whereby we more strictly bind ourselves to necessary duties: or, to other things, so far and so long as they may fitly conduce thereunto.[2]

[1] Ps. 76:11; Jer. 44:25-26
[2] Deut. 23:21-23; Ps. 50:14; Gen. 28: 20-22; 1 Sam. 1:11; Ps. 66:13-14; 132:2-5

7. No man may vow to do any thing forbidden in the Word of God, or what would hinder any duty therein commanded,

or which is not in his own power, and for the performance whereof he hath no promise of ability from God.[1] In which respects, popish monastical vows of perpetual single life, professed poverty, and regular obedience, are so far from being degrees of higher perfection, that they are superstitious and sinful snares, in which no Christian may entangle himself.[2]

[1] Acts 23:12, 14; Mark 6:26; Numb. 30:5, 8, 12-13
[2] Matt. 19:11-12; 1 Cor. 7:2, 9; Eph. 4:28; 1 Pet. 4:2; 1 Cor. 7:23

XXI. Of Religious Worship, and the Sabbath Day

7. As it is the law of nature, that, in general, a due proportion of time be set apart for the worship of God; so, in His Word, by a positive, moral, and perpetual commandment binding all men in all ages, He hath particularly appointed one day in seven, for a Sabbath, to be kept holy unto Him:[1] which, from the beginning of the world to the resurrection of Christ, was the last day of the week; and, from the resurrection of Christ, was changed into the first day of the week,[2] which, in Scripture, is called the Lord's Day,[3] and is to be continued to the end of the world, as the Christian Sabbath.[4]

[1] Exod. 20:8, 10-11; Isa. 56:2, 4, 6-7
[2] Gen. 2:2-3; 1 Cor. 16:1-2; Acts 20:7
[3] Rev. 1:10
[4] Exod. 20:8, 10; Matt. 5:17-18

8. This Sabbath is then kept holy unto the Lord, when men, after a due preparing of their hearts, and ordering of their common affairs beforehand, do not

Q. 57: Which is the fourth commandment?

A.: The fourth commandment is, "Remember the sabbath day, to keep it holy. Six days shalt thou labour, and do all thy work: but the seventh day is the sabbath of the LORD thy God: in it thou shalt not do any work, thou, nor thy son, nor thy daughter, thy manservant, nor thy maidservant, nor thy cattle, nor thy stranger that is within thy gates: for in six days the LORD made heaven and earth, the sea, and all that in them is, and rested the seventh day: wherefore the LORD blessed the sabbath day, and hallowed it."[1]

[1] Exod. 20:8-11

Q. 58: What is required in the fourth commandment?

A.: The fourth commandment requireth the keeping holy to God such set times as he hath appointed in His Word; expressly one whole day in seven, to be a holy sabbath to Himself.[1]

[1] Deut. 5:12-14

Q. 115: Which is the fourth commandment?

A.: The fourth commandment is, Remember the sabbath day, to keep it holy. Six days shalt thou labour, and do all thy work: but the seventh day is the sabbath of the LORD thy God: in it thou shalt not do any work, thou, nor thy son, nor thy daughter, thy manservant, nor thy maidservant, nor thy cattle, nor thy stranger that is within thy gates: for in six days the LORD made heaven and earth, the sea, and all that in them is, and rested the seventh day: wherefore the LORD blessed the sabbath day, and hallowed it.[1]

[1] Exod. 20:8-11

Q. 116: What is required in the fourth commandment?

A.: The fourth commandment requireth of all men the sanctifying or keeping holy to God such set times as He hath appointed in His Word, expressly one whole day in seven; which was the seventh from the beginning of the world to the resurrection of Christ, and the first day of the week ever since, and so to continue to the end of the world; which is the Christian sabbath,[1] and in the New Testament called the Lord's day.[2]

[1] Deut. 5:12-14; Gen. 2:2-3; 1 Cor. 16:1-2; Acts 20:7; Matt. 5:17-18; Isa. 56:2, 4, 6-7
[2] Rev. 1:10

Q. 117: How is the sabbath or the Lord's day to be sanctified?

A.: The sabbath or Lord's day is to be sanctified by a holy resting all the day,[1] not only from such works as are at all times sinful, but even from such worldly employments and recreations as are on other days lawful;[2] and making it our delight to spend the whole time (except so much of it as is to be taken up in works of necessity and mercy[3]) in the public and private exercises of God's worship:[4] and, to that end, we are to prepare our hearts, and with such foresight, diligence, and moderation, to dispose and seasonably dispatch our worldly business, that we may be the more free and fit for the duties of that day.[5]

[1] Exod. 20:8, 10
[2] Exod. 16:25-28; Neh. 13:15-22; Jer. 17:21-22
[3] Matt. 12:1-13
[4] Isa. 58:13; Luke 4:16; Acts 20:7; 1 Cor. 16:1-2; Ps. 92 title; Isa. 66:23; Lev. 23:3
[5] Exod. 20:8; Luke 23:54, 56; 16:22, 25-26, 29; Neh. 13:19

Belgic Confession (1561)	Heidelberg Catechism (1563)	Second Helvetic Confession (1566)	Canons of Dort (1619)

Westminster Confession of Faith (1647)	Westminster Shorter Catechism (1647)	Westminster Larger Catechism (1648)
only observe a holy rest, all the day, from their own works, words, and thoughts about their worldly employments and recreations,[1] but also are taken up, the whole time, in the public and private exercises of His worship, and in the duties of necessity and mercy.[2]	*Q. 59: Which day of the seven hath God appointed to be the weekly sabbath?* A.: From the beginning of the world to the resurrection of Christ, God appointed the seventh day of the week to be the weekly sabbath; and the first day of the week ever since, to continue to the end of the world, which is the Christian sabbath.[1]	*Q. 118: Why is the charge of keeping the sabbath more specially directed to governors of families, and other superiors?* A.: The charge of keeping the sabbath is more specially directed to governors of families, and other superiors, because they are bound not only to keep it themselves, but to see that it be observed by all those that are under their charge; and because they are prone ofttimes to hinder them by employments of their own.[1]

<table>
<tr><td>

[1] Exod. 20:8; 16:23, 25-26, 29-30; 31:15-17; Isa. 58:13; Neh. 13:15-22
[2] Isa. 58:13; Matt. 12:1-13

</td><td>

[1] Gen. 2:2-3; 1 Cor. 16:1-2; Acts 20:7

Q. 60: How is the sabbath to be sanctified?
A.: The sabbath is to be sanctified by a holy resting all that day,[1] even from such worldly employments and recreations as are lawful on other days;[2] and spending the whole time in the public and private exercises of God's worship,[3] except so much as is to be taken up in the works of necessity and mercy.[4]

[1] Exod. 20:8, 10; 16:25-28
[2] Neh. 13:15-22
[3] Luke 4:16; Acts 20:7; Ps. 92 title; Isa. 66:23
[4] Matt. 12:1-31

Q. 61: What is forbidden in the fourth commandment?
A.: The fourth commandment forbiddeth the omission or careless performance, of the duties required,[1] and the profaning the day by idleness,[2] or doing that which is in itself sinful,[3] or by unnecessary thoughts, words, or works, about our worldly employments or recreations.[4]

[1] Ezek. 22:26; Amos 8:5; Mal. 1:13
[2] Acts 20:7, 9
[3] Ezek. 23:38
[4] Jer. 17:24-26; Isa. 58:13

Q. 62: What are the reasons

</td><td>

[1] Exod. 20:10; Josh. 24:15; Neh. 13:15-17; Jer. 17:20-22; Exod. 23:12

Q. 119: What are the sins forbidden in the fourth commandment?
A.: The sins forbidden in the fourth commandment are, all omissions of the duties required,[1] all careless, negligent, and unprofitable performing of them, and being weary of them;[2] all profaning the day by idleness, and doing that which is in itself sinful;[3] and by all needless works, words, and thoughts, about our worldly employments and recreations.[4]

[1] Ezek. 22:26
[2] Acts 20:7, 9; Ezek. 33:30-32; Amos 8:5; Mal. 1:13
[3] Ezek. 23:38
[4] Jer. 17:24, 27; Isa. 58:13

Q. 120: What are the reasons annexed to the fourth commandment, the more to enforce it?
A.: The reasons annexed to the fourth commandment, the more to enforce it, are taken from the equity of it, God allowing us six days of seven for our own affairs, and reserving but one for Himself, in these words, *Six days shalt thou labor, and do all thy work;*[1] from God's challenging a special propriety in that day, *The seventh day is the sabbath of the LORD thy God;*[2] from the example of God, who *in six days made heaven and earth, the sea, and all that in them is, and rested the seventh day;* and from that blessing which God put upon that day, not only in sanctifying it to be a day for His service, but in ordaining it to be a means of blessing to us in our sanctifying it: *Wherefore the LORD blessed the sabbath day, and hallowed it.*[3]

[1] Exod. 20:9
[2] Exod. 20:10
[3] Exod. 20:11

Q. 121: Why is the word "remember" set in the beginning of the fourth commandment?
A.: The word *remember* is set in the beginning of the fourth commandment,[1] partly, because of the great benefit of remembering it, we being thereby helped in our preparation to keep it,[2] and, in keeping it, better to keep all the rest of the commandments,[3] and to continue a thankful remembrance of the two great benefits of creation and redemption, which contain a short abridgment of religion;[4] and partly, because we are very ready to forget it,[5] for that there is less light of nature for it,[6] and yet it restraineth our natural liberty in things at other times lawful;[7] that it cometh but once in seven days, and many worldly businesses come between, and too often take off our minds from thinking of it, either to prepare for it, or to sanctify it;[8] and that Satan with his instruments much labours to blot out the glory, and even the memory of it, to bring in all irreligion and impiety.[9]

[1] Exod. 20:8
[2] Exod. 16:23; Luke 23:54, 56; Mark 15:42; Neh. 13:19
[3] Ps. 92 title, 13-14; Ezek. 20:12, 19-20
[4] Gen. 2:2-3; Ps. 118:22, 24; Acts 4:10-11; Rev. 1:10

</td></tr>
</table>

Belgic Confession (1561)	Heidelberg Catechism (1563)	Second Helvetic Confession (1566)	Canons of Dort (1619)

The Fifth Commandment

Belgic Confession (1561)	Heidelberg Catechism (1563)	Second Helvetic Confession (1566)	Canons of Dort (1619)
	Q. 104: What doth God require in the fifth commandment? A.: That I show all honor, love and fidelity, to my father and mother and all in authority over me, and submit myself to their good instruction and correction, with due obedience;[1] and also patiently bear with their weaknesses and infirmities,[2] since it pleases God to govern us by their hand.[3] --- [1] Eph. 6:1-2, etc.; Col. 3:18, 20; Eph. 5:22; Rom. 1:31 [2] Prov. 23:22 [3] Eph. 6:5-6; Col. 3:19, 21; Rom. 13:1-8; Matt. 22:21		

Westminster Confession of Faith (1647)	Westminster Shorter Catechism (1647)	Westminster Larger Catechism (1648)

annexed to the fourth commandment?

A.: The reasons annexed to the fourth commandment are, God's allowing us six days of the week for our own employments,[1] His challenging a special propriety in the seventh, His own example, and His blessing the sabbath day.[2]

[1] Exod. 20:9
[2] Exod. 20:11

[5] Ezek. 22:26
[6] Neh. 9:14
[7] Exod. 34:21
[8] Deut. 5:14-15; Amos 8:5
[9] Lam. 1:7; Jer. 17:21-23; Neh. 13:15-23

Q. 63: Which is the fifth commandment?

A.: The fifth commandment is, "Honour thy father and thy mother: that thy days may be long upon the land which the LORD thy God giveth thee."[1]

[1] Exod. 20:12

Q. 64: What is required in the fifth commandment?

A.: The fifth commandment requireth the preserving the honour, and performing the duties, belonging to everyone in their several places and relations, as superiors,[1] inferiors,[2] or equals.[3]

[1] Eph. 5:21
[2] 1 Pet. 2:17
[3] Rom. 12:10

Q. 65: What is forbidden in the fifth commandment?

A.: The fifth commandment forbiddeth the neglecting of, or doing anything against, the honour and duty which belongeth to every one in their several places and relations.[1]

[1] Matt. 15:4-6; Ezek. 34:2-4; Rom. 13:8

Q. 123: Which is the fifth commandment?

A.: The fifth commandment is, *Honour thy father and thy mother: that thy days may be long upon the land which the LORD thy God giveth thee.*[1]

[1] Exod. 20:12

*Q. 124: Who are meant by **father** and **mother** in the fifth commandment?*

A.: By *father* and *mother*, in the fifth commandment, are meant, not only natural parents,[1] but all superiors in age[2] and gifts;[3] and especially such as, by God's ordinance, are over us in place of authority, whether in family,[4] Church,[5] or commonwealth.[6]

[1] Prov. 23:22, 25; Eph. 6:1-2
[2] 1 Tim. 5:1-2
[3] Gen. 4:20-22; Gen. 45:8
[4] 2 Ki. 5:13
[5] 2 Ki. 2:12; 13:14; Gal. 4:19
[6] Isa. 49:23

*Q. 125: Why are superiors styled **Father** and **Mother**?*

A.: Superiors are styled *Father* and *Mother*, both to teach them in all duties toward their inferiors, like natural parents, to express love and tenderness to them, according to their several relations;[1] and to work inferiors to a greater willingness and cheerfulness in performing their duties to their superiors, as to their parents.[2]

[1] Eph. 6:4; 2 Cor. 12:14; 1 Thes. 2:7-8, 11; Num. 11:11-12
[2] 1 Cor. 4:14-16; 2 Ki. 5:13

Q. 126: What is the general scope of the fifth commandment?

A.: The general scope of the fifth commandment is, the performance of those duties which we mutually owe in our several relations, as inferiors, superiors, or equals.[1]

[1] Eph. 5:21; 1 Pet. 2:17; Rom. 12:10

Q. 127: What is the honour that inferiors owe to their superiors?

A.: The honour which inferiors owe to their superiors is, all due reverence in heart,[1] word,[2] and behaviour;[3] prayer and thanksgiving for them;[4] imitation of their virtues and graces;[5] willing obedience

Belgic Confession (1561)	Heidelberg Catechism (1563)	Second Helvetic Confession (1566)	Canons of Dort (1619)

Westminster Confession of Faith (1647)	Westminster Shorter Catechism (1647)	Westminster Larger Catechism (1648)

| | **Q. 66:** *What is the reason annexed to the fifth commandment?* | to their lawful commands and counsels;[6] due submission to their corrections;[7] fidelity to,[8] defense[9] and maintenance of their persons and authority, according to their several ranks, and the nature of their places;[10] bearing with their infirmities, and covering them in love,[11] that so they may be an honour to them and to their government.[12] |

A.: The reason annexed to the fifth commandment is, a promise of long life and prosperity (as far as it shall serve for God's glory and their own good) to all such as keep this commandment.[1]

[1] Deut. 5:16; Eph. 6:2-3

[1] Mal. 1:6; Lev. 19:3
[2] Prov. 31:28; 1 Pet. 3:6
[3] Lev. 19:32; 1 Ki. 2:19
[4] 1 Tim. 2:1-2
[5] Heb. 13:7; Phil. 3:17
[6] Eph. 6:1-2, 5-7; 1 Pet. 2:13-14; Rom. 13:1-5; Heb. 13:17; Prov. 4:3-4; 23:22; Exod. 18:19, 24
[7] Heb. 12:9; 1 Pet. 2:18-20
[8] Titus 2:9-10
[9] 1 Sam. 26:15-16; 2 Sam. 18:3; Esth. 6:2
[10] Matt. 22:21; Rom. 13:6-7; 1 Tim. 5:17-18; Gal. 6:6; Gen. 45:11; 47:12
[11] 1 Pet. 2:18; Prov. 23:22; Gen. 9:23
[12] Ps. 127:3-5; Prov. 31:23

Westminster Larger Catechism (cont.)

Q. 128: *What are the sins of inferiors against their superiors?*

A.: The sins of inferiors against their superiors are, all neglect of the duties required toward them;[1] envying at,[2] contempt of,[3] and rebellion[4] against, their persons[5] and places,[6] in their lawful counsels,[7] commands, and corrections;[8] cursing, mocking,[9] and all such refractory and scandalous carriage, as proves a shame and dishonour to them and their government.[10]

[1] Matt. 15:4-6
[2] Numb. 11:28-29
[3] 1 Sam. 8:7; Isa. 3:5
[4] 2 Sam. 15:1-12
[5] Exod. 21:15
[6] 1 Sam. 10:27
[7] 1 Sam. 2:25
[8] Deut. 21:18-21
[9] Prov. 30:11, 17
[10] Prov. 19:26

Q. 129: *What is required of superiors towards their inferiors?*

A.: It is required of superiors, according to that power they receive from God, and that relation wherein they stand, to love,[1] pray for,[2] and bless their inferiors;[3] to instruct,[4] counsel, and admonish them;[5] countenancing,[6] commending,[7] and rewarding such as do well;[8] and discountenancing,[9] reproving, and chastising such as do ill;[10] protecting,[11] and providing for them all things necessary for soul[12] and body;[13] and by grave, wise, holy, and exemplary carriage, to procure glory to God,[14] honour to themselves,[15] and so to preserve that authority which God hath put upon them.[16]

[1] Col. 3:19; Titus 2:4
[2] 1 Sam. 12:23; Job 1:5
[3] 1 Ki. 8:55-56; Heb. 7:7; Gen. 49:28
[4] Deut. 6:6-7
[5] Eph. 6:4
[6] 1 Pet. 3:7
[7] 1 Pet. 2:14; Rom. 13:3
[8] Esth. 6:3
[9] Rom. 13:3-4
[10] Prov. 29:15; 1 Pet. 2:14
[11] Job 29:12-17; Isa. 1:10, 17
[12] Eph. 6:4
[13] 1 Tim. 5:8
[14] 1 Tim. 4:12; Titus 2:3-5
[15] 1 Ki. 3:28
[16] Titus 2:15

Q. 130: *What are the sins of superiors?*

A.: The sins of superiors are, besides the neglect of the duties required of them,[1] an inordinate seeking of themselves,[2] their own glory;[3] ease, profit, or pleasure;[4] commanding things unlawful,[5] or not in the power of inferiors to perform;[6] counselling,[7] encouraging,[8] or favouring them in that which is evil;[9] dissuading, discouraging, or discountenancing them in that which is good;[10] correcting them unduly;[11] careless exposing, or leaving them to wrong, temptation, and danger;[12] provoking them to wrath;[13] or any way dishonouring themselves, or lessening their authority, by an unjust, indiscreet, rigorous, or remiss behavior.[14]

[1] Ezek. 34:2-4
[2] Phil. 2:21
[3] John 5:44; 7:18
[4] Isa. 56:10-11; Deut. 17:17
[5] Dan. 3:4-6; Acts 4:17-18
[6] Exod. 5:10-18; Matt. 23:2, 4
[7] Matt. 14:8; Mark 6:24
[8] 2 Sam. 13:28
[9] 1 Sam. 3:13
[10] John 7:46-49; Col. 3:21; Exod. 5:17
[11] 1 Pet. 2:18-20; Heb. 12:10; Deut. 25:3
[12] Gen. 38:11, 26; Acts 18:17
[13] Eph. 6:4
[14] Gen. 9:21; 1 Ki. 12:13-16; 1:6; 1 Sam. 2:29-31

Q. 131: *What are the duties of equals?*

A.: The duties of equals are, to regard the dignity and worth of each other,[1] in giving honour to go one before another;[2] and to rejoice in each other's gifts and advancement, as their own.[3]

[1] 1 Pet. 2:17
[2] Rom. 12:10
[3] Rom. 12:15-16; Phil. 2:3-4

Q. 132: *What are the sins of equals?*

A.: The sins of equals are, besides the neglect of the duties required,[1] the undervaluing of the worth,[2] envying the gifts,[3] grieving at the advancement of prosperity one of another;[4] and usurping preeminence one over another.[5]

[1] Rom. 13:8
[2] 2 Tim. 3:3
[3] Acts 7:9; Gal. 5:26
[4] Numb. 12:2; Esth. 6:12-13
[5] 3 John 9; Luke 22:24

Belgic Confession (1561)	Heidelberg Catechism (1563)	Second Helvetic Confession (1566)	Canons of Dort (1619)

The Sixth Commandment

Q. 105: What doth God require in the sixth commandment?

A.: That neither in thoughts, nor words, nor gestures, much less in deeds, I dishonor, hate, wound, or kill my neighbor, by myself or by another;[1] but that I lay aside all desire of revenge;[2] also, that I hurt not myself, nor wilfully expose myself to any danger.[3] Wherefore also the magistrate is armed with the sword to prevent murder.[4]

---

[1] Matt. 5:21-22; Prov. 12:18; Matt. 26:52
[2] Eph. 4:26; Rom. 12:19; Matt. 5:39-40
[3] Matt. 4:5-7; Col. 2:23
[4] Gen. 9:6; Matt. 26:52; Rom. 13:4

Q. 106: But this commandment seems only to speak of murder?

A.: In forbidding murder, God teaches us that He abhors the causes thereof, such as envy,[1] hatred,[2] anger, and desire of revenge; and that He accounts all these as murder.[3]

---

[1] James 1:20; Gal. 5:20
[2] Rom. 1:29; 1 John 2:9
[3] 1 John 3:15

Q. 107: But is it enough that we do not kill any man in the manner mentioned above?

Westminster Confession of Faith (1647)	Westminster Shorter Catechism (1647)	Westminster Larger Catechism (1648)

Westminster Larger Catechism (cont.)

Q. 133: What is the reason annexed to the fifth commandment, the more to enforce it?

A.: The reason annexed to the fifth commandment, in these words, *That thy days may be long upon the land which the Lord thy God giveth thee,*[1] is an express promise of long life and prosperity, as far as it shall serve for God's glory and their own good, to all such as keep this commandment.[2]

[1] Exod. 20:12
[2] Deut. 5:16; 1 Ki. 8:25; Eph. 6:2-3

Q. 67: Which is the sixth commandment?

A.: The sixth commandment is, "Thou shalt not kill."[1]

[1] Exod. 20:13

Q. 68: What is required in the sixth commandment?

A.: The sixth commandment requireth all lawful endeavours to preserve our own life,[1] and the life of others.[2]

[1] Eph. 5:28-29
[2] 1 Ki. 18:4

Q. 69: What is forbidden in the sixth commandment?

A.: The sixth commandment forbiddeth the taking away of our own life, or the life of our neighbour unjustly, or whatsoever tendeth thereunto.[1]

[1] Acts 16:28; Gen. 9:6

Q. 134: Which is the sixth commandment?

A.: The sixth commandment is, *Thou shalt not kill.*[1]

[1] Exod. 20:13

Q. 135: What are the duties required in the sixth commandment?

A.: The duties required in the sixth commandment are, all careful studies, and lawful endeavors, to preserve the life of ourselves[1] and others[2] by resisting all thoughts and purposes,[3] subduing all passions,[4] and avoiding, all occasions,[5] temptations,[6] and practices, which tend to the unjust taking away the life of any;[7] by just defense thereof against violence,[8] patient bearing of the hand of God,[9] quietness of mind,[10] cheerfulness of spirit;[11] a sober use of meat,[12] drink,[13] physic,[14] sleep,[15] labour,[16] and recreations;[17] by charitable thoughts,[18] love,[19] compassion,[20] meekness, gentleness, kindness;[21] peaceable,[22] mild and courteous speeches and behaviour;[23] forbearance, readiness to be reconciled, patient bearing and forgiving of injuries, and requiting good for evil;[24] comforting and succouring the distressed, and protecting and defending the innocent.[25]

[1] Eph. 5:28-29
[2] 1 Ki. 18:4
[3] Jer. 26:15-16; Acts 23:12, 16-17, 21, 27
[4] Eph. 4:26-27
[5] 2 Sam. 2:22; Deut. 22:8
[6] Matt. 4:6-7; Prov. 1:10-11, 15-16
[7] 1 Sam. 24:12; 26:9-11; Gen. 37:21-22
[8] Ps. 82:4; Prov. 24:11-12; 1 Sam. 14:45
[9] James 5:7-11; Heb. 12:9
[10] 1 Thes. 4:11; 1 Pet. 3:3-4; Ps. 37:8-11
[11] Prov. 17:22
[12] Prov. 25:16, 27
[13] 1 Tim. 5:23
[14] Isa. 38:21
[15] Ps. 127:2
[16] Eccl. 5:12; 2 Thes. 3:10, 12; Prov. 16:26
[17] Eccl. 3:4, 11
[18] 1 Sam. 19:4-5; 22:13-14
[19] Rom. 13:10
[20] Luke 10:33-34
[21] Col. 3:12-13
[22] James 3:17
[23] 1 Pet. 3:8-11; Prov. 15:1; Judg. 8:1-3
[24] Matt. 5:24; Eph. 4:2, 32; Rom. 12:17, 20-21
[25] 1 Thes. 5:14; Job 31:19-20; Matt. 25:35-36; Prov. 31:8-9

Q. 136: What are the sins forbidden in the sixth commandment?

A.: The sins forbidden in the sixth commandment are, all taking away the life of ourselves,[1] or of others,[2] except in case of public justice,[3] lawful war,[4] or necessary defense;[5] the neglecting or withdrawing the lawful and necessary means of preservation of life;[6]

Belgic Confession (1561)	Heidelberg Catechism (1563)	Second Helvetic Confession (1566)	Canons of Dort (1619)
	A.: No, for when God forbids envy, hatred, and anger, He commands us to love our neighbor as ourselves;[1] to show patience,[2] peace, meekness,[3] mercy,[4] and all kindness towards him, and prevent his hurt as much as in us lies;[5] and that we do good, even to our enemies.[6] [1] Matt. 22:39; Matt. 7:12 [2] Rom. 12:10 [3] Eph. 4:2; Gal. 6:1-2; Matt. 5:5; Rom. 12:18 [4] Exod. 23:5 [5] Matt. 5:45 [6] Rom. 12:20		

The Seventh Commandment

Belgic Confession (1561)	Heidelberg Catechism (1563)	Second Helvetic Confession (1566)	Canons of Dort (1619)
	Q. 108: *What doth the seventh commandment teach us?* A.: That all uncleanness is accursed of God;[1] and that therefore we must with all our hearts detest the same,[2] and live chastely and temperately,[3] whether in holy wedlock or in single life.[4] [1] Lev. 18:27 [2] Deut. 29:20-23 [3] 1 Thes. 4:3-4 [4] Heb. 13:4; 1 Cor. 7:4-9 Q. 109: *Doth God forbid in this commandment only adultery and such like gross sins?* A.: Since both our body and soul are temples of the Holy Ghost, He commands us to preserve them pure and holy; therefore He forbids all unchaste actions,		

Westminster Confession of Faith (1647)	Westminster Shorter Catechism (1647)	Westminster Larger Catechism (1648)
		sinful anger,[7] hatred,[8] envy,[9] desire of revenge;[10] all excessive passions,[11] distracting cares;[12] immoderate use of meat, drink,[13] labour,[14] and recreations;[15] provoking words,[16] oppression,[17] quarreling,[18] striking, wounding,[19] and whatsoever else tends to the destruction of the life of any.[20]

[1] Acts 16:28
[2] Gen. 9:6
[3] Numb. 35:31,33
[4] Jer. 48:10; Deut. 20
[5] Exod. 22:2-3
[6] Matt. 25:42-43; James 2:15-16; Eccl. 6:1-2
[7] Matt. 5:22
[8] 1 John 3:15; Lev. 19:17
[9] Prov. 14:30
[10] Rom. 12:19
[11] Eph. 4:31
[12] Matt. 6:31, 34
[13] Luke 21:34; Rom. 13:13
[14] Eccl. 12:12; 2:22-23
[15] Isa. 5:12
[16] Prov. 15:1; 12:18
[17] Ezek. 18:18; Exod. 1:14
[18] Gal. 5:15; Prov. 23:29
[19] Numb. 35:16-18, 21
[20] Exod. 21:18-36

Westminster Shorter Catechism (1647)

Q. 70: Which is the seventh commandment?

A.: The seventh commandment is, "Thou shalt not commit adultery."[1]

[1] Exod. 20:14

Q. 71: What is required in the seventh commandment?

A.: The seventh commandment requireth the preservation of our own and our neighbour's chastity, in heart, speech, and behaviour.[1]

[1] 1 Cor. 7:2-3, 5, 34, 36; Col. 4:6; 1 Pet. 3:2

Q. 72: What is forbidden in the seventh commandment?

A.: The seventh commandment forbiddeth all unchaste thoughts, words, and actions.[1]

[1] Matt. 15:19; 5:28; Eph. 5:3-4

Westminster Larger Catechism (1648)

Q. 137: Which is the seventh commandment?

A.: The seventh commandment is, *Thou shalt not commit adultery.*[1]

[1] Exod. 20:14

Q. 138: What are the duties required in the seventh commandment?

A.: The duties required in the seventh commandment are, chastity in body, mind, affections,[1] words,[2] and behaviour;[3] and the preservation of it in ourselves and others;[4] watchfulness over the eyes and all the senses;[5] temperance,[6] keeping of chaste company,[7] modesty in apparel;[8] marriage by those that have not the gift of continency,[9] conjugal love,[10] and cohabitation;[11] diligent labour in our callings;[12] shunning all occasions of uncleanliness, and resisting temptations thereunto.[13]

[1] 1 Thes. 4:4; Job 31:1; 1 Cor. 7:34
[2] Col. 4:6
[3] 1 Pet. 2:3
[4] 1 Cor. 7:2, 35-36
[5] Job 31:1
[6] Acts 24:24-25
[7] Prov. 2:16-20
[8] 1 Tim. 2:9
[9] 1 Cor. 7:2, 9
[10] Prov. 5:19-20
[11] 1 Pet. 3:7
[12] Prov. 31:11, 27-28
[13] Prov. 5:8; Gen. 39:8-10

Q. 139: What are the sins forbidden in the seventh commandment?

A.: The sins forbidden in the seventh commandment, besides the

Belgic Confession (1561)	Heidelberg Catechism (1563)	Second Helvetic Confession (1566)	Canons of Dort (1619)
	gestures,[1] words, thoughts, desires,[2] and whatever can entice men thereto.[3] ___ [1] Eph. 5:3; 1 Cor. 6:18 [2] Matt. 5:28 [3] Eph. 5:18; 1 Cor. 15:33		

The Eighth Commandment

Belgic Confession (1561)	Heidelberg Catechism (1563)	Second Helvetic Confession (1566)	Canons of Dort (1619)
	Q. 110: What doth God forbid in the eighth commandment? A.: God forbids not only those thefts[1] and robberies[2] which are punishable by the magistrate; but He comprehends under the name of theft all wicked tricks and devices, whereby we design to appropriate to ourselves the goods which belong to our neighbor;[3] whether it be by force, or under the appearance of right, as by unjust weights,[4] ells, measures,[5] fraudulent merchandise, false coins, usury,[6] or by any other way forbidden by God; as also all covet-		

Westminster Confession of Faith (1647)	Westminster Shorter Catechism (1647)	Westminster Larger Catechism (1648)

neglect of the duties required,[1] are, adultery, fornication,[2] rape, incest,[3] sodomy, and all unnatural lusts;[4] all unclean imaginations, thoughts, purposes, and affections;[5] all corrupt or filthy communications, or listening thereunto;[6] wanton looks,[7] impudent or light behaviour, immodest apparel;[8] prohibiting of lawful,[9] and dispensing with unlawful marriages;[10] allowing, tolerating, keeping of stews, and resorting to them;[11] entangling vows of single life,[12] undue delay of marriage;[13] having more wives or husbands than one at the same time;[14] unjust divorce,[15] or desertion;[16] idleness, gluttony, drunkenness,[17] unchaste company;[18] lascivious songs, books, pictures, dancings, stage plays;[19] and all other provocations to, or acts of uncleanness, either in ourselves or others.[20]

[1] Prov. 5:7
[2] Heb. 13:4; Gal. 5:19
[3] 2 Sam. 13:14; 1 Cor. 5:1
[4] Rom. 1:24, 26-27; Lev. 20:15-16
[5] Matt. 5:28; 15:19; Col. 3:5
[6] Eph. 5:3-4; Prov. 7:5, 21-22
[7] Isa. 3:16; 2 Pet. 2:14
[8] Prov. 7:10, 13
[9] 1 Tim. 4:3
[10] Lev. 18:1-21; Mark 6:18; Mal. 2:11-12
[11] 1 Ki. 15:12; 2 Ki. 23:7; Deut. 23:17-18; Lev. 19:29; Jer. 5:7; Prov. 7:24-27
[12] Matt. 19:10-11
[13] 1 Cor. 7:7-9; Gen. 38:26
[14] Mal. 2:14-15; Matt. 19:5
[15] Mal. 2:16; Matt. 5:32
[16] 1 Cor. 7:12-13
[17] Ezek. 16:49; Prov. 23:30-33
[18] Gen. 39:10; Prov. 5:8
[19] Eph. 5:4; Ezek. 23:14-17; Isa. 23:15-17; 3:16; Mark 6:22; Rom. 13:13; 1 Pet. 4:3
[20] 2 Ki. 9:30; Jer. 4:30; Ezek. 23:40

Q. 73: Which is the eighth commandment?

A.: The eighth commandment is, "Thou shalt not steal."[1]

[1] Exod. 20:15

Q. 74: What is required in the eighth commandment?

A.: The eighth commandment requireth the lawful procuring and furthering the wealth and outward estate of ourselves and others.[1]

[1] Gen. 30:30; 1 Tim. 5:8; Lev. 25:35; Deut. 22:1-5; Exod. 23:4-5; Gen. 47:14, 20

Q. 75: What is forbidden in the eighth commandment?

A.: The eighth command-

Q. 140: Which is the eighth commandment?

A.: The eighth commandment is, Thou shalt not steal.[1]

[1] Exod. 20:15

Q. 141: What are the duties required in the eighth commandment?

A.: The duties required in the eighth commandment are, truth, faithfulness, and justice in contracts and commerce between man and man;[1] rendering to everyone his due;[2] restitution of goods unlawfully detained from the right owners thereof;[3] giving and lending freely, according to our abilities, and the necessities of others;[4] moderation of our judgments, wills, and affections concerning worldly goods;[5] a provident care and study to get,[6] keep, use, and dispose these things which are necessary and convenient for the sustentation of our nature, and suitable to our condition;[7] a lawful calling,[8] and diligence in it;[9] frugality;[10] avoiding unnecessary lawsuits,[11] and suretyship, or other like engagements;[12] and an endeavour, by all just and lawful means, to procure, preserve, and further the wealth and outward estate of others, as well as our own.[13]

[1] Ps. 15:2, 4; Zech. 7:4, 10; 8:16-17
[2] Rom. 13:7
[3] Lev. 6:2-5; Luke 19:8
[4] Luke 6:30, 38; 1 John 3:17; Eph. 4:28; Gal. 6:10
[5] 1 Tim. 6:6-9; Gal. 6:14

Belgic Confession (1561)	Heidelberg Catechism (1563)	Second Helvetic Confession (1566)	Canons of Dort (1619)
	ousness,[7] all abuse and waste of His gifts. [1] 1 Cor. 6:10 [2] 1 Cor. 5:10 [3] Luke 3:14; 1 Thes. 4:6 [4] Prov. 11:1 [5] Ezek. 45:9-11; Deut. 25:13 [6] Ps. 15:5; Luke 6:35 [7] 1 Cor. 6:10 *Q. 111: But what doth God require in this commandment?* A.: That I promote the advantage of my neighbor in every instance I can or may, and deal with him as I desire to be dealt with by others;[1] further also that I faithfully labor, so that I may be able to relieve the needy.[2] [1] Matt. 7:12 [2] Prov. 5:16; Eph. 4:28		

The Ninth Commandment

Belgic Confession (1561)	Heidelberg Catechism (1563)	Second Helvetic Confession (1566)	Canons of Dort (1619)
	Q. 112: What is required in the ninth commandment? A.: That I bear false witness against no man[1] nor falsify any man's words;[2] that I be no backbiter nor slanderer;[3] that I do not judge, nor join in condemning any man rashly or unheard;[4] but that I avoid all sorts of lies and deceit,[5] as the proper works of the devil,[6] unless I would bring down upon me		

Westminster Confession of Faith (1647)	Westminster Shorter Catechism (1647)	Westminster Larger Catechism (1648)

ment forbiddeth whatsoever doth or may unjustly hinder our own or our neighbour's wealth or outward estate.[1]

----

[1] Prov. 21:17; 23:20-21; 28:19; Eph. 4:28

---

[6] 1 Tim. 5:8
[7] Prov. 27:23-27; Eccl. 2:24; 3:12-13; 1 Tim. 6:17-18; Isa. 38:1; Matt. 11:8
[8] 1 Cor. 7:20; Gen 2:15; 3:19
[9] Eph. 4:28; Prov. 10:4
[10] John 6:12; Prov. 21:20
[11] 1 Cor. 6:1-9
[12] Prov. 6:1-6; 11:15
[13] Lev. 25:35; Deut. 22:1-4; Exod. 23:4-5; Gen. 47:14, 20; Phil. 2:4; Matt. 22:39

Q. 142: What are the sins forbidden in the eighth commandment?

A.: The sins forbidden in the eighth commandment, besides the neglect of the duties required,[1] are, theft,[2] robbery,[3] man-stealing,[4] and receiving anything that is stolen;[5] fraudulent dealing,[6] false weights and measures,[7] removing land-marks,[8] injustice and unfaithfulness in contracts between man and man,[9] or in matters of trust;[10] oppression,[11] extortion,[12] usury,[13] bribery,[14] vexatious law-suits,[15] unjust inclosures and depopulations;[16] ingrossing commodities to enhance the price;[17] unlawful callings,[18] and all other unjust or sinful ways of taking or withholding from our neighbour what belongs to him, or of enriching ourselves;[19] covetousness;[20] inordinate prizing and affecting worldly goods;[21] distrustful and distracting cares and studies in getting, keeping, and using them;[22] envying at the prosperity of others;[23] as likewise idleness,[24] prodigality, wasteful gaming; and all other ways whereby we do unduly prejudice our own outward estate,[25] and defrauding ourselves of the due use and comfort of that estate which God hath given us.[26]

----

[1] James 2:15-16; 1 John 3:17
[2] Eph. 4:28
[3] Ps. 62:10
[4] 1 Tim. 1:10
[5] Prov. 29:24; Ps. 50:18
[6] 1 Thes. 4:6
[7] Prov. 11:1; 20:10
[8] Deut. 19:14; Prov. 23:10
[9] Amos 8:5; Ps. 37:21
[10] Luke 16:10-12
[11] Ezek. 22:29; Lev. 25:17
[12] Matt. 23:25; Ezek. 22:12
[13] Ps. 15:5
[14] Job 15:34
[15] 1 Cor. 6:6-8; Prov. 3:29-30
[16] Isa. 5:8; Micah 2:2
[17] Prov. 11:26
[18] Acts 19:19, 24-25
[19] Job 20:19; James 5:4; Prov. 21:6
[20] Luke 12:15
[21] 1 Tim. 6:5; Col. 3:2; Prov. 23:5; Ps. 62:10
[22] Matt. 6:25, 31, 34; Eccl. 5:12
[23] Ps. 73:3; 37:1,7
[24] 2 Thes. 3:11; Prov. 18:9
[25] Prov. 21:17; 23:20-21; 28:19
[26] Eccl. 4:8; 6:2; 1 Tim. 5:8

Q. 76: Which is the ninth commandment?

A.: The ninth commandment is, "Thou shalt not bear false witness against thy neighbor."[1]

----

[1] Exod. 20:16

Q. 77: What is required in the ninth commandment?

A.: The ninth commandment requireth the maintaining and promoting of truth between man and

---

Q. 143: Which is the ninth commandment?

A.: The ninth commandment is, *Thou shalt not bear false witness against thy neighbour.*[1]

----

[1] Exod. 20:16

Q. 144: What are the duties required in the ninth commandment?

A.: The duties required in the ninth commandment are, the preserving and promoting of truth between man and man,[1] and the good name of our neighbour, as well as our own;[2] appearing and standing for the truth;[3] and from the heart,[4] sincerely,[5] freely,[6] clearly,[7] and fully,[8] speaking the truth, and only the truth, in matters of judgment and justice,[9] and in all other things whatsoever;[10] a charitable esteem of our neighbours;[11] loving, desiring, and rejoicing in their good name;[12] sorrowing for,[13] and covering of their infirmities;[14] freely

Belgic Confession (1561)	Heidelberg Catechism (1563)	Second Helvetic Confession (1566)	Canons of Dort (1619)
	the heavy wrath of God; likewise, that in judgment and all other dealings I love the truth, speak it uprightly and confess it;[7] also that I defend and promote, as much as I am able, the honor and good character of my neighbor.[8] [1] Prov. 19:5, 9; Prov. 21:28 [2] Ps. 15:3 [3] Rom. 1:29-30 [4] Matt. 7:1, etc.; Luke 6:37 [5] Lev. 19:11 [6] Prov. 12:22; Prov. 13:5 [7] 1 Cor. 13:6; Eph. 4:25 [8] 1 Pet. 4:8		

Westminster Confession of Faith (1647)	Westminster Shorter Catechism (1647)	Westminster Larger Catechism (1648)
	man,[1] and of our own and our neighbour's good name,[2] especially in witness-bearing.[3] [1] Zech. 8:16 [2] 3 John 12 [3] Prov. 14:5, 25	acknowledging of their gifts and graces,[15] defending their innocency;[16] a ready receiving of a good report,[17] and unwillingness to admit of an evil report,[18] concerning them; discouraging tale-bearers,[19] flatterers,[20] and slanderers;[21] love and care of our own good name, and defending it when need requireth;[22] keeping of lawful promises;[23] studying and practicing of whatsoever things are true, honest, lovely, and of good report.[24]

Q. 78: What is forbidden in the ninth commandment?

A.: The ninth commandment forbiddeth whatsoever is prejudicial to truth, or injurious to our own or our neighbour's, good name.[1]

[1] 1 Sam. 17:28; Lev. 19:16; Ps. 15:3

[1] Zech. 8:16
[2] 3 John 12
[3] Prov. 31:8-9
[4] Ps. 15:2
[5] 1 Chron. 19:9
[6] 1 Sam. 19:4-5
[7] Josh. 7:19
[8] 2 Sam. 14:18-20
[9] Lev. 19:15; Prov. 14:5, 25
[10] 2 Cor. 1:17-18; Eph. 4:25
[11] Heb. 6:9; 1 Cor. 13:7
[12] Rom. 1:8; 2 John 4; 3 John 3-4

[13] 2 Cor. 2:4; 12:21
[14] Prov. 17:9; 1 Pet. 4:8
[15] 1 Cor. 1:4-5, 7; 2 Tim. 1:4-5
[16] 1 Sam. 22:14
[17] 1 Cor. 13:6-7
[18] Ps. 15:3
[19] Prov. 25:23
[20] Prov. 26:24-25
[21] Ps. 101:5
[22] Prov. 22:1; John 8:49
[23] Ps. 15:4
[24] Phil. 4:8

Westminster Larger Catechism (cont.)

Q. 145: What are the sins forbidden in the ninth commandment?

A.: The sins forbidden in the ninth commandment are, all prejudicing the truth, and the good name of our neighbours, as well as our own,[1] especially in public judicature;[2] giving false evidence,[3] suborning false witnesses,[4] wittingly appearing and pleading for an evil cause, out-facing and over-bearing the truth;[5] passing unjust sentence,[6] calling evil good, and good evil; rewarding the wicked according to the work of the righteous, and the righteous according to the work of the wicked;[7] forgery,[8] concealing the truth, undue silence in a just cause,[9] and holding our peace when iniquity calleth for either a reproof from ourselves,[10] or complaint to others;[11] speaking the truth unseasonably,[12] or maliciously to a wrong end,[13] or perverting it to a wrong meaning,[14] or in doubtful and or equivocal expressions, to the prejudice of truth or justice;[15] speaking untruth,[16] lying,[17] slandering,[18] backbiting,[19] detracting,[20] tale-bearing,[21] whispering,[22] scoffing,[23] reviling,[24] rash,[25] harsh,[26] and partial censuring;[27] misconstructing intentions, words, and actions;[28] flattering,[29] vain-glorious boasting,[30] thinking or speaking too highly or too meanly of ourselves or others;[31] denying the gifts and graces of God;[32] aggravating smaller faults;[33] hiding, excusing, or extenuating of sins, when called to a free confession;[34] unnecessary discovering of infirmities;[35] raising false rumours,[36] receiving and countenancing evil reports,[37] and stopping our ears against just defense;[38] evil suspicion;[39] envying or grieving at the deserved credit of any,[40] endeavouring or desiring to impair it,[41] rejoicing in their disgrace and infamy;[42] scornful contempt,[43] fond admiration;[44] breach of lawful promises;[45] neglecting such things as are of good report,[46] and practicing, or not avoiding ourselves, or not hindering what we can in others, such things as procure an ill name.[47]

[1] 1 Sam. 17:28; 2 Sam. 16:3; 1:9-10, 15-16
[2] Lev. 19:15; Hab. 1:4
[3] Prov. 19:5; 6:16, 19
[4] Acts 6:13
[5] Jer. 9:3, 5; Acts 24:2, 5; Ps. 12:3-4; 52:1-4
[6] Prov. 17:15; 1 Ki. 21:9-14
[7] Isa. 5:23
[8] Ps. 119:69; Luke 19:8; 16:5-7
[9] Lev. 5:1; Deut. 13:8; Acts 5:3, 8-9; 2 Tim. 4:6
[10] 1 Ki. 1:6; Lev. 19:17
[11] Isa. 59:4
[12] Prov. 29:11
[13] 1 Sam. 22:9-10; Ps. 52:1-5
[14] Ps. 56:5; John 2:19; Matt. 26:60-61
[15] Gen. 3:5; 26:7,9
[16] Isa. 59:13
[17] Lev. 19:11; Col. 3:9
[18] Ps. 50:20
[19] Ps. 15:3
[20] James 4:11; Jer. 38:4
[21] Lev. 19:16
[22] Rom. 1:29-30
[23] Gen. 21:9; Gal. 4:29

[24] 1 Cor. 6:10
[25] Matt. 7:1
[26] Acts 28:4
[27] Gen. 38:24; Rom. 2:1
[28] Neh. 6:6-8; Rom. 3:8; Ps. 69:10; 1 Sam. 1:13-15; 2 Sam. 10:3
[29] Ps. 12:2-3
[30] 2 Tim. 3:2
[31] Luke 18:9, 11; Rom. 12:16; 1 Cor. 4:6; Acts 12:22; Exod. 4:10-14
[32] Job 27:5-6; 4:6
[33] Matt. 7:3-5
[34] Prov. 28:13; 30:20; Gen. 3:12-13; Jer. 2:35; 2 Ki. 5:25; Gen. 4:9
[35] Gen. 9:22; Prov. 25:9-10
[36] Exod. 23:1
[37] Prov. 29:12
[38] Acts 7:56-57; Job 31:13-14
[39] 1 Cor. 13:5; 1 Tim. 6:4
[40] Numb. 11:29; Matt. 21:15
[41] Ezra 4:12-13
[42] Jer. 48:27
[43] Ps. 35:15-16, 21; Matt. 27:28-29
[44] Jude 16; Acts 12:22
[45] Rom. 1:31; 2 Tim. 3:3
[46] 1 Sam. 2:24
[47] 2 Sam. 13:12-13; Prov. 5:8-9; 6:33

Belgic Confession (1561)	Heidelberg Catechism (1563)	Second Helvetic Confession (1566)	Canons of Dort (1619)

The Tenth Commandment and Application

Q. 113: What doth the tenth commandment require of us?

A.: That even the smallest inclination or thought contrary to any of God's commandments never rise in our hearts; but that at all times we hate all sin with our whole heart, and delight in all righteousness.[1]

---
[1] Rom. 7:7, etc.

Q. 114: But can those who are converted to God perfectly keep these commandments?

A.: No, but even the holiest men, while in this life, have only a small beginning of this obedience;[1] yet so, that with a sincere resolution they begin to live, not only according to some, but all the commandments of God.[2]

---
[1] Rom. 7:14
[2] Rom. 7:22, 15, etc.; James 3:2

Q. 115: Why will God then have the ten commandments so strictly preached, since no man in this life can keep them?

A.: First, that all our lifetime we may learn more and more to know our sinful nature,[1] and thus become the more earnest in seeking the remission of sin and righteousness in Christ;[2] likewise, that we constantly endeavor and pray to God for the grace of the Holy Spirit, that we may become more and more con-

Westminster Confession of Faith (1647)	Westminster Shorter Catechism (1647)	Westminster Larger Catechism (1648)

Q. 79: Which is the tenth commandment?

A.: The tenth commandment is, "Thou shalt not covet thy neighbour's house, thou shalt not covet thy neighbour's wife, nor his manservant, nor his maidservant, nor his ox, nor his ass, nor any thing that is thy neighbour's."[1]

[1] Exod. 20:17

Q. 80: What is required in the tenth commandment?

A.: The tenth commandment requireth full contentment with our own condition,[1] with a right and charitable frame of spirit toward our neighbour, and all that is his.[2]

[1] Heb. 13:5; 1 Tim. 6:6
[2] Job 31:29; Rom. 12:15; 1 Tim. 1:5; 1 Cor. 13:4-7

Q. 81: What is forbidden in the tenth commandment?

A.: The tenth commandment forbiddeth all discontentment with our own estate,[1] envying or grieving at the good of our neighbour,[2] and all inordinate motions and affections to anything that is his.[3]

[1] 1 Ki. 21:4; Esth. 5:13; 1 Cor. 10:10
[2] Gal. 5:26; James 3:14, 16
[3] Rom. 7:7-8; 13:9; Deut. 5:21

Q. 82: Is any man able perfectly to keep the commandments of God?

A.: No mere man since the fall is able in this life perfectly to keep the commandments of God,[1] but doth daily break them in thought, word, and deed.[2]

Q. 146: Which is the tenth commandment?

A.: The tenth commandment is, *Thou shalt not covet thy neighbour's house, thou shalt not covet thy neighbour's wife, nor his manservant, nor his maidservant, nor his ox, nor his ass, nor any thing that is thy neighbour's.*[1]

[1] Exod. 20:17

Q. 147: What are the duties required in the tenth commandment?

A.: The duties required in the tenth commandment are, such a full contentment with our own condition,[1] and such a charitable frame of the whole soul toward our neighbour, as that all our inward motions and affections touching him, tend unto, and further all that good which is his.[2]

[1] Heb. 13:5; 1 Tim. 6:6
[2] Job 31:29; Rom. 12:15; Ps. 122:7-9; 1 Tim. 1:5; Esth. 10:3; 1 Cor. 13:4-7

Q. 148: What are the sins forbidden in the tenth commandment?

A.: The sins forbidden in the tenth commandment are, discontentment with our own estate;[1] envying[2] and grieving at the good of our neighbour,[3] together with all inordinate motions and affections to anything that is his.[4]

[1] 1 Ki. 21:4; Esth. 5:13; 1 Cor. 10:10
[2] Gal. 5:26; James 3:14, 16
[3] Ps. 112:9-10; Neh. 2:10
[4] Rom. 7:7-8; 13:9; Col. 3:5; Deut. 5:21

Q. 149: Is any man able perfectly to keep the commandments of God?

A.: No man is able, either of himself,[1] or by any grace received in this life, perfectly to keep the commandments of God;[2] but doth daily break them, in thought,[3] word, and deed.[4]

[1] James 3:2; John 15:5; Rom. 8:3
[2] Eccl. 7:20; 1 John 1:8, 10; Gal. 5:17; Rom. 7:18-19
[3] Gen. 6:5; 8:21
[4] Rom. 3:9-19; James 3:2-13

Q. 150: Are all transgressions of the law of God equally heinous in themselves, and in the sight of God?

A.: All transgressions of the law of God are not equally heinous; but some sins in themselves, and by reason of several aggravations, are more heinous in the sight of God than others.[1]

[1] John 19:11; Ezek. 8:6, 13, 15; 1 John 5:16; Ps. 78:17, 32, 56

Q. 151: What are those aggravations that make some sins more heinous than others?

A.: Sins receive their aggravations, 1. From the persons offending:[1] if they be of riper age,[2] greater experience or grace,[3] eminent for profession,[4] gifts,[5] place,[6] office,[7] guides to others,[8] and whose example is likely to be followed by others.[9]

2. From the parties offended:[10] if immediately against God,[11] His attributes,[12] and worship;[13] against Christ, and His grace;[14] the Holy Spirit,[15] His witness,[16] and workings;[17] against superiors, men of

Belgic Confession (1561)	Heidelberg Catechism (1563)	Second Helvetic Confession (1566)	Canons of Dort (1619)
	formable to the image of God, till we arrive at the perfection proposed to us in a life to come.[3] [1] 1 John 1:9; Rom. 3:20; Rom. 5:13; Rom. 7:7 [2] Rom. 7:24 [3] 1 Cor. 9:24; Phil. 3:12-14		

Westminster Confession of Faith (1647)	Westminster Shorter Catechism (1647)	Westminster Larger Catechism (1648)

Westminster Shorter Catechism (1647)

[1] Eccl. 7:20; 1 John 1:8, 10; Gal. 5:17
[2] Gen. 6:5; 8:21; Rom. 3:9-21; James 3:2-13

Q. 83: Are all transgressions of the law equally heinous?

A.: Some sins in themselves, and by reason of several aggravations, are more heinous in the sight of God than others.[1]

[1] Ezek. 8:6, 13, 15; 1 John 5:16; Ps. 78:17, 32, 56

Westminster Larger Catechism (1648)

eminency,[18] and such as we stand especially related and engaged unto;[19] against any of the saints,[20] particularly weak brethren,[21] the souls of them, or any other,[22] and the common good of all or many.[23]

3. From the nature and quality of the offense:[24] if it be against the express letter of the law,[25] break many commandments, contain in it many sins;[26] if not only conceived in the heart, but breaks forth in words and actions,[27] scandalize others,[28] and admit of no reparation;[29] if against means,[30] mercies,[31] judgments,[32] light of nature,[33] conviction of conscience,[34] public or private admonition,[35] censures of the church,[36] civil punishments,[37] and our prayers, purposes, promises,[38] vows,[39] covenants,[40] and engagements to God or men;[41] if done deliberately,[42] wilfully,[43] presumptuously,[44] impudently,[45] boastingly,[46] maliciously,[47] frequently,[48] obstinately,[49] with delight,[50] continuance,[51] or relapsing, after repentance.[52]

4. From circumstances of time[53] and place:[54] if on the Lord's day,[55] or other times of divine worship,[56] or immediately before[57] or after these,[58] or other helps to prevent or remedy such miscarriages;[59] if in public, or in the presence of others, who are thereby likely to be provoked or defiled.[60]

[1] Jer. 2:8
[2] Job 32:7, 9; Eccl. 4:13
[3] 1 Ki. 11:4, 9
[4] 2 Sam. 12:14; 1 Cor. 5:1
[5] James 4:17; Luke 12:47-48
[6] Jer. 5:4-5
[7] 2 Sam. 12:7-9; Ezek. 8:11-12
[8] Rom. 2:17-24
[9] Gal. 2:11-14
[10] Matt. 21:38-39
[11] 1 Sam. 2:25; Acts 5:4; Ps. 51:4
[12] Rom. 2:4
[13] Mal. 1:8, 14
[14] Heb. 2:2-3; 12:25
[15] Heb. 10:29; Matt. 12:31-32
[16] Eph. 4:30
[17] Heb. 6:4-6
[18] Jude 8; Numb. 12:8-9; Isa. 3:5
[19] Prov. 30:17; 2 Cor. 12:15; Ps. 55:12-15
[20] Zeph. 2:8, 10-11; Matt. 18:6; 1 Cor. 6:8; Rev. 17:6.
[21] 1 Cor. 8:11-12; Rom. 14:13, 15, 21
[22] Ezek. 13:19; 1 Cor. 8:12; Rev. 18:12-18; Matt. 23:15
[23] 1 Thes. 2:15-16; Josh. 22:20
[24] Prov. 6:30-33
[25] Ezra 9:10-12; 1 Ki. 11:9-10
[26] Col. 3:5; 1 Tim. 6:10; Prov. 5:8-12; 6:32-33; Josh. 7:21
[27] James 1:14-15; Matt. 5:22; Micah 2:1
[28] Matt. 18:7; Rom. 2:23-24
[29] Deut. 22:22, 28-29; Prov. 6:32-35
[30] Matt. 11:21-24; John 15:22
[31] Isa. 1:3; Deut. 32:6
[32] Amos 4:8-11; Jer. 5:3
[33] Rom. 1:26-27
[34] Rom. 1:32; Dan. 5:22; Titus 3:10-11
[35] Prov. 29:1
[36] Titus 3:10; Matt. 18:17
[37] Prov. 27:22; 23:35
[38] Ps. 78:34-37; Jer. 2:20; 42:5-6, 20-21
[39] Eccl. 5:4-6; Prov. 20:25
[40] Lev. 26:25
[41] Prov. 2:17; Ezek. 17:18-19
[42] Ps. 36:4
[43] Jer. 6:16
[44] Numb. 15:30; Exod. 21:14
[45] Jer. 3:3; Prov. 7:13
[46] Ps. 52:1
[47] 3 John 10
[48] Numb. 14:22
[49] Zech. 7:11-12
[50] Prov. 2:14
[51] Isa. 57:17
[52] Jer. 34:8-11; 2 Pet. 2:20-22
[53] 2 Ki. 5:26
[54] Jer. 7:10; Isa. 26:10
[55] Ezek. 23:37-39
[56] Isa. 58:3-7
[57] 1 Cor. 11:20-21
[58] Jer. 7:8-10; Prov. 7:14-15; John 13:27, 30
[59] Ezra 9:13-14
[60] 2 Sam. 16:22; 1 Sam. 2:22-24

Q. 152: What doth every sin deserve at the hands of God?

A.: Every sin, even the least, being against the sovereignty,[1] goodness,[2] and holiness of God,[3] and against His righteous law,[4] deserveth His wrath and curse,[5] both in this life,[6] and that which is to come,[7] and cannot be expiated but by the blood of Christ.[8]

[1] James 2:10-11
[2] Exod. 20:1-2
[3] Hab. 1:13; Lev. 10:3; 11:44-45
[4] 1 John 3:4; Rom. 7:12
[5] Eph. 5:6; Gal. 3:10
[6] Lam. 3:39; Deut. 28:15-68
[7] Matt. 25:41
[8] Heb. 9:22; 1 Pet. 1:18-19

Belgic Confession (1561)	Heidelberg Catechism (1563)	Second Helvetic Confession (1566)	Canons of Dort (1619)

Christian Liberty

XXVII. Of Rites, Ceremonies, and Things Indifferent

1. Unto the ancient people were given in old time certain ceremonies, as a kind of schooling to those who were kept under the law, as under a schoolmaster or tutor. But Christ, the deliverer, being once come, and the law taken away, we who believe are no more under the law (Rom. 6:14), and the ceremonies have vanished out of use. And the apostles were so far from retaining them, or repairing them, in the Church of Christ, that they witnessed plainly that they would not lay any burden upon the Church (Acts 15:28). Wherefore we should seem to bring in and set up Judaism again if we should multiply ceremonies or rites in the Church according to the manner of the Jewish Church. And thus we are not of their judgment who would have the Church of Christ bound by many and divers rites, as it were by a certain schooling. For if the apostles would not thrust upon the Christian people the ceremonies and rites which were appointed by God, who is there, I pray you, that is well in his wits, that will thrust upon it the inventions devised by man? The greater the heap of ceremonies in the Church, so much the more is taken, not only from Christian liberty, but also from Christ, and from faith in Him; while the people seek those things in ceremonies which they should seek in the only Son of God, Jesus Christ, through faith. Wherefore a few moderate and simple rites, that are not contrary to the Word of God, do suffice the godly.

2. And in that there is found diversity of rites in the churches, let no man say, therefore, that the churches do not agree. Socrates says, in his *Church History*, "It were not possible to set down in writing all the ceremonies of the churches which are observed throughout cities and countries. No religion does keep everywhere the same ceremonies, although they admit and receive one and the self-same doctrine touching them; for even they who have one and the self-same faith do disagree among themselves about ceremonies." Thus much says Socrates; and we, at this day, having diversities in the celebration of the Lord's Supper, and in certain other things, in our churches, yet we do not disagree in doctrine and faith; neither is the unity and society of our churches rent asunder. For the churches have always used their liberty in such rites, as

Westminster Confession of Faith (1647)	Westminster Shorter Catechism (1647)	Westminster Larger Catechism (1648)

XX. Of Christian Liberty, and Liberty of Conscience

1. The liberty which Christ hath purchased for believers under the gospel consists in their freedom from the guilt of sin, the condemning wrath of God, the curse of the moral law;[1] and, in their being delivered from this present evil world, bondage to Satan, and dominion of sin;[2] from the evil of afflictions, the sting of death, the victory of the grave, and everlasting damnation;[3] as also, in their free access to God,[4] and their yielding obedience unto Him, not out of slavish fear, but a child-like love and willing mind.[5] All which were common also to believers under the law.[6] But, under the New Testament, the liberty of Christians is further enlarged, in their freedom from the yoke of the ceremonial law, to which the Jewish Church was subjected;[7] and in greater boldness of access to the throne of grace,[8] and in fuller communications of the free Spirit of God, than believers under the law did ordinarily partake of.[9]

[1] Titus 2:14; 1 Thes. 1:10; Gal. 3:13
[2] Gal. 1:4; Col. 1:13; Acts 26:18; Rom. 6:14
[3] Rom. 8:28; Ps. 119:71; 1 Cor. 15:54-57; Rom. 8:1
[4] Rom. 5:1-2
[5] Rom. 8:14-15; 1 John 4:18
[6] Gal. 3:9, 14
[7] Gal. 4:1-3, 6-7; 5:1; Acts 15:10-11
[8] Heb. 4:14, 16; Heb. 10:19-22
[9] John 7:38-39; 2 Cor. 3:13, 17-18

2. God alone is Lord of the conscience,[1] and hath left it free from the doctrines and commandments of men, which are, in any thing, contrary to His Word; or beside it, in matters of faith, or worship.[2] So that, to believe such doctrines, or to obey such commands, out of conscience, is to betray true liberty of conscience;[3] and the requiring of an implicit faith, and an absolute and blind obedience, is to destroy liberty of conscience, and reason also.[4]

[1] James 4:12; Rom. 14:4
[2] Acts 4:19; 5:29; 1 Cor. 7:23; Matt. 23:8-10; 2 Cor. 1:24; Matt. 15:9
[3] Col. 2:20, 22-23; Gal. 1:10; 2:4-5; 5:1
[4] Rom. 10:17; 14:23; Isa. 8:20; Acts 17:11; John 4:22; Hos. 5:11; Rev. 13:12, 16-17; Jer. 8:9

3. They who, upon pretense of Christian liberty, do practice any sin, or cherish any lust, do thereby destroy the end of Christian liberty, which is, that being delivered out of the hands of our enemies, we might serve the Lord without

Belgic Confession (1561)	Heidelberg Catechism (1563)	Second Helvetic Confession (1566)	Canons of Dort (1619)
		being things indifferent, which we also do at this day. 3. But yet, notwithstanding, we admonish men to take heed that they count not among things indifferent such as are not indeed indfferent, as some used to count the mass and the use of images in the Church for things indifferent. "That is indifferent" (says Jerome to Augustine), "which is neither good nor evil; so that, whether you do it or do it not, you are never the more just or unjust thereby." Therefore, when things indifferent are wrested to the confession of faith, they cease to be free; as Paul does show that it is lawful for a man to eat flesh if no man do admonish him that it was offered to idols (1 Cor. 10:27-28), for then it is unlawful, because he that eats it does seem to approve idolatry by eating of it (1 Cor. 8:10).	

Prayer and Fasting

Belgic Confession (1561)	Heidelberg Catechism (1563)	Second Helvetic Confession (1566)	Canons of Dort (1619)
	Q. 116: Why is prayer necessary for Christians? A.: Because it is the chief part of thankfulness which God requires of us;[1] and also, because God will give His grace and Holy Spirit to those only, who with sincere desires continually ask	XXIII. Of the Prayers of the Church, of Singing, and of Canonical Hours 1. True it is that a man may lawfully pray privately in any tongue that he does understand; but public prayers ought, in the holy assemblies, to be made in the vulgar tongue, or such a language as is known to all. Let all the prayers of the faithful be poured forth to God alone, through the mediation of Christ only, out of a true faith and pure love. As for invocation of saints, or using them as intercessors to entreat for us, the priest-	

Westminster Confession of Faith (1647)	Westminster Shorter Catechism (1647)	Westminster Larger Catechism (1648)
fear, in holiness and righteousness before Him, all the days of our life.[1] [1] Gal. 5:13; 1 Pet. 2:16; 2 Pet. 2:19; John 8:34; Luke 1:74-75 4. And because the powers which God hath ordained, and the liberty which Christ hath purchased, are not intended by God to destroy, but mutually to uphold and preserve one another, they who, upon pretense of Christian liberty, shall oppose any lawful power, or the lawful exercise of it, whether it be civil or ecclesiastical, resist the ordinance of God.[1] And, for their publishing of such opinions, or maintaining of such practices, as are contrary to the light of nature, or to the known principles of Christianity (whether concerning faith, worship, or conversation), or to the power of godliness; or, such erroneous opinions or practices, as either in their own nature, or in the manner of publishing or maintaining them, are destructive to the external peace and order which Christ hath established in the Church, they may lawfully be called to account,[2] and proceeded against, by the censures of the Church, and by the power of the civil magistrate.[3] [1] Matt. 12:25; 1 Pet. 2:13-14, 16; Rom. 13:1-8; Heb. 13:17 [2] Rom. 1:32; 1 Cor. 5:1, 5, 11, 13; 2 John 10-11; 2 Thes. 3:14; 1 Tim. 6:3-5; Titus 1:10-11, 13; 3:10; Matt. 18:15-17; 1 Tim. 1:19-20; Rev. 2:2, 14-15, 20; Rev. 3:9 [3] Deut. 13:6-12; Rom. 13:3-4; 2 John 10-11; Ezra 7:23, 25-28; Rev. 17:12, 16-17; Neh. 13:15, 17, 21-22, 25, 30; 2 Ki. 23:5-6, 9, 20-21; 2 Chron. 34:33; 15:12-13, 16; Dan. 3:29; 1 Tim. 2:2; Isa. 49:23; Zech. 13:2-3		

Westminster Confession of Faith	Westminster Shorter Catechism	Westminster Larger Catechism
XXI. Of Religious Worship, and the Sabbath Day 3. Prayer, with thanksgiving, being one special part of religious worship,[1] is by God required of all men:[2] and, that it may be accepted, it is to be made in the name of the Son,[3] by the help of His Spirit,[4] according to His will,[5] with understanding, reverence, humility, fervency, faith, love and perseverance;[6] and, if vocal, in a known tongue.[7]	*Q. 98: What is prayer?* A.: Prayer is an offering up of our desires unto God,[1] for things agreeable to His will,[2] in the name of Christ,[3] with confession of our sins,[4] and thankful acknowledgment of His mercies.[5] [1] Ps. 62:8	*Q. 178: What is prayer?* A.: Prayer is an offering up of our desires unto God,[1] in the name of Christ,[2] by the help of His Spirit;[3] with confession of our sins,[4] and thankful acknowledgment of His mercies.[5] [1] Ps. 62:8 [2] John 16:23 [3] Rom. 8:26 [4] Ps. 32:5-6; Dan. 9:4 [5] Phil. 4:6

Belgic Confession (1561)	Heidelberg Catechism (1563)	Second Helvetic Confession (1566)	Canons of Dort (1619)
	them of Him, and are thankful for them.[2] [1] Ps. 50:14-15 [2] Matt. 7:7; Luke 11:9, 13; Matt. 13:2; Ps. 50:15 Q. 117: *What are the requisites of that prayer which is acceptable to God and which He will hear?* A.: First, that we from the heart pray to the one true God only, who hath manifested Himself in His Word,[1] for all things He hath commanded us to ask of Him;[2] secondly, that we rightly and thoroughly know our need and misery, that so we may deeply humble ourselves in the presence of His divine majesty;[3] thirdly, that we be fully persuaded that He, notwithstanding that we are unworthy of it,[4] will, for the sake of Christ our Lord, certainly hear our prayer,[5] as He has promised us in His Word.[6] [1] John 4:22-23 [2] Rom. 8:26; 1 John 5:14 [3] John 4:23-24; Ps. 145:18 [4] 2 Chron. 20:12 [5] Ps. 2:11; Ps. 34:18-19; Isa. 66:2 [6] Rom. 10:13; Rom. 8:15-16; James 1:6; John 14:13; Dan. 9:17-18; Matt. 7:8; Ps. 143:1	hood of our Lord Christ and true religion will not permit us. Prayer must be made for the magistracy, for kings, and all that are placed in authority, for ministers of the Church, and for all necessities of churches; and especially in any calamity of the Church prayer must be made, both privately and publicly, without ceasing. 2. Moreover, we must pray willingly, and not by constraint, nor for any reward; neither must we superstitiously tie prayer to any place, as though it were not lawful to pray but in the church. There is no necessity that public prayers should be in form and time the same or alike in all churches. Let all churches use their liberty. Socrates, in his *History*, says, "In any country or nation whatsoever, you shall not find two churches which do wholly agree in prayer." The authors of this difference, I think, were those who had the government of the churches in several ages. But if any do agree, it deserves great commendation, and is to be imitated by others. 3. Besides this, there must be a mean and measure, as in every other thing, so also in public prayers, that they be not over-long and tedious. Let, therefore, most time be given to the teaching of the gospel in such holy assemblies; and let there be diligent heed taken that the people in the assemblies be not wearied with over-long prayers, so that, when the preaching of the gospel should be heard, they, through wearisomeness, either desire to go forth themselves or to have the assembly wholly dismissed. For unto such the sermons seem to be over-long which otherwise are brief enough. Yea, and the preachers ought to keep a mean. *XXIV. Of Holydays, Fasts, and Choice of Meats* 4. Now, the more sharply the Church of Christ does condemn surfeiting, drunkenness, and all kinds of lusts and intemperance, so much the more earnestly does it commend unto us Christian fasting. For fasting is nothing else than the abstinence and temperance of the godly and a watching and chastising of our flesh, taken up for present necessity, whereby we are humbled before God, and withdraw from the flesh those things with which it is cherished, to the end that it may the more willingly and easily obey the Spirit. Wherefore they do not fast at all that have no regard for those things, but imagine that they fast if they stuff their bellies once a day, and for a set or prescribed time do abstain from certain meats, thinking that by this very work wrought they please God and acquire merit. Fasting is a help of the prayers of the saints and all virtues; but the fasts wherein the Jews fasted	

Westminster Confession of Faith (1647)	Westminster Shorter Catechism (1647)	Westminster Larger Catechism (1648)

[1] Phil. 4:6
[2] Ps. 65:2
[3] John 14:13-14; 1 Pet. 2:5
[4] Rom. 8:26
[5] 1 John 5:14
[6] Ps. 47:7; Eccl. 5:1-2; Heb. 12:28; Gen. 18:27; James 5:16; 1:6-7; Mark 11:24; Matt. 6:12, 14-15; Col. 4:2; Eph. 6:18
[7] 1 Cor. 14:14

4. Prayer is to be made for things lawful;[1] and for all sorts of men living, or that shall live hereafter:[2] but not for the dead,[3] nor for those of whom it may be known that they have sinned the sin unto death.[4]

[1] 1 John 5:14
[2] 1 Tim. 2:1-2; John 17:20; 2 Sam. 7:29; Ruth 4:12
[3] 2 Sam. 12:21-23; Luke 16:25-26; Rev. 14:13
[4] 1 John 5:16

[2] 1 John 5:14
[3] John 16:23
[4] Ps. 32:5-6; Dan. 9:4
[5] Phil. 4:6

Q. 179: Are we to pray unto God only?
A.: God only being able to search the hearts,[1] hear the requests,[2] pardon the sins,[3] and fulfil the desires of all;[4] and only to be believed in,[5] and worshipped with religious worship;[6] prayer, which is a special part thereof,[7] is to be made by all to Him alone,[8] and to none other.[9]

[1] 1 Ki. 8:39; Acts 1:24; Rom. 8:27
[2] Ps. 65:2
[3] Micah 7:18
[4] Ps. 145:18-19
[5] Rom. 10:14
[6] Matt. 4:10
[7] 1 Cor. 1:2
[8] Ps. 50:15
[9] Rom. 10:14

Westminster Larger Catechism (cont.)

Q. 180: What is it to pray in the name of Christ?
A.: To pray in the name of Christ is, in obedience to His command, and in confidence on His promises, to ask mercy for His sake;[1] not by bare mentioning of His name,[2] but by drawing our encouragement to pray, and our boldness, strength, and hope of acceptance in prayer, from Christ and His mediation.[3]

[1] John 14:13-14; 16:24; Dan. 9:17
[2] Matt. 7:21
[3] Heb. 4:14-16; 1 John 5:13-15

Q. 181: Why are we to pray in the name of Christ?
A.: The sinfulness of man, and his distance from God by reason thereof, being so great, as that we can have no access into His presence without a mediator;[1] and there being none in heaven or earth appointed to, or fit for, that glorious work but Christ alone,[2] we are to pray in no other name but His only.[3]

[1] John 14:6; Isa. 59:2; Eph. 3:12
[2] John 6:27; Heb. 7:25-27; 1 Tim. 2:5
[3] Col. 3:17; Heb. 13:15

Q. 182: How doth the Spirit help us to pray?
A.: We not knowing what to pray for as we ought, the Spirit helpeth our infirmities, by enabling us to understand both for whom, and what, and how prayer is to be made; and by working and quickening in our hearts (although not in all persons, nor at all times, in the same measure) those apprehensions, affections, and graces which are requisite for the right performance of that duty.[1]

[1] Rom. 8:26-27; Ps. 10:17; Zech. 12:10

Q. 183: For whom are we to pray?
A.: We are to pray for the whole Church of Christ upon earth;[1] for magistrates,[2] and ministers;[3] for ourselves,[4] our brethren,[5] yea, our enemies;[6] and for all sorts of men living,[7] or that shall live hereafter;[8] but not for the dead,[9] nor for those that are known to have sinned the sin unto death.[10]

[1] Eph. 6:18; Ps. 28:9
[2] 1 Tim. 2:1-2

[3] Col. 4:3
[4] Gen. 32:11
[5] James 5:16
[6] Matt. 5:44
[7] 1 Tim. 2:1-2
[8] John 17:20; 2 Sam. 7:29
[9] 2 Sam. 12:21-23
[10] 1 John 5:16

Q. 184: For what things are we to pray?
A.: We are to pray for all things tending to the glory of God,[1] the welfare of the Church,[2] our own[3] or other's good;[4] but not for anything that is unlawful.[5]

[1] Matt. 6:9
[2] Ps. 51:18; 122:6
[3] Matt. 7:11
[4] Ps. 125:4
[5] 1 John 5:14

Q. 185: How are we to pray?
A.: We are to pray with an awful apprehension of the majesty of God,[1] and deep sense of our own unworthiness,[2] necessities,[3] and sins;[4] with penitent,[5] thankful,[6] and enlarged hearts;[7] with understanding,[8] faith,[9] sincerity,[10] fervency,[11] love,[12] and perseverance,[13] waiting upon Him,[14] with humble submission to His will.[15]

[1] Eccl. 5:1
[2] Gen. 18:27; 32:10
[3] Luke 15:17-19
[4] Luke 18:13-14
[5] Ps. 51:17
[6] Phil. 4:6
[7] 1 Sam. 1:15; 2:1
[8] 1 Cor. 14:15
[9] Mark 11:24; James 1:6
[10] Ps. 145:18; 17:1
[11] James 5:16
[12] 1 Tim. 2:8
[13] Eph. 6:18
[14] Micah 7:7
[15] Matt. 26:39

Belgic Confession (1561)	Heidelberg Catechism (1563)	Second Helvetic Confession (1566)	Canons of Dort (1619)

Second Helvetic Confession (cont.)

from meat, and not from wickedness, pleased God nothing at all, as we may see in the books of the prophets.

5. Now, fasting is either public or private. In olden times they celebrated public fasts in troublesome times and in the afflictions of the Church; wherein they abstained altogether from meat till the evening, and bestowed all that time in holy prayers, the worship of God, and repentance. These differed little from mournings and lamentations; and of these there is often mention made in the prophets, and especially in the second chapter of Joel. Such a fast should be kept at this day, when the Church is in distress. Private fasts are used by every one of us, according as every one feels the spirit weakened in him; for so he withdraws that which might cherish and strengthen the flesh.

6. All fasts ought to proceed from a free and willing spirit, and such a one as is truly humbled, and not framed to win applause and the liking of men, much less to the end that a man might merit righteousness by them. But let every one fast to this end, that he may deprive the flesh of that which would cherish it, and that he may the more zealously serve God.

7. The fast of Lent has testimony of antiquity, but none out of the apostles' writings; and therefore ought not, nor cannot, be imposed on the faithful. It is certain that in old time there were divers manners and uses of this fast; whereupon Irenaeus, a most ancient writer, says, "Some think that this fast should be observed one day only, others two days, but others more, and some forty days. This diversity in keeping this fast began not in our times, but long before us; by those, as I suppose, who, not simply holding that which was delivered them from the beginning, fell shortly after into another custom, either through negligence or ignorance." Moreover, Socrates, the historian, says,

"Because no ancient record is found concerning this matter, I think the apostles left this to every man's own judgment, that every one might work that which is good, without fear or constraint."

8. Now, as concerning the choice of meats, we suppose that, in fasting, all things should be denied to the flesh whereby the flesh is made more lusty, wherein it does most immoderately delight, and whereby it is most of all pampered, whether they be fish, spices, dainties, or excellent wines. Otherwise we know that all the creatures of God were made for the use and service of men. All things which God made are good (Gen. 1:31), and are to be used in the fear of God, and with due moderation, without putting any difference between them. For the apostle says, "Unto the pure all things are pure" (Titus 1:15), and also, "Whatsoever is sold in the shambles, that eat, asking no question for conscience sake" (1 Cor. 10:25). The same apostle calls the doctrine of those who teach to abstain from meats "doctrines of devils"; for that God created meats "to be received with thanksgiving of them which believe and know the truth. For every creature of God is good, and nothing to be refused, if it be received with thanksgiving" (1 Tim. 4:1, 3-4). The same apostle, in the epistle to the Colossians, reproves those who, by an overmuch abstinence, will get unto themselves an opinion of holiness (Col. 2:20-23). Therefore we do altogether mislike the Tatians and the Encratites, and all the disciples of Eustathius (of Sebaste), against whom the Gangrian Synod was assembled.

The Lord's Prayer

Q. 118: What hath God commanded us to ask of Him?

A.: All things necessary for soul and body,[1] which Christ our Lord has comprised in that prayer He Himself has taught us.[2]

[1] James 1:17; Matt. 6:33
[2] Matt. 6:9-10, etc.; Luke 11:2, etc.

Westminster Confession of Faith (1647)	Westminster Shorter Catechism (1647)	Westminster Larger Catechism (1648)
	Q. 99: What rule hath God given for our direction in prayer? A.: The whole Word of God is of use to direct us in prayer;[1] but the special rule of direction is that form of prayer which Christ taught His disciples, commonly called *the Lord's prayer.*[2] ――― [1] 1 John 5:14 [2] Matt. 6:9-13; Luke 11:2-4	*Q. 186: What rule hath God given for our direction in the duty of prayer?* A.: The whole Word of God is of use to direct us in the duty of prayer;[1] but the special rule of direction is that form of prayer which our Savior Christ taught His disciples, commonly called *the Lord's prayer.*[2] ――― [1] 1 John 5:14 [2] Matt. 6:9-13; Luke 11:2-4 *Q. 187: How is the Lord's prayer to be used?* A.: The Lord's prayer is not only for direction, as a pattern, according to which we are to make

Belgic Confession (1561)	Heidelberg Catechism (1563)	Second Helvetic Confession (1566)	Canons of Dort (1619)
	Q. 119: What are the words of that prayer? A.: *Our Father which art in heaven, hallowed be Thy name. Thy kingdom come. Thy will be done in earth, as it is in heaven. Give us this day our daily bread. And forgive us our debts, as we forgive our debtors. And lead us not into temptation, but deliver us from evil: for Thine is the kingdom, and the power, and the glory, for ever. Amen.*[1]		

[1] Matt. 6:9-13

Q. 120: Why hath Christ commanded us to address God thus: "Our Father"?

A.: That immediately, in the very beginning of our prayer, He might excite in us a childlike reverence for and confidence in God, which are the foundation of our prayer, namely, that God is become our Father in Christ,[1] and will much less deny us what we ask of Him in true faith than our parents will refuse us earthly things.[2]

[1] Matt. 6:9
[2] Matt. 7:9-11; Luke 11:11; Isa. 49:15

Q. 121: Why is it here added, "which art in heaven"?

A.: Lest we should form any earthly conceptions of God's heavenly majesty,[1] and that we may expect from His almighty power all things necessary for soul and body.[2]

[1] Jer. 23:24
[2] Acts 17:24; Rom. 10:12

Westminster Confession of Faith (1647)	Westminster Shorter Catechism (1647)	Westminster Larger Catechism (1648)
	Q. 100: What doth the preface of the Lord's prayer teach us? A.: The preface of the Lord's prayer (which is, *Our Father which art in heaven*[1]) teacheth us to draw near to God with all holy reverence and confidence, as children to a father, able and ready to help us;[2] and that we should pray with and for others.[3] [1] Matt. 6:9 [2] Rom. 8:15; Luke 11:13 [3] Acts 12:5; 1 Tim. 2:1-2	other prayers; but may also be used as a prayer, so that it be done with understanding, faith, reverence, and other graces necessary to the right performance of the duty of prayer.[1] [1] Matt. 6:9 compared with Luke 11:2
		Q. 188: Of how many parts doth the Lord's prayer consist? A.: The Lord's prayer consists of three parts; a preface, petitions, and a conclusion.
	Q. 101: What do we pray for in the first petition? A.: In the first petition (which is, *Hallowed be Thy name*[1]) we pray, that God would enable us and others to glorify Him in all that whereby He maketh Himself known;[2] and that He would dispose all things to His own glory.[3] [1] Matt. 6:9 [2] Ps. 67:2-3 [3] Ps. 83	*Q. 189: What doth the preface of the Lord's prayer teach us?* A.: The preface of the Lord's prayer (contained in these words, *Our Father which art in heaven*,[1]) teacheth us, when we pray, to draw near to God with confidence of His fatherly goodness, and our interest therein;[2] with reverence, and all other child-like dispositions,[3] heavenly affections,[4] and due apprehensions of His sovereign power, majesty, and gracious condescension;[5] as also, to pray with and for others.[6] [1] Matt. 6:9 [2] Luke 11:13; Rom. 8:15 [3] Isa. 64:9 [4] Ps. 123:1; Lam. 3:41 [5] Isa. 63:15-16; Neh. 1:4-6 [6] Acts 12:5
	Q. 102: What do we pray for in the second petition? A.: In the second petition (which is, *Thy kingdom come*[1]) we pray, that Satan's kingdom may be destroyed;[2] and that the kingdom of grace may be advanced,[3] ourselves and others brought into it, and kept in it;[4] and that the kingdom of glory may be hastened.[5] [1] Matt. 6:10 [2] Ps. 68:1, 18 [3] Rev. 12:10-11 [4] 2 Thes. 3:1; Rom. 10:1; John 17:9, 20 [5] Rev. 22:20	*Q. 190: What do we pray for in the first petition?* A.: In the first petition, (which is, *Hallowed be Thy name*[1]), acknowledging the utter inability and indisposition that is in ourselves and all men to honour God aright,[2] we pray, that God would by His grace enable and incline us and others to know, to acknowledge, and highly to esteem Him,[3] His titles,[4] attributes,[5] ordinances, Word,[6] works, and whatsoever He is pleased to make Himself known by;[7] and to glorify Him in thought, word,[8] and deed:[9] that He would prevent and remove atheism,[10] ignorance,[11] idolatry,[12] profaneness,[13] and whatsoever is dishonourable to Him;[14] and, by His over-ruling providence, direct and dispose of all things to His own glory.[15] [1] Matt. 6:9 [2] 2 Cor. 3:5; Ps. 51:15 [3] Ps. 67:2-3 [4] Ps. 83:18 [5] Ps. 86:10-13, 15 [6] 2 Thes. 3:1; Ps. 147:19-20; 138:1-3; 2 Cor. 2:14-15 [7] Ps. 145; 8 [8] Ps. 103:1; 19:14 [9] Phil. 1:9, 11 [10] Ps. 67:1-4 [11] Eph. 1:17-18 [12] Ps. 97:7 [13] Ps. 74:18, 22-23 [14] 2 Ki. 19:15-16 [15] 2 Chron. 20:6, 10-12; Ps. 83; 140:4, 8
	Q. 103: What do we pray for in the third petition? A.: In the third petition (which is, *Thy will be done in earth, as it is in heaven*[1]) we pray, that God, by His	

Belgic Confession (1561)	Heidelberg Catechism (1563)	Second Helvetic Confession (1566)	Canons of Dort (1619)
	Q. 122: Which is the first petition? A.: *"Hallowed be Thy name";*[1] that is, grant us, first, rightly to know Thee,[2] and to sanctify, glorify and praise Thee in all Thy works, in which Thy power, wisdom, goodness, justice, mercy and truth, are clearly displayed;[3] and further also, that we may so order and direct our whole lives, our thoughts, words and actions, that Thy Name may never be blasphemed, but rather honored and praised on our account.[4] [1] Matt. 6:9 [2] John 17:3; Jer. 9:23-24; Matt. 16:17; James 1:5 [3] Ps. 119:137-138; Luke 1:46; Ps. 145:8-9 [4] Ps. 115:1; Ps. 71:8 *Q. 123: Which is the second petition?* A.: *"Thy kingdom come";*[1] that is, rule us so by Thy Word and Spirit, that we may submit ourselves more and more to Thee,[2] preserve and increase Thy Church,[3] destroy the works of the devil,[4] and all violence which would exalt itself against Thee; and also, all wicked counsels devised against Thy holy Word; till the full perfection of Thy kingdom take place,[5] wherein Thou shalt be all in all.[6] [1] Matt. 6:10 [2] Ps. 119:5 [3] Ps. 51:18 [4] 1 John 3:8; Rom. 16:20 [5] Rev. 22:17, 20 [6] 1 Cor. 15:15, 28 *Q. 124: Which is the third petition?* A.: *"Thy will be done on*		

Westminster Confession of Faith (1647)	Westminster Shorter Catechism (1647)	Westminster Larger Catechism (1648)

grace, would make us able and willing to know, obey, and submit to His will in all things,[2] as the angels do in heaven.[3]

---

[1] Matt. 6:10
[2] Ps. 67; 119:36; Matt. 26:39; 2 Sam. 15:25; Job 1:21
[3] Ps. 103:20-21

Q. 104: What do we pray for in the fourth petition?

A.: In the fourth petition (which is, *Give us this day our daily bread*[1]) we pray, that of God's free gift we may receive a competent portion of the good things of this life, and enjoy His blessing with them.[2]

---

[1] Matt. 6:11
[2] Prov. 30:8-9; Gen. 28:20; 1 Tim. 4:4-5

Q. 105: What do we pray for in the fifth petition?

A.: In the fifth petition (which is, *And forgive us our debts, as we forgive our debtors*[1]) we pray, that God, for Christ's sake, would freely pardon all our sins;[2] which we are the rather encouraged to ask, because by His grace we are enabled from the heart to forgive others.[3]

---

[1] Matt. 6:12
[2] Ps. 51:1-2, 7, 9; Dan. 9:17-19
[3] Luke 11:4; Matt. 18:35

Q. 106: What do we pray for in the sixth petition?

A.: In the sixth petition (which is, *And lead us not into temptation, but deliver us from evil*[1]) we pray, that God would either keep us from being tempted to sin,[2] or support and deliver us when we are tempted.[3]

---

[1] Matt. 6:13
[2] Matt. 26:41
[3] 1 Cor. 12:7-8

Q. 191: What do we pray for in the second petition?

A.: In the second petition (which is, *Thy kingdom come*[1]), acknowledging ourselves and all mankind to be by nature under the dominion of sin and Satan,[2] we pray, that the kingdom of sin and Satan may be destroyed,[3] the gospel propagated throughout the world,[4] the Jews called,[5] the fulness of the Gentiles brought in;[6] the Church furnished with all gospel-officers and ordinances,[7] purged from corruption,[8] countenanced and maintained by the civil magistrate;[9] that the ordinances of Christ may be purely dispensed, and made effectual to the converting of those that are yet in their sins, and the confirming, comforting, and building up of those that are already converted;[10] that Christ would rule in our hearts here,[11] and hasten the time of His second coming, and our reigning with Him for ever;[12] and that He would be pleased so to exercise the kingdom of His power in all the world, as may best conduce to these ends.[13]

---

[1] Matt. 6:10
[2] Eph. 2:2-3
[3] Ps. 67:1, 18; Rev. 12:10-11
[4] 2 Thes. 3:1
[5] Rom. 10:1
[6] John 17:9, 20; Rom. 11:25-26; Ps. 67
[7] Matt. 9:38; 2 Thes. 3:1
[8] Mal. 1:11; Zeph. 3:9
[9] 1 Tim. 2:1-2
[10] Acts 4:29-30; Eph. 6:18-20; Rom. 15:29-30, 32; 2 Thes. 1:11; 2:16-17
[11] Eph. 3:14-20
[12] Rev. 22:20
[13] Isa. 64:1-2; Rev. 4:8-11

Q. 192: What do we pray for in the third petition?

A.: In the third petition, (which is, *Thy will be done in earth, as it is in heaven*[1]), acknowledging, that by nature we and all men are not only utterly unable and unwilling to know and do the will of God,[2] but prone to rebel against His Word,[3] to repine and murmur against His providence,[4] and wholly inclined to do the will of the flesh, and of the devil,[5] we pray, that God would by His Spirit take away from ourselves and others all blindness,[6] weakness,[7] indisposedness,[8] and perverseness of heart;[9] and by His grace make us able and willing to know, do, and submit to His will in all things,[10] with the like humility,[11] cheerfulness,[12] faithfulness,[13] diligence,[14] zeal,[15] sincerity,[16] and constancy,[17] as the angels do in heaven.[18]

---

[1] Matt. 6:10
[2] Rom. 7:18; Job 21:14; 1 Cor. 2:14
[3] Rom. 8:7
[4] Exod. 17:7; Numb. 14:2
[5] Eph. 2:2
[6] Eph. 1:17-18
[7] Eph. 3:16
[8] Matt. 26:40-41
[9] Jer. 31:18-19

Belgic Confession (1561)	Heidelberg Catechism (1563)	Second Helvetic Confession (1566)	Canons of Dort (1619)
	earth as it is in heaven";[1] that is, grant that we and all men may renounce our own will,[2] and without murmuring obey Thy will,[3] which is only good; that so every one may attend to and perform the duties of his station and calling[4] as willingly and faithfully as the angels do in heaven.[5] [1] Matt. 6:10 [2] Matt. 16:24; Titus 2:12 [3] Luke 22:42 [4] 1 Cor. 7:24; Eph. 4:1 [5] Ps. 103:20 *Q. 125: Which is the fourth petition?* A.: *"Give us this day our daily bread"*;[1] that is, be pleased to provide us with all things necessary for the body,[2] that we may thereby acknowledge Thee to be the only fountain of all good,[3] and that neither our care nor industry, nor even Thy gifts, can profit us without Thy blessing,[4] and therefore that we may withdraw our trust from all creatures and place it alone in Thee.[5] [1] Matt. 6:11 [2] Ps. 145:15; Matt. 6:25, etc. [3] Acts 17:25; Acts 14:17 [4] 1 Cor. 15:58; Deut. 8:3; Ps. 127:1-2 [5] Ps. 62:11; Ps. 55:22 *Q. 126: Which is the fifth petition?* A.: *"And forgive us our debts as we forgive our debtors"*;[1] that is, be pleased for the sake of Christ's blood, not to impute to us poor sinners our transgressions, nor that depravity which always cleaves to us;[2] even as we feel this		

Westminster Confession of Faith (1647)	Westminster Shorter Catechism (1647)	Westminster Larger Catechism (1648)
	Q. 107: What doth the conclusion of the Lord's prayer teach us? A.: The conclusion of the Lord's prayer (which is, *For Thine is the kingdom, and the power, and the glory, for ever, Amen*[1]) teacheth us to take our encouragement in prayer from God only,[2] and in our prayers to praise Him, ascribing kingdom, power, and glory to Him.[3] And, in testimony of our desire, and assurance to be heard, we say, Amen.[4] [1] Matt. 6:13 [2] Dan. 9:4, 7-9, 16-19 [3] 1 Chron. 29:10-13 [4] 1 Cor. 14:16; Rev. 22:20-21	[10] Ps. 119:1, 8, 35-36; Acts 21:14 [11] Micah 6:8 [12] Ps. 100:2; Job 1:21; 2 Sam. 15:25-26 [13] Isa. 38:3 [14] Ps. 119:4-5 [15] Rom. 12:11 [16] Ps. 119:80 [17] Ps. 119:112 [18] Isa. 6:2-3; Ps. 103:20-21; Matt. 18:10 *Q. 193: What do we pray for in the fourth petition?* A.: In the fourth petition, (which is, *Give us this day our daily bread*[1]), acknowledging, that in Adam, and by our own sin, we have forfeited our right to all the outward blessings of this life, and deserve to be wholly deprived of them by God, and to have them cursed to us in the use of them;[2] and that neither they of themselves are able to sustain us,[3] nor we to merit,[4] or by our own industry to procure them;[5] but prone to desire,[6] get,[7] and use them unlawfully;[8] we pray for ourselves and others, that both they and we, waiting upon the providence of God from day to day in the use of lawful means, may, of His free gift, and as to His fatherly wisdom shall seem best, enjoy a competent portion of them;[9] and have the same continued

Westminster Larger Catechism (cont.)

and blessed unto us in our holy and comfortable use of them,[10] and contentment in them;[11] and be kept from all things that are contrary to our temporal support and comfort.[12]

[1] Matt. 6:11
[2] Gen. 2:17; 3:17; Rom. 8:20-22; Jer. 5:25; Deut. 28:15-68
[3] Deut. 8:3
[4] Gen. 32:10
[5] Deut. 8:17-18
[6] Jer. 6:13; Mark 7:21-22
[7] Hos. 12:7
[8] James 4:3
[9] Gen. 43:12-14; Gen. 28:20; Eph. 4:28; 2 Thes. 3:11-12; Phil. 4:6
[10] 1 Tim. 4:3-5
[11] 1 Tim. 6:6-8
[12] Prov. 30:8-9

Q. 194: What do we pray for in the fifth petition?

A.: In the fifth petition, (which is, *Forgive us our debts, as we forgive our debtors*[1]), acknowledging, that we and all others are guilty both of original and actual sin, and thereby become debtors to the justice of God; and that neither we, nor any other creature, can make the least satisfaction for that debt;[2] we pray for ourselves and others, that God of His free grace would, through the obedience and satisfaction of Christ, apprehended and applied by faith, acquit us both from the guilt and punishment of sin,[3] accept us in His Beloved;[4] continue His favour and grace to us,[5] pardon our daily failings,[6] and fill us with peace and joy, in giving us daily more and more assurance of forgiveness;[7] which we are the rather emboldened to ask, and encouraged to expect, when we have this testimony in ourselves, that we from the heart forgive others their offenses.[8]

[1] Matt. 6:12

[2] Rom. 3:9-22; Matt. 18:24-25; Ps. 130:3-4
[3] Rom. 3:24-26; Heb. 9:22
[4] Eph. 1:6-7
[5] 2 Pet. 1:2
[6] Hosea 14:2; Jer. 14:7
[7] Rom. 15:13; Ps. 51:7-10, 12
[8] Luke 11:4; Matt. 6:14-15; Matt. 18:35

Q. 195: What do we pray for in the sixth petition?

A.: In the sixth petition, (which is, *And lead us not into temptation, but deliver us from evil*[1]), acknowledging, that the most wise, righteous, and gracious God, for divers holy and just ends, may so order things, that we may be assaulted, foiled, and for a time led captive by temptations;[2] that Satan,[3] the world,[4] and the flesh, are ready powerfully to draw us aside, and ensnare us;[5] and that we, even after the pardon of our sins, by reason of our corruption,[6] weakness, and want of watchfulness,[7] are not only subject to be tempted, and forward to expose ourselves unto temptations,[8] but also of ourselves unable and unwilling to resist them, to recover out of them, and to improve them;[9] and worthy to be left under the power of them;[10] we pray, that God would so over-rule the world and all in it,[11] subdue the flesh,[12] and restrain Satan,[13] order all things,[14] bestow and bless all means of grace,[15] and quicken us to watchfulness in the use of them, that we and all His people may by His providence be kept from being tempted to sin;[16] or, if tempted, that by His Spirit we may be powerfully supported and enabled to stand in the hour of temptation;[17] or when fallen, raised again and recovered out of it,[18] and have a sanctified use and improvement thereof;[19] that our sanctification and salvation may be perfected,[20] Satan trodden under our feet,[21] and we fully freed from sin, temptation, and all evil, for ever.[22]

Belgic Confession (1561)	Heidelberg Catechism (1563)	Second Helvetic Confession (1566)	Canons of Dort (1619)

Heidelberg Catechism (cont.)

evidence of Thy grace in us, that it is our firm resolution from the heart to forgive our neighbor.[3]

---
[1] Matt. 6:12
[2] Ps. 51:1; 1 John 2:1-2
[3] Matt. 6:14-15

Q. 127: Which is the sixth petition?

A.: *"And lead us not into temptation, but deliver us from evil"*;[1] that is, since we are so weak in ourselves that we cannot stand a moment;[2] and besides this, since our mortal enemies, the devil,[3] the world,[4] and our own flesh,[5] cease not to assault us, do Thou therefore preserve and strengthen us by the power of Thy Holy Spirit, that we may not be overcome in this spiritual warfare, but constantly and strenuously may resist our foes[6] till at last we obtain a complete victory.[7]

---
[1] Matt. 6:13
[2] Rom. 8:26; Ps. 103:14
[3] 1 Pet. 5:8
[4] Eph. 6:12; John 15:19
[5] Rom. 7:23; Gal. 5:17
[6] Matt. 26:41; Mark 13:33
[7] 1 Thes. 3:13; 1 Thes. 5:23

Q. 128: How dost thou conclude thy prayer?

A.: *"For Thine is the kingdom, and the power, and the glory, forever"*;[1] that is, all these we ask of Thee, because Thou, being our King and almighty, art willing and able to give us all good;[2] and all this we pray for, that thereby not we, but Thy holy Name, may be glorified for ever.[3]

---
[1] Matt. 6:13
[2] Rom. 10:12; 2 Pet. 2:9
[3] John 14:13; Ps. 115:1; Phil. 4:20

Q. 129: What doth the word "Amen" signify?

A.: *"Amen"* signifies it shall truly and certainly be, for my prayer is more assuredly heard of God than I feel in my heart that I desire these things of Him.[1]

---
[1] 2 Cor. 1:20; 2 Tim. 2:13

Westminster Confession of Faith (1647)	Westminster Shorter Catechism (1647)	Westminster Larger Catechism (1648)

Westminster Larger Catechism (cont.)

[1] Matt. 6:13
[2] 2 Chron. 32:31
[3] 1 Chron. 21:1
[4] Luke 21:34; Mark 4:19
[5] James 1:14
[6] Gal. 5:17
[7] Matt. 26:41
[8] Matt. 26:69-72; Gal. 2:11-14; 2 Chron. 18:3; 19:2
[9] Rom. 7:23-24; 1 Chron. 21:1-4; 2 Chron. 16:7-10
[10] Ps. 81:11-12
[11] John 17:15
[12] Ps. 51:10; 119:133
[13] 2 Cor. 12:7-8
[14] 1 Cor. 10:12-13
[15] Heb. 13:20-21
[16] Matt. 26:41; Ps. 19:13
[17] Eph. 3:14-17; 1 Thes. 3:13; Jude 24
[18] Ps. 51:12
[19] 1 Pet. 5:8-10
[20] 2 Cor. 13:7, 9
[21] Rom. 16:20; Zech. 3:2; Luke 22:31-32
[22] John 17:15; 1 Thes. 5:23

Q. 196: What doth the conclusion of the Lord's prayer teach us?

A.: The conclusion of the Lord's prayer, (which is, *For Thine is the kingdom, and the power, and the glory, for ever. Amen*[1]), teacheth us to enforce our petitions with arguments,[2] which are to be taken, not from any worthiness in ourselves, or in any other creature, but from God;[3] and with our prayers to join praises,[4] ascribing to God alone eternal sovereignty, omnipotency, and glorious excellency;[5] in regard whereof, as He is able and willing to help us,[6] so we by faith are emboldened to plead with Him that He would,[7] and quietly to rely upon Him, that He will fulfil our requests.[8] And, to testify this is our desire and assurance, we say, Amen.[9]

[1] Matt. 6:13
[2] Rom. 15:30
[3] Dan. 9:4, 7-9, 16-19
[4] Phil. 4:6
[5] 1 Chron. 29:10-13
[6] Eph. 3:20-21; Luke 11:13
[7] 2 Chron. 20:6, 11
[8] 2 Chron. 14:11
[9] 1 Cor. 14:16; Rev. 22:20-21

Ecclesiology:
The Doctrine of
the Church

Belgic Confession (1561)	Heidelberg Catechism (1563)	Second Helvetic Confession (1566)	Canons of Dort (1619)

The Doctrine of the Church

Article 27

The Catholic Christian Church

We believe and profess one catholic or universal Church,[1] which is a holy congregation of true Christian believers, all expecting their salvation in Jesus Christ, being washed by His blood, sanctified and sealed by the Holy Ghost.

This Church hath been from the beginning of the world, and will be to the end thereof;[2] which is evident from this, that Christ is an eternal king, which, without subjects He cannot be.[3] And this holy Church is preserved or supported by God against the rage of the whole world;[4] though she sometimes (for a while) appears very small, and, in the eyes of men, to be reduced to nothing;[5] as during the perilous reign of Ahab, when nevertheless *the Lord reserved unto Him seven thousand men, who had not bowed their knees to Baal.*[6]

Furthermore, this holy Church is not confined, bound, or limited to a certain place or to certain persons, but is spread and dispersed over the whole world; and yet is joined and united with heart and will,[7] by the power of faith, in one and the same spirit.[8]

---

[1] Isa. 2:2; Ps. 46:5; 102:14; Jer. 31:36
[2] Matt. 28:20; 2 Sam. 7:16

Q. 54: What believest thou concerning the "holy catholic Church" of Christ?

A.: That the Son of God[1] from the beginning to the end of the world,[2] gathers,[3] defends, and preserves to Himself[4] by His Spirit and Word,[5] out of the whole human race,[6] a Church chosen to everlasting life,[7] agreeing in true faith; and that I am and for ever shall remain, a living member thereof.[8]

---

[1] John 10:11
[2] Gen. 26:4
[3] Rom. 9:24; Eph. 1:10
[4] John 10:16
[5] Isa. 59:21
[6] Deut. 10:14-15
[7] Acts 13:48
[8] 1 Cor. 1:8-9; Rom. 8:35, etc.

XVII. Of the Catholic and Holy Church of God, and of the One Only Head of the Church

1. Forasmuch as God from the beginning would have men to be saved, and to come to the knowledge of the truth (1 Tim. 2:4), therefore it is necessary that there always should have been, and should be at this day, and to the end of the world, a Church — that is, a company of the faithful called and gathered out of the world; a communion (I say) of all saints, that is, of them who truly know and rightly worship and serve the true God, in Jesus Christ the Savior, by the word of the Holy Spirit, and who by faith are partakers of all those good graces which are freely offered through Christ. These all are citizens of one and the same city, living under one Lord, under the same laws, and in the same fellowship of all good things; for the apostle calls them "fellowcitizens with the saints, and of the household of God" (Eph. 2:19); terming the faithful upon the earth saints (1 Cor. 4:1), who are sanctified by the blood of the Son of God. Of these is that article of our Creed wholly to be understood, "I believe an holy catholic Church; the communion of saints."

2. And, seeing that there is always but "one God, and one mediator between God and men, the man Christ Jesus" (1 Tim. 2:5); also, one shepherd of the whole flock, one Head of this body, and, to conclude, one Spirit, one salvation, one faith, one testament, or covenant, — it follows necessarily that there is but one Church, which we therefore call *catholic* because it is universal, spread abroad through all the parts and quarters of the world, and reaches unto all times, and is not limited within the compass either of time or place. Here, therefore, we must condemn the Donatists who pinned up the Church within the corners of Africa; neither do we assent to the Roman clergy who vaunt that the Church of Rome alone is in a manner catholic.

3. The Church is divided by some into divers parts or sorts; not that it is rent and divided from itself, but rather distinguished in respect of the diversity of the members that are in it. One part thereof they make to be the Church militant, the other the Church triumphant. The militant wars still on earth, and fights against the flesh, the world, and the prince of the world, the devil; against sin and against death. The other, being already set at liberty, is now in

Westminster Confession of Faith (1647)	Westminster Shorter Catechism (1647)	Westminster Larger Catechism (1648)

XXV. Of the Church

1. The catholic or universal Church, which is invisible, consists of the whole number of the elect, that have been, are, or shall be gathered into one, under Christ the Head thereof; and is the spouse, the body, the fulness of Him that filleth all in all.[1]

[1] Eph. 1:10, 22-23; 5:23, 27, 32; Col. 1:18

2. The visible Church, which is also catholic or universal under the gospel (not confined to one nation, as before under the law), consists of all those throughout the world that profess the true religion,[1] and of their children,[2] and is the kingdom of the Lord Jesus Christ,[3] the house and family of God,[4] out of which there is no ordinary possibility of salvation.[5]

[1] 1 Cor. 1:2; 12:12-13; Ps. 2:8; Rev. 7:9; Rom. 15:9-12
[2] 1 Cor. 7:14; Acts 2:39; Ezek. 16:20-21; Rom. 11:16; Gen. 3:15; 17:7
[3] Matt. 13:47; Isa. 9:7
[4] Eph. 2:19; 3:15
[5] Acts 2:47

3. Unto this catholic visible Church Christ hath given the ministry, oracles, and ordinances of God, for the gathering and perfecting of the saints, in this life, to the end of the world, and doth, by His own presence and Spirit, according to His promise, make them effectual thereunto.[1]

[1] 1 Cor. 12:28; Eph. 4:11-13; Matt. 28:19-20; Isa. 59:21

4. This catholic Church hath been sometimes more, sometimes less visible.[1] And particular Churches, which are members thereof, are more or less pure, according as the doctrine of the gospel is taught and embraced, ordinances administered, and public worship performed more or less purely in them.[2]

[1] Rom. 11:3-4; Rev. 12:6, 14
[2] Rev. 2; 3; 1 Cor. 5:6-7

5. The purest Churches under heaven are subject both to mixture and error;[1] and some have so degenerated, as to become no Churches of Christ, but synagogues of Satan.[2] Nevertheless, there shall be always a Church on earth to worship God according to His will.[3]

[1] 1 Cor. 13:12; Rev. 2; 3; Matt. 13:24-30, 47
[2] Rev. 18:2; Rom. 11:18-22
[3] Matt. 16:18; Ps. 72:17; 102:28; Matt. 28:19-20

Q. 61: Are all they saved who hear the gospel, and live in the Church?

A.: All that hear the gospel, and live in the visible Church, are not saved; but they only who are true members of the Church invisible.[1]

[1] John 12:38-40; Rom. 9:6; Matt. 22:14; 7:21; Rom. 11:7

Q. 62: What is the visible Church?

A.: The visible Church is a society made up of all such as in all ages and places of the world do profess the true religion,[1] and of their children.[2]

[1] 1 Cor. 1:2; 12:13; Rom. 15:9-12; Rev. 7:9; Ps. 2:8; 22:27-31; 45:17; Matt. 28:19-20; Isa. 59:21
[2] 1 Cor. 7:14; Acts 2:39; Rom. 11:16; Gen. 17:7

Q. 63: What are the special privileges of the visible Church?

A.: The visible Church hath the privilege of being under God's special care and government;[1] of being protected and preserved in all ages, notwithstanding the opposition of all enemies;[2] and of enjoying the communion of saints, the ordinary means of salvation,[3] and offers of grace by Christ to all the members of it in the ministry of the gospel, testifying, that whosoever believes in Him shall be saved,[4] and excluding none that will come unto Him.[5]

[1] Isa. 4:5-6; 1 Tim. 4:10
[2] Ps. 115:1-2, 9; Isa. 31:4-5; Zech. 12:2-4, 8-9
[3] Acts 2:39, 42
[4] Ps. 147:19-20; Rom. 9:4; Eph. 4:11-12; Mark 16:15-16
[5] John 6:37

Q. 64: What is the invisible Church?

A.: The invisible Church is the whole number of the elect, that have been, are, or shall be gathered into one under Christ the head.[1]

[1] Eph. 1:10, 22-23; John 10:16; 11:52

Belgic Confession (1561)	Heidelberg Catechism (1563)	Second Helvetic Confession (1566)	Canons of Dort (1619)

[3] Luke 1:32-33; Ps. 89:37-38; 110:2-4

[4] Matt. 16:18; John 16:33; Gen. 22:17; 2 Tim. 2:19

[5] Luke 12:32; Isa. 1:9; Rev. 12:6,14; Luke 17:21; Matt. 16:18

[6] Rom. 12:4; 11:2,4; 1 Ki. 19:18; Isa. 1:9; Rom. 9:29

[7] Acts 4:32

[8] Eph. 4:3-4

Article 28

Every One is Bound to Join Himself to the True Church

We believe, since this holy congregation is an assembly of those who are saved, and out of it there is no salvation,[1] that no person of whatsoever state or condition he may be, ought to withdraw himself to live in a separate state from it;[2] but that all men are in duty bound to join and unite themselves with it; maintaining the unity of the Church;[3] submitting themselves to the doctrine and discipline thereof; bowing their necks under the yoke of Jesus Christ;[4] and as mutual members of the same body,[5] serving to the edification of the brethren, according to the talents God has given them.

And that this may be the more effectually observed, it is the duty of all believers, according to the Word of God, to separate themselves from those who do not belong to the Church,[6] and to join themselves to this congregation, wheresoever God hath established it,[7] even though the magistrates and edicts of princes be against it; yea, though they should suffer death or any other corporal

Second Helvetic Confession

heaven, and triumphs over all those things overcome, and continually rejoices before the Lord. Yet these two Churches have, notwithstanding, a communion and fellowship between themselves.

4. Moreover, the Church militant upon the earth has evermore had many particular Churches, which must all, notwithstanding, be referred to the unity of the catholic Church. This militant Church was otherwise ordered and governed before the law, among the patriarchs; otherwise under Moses, by the law; and otherwise of Christ, by the gospel. There are but two sorts of people, for the most part, mentioned: to wit, the Israelites and the Gentiles; or they who, of the Jews and Gentiles, were gathered to make a Church. There are also two Testaments, the Old and the New. Yet both these sorts of people have had, and still have, one fellowship, one salvation, in one and the same Messiah; in whom, as members of one body, they are all joined together under one head, and by one faith are all partakers of one and the same spiritual meat and drink. Yet here we do acknowledge a diversity of times, and a diversity in the pledges and signs of Christ promised and exhibited; and that now, the ceremonies being abolished, the light shines unto us more clearly, our gifts and graces are more abundant, and our liberty is more full and ample.

5. This holy Church of God is called "the temple of the living God" (2 Cor. 6:16), builded of "lively stones, . . . a spiritual house" (1 Pet. 2:5), founded upon a rock (Matt. 16:18), "which cannot be moved" (Heb. 12:28), upon a foundation besides which none can be laid (1 Cor. 3:11). Whereupon it is called "the pillar and ground of the truth" (1 Tim. 3:15), that does not err, so long as it relies upon the rock Christ, and upon the foundation of the prophets and apostles. And no marvel if it do err, so often as it forsakes Him who is the alone truth. This Church is also called "a virgin" (2 Cor. 11:2), and the "spouse" of Christ (Songs 4:8), and his "beloved" (Songs 5:16). For the apostle says, "I have espoused you to one husband, that I may present you as a chaste virgin to Christ" (2 Cor. 11:2). The Church is called a flock of sheep under one shepherd, even Christ (Ezek. 34:22-23; John 10:16); also, the body of Christ (Col. 1:24), because the faithful are the lively members of Christ, having Him for their head.

6. It is the head which has the preeminence in the body, and from whence the whole body receives life; by whose spirit it is governed in all things; of whom, also, it receives increase, that it may grow up. Also, there is but one head to the body, which has agreement with the body; and therefore the Church cannot have any other head besides Christ. For as the Church is a spiritual body, so must it needs have a spiritual head like unto itself. Neither can it be governed by any other spirit than by the Spirit of Christ. Wherefore Paul says, "And He is the head of the body, the Church: who is the beginning, the firstborn from the dead; that in all things he might have the pre-eminence" (Col. 1:18). And in another place, "Christ," saith he, "is the head of the Church: and He is the saviour of the body" (Eph. 5:23). And again, "and gave Him to be the head over all things to the Church, which is His body, the fullness of Him that filleth all in all" (Eph. 1:22-23). Again, "may grow up into Him in all things, which is the head, even Christ: from whom the whole body fitly joined together. . . maketh increase" (Eph. 4:15-16). And therefore we do not allow of the doctrine of the Romish prelates, who would make the pope the general pastor and supreme head of the Church militant here on earth, and the very vicar of Jesus Christ, who has (as they say) all fullness of power and sovereign authority in the Church. For we hold and teach that Christ our Lord is, and remains still, the only universal pastor, and highest bishop, before God His Father; and that in the Church He performs all the duties of a pastor or bishop, even to the world's end; and

Westminster Confession of Faith (1647)	Westminster Shorter Catechism (1647)	Westminster Larger Catechism (1648)
6. There is no other head of the Church but the Lord Jesus Christ.[1] Nor can the pope of Rome, in any sense, be head thereof, but is that Antichrist, that man of sin, and son of perdition, that exalteth himself, in the Church, against Christ and all that is called God.[2]		

[1] Col. 1:18; Eph. 1:22
[2] Matt. 23:8-10; 2 Thes. 2:3-4, 8-9; Rev. 13:6

Belgic Confession (1561)	Heidelberg Catechism (1563)	Second Helvetic Confession (1566)	Canons of Dort (1619)

punishment.[8] Therefore all those who separate themselves from the same, or do not join themselves to it, act contrary to the ordinance of God.

---

[1] 1 Pet. 3:20; Joel 2:32
[2] Acts 2:40; Isa. 52:11
[3] Ps. 22:23; Eph. 4:3,12; Heb. 2:12
[4] Ps. 2:10-12; Matt. 11:29
[5] Eph. 4:12,16; 1 Cor. 12:12, etc.
[6] Acts 2:40; Isa. 52:11; 2 Cor. 6:17; Rev. 18:4
[7] Matt. 12:30; 24:28; Isa. 49:22; Rev. 17:14
[8] Dan. 3:17-18; 6:8-10; Rev. 14:14; Acts 4:17,19; 17:7; 18:13

Article 29

The Marks of the True Church, and Wherein She Differs From the False Church

We believe that we ought diligently and circumspectly to discern from the Word of God which is the true Church, since all sects which are in the world assume to themselves the name of the Church. But we speak here not of hypocrites, who are mixed in the Church with the good, yet are not of the Church, though externally in it;[1] but we say that the body and communion of the true Church must be distinguished from all sects who call themselves the Church.

The marks by which the true Church is known are these: if the pure doctrine of the gospel is preached therein;[2] if she maintains the pure administration of the sacraments as instituted by Christ;[3] if church discipline is exercised in punishing of sin;[4] in short, if all things are managed according to

Second Helvetic Confession (cont.)

therefore stands not in need of any other to supply His room. For he is said to have a substitute, who is absent; but Christ is present with His Church, and is the head that gives life thereunto. He did straitly forbid His apostles and their successors all superiority or dominion in the Church. They, therefore, that by gainsaying set themselves against so manifest a truth, and bring another kind of government into the Church, who sees not that they are to be counted in the number of them of the apostles of Christ prophesied as in Peter, (2 Pet. 2:1), and Paul, (Acts 20:29; 2 Cor. 11:13; 2 Thes. 2:8-9), and in many other places?

7. Now, by taking away the Romish head we do not bring any confusion or disorder into the Church. For we teach that the government of the Church which the apostles set down is sufficient to keep the Church in due order; which, from the beginning, while as yet it wanted such a Romish head as is now pretended to keep it in order, was not disordered or full of confusion. The Romish head doth maintain indeed his tyranny and corruption which have been brought into the Church; but in the meantime he hinders, resists, and, with all the might he can make, cuts off the right and lawful reformation of the Church.

8. They object against us that there have been great strifes and dissensions in our Churches since they did sever themselves from the Church of Rome; and that therefore they cannot be true churches. As though there were never in the Church of Rome any sects, any contentions and quarrels; and that, in matters of religion, maintained not so much in the schools as in the holy chairs, even in the audience of the people. We know that the apostle said, "God is not the author of confusion, but of peace" (1 Cor. 14:33), and, "Whereas there is among you envying, and strife, and divisions, are ye not carnal?" (1 Cor. 3:3). Yet may we not deny that God was in that Church planted by the apostle; and that the Apostolic Church was a true Church, howsoever there were strifes and dissensions in it. The apostle Paul reprehended Peter, an apostle (Gal. 2:11), and Barnabas fell at variance with Paul (Acts 15:39). Great contention arose in the Church of Antioch between them that preached one and the same Christ, as Luke records in the Acts of the Apostles (chap. 15:2). And there have at all times been great contentions in the Church, and the most excellent doctors of the Church have, about no small matters, differed in opinion; yet so as, in the meantime, the Church ceased not to be the Church for all these contentions. For thus it pleases God to use the dissensions that arise in the Church, to the glory of His Name, to the setting forth of the truth, and to the end that such as are not approved might be manifest (1 Cor. 11:19).

9. Now, as we acknowledge no other head of the Church than Christ, so do we not acknowledge every church to be the true Church which vaunts herself so to be; but we teach that to be the true Church indeed in which the marks and tokens of the true Church are to be found. Firstly and chiefly, the lawful and sincere preaching of the Word of God as it is left unto us in the writings of the prophets and the apostles, which do all seem to lead us unto Christ, who in the gospel has said, "My sheep hear my voice, and I know them, and they follow me: and I give unto them eternal life. A stranger will they not follow, but will flee from him: for they know not the voice of strangers" (John 10:5, 27-28).

10. And they that are such in the Church of God have all but one faith and one spirit; and therefore they worship but one God, and Him alone they serve in Spirit and in truth, loving Him with all their hearts and with all their strength, praying unto Him alone through Jesus Christ, the only Mediator and Intercessor; and they seek not life or justice but only in Christ, and

Westminster Confession of Faith (1647)	Westminster Shorter Catechism (1647)	Westminster Larger Catechism (1648)

Belgic Confession (cont.)

the pure Word of God, all things contrary thereto rejected,[5] and Jesus Christ acknowledged as the only Head of the Church.[6] Hereby the true Church may certainly be known, from which no man has a right to separate himself.

With respect to those who are members of the Church, they may be known by the marks of Christians, namely, by faith;[7] and when they have received Jesus Christ the only Savior,[8] they avoid sin, follow after righteousness,[9] love the true God and their neighbor, neither turn aside to the right or left, and crucify the flesh with the works thereof.[10] But this is not to be understood as if there did not remain in them great infirmities; but they fight against them through the Spirit all the days of their life,[11] continually taking their refuge in the blood, death, passion, and obedience of our Lord Jesus Christ, *in whom they have remission of sins through faith in Him.*[12]

As for the false Church, she ascribes more power and authority to herself and her ordinances than to the Word of God,[13] and will not submit herself to the yoke of Christ.[14] Neither does she administer the sacraments, as appointed by Christ in His Word, but adds to and takes from them as she thinks

proper; she relieth more upon men than upon Christ; and persecutes those who live holily according to the Word of God,[15] and rebuke her for her errors, covetousness, and idolatry.[16] These two Churches are easily known and distinguished from each other.

---

[1] Matt. 13:22; 2 Tim. 2:18-20; Rom. 9:6
[2] John 10:27; Eph. 2:20; Acts 17:11-12; Col. 1:23; John 8:47
[3] Matt. 28:19; Luke 22:19; 1 Cor. 11:23
[4] Matt. 18:15-18; 2 Thes. 3:14-15
[5] Matt. 28:2; Gal. 1:6-8
[6] Eph. 1:22-23; John 10:4-5,14
[7] Eph. 1:13; John 17:20
[8] 1 John 4:2
[9] 1 John 3:8-10
[10] Rom. 6:2; Gal. 5:24
[11] Rom. 7:6, 17; Gal. 5:17
[12] Col. 1:14
[13] Col. 2:18-19
[14] Ps. 2:3
[15] Rev. 12:4; John 16:2
[16] Rev. 17:3-4, 6

Second Helvetic Confession (cont.)

by faith in Him; because they do acknowledge Christ the only Head and foundation of His Church, and, being surely founded on Him, do daily repair themselves by repentance, and do with patience bear the cross laid upon them; and, besides, by unfeigned love joining themselves to all the members of Christ, do thereby declare themselves to be the disciples of Christ, by continuing in the bond of peace and holy unity. They do withal communicate in the sacraments ordained by Christ, and delivered unto us by His apostles, using them in no other manner than as they received them from the Lord Himself. That saying of the apostle Paul is well known to all, "I have received of the Lord that which also I delivered unto you" (1 Cor. 11:23). For which cause we condemn all such churches, as strangers from the true Church of Christ, which are not such as we have heard they ought to be, howsoever, in the meantime, they brag of the succession of bishops, of unity, and of antiquity. Moreover, we have in charge from the apostles of Christ to "flee from idolatry" (1 Cor. 10:14; 1 John 5:21), and to come out of Babylon, and to have no fellowship with her, unless we mean to be partakers with her of all God's plagues laid upon her (Rev. 18:4; 2 Cor. 6:17).

11. But as for communicating with the true Church of Christ, we so highly esteem it that we say plainly that none can live before God who do not communicate with the true Church of God, but separate themselves from the same. For as without the ark of Noah there was no escaping when the world perished in the flood; even so do we believe that without Christ, who in the Church offers Himself to be enjoyed of the elect, there can be no certain salvation; and therefore we

teach that such as would be saved must in no wise separate themselves from the true Church of Christ.

12. But as yet we do not so strictly shut up the Church within those marks before mentioned, as thereby to exclude all those out of the Church who either do not participate of the sacraments (not willingly, nor upon contempt; but who, being constrained by necessity, do against their will abstain from them, or else do want them), or in whom faith does sometimes fail, though not quite decay, nor altogether die; or in whom some slips and errors of infirmity may be found. For we know that God had some friends in the world that were not of the commonwealth of Israel. We know what befell the people of God in the captivity of Babylon, where they were without their sacrifices seventy years. We know what happened to St. Peter, who denied his Master, and what is wont daily to happen among the faithful and chosen of God who go astray and are full of infirmities. We know, moreover, what manner of churches the churches in Galatia and Corinth were in the apostles' time, in which St. Paul condemns many and heinous crimes; yet he calls them holy Churches of Christ (1 Cor. 1:2; Gal. 1:2).

13. Yea, and it happens sometimes that God in His just judgment suffers the truth of His Word, and the catholic faith, and His own true worship, to be so obscured and defaced that the Church seems almost quite razed out, and not so much as a face of a Church to remain; as we see fell out in the days of Elijah (1 Ki. 19:10, 14), and at other times. And yet, in the meantime, the Lord has in this world, even in this darkness, His true worshippers, and those not a few, but even seven

Belgic Confession (1561)	Heidelberg Catechism (1563)	Second Helvetic Confession (1566)	Canons of Dort (1619)

Second Helvetic Confession (cont.)

thousand and more (1 Ki. 19:18; Rev. 7:4, 9). For the apostle cries, "The foundation of God standeth sure, having this seal, The Lord knoweth them that are His," etc. (2 Tim. 2:19). Whereupon the Church of God may be termed invisible; not that the men whereof it consists are invisible, but because, being hidden from our sight, and known only unto God, it cannot be discerned by the judgment of man.

14. Again, not all that are reckoned in the number of the Church are saints, and lively and true members of the Church. For there are many hypocrites, who outwardly do hear the Word of God, and publicly receive the sacraments, and do seem to pray unto God alone through Christ, to confess Christ to be their only righteousness, and to worship God, and to exercise the duties of charity to the brethren, and for a while through patience to endure in troubles and calamities. And yet they are altogether destitute of the inward illumination of the Spirit of God, of faith and sincerity of heart, and of perseverance or continuance to the end. And these men are, for the most part, at length laid open in their true character. For the apostle John says, "They went out from us, but they were not of us: for if they had been of us, they would no doubt have continued with us" (1 John 2:19). Yet these men, while they do pretend religion, are accounted to be in the Church. Even as traitors in a commonwealth, before they be detected, are accounted in the number of good citizens; and as the cockle and darnel and chaff are found among the wheat; and as wens and swellings are in a perfect body, when they are rather diseases and deformities than true members of the body. And therefore the Church is very well compared to a drag-net, which draws up fishes of all sorts; and to a field, wherein is found both darnel and good corn (Matt. 13:26, 47). Hence we must be very careful not to judge rashly before the time, nor to exclude, and cast off or cut away, those whom the Lord would not have excluded nor cut off, or whom, without some damage to the Church, we cannot separate from it. Again, we must be very vigilant lest the godly, falling fast asleep, the wicked grow stronger, and do some mischief in the Church.

15. Furthermore, we teach that it is carefully to be marked, wherein especially the truth and unity of the Church consists, lest that we either rashly breed or nourish schisms in the Church. It consists not in outward rites and ceremonies, but rather in the truth and unity of the catholic faith. This catholic faith is not taught us by the ordinances or laws of men, but by the holy Scriptures, a compendious and short sum whereof is the Apostles' Creed. And, therefore, we read in the ancient writers that there were manifold diversities of ceremonies, but that those were always free; neither did any man think that the unity of the Church was thereby broken or dissolved. We say, then, that the true unity of the Church does consist in several points of doctrine, in the true and uniform preaching of the gospel, and in such rites as the Lord Himself has expressly set down. And here we urge that saying of the apostle very earnestly, "Let us therefore, as many as be perfect, be thus minded: and if in any thing ye be otherwise minded, God shall reveal even this unto you. Nevertheless, whereto we have already attained, let us walk by the same rule, let us mind the same thing" (Phil. 3:15-16).

Westminster Confession of Faith (1647)	Westminster Shorter Catechism (1647)	Westminster Larger Catechism (1648)

Belgic Confession (1561)	Heidelberg Catechism (1563)	Second Helvetic Confession (1566)	Canons of Dort (1619)

Union with Christ and the Communion of Saints

Q. 32: But why art thou called a Christian?

A.: Because I am a member of Christ by faith,[1] and thus am partaker of His anointing,[2] that so I may confess His name,[3] and present myself a living sacrifice of thankfulness to Him;[4] and also that with a free and good conscience I may fight against sin and Satan in this life,[5] and afterwards reign with Him eternally over all creatures.[6]

[1] 1 Cor. 6:15
[2] 1 John 2:27; Joel 2:28
[3] Matt. 10:32
[4] Rom. 12:1
[5] Eph. 6:11-12; 1 Tim. 1:18-19
[6] 2 Tim. 2:12

Q. 52: What comfort is it to thee that "Christ shall come again to judge the quick and the dead"?

A.: That in all my sorrows and persecutions, with uplifted head I look for the very same person, who before offered Himself for my sake to the tribunal of God, and has removed all curse from me, to come as judge from heaven,[1] who shall cast all His and my enemies into everlasting condemnation,[2] but shall translate me with all His chosen ones to Himself, into heavenly joys and glory.[3]

[1] Luke 21:28; Rom. 8:23-24; 1 Thes. 4:16
[2] 2 Thes. 1:6-9; Matt. 25:41
[3] Matt. 25:34

Westminster Confession of Faith (1647)	Westminster Shorter Catechism (1647)	Westminster Larger Catechism (1648)

XXVI. Of the Communion of Saints

1. All saints, that are united to Jesus Christ their Head, by His Spirit, and by faith, have fellowship with Him in His grace, sufferings, death, resurrection, and glory;[1] and, being united to one another in love, they have communion in each other's gifts and graces,[2] and are obliged to the performance of such duties, public and private, as do conduce to their mutual good, both in the inward and outward man.[3]

[1] 1 John 1:3; Eph. 3:16-19; John 1:16; Eph. 2:5-6; Phil. 3:10; Rom. 6:5-6; 2 Tim. 2:12
[2] Eph. 4:15-16; 1 Cor. 12:7; 3:21-23; Col. 2:19
[3] 1 Thes. 5:11, 14; Rom. 1:11-12, 14; 1 John 3:16-18; Gal. 6:10

2. Saints by profession are bound to maintain a holy fellowship and communion in the worship of God, and in performing such other spiritual services as tend to their mutual edification;[1] as also in relieving each other in outward things, according to their several abilities and necessities. Which communion, as God offereth opportunity, is to be extended unto all those who, in every place, call upon the name of the Lord Jesus.[2]

[1] Heb. 10:24-25; Acts 2:42, 46; Isa. 2:3; 1 Cor. 11:20
[2] Acts 2:44-45; 2 Cor. 8; 9; 1 John 3:17; Acts 11:29-30

3. This communion which the saints have with Christ doth not make them in any wise partakers of the substance of His Godhead; or to be equal with Christ in any respect: either of which to affirm is impious and blasphemous.[1] Nor doth their communion one with another, as saints, take away, or infringe the title or propriety which each man hath in his goods and possessions.[2]

[1] Col. 1:18-19; 1 Cor. 8:6; Isa. 42:8; 1 Tim. 6:15-16; Ps. 45:7; Heb. 1:8-9
[2] Exod. 20:15; Eph. 4:28; Acts 5:4

Q. 37: What benefits do believers receive from Christ at death?
A.: The souls of believers are at their death made perfect in holiness,[1] and do immediately pass into glory;[2] and their bodies, being still united to Christ,[3] do rest in their graves[4] till the resurrection.[5]

[1] Heb. 12:23
[2] 2 Cor. 5:1, 6, 8; Phil. 1:23; Luke 23:43
[3] 1 Thes. 4:14
[4] Isa. 57:2
[5] Job 19:26-27

Q. 38: What benefits do believers receive from Christ at the resurrection?
A.: At the resurrection, believers, being raised up in glory,[1] shall be openly acknowledged and acquitted in the day of judgment,[2] and made perfectly blessed in the full enjoying of God[3] to all eternity.[4]

[1] 1 Cor. 15:43
[2] Matt. 25:23; 10:32
[3] 1 John 3:2; 1 Cor. 13:12
[4] 1 Thes. 4:17-18

Q. 65: What special benefits do the members of the invisible Church enjoy by Christ?
A.: The members of the invisible Church by Christ enjoy union and communion with Him in grace and glory.[1]

[1] John 17:21; Eph. 2:5-6; John 17:24

Q. 66: What is that union which the elect have with Christ?
A.: The union which the elect have with Christ is the work of God's grace,[1] whereby they are spiritually and mystically, yet really and inseparably, joined to Christ as their Head and Husband;[2] which is done in their effectual calling.[3]

[1] Eph. 1:22; 2:6-8
[2] 1 Cor. 6:17; John 10:28; Eph. 5:23, 30
[3] 1 Pet. 5:10; 1 Cor. 1:9

Q. 82: What is the communion in glory which the members of the invisible Church have with Christ?
A.: The communion in glory which the members of the invisible Church have with Christ, is in this life,[1] immediately after death,[2] and at last perfected at the resurrection and day of judgment.[3]

[1] 2 Cor. 3:18
[2] Luke 23:43
[3] 1 Thes. 4:17

Q. 83: What is the communion in glory with Christ which the members of the invisible Church enjoy in this life?
A.: The members of the invisible Church have communicated to them in this life the first fruits of glory with Christ, as they are members of Him their Head, and so in Him are interested in that glory which He is fully possessed of;[1] and as an earnest thereof, enjoy the sense of God's love,[2] peace of conscience, joy in the Holy Ghost, and hope of glory;[3] as, on the contrary, sense of God's revenging wrath, horror of conscience, and a fearful expectation of judgment, are to the wicked the beginning of their torments which they shall endure after death.[4]

[1] Eph. 2:5-6
[2] Rom. 5:5; 2 Cor. 1:22
[3] Rom. 5:1-2; 14:17
[4] Gen. 4:13; Matt. 27:4; Heb. 10:27; Rom. 2:9; Mark 9:44

Belgic Confession (1561)	Heidelberg Catechism (1563)	Second Helvetic Confession (1566)	Canons of Dort (1619)

Q. 55: What do you understand by "the communion of saints"?

A.: First, that all and every one who believes, being members of Christ, are in common, partakers of Him, and of all His riches and gifts;[1] secondly, that every one must know it to be his duty, readily and cheerfully to employ his gifts, for the advantage and salvation of other members.[2]

---
[1] John 1:3-4; Rom. 8:32; 1 Cor. 12:13
[2] 1 Cor. 13:5; Phil. 2:4-6

Q. 57: What comfort doth the "resurrection of the body" afford thee?

A.: That not only my soul after this life shall be immediately taken up to Christ its Head;[1] but also, that this my body, being raised by the power of Christ, shall be reunited with my soul, and made like unto the glorious body of Christ.[2]

---
[1] Luke 23:43; Phil. 1:23
[2] 1 Cor. 15:53; Job 19:25-26

Q. 58: What comfort takest thou from the article of "life everlasting"?

A.: That since I now feel in my heart the beginning of eternal joy,[1] after this life I shall inherit perfect salvation,[2] which "eye hath not seen, nor ear heard, neither have entered into the heart of man" to conceive,[3] and that, to praise God therein for ever.

---
[1] 2 Cor. 5:2-3, 6; Rom. 14:17
[2] Ps. 10:11
[3] 1 Cor. 2:9

The Government and Office-bearers of the Church

Article 30

The Government of and Offices in the Church

We believe that this true Church must be governed by the spiritual policy which our Lord hath taught us in His Word namely, that there must be ministers or pastors to preach the Word of God, and to administer the sacraments;[1] also elders and deacons, who, together with the pastors, form the council of the Church;[2] that by these means the true religion may be preserved, and the true doctrine everywhere propagated, likewise transgressors punished and restrained by spiritual means;[3] also that the poor and dis-

Q. 82: Are they also to be admitted to this supper, who, by confession and life, declare themselves unbelieving and ungodly?

A.: No; for by this, the covenant of God would be profaned and His wrath kindled against the whole congregation;[1] therefore it is the duty of the Christian Church, according to the appointment of Christ and His apostles, to exclude such persons[2] by the keys of the kingdom of heaven till they show amendment of life.

---
[1] 1 Cor. 10:21; 1 Cor. 11:30-31; Isa. 1:11, 13; Jer. 7:21; Ps. 50:16, 22
[2] Matt. 18:17-18

XIV. Of Repentance, and the Conversion of Man

5. As concerning the keys of the kingdom of heaven, which the Lord committed to His apostles, they [the papists] prate many strange things; and of these keys they make swords, spears, scepters, and crowns, and full power over mighty kingdoms, yea, and over men's souls and bodies. But we, judging uprightly, according to the Word of God, do say that all ministers, truly called, have and exercise the keys, or the use of them, when they preach the gospel; that is to say, when they teach, exhort, reprove, and keep in order the people committed to their charge. For they do open the kingdom of God to the obedient, and shut it against the disobedient. These keys did the Lord promise to the apostles, in Matt. 16:19; and delivered them, in John 20:23; Mark 16:15-16; Luke 24:47, when He sent forth His disciples, and commanded them to preach the gospel in all the world, and to remit sins. The apostle, in the epistle to the Corinthians, says that the Lord "hath given to us the ministry of reconciliation" (2 Cor. 5:18). And what this was he straightway makes plain and says, "the word of reconciliation" (ver. 19). And yet more plainly expounding his words, he

Westminster Confession of Faith (1647)	Westminster Shorter Catechism (1647)	Westminster Larger Catechism (1648)

Westminster Larger Catechism (cont.)

Q. 86: What is the communion in glory with Christ, which the members of the invisible Church enjoy immediately after death?

A.: The communion in glory with Christ, which the members of the invisible Church enjoy immediately after death, is, in that their souls are then made perfect in holiness,[1] and received into the highest heavens,[2] where they behold the face of God in light and glory,[3] waiting for the full redemption of their bodies,[4] which even in death continue united to Christ,[5] and rest in their graves as in their beds,[6] till at the last day they be again united to their souls.[7] Whereas the souls of the wicked are at their death cast into hell, where they remain in torments and utter darkness, and their bodies kept in their graves, as in their prisons, till the resurrection and judgment of the great day.[8]

[1] Heb. 12:23
[2] 2 Cor. 5:1, 6, 8; Phil. 1:23; Acts 3:21; Eph. 4:10
[3] 1 John 3:2; 1 Cor. 13:12
[4] Rom. 8:23; Ps. 16:9
[5] 1 Thes. 4:14
[6] Isa. 57:2
[7] Job 19:26-27
[8] Luke 16:23-24; Acts 1:25; Jude 6-7

Q. 90: What shall be done to the righteous at the day of judgment?

A.: At the day of judgment, the righteous, being caught up to Christ in the clouds,[1] shall be set on His right hand, and there openly acknowledged and acquitted,[2] shall join with Him in the judging of reprobate angels and men,[3] and shall be received into heaven,[4] where they shall be fully and for ever freed from all sin and misery;[5] filled with inconceivable joys,[6] made perfectly holy and happy both in body and soul, in the company of innumerable saints and holy angels,[7] but especially in the immediate vision and fruition of God the Father, of our Lord Jesus Christ, and of the Holy Spirit, to all eternity.[8] And this is the perfect and full communion, which the members of the invisible Church shall enjoy with Christ in glory, at the resurrection and day of judgment.

[1] 1 Thes. 4:17
[2] Matt. 25:33; 10:32
[3] 1 Cor. 6:2-3
[4] Matt. 25:34, 46
[5] Eph. 5:27; Rev. 14:13
[6] Ps. 16:11
[7] Heb. 12:22-23
[8] 1 John 3:2; 1 Cor. 13:12; 1 Thes. 4:17-18

I. Of the Holy Scripture

6. The whole counsel of God concerning all things necessary for His own glory, man's salvation, faith and life, is either expressly set down in Scripture, or by good and necessary consequence may be deduced from Scripture; unto which nothing at any time is to be added, whether by new revelations of the Spirit, or traditions of men.[1] Nevertheless, we acknowledge the inward illumination of the Spirit of God to be necessary for the saving understanding of such things as are revealed in the Word;[2] and that there are some circumstances concerning the worship of God, and government of the Church, common to human actions and societies, which are to be ordered by the light of nature, and Christian prudence, according to the general rules of the Word, which are always to be observed.[3]

[1] 2 Tim. 3:15-17; Gal. 1:8-9; 2 Thes. 2:2
[2] John 6:45; 1 Cor. 2:9-12
[3] 1 Cor. 11:13-14; 14:26, 40

Belgic Confession (1561)	Heidelberg Catechism (1563)	Second Helvetic Confession (1566)	Canons of Dort (1619)

tressed may be relieved and comforted, according to their necessities. By these means everything will be carried on in the Church with good order and decency, when faithful men are chosen, according to the rule prescribed by St. Paul in his epistle to Timothy.[4]

[1] Eph. 4:11; 1 Cor. 4:1-2; 2 Cor. 5:20; John 20:23; Acts 26:17-18; Luke 10:16
[2] Acts 6:3; 14:23
[3] Matt. 18:17; 1 Cor. 5:4-5
[4] 1 Tim. 3:1; Titus 1:5

Article 31

The Ministers, Elders, and Deacons

We believe that the ministers of God's Word,[1] and the elders and deacons,[2] ought to be chosen to their respective offices by a lawful election of the Church, with calling upon the name of the Lord, and in that order which the Word of God teacheth. Therefore every one must take heed not to intrude himself by indecent means, but is bound to wait till it shall please God to call him;[3] that he may have testimony of his calling, and be certain and assured that it is of the Lord. As for the ministers of God's Word, they have equally the same power and authority wheresoever they are, as they are all ministers of Christ,[4] the only universal Bishop, and the only Head of the Church.[5] Moreover, that this holy ordinance of God may not be violated or slighted, we say that every one ought to esteem the ministers of

Q. 83: What are the keys of the kingdom of heaven?[1]
A.: The preaching of the holy gospel, and Christian discipline,[2] or excommunication out of the Christian Church;[3] by these two, the kingdom of heaven is opened to believers and shut against unbelievers.

[1] Matt. 16:19
[2] John 20:23
[3] Matt. 18:15-18

Q. 84: How is the kingdom of heaven opened and shut by the preaching of the holy gospel?
A.: Thus: when according to the command of Christ[1] it is declared and publicly testified to all and every believer, that, whenever they receive the promise of the gospel by a true faith,[2] all their sins are really forgiven them of God for the sake of Christ's merits; and on the contrary, when it is declared and testified to all unbelievers, and such as do not sincerely repent, that they stand exposed to the wrath of God and eternal condemnation,[3] so long as they are unconverted;[4] according to which testimony of the gospel, God will judge them both in this and in the life to come.

[1] Matt. 28:19
[2] John 3:18, 36; Mark 16:16
[3] 2 Thes. 1:7-9
[4] John 20:21-23; Matt. 16:19; Rom. 2:2, 13-17

Q. 85: How is the kingdom of heaven shut and opened by Christian discipline?

adds, that the ministers of Christ do, as it were, go on an embassage in Christ's name, as if God Himself should by His ministers exhort the people to be reconciled to God (ver. 20); to wit, by faithful obedience. They use the keys, therefore, when they persuade to faith and repentance. Thus do they reconcile men to God; thus they forgive sins; thus they open the kingdom of heaven and bring in the believers; much differing herein from those of whom the Lord spake in the gospel, "Woe unto you, lawyers! for ye have taken away the key of knowledge: ye entered not in yourselves, and them that were entering in ye hindered" (Luke 11:52).

6. Rightly, therefore, and effectually do ministers absolve, when they preach the gospel of Christ, and thereby remission of sins; which is promised to every one that believes, even as every one is baptized; and to testify of it that it does particularly appertain to all. Neither do we imagine that this absolution is made any whit more effectual for that which is mumbled into some priest's ear, or upon some man's head particularly; yet we judge that men must be taught diligently to seek remission of sins in the blood of Christ, and that every one is to be put in mind that forgiveness of sins does belong unto him.

XVIII. *Of the Ministers of the Church, Their Institution and Offices*

1. God has always used His ministers for the gathering or erecting of a Church to Himself, and for the governing and preservation of the same; and still He does, and always will, use them so long as the Church remains on earth. Therefore, the first beginning, institution and office of the ministers, is a most ancient ordinance of God Himself, not a new device appointed by men. True it is that God can, by His power, without any means, take unto Himself a Church from among men; but He had rather deal with men by the ministry of men. Therefore ministers are to be considered, not as ministers by themselves alone, but as the ministers of God, by whose means God does work the salvation of mankind. For which cause we give counsel to beware that we do not so attribute the things appertaining to our conversion and instruction unto the secret virtue of the Holy Spirit as to make void the ecclesiastical ministry. For it behooves us always to have in mind the words of the apostle, "How shall they believe in Him of whom they have not heard? and how shall they hear without a preacher? So then faith cometh by hearing, and hearing by the word of God" (Rom. 10:14, 17). And that also which the Lord says, in the gospel,

Westminster Confession of Faith (1647)	Westminster Shorter Catechism (1647)	Westminster Larger Catechism (1648)

XXX. Of Church Censures

1. The Lord Jesus, as King and Head of His Church, hath therein appointed a government, in the hand of Church officers, distinct from the civil magistrate.[1]

[1] Isa. 9:6-7; 1 Tim. 5:17; 1 Thes. 5:12; Acts 20:17-18; Heb. 13:7, 17, 24; 1 Cor. 12:28; Matt. 28:18-20

2. To these officers the keys of the kingdom of heaven are committed; by virtue whereof, they have power, respectively, to retain, and remit sins; to shut that kingdom against the impenitent, both by the Word, and censures; and to open it unto penitent sinners, by the ministry of the gospel; and by absolution from censures, as occasion shall require.[1]

[1] Matt. 16:19; 18:17-18; John 20:21-23; 2 Cor. 2:6-8

3. Church censures are necessary, for the reclaiming and gaining of offending brethren, for deterring of others from the like offenses, for purging out of that leaven which might infect the whole lump, for vindicating the honor of Christ, and the holy profession of the gospel, and for preventing the wrath of God, which might justly fall upon the Church, if they should suffer His covenant, and the seals thereof, to be profaned by notorious and obstinate offenders.[1]

[1] 1 Cor. 5; 1 Tim. 5:20; Matt. 7:6; 1 Tim. 1:20; 1 Cor. 11:27-34; Jude 23

4. For the better attaining of these ends, the officers of the Church are to proceed by admonition, suspension from the sacrament of the Lord's Supper for a season; and by excommunication from the Church, according to the nature of the crime, and demerit of the person.[1]

[1] 1 Thes. 5:12; 2 Thes. 3:6, 14-15; 1 Cor. 5:4-5, 13; Matt. 18:17; Titus 3:10

XXXI. Of Synods and Councils

1. For the better government, and further edification of the Church, there ought to be such assemblies as are commonly called synods or councils.[1]

[1] Acts 15:2, 4, 6

2. As magistrates may lawfully call a synod of ministers, and other fit persons, to consult and advise with, about matters of religion;[1] so, if magistrates be open enemies to the Church, the ministers of Christ, of themselves, by virtue of their office, or they, with other fit persons upon delegation from their Churches, may meet together in such assemblies.[2]

Belgic Confession (1561)	Heidelberg Catechism (1563)	Second Helvetic Confession (1566)	Canons of Dort (1619)

Belgic Confession (1561)

God's Word and the elders of the Church very highly for their work's sake, and be at peace with them without murmuring, strife, or contention,[6] as much as possible.

[1] 1 Tim. 5:22
[2] Acts 6:3
[3] Jer. 23:21; Heb. 5:4; Acts 1:23; 13:2
[4] 1 Cor. 4:1; 3:9; 2 Cor. 5:20; Acts 26:16-17
[5] 1 Pet. 2:25; 5:4; Isa. 61:1; Eph. 1:22; Col. 1:18
[6] 1 Thes. 5:12-13; 1 Tim. 5:17; Heb. 13:17

Article 32

The Order and Discipline of the Church

In the meantime we believe, though it is useful and beneficial, that those who are rulers of the Church institute and establish certain ordinances among themselves for maintaining the body of the Church; yet they ought studiously to take care that they do not depart from those things which Christ, our only Master, hath instituted.[1] And therefore, we reject all human inventions, and all laws which man would introduce into the worship of God, thereby to bind and compel the conscience in any manner whatever.[2]

Therefore we admit only of that which tends to nourish and preserve concord and unity, and to keep all men in obedience to God. For this purpose excommunication or church discipline is requisite, with the several circumstances belonging to it, according to the Word of God.[3]

Heidelberg Catechism (1563)

A.: Thus: when according to the command of Christ[1] those, who under the name of Christians, maintain doctrines or practices inconsistent therewith,[2] and will not, after having been often brotherly admonished, renounce their errors and wicked course of life, are complained of to the Church or to those[3] who are thereunto appointed by the Church;[4] and if they despise their admonition, are by them forbidden the use of the sacraments;[5] whereby they are excluded from the Christian Church and by God Himself from the kingdom of Christ; and when they promise and show real amendment, are again received as members of Christ and His Church.[6]

[1] Matt. 18:15
[2] 1 Cor. 5:12
[3] Matt. 18:15-18
[4] Rom. 12:7-9; 1 Cor. 12:28; 1 Tim. 5:17; 2 Thes. 3:14
[5] Matt. 18:17; 1 Cor. 5:3-5
[6] 2 Cor. 2:6-8, 10-11; Luke 15:18

Second Helvetic Confession (1566)

"Verily, verily, I say unto you, he that receiveth whomsoever I send receiveth Me; and he that receiveth Me receiveth Him that sent Me" (John 13:20). Likewise what a man of Macedonia, appearing in a vision to Paul, being then in Asia, said unto him, "Come over into Macedonia, and help us" (Acts 16:9). And in another place the same apostle says, "We are labourers together with God; ye are God's husbandry, ye are God's building" (1 Cor. 3:9).

2. Yet, on the other side, we must take heed that we do not attribute too much to the ministers and ministry; herein remembering also the words of our Lord in the gospel, "No man can come to Me, except the Father which hath sent Me draw him" (John 6:44), and the words of the apostle, "Who then is Paul, and who is Apollos, but ministers by whom ye believed, even as the Lord gave to every man? So then neither is he that planteth any thing, neither he that watereth; but God that giveth the increase" (1 Cor. 3:5, 7). Therefore let us believe that God does teach us by His Word, outwardly through His ministers, and does inwardly move and persuade the hearts of His elect unto belief by His Holy Spirit; and that therefore we ought to render all the glory of this whole benefit unto God. But we have spoken of this matter in the first chapter of this our Declaration.

3. God has used for His ministers, even from the beginning of the world, the best and most eminent men in the world (for, although some of them were inexperienced in worldly wisdom or philosophy, yet surely in true divinity they were most excellent) — namely, the patriarchs, to whom He spake very often by His angels. For the patriarchs were the prophets or teachers of their age, whom God, for this purpose, would have to live many years, that they might be, as it were, fathers and lights of the world. They were followed by Moses and the prophets renowned throughout all the world.

4. Then, after all these, our heavenly Father sent His only-begotten Son, the most perfect teacher of the world; in whom is hidden the wisdom of God, and from whom we derive that most holy, perfect, and pure doctrine of the gospel. For He chose unto Himself disciples, whom He made apostles; and they, going out into the whole world, gathered together churches in all places by the preaching of the gospel. And afterward they ordained pastors and teachers in all churches, by the commandment of Christ; who, by such as succeeded them, has taught and governed the Church unto this day. Therefore, as God gave unto His ancient people the patriarchs, together

Westminster Confession of Faith (1647)	Westminster Shorter Catechism (1647)	Westminster Larger Catechism (1648)

[1] Isa. 49:23; 1 Tim. 2:1-2; 2 Chron. 19:8-11; 29:1-36; 30:1-27; Mal. 2:4-5; Prov. 11:14.
[2] Acts 15:2, 4, 22-23, 25

3. It belongeth to synods and councils, ministerially to determine controversies of faith, and cases of conscience; to set down rules and directions for the better ordering of the public worship of God, and government of His Church; to receive complaints in cases of maladministration, and authoritatively to determine the same: which decrees and determinations, if consonant to the Word of God, are to be received with reverence and submission; not only for their agreement with the Word, but also for the power whereby they are made, as being an ordinance of God appointed thereunto in His Word.[1]

[1] Acts 15:15, 19, 24, 27-31; 16:4; Matt. 18:17-20

4. All synods or councils, since the apostles' times, whether general or particular, may err; and many have erred. Therefore they are not to be made the rule of faith or practice; but to be used as a help in both.[1]

[1] Eph. 2:20; Acts 17:11; 1 Cor. 2:5; 2 Cor. 1:24

5. Synods and councils are to handle, or conclude, nothing but that which is ecclesiastical; and are not to intermeddle with civil affairs which concern the commonwealth, unless by way of humble petition in cases extraordinary; or, by way of advice, for satisfaction of conscience, if they be thereunto required by the civil magistrate.[1]

[1] Luke 12:13-14; John 18:36

Belgic Confession (1561)	Heidelberg Catechism (1563)	Second Helvetic Confession (1566)	Canons of Dort (1619)
[1] Col. 2:6-7 [2] 1 Cor. 7:23; Matt. 15:9; Isa. 29:13; Gal. 5:1; Rom. 16:17-18 [3] Matt. 18:17; 1 Cor. 5:5; 1 Tim. 1:20		with Moses and the prophets, so also to His people under the new covenant He sent His only-begotten Son, and, with Him, the apostles and teachers of this Church. 5. Furthermore, the ministers of the new covenant are termed by divers names; for they are called apostles, prophets, evangelists, bishops, elders, pastors, and teachers (1 Cor. 12:28; Eph. 6:11). The apostles remained in no certain place, but gathered together divers churches throughout the whole world; which Churches,	

Second Helvetic confession (cont.)

when they were once established, there ceased to be any more apostles, and in their places were particular pastors appointed in every church. The prophets, in old time, did foresee and foretell things to come; and, besides, did interpret the Scriptures; and such are found some among us at this day. They were called evangelists, who were the penmen of the history of the gospel, and were also preachers of the gospel of Christ; as the apostle Paul gives in charge unto Timothy, "do the work of an evangelist" (2 Tim. 4:5). Bishops are the overseers and watchmen of the Church, who distribute food and other necessities to the Church. The elders are the ancients and, as it were, the senators and fathers of the Church, governing it with wholesome counsel. The pastors both keep the Lord's flock, and also provide things necessary for it. The teachers do instruct and teach the true faith and godliness. Therefore the Church ministers that now are may be called bishops, elders, pastors, and teachers.

6. But in process of time there were many more names of ministers brought into the Church. For some were created patriarchs, others archbishops, others suffragans; also, metropolitans, archdeacons, deacons, subdeacons, acolytes, exorcists, choristers, porters, and I know not what others, as cardinals, provosts, and priors; abbots, greater and lesser; orders, higher and lower. But touching all these, we little heed what they have been in times past, or what they are now; it is sufficient for us that, so much as concerns ministers, we have the doctrine of the apostles.

7. We, therefore, knowing certainly that monks, and the orders or sects of them, are instituted neither by Christ nor by His apostles, we teach that they are so far from being profitable that they are pernicious and hurtful unto the Church of God. For, although in former times they were tolerable (when they lived solitarily, getting their livings with their own hands, and were burdensome to none, but did in all places obey their pastors, even as laymen), yet what kind of men they be now all the world sees and perceives. They pretend I know not what vows, but they lead a life altogether disagreeing from their vows; so that the very best of them may justly be numbered among those of whom the apostle speaks: "We hear that there are some which walk among you disorderly, working not at all, but are busybodies," etc. (2 Thes. 3:11). Therefore, we have no such in our churches; and, besides, we teach that they should not be suffered to rout in the Churches of Christ.

8. Furthermore, no man ought to usurp the honor of the ecclesiastical ministry; that is to say, greedily to pluck it to himself by bribes, or any evil shifts, or of his own accord. But let the ministers of the Church be called and chosen by a lawful and ecclesiastical election and vocation; that is to say, let them be chosen religiously by the Church, and that in due order, without any tumult, seditions, or contention. But we must have an eye to this, that not every one that will should be elected, but such men as are fit and have sufficient learning, especially in the Scriptures, and godly eloquence, and wise simplicity; to conclude, such men as are of good report for moderation and honesty of life, according to that apostolic rule which St. Paul gives in the 1st Epistle to Timothy 3:2-7, and to Titus 1:7-9. And those who are chosen let them be ordained by the elders with public prayer, and laying on of hands. We do here, therefore, condemn all those who run of their own accord, being neither chosen, sent, nor ordained. We do also utterly disallow unfit ministers, and such as are not furnished with gifts requisite for a pastor.

9. In the meantime we are not ignorant that the innocent simplicity of certain pastors in the primitive Church did sometimes more profit the Church than the manifold, exquisite, and nice learning of some others that were over-lofty and high-minded. And for this cause we also, at this day, do not reject the honest simplicity of certain men, who yet are not destitute of all knowledge and learning.

10. The apostles of Christ do term all those who believe in Christ "priests"; not in regard to their ministry, but because that all the faithful, being made kings and priests, may, through Christ, offer up spiritual sacrifices unto God (Exod. 19:6; 1 Pet. 2:5, 9; Rev. 1:6). The ministry, then, and the priesthood are things far different one from the other. For the priesthood, as we said even now, is common to all Christians; not so is the ministry. And we have not taken away the ministry of the Church because we have thrust the popish priesthood out of the Church of Christ. For surely in the new covenant of Christ there is no longer any such priesthood as was in the ancient Church of the Jews; which had an external anointing, holy garments, and very many ceremonies which were figures and types of Christ, who, by His coming, fulfilled and abolished them (Heb. 9:10-11). And He Himself remains the only priest forever; and we do not communicate

Westminster Confession of Faith (1647)	Westminster Shorter Catechism (1647)	Westminster Larger Catechism (1648)

Second Helvetic Confession (cont.)

the name of priest to any of the ministers, lest we should detract anything from Christ. For the Lord Himself has not appointed in the Church any priests of the New Testament, who, having received authority from the suffragan, may offer up the host every day, that is, the very flesh and the very blood of our Savior, for the quick and the dead; but ministers who may teach and administer the sacraments. Paul declares plainly and shortly what we are to think of the ministers of the New Testament, or of the Church of Christ, and what we must attribute unto them: "Let a man," says he, "so account of us, as of the ministers of Christ, and stewards of the mysteries of God" (1 Cor. 4:1). So that the apostle wants us to esteem ministers as ministers. Now the apostle calls them as it were under-rowers, who have an eye only to their pilot; that is to say, men that live not unto themselves, nor according to their own will, but for others — to wit, their masters, at whose commandment and beck they ought to be. For the minister of the Church is commanded wholly, and in all parts of his duty, not to please himself, but to execute that only which he has received in commandment from his Lord. And in this place it is expressly declared who is our Master, even Christ; to whom the ministers are in subjection in all the functions of their ministry. He adds further that the ministers of the Church are "stewards of the mysteries of God" (1 Cor. 4:1). Now the mysteries of God Paul in many places, and especially in Ephesians 3:4, does call "the mystery of Christ." And the sacraments of Christ are also called mysteries by the ancient writers. Therefore for this purpose are the ministers called — namely, to preach the gospel of Christ unto the faithful, and to administer the sacraments. We read, also, in another place in the gospel, of "that faithful and wise steward, whom his lord shall make ruler over His household, to give them their portion of meat in due season" (Luke 12:42). Again, in another place of the gospel, a man goes into a strange country, and, leaving his house, gives unto his servants authority therein, commits to them his substance, and appoints every man his work (Matt. 25:14).

11. This is now a fit place to speak somewhat also of the power and office of the ministers of the Church. And concerning their power some have disputed over busily, and would bring all things, even the very greatest, under their jurisdiction; and that against the commandment of God, who forbade unto His disciples all dominion, and highly commended humility (Luke 22:26; Matt. 18:3). Indeed, there is one kind of power which is mere and absolute power, called the power of right. According to this power all things in the whole world are subject unto Christ, who is Lord of all; even as He Himself witnesses, saying, "All power is given unto Me in heaven and in earth" (Matt. 28:18), and again, "I am the first and the last:... and, behold, I am alive for evermore...and have the keys of hell and of death" (Rev. 1:17-18); also, "He that hath the key of David, He that openeth, and no man shutteth; and shutteth, and no man openeth" (Rev. 3:7).

12. This power the Lord reserves to Himself, and does not transfer it to any other, that He might sit idly by, and look on

His ministers while they wrought. For Isaiah says, "And the key of the house of David will I lay upon His shoulder" (Isa. 22:22); and again, "The government shall be upon His shoulder" (Isa. 9:6). For He does not lay the government on other men's shoulders, but does still keep and use His own power, thereby governing all things. Furthermore, there is another power, that of office, or ministerial power, limited by Him who has full and absolute power and authority. And this is more like a service than a dominion. For we see that a master does give unto the steward of his house authority and power over his house, and for that cause delivers him the keys, that he may admit or exclude such as his master will have admitted or excluded. According to this power does the minister, by his office, that which the Lord has commanded him to do; and the Lord does ratify and confirm that which he does, and will have the deeds of His ministers to be acknowledged and esteemed by His own deeds. Unto which end are those speeches in the gospel: "I will give unto thee the keys of the kingdom of heaven: and whatsoever thou shalt bind on earth shall be bound in heaven: and whatsoever thou shalt loose on earth shall be loosed in heaven" (Matt. 16:19). Again, "Whose soever sins ye remit, they are remitted unto them; and whose soever sins ye retain, they are retained" (John 20:23). But if the minister deal not in all things as the Lord has commanded him, but pass the limits and bounds of faith, then the Lord does make void that which he does. Wherefore the ecclesiastical power of the ministers of the Church is that function whereby they do indeed govern the Church of God, but yet so do all things in the Church as He has prescribed in His Word; which thing being so done, the faithful do esteem them as done of the Lord Himself. But touching the keys we have spoken somewhat before.

13. Now the power, or function, that is given to the ministers of the Church is the same and alike in all. Certainly, in the beginning, the bishops or elders did, with a common consent and labor, govern the Church; no man lifted up himself above another, none usurped greater power or authority over his fellow bishops. For they remembered the words of the Lord, "He that is greatest among you, let him be as the younger; and he that is chief, as he that doth serve" (Luke 22:26). They kept themselves by humility, and did mutually aid one another in the government and preservation of the Church. Notwithstanding, for order's sake, some one of the ministers called the assembly together, propounded unto the assembly the matters to be consulted of, gathered together the voices or sentences of the rest, and, to be brief, as much as lay in him, provided that there might arise no confusion.

14. So did St. Peter, as we read in the Acts of the Apostles (11:4-18), who yet for all that neither was above the rest, nor had greater authority than the rest. Very true, therefore, is that saying of Cyprian the martyr, in his book De Simplicitate Clericorum: "The same doubtless were the rest of the apostles that Peter was, having an equal fellowship with him both in honor and power: but the beginning hereof proceedeth from unity, to signify unto us that there is but one Church." St. Jerome also, in

Belgic Confession (1561)	Heidelberg Catechism (1563)	Second Helvetic Confession (1566)	Canons of Dort (1619)

Second Helvetic Confession (cont.)

his commentary upon the epistle of Paul to Titus, has a saying not much unlike this: "Before that, by the instinct of the devil, there arose parties in religion, the churches were governed by the common advice of the elders; but after that every one thought that whom he had baptized were his own, and not Christ's, it was decreed that one of the elders should be chosen, and set over the rest, who should have the care of the whole Church laid upon him, and by whose means all schisms should be removed." Yet Jerome does not avouch this as an order set down of God; for straightway he adds, "Even as the elders knew, by the continual custom of the Church, that they were subject to him that is set over them, so the bishops must know that they are above the elders rather by custom than by the prescript rule of God's truth, and that they ought to have the government of the Church in common with them." Thus far Jerome. Now, therefore, no man can forbid by any right that we may return to the old appointment of God, and rather receive that than the custom devised by men.

15. The offices of the ministers are divers; yet, notwithstanding, most men do restrain them to two, in which all the rest are comprehended: to the teaching of the gospel of Christ, and to the lawful administration of the sacraments. For it is the duty of the ministers to gather together a holy assembly, therein to expound the Word of God, and also to apply the general doctrine to the state and use of the Church; to the end that the doctrine which they teach may profit the hearers, and may build up the faithful. The minister's duty, I say, is to teach the unlearned, and to exhort; yea, and to urge them to go forward in the way of the Lord who do stand still, or linger and go slowly on; moreover, to comfort and to strengthen those which are fainthearted, and to arm them against the manifold temptations of Satan; to rebuke offenders; to bring them home that go astray; to raise them that are fallen; to convince the gainsayers; to chase away the wolf from the Lord's flock; to rebuke wickedness and wicked men wisely and severely; not to wink at nor to pass over great wickedness. And, besides, to administer the sacraments, and to commend the right use of them, and to prepare all men by wholesome doctrine to receive them; to keep together all the faithful in a holy unity; and to encounter schisms. To conclude, to catechize the ignorant, to commend the necessity of the poor to the Church, to visit and instruct those that are sick, or entangled with divers temptations, and so keep them in the way of life. Besides all this, to provide diligently that there be public prayers and supplications made in time of necessity, together with fastings, that is, a holy abstinency, and most carefully to look to those things which belong to the tranquility, peace, and safety of the Church.

16. And to the end that the minister may perform all these things the better, and with more ease, it is required of him that he be one that fears God, prays diligently, gives himself much to the reading of the Scripture, and, in all things, and at all times, is watchful, and does show forth a good example unto all men of holiness of life.

17. And seeing that there must be discipline in the Church, and that, among the ancient Fathers, excommunication was in use; and there were ecclesiastical judgments among the people of God, wherein this discipline was exercised by godly men, it belongs also to the minister's duty, for the edifying of the Church, to moderate this discipline, according to the condition of the time and public estate, and according to necessity. This rule is always to be holden, that "all things be done decently and in order" (1 Cor. 14:40), without any oppression or tumult. For the apostle witnesses, that power was given to him of God, to edify and not to destroy (2 Cor. 10:8). And the Lord Himself forbade the cockle to be plucked up in the Lord's field, because there would be danger lest the wheat also be plucked up with it (Matt. 13:29).

18. But as for the error of the Donatists, we do here utterly detest it; who esteem the doctrine and administration of the sacraments to be either effectual or not effectual, according to the good or evil life of the ministers. For we know that the voice of Christ is to be heard, though it be out of the mouths of evil ministers; forasmuch as the Lord Himself said, "All therefore whatsoever they bid you observe, that observe and do; but do not ye after their works: for they say, and do not" (Matt. 23:3). We know that the sacraments are sanctified by the institution, and through the word of Christ; and that they are effectual to the godly, although they be administered by ungodly ministers, of which matter Augustine, that blessed servant of God, did reason diversely out of the Scriptures against the Donatists. Yet, notwithstanding there ought to be a discipline among the ministers — for there should be intelligent inquiry in the synods touching the life and doctrine of the ministers — those that offend should be rebuked by the elders, and be brought into the way, if they be not past recovery; or else be deposed, and, as wolves, be driven from the Lord's flock by the true pastors if they be incurable. For, if they be false teachers, they are in no wise to be tolerated. Neither do we disallow of general councils, if that they be taken up according to the example of the apostles, to the salvation of the Church, and not to the destruction thereof.

19. The faithful ministers also are worthy (as good workmen) of their reward; neither do they offend when they receive a stipend, and all things that be necessary for themselves and their family. For the apostle shows that these things are for just cause given by the Church, and received by the ministers, in 1 Corinthians 9:14, and in 1 Timothy 5:17-18, and in other places also.

20. The Anabaptists likewise are confuted by this apostolical doctrine, who condemn and rail upon those ministers who live upon the ministry.

XXII. Of Holy and Ecclesiastical Meetings

1. Although it be lawful for all men privately at home to read the Holy Scriptures, and by instruction to edify one another in the true religion, yet that the Word of God may be lawfully preached to the people, and prayers and supplications publicly made, also that the sacraments may be lawfully administered,

Westminster Confession of Faith (1647)	Westminster Shorter Catechism (1647)	Westminster Larger Catechism (1648)

Second Helvetic Confession (cont.)

and that collections may be made for the poor, and to defray all necessary charges, or to supply the wants of the Church, it is very needful that there should be holy meetings and ecclesiastical assemblies. For it is manifest that, in the apostolic and primitive Church, there were such assemblies, frequented by godly men. So many, then, as do despise them, and separate themselves from them, they are contemners of true religion, and are to be urged by the pastors and godly magistrates to abstain from stubbornly absenting themselves from sacred assemblies. Now, ecclesiastical assemblies must not be hidden and secret, but public and common; except persecution by the enemies of Christ and the Church will not suffer them to be public; for we know what manner of assemblies the primitive Church had formerly in secret corners, being under the tyranny of Roman emperors. But let those places where the faithful meet together be decent, and in all respects fit for God's Church. Therefore, let houses be chosen for that purpose, or churches, that are large and fair, so that they be purged from all such things as do not beseem the Church. And let all things be ordered as is most meet for comeliness, necessity, and godly decency, that nothing be wanting which is requisite for rites and orders, and the necessary uses of the Church.

2. And as we believe that God does not dwell in temples made with hands, so we know that by reason of the Word of God, and holy exercises therein celebrated, places dedicated to God and His worship are not profane, but holy; and that therefore such as are conversant in them ought to behave themselves reverently and modestly, as they who are in a sacred place, in the presence of God and His holy angels. All excess of apparel, therefore, is to be abandoned in churches and places where Christians meet for prayer, together with all pride and whatsoever else does not beseem Christian humility, discipline, and modesty. For the true ornament of churches does not consist in ivory, gold, and precious stones; but in the sobriety, godliness, and virtues of those who are in the Church. "Let all things be done decently and in order" in the Church (1 Cor. 14:40). To conclude, "Let all things be done unto edifying" (ver. 26). Therefore, let all strange tongues keep silence in the holy assemblies, and let all things be uttered in the vulgar tongue, which is understood of all men in the company.

XXIII. Of the Prayers of the Church, of Singing, and of Canonical Hours

1. True it is that a man may lawfully pray privately in any tongue that he does understand; but public prayers ought, in the holy assemblies, to be made in the vulgar tongue, or such a language as is known to all. Let all the prayers of the faithful be poured forth to God alone, through the mediation of Christ only, out of a true faith and pure love. As for invocation of saints, or using them as intercessors to entreat for us, the priesthood of our Lord Christ and true religion will not permit us. Prayer must be made for the magistracy, for kings, and all that are placed in authority, for ministers of the Church, and for all necessities of churches; and especially in

any calamity of the Church prayer must be made, both privately and publicly, without ceasing.

2. Moreover, we must pray willingly, and not by constraint, nor for any reward; neither must we superstitiously tie prayer to any place, as though it were not lawful to pray but in the Church. There is no necessity that public prayers should be in form and time the same or alike in all churches. Let all churches use their liberty. Socrates, in his *History*, says, "In any country or nation whatsoever, you shall not find two churches which do wholly agree in prayer." The authors of this difference, I think, were those who had the government of the churches in several ages. But if any do agree, it deserves great commendation, and is to be imitated by others.

3. Besides this, there must be a mean and measure, as in every other thing, so also in public prayers, that they be not over-long and tedious. Let, therefore, most time be given to the teaching of the gospel in such holy assemblies; and let there be diligent heed taken that the people in the assemblies be not wearied with over-long prayers, so that, when the preaching of the gospel should be heard, they, through wearisomeness, either desire to go forth themselves or to have the assembly wholly dismissed. For unto such the sermons seem to be over-long which otherwise are brief enough. Yea, and the preachers ought to keep a mean.

4. Likewise the singing in sacred assemblies ought to be moderated where it is in use. That song which they call the Gregorian Chant has many gross things in it; wherefore it is upon good cause rejected by our Church, and most other Reformed churches. If there be any churches which have faithful prayer in good manner, without any singing, they are not therefore to be condemned, for all churches have not the advantage and opportunity of sacred music. And certain it is by testimonies of antiquity that, as the custom of singing is very ancient in the Eastern churches, so it was long ere it was received in the Western churches.

5. In ancient times there were no such things as canonical hours; that is, fixed prayers framed for certain hours in the day, and therein chanted or often repeated, as the papists' manner is, which may be proved by many of their lessons, appointed in their hours, and divers other arguments. Moreover, they have many absurd things (of which I say no more) that are well omitted by our churches and replaced by matters more wholesome for the universal Church of God.

XXIV. Of Holy Days, Fasts, and Choice of Meats

1. Although religion be not tied unto time, yet can it not be planted and exercised without a due dividing and allotting-out of time. Every Church, therefore, does choose unto itself a certain time for public prayers, and for the preaching of the gospel, and for the celebration of the sacraments; and it is not lawful for any one to overthrow this appointment of the Church at his own pleasure. For except some due time and leisure were

Belgic Confession (1561)	Heidelberg Catechism (1563)	Second Helvetic Confession (1566)	Canons of Dort (1619)

Second Helvetic Confession (cont.)

allotted to the outward exercise of religion, without doubt men would be quite drawn from it by their own affairs.

2. In regard hereof, we see that in the ancient churches there were not only certain set hours in the week appointed for meetings, but that also the Lord's Day itself, ever since the apostles' time, was consecrated to religious exercises and to a holy rest; which also is now very well observed by our churches, for the worship of God and the increase of charity. Yet herein we give no place unto the Jewish observation of the day, or to any superstitions. For we do not account one day to be holier than another, nor think that mere rest is of itself acceptable to God. Besides, we do celebrate and keep the Lord's Day, and not the Jewish Sabbath, and that with a free observation.

3. Moreover, if the Churches do religiously celebrate the memory of the Lord's nativity, circumcision, passion, resurrection, and of His ascension into heaven, and the sending of the Holy Spirit upon His disciples, according to Christian liberty, we do very well approve of it. But as for festival days, ordained for men or saints departed, we cannot allow of them. For, indeed, festival days must be referred to the first table of the law, and belong peculiarly unto God. To conclude, those festival days which are appointed for saints, and abrogated by us, have in them many gross things, unprofitable and not to be tolerated. In the meantime, we confess that the remembrance

of saints, in due time and place, may be to good use and profit commended unto the people in sermons, and the holy examples of holy men set before their eyes to be imitated by all.

XXV. Of Catechizing, of Comforting and Visiting the Sick

1. The Lord enjoined His ancient people to take great care and diligence in instructing the youth well, even from their infancy; and, moreover, commanded expressly in His law that they should teach them, and declare the mystery of the sacrament unto them. Now, forasmuch as is evident by the writings of the evangelists and apostles, that God has no less care of the youth of His new people (seeing He says, "Suffer little children, and forbid them not, to come unto Me; for of such is the kingdom of heaven" (Matt. 19:14), therefore the pastors do very wisely who do diligently and betimes catechize their youth, laying the first grounds of faith, and faithfully teaching the rudiments of our religion, by expounding the Ten Commandments, the Apostles' Creed, the Lord's Prayer, and the doctrine of the sacraments, with other like principles and chief heads of our religion. And here let the Church perform her faithfulness and diligence in bringing the children to be catechized, as being desirous and glad to have her children well instructed.

2. Seeing that men do never lie open to more grievous temptations than when they are exercised with infirmities, or else

---

The Means of Grace: Word and Sacrament

Article 33
The Sacraments

We believe that our gracious God, on account of our weakness and infirmities, hath ordained the sacraments for us, thereby to seal unto us His promises,[1] and to be pledges of the good will and grace of God toward us, and also to nourish and strengthen our faith, which He hath joined to the Word of the gospel, the better to present to our senses, both that which He signifies to us by His Word, and that which He works in-

Q. 65: Since then we are made partakers of Christ and all His benefits by faith only, whence doth this faith proceed?

A.: From the Holy Ghost, who works faith[1] in our hearts by the preaching of the gospel, and confirms it by the use of the sacraments.[2]

[1] Eph. 2:8; Eph. 6:23; Phil. 1:29
[2] Matt. 28:19; Rom. 4:11

Q. 66: What are the sacraments?

A.: The sacraments are holy visible signs and seals, appointed of God

XIII. Of the Gospel of Jesus Christ: also of Promises; of the Spirit and of the Letter

3. And although, after this manner, our fathers had the gospel in the writings of the prophets, by which they attained salvation in Christ through faith, yet the gospel is properly called "glad and happy tidings"; wherein, first by John the Baptist, then by Christ the Lord Himself, and afterwards by the apostles and their successors, is preached to us in the world, that God has now performed that which He promised from the beginning of the world, and has sent, yea, and even given unto us, His only Son, and, in Him, reconciliation with the Father, remission of sins, all fullness, and everlasting life. The history, therefore, set down by the four evangelists, declaring how these things were done or fulfilled in Christ, and what He taught and did, and that they who believe in Him have all fullness — this, I say, is truly called the gospel. The preaching, also, and Scripture of the apostles, in which they ex-

HEAD III & IV
Article 17

As the almighty operation of God, whereby He prolongs and supports this our natural life, does not exclude, but requires the use of means, by which God of His infinite mercy and goodness hath chosen to exert His influence, so also the beforementioned supernatural operation of God, by which we are regenerated, in no wise excludes or subverts the use of the gospel, which the most wise God has ordained to be the seed

Westminster Confession of Faith (1647)	Westminster Shorter Catechism (1647)	Westminster Larger Catechism (1648)

Second Helvetic Confession (cont.)

are sick and brought low by diseases, it behooves the pastors of the churches to be never more vigilant and careful for the safety of the flock than in such diseases and infirmities. Therefore let them visit the sick betimes, and let them be quickly sent for by the sick, if the matter shall so require; let them comfort and confirm them in the true faith; finally, let them strengthen them against the dangerous suggestions of Satan. In like manner, let them pray with the sick person at home in his house; and, if need be, let them make prayers for the sick in the public meeting; and let them be careful that they have a happy passage out of this life. As for popish visiting with the extreme unction, we have said before that we do not like it, because it has many absurd things in it, and such as are not approved by the canonical Scriptures.

XXVIII. Of the Goods of the Church, and the Right Use of Them

1. The Church of Christ has riches through the bountifulness of princes, and the liberality of the faithful, who have given their goods to the Church. For the Church has need of such goods; and has had goods from ancient time for the maintenance of things necessary for the Church. Now, the true use of the ecclesiastical goods was, and now is, to maintain learning in schools

and in holy assemblies, with all the service, rites, and buildings of the Church; finally, to maintain teachers, scholars, and ministers, with other necessary things, and chiefly for the succor and relief of the poor. But for the lawful dispensing of these ecclesiastical goods let men be chosen that fear God — wise men, and such as are of good report in the government of their families.

2. But if the goods of the Church, by injury of the time, and the boldness, ignorance, or covetousness of some, be turned to any abuse, let them be restored again, by godly and wise men, unto their holy use; for they must not connive at so impious an abuse. Therefore, we teach that schools and colleges, whereinto corruption is crept in doctrine, in the service of God, and in manners, must be reformed; and that there provision should be made, piously, faithfully, and wisely, for the relief of the poor.

XXVII. Of the Word and Sacraments

1. Sacraments are holy signs and seals of the covenant of grace,[1] immediately instituted by God,[2] to represent Christ and His benefits; and to confirm our interest in Him;[3] as also, to put a visible difference between those that belong unto the Church and the rest of the world;[4] and solemnly to engage them to the service of God in Christ, according to His Word.[5]

[1] Rom. 4:11; Gen. 17:7, 10
[2] Matt. 28:19; 1 Cor. 11:23
[3] 1 Cor. 10:16; 11:25-26; Gal. 3:27
[4] Rom. 15:8; Exod. 12:48; Gen. 34:14
[5] Rom. 6:3-4; 1 Cor. 10:16, 21

2. There is, in every sacrament, a spiritual relation, or sacramental union, between the sign and the thing signified: whence it comes to pass, that the names and effects of the one are attributed to the other.[1]

[1] Gen. 17:10; Matt. 26:27-28; Titus 3:5

Q. 85: What doth God require of us, that we may escape His wrath and curse, due to us for sin?

A.: To escape the wrath and curse of God, due to us for sin, God requireth of us faith in Jesus Christ, repentance unto life,[1] with diligent use of all the outward means whereby Christ communicateth to us the benefits of redemption.[2]

[1] Acts 20:21
[2] Prov. 2:1-5; 8:33-36; Isa. 55:3

Q. 88: What are the outward and ordinary means whereby Christ communicateth to us the benefits of redemption?

A.: The outward and ordi-

Q. 153: What doth God require of us, that we may escape His wrath and curse due to us by reason of the transgression of the law?

A.: That we may escape the wrath and curse of God due to us by reason of the transgression of the law, He requireth of us repentance toward God, and faith toward our Lord Jesus Christ,[1] and the diligent use of the outward means whereby Christ communicates to us the benefits of His mediation.[2]

[1] Acts 20:21; Matt. 3:7-8; Luke 13:3, 5; Acts 16:30-31; John 3:16, 18
[2] Prov. 2:1-5; 8:33-36

Q. 154: What are the outward means whereby Christ communicates to us the benefits of His mediation?

A.: The outward and ordinary means whereby Christ communicates to His Church the benefits of His mediation, are all His ordinances; especially the Word, sacraments, and prayer; all

Belgic Confession (1561)	Heidelberg Catechism (1563)	Second Helvetic Confession (1566)	Canons of Dort (1619)

Belgic Confession (1561)

wardly in our hearts, thereby assuring and confirming in us the salvation which He imparts to us. For they are visible signs and seals of an inward and invisible thing, by means whereof God worketh in us by the power of the Holy Ghost. Therefore the signs are not in vain or insignificant, so as to deceive us. For Jesus Christ is the true object presented by them, without whom they would be of no moment.[2]

Moreover, we are satisfied with the number of sacraments which Christ our Lord hath instituted, which are two only, namely, the sacrament of baptism, and the holy supper of our Lord Jesus Christ.[3]

[1] Rom. 4:11; Gen. 9:13; 17:11
[2] Col. 2:11,17; 1 Cor. 5:7
[3] Matt. 26:36; 28:19

Heidelberg Catechism (1563)

for this end, that by the use thereof He may the more fully declare and seal to us the promise of the gospel, namely, that He grants us freely the remission of sin and life eternal for the sake of that one sacrifice of Christ accomplished on the cross.[1]

[1] Gen. 17:11; Rom. 4:11; Lev. 6:25; Acts 22:16; Acts 2:38; Matt. 26:28

Q. 67: Are both Word and sacraments, then, ordained and appointed for this end, that they may direct our faith to the sacrifice of Jesus Christ on the cross as the only ground of our salvation?
A.: Yes, indeed, for the Holy Ghost teaches us in the gospel, and assures us by the sacraments, that the whole of our salvation depends upon that one sacrifice of Christ which He offered for us on the cross.[1]

[1] Rom. 6:3; Gal. 3:27

Q. 68: How many sacraments has Christ instituted in the new covenant, or testament?
A.: Two, namely, holy baptism and the holy supper.[1]

[1] 1 Cor. 10:2-4

Second Helvetic Confession (1566)

pound unto us how the Son was given us of the Father, and, in Him, all things pertaining to life and salvation, is truly called the doctrine of the gospel; so as even at this day it loses not that worthy name, if it be sincere.

4. The same preaching of the gospel is by the apostle termed the Spirit, and "the ministration of the spirit" (2 Cor. 3:8), because it lives and works through faith in the ears, yea, in the hearts, of the faithful, through the illumination of the Holy Spirit. For the letter, which is opposed unto the Spirit, does indeed signify every outward thing, but more especially the doctrine of the law, which, without the Spirit and faith, works wrath, and stirs up sin in the minds of them that do not truly believe. For which cause it is called by the apostle "the ministration of death" (2 Cor. 3:7); for hitherto pertains that saying of the apostle, "the letter killeth, but the spirit giveth life" (ver. 6). The false apostles preached the gospel, corrupted by mingling of the law therewith; as though Christ could not save without the law. Such, also, were the Ebionites said to be, who came from Ebion the heretic; and the Nazarites, who beforetime were called Mineans. All whom we do condemn, sincerely preaching the word, and teaching that believers are justified through the Spirit (or Christ) only, and not through the law. But of this matter there shall follow a fuller exposition, under the title of justification.

5. And although the doctrine of the gospel, compared with the Pharisees' doctrine of the law, might seem (when it was first preached by Christ) to be a new doctrine (which thing also Jeremiah prophesied of the New Testament); yet, indeed, it not only was, and as yet is (though the papists call it new, in regard of popish doctrine, which has of long time been received) an ancient doctrine, but also the most ancient in the world. For God from all eternity foreordained to save the world by Christ, and this His predestination and eternal counsel has He opened to the world by the gospel (2 Tim. 1:9-10). Whereby it appears that the evangelical doctrine and religion were the most ancient of all that ever were or are; wherefore we say, that all they [the papists] err foully, and speak things unworthy the eternal counsel of God, who term the evangelical doctrine and religion a newly concocted faith, scarce thirty years old; to whom that saying of Isaiah does very well agree — "Woe unto them that call evil good, and good evil; that put darkness for light, and light for darkness; that put bitter for sweet, and sweet for bitter!" (v. 20).

XIX. Of the Sacraments of the Church of Christ
1. God even from the beginning added unto the preaching of the Word His sacraments, or sacra-

Canons of Dort (1619)

of regeneration and food of the soul. Wherefore, as the apostles, and teachers who succeeded them, piously instructed the people concerning this grace of God, to His glory, and the abasement of all pride, and in the meantime, however, neglected not to keep them by the sacred precepts of the gospel in the exercise of the Word, sacraments and discipline; so even to this day, be it far from either instructors or instructed to presume to tempt God in the Church by separating what He of His good pleasure hath most intimately joined together. For grace is conferred by means of admonitions; and the more readily we perform our duty, the more eminent usually is this blessing of God working in us, and the more directly is His work advanced; to whom alone all the glory both of means, and of their saving fruit and efficacy is forever due. Amen.

Head V

Article 14
And as it hath pleased God, by the preaching of the gospel, to begin this work of grace in us, so He preserves, continues, and perfects it by the hearing and reading of His Word, by meditation thereon, and by the exhortations, threatenings, and promises thereof, as well as by the use of the sacraments.

Westminster Confession of Faith (1647)	Westminster Shorter Catechism (1647)	Westminster Larger Catechism (1648)
3. The grace which is exhibited in or by the sacraments rightly used, is not conferred by any power in them; neither doth the efficacy of a sacrament depend upon the piety or intention of him that doth administer it,[1] but upon the work of the Spirit,[2] and the word of institution, which contains, together with a precept authorizing the use thereof, a promise of benefit to worthy receivers.[3] [1] Rom. 2:28-29; 1 Pet. 3:21 [2] Matt. 3:11; 1 Cor. 12:13 [3] Matt. 26:27-28; 28:19-20 4. There be only two sacraments ordained by Christ our Lord in the gospel; that is to say, baptism, and the supper of the Lord, neither of which may be dispensed by any, but by a minister of the Word lawfully ordained.[1] [1] Matt. 28:19; 1 Cor. 11:20, 23; 4:1; Heb. 5:4 5. The sacraments of the Old Testament, in regard of the spiritual things thereby signified and exhibited, were, for substance, the same with those of the New.[1] [1] 1 Cor. 10:1-4.	nary means whereby Christ communicateth to us the benefits of redemption, are His ordinances, especially the Word, sacraments, and prayer; all which are made effectual to the elect for salvation.[1] [1] Matt. 28:19-20; Acts 2:42, 46-47 *Q. 89: How is the Word made effectual to salvation?* A.: The Spirit of God maketh the reading, but especially the preaching of the Word, an effectual means of convincing and converting sinners, and of building them up in holiness and comfort, through faith, unto salvation.[1] [1] Neh. 8:8; 1 Cor. 14:24-25; Acts 26:18; Ps. 19:8; Acts 20:32; Rom. 15:4; 2 Tim. 3:15-17; Rom. 10:13-17; 1:16 *Q. 90: How is the Word to be read and heard, that it may become effectual to salvation?* A.: That the Word may become effectual to salvation, we must attend thereunto with diligence,[1] preparation,[2] and prayer;[3] receive it with faith and love,[4] lay it up in our hearts,[5] and practice it in our lives.[6] [1] Prov. 8:34 [2] 1 Pet. 2:1-2 [3] Ps. 119:18 [4] Heb. 4:2; 2 Thes. 2:10 [5] Ps. 119:11 [6] Luke 8:15; James 1:25 *Q. 91: How do the sacraments become effectual means of salvation?* A.: The sacraments become effectual means of salvation, not from any virtue in them, or in him that doth administer them; but only by the blessing of Christ,[1] and the working of His Spirit in them that by faith receive them.[2] [1] 1 Pet. 3:21; Matt. 3:11; 1 Cor. 3:6-7 [2] 1 Cor. 12:13	which are made effectual to the elect for their salvation.[1] [1] Matt. 28:19-20; Acts 2:42, 46-47 *Q. 155: How is the Word made effectual to salvation?* A.: The Spirit of God maketh the reading, but especially the preaching of the Word, an effectual means of enlightening,[1] convincing, and humbling sinners;[2] of driving them out of themselves, and drawing them unto Christ;[3] of conforming them to His image,[4] and subduing them to His will;[5] of strengthening them against temptations and corruptions;[6] of building them up in grace,[7] and establishing their hearts in holiness and comfort through faith unto salvation.[8] [1] Neh. 8:8; Acts 26:18; Ps. 19:8 [2] 1 Cor. 14:24-25; 2 Chron. 34:18-19, 26-28 [3] Acts 2:37, 41; 8:27-39 [4] 2 Cor. 3:18 [5] 2 Cor. 10:4-6; Rom. 6:17 [6] Matt. 4:4, 7, 10; Eph. 6:16-17; Ps. 19:11; 1 Cor. 10:11 [7] Acts 20:32; 2 Tim. 3:15-17 [8] Rom. 16:25; 1 Thes. 3:2, 10-11, 13; Rom. 15:4; 10:13-17; 1:16 *Q. 156: Is the Word of God to be read by all?* A: Although all are not to be permitted to read the Word publicly to the congregation,[1] yet all sorts of people are bound to read it apart by themselves,[2] and with their families,[3] to which end, the Holy Scriptures are to be translated out of the original into vulgar languages.[4] [1] Deut. 31:9, 11-13; Neh. 8:2-3; 9:3-5 [2] Deut. 17:19; Rev. 1:3; John 5:39; Isa. 34:16 [3] Deut. 6:6-9; Gen. 18:17, 19; Ps. 78:5-7 [4] 1 Cor. 14:6, 9, 11-12, 15-16, 24, 27-28 *Q. 157: How is the Word of God to be read?* A: The Holy Scriptures are to be read with a high and reverent esteem of them;[1] with a firm persuasion that they are the very Word of God,[2] and that He only can enable us to understand them;[3] with desire to know, believe, and obey the will of God revealed in them;[4] with diligence,[5] and attention to the matter and scope of them;[6] with meditation,[7] application,[8] self-denial,[9] and prayer.[10] [1] Ps. 19:10; Neh. 8:3-10; Exod. 24:7; 2 Chron. 34:27; Isa. 66:2 [2] 2 Pet. 1:19-21 [3] Luke 24:45; 2 Cor. 3:13-16 [4] Deut. 17:10, 20 [5] Acts 17:11 [6] Acts 8:30, 34; Luke 10:26-28 [7] Ps. 1:2; 119:97 [8] 2 Chron. 34:21 [9] Prov. 3:5; Deut. 33:3 [10] Prov. 2:1-6; Ps. 119:18; Neh. 7:6, 8

Belgic Confession (1561)	Heidelberg Catechism (1563)	Second Helvetic Confession (1566)	Canons of Dort (1619)

Second Helvetic Confession (cont.)

mental signs, in His Church. And to this does the holy Scripture plainly testify. Sacraments are mystical symbols, or holy rites, or sacred actions, ordained by God Himself, consisting of His Word, of outward signs, and of things signified; whereby He keeps in continual memory, and recalls to mind, in His Church, His great benefits bestowed upon man; and whereby He seals up His promises, and outwardly represents, and, as it were, offers unto our sight those things which inwardly He performs unto us, and therewithal strengthens and increases our faith through the working of God's Spirit in our hearts; lastly, whereby He does separate us from all other people and religions, and consecrates and binds us wholly unto Himself, and gives us to understand what He requires of us.

2. These sacraments are either of the Old Church or of the New. The sacraments of the Old were Circumcision, and the Paschal Lamb, which was offered up; under which name, reference is made to the sacrifices which were in use from the beginning of the world. The sacraments of the New Church are baptism and the supper of the Lord.

3. Some there are who reckon seven sacraments of the New Church. Of which number we grant that repentance, matrimony, and the ordination of ministers (we mean not the popish, but the apostolical ordination) are very profitable, but no sacraments. As for confirmation and extreme unction, they are mere devices of men, which the Church may very well spare, without any damage or inconvenience at all; and, therefore, we have them not in our churches, because there are certain things in them which we can by no means allow of.[1] As for that merchandise which the Romish prelates use in ministering their sacraments, we utterly abhor it.

4. The author and institutor of all sacraments is not any man, but God alone; for man can by no means ordain sacraments, because they belong to the worship of God, and it is not for man to appoint and prescribe a service of God, but to embrace and retain that which is taught unto him by the Lord. Besides, the sacramental signs have God's promises annexed to them, which necessarily require faith. Now faith stays itself only upon the Word of God; and the Word of God is resembled to writings or letters, the sacraments to seals, which the Lord alone sets to His own letters. And as the Lord is the author of the sacraments, so He continually works in that Church where they are rightly used; so that the faithful, when they receive them from the ministers, do know that the Lord works in His own ordinance, and therefore they receive them as from the hand of God; and the minister's faults (if there be any notorious in them) cannot hurt them, seeing they do acknowledge the goodness of the sacraments to depend upon the ordinance of the Lord. For which cause they put a difference, in the administration of the sacraments, between the Lord Himself and His minister; confessing that the substance of the sacraments is given them by the Lord, and the outward signs by the ministers of the Lord.

4. But the principal thing, which in all sacraments is offered by the Lord, and chiefly regarded by the godly of all ages (which

some have called the substance and matter of the sacraments), is Christ our Savior — that only sacrifice (Heb. 10:12); and that Lamb of God slain from the foundation of the world (Rev. 13:8); that rock, also, of which all our fathers drank (1 Cor. 10:4), by whom all the elect are circumcised with the circumcision made without hands, through the Holy Spirit (Col. 2:11-12), and are washed from all their sins (Rev. 1:5), and are nourished with the very body and blood of Christ unto eternal life (John 6:54).

5. Now, in respect of that which is the chief thing, and the very matter and substance of the sacraments, the sacraments of both covenants are equal. For Christ, the only Mediator and Savior of the faithful, is the chief thing and substance in them both. One and the same God is author of them both. They were given unto both churches as signs and seals of the grace and promises of God; which should call to mind and renew the memory of God's great benefits to them, and should distinguish the faithful from all the religions in the world; lastly, which should be received spiritually by faith, and should bind the receivers unto the Church, and admonish them of their duty. In these, I say, and such like things, the sacraments of both Churches are not unequal, although in the outward signs they are diverse.

6. And, indeed, we do yet put a greater difference between them; for ours are more firm and durable, as those which are not to be changed to the end of the world. Again, ours testify that the substance and promise are already fulfilled and performed in Christ, whereas the other did only signify that they should be fulfilled. And again, ours are more simple, and nothing so painful, nothing so sumptuous, nor so full of ceremonies. Moreover, they belong to greater people, that is dispersed through the face of the whole earth; and because they are more excellent, and do by the Spirit of God stir up in us a greater measure of faith, therefore a more plentiful measure of the Spirit does follow them.

7. But now, since Christ the true Messiah is exhibited unto us, and the abundance of grace is poured forth upon the people of the New Testament, the sacraments of the Old Law are surely abrogated and have ceased; and in their stead the sacraments of the New Testament are placed — namely, for circumcision, baptism; and for the Paschal Lamb and sacrifices, the supper of the Lord.

8. And as in the old Church the sacraments consisted of the Word, the sign, and the thing signified; so even at this day they are composed, as it were, of the same parts. For the Word of God makes them sacraments, which before were none; for they are consecrated by the Word, and declared to be sanctified by Him who first ordained them. To sanctify or consecrate a thing is to dedicate it unto God, and unto holy uses; that is, to take it from the common and ordinary use, and to appoint it to some holy use. For the signs in the sacraments are drawn from common use, things external and visible. As in baptism, the outward sign is the element of water, and that visible washing which is done by the minister; but the thing signified is regeneration and the cleansing from sins. Like-

Westminster Confession of Faith (1647)	Westminster Shorter Catechism (1647)	Westminster Larger Catechism (1648)
	Q. 92: What is a sacrament? A.: A sacrament is a holy ordinance instituted by Christ; wherein, by sensible signs, Christ, and the benefits of the new covenant, are represented, sealed, and applied to believers.[1] [1] Gen. 17:7, 10; Exod. 12; 1 Cor. 11:23, 26 *Q. 93: Which are the sacraments of the New Testament?* A.: The sacraments of the New Testament are, baptism,[1] and the Lord's Supper.[2] [1] Matt. 28:19 [2] Matt. 26:26-28	*Q. 158: By whom is the Word of God to be preached?* A.: The Word of God is to be preached only by such as are sufficiently gifted,[1] and also duly approved and called to that office.[2] [1] 1 Tim. 3:2, 6; Eph. 4:8-11; Hosea 4:6; Mal. 2:7; 2 Cor. 3:6 [2] Jer. 14:15; Rom. 10:15; Heb. 5:4; 1 Cor. 12:28-29; 1 Tim. 3:10; 4:14; 5:22 *Q. 159: How is the Word of God to be preached by those that are called thereunto?* A.: They that are called to labor in the ministry of the Word, are to preach sound doctrine,[1] diligently,[2] in season and out of season;[3] plainly,[4] not in the enticing words of man's wisdom, but in demonstration of the Spirit, and of power;[5] faithfully,[6] making known the whole counsel of God;[7] wisely,[8] applying themselves to the necessities and capacities of the hearers;[9] zealously,[10]

Westminster Larger Catechism (cont.)

with fervent love to God[11] and the souls of His people;[12] sincerely,[13] aiming at His glory,[14] and their conversion,[15] edification,[16] and salvation.[17]

[1] Titus 2:1, 8
[2] Acts 18:25
[3] 2 Tim. 4:2
[4] 1 Cor. 14:19
[5] 1 Cor. 2:4
[6] Jer. 23:28; 1 Cor. 4:1-2
[7] Acts 20:27
[8] Col. 1:28; 2 Tim. 2:15
[9] 1 Cor. 3:2; Heb. 5:12-14; Luke 12:42
[10] Acts 18:25
[11] 2 Cor. 5:13-14; Phil. 1:15-17
[12] Col. 4:12; 2 Cor. 12:15
[13] 2 Cor. 2:17; 4:2
[14] 1 Thes. 2:4-6; John 7:18
[15] 1 Cor. 9:19-22
[16] 2 Cor. 12:19; Eph. 4:12
[17] 1 Tim. 4:16; Acts 26:16-18

Q. 160: What is required of those that hear the Word preached?
A.: It is required of those that hear the Word preached, that they attend upon it with diligence,[1] preparation,[2] and prayer;[3] examine what they hear by the Scriptures;[4] receive the truth with faith,[5] love,[6] meekness,[7] and readiness of mind,[8] as the Word of God;[9] meditate,[10] and confer of it;[11] hide it in their hearts,[12] and bring forth the fruit of it in their lives.[13]

[1] Prov. 8:34
[2] 1 Pet. 2:1-2; Luke 8:18
[3] Ps. 119:18; Eph. 6:18-19
[4] Acts 17:11
[5] Heb. 4:2
[6] 2 Thes. 2:10
[7] James 1:21
[8] Acts 17:11
[9] 1 Thes. 2:13
[10] Luke 9:44; Heb. 2:1
[11] Luke 24:14; Deut. 6:6-7
[12] Prov. 2:1; Ps. 119:11
[13] Luke 8:15; James 1:25

Q. 161: How do the sacraments become effectual means of salvation?
A.: The sacraments become effectual means of salvation, not by any power in themselves, or any virtue derived from the piety or intention of him by whom they are administered, but only by the working of the Holy Ghost, and the blessing of Christ, by whom they are instituted.[1]

[1] 1 Pet. 3:21; Acts 8:13, 23; 1 Cor. 3:6-7; 12:13

Q. 162: What is a sacrament?
A.: A sacrament is a holy ordinance instituted by Christ in His Church,[1] to signify, seal, and exhibit[2] unto those that are within the covenant of grace,[3] the benefits of His mediation;[4] to strengthen and increase their faith, and all other graces;[5] to oblige them to obedience;[6] to testify and cherish their love and communion one with another;[7] and to distinguish them from those that are without.[8]

[1] Gen. 17:7, 10; Exod. 12; Matt. 28:19; 26:26-28
[2] Rom. 4:11; 1 Cor. 11:24-25
[3] Rom. 15:8; Exod. 12:48
[4] Acts 2:38; 1 Cor. 10:16
[5] Rom. 4:11; Gal. 3:27
[6] Rom. 6:3-4; 1 Cor. 10:21
[7] Eph. 4:2-5; 1 Cor. 12:13
[8] Eph. 2:11-12; Gen. 34:14

Q. 163: What are the parts of a sacrament?
A.: The parts of a sacrament are two; the one an outward and sensible sign, used according to Christ's own appointment; the other an inward and spiritual grace thereby signified.[1]

[1] Matt. 3:11; 1 Pet. 3:21; Rom. 2:28-29

Q. 164: How many sacraments hath Christ instituted in His Church under the New Testament?

Belgic Confession (1561)	Heidelberg Catechism (1563)	Second Helvetic Confession (1566)	Canons of Dort (1619)

Second Helvetic Confession (cont.)

wise, in the Lord's Supper, the outward sign is bread and wine, taken from things commonly used for meat and drink; but the thing signified is the body of Christ which was given, and His blood which was shed for us, or the communion of the body and blood of the Lord. Wherefore, the water, bread, and wine, considered in their own nature, and out of this holy use and institution of the Lord, are only that which they are called, and which we find them to be. But let the Word of God be added to them, together with invocation upon His holy name, and the renewing of their first institution and sanctification, and then these signs are consecrated, and declared to be sanctified by Christ. For Christ's first institution and consecration of the sacraments stands yet in force in the Church of God, in such sort that they who celebrate the sacraments no otherwise than the Lord Himself from the beginning has appointed, have still, even to this day, the use and benefit of that first and most excellent consecration. And for this cause, in the administration of the sacraments, the very words of Christ are repeated.

9. And as we learn out of the Word of God that these signs were appointed unto another end and use than the common one, therefore we teach that they now, in this their holy use, do take upon them the names of things signified, and are not still called bare water, bread, or wine; but that the water is called "washing of regeneration" (Titus 3:5), and the bread and wine "the body of Christ" (1 Cor. 10:16), or the pledges and sacraments of His body and blood. Not that the signs are turned into the things signified, or cease to be that which in their own nature they are (for then they could not be sacraments, which should consist only of the thing signified, and have no signs); but therefore do the signs bear the names of things, because they are mystical tokens of holy things, and because the signs and the things signified are sacramentally joined together; joined together, I say, or united by a mystical signification, and by the purpose and will of Him who first instituted them. For the water, bread, and wine are not common, but holy signs. And He that instituted water in baptism did not institute it with that mind and purpose that the faithful should only be dipped in the water of baptism; and he which commanded the bread to be eaten and the wine to be drunk in the supper did not mean that the faithful should only receive bread and wine without any further mystery, as they eat bread at home in their houses: but that they should spiritually be partakers of the things signified, and by faith be truly purged from their sins, and be partakers of Christ also.

10. And, therefore, we cannot allow of them who attribute the consecration of the sacraments to I know not what syllables; to the rehearsal of certain words pronounced by him that is consecrated,[2] and that has an intent of consecrating; or to some other accidental things, which are not left unto us either by the word, or by the example, of Christ or His apostles. We do also mislike the doctrine of those that speak no otherwise of the sacraments than of common signs, not sanctified, nor effectual. We condemn them also who, because of the invisible things, do despise the visible, and think the signs superfluous, because they do already enjoy the things themselves; such were the Messalians, as it is recorded. We do disallow their doctrine also who teach that grace and the things signified are to be so tied to and included in the signs that whosoever do outwardly receive the signs must needs inwardly participate in the grace, and in the things signified, what manner of men soever they be.

11. Notwithstanding, as we esteem not the goodness of the sacraments by the worthiness or unworthiness of the ministers, so likewise we do not weigh them by the condition of the receivers. For we know that the goodness of the sacraments does depend upon the faithfulness, or truth, and the mere goodness of God. For even as God's Word remains the true Word of God; wherein not only bare words are uttered when it is preached, but therewithal the things signified by the words are offered of God, although the wicked and unbelievers hear and understand the words, yet enjoy not the things signified, because they receive them not by a true faith; even so the sacraments, consisting of the Word, the signs, and the things signified, continue true and perfect sacraments, not only because they are holy things, but also because God offers the things signified, howsoever the unbelievers receive not the things which are offered. This comes to pass, not by any fault in God, the author and offerer of them, but by the fault of men, who do receive them without faith, and unlawfully — "whose unbelief" cannot "make the faith of God without effect" (Rom. 3:3).

12. Now, forasmuch as in the beginning, where we showed what the sacraments were, we did also, by the way, set down to what end they were ordained, it will not be necessary to trouble ourselves with repeating any thing which has been already handled. Next, therefore, in order, it remains to speak severally of the sacraments of the Christian Church.

---

[1] Confirmation, with preparatory catechetical instruction, has afterwards been introduced in many Reformed churches in Europe, to supplement infant baptism.

[2] According to the reading, *a corsecrato*. But other editions read *a consecratore*, by him who consecrates.

Westminster Confession of Faith (1647)	Westminster Shorter Catechism (1647)	Westminster Larger Catechism (1648)

Westminster Larger Catechism (cont.)

A.: Under the New Testament Christ hath instituted in His Church only two sacraments, baptism and the Lord's Supper.[1]

[1] Matt. 28:19; 1 Cor. 11:20, 23; Matt. 26:26-28

Q. 176: *Wherein do the sacraments of baptism and the Lord's Supper agree?*

A.: The sacraments of baptism and the Lord's Supper agree, in that the author of both is God;[1] the spiritual part of both is Christ and His benefits;[2] both are seals of the same covenant,[3] are to be dispensed by ministers of the gospel, and by none other;[4] and to be continued in the Church of Christ until His second coming.[5]

[1] Matt. 28:19; 1 Cor. 11:23
[2] Rom. 6:3-4; 1 Cor. 10:16
[3] Rom. 4:11; Col. 2:12; Matt. 26:27-28
[4] John 1:33; Matt. 28:19; 1 Cor. 11:23; 4:1; Heb. 5:4
[5] Matt. 28:19-20; 1 Cor. 11:26

Q. 177: *Wherein do the sacraments of baptism and the Lord's Supper differ?*

A.: The sacraments of baptism and the Lord's Supper differ, in that baptism is to be administered but once, with water, to be a sign and seal of our regeneration and ingrafting into Christ,[1] and that even to infants;[2] whereas the Lord's Supper is to be administered often, in the elements of bread and wine, to represent and exhibit Christ as spiritual nourishment to the soul,[3] and to confirm our continuance and growth in Him,[4] and that only to such as are of years and ability to examine themselves.[5]

[1] Matt. 3:11; Titus 3:5; Gal. 3:27
[2] Gen. 17:7, 9; Acts 2:38-39; 1 Cor. 7:14
[3] 1 Cor. 11:23-26
[4] 1 Cor. 10:16
[5] 1 Cor. 11:28-29

Belgic Confession (1561)	Heidelberg Catechism (1563)	Second Helvetic Confession (1566)	Canons of Dort (1619)

Holy Baptism

Article 34

Holy Baptism

We believe and confess that Jesus Christ, who is the end of the law,[1] hath made an end, by the shedding of His blood, of all other sheddings of blood which men could or would make as a propitiation or satisfaction for sin; and that He, having abolished circumcision, which was done with blood, hath instituted the sacrament of baptism[2] instead thereof, by which we are received into the Church of God, and separated from all other people and strange religions, that we may wholly belong to Him whose ensign and banner we bear, and which serves as a testimony unto us that He will forever be our gracious God and Father.

Therefore He has commanded all those who are His to be baptized with pure water, *in the name of the Father, and of the Son, and of the Holy Ghost,*[3] thereby signifying to us, that as water washeth away the filth of the body, when poured upon it, and is seen on the body of the baptized, when sprinkled upon him, so doth the blood of Christ, by the power of the Holy Ghost, internally sprinkle the soul, cleanse it from its sins, and regenerate us from children of wrath unto children of God.[4] Not that this is effected by the external water, but by the sprinkling of the precious

Q. 69: How art thou admonished and assured by holy baptism that the one sacrifice of Christ upon the cross is of real advantage to thee?

A.: Thus: That Christ appointed this external washing with water,[1] adding thereto this promise,[2] that I am as certainly washed by His blood and Spirit from all the pollution of my soul, that is, from all my sins,[3] as I am washed externally with water, by which the filthiness of the body is commonly washed away.

---
[1] Matt. 28:19; Acts 2:38
[2] Mark 16:16; Matt. 3:11; Rom. 6:3
[3] Mark 1:4; Luke 3:3

Q. 70: What is it to be washed with the blood and Spirit of Christ?

A.: It is to receive of God the remission of sins freely, for the sake of Christ's blood which He shed for us by His sacrifice upon the cross;[1] and also to be renewed by the Holy Ghost, and sanctified to be members of Christ, that so we may more and more die unto sin, and lead holy and unblamable lives.[2]

---
[1] Heb. 12:24; 1 Pet. 1:2
[2] John 1:33; Rom. 6:4; Col. 2:11

Q. 71: Where has Christ promised us, that He will as certainly wash us by His blood and Spirit, as we are washed with the water of baptism?

XX. Of Holy Baptism

1. Baptism was instituted and consecrated by God; and the first that baptized was John, who dipped Christ in the water in Jordan. From him it came to the apostles, who also did baptize with water. The Lord, in plain words, commanded them to preach the gospel and to baptize "in the name of the Father, and of the Son, and of the Holy Ghost" (Matt. 28:19). And Peter also, when divers demanded of him what they ought to do, said to them, in the Acts, "Repent, and be baptized every one of you in the name of Jesus Christ for the remission of sins, and ye shall receive the gift of the Holy Ghost" (Acts 2:38). Hence baptism is called by some a sign of initiation for God's people, whereby the elect of God are consecrated unto God.

2. There is but one baptism in the Church of God; for it is sufficient to be once baptized or consecrated unto God. For baptism once received does continue all a man's life, and is a perpetual sealing of our adoption unto us. For to be baptized in the name of Christ is to be enrolled, entered, and received into the covenant and family, and so into the inheritance, of the sons of God; yea, and in this life to be called after the name of God; that is to say, to be called a son of God; to be purged also from the filthiness of sins, and to be endued with the manifold grace of God, in order to lead a new and innocent life. Baptism, therefore, does call to mind and keep in remembrance the great benefit of God performed to mankind. For we are all born in the pollution of sin and are the children of wrath. But God, who is rich in mercy, does freely purge us from our sins by the blood of His Son, and in Him does adopt us to be His sons, and by a holy covenant does join us to Himself, and does enrich us with divers gifts, that we might live a new life. All these things are sealed up unto us in baptism. For inwardly we are regenerated, purified, and renewed of God through the Holy Spirit; and outwardly we receive the sealing of most notable gifts by the water, by which also those great benefits are represented, and, as it were, set before our eyes to be looked upon. And therefore are we baptized, that is, washed or sprinkled with visible water. For the water makes clean that which is filthy, and refreshes and cools the bodies that fail and faint. And the grace of God deals in like manner with the soul; and that invisibly and spiritually.

Westminster Confession of Faith (1647)	Westminster Shorter Catechism (1647)	Westminster Larger Catechism (1648)

XXVIII: Of Baptism

1. Baptism is a sacrament of the New Testament, ordained by Jesus Christ,[1] not only for the solemn admission of the party baptized into the visible Church;[2] but also to be unto him a sign and seal of the covenant of grace,[3] of his ingrafting into Christ,[4] of regeneration,[5] of remission of sins,[6] and of his giving up unto God, through Jesus Christ, to walk in the newness of life.[7] Which sacrament is, by Christ's own appointment, to be continued in His Church until the end of the world.[8]

[1] Matt. 28:19
[2] 1 Cor. 12:13
[3] Rom. 4:11; Col. 2:11-12
[4] Gal. 3:27; Rom. 6:5
[5] Titus 3:5
[6] Mark 1:4
[7] Rom. 6:3-4
[8] Matt. 28:19-20

2. The outward element to be used in this sacrament is water, wherewith the party is to be baptized, in the name of the Father, and of the Son, and of the Holy Ghost, by a minister of the gospel, lawfully called thereunto.[1]

[1] Matt. 3:11; John 1:33; Matt. 28:19-20

3. Dipping of the person into the water is not necessary; but baptism is rightly administered by pouring, or sprinkling water upon the person.[1]

[1] Heb. 9:10, 19-22; Acts 2:41; 16:33; Mark 7:4

4. Not only those that do actually profess faith in and obedience unto Christ,[1] but also the infants of one, or both, believing parents, are to be baptized.[2]

[1] Mark 16:15-16; Acts 8:37-38
[2] Gen. 17:7, 9; Gal. 3:9, 14; Col. 2:11-12; Acts 2:38-39; Rom. 4:11-12; 1 Cor. 7:14; Matt. 28:19; Mark 10:13-16; Luke 18:15

5. Although it be a great sin to contemn or neglect this ordinance,[1] yet grace and salvation are not so inseparably annexed unto it, as that no person can be regenerated, or saved, without it;[2] or, that all that are baptized are undoubtedly regenerated.[3]

[1] Luke 7:30; Exod. 4:24-26
[2] Rom. 4:11; Acts 10:2, 4, 22, 31, 45, 47
[3] Acts 8:13, 23

6. The efficacy of baptism is not tied to that

Q. 94: What is baptism?

A.: Baptism is a sacrament, wherein the washing with water in the name of the Father, and of the Son, and of the Holy Ghost,[1] doth signify and seal our ingrafting into Christ, and partaking of the benefits of the covenant of grace, and our engagement to be the Lord's.[2]

[1] Matt. 28:19
[2] Rom. 6:4; Gal. 3:27

Q. 95: To whom is baptism to be administered?

A.: Baptism is not to be administered to any that are out of the visible church, till they profess their faith in Christ, and obedience to Him;[1] but the infants of such as are members of the visible church are to be baptized.[2]

[1] Acts 8:36-37; 2:38
[2] Acts 2:38-39; Gen. 17:10; Col. 2:11-12; 1 Cor. 7:14

Q. 165: What is baptism?

A.: Baptism is a sacrament of the New Testament, wherein Christ hath ordained the washing with water in the name of the Father, and of the Son, and of the Holy Ghost,[1] to be a sign and seal of ingrafting into Himself,[2] of remission of sins by His blood,[3] and regeneration by His Spirit;[4] of adoption,[5] and resurrection unto everlasting life;[6] and whereby the parties baptized are solemnly admitted into the visible church,[7] and enter into an open and professed engagement to be wholly and only the Lord's.[8]

[1] Matt. 28:19
[2] Gal. 3:27
[3] Mark 1:4; Rev. 1:5
[4] Titus 3:5; Eph. 5:26
[5] Gal. 3:26-27
[6] 1 Cor. 15:29; Rom. 6:5
[7] 1 Cor. 12:13
[8] Rom. 6:4

Q. 166: Unto whom is baptism to be administered?

A.: Baptism is not to be administered to any that are out of the visible church, and so strangers from the covenant of promise, till they profess their faith in Christ, and obedience to Him,[1] but infants descending from parents, either both, or but one of them, professing faith in Christ, and obedience to Him, are in that respect within the covenant, and to be baptized.[2]

[1] Acts 8:36-38
[2] Gen. 17:7, 9; Gal. 3:9, 14; Col. 2:11-12; Acts 2:38-39; Rom. 4:11-12; 1 Cor. 7:14; Matt. 28:19; Luke 18:15-16; Rom. 11:16

Q. 167: How is our baptism to be improved by us?

A.: The needful but much neglected duty of improving our baptism, is to be performed by us all our life long, especially in the time of temptation, and when we are present at the administration of it to others;[1] by serious and thankful consideration of the nature of it, and of the ends for which Christ instituted it, the privileges and benefits conferred and sealed thereby, and our solemn vow made therein;[2] by being humbled for our sinful defilement, our falling short of, and walking contrary to, the grace of baptism, and our engagements;[3] by growing up to assurance of pardon of sin, and of all other blessings sealed to us in that sacrament;[4] by drawing strength from the death and resurrection of Christ, into whom we are baptized, for the mortifying of sin, and quickening of grace;[5] and by

Belgic Confession (1561)	Heidelberg Catechism (1563)	Second Helvetic Confession (1566)	Canons of Dort (1619)
blood of the Son of God;[5] who is our Red Sea, through which we must pass to escape the tyranny of Pharaoh, that is, the devil, and to enter into the spiritual land of Canaan. Therefore the ministers, on their part, administer the sacrament, and that which is visible,[6] but our Lord giveth that which is signified by the sacrament, namely, the gifts and invisible grace; washing, cleansing, and purging our souls of all filth and unrighteousness;[7] renewing our hearts and filling them with all comfort; giving unto us a true assurance of His fatherly goodness; putting on us the new man, and putting off the old man with all his deeds.[8] Therefore we believe that every man who is earnestly studious of obtaining life eternal ought to be but once baptized with this only baptism, without ever repeating the same,[9] since we cannot be born twice. Neither doth this baptism only avail us at the time when the water is poured upon us and received by us, but also through the whole course of our life.[10] Therefore we detest the error of the Anabaptists, who are not content with the one only baptism they have once received, and moreover condemn the baptism of the infants of believers, whom we believe ought to be baptized and sealed with the sign of the covenant,[11] as the children in Israel formerly were circumcised[12] upon the same promises which are made unto our children. And indeed, Christ shed	A.: In the institution of baptism, which is thus expressed: "Go ye therefore, and teach all nations, baptizing them in the name of the Father, and of the Son, and of the Holy Ghost,"[1] "He that believeth and is baptized, shall be saved; but he that believeth not shall be damned."[2] This promise is also repeated, where the Scripture calls baptism the washing of regeneration[3] and the washing away of sins.[4] [1] Matt. 28:19 [2] Mark 16:16 [3] Titus 3:5 [4] Acts 22:16 Q. 72: *Is then the external baptism with water the washing away of sin itself?* A.: Not at all; for the blood of Jesus Christ only,[1] and the Holy Ghost cleanse us from all sin.[2] [1] Matt. 3:11; 1 Pet. 3:21 [2] 1 John 1:7; 1 Cor. 6:11 Q. 73: *Why then doth the Holy Ghost call baptism "the washing of regeneration" and the "washing away of sins"?* A.: God speaks thus not without great cause, to wit, not only thereby to teach us that as the filth of the body is purged away by water, so our sins are removed by the blood and Spirit of Jesus Christ;[1] but especially that by this divine pledge and sign He may assure us that we are spiritually cleansed from our sins as really as we are externally washed with water.[2] [1] Rev. 1:5; 1 Cor. 6:11 [2] Mark 16:16; Gal. 3:27	3. Moreover, by the sacrament of baptism God does separate us from all other religions and nations, and does consecrate us a peculiar people to Himself. We, therefore, by being baptized, do confess our faith, and are bound to give unto God obedience, mortification of the flesh, and newness of life; yea, and we are soldiers enlisted for the holy warfare of Christ, that all our life long we should fight against the world, Satan, and our own flesh. Moreover, we are baptized into one body of the Church, that we might well agree with all the members of the Church in the same religion and mutual duties. 4. We believe that the most perfect form of baptism is that by which Christ was baptized, and which the apostles did use. Those things, therefore, which by man's device were added afterwards and used in the Church we do not consider necessary to the perfection of baptism. Of this kind is exorcism, the use of lights, oil, spittle, and such other things; as, namely, that baptism is twice every year consecrated with divers ceremonies. But we believe that the baptism of the Church, which is but one, was sanctified in God's first institution of it, and is consecrated by the Word, and is now of full force, by the first blessing of God upon it. 5. We teach that baptism should not be ministered in the Church by women or midwives. For Paul secludes women from ecclesiastical callings; but baptism belongs to ecclesiastical offices. 6. We condemn the Anabaptists, who deny that young infants, born of faithful parents, are to be baptized. For, according to the doctrine of the gospel, "for of such is the kingdom of God" (Luke 18:16), and they are written in the covenant of God (Acts 3:25). Why, then, should not the sign of the covenant of God be given to them? Why should they not be consecrated by holy baptism, who are God's peculiar people and are in the Church of God? We condemn also the Anabaptists in the rest of those peculiar opinions which they hold against the Word of God. We therefore are not Anabaptists, neither do we agree with them in any point that is theirs.	

Westminster Confession of Faith (1647)	Westminster Shorter Catechism (1647)	Westminster Larger Catechism (1648)
moment of time wherein it is administered;[1] yet, notwithstanding, by the right use of this ordinance, the grace promised is not only offered, but really exhibited, and conferred, by the Holy Ghost, to such (whether of age or infants) as that grace belongeth unto, according to the counsel of God's own will, in His appointed time.[2] --- [1] John 3:5, 8 [2] Gal. 3:27; Titus 3:5; Eph. 5:25-26; Acts 2:38, 41 7. The sacrament of baptism is but once to be administered unto any person.[1] --- [1] Titus 3:5		endeavouring to live by faith,[6] to have our conversation in holiness and righteousness,[7] as those that have therein given up their names to Christ;[8] and to walk in brotherly love, as being baptized by the same Spirit into one body.[9] --- [1] Col. 2:11-12; Rom. 6:4, 6, 11 [2] Rom. 6:3-5 [3] 1 Cor. 1:11-13; Rom. 6:2-3 [4] Rom. 4:11-12; 1 Pet. 3:21 [5] Rom. 6:3-5 [6] Gal. 3:26-27 [7] Rom. 6:22 [8] Acts 2:38 [9] 1 Cor. 12:13, 25-27

Belgic Confession (1561)	Heidelberg Catechism (1563)	Second Helvetic Confession (1566)	Canons of Dort (1619)
His blood no less for the washing of the children of the faithful than for adult persons;[13] and therefore, they ought to receive the sign and sacrament of that which Christ hath done for them; as the Lord commanded in the law, that they should be made partakers of the sacrament of Christ's suffering and death shortly after they were born, by offering for them a lamb, which was a sacrament of Jesus Christ.[14] Moreover, what circumcision was to the Jews, that baptism is to our children. And for this reason Paul calls baptism the *circumcision of Christ*.[15]	Q. 74: *Are infants also to be baptized?* A.: Yes, for since they, as well as the adult, are included in the covenant[1] and church of God;[2] and since redemption from sin[3] by the blood of Christ, and the Holy Ghost, the author of faith, is promised to them[4] no less than to the adult; they must therefore by baptism, as a sign of the covenant, be also admitted into the Christian church, and be distinguished from the children of unbelievers[5] as was done in the old covenant or testament by circumcision,[6] instead of which baptism is instituted in the new covenant.[7]		

Belgic footnotes:
[1] Rom. 10:4
[2] Col. 2:11; 1 Pet. 3:21; 1 Cor. 10:2
[3] Matt. 28:19
[4] 1 Cor. 6:11; Titus 3:5; Heb. 9:14; 1 John 1:7; Rev. 1:6
[5] John 19:34
[6] Matt. 3:11; 1 Cor. 3:5,7; Rom. 6:3
[7] Eph. 5:26; Acts 22:16; 1 Pet. 3:21
[8] Gal. 3:27; 1 Cor. 12:13; Eph. 4:22-24
[9] Mark 16:16; Matt. 28:19; Eph. 4:5; Heb. 6:2
[10] Acts 2:38; 8:16
[11] Matt. 19:14; 1 Cor. 7:14
[12] Gen. 17:11-12
[13] Col. 2:11-12
[14] John 1:29; Lev. 12:6
[15] Col. 2:11

Heidelberg footnotes:
[1] Gen. 17:7; Acts 2:39
[2] 1 Cor. 7:14; Joel 2:16
[3] Matt. 19:14
[4] Luke 1:14-15; Ps. 22:10; Acts 2:39
[5] Acts 10:47; 1 Cor. 12:13; 1 Cor. 7:14
[6] Gen. 17:14
[7] Col. 2:11-13

The Lord's Supper

| Article 35 **The Holy Supper of Our Lord Jesus Christ** We believe and confess that our Savior Jesus Christ did ordain and institute the sacrament of the Holy Supper,[1] to nourish and support those | Q. 75: *How art thou admonished and assured in the Lord's Supper that thou art a partaker of that one sacrifice of Christ, accomplished on the cross, and of all His benefits?* A.: Thus: That Christ has commanded me | **XXI. Of the Holy Supper of the Lord** 1. The Supper of the Lord (which is called the Lord's Table, and the Eucharist, that is, a Thanksgiving) is, therefore, commonly called a supper, because it was instituted by Christ at His last supper, and does as yet represent the same, and because in it the faithful are spiritually fed and nourished. For the author of the Supper of the Lord is not an angel or man, but the very Son of | |

Westminster Confession of Faith (1647)	Westminster Shorter Catechism (1647)	Westminster Larger Catechism (1648)

XXIX: Of the Lord's Supper

1. Our Lord Jesus, in the night wherein He was betrayed, instituted the sacrament of His body and blood, called the Lord's Supper, to be observed in His Church, unto the end of the world, for the perpetual remembrance of the sacrifice of Himself in His death; the sealing all benefits thereof unto true believers, their spiritual nourishment and growth in Him, their further en-

Q. 96: What is the Lord's Supper?

A.: The Lord's Supper is a sacrament, wherein, by giving and receiving bread and wine, according to Christ's appointment, His death is shewed forth; and the worthy receivers are, not after

Q. 168: What is the Lord's Supper?

A.: The Lord's Supper is a sacrament of the New Testament,[1] wherein, by giving and receiving bread and wine according to the appointment of Jesus Christ, His death is shewed forth; and they that worthily communicate feed upon His body and blood, to their spiritual nourishment and growth in grace;[2] have their union and communion with Him confirmed;[3]

Belgic Confession (1561)	Heidelberg Catechism (1563)	Second Helvetic Confession (1566)	Canons of Dort (1619)

Belgic Confession (1561)

whom He hath already regenerated and incorporated into His family, which is His Church.

Now those who are regenerated have in them a twofold life,[2] the one corporal and temporal, which they have from the first birth, and is common to all men; the other spiritual and heavenly, which is given them in their second birth,[3] which is effected by the word of the gospel,[4] in the communion of the body of Christ; and this life is not common, but is peculiar to God's elect.[5] In like manner God hath given us, for the support of the bodily and earthly life, earthly and common bread, which is subservient thereto, and is common to all men, even as life itself. But for the support of the spiritual and heavenly life which believers have, He hath sent a living bread, which descended from heaven, namely, Jesus Christ,[6] who nourishes and strengthens the spiritual life of believers, when they eat Him, that is to say, when they apply and receive Him by faith, in the Spirit.[7]

Christ, that He might represent unto us this spiritual and heavenly bread, hath instituted an earthly and visible bread as a sacrament of His body, and wine as a sacrament of His blood,[8] to testify by them unto us, that, as certainly as we receive and hold this sacrament in our hands, and eat and drink the same with our mouths, by which our life is afterwards nourished, we also do as certainly receive by

Heidelberg Catechism (1563)

and all believers to eat of this broken bread and to drink of this cup in remembrance of Him, adding these promises:[1] first, that His body was offered and broken on the cross for me, and His blood shed for me, as certainly as I see with my eyes the bread of the Lord broken for me and the cup communicated to me; and further, that He feeds and nourishes my soul to everlasting life, with His crucified body and shed blood, as assuredly as I receive from the hands of the minister, and taste with my mouth the bread and cup of the Lord, as certain signs of the body and blood of Christ.

---
[1] Matt. 26:26-28; Mark 14:22-24; Luke 22:19-20; 1 Cor. 10:16-17; 1 Cor. 11:23-25

Q. 76: What is it then to eat the crucified body, and drink the shed blood of Christ?

A.: It is not only to embrace with a believing heart all the sufferings and death of Christ, and thereby to obtain the pardon of sin and life eternal;[1] but also, besides that, to become more and more united to His sacred body, by the Holy Ghost, who dwells both in Christ and in us;[2] so that we, though Christ is in heaven[3] and we on earth, are notwithstanding "flesh of His flesh, and bone of His bone";[4] and that we live, and are governed forever by one spirit, as mem-

Second Helvetic Confession (1566)

God, our Lord Jesus Christ, who did first of all consecrate it to His Church. And the same blessing and consecration does still remain among all those who celebrate no other but that very supper, which the Lord did institute, and at that do recite the words of the Supper of the Lord, and in all things look unto the one Christ by a true faith; at whose hands, as it were, they do receive that which they do receive by the ministry of the ministers of the Church.

2. The Lord, by this sacred rite, would have that great benefit to be kept in fresh remembrance which He procured for mankind; to wit, that by giving up His body to death and shedding His blood He has forgiven us all our sins, and redeemed us from eternal death and the power of the devil, and now feeds us with His flesh, and gives us His blood to drink; which things, being apprehended spiritually by a true faith, do nourish us up to life everlasting. And this so great a benefit is renewed so oft as the Supper is celebrated. For the Lord said, "This do in remembrance of me" (Luke 22:19).

3. By this holy Supper also it is sealed unto us, that the very body of Christ was truly given up for us, and His blood shed for the remission of our sins, lest our faith might somewhat waver. And this is outwardly represented unto us by the minister in the sacrament, after a visible manner, and, as it were, laid before our eyes to be seen, which is inwardly in the soul invisibly performed by the Holy Spirit. Outwardly, bread is offered by the minister, and the words of the Lord are heard: "Take, eat; this is my body;" and, "Drink ye all of it; for this is my blood" (Matt. 26:26-28; Luke 22:17-20). Therefore the faithful do receive that which is given by the ministers of the Lord, and do eat the bread of the Lord, and do drink of the Lord's cup. And at the same time inwardly, by the working of Christ through the Holy Spirit, they receive also the flesh and blood of the Lord, and do feed on them unto life eternal. For the flesh and blood of Christ is true meat and drink unto life eternal; yea, Christ Himself, in that He was delivered for us, and is our Savior, is that special thing and substance of the Supper; and therefore we suffer nothing to be put in His place.

4. But that it may the better and more plainly be understood how the flesh and blood of Christ are the meat and drink of the faithful, and are received by the faithful unto life eternal, we will add, moreover, these few things:

5. Eating is of divers sorts. (1.) There is a *corporal* eating, whereby meat is taken into a man's

Westminster Confession of Faith (1647)	Westminster Shorter Catechism (1647)	Westminster Larger Catechism (1648)

gagement in and to all duties which they owe unto Him; and, to be a bond and pledge of their communion with Him, and with each other, as members of His mystical body.[1]

[1] 1 Cor. 11:23-26; 10:16-17, 21; 12:13

2. In this sacrament, Christ is not offered up to His Father; nor any real sacrifice made at all, for remission of sins of the quick or dead;[1] but only a commemoration of that one offering up of Himself, by Himself, upon the cross, once for all, and a spiritual oblation of all possible praise unto God, for the same;[2] so that the popish sacrifice of the mass (as they call it) is most abominably injurious to Christ's one, only sacrifice, the alone propitiation for all the sins of His elect.[3]

[1] Heb. 9:22, 25-26, 28
[2] 1 Cor. 11:24-26; Matt. 26:26-27
[3] Heb. 7:23-24, 27; 10:11-12, 14, 18

3. The Lord Jesus hath, in this ordinance, appointed His ministers to declare His word of institution to the people; to pray, and bless the elements of bread and wine, and thereby to set them apart from a common to a holy use; and to take and break the bread, to take the cup, and (they communicating also themselves) to give both to the communicants;[1] but to none who are not then present in the congregation.[2]

[1] Matt. 26:26-28; Mark 14:22-24; Luke 22:19-20; 1 Cor. 11:23-26
[2] Acts 20:7; 1 Cor. 11:20

4. Private masses, or receiving this sacrament by a priest, or any other, alone;[1] as likewise, the denial of the cup to the people,[2] worshipping the elements, the lifting them up, or carrying them about, for adoration, and the reserving them for any pretended religious use, are all contrary to the nature of this sacrament, and to the institution of Christ.[3]

[1] 1 Cor. 10:6
[2] Mark 14:23; 1 Cor. 11:25-29
[3] Matt. 15:9

5. The outward elements in this sacrament, duly set apart to the uses ordained by Christ, have such relation to Him crucified, as that, truly, yet sacramentally only, they are sometimes called by the name of the things they represent, to wit, the body and blood of Christ;[1] albeit, in substance and nature, they still remain truly and only bread and wine, as they were before.[2]

[1] Matt. 26:26-28
[2] 1 Cor. 11:26-28; Matt. 26:29

6. That doctrine which maintains a change of

a corporal and carnal manner, but by faith, made partakers of His body and blood, with all His benefits, to their spiritual nourishment, and growth in grace.[1]

[1] 1 Cor. 11:23-26; 1 Cor. 10:16

Q. 97: What is required for the worthy receiving of the Lord's Supper?

A.: It is required of them that would worthily partake of the Lord's Supper, that they examine themselves of their knowledge to discern the Lord's body,[1] of their faith to feed upon Him,[2] of their repentance,[3] love,[4] and new obedience;[5] lest, coming unworthily, they eat and drink judgment to themselves.[6]

[1] 1 Cor. 11:28-29
[2] 2 Cor. 13:5
[3] 1 Cor. 11:31
[4] 1 Cor. 10:16-17
[5] 1 Cor. 5:7-8
[6] 1 Cor. 11:28-29

testify and renew their thankfulness,[4] and engagement to God,[5] and their mutual love and fellowship each with other, as members of the same mystical body.[6]

[1] Luke 22:20
[2] Matt. 26:26-28; 1 Cor. 11:23-26
[3] 1 Cor. 10:16
[4] 1 Cor. 11:24
[5] 1 Cor. 10:14-16, 21
[6] 1 Cor. 10:17

Q. 169: How hath Christ appointed bread and wine to be given and received in the sacrament of the Lord's Supper?

A.: Christ hath appointed the ministers of His Word, in the administration of this sacrament of the Lord's Supper, to set apart the bread and wine from common use, by the word of institution, thanksgiving, and prayer; to take and break the bread, and to give both the bread and the wine to the communicants, who are, by the same appointment, to take and eat the bread, and to drink the wine, in thankful remembrance that the body of Christ was broken and given, and His blood shed, for them.[1]

[1] 1 Cor. 11:23-24; Matt. 26:26-28; Mark 14:22-24; Luke 22:19-20

Q. 170: How do they that worthily communicate in the Lord's Supper feed upon the body and blood of Christ therein?

A.: As the body and blood of Christ are not corporally or carnally present in, with, or under the bread and wine in the Lord's Supper,[1] and yet are spiritually present to the faith of the receiver, no less truly and really than the elements themselves are to their outward senses;[2] so they that worthily communicate in the sacrament of the Lord's Supper, do therein feed upon the body and blood of Christ, not after a corporal and carnal, but in a spiritual manner; yet truly and really,[3] while by faith they receive and apply unto themselves Christ crucified, and all the benefits of His death.[4]

[1] Acts 3:21
[2] Matt. 26:26, 28
[3] 1 Cor. 11:24-29
[4] 1 Cor. 10:16

Q. 171: How are they that receive the sacrament of the Lord's Supper to prepare themselves before they come unto it?

A.: They that receive the sacrament of the Lord's Supper are, before they come, to prepare themselves thereunto, by examining themselves[1] of their being in Christ,[2] of their sins and wants;[3] of the truth and measure of their

Belgic Confession (1561)	Heidelberg Catechism (1563)	Second Helvetic Confession (1566)	Canons of Dort (1619)

Belgic Confession (1561)

faith (which is the hand and mouth of our soul) the true body and blood of Christ our only Savior in our souls, for the support of our spiritual life.[9]

Now as it is certain and beyond all doubt that Jesus Christ hath not enjoined to us the use of His sacraments in vain, so He works in us all that He represents to us by these holy signs, though the manner surpasses our understanding, and cannot be comprehended by us, as the operations of the Holy Ghost are hidden and incomprehensible. In the meantime we err not when we say that what is eaten and drunk by us is the proper and natural body, and the proper blood, of Christ.[10] But the manner of our partaking of the same is not by the mouth, but by the Spirit through faith. Thus, then, though Christ always sits at the right hand of His Father in the heavens,[11] yet doth He not, therefore, cease to make us partakers of Himself by faith. This feast is a spiritual table, at which Christ communicates Himself with all His benefits to us, and gives us there to enjoy both Himself and the merits of His sufferings and death,[12] nourishing, strengthening, and comforting our poor comfortless souls, by the eating of His flesh, quickening and refreshing them by the drinking of His blood.[13]

Further, though the sacraments are connected with the thing signified, nevertheless both are not received by all men; the ungodly in-

Heidelberg Catechism (1563)

bers of the same body are by one soul.[5]

[1] John 6:35, 40, 47-48, 50-51, 53-54
[2] John 6:55-56
[3] Acts 3:21; Acts 1:9-11; 1 Cor. 11:26
[4] Eph. 5:29-32; 1 Cor. 6:15, 17, 19; 1 John 3:24
[5] John 6:56-58; Eph. 4:15-16

Q. 77: Where has Christ promised that He will as certainly feed and nourish believers with His body and blood, as they eat of this broken bread, and drink of this cup?

A.: In the institution of the supper, which is thus expressed: "The Lord Jesus the same night in which He was betrayed took bread: and when He had given thanks, He brake it, and said, Take, eat: this is My body, which is broken for you; this do in remembrance of Me.[1] After the same manner also He took the cup, when He had supped, saying, This cup is the new testament in My blood;[2] this do ye, as often as ye drink it, in remembrance of Me. For, as often as ye eat this bread, and drink this cup, ye do show the Lord's death till He come."[3] This promise is repeated by the holy apostle Paul, where he says: "The cup of blessing which we bless, is it not the communion of the blood of Christ? For we, being many, are one bread and one body: for we are all partakers of that one bread."[4]

[1] 1 Cor. 11:23; Matt. 26:26; Mark 14:22; Luke 22:19
[2] Exod. 24:8; Heb. 9:20
[3] Exod. 13:9; 1 Cor. 11:26
[4] 1 Cor. 10:16-17

Second Helvetic Confession (1566)

mouth, chewed with the teeth, swallowed down, and digested. After this manner did the Capernaites in times past think that they should eat the flesh of the Lord; but they are confuted by him (John 6:30-63). For as the flesh of Christ could not be eaten bodily, without great wickedness and cruelty, so is it not food for the body, as all men do confess. We therefore disallow that canon in the pope's decrees, *Ego Berengarius (De Consecrat. Dist. 2)*. For neither did godly antiquity believe, neither yet do we believe, that the body of Christ can be eaten corporally and essentially, with a bodily mouth.

6. (2.) There is also a *spiritual* eating of Christ's body; not such a one whereby it may be thought that the very meat is changed into the spirit, but whereby (the Lord's body and blood remaining in their own essence and property) those things are spiritually communicated unto us, not after a corporal, but after a spiritual manner, through the Holy Spirit, who does apply and bestow upon us those things (to wit, remission of sins, deliverance, and life eternal) which are prepared for us by the flesh and blood of our Lord, sacrificed for us; so that Christ does now live in us, as we live in Him; and does cause us to apprehend Him by true faith to this end, that He may become unto us such a spiritual meat and drink, that is to say, our life. For even as corporal meat and drink do not only refresh and strengthen our bodies, but also do keep them in life; even so the flesh of Christ delivered for us, and his blood shed for us, do not only refresh and strengthen our souls, but also do preserve them alive, not so far as they be corporally eaten and drunken, but so far as they are communicated unto us spiritually by the Spirit of God, the Lord saying, "The bread that I will give is My flesh, which I will give for the life of the world" (John 6:51); also it is the spirit that gives life: "the flesh" (to wit, corporally eaten) "profiteth nothing: the words that I speak unto you, they are spirit, and they are life" (John 6:63). And as we must by eating receive the meat into our bodies, to the end that it may work in us, and show its efficacy in us (because, while it is without us, it profiteth us not at all); even so it is necessary that we receive Christ by faith, that He may be made ours, and that He live in us, and we in Him. For He says, "I am the bread of life; he that cometh to Me shall never hunger; and he that believeth on Me shall never thirst" (John 6:35); and also, "This is the bread which cometh down from heaven, that a man may eat thereof, and not die" (John 6:50).

7. From all this it appears manifestly, that by spiritual meat we mean not any imaginary thing,

Westminster Confession of Faith (1647)	Westminster Shorter Catechism (1647)	Westminster Larger Catechism (1648)

the substance of bread and wine, into the substance of Christ's body and blood (commonly called transubstantiation) by consecration of a priest, or by any other way, is repugnant, not to Scripture alone, but even to common sense, and reason; overthroweth the nature of the sacrament, and hath been, and is, the cause of manifold superstitions; yea, of gross idolatries.[1]

---
[1] Acts 3:21; 1 Cor. 11:24-26; Luke 24:6, 39

7. Worthy receivers, outwardly partaking of the visible elements, in this sacrament,[1] do then also, inwardly by faith, really and indeed, yet not carnally and corporally but spiritually, receive and feed upon, Christ crucified, and all benefits of His death, the body and blood of Christ being then, not corporally or carnally, in, with, or under the bread and wine; yet, as really, but spiritually, present to the faith of believers in that ordinance, as the elements themselves are to their outward senses.[2]

---
[1] 1 Cor. 11:28
[2] 1 Cor. 10:16

8. Although ignorant and wicked men receive the outward elements in this sacrament, yet, they receive not the thing signified thereby; but, by their unworthy coming thereunto, are guilty of the body and blood of the Lord, to their own damnation. Wherefore, all ignorant and ungodly persons, as they are unfit to enjoy communion with Him, so are they unworthy of the Lord's table; and cannot, without great sin against Christ, while they remain such, partake of these holy mysteries,[1] or be admitted thereunto.[2]

---
[1] 1 Cor. 11:27-29; 2 Cor. 6:14-16
[2] 1 Cor. 5:6-7, 13; 2 Thes. 3:6, 14-15; Matt. 7:6

knowledge,[4] faith,[5] repentance;[6] love to God and the brethren,[7] charity to all men,[8] forgiving those that have done them wrong;[9] of their desires after Christ,[10] and of their new obedience;[11] and by renewing the exercise of these graces,[12] by serious meditation,[13] and fervent prayer.[14]

---
[1] 1 Cor. 11:28
[2] 2 Cor. 13:5
[3] 1 Cor. 5:7; Exod. 12:15
[4] 1 Cor. 11:29
[5] 1 Cor. 13:5; Matt. 26:28
[6] Zech. 12:10; 1 Cor. 11:31
[7] 1 Cor. 10:16-17; Acts 2:46-47
[8] 1 Cor. 5:8; 11:18, 20
[9] Matt. 5:23-24
[10] Isa. 55:1; John 7:37
[11] 1 Cor. 5:7-8
[12] 1 Cor. 11:25-26, 28; Heb. 10:21, 22, 24; Ps. 26:6
[13] 1 Cor. 11:24-25
[14] 2 Chron. 30:18-19; Matt. 26:26

Q. 172: May one who doubteth of his being in Christ, or of his due preparation, come to the Lord's Supper?

A.: One who doubteth of his being in Christ, or of his due preparation to the sacrament of the Lord's Supper, may have true interest in Christ, though he be not yet assured thereof;[1] and in God's account hath it, if he be duly affected with the apprehension of the want of it,[2] and unfeignedly desires to be found in Christ,[3] and to depart from iniquity;[4] in which case (because promises are made, and this sacrament is appointed, for the relief even of weak and doubting Christians[5]) he is to bewail his unbelief,[6] and labor to have his doubts resolved;[7] and, so doing, he may and ought to come to the Lord's Supper, that he may be further strengthened.[8]

---
[1] Isa. 1:10; 1 John 5:13; Ps. 88; 77:1-12; Jonah 2:4, 7
[2] Isa. 54:7-10; Matt. 5:3-4; Ps. 31:22; 73:13, 22-23
[3] Phil. 3:8-9; Ps. 10:17; 42:1-2, 5, 11
[4] 2 Tim. 2:19; Isa. 50:10; Ps. 66:18-20
[5] Isa. 40:11, 29, 31; Matt. 11:28; 12:20; 26:28
[6] Mark 9:24
[7] Acts 2:37; 16:30
[8] Rom. 4:11; 1 Cor. 11:28

Q. 173: May any who profess the faith, and desire to come to the Lord's Supper, be kept from it?

A.: Such as are found to be ignorant or scandalous, notwithstanding their profession of the faith, and desire to come to the Lord's Supper, may and ought to be kept from that sacrament, by the power which Christ hath left in His church,[1] until they receive instruction, and manifest their reformation.[2]

---
[1] 1 Cor. 11:27-31; Matt. 7:6; 1 Cor. 5; Jude 23; 1 Tim. 5:22
[2] 2 Cor. 2:7

Belgic Confession (1561)	Heidelberg Catechism (1563)	Second Helvetic Confession (1566)	Canons of Dort (1619)

Belgic Confession (1561)

deed receives the sacrament to his condemnation,[14] but he doth not receive the truth of the sacrament. As Judas and Simon the sorcerer, both indeed received the sacrament, but not Christ who was signified by it, of whom believers only are made partakers.

Lastly, we receive this holy sacrament in the assembly of the people of God, with humility and reverence,[15] keeping up among us a holy remembrance of the death of Christ our Savior, with thanksgiving, making there confession of our faith and of the Christian religion. Therefore no one ought to come to this table without having previously rightly examined himself; lest by eating of this bread and drinking of this cup he eat and drink judgment to himself.[16] In a word, we are excited by the use of this holy sacrament to a fervent love towards God and our neighbor.

Therefore we reject all mixtures and damnable inventions, which men have added unto and blended with the sacraments, as profanations of them, and affirm that we ought to rest satisfied with the ordinance which Christ and His apostles have taught us, and that we must speak of them in the same manner as they have spoken.

[1] Matt. 26:26; Mark 14:22; Luke 22:19; 1 Cor. 11:23-25
[2] John 3:6
[3] John 3:5
[4] John 5:23,25
[5] 1 John 5:12; John 10:28
[6] John 6:32-33,51
[7] John 6:63
[8] Mark 6:26

Heidelberg Catechism (1563)

Q. 78: *Do then the bread and wine become the very body and blood of Christ?*

A.: Not at all; but as the water in baptism is not changed into the blood of Christ, neither is the washing away of sin itself, being only the sign and confirmation thereof appointed of God;[1] so the bread in the Lord's Supper is not changed into the very body of Christ,[2] though agreeably to the nature and properties of sacraments,[3] it is called the body of Christ Jesus.

[1] 1 Cor. 10:1-4; 1 Pet. 3:21; John 6:35, 62-63
[2] 1 Cor. 10:16, etc.; 1 Cor. 11:20, etc.
[3] Gen. 17:10-11, 14; Exod. 12:26-27, 43, 48; Acts 7:8; Matt. 26:26; Mark 14:24

Q. 79: *Why then doth Christ call the bread His body, and the cup His blood, or the new covenant in His blood; and Paul, the "communion of the body and blood of Christ"?*

A.: Christ speaks thus not without great reason, namely, not only thereby to teach us that as bread and wine support this temporal life, so His crucified body and shed blood are the true meat and drink whereby our souls are fed to eternal life;[1] but more especially by these visible signs and pledges to assure us that we are as really partakers of His true body and blood (by the operation of the Holy Ghost) as we receive by the mouths of our bodies these holy signs in remembrance of Him;[2] and

Second Helvetic Confession (1566)

but the very body of our Lord Jesus, given to us; which yet is received by the faithful not corporally, but spiritually by faith, in which point we do wholly follow the doctrine of our Lord and Savior Christ, in the 6th chapter of John. And this eating of the flesh and drinking of the blood of the Lord is so necessary to salvation that without it no man can be saved. But this spiritual eating and drinking takes place also without the Supper of the Lord, even so often as, and wheresoever, a man does believe in Christ. To which purpose that sentence of St. Augustine does happily belong, "Why dost thou prepare thy teeth and belly? Believe, and thou hast eaten."

8. (3.) Besides that former spiritual eating, there is a *sacramental* eating of the body of the Lord; whereby the believer not only is partaker, spiritually and internally, of the true body and blood of the Lord, but also, by coming to the table of the Lord, does outwardly receive the visible sacraments of the body and blood of the Lord. True it is, that by faith the believer did before receive the food that gives life, and still receives the same; but yet, when he receives the sacrament, he receives something more. For he goes on in continual communication of the body and blood of the Lord, and his faith is daily more and more kindled, more strengthened and refreshed, by the spiritual nourishment. For while we live, faith has continual increasings; and he that outwardly does receive the sacrament with a true faith, the same does not only receive the sign, but also does enjoy (as we said) the thing itself. Moreover, the same does obey the Lord's institution and commandment, and with a joyful mind gives thanks for his redemption and that of all mankind, and makes a faithful remembrance of the Lord's death, and does witness the same before the Church, of which body he is a member. This also is sealed to those who receive the sacrament, that the body of the Lord was given, and His blood shed, not only for men in general, but particularly for every faithful communicant, whose meat and drink he is, to life eternal.

9. But as for him that without faith comes to this holy table of the Lord, he is made partaker of the outward sacrament only; but the matter of the sacrament, from whence comes life unto salvation, he receives not at all; and such men do unworthily eat of the Lord's table. "Wherefore whosoever shall eat this bread, and drink this cup of the Lord, unworthily, shall be guilty of the body and blood of the Lord. . . . and drinketh damnation to himself" (1 Cor. 11:27-29). For when they do not approach with true faith, they do despite unto the death of Christ, and therefore eat and drink condemnation to themselves.

Westminster Confession of Faith (1647)	Westminster Shorter Catechism (1647)	Westminster Larger Catechism (1648)

Westminster Larger Catechism (cont.)

Q. 174: What is required of them that receive the sacrament of the Lord's Supper in the time of the administration of it?

A.: It is required of them that receive the sacrament of the Lord's Supper, that, during the time of the administration of it, with all holy reverence and attention they wait upon God in that ordinance,[1] diligently observe the sacramental elements and actions,[2] heedfully discern the Lord's body,[3] and affectionately meditate on His death and sufferings,[4] and thereby stir up themselves to a vigorous exercise of their graces;[5] in judging themselves,[6] and sorrowing for sin;[7] in earnest hungering and thirsting after Christ,[8] feeding on Him by faith,[9] receiving of His fulness,[10] trusting in His merits,[11] rejoicing in His love,[12] giving thanks for His grace;[13] in renewing of their covenant with God,[14] and love to all the saints.[15]

[1] Lev. 10:3; Heb. 12:28; Ps. 5:7; 1 Cor. 11:17, 26-27
[2] Exod. 24:8; Matt. 26:28
[3] 1 Cor. 11:29
[4] Luke 22:19
[5] 1 Cor. 11:26; 10:3-5, 11, 14
[6] 1 Cor. 11:31
[7] Zech. 12:10
[8] Rev. 22:17
[9] John 6:35
[10] John 1:16
[11] Phil. 1:16
[12] Ps. 63:4-5; 2 Chron. 30:21
[13] Ps. 22:26
[14] Jer. 50:5; Ps. 50:5
[15] Acts 2:42

Q. 175: What is the duty of Christians, after they have received the sacrament of the Lord's Supper?

A.: The duty of Christians, after they have received the sacrament of the Lord's Supper, is seriously to consider how they have behaved themselves therein, and with what success;[1] if they find quickening and comfort, to bless God for it,[2] beg the continuance of it,[3] watch against relapses,[4] fulfil their vows,[5] and encourage themselves to a frequent attendance on that ordinance;[6] but if they find no present benefit, more exactly to review their preparation to, and carriage at, the sacrament;[7] in both which, if they can approve themselves to God and their own consciences, they are to wait for the fruit of it in due time;[8] but, if they see they have failed in either, they are to be humbled,[9] and to attend upon it afterwards with more care and diligence.[10]

[1] Ps. 28:7; 85:8; 1 Cor. 11:17, 30-31
[2] 2 Chron. 30:21-23, 25-26; Acts 2:42, 46-47
[3] Ps. 36:10; Songs 3:4; 1 Chron. 29:18
[4] 1 Cor. 10:3-5, 12
[5] Ps. 50:14
[6] 1 Cor. 11:25-26; Acts 2:42, 46
[7] Songs 5:1-6; Eccl. 5:1-6
[8] Ps. 123:1-2; 42:5, 8; 43:3-5
[9] 2 Chron. 30:18-19; Isa. 1:16, 18
[10] 2 Cor. 7:11; 1 Chron. 15:12-14

Belgic Confession (1561)	Heidelberg Catechism (1563)	Second Helvetic Confession (1566)	Canons of Dort (1619)

Belgic Confession (1561)

[9] 1 Cor. 10:16-17; Eph. 3:17; John 6:35
[10] John 6:55-56; 1 Cor. 10:16
[11] Acts 3:21; Mark 16:19; Matt. 26:11
[12] Matt. 26:26, etc.; Luke 22:19-20; 1 Cor. 10:2-4
[13] Isa. 55:2; Rom. 8:22-23
[14] 1 Cor. 11:29; 2 Cor. 6:14-15; 1 Cor. 2:14
[15] Acts 2:42; 20:7
[16] 1 Cor. 11:27-28

Heidelberg Catechism (1563)

that all His sufferings and obedience are as certainly ours, as if we had in our own persons suffered and made satisfaction for our sins to God.[3]

[1] John 6:51, 55-56
[2] 1 Cor. 10:16-17; 1 Cor. 11:26-28; Eph. 5:30
[3] Rom. 5:9, 18-19; Rom. 8:4

Q. 80: What difference is there between the Lord's Supper and the popish mass?
A.: The Lord's Supper testifies to us that we have a full pardon of all sin by the only sacrifice of Jesus Christ, which He Himself has once accomplished on the cross;[1] and that we by the Holy Ghost are ingrafted into Christ,[2] who, according to His human nature is now not on earth, but in heaven, at the right hand of God His Father,[3] and will there be worshipped by us[4] — but the mass teaches that the living and dead have not the pardon of sins through the sufferings of Christ, unless Christ is also daily offered for them by the priests; and further, that Christ is bodily under the form of bread and wine, and therefore is to be worshipped in them; so that the mass, at bottom, is nothing else than a denial of the one sacrifice and sufferings of Jesus Christ, and an accursed idolatry.[5]

[1] Heb. 7:27; Heb. 9:12, 26; Matt. 26:28; Luke 22:19-20; 2 Cor. 5:21
[2] 1 Cor. 12:13
[3] Heb. 1:3; Heb. 8:1, etc.
[4] John 4:21-23; Col. 3:1; Phil. 3:20; Luke 24:52-53; Acts 7:55
[5] Isa. 1:11, 14; Matt. 15:9; Col. 2:22-23; Jer. 2:13

Second Helvetic Confession (1566)

10. We do not, therefore, so join the body of the Lord and His blood with the bread and wine, as though we thought that the bread is the body of Christ, more than after a sacramental manner; or that the body of Christ does lie hid corporally under the bread, so that it ought to be worshipped under the form of bread; or yet that whosoever he be who receives the sign, receives also the thing itself. The body of Christ is in the heavens, at the right hand of his Father; and therefore our hearts are to be lifted up on high, and not to be fixed on the bread, neither is the Lord to be worshipped in the bread. Yet the Lord is not absent from His Church when she celebrates the Supper. The sun, being absent from us in the heavens, is yet, notwithstanding, present among us effectually; how much more Christ, the Sun of Righteousness, though in body He be absent from us in the heavens, yet is present among us, not corporally, but spiritually, by His lively operation, and so as He Himself promised, in His Last Supper, to be present among us (John 14, 15 and 16). Whereupon it follows that we have not the Supper without Christ, and yet that we may have meanwhile an unbloody and mystical supper, even as all antiquity called it.

11. Moreover, we are admonished, in the celebration of the Supper of the Lord, to be mindful of the body whereof we are members; and that, therefore, we should be at concord with our brethren, that we live holily, and not pollute ourselves with wickedness and strange religions; but, persevering in the true faith to the end of our life, give diligence to excel in holiness of life. It is therefore very requisite that, purposing to come to the Supper of the Lord, we do examine ourselves, according to the commandment of the apostle: first, with what faith we are indued, whether we believe that Christ is come to save sinners and to call them to repentance, and whether each man believes that he is in the number of them that are delivered by Christ and saved; and whether he has purposed to change this wicked life, to live holily, and to persevere through God's assistance, in the true religion, and in concord with his brethren, and to give worthy thanks to God for his delivery.

12. We think that rite, manner, or form of the Supper to be the most simple and excellent which comes nearest to the first institution of the Lord and to the apostles' doctrine, which does consist in declaring the Word of God, in godly prayers, in the action itself that the Lord used, and the repeating of it; in the eating of the Lord's body and drinking of His blood; in the wholesome

Canons of Dort (1619)

Westminster Confession of Faith (1647)	Westminster Shorter Catechism (1647)	Westminster Larger Catechism (1648)

Belgic Confession (1561)	Heidelberg Catechism (1563)	Second Helvetic Confession (1566)	Canons of Dort (1619)

Heidelberg Catechism (cont.)

Q. 81: For whom is the Lord's Supper instituted?

A.: For those who are truly sorrowful for their sins,[1] and yet trust that these are forgiven them for the sake of Christ; and that their remaining infirmities are covered by His passion and death;[2] and who also earnestly desire to have their faith more and more strengthened, and their lives more holy;[3] but hypocrites, and such as turn not to God with sincere hearts, eat and drink judgment to themselves.[4]

[1] Matt. 5:3, 6; Luke 7:37-38; Luke 15:18-19
[2] Ps. 103:3
[3] Ps. 116:12-14; 1 Pet. 2:11-12
[4] 1 Cor. 10:20, etc.; 1 Cor. 11:28, etc.; Titus 1:16; Ps. 50:15-16

Q. 82: Are they also to be admitted to this supper, who, by confession and life, declare themselves unbelieving and ungodly?

A.: No; for by this, the covenant of God would be profaned and His wrath kindled against the whole congregation;[1] therefore it is the duty of the Christian church, according to the appointment of Christ and His apostles, to exclude such persons[2] by the keys of the kingdom of heaven till they show amendment of life.

[1] 1 Cor. 10:21; 1 Cor. 11:30-31; Isa. 1:11, 13; Jer. 7:21; Ps. 50:16, 22
[2] Matt. 18:17-18

remembrance of the Lord's death, and faithful giving of thanks; and in a holy fellowship in the union of the body of the Church.

13. We therefore disallow those who have taken from the faithful one part of the sacrament, to wit, the Lord's cup. For these do very grievously offend against the institution of the Lord, who says, "Drink ye all of it" (Matt. 26:27); which He did not so plainly say of the bread.

14. What manner of mass it was that the fathers used, whether it were tolerable or intolerable, we do not now dispute. But this we say freely, that the mass which is now used throughout the Roman Church is quite abolished out of our churches for many and just causes, which, for brevity's sake, we will not now particularly recite. Truly we could not approve of it, because they have changed a most wholesome action into a vain spectacle; also because the mass is made a meritorious matter, and is said for money; likewise because in it the priest is said to make the very body of the Lord, and to offer the same really, even for the remission of the sins of the quick and the dead. Add this also, that they do it for the honor, worship, and reverence of the saints in heaven (and for the relief of souls in purgatory), etc.

Civil Authorities

Article 36
The Magistrates

We believe that our gracious God, because of the depravity of mankind, hath appointed kings, princes, and magistrates,[1] willing that the world should be governed by certain laws and policies; to the end that the dissoluteness of men might be restrained, and all things carried on among them with good order and decency. For

Q. 101: May we then swear religiously by the name of God?

A.: Yes, either when the magistrates demand it of the subjects or when necessity requires us thereby to confirm fidelity and truth to the glory of God and the safety of our neighbor;[1] for such an oath is founded on God's Word,[2] and therefore was justly used by the saints, both in the Old and New Testament.[3]

XXX. Of the Magistracy

1. The magistracy, of what sort soever it be, is ordained of God Himself, for the peace and quietness of mankind; and so that He should have the chief place in the world. If the magistrate be an adversary to the Church, he may hinder and disturb it very much; but if he be a friend and a member of the Church, he is a most useful and excellent member thereof; he may profit it very much, and finally may help and further it very excellently.

2. The chief duty of the civil magistrate is to procure and maintain peace and public tranquility; which, doubtless, he shall never do more happily than when he shall be truly seasoned with the fear of God and true religion — namely, when he

Westminster Confession of Faith (1647)	Westminster Shorter Catechism (1647)	Westminster Larger Catechism (1648)

XXIII. Of the Civil Magistrate

1. God, the supreme Lord and King of all the world, hath ordained civil magistrates, to be, under Him, over the people, for His own glory, and the public good; and, to this end, hath armed them with the power of the sword, for the defense and encouragement of them that are good, and for the punishment of evil doers.[1]

[1] Rom. 13:1-4; 1 Pet. 2:13-14

2. It is lawful for Christians to accept and execute the office of a magistrate, when called thereunto;[1] in the managing whereof, as they ought especially to maintain piety, justice, and peace, according to the wholesome laws of each commonwealth;[2] so, for that end, they may

Belgic Confession (1561)	Heidelberg Catechism (1563)	Second Helvetic Confession (1566)	Canons of Dort (1619)

Belgic Confession (1561)

this purpose He hath invested the magistracy with the sword, *for the punishment of evil doers,* and for the praise of them that do well. And their office is, not only to have regard unto and watch for the welfare of the civil state, but also that they protect the sacred ministry, and thus may remove and prevent all idolatry and false worship;[2] that the kingdom of antichrist may be thus destroyed, and the kingdom of Christ promoted. They must, therefore, countenance the preaching of the word of the gospel everywhere, that God may be honored and worshipped by every one, as He commands in His Word.

Moreover, it is the bounden duty of every one, of what state, quality, or condition soever he may be, to subject himself to the magistrates;[3] to pay tribute,[4] to show due honor and respect to them, and to obey them in all things which are not repugnant to the Word of God;[5] to supplicate for them in their prayers, that God may rule and guide them in all their ways, and that we may lead a quiet and peaceable life in all godliness and honesty.[6]

Wherefore we detest the error of the Anabaptists and other seditious people, and in general all those who reject the higher powers and magistrates, and would subvert justice,[7] introduce a community of goods, and confound that decency and good order which God hath established among men.[8]

Heidelberg Catechism (1563)

Q. 104: What doth God require in the fifth commandment?
A.: That I show all honor, love and fidelity, to my father and mother and all in authority over me, and submit myself to their good instruction and correction, with due obedience;[1] and also patiently bear with their weaknesses and infirmities,[2] since it pleases God to govern us by their hand.[3]

---
[1] Eph. 6:1-2, etc.; Col. 3:18, 20; Eph. 5:22; Rom. 1:31
[2] Prov. 23:22
[3] Eph. 6:5-6; Col. 3:19, 21; Rom. 13:1-8; Matt. 22:21

Q. 105: What doth God require in the sixth commandment?
A.: That neither in thoughts, nor words, nor gestures, much less in deeds, I dishonor, hate, wound, or kill my neighbor, by myself or by another;[1] but that I lay aside all desire of revenge;[2] also, that I hurt not myself, nor wilfully expose myself to any danger.[3] Wherefore also the magistrate is armed with the sword to prevent murder.[4]

---
[1] Matt. 5:21-22, Prov. 12:18, Matt. 26:52
[2] Eph. 4:26, Rom. 12:19, Matt. 5:39-40
[3] Matt. 4:5-7, Col. 2:23
[4] Gen. 9:6, Matt. 26:52, Rom. 13:4

Second Helvetic Confession (1566)

shall, after the example of the most holy kings and princes of the people of the Lord, advance the preaching of the truth, and the pure and sincere faith, and shall root out lies and superstition, with all impiety and idolatry, and shall defend the Church of God. For indeed we teach that the care of religion does chiefly appertain to the holy magistrate.

3. Let him, therefore, hold the Word of God in his hands, and look that nothing be taught contrary thereunto. In like manner, let him govern the people, committed to him of God, with good laws, made according to the Word of God in his hands, and look that nothing be taught contrary thereunto. Let him hold them in discipline and in duty and in obedience. Let him exercise judgment by judging uprightly; let him not respect any man's person, or receive bribes. Let him protect widows, fatherless children, and those that be afflicted, against wrong; let him repress, yea, and cut off, such as are unjust, whether in deceit or by violence. "For he beareth not the sword in vain" (Rom. 13:4). Therefore let him draw forth this sword of God against all malefactors, seditious persons, thieves, murderers, oppressors, blasphemers, perjured persons, and all those whom God has commanded him to punish or even to execute. Let him suppress stubborn heretics (who are heretics indeed), who cease not to blaspheme the majesty of God, and to trouble the Church, yea, and finally to destroy it.

4. And if it be necessary to preserve the safety of the people by war, let him do it in the name of God; provided he have first sought peace by all means possible, and can save his subjects in no way but by war. And while the magistrate does these things in faith, he serves God with those works which are good, and shall receive a blessing from the Lord.

5. We condemn the Anabaptists, who, as they deny that a Christian man should bear the office of a magistrate, deny also that any man can justly be put to death by the magistrate, or that the magistrate may make war, or that oaths should be administered by the magistrate, and such like things.

6. For as God will work the safety of His people by the magistrate, whom it is given to be, as it were, a father of the world, so all subjects are commanded to acknowledge this benefit of God in the magistrate. Therefore let them honor and reverence the magistrate as the minister of God; let them love him, favor him, and pray for him as their father; and let them obey all his just and equal commandments. Finally, let them pay all

Westminster Confession of Faith (1647)	Westminster Shorter Catechism (1647)	Westminster Larger Catechism (1648)

lawfully, now under the new testament, wage war, upon just and necessary occasion.[3]

[1] Prov. 8:15-16; Rom. 13:1-4
[2] Ps. 2:10-12; 1 Tim. 2:2; Ps. 82:3-4; 2 Sam. 23:3; 1 Pet. 2:13
[3] Luke 3:14; Rom. 13:4; Matt. 8:9-10; Acts 10:1-2; Rev. 17:14, 16

3. The civil magistrate may not assume to himself the administration of the Word and sacraments, or the power of the keys of the kingdom of heaven;[1] yet he hath authority, and it is his duty, to take order that unity and peace be preserved in the Church, that the truth of God be kept pure and entire, that all blasphemies and heresies be suppressed, all corruptions and abuses in worship and discipline prevented or reformed, and all the ordinances of God duly settled, administered, and observed.[2] For the better effecting whereof, he hath power to call synods, to be present at them and to provide that whatsoever is transacted in them be according to the mind of God.[3]

[1] 2 Chron. 26:18; Matt. 18:17; 16:19; 1 Cor. 12:28-29; Eph. 4:11-12; 1 Cor. 4:1-2; Rom. 10:15; Heb. 5:4
[2] Isa. 49:23; Ps. 122:9; Ezra 7:23, 25-28; Lev. 24:16; Deut. 13:5-6, 12; 2 Ki. 18:4; 1 Chron. 13:1-9; 2 Ki. 24:1-26; 2 Chron. 34:33; 15:12-13
[3] 2 Chron. 19:8-11; 2 Chron. 29; 30; Matt. 2:4-5

4. It is the duty of people to pray for magistrates,[1] to honor their persons,[2] to pay them tribute or other dues,[3] to obey their lawful commands, and to be subject to their authority, for conscience' sake.[4] Infidelity, or difference in religion, doth not make void the magistrates' just and legal authority, nor free the people from their due obedience to them;[5] from which ecclesiastical persons are not exempted,[6] much less hath the pope any power and jurisdiction over them in their dominions, or over any of their people; and, least of all, to deprive them of their dominions, or lives, if he shall judge them to be heretics, or upon any other pretence whatsoever.[7]

[1] 1 Tim. 2:1-2
[2] 1 Pet. 2:17
[3] Rom. 13:6-7
[4] Rom. 13:5; Titus 3:1
[5] 1 Pet. 2:13-14, 16
[6] Rom. 13:1; 1 Ki. 2:35; Acts 25:9-11; 2 Pet. 2:1, 10-11; Jude 8-11
[7] 2 Thes. 2:4; Rev. 13:15-17

XXXI: Of Synods and Councils

2. As magistrates may lawfully call a synod of ministers, and other fit persons, to consult and advise with, about matters of religion;[1] so, if magistrates be open enemies to the Church, the ministers of Christ, of themselves, by virtue of

Belgic Confession (1561)	Heidelberg Catechism (1563)	Second Helvetic Confession (1566)	Canons of Dort (1619)
[1] Exod. 18:20, etc.; Rom. 13:1; Prov. 8:15; Jer. 21:12; 22:2-3; Ps. 82:1, 6; 101:2; Deut. 1:15-16; 16:18; 17:15; Dan. 2:21, 37; 5:18 [2] Isa. 49:23, 25; 1 Ki. 15:12; 2 Ki. 23:2-4 [3] Titus 3:1; Rom. 13:1 [4] Mark 12:17; Matt. 17:24 [5] Acts 4:17-19; 5:29; Hos. 5:11 [6] Jer. 29:7; 1 Tim. 2:1-2 [7] 2 Pet. 2:10 [8] Jude 8, 10		customs and tributes, and all other duties of the like sort, faithfully and willingly. And if the common safety of the country and justice require it, and the magistrate do of necessity make war, let them even lay down their life, and spend their blood for the common safety and defense of the magistrate; and that in the name of God, willingly, valiantly, and cheerfully. For he that opposes himself against the magistrate does provoke the wrath of God against him.

7. We condemn, therefore, all contemners of magistrates, rebels, enemies of the commonwealth, seditious villains, and, in a word, all such as do either openly or closely refuse to perform those duties which they owe.

The Conclusion. We beseech God, our most merciful Father in heaven, that He will bless the rulers of the people, and us, and His whole people, through Jesus Christ, our only Lord and Savior; to whom be praise and glory and thanksgiving, both now and forever. Amen. | |

Celibacy, Marriage, Divorce, and Family Life

		XXIX. Of Single Life, Wedlock, and Household Government

1. Such as have the gift of chastity given unto them from above, so that they can with the heart or whole mind be pure and continent, and not be grievously burned with lust, let them serve the Lord in that calling, as long as they shall feel themselves endued with that heavenly gift; and let them not lift up themselves above others, but let them serve the Lord daily in simplicity and humility. For such are more apt for attending to heavenly things than they who are distracted with the private affairs of a family. But if, again, the gift be taken away, and they feel a continual burning, let them call to mind the words of the apostle, "It is better to marry than to burn" (1 Cor. 7:9).

2. For wedlock (which is the medicine of incontinency, and continency itself) was ordained by the Lord God Himself, who blessed it most bountifully, and willed man and woman to cleave one to the other inseparably, and to live together in great concord (Gen. 2:24; Matt. 14:5-6). Whereupon we know the apostle said, "Marriage is honourable in all, and the bed undefiled" (Heb. 13:4). And again, "If a virgin marry, she hath not sinned" (1 Cor. 7:28). We therefore condemn | |

Westminster Confession of Faith (1647)	Westminster Shorter Catechism (1647)	Westminster Larger Catechism (1648)

their office, or they, with other fit persons upon delegation from their Churches, may meet together in such assemblies.[2]

[1] Isa. 49:23; 1 Tim. 2:1-2; 2 Chron. 19:8-11; 29:1-36; 30:1-27; Mal. 2:4-5; Prov. 11:14.
[2] Acts 15:2, 4, 22-23, 25

5. Synods and councils are to handle, or conclude nothing, but that which is ecclesiastical, and are not to intermeddle with civil affairs which concern the commonwealth, unless by way of humble petition in cases extraordinary; or, by way of advice, for satisfaction of conscience, if they be thereunto required by the civil magistrate.[1]

[1] Luke 12:13-14; John 18:36

XXIV. Of Marriage and Divorce

1. Marriage is to be between one man and one woman: neither is it lawful for any man to have more than one wife, nor for any woman to have more than one husband, at the same time.[1]

[1] Gen. 2:24; Matt. 19:5-6; Prov. 2:17

2. Marriage was ordained for the mutual help of husband and wife,[1] for the increase of mankind with a legitimate issue, and of the Church with a holy seed;[2] and for preventing of uncleanness.[3]

[1] Gen. 2:18
[2] Mal. 2:15
[3] 1 Cor. 7:2, 9

3. It is lawful for all sorts of people to marry, who are able with judgment to give their consent.[1] Yet is it the duty of Christians to marry only in the Lord.[2] And therefore such as profess the true Reformed religion should not marry with infidels, papists, or other idolaters; neither should such as are godly be unequally yoked, by marrying with such as are notoriously wicked in their life, or maintain damnable heresies.[3]

[1] Heb. 13:4; 1 Tim. 4:3; 1 Cor. 7:36-38; Gen. 24:57-58
[2] 1 Cor. 7:39

Belgic Confession (1561)	Heidelberg Catechism (1563)	Second Helvetic Confession (1566)	Canons of Dort (1619)
		polygamy, and those who condemn second marriages. We teach that marriages ought to be contracted lawfully, in the fear of the Lord, and not against the laws which forbid certain degrees to join in matrimony, lest the marriages should be incestuous. Let marriages be made with consent of the parents, or such as are instead of parents; and for that end especially for which the Lord ordained marriages. And let them be confirmed publicly in the Church, with prayer and blessing. Moreover, let them be kept holy, with peace, faithfulness, dutifulness, love, and purity of the persons coupled together. Therefore let them take heed of brawlings, debates, lusts, and adulteries. Let lawful judgments and holy judges be established in the Church, who may maintain marriages, and may repress all dishonesty and shamefulness, and before whom controversies in matrimony may be decided and ended. 3. Let children also be brought up by the parents in the fear of the Lord; and let parents provide for their children, remembering the saying of the apostle, "If any provide not for his own... [he] hath denied the faith, and is worse than an infidel" (1 Tim. 5:8). But especially let them teach their children honest arts and occupations, whereby they may maintain themselves. Let them keep them from idleness, and plant in them a true confidence in God in all these things; lest they, through distrust, or overmuch careless security, or filthy covetousness, wax loose, and in the end come to no good. 4. Now, it is most certain that those works which parents do in true faith, by the duties of marriage, and government of their families, are, before God, holy and good works indeed, and do please God no less than prayers, fastings, and alms-deeds. For so the apostle has taught in his epistles, especially in those to Timothy and Titus. And with the same apostle we account the doctrine of such as forbid marriage, or do openly dispraise or secretly discredit it as not holy or clean, among the "doctrines of devils" (1 Tim. 4:1). 5. And we do detest unclean single life, licentious lusts, and fornication, both open and secret, and the continency of dissembling hypocrites, when they are, of all men, most incontinent. All these God will judge. We do not disallow riches, nor contemn rich men, if they be godly and use their riches well; but we reprove the sect of the Apostolicals, etc.	

Westminster Confession of Faith (1647)	Westminster Shorter Catechism (1647)	Westminster Larger Catechism (1648)
[3] Gen. 34:14; Exod. 34:16; Deut. 7:3-4; 1 Ki. 11:4; Neh. 13:25-27; Mal. 2:11-12; 2 Cor. 6:14		

[3] Gen. 34:14; Exod. 34:16; Deut. 7:3-4; 1 Ki. 11:4; Neh. 13:25-27; Mal. 2:11-12; 2 Cor. 6:14

4. Marriage ought not to be within the degrees of consanguinity or affinity forbidden by the Word.[1] Nor can such incestuous marriages ever be made lawful by any law of man or consent of parties, so as those persons may live together as man and wife.[2] The man may not marry any of his wife's kindred, nearer in blood than he may of his own; nor the woman of her husband's kindred, nearer in blood than of her own.[3]

[1] Lev. 18; 1 Cor. 5:1; Amos 2:7
[2] Mark 6:18; Lev. 18:24-28
[3] Lev. 20:19-21

5. Adultery or fornication committed after a contract, being detected before marriage, giveth just occasion to the innocent party to dissolve that contract.[1] In the case of adultery after marriage, it is lawful for the innocent party to sue out a divorce;[2] and, after the divorce, to marry another, as if the offending party were dead.[3]

[1] Matt. 1:18-20
[2] Matt. 5:31-32
[3] Matt. 19:9; Rom. 7:2-3

6. Although the corruption of man be such as is apt to study arguments unduly to put asunder those whom God hath joined together in marriage; yet, nothing but adultery, or such wilful desertion as can no way be remedied by the Church, or civil magistrate, is cause sufficient of dissolving the bond of marriage,[1] wherein, a public and orderly course of proceeding is to be observed; and the persons concerned in it not left to their own wills, and discretion, in their own case.[2]

[1] Matt. 19:8-9; 1 Cor. 7:15; Matt. 19:6
[2] Deut. 24:1-4

Eschatology:
The Doctrine of the
Last Things

Belgic Confession (1561)	Heidelberg Catechism (1563)	Second Helvetic Confession (1566)	Canons of Dort (1619)

Resurrection from the Dead

Article 37

The Last Judgment

For all the dead shall be raised out of the earth, and their souls joined and united with their proper bodies in which they formerly lived.[1] As for those who shall then be living, they shall not die as the others, but be changed in the twinkling of an eye, and from corruptible become incorruptible.[2]

---

[1] John 5:28-29; 6:54; Dan. 12:2; Job 19:26-27
[2] 1 Cor. 15:51-53

Q. 57: What comfort doth the "resurrection of the body" afford thee?

A.: That not only my soul after this life shall be immediately taken up to Christ its Head;[1] but also, that this my body, being raised by the power of Christ, shall be reunited with my soul, and made like unto the glorious body of Christ.[2]

---

[1] Luke 23:43, Phil. 1:23
[2] 1 Cor. 15:53, Job 19:25-26

XXVI. Of the Burial of the Faithful, and of the Care which is to be had for such as are Dead; of Purgatory, and the Appearing of Spirits

1. The Scripture directs that the bodies of the faithful, as being temples of the Holy Spirit, which we truly believe shall rise again at the last day, should be honorably, without any superstition, committed to the earth; and, besides, that we should make honorable mention of those who died in the Lord, and perform all duties of love to those they leave behind, as their widows and fatherless children. Other care for the dead we do not enjoin. Therefore, we do greatly mislike the Cynics, who neglected the bodies of the dead, or did carelessly and disdainfully cast them into the earth, never speaking so much as a good word of the deceased, nor any whit regarding those whom they left behind them.

2. Again, we disapprove of those who are too much and preposterously officious to the dead; who, like the heathen, do greatly lament and bewail their dead (although we do not censure that moderate mourning which the apostle does allow [1 Thes. 4:13], since it is unnatural not to be touched with sorrow); and who do sacrifice for the dead, and mumble certain prayers, not without their penny for their pains; thinking by these prayers to deliver their friends from torments, wherein, being wrapped by death, they suppose they may be rid of them again by such lamentable songs.

3. For we believe that the faithful, after bodily death, do go directly unto Christ, and, therefore, do not stand in need of helps or prayers for the dead, or any other such duty of them that are alive. In like manner, we believe that the unbelievers are cast headlong into hell, from whence there is no return opened to the wicked by any offices of those who live.

4. But as touching that which some teach concerning the fire of purgatory, it is directly contrary to the Christian faith ("I believe in the forgiveness of sins, and the life everlasting"), and to the absolute purgation of sins made by Christ, and to these sayings of Christ our Lord: "Verily, verily, I say unto you, he that heareth My word, and believeth on Him that sent Me, hath everlasting life, and shall not come into condemnation; but is passed from death unto life" (John 5:24). Again, "He that is washed needeth not save to wash his

Westminster Confession of Faith (1647)	Westminster Shorter Catechism (1647)	Westminster Larger Catechism (1648)

XXXII: Of the State of Men after Death, and of the Resurrection of the Dead

1. The bodies of men, after death, return to dust, and see corruption,[1] but their souls, which neither die nor sleep, having an immortal subsistence, immediately return to God who gave them;[2] the souls of the righteous, being then made perfect in holiness, are received into the highest heavens, where they behold the face of God, in light and glory, waiting for the full redemption of their bodies.[3] And the souls of the wicked are cast into hell, where they remain in torments and utter darkness, reserved to the judgment of the great day.[4] Beside these two places, for souls separated from their bodies, the Scripture acknowledgeth none.

[1] Gen. 3:19; Acts 13:36
[2] Luke 23:43; Eccl. 12:7
[3] Heb. 12:23; 2 Cor. 5:1, 6, 8; Phil. 1:23; Acts 3:21; Eph. 4:10
[4] Luke 16:23-24; Acts 1:25; Jude 6-7; 1 Pet. 3:19

2. At the last day, such as are found alive shall not die, but be changed;[1] and all the dead shall be raised up, with the selfsame bodies, and none other (although with different qualities), which shall be united again to their souls forever.[2]

[1] 1 Thes. 4:17; 1 Cor. 15:51-52
[2] Job 19:26-27; 1 Cor. 15:42-44

3. The bodies of the unjust shall, by the power of Christ, be raised to dishonor; the bodies of the just, by His Spirit, unto honor, and be made conformable to His own glorious body.[1]

[1] Acts 24:15; John 5:28-29; 1 Cor. 15:43; Phil. 3:21

Q. 37: What benefits do believers receive from Christ at death?

A.: The souls of believers are at their death made perfect in holiness,[1] and do immediately pass into glory;[2] and their bodies, being still united to Christ,[3] do rest in their graves[4] till the resurrection.[5]

[1] Heb. 12:23
[2] 2 Cor. 5:1, 6, 8; Phil. 1:23; Luke 23:43
[3] 1 Thes. 4:14
[4] Isa. 57:2
[5] Job 19:26-27

Q. 84: Shall all men die?

A.: Death being threatened as the wages of sin,[1] it is appointed unto all men once to die;[2] for that all have sinned.[3]

[1] Rom. 6:23
[2] Heb. 9:27
[3] Rom. 5:12

Q. 85: Death, being the wages of sin, why are not the righteous delivered from death, seeing all their sins are forgiven in Christ?

A.: The righteous shall be delivered from death itself at the last day, and even in death are delivered from the sting and curse of it;[1] so that, although they die, yet it is out of God's love,[2] to free them perfectly from sin and misery,[3] and to make them capable of further communion with Christ in glory, which they then enter upon.[4]

[1] 1 Cor. 15:26, 55-57; Heb. 2:15
[2] Isa. 57:1-2; 2 Ki. 22:20
[3] Rev. 14:13; Eph. 5:27
[4] Luke 23:43; Phil. 1:23

Q. 86: What is the communion in glory with Christ, which the members of the invisible church enjoy immediately after death?

A.: The communion in glory with Christ, which the members of the invisible church enjoy immediately after death, is, in that their souls are then made perfect in holiness,[1] and received into the highest heavens,[2] where they behold the face of God in light and glory,[3] waiting for the full redemption of their bodies,[4] which even in death continue united to Christ,[5] and rest in their graves as in their beds,[6] till at the last day they be again united to their souls.[7] Whereas the souls of the wicked are at their death cast into hell, where they remain in torments and utter darkness, and their bodies kept in their graves, as in their prisons, till the resurrection and judgment of the great day.[8]

[1] Heb. 12:23
[2] 2 Cor. 5:1, 6, 8; Phil. 1:23; Acts 3:21; Eph. 4:10
[3] 1 John 3:2; 1 Cor. 13:12
[4] Rom. 8:23; Ps. 16:9
[5] 1 Thes. 4:14
[6] Isa. 57:2
[7] Job 19:26-27
[8] Luke 16:23-24; Acts 1:25; Jude 6-7

Q. 87: What are we to believe concerning the resurrection?

A.: We are to believe, that at the last day there shall be a general resurrection of the dead, both

Belgic Confession (1561)	Heidelberg Catechism (1563)	Second Helvetic Confession (1566)	Canons of Dort (1619)
		feet, but is clean every whit: and ye are clean" (John 13:10). 5. Now, that which is recorded of the spirits or souls of the dead sometimes appearing to them that are alive, and craving certain duties of them whereby they may be set free: we count those apparitions among the delusions, crafts, and deceits of the devil, who, as he can transform himself into an angel of light, so he labors tooth and nail either to overthrow the true faith, or else to call it into doubt. The Lord, in the Old Testament, forbade us to inquire the truth of the dead, and to have any thing to do with spirits (Deut. 18:10-11). And to the glutton, being bound in torments, as the truth of the gospel does declare, is denied any return to his brethren on earth; the oracle of God pronouncing and saying, "They have Moses and the prophets; . . . neither will they be persuaded, though one rose from the dead" (Luke 16:29, 31).	

The Last Judgment and Eternity

Belgic Confession (1561)	Heidelberg Catechism (1563)	Second Helvetic Confession (1566)	Canons of Dort (1619)
Article 37 **The Last Judgment** Finally, we believe, according to the Word of God, when the time appointed by the Lord (which is unknown to all creatures)[1] is come, and the number of the elect complete, that our Lord Jesus Christ will come from heaven, corporally and visibly, as He ascended,[2] with great glory and majesty, to declare Himself Judge of the quick and the dead,[3] burning this old world with fire and flame to cleanse it.[4] And then all men will personally appear before this great Judge, both men and women and children, that have been from the beginning of the world to the end thereof,[5] be-	*Q. 58: What comfort takest thou from the article of "life everlasting"?* A.: That since I now feel in my heart the beginning of eternal joy,[1] after this life I shall inherit perfect salvation,[2] which "eye hath not seen, nor ear heard, neither have entered into the heart of man" to conceive,[3] and that, to praise God therein for ever. [1] 2 Cor. 5:2-3, 6; Rom. 14:17 [2] Ps. 10:11 [3] 1 Cor. 2:9 *Q. 123: Which is the second petition?* A.: "Thy kingdom come";[1] that is, rule us so by Thy Word and Spirit, that we may submit ourselves more and more to Thee;[2] pre-		

Westminster Confession of Faith (1647)	Westminster Shorter Catechism (1647)	Westminster Larger Catechism (1648)
		of the just and unjust:[1] when they that are then found alive shall in a moment be changed; and the selfsame bodies of the dead which were laid in the grave, being then again united to their souls for ever, shall be raised up by the power of Christ.[2] The bodies of the just, by the Spirit of Christ, and by virtue of His resurrection as their Head, shall be raised in power, spiritual, incorruptible, and made like to His glorious body;[3] and the bodies of the wicked shall be raised up in dishonor by Him, as an offended judge.[4]

[1] Acts 24:15
[2] 1 Cor. 15:51-53; 1 Thes. 4:15-17; John 5:28-29
[3] 1 Cor. 15:21-23, 42-44; Phil. 3:21
[4] John 5:27-29; Matt. 25:33

XXXIII: Of the Last Judgment

1. God hath appointed a day, wherein He will judge the world, in righteousness, by Jesus Christ,[1] to whom all power and judgment is given of the Father.[2] In which day, not only the apostate angels shall be judged,[3] but likewise all persons that have lived upon earth shall appear before the tribunal of Christ, to give an account of their thoughts, words, and deeds; and to receive according to what they have done in the body, whether good or evil.[4]

[1] Acts 17:31
[2] John 5:22, 27
[3] 1 Cor. 6:3; Jude 6; 2 Pet. 2:4
[4] 2 Cor. 5:10; Eccl. 12:14; Rom. 2:16; 14:10, 12; Matt. 12:36-37

2. The end of God's appointing this day is for the manifestation of the glory of His mercy, in the eternal salvation of the elect; and of His justice, in the damnation of the reprobate, who are wicked and disobedient. For then shall the righteous go into everlasting life, and receive that fulness of joy and refreshing, which shall come from the presence of the Lord; but the wicked who know not God, and obey not the gospel of Jesus Christ, shall be cast into eternal

---

Q. 38: What benefits do believers receive from Christ at the resurrection?

A.: At the resurrection, believers, being raised up in glory,[1] shall be openly acknowledged and acquitted in the day of judgment,[2] and made perfectly blessed in the full enjoying of God[3] to all eternity.[4]

[1] 1 Cor. 15:43
[2] Matt. 25:23; 10:32
[3] 1 John 3:2; 1 Cor. 13:12
[4] 1 Thes. 4:17-18

Q. 88: What shall immediately follow after the resurrection?

A.: Immediately after the resurrection shall follow the general and final judgment of angels and men;[1] the day and hour whereof no man knoweth, that all may watch and pray, and be ever ready for the coming of the Lord.[2]

[1] 2 Pet. 2:4; Jude 6-7, 14-15; Matt. 25:46
[2] Matt. 24:36, 42, 44; Luke 21:35-36

Q. 89: What shall be done to the wicked at the day of judgment?

A.: At the day of judgment, the wicked shall be set on Christ's left hand,[1] and, upon clear evidence, and full conviction of their own consciences,[2] shall have the fearful but just sentence of condemnation pronounced against them;[3] and thereupon shall be cast out from the favorable presence of God, and the glorious fellowship with Christ, His saints, and all His holy angels, into hell, to be punished with unspeakable torments, both of body and soul, with the devil and his angels for ever.[4]

[1] Matt. 25:33
[2] Rom. 2:15-16
[3] Matt. 25:41-43
[4] Luke 16:26; 2 Thes. 1:8-9

Belgic Confession (1561)	Heidelberg Catechism (1563)	Second Helvetic Confession (1566)	Canons of Dort (1619)
ing summoned by the voice of the archangel, and by the sound of the trumpet of God.[6] Then the books (that is to say, the consciences) shall be opened, and the dead judged according to what they shall have done in this world, whether it be good or evil.[7] Nay, all men shall give an account of every idle word they have spoken, which the world only counts amusement and jest;[8] and then the	serve and increase Thy church;[3] destroy the works of the devil,[4] and all violence which would exalt itself against Thee; and also, all wicked counsels devised against Thy holy Word; till the full perfection of Thy kingdom take place,[5] wherein Thou shalt be all in all.[6] ___ [1] Matt. 6:10 [2] Ps. 119:5 [3] Ps. 51:18 [4] 1 John 3:8; Rom. 16:20 [5] Rev. 22:17, 20 [6] 1 Cor. 15:15, 28		

Belgic Confession (cont.)

secrets and hypocrisy of men shall be disclosed and laid open before all.[9]

And, therefore, the consideration of this judgment is justly terrible and dreadful to the wicked and ungodly,[10] but most desirable and comfortable to the righteous and the elect; because then their full deliverance shall be perfected, and there they shall receive the fruits of their labor and trouble which they have borne.[11] Their innocence shall be known to all, and they shall see the terrible vengeance which God shall execute on the wicked,[12] who most cruelly persecuted, oppressed, and tormented them in this world;[13] and who shall be convicted by the testimony of their own consciences,[14] and, being immortal, shall be tormented in that everlasting fire[15] which is prepared for the devil and his angels.[16]

But on the contrary, the faithful and elect shall be crowned with glory and honor;[17] and the Son of God will confess their names before God His Father, and His elect angels;[18] all tears shall be wiped from their eyes;[19] and their cause, which is now condemned by many judges and magistrates as heretical and impious, will then be known to be the cause of the Son of God.[20] And for a gracious reward, the Lord will cause them to possess such a glory as never entered into the heart of man to conceive.[21]

Therefore we expect that great day with a most ardent

desire, to the end that we may fully enjoy the promises of God in Christ Jesus our Lord.[22] Amen.

Even so, come, Lord Jesus (Rev. 22:20).

___
[1] Matt. 24:36; 25:13; 1 Thes. 5:1-2; Rev. 6:11; Acts 1:7; 2 Pet. 3:10
[2] Acts 1:11
[3] 2 Thes. 1:7-8; Acts 17:31; Matt. 24:30; 25:31; Jude 15; 1 Pet. 4:5; 2 Tim. 4:1
[4] 2 Pet. 3:7,10; 2 Thes. 1:8
[5] Rev. 20:12-13; Acts 17:31; Heb. 6:2; 9:27; 2 Cor. 5:10; Rom. 14:10
[6] 1 Cor. 15:42; Rev. 20:12-13; 1 Thes. 4:16
[7] Rev. 20:12-13; 1 Cor. 4:5; Rom. 14:11-12; Job 34:11; John 5:24; Dan. 12:2; Ps. 62:13; Matt. 11:22; 23:33; John 5:29; Rom. 2:5-6; 2 Cor. 5:10; Heb. 6:2; 9:27
[8] Rom. 2:5; Jude 15; Matt. 12:36
[9] 1 Cor. 4:5; Rom. 2:1-2,16; Matt. 7:1-2
[10] Rev. 6:15-16; Heb. 10:27
[11] Luke 21:28; 1 John 3:2; 4:17; Rev. 14:7; 2 Thes. 1:5-7; Luke 14:14
[12] Dan. 7:26
[13] Matt. 25:46; 2 Thes. 1:6-8; Mal. 4:3
[14] Rom. 2:15
[15] Rev. 21:8; 2 Pet. 2:9
[16] Mal. 4:1; Matt. 25:41
[17] Matt. 25:34; 13:43
[18] Matt. 10:32
[19] Isa. 25:8; Rev. 21:4
[20] Isa. 66:5
[21] Isa. 64:4; 1 Cor. 2:9
[22] Heb. 10:36-38

Westminster Confession of Faith (1647)	Westminster Shorter Catechism (1647)	Westminster Larger Catechism (1648)
torments, and be punished with everlasting destruction from the presence of the Lord, and from the glory of His power.[1] ―――――― [1] Matt. 25:31-46; Rom. 2:5-6; Rom. 9:22-23; Matt. 25:21; Acts 3:19; 2 Thes. 1:7-10 3. As Christ would have us to be certainly persuaded that there shall be a day of judgment, both to deter all men from sin, and for the greater consolation of the godly in their adversity;[1] so will He have that day unknown to men, that they may shake off all carnal security, and be always watchful, because they know not at what hour the Lord will come; and may be ever prepared to say, Come Lord Jesus, come quickly. Amen.[2] ―――――― [1] 2 Pet. 3:11, 14; 2 Cor. 5:10-11; 2 Thes. 1:5-7; Luke 21:7, 28; Rom. 8:23-25 [2] Matt. 24:36, 42-44; Mark 13:35-37; Luke 12:35-36; Rev. 22:20		Q. 90: *What shall be done to the righteous at the day of judgment?* A.: At the day of judgment, the righteous, being caught up to Christ in the clouds,[1] shall be set on His right hand, and there openly acknowledged and acquitted,[2] shall join with Him in the judging of reprobate angels and men,[3] and shall be received into heaven,[4] where they shall be fully and for ever freed from all sin and misery;[5] filled with inconceivable joys,[6] made perfectly holy and happy both in body and soul, in the company of innumerable saints and holy angels,[7] but especially in the immediate vision and fruition of God the Father, of our Lord Jesus Christ, and of the Holy Spirit, to all eternity.[8] And this is the perfect and full communion, which the members of the invisible church shall enjoy with Christ in glory, at the resurrection and day of judgment. ―――――― [1] 1 Thes. 4:17 [2] Matt. 25:33; 10:32 [3] 1 Cor. 6:2-3 [4] Matt. 25:34, 46 [5] Eph. 5:27; Rev. 14:13 [6] Ps. 16:11 [7] Heb. 12:22-23 [8] 1 John 3:2; 1 Cor. 13:12; 1 Thes. 4:17-18

SELECTED BIBLIOGRAPHY

Joel R. Beeke

The following annotated bibliography, citing English sources only, follows the pattern of the oldest Reformed doctrinal standard included in this harmony, the Belgic Confession of Faith. *With few exceptions, the works cited are confined to those that would be of value to readers of Reformed persuasion.*

Article 1 — The Doctrine of God

The classic work on God's undeniable existence and attributes is Stephen Charnock's (1628-1680) fourteen massive *Discourses on the Existence and Attributes of God* (1682; reprint 2 vols., Grand Rapids: Baker, 1979). *Discourses* is marked by sound Puritan theology, profound thought, and humble adoration of God. Charnock intended to preach an entire "body of divinity," but he came no further than the attributes of God before being taken into the very presence of God at the age of fifty-two.

Another significant Puritan work on God's attributes is William Bates (1625-1699), *The Harmony of the Divine Attributes* in the Contrivance and Accomplishment of Man's Redemption (1674; reprint Harrisonburg, VA: Sprinkle, 1985). Bates focuses on God's justice, holiness, power, and mercy. He stresses practical piety and is a master of the Puritan "plain style" of preaching.

Two nineteenth-century works are quite helpful: Robert Phillip, *The Eternal; or, The Attributes of Jehovah* (London: Ward, 1846), and Alexander Carson, *The Knowledge of Jesus the Most Excellent of the Sciences* (New York: Edward Fletcher, 1851). Carson's volume is misnamed; it contains a classic presentation of God's attributes with little focus on Christ until the last chapter.

Standard Reformed dogmatics often have valuable sections on the doctrine of God. Herman Hoeksema, *Reformed Dogmatics* (Grand Rapids: Reformed Free, 1966) is particularly moving on God's attributes. Herman Bavinck, *The Doctrine of God* (Grand Rapids: Eerdmans, 1951) is unsurpassed among the systematicians for a thorough treatment.

Carl Henry, *God, Revelation and Authority*, 6 vols. (Waco, TX: Word, 1976-1983) is too difficult for most readers, but it contains some valuable material on the doctrine of God for the discerning, especially in Volumes 2, 5, and 6.

The best twentieth-century works on God's attributes are A. W. Tozer, *The Knowledge of the Holy* (New York: Harper & Brothers, 1961); Arthur W. Pink, *The Attributes of God* (Swengel, PA: Reiner, 1968); J. I. Packer, *Knowing God* (Downers Grove, IL: InterVarsity, 1973); C. Samuel Storms, *The Grandeur of God: A Theological and Devotional Study of the Divine Attributes* (Grand Rapids: Baker, 1984). Tozer is the most inspiring; Pink, the most experimental; Packer, the most practical; Storms, the most theological.

If you have never read a book (other than the Bible) about God and His attributes, begin with Packer's. It's already a classic. Part 1 deals with the blessings and benefits of knowing God; Part 2 with who God is in His attributes; Part 3 with the effect God's being and attributes should have on our lives.

Article 2 — By What Means God is Made Known Unto Us

John Calvin's *Institutes of the Christian Religion* (Vols. 20-21 of Library of Christian Classics; edited by John T. McNeill; translated by Ford Lewis Battles; Philadelphia: Westminster Press, 1960) is the all-time classic on the Reformed doctrine of the knowledge of God. The entire structure of *Institutes* is organized around how God is to be known as Father, Son, and Spirit. The best secondary source for Calvin's view of the knowledge of God is B. B. Warfield, "Calvin's Doctrine of the Knowledge of God," in *Calvin and Augustine* (edited by Samuel Craig; reprint Philadelphia: Presbyterian and Reformed, 1956). E. A. Dowey, Jr., *The Knowledge of God in Calvin's Theology* (1952; reprint New York: Columbia University Press, 1965), and T. H. L. Parker, *The Doctrine of the Knowledge of God: A Study in the Theology of John Calvin* (Edinburgh: Oliver and Boyd, 1952) are tinged with neo-orthodoxy. Serious students could also consult the unpublished dissertation of Kenneth Kantzer, "The Knowledge of God and the Word of God in John Calvin" (Harvard, 1950).

Additional, older works on divine revelation that are still helpful include John Brown, *A Compendious View of Natural and Revealed Religion* (Philadelphia: David Hogan, 1819), Books 1 and 2; Thomas Halyburton, "A Treatise on Natural and Revealed Religion," *The Works of the Rev. Thomas Halyburton* (London: Thomas & Tegg, 1835), pp. 254-503; George P. Fisher, *The Nature and Method of Revelation* (New York: Charles Scribner's Sons, 1890).

For twentieth-century works on the doctrine of revelation, Leon Morris's *I Believe in Revelation* (Grand Rapids: Eerdmans, 1976) is the best introductory review. Arthur W. Pink's *The Doctrine of Revelation* (Grand Rapids: Baker, 1975) focuses on God's revelation of Himself in creation, the moral nature of man, history, the Incarnation, and the Scriptures. This is the most edifying work on revelation from a popular, experimental, Reformed perspective. *The Bible: The Living Word of Revelation,* edited by Merrill Chapin Tenney (Grand Rapids: Zondervan, 1968), consists of ten essays by Evangelical Theological Society members, the bulk of which stress aspects of the doctrine of revelation, the mode of divine communication, or ramifications of inerrancy.

For in-depth Reformed works on the doctrine of revelation, consult Benjamin B. Warfield, *Revelation and Inspiration* (New York: Oxford, 1927); William Masselink, *General Revelation and Common Grace* (Grand Rapids: Eerdmans, 1953); Herman Bavinck, *The Philosophy of Revelation* (Grand Rapids: Baker, 1959); Gordon H. Clark, *Religion, Reason and Revelation* (Nutley, NJ: Presbyterian and Reformed, 1961); Cornelius VanTil, *An Introduction to Systematic Theology: Defense of the Faith* (Nutley, NJ: Presbyterian and Reformed,

1974); John H. Frame, *The Doctrine of the Knowledge of God* (Phillipsburg, NJ: Presbyterian and Reformed, 1987). G. C. Berkouwer interacts with Dutch Reformed theologians in his thought-provoking *General Revelation* (Grand Rapids: Eerdmans, 1955). Especially enlightening are Chapters 7 and 10, the latter titled, "The Controversy Regarding Article II of the Belgic Confession." As usual, however, Berkouwer asks more questions than he answers.

The most valuable study in the historical development of the doctrine of revelation is Bruce A. DeMarest, *General Revelation: Historical Views and Contemporary Issues* (Grand Rapids: Zondervan, 1982). For the post-Reformation era, see Richard Muller, *Post-Reformation Reformed Dogmatics,* Chapter 5 of Volume 1 (Grand Rapids: Baker, 1987). Also quite helpful, more detailed, and extending treatment up to 1960, is H. D. McDonald, *Theories of Revelation: An Historical Study 1700-1960* (2 vols. in 1; reprint Grand Rapids: Baker, 1979 — formerly published as *Ideas of Revelation, An Historical Study, A.D. 1700 to A.D. 1860,* and *Theories of Revelation, An Historical Study, 1860-1960*). For twentieth-century views on revelation, John Baillie, *The Idea of Revelation in Recent Thought* (New York: Columbia University Press, 1956), though often cited, is too liberal to be of much help. Of more value, though somewhat dated, is a work edited by Carl Henry, *Revelation and the Bible: Contemporary Evangelical Thought* (Grand Rapids: Baker, 1958).

Where should you start reading? Begin with Psalm 19 and Romans 1. Search the Scriptures and nature, in which God has richly revealed Himself. Peruse Calvin, Morris, Pink, and DeMarest.

Article 3 — The Inspiration of the Scriptures

Articles 3-7 of the Belgic Confession address the doctrine of God's special revelation deposited in the Holy Scriptures. Concerning this doctrine, Solomon's admonition is timely: "Of making many books there is no end." The last two decades in particular have produced an endless stream of tomes at all levels about the written Word of God. For our purposes, we wish to highlight some of the best works, past and present, under the following divisions: the inspiration of the Scriptures (Article 3), the canonicity of the Scriptures (Article 4), the authority of the Scriptures (Article 5), the inferiority of the Apocrypha compared to the Scriptures (Article 6), and the sufficiency and inerrancy of the Scriptures (Article 7).

Nineteenth-century works on the Bible's divine inspiration include Robert Haldane, *The Books of the Old and New Testaments Proved to be Canonical and Their Verbal Inspiration Maintained and Established* (Boston: American Doctrinal Tract Society, 1835); Archibald Alexander, *Evidences of the Authenticity, Inspiration and Canonical Authority of the Holy Scriptures* (Philadelphia: Presbyterian Board of Publications, 1836); Louis Gaussen, *Theopneustia: The Plenary Inspiration of the Holy Scriptures* (1840; reprint Grand Rapids: Kregel, 1971); James Bannerman, *Inspiration: The Infallible Truth and Divine Authority of the Holy Scriptures* (Edinburgh: T. & T. Clark, 1865). Haldane reacts to German rationalism with verbal inspiration; Alexander's work presents numerous "evidences" but lacks his customary depth of thought; Gaussen's treatise is the nineteenth-century classic; Bannerman excels on the history of the doctrine of inspiration.

The twentieth-century classic is B. B. Warfield, *The Inspiration and Authority of the Bible,* edited by Samuel G. Craig (Philadelphia: Presbyterian and Reformed, 1970), which contains the bulk of articles (many of which have never been surpassed exegetically or theologically) in *Revelation and Inspiration* (New York: Oxford, 1927), as well as a superior 65-page introduction by Cornelius Van Til. Warfield is essential reading for understanding the "old Princeton" position on divine inspiration.

Edward J. Young, *Thy Word is Truth* (Grand Rapids: Eerdmans, 1957) does a marvelous job of combining doctrinal accuracy with popular readability. He also effectively addresses inerrancy, individual "problem texts," and modern views of Scripture.

Other helpful volumes on the popular level include: Theodore Engelder, *Scripture Cannot Be Broken* (St. Louis: Concordia, 1945), a vigorous defense of verbal-plenary inspiration; A. W. Pink, *The Divine Inspiration of the Bible* (Swengel, PA: Reiner, 1971), which aims for personal edification more than doctrinal depth; Brian Edwards, *Nothing but the Truth* (Welwyn, England: Evangelical Press, 1978), which excels for those unfamiliar with doctrinal terms and recent debate; James I. Packer, *God Has Spoken* (Downers Grove, IL: InterVarsity Press, 1979), which stresses the joy of Bible study and examines what Scripture says about itself. Packer's work includes the 1978 *Chicago Statement on Biblical Inerrancy.*

Robert Preus, *The Inspiration of Scripture,* 2nd edition (Edinburgh: Oliver and Boyd, 1957) is an able monograph on the theology of seventeenth-century Lutheran dogmaticians. For an in-depth seventeenth-century Reformed dogmatician on inspiration, see Francis Turretin, *The Doctrine of Scripture,* edited and translated by John W. Beardslee III (Grand Rapids: Baker, 1981).

Where should you begin reading? Study 2 Timothy 3:16 and 2 Peter 1:21 with the assistance of reputable commentaries. Then read Young and Edwards.

Article 4 — The Canon of the Scriptures

The beginning reader should consult William J. McRae, *The Birth of the Bible* (Scarborough: Everyday Publications, 1984) or Neil Lightfoot, *How We Got Our Bible* (Grand Rapids: Baker, 1963) for a simple treatment of the establishment of the sacred canon of Scripture. On a somewhat higher level, R. Laird Harris, *Inspiration and Canonicity of the Bible* (Grand Rapids: Zondervan, 1957) is a basic, reliable work on canonization that covers most major issues. Harris lucidly argues that inspiration is the core principle of canonicity. Also, Roland K. Harrison, "The Canon of the Old Testament" and Everett F. Harrison, "The Canon of the New Testament"— articles found in most modern editions of *Young's Analytical Concordance* — are clear, concise, and sound. For a more scholarly approach to canonization, a diligent reading of William Cunningham's essay on canonicity in his *Theological Lectures* (London: Nisbet, 1878), as well as William Henry Green, *General Introduction to the Old Testament: The Canon* (London: John Murray, 1899) will reap rewards, notwithstanding their datedness. For a more recent scholarly work, consult Bruce Metzger, *The Canon of the New Testament* (Oxford: University Press, 1987).

Numerous works of "Biblical introduction" survey the

Old and New Testament canon and text, covering each book's author, date and setting, theme and purpose, survey and outline. Most helpful at a simple level are William Hendriksen, *Survey of the Bible* (reprint Grand Rapids: Baker, 1976), which is reliable and short; William Deal, *Pictorial Introduction to the Bible* (Grand Rapids: Baker, 1982), which excels in practical lessons to be gleaned from each Bible book. For an intermediate level, consult John Raven, *Old Testament Introduction* (New York: Revell, 1910), which has been a conservative, somewhat dry, standard text for half a century; Edward J. Young, *An Introduction to the Old Testament* (Grand Rapids: Eerdmans, 1960) usurps Raven as the most reliable guide to treat the major critical problems; Gleason Archer, *A Survey of Old Testament Introduction* (Chicago: Moody, 1964) ably defends the conservative evangelical position; Lawrence O. Richards, *Teacher's Commentary* (Wheaton: Victor Books, 1987) is weak on theology but excels as a practical guide for Sunday school teachers, Christian educators, and leaders of Bible-group studies. For a scholarly level, see the generally reliable works of Theodor Zahn, *Introduction to the New Testament*, 3 volumes (1909; reprint Grand Rapids: Kregel, 1953); Roland K. Harrison, *Introduction to the Old Testament* (Grand Rapids: Eerdmans, 1969); Everett F. Harrison, *Introduction to the New Testament* (Grand Rapids: Eerdmans, 1971); Donald Guthrie, *New Testament Introduction*, 4th revised edition (Downers Grove, IL: InterVarsity, 1990); D. A. Carson, Douglas J. Moo, and Leon Morris, *An Introduction to the New Testament* (Grand Rapids: Zondervan, 1992); Raymond B. Dillard and Tremper Logman III, *An Introduction to the Old Testament* (Grand Rapids: Zondervan, 1995).

Begin with R. Laird Harris.

Article 5 — The Authority of Scripture

The two most helpful books on biblical authority are *The Infallible Word: A Symposium by the Members of the Faculty of Westminster Theological Seminary*, edited by Ned Stonehouse and Paul Woolley (Philadelphia: Presbyterian and Reformed, 1946) and Bernard Ramm, *The Pattern of Religious Authority* (Grand Rapids: Eerdmans, 1957). The symposium contains an excellent series of Reformed essays dealing with the general character of biblical authority and canonicity. It concludes by stressing the relevancy and distinctive characteristics of these doctrines as well as the importance of preaching them.

Ramm addresses issues on authority that confront the conservative evangelical. He distinguishes between the "grounds of accepting an authority" and "the right of authority," and claims that reason, intuition, or inclination are modes of perceiving or receiving an authority but do not constitute the right of the authority received. He argues that the believer's doctrine of authority is threefold: the authority of the Scriptures, of the Holy Spirit, and of Christ. This threefold delineation is contrasted with Roman Catholicism, modernism, and neo-orthodoxy.

Helpful articles by John Gerstner, James Packer, Francis Schaeffer, R. C. Sproul, and others can be found in *The Foundation of Biblical Authority*, edited by James M. Boice (Grand Rapids: Zondervan, 1978), which is the first major publication of the International Council on Biblical Inerrancy (ICBI), founded in 1977. Volume 4 of Carl Henry, *God, Revelation and Authority* (Waco, TX: Word, 1979) contains a massive technical treatment of biblical authority. Meredith Kline, *The Structure of Biblical Authority* (Grand Rapids: Eerdmans, 1972) argues that our understanding of authority can be forwarded by relating the concept of canon to the treaty documents of the ancient Near East. John D. Woodbridge, *Biblical Authority: A Critique of the Rogers/McKim Proposal* (Grand Rapids: Zondervan, 1982) effectively exposes the sloppy scholarship of Rogers and McKim, and it positively addresses the issue of biblical authority for our day from a conservative, evangelical perspective.

For historical studies on biblical authority, consult Rupert Eric Davies, *The Problem of Authority in the Continental Reformers: A Study in Luther, Zwingli, and Calvin* (London: Epworth Press, 1946); Henry Jackson Forstman, *Calvin's Doctrine of Biblical Authority* (Stanford: Stanford University Press, 1962), which includes a helpful epilogue on "Calvin, Calvinism, and the Contemporary Situation" as well as an excellent bibliography.

Where should you begin? Read a persuasive, little book by D. Martyn Lloyd-Jones titled *Authority* (London: InterVarsity, 1966), which is a clarion call to return to the authority of Christ, the Word, and the Holy Spirit.

Article 6 — The Apocrypha

Sources for the Apocrypha include:

(1) *King James Version*: Most KJV pulpit Bibles include the Apocrypha, as does Thomas Nelson's 1990 reprint of the 1611 KJV.

(2) *Geneva Bible*: See the 1969 facsimile of the 1560 edition published by the University of Wisconsin Press.

(3) *Reims-Douay*: The apocryphal books are interspersed with the canonical books in keeping with the Roman Catholic tradition.

(4) *Revised Version*: The Apocrypha was published in 1894 as a sequel to the RV of 1881 (see *The World's Classic Series*, vol. 294 [Oxford University Press]).

(5) *Revised Standard Version*: "The Oxford Annotated Apocrypha," edited by Bruce Metzger (New York: Oxford, 1965; also printed as part of *The New Oxford Annotated Bible with the Apocrypha* [1973]), is a very helpful edition.

The Apocrypha and Pseudepigrapha, edited by Robert H. Charles in two volumes with introductions and explanatory notes (Oxford: 1913, reprint: Clarendon Press, 1963), is the standard critical work. William Oesterley, *An Introduction to the Books of the Apocrypha* (London: SPCK, 1946) has been superseded by Bruce M. Metzger, *An Introduction to the Apocrypha* (New York: Oxford, 1957). Metzger provides a comprehensive examination of the books of the Apocrypha, together with an evaluation of their history and significance. David Russell, *Between the Testaments* (London: SCM Press, 1960) and Herbert Andrews, *An Introduction to the Apocryphal Books of the Old and New Testament*, revised and edited by Charles F. Pfeiffer (Grand Rapids: Baker, 1964) address the cultural and literary background of the Apocrypha. Roland K. Harrison, *Introduction to the Old Testament* (Grand Rapids: Eerdmans, 1969) provides a special, 100-page supplement on the Apocrypha.

Where should you begin? Read the Apocrypha and E. J. Goodspeed, *The Story of the Apocrypha* (Chicago, 1939), followed by Harrison and Metzger's *Introduction*.

Article 7 — Scripture's Sufficiency and Inerrancy

Sufficiency

Numerous books touch on the sufficiency of Scripture, but none addresses both the long-standing and contemporary issues involved in such an able, engaging, and readable manner as Noel Weeks, *The Sufficiency of Scripture* (Edinburgh: Banner of Truth Trust, 1988). The first part deals with basic issues such as authority, revelation, providence, inerrancy, and contextualization; the remainder of the volume addresses specific points of contention, such as creation, the interpretation of prophecy, women in church offices, psychology, and Bible translation.

James I. Packer, *Beyond the Battle for the Bible* (Westchester, IL: Cornerstone, 1980) deals with the sufficiency of Scripture in a lengthy chapter on how to use Scripture in public and private. It also addresses the current debate on inerrancy.

Inerrancy

A helpful, readable book that defends inerrancy on the basis of Christ's view of Scripture is Robert P. Lightner, *The Saviour and the Scriptures* (Philadelphia: Presbyterian and Reformed, 1966). *God's Inerrant Word*, edited by John W. Montgomery (Minneapolis: Bethany, 1974), is a collection of superior essays written prior to Lindsell's books.

Harold Lindsell, *The Battle for the Bible* (Grand Rapids: Zondervan, 1976) gave the inerrancy debate fresh impetus by documenting evidence of substantial erosion of commitment to this doctrine in evangelical denominations and schools. In a sequel volume, *The Bible in the Balance* (Grand Rapids: Zondervan, 1979), Lindsell fleshes out his arguments, answers his critics, and cites further inerrancy erosion in churches and schools.

Some of the best material on the Reformed view of inerrancy can be found in several collections of essays published in the 1980s, including *Inerrancy and Common Sense*, edited by Roger R. Nicole and J. Ramsey Michaels (Grand Rapids: Baker, 1980); *Inerrancy*, edited by Norman L. Geisler (Grand Rapids: Zondervan, 1980); *Scripture and Truth*, edited by D. A. Carson and John D. Woodbridge (Grand Rapids: Zondervan, 1983); *Inerrancy and the Church*, edited by John D. Hannah (Chicago: Moody Press, 1984); *Challenges to Inerrancy: A Theological Response*, edited by Gordon R. Lewis and Bruce Demarest (Chicago: Moody Press, 1984); *Hermeneutics, Inerrancy, and the Bible*, edited by Earl D. Radmacher and Robert D. Preus (Grand Rapids: Zondervan, 1984); *Evangelicals and Inerrancy*, edited by Ronald Youngblood (New York: Thomas Nelson, 1984); *Inerrancy and Hermeneutics*, edited by Harvie Conn (Grand Rapids: Baker, 1988).

A word of warning: Avoid G. C. Berkouwer, *Holy Scripture*, translated by Jack Rogers (Grand Rapids: Eerdmans, 1975). Berkouwer qualifies inerrancy by disassociating it from historical and scientific exactness. He neglects to spell out the dangerous consequences of tolerating arbitrary rejection of selected Scriptures.

Where should you begin reading on inerrancy? For a brief, nontechnical starter, read John H. Gerstner, *Bible Inerrancy Primer* (Grand Rapids: Baker, 1965).

Articles 8-9 — The Trinity

During the earliest centuries of church history, the Christian doctrine of God as "three persons in one substance or essence" assumed the shape that has been largely retained ever since. Athanasius and the Cappadocians in the fourth century, and later, Augustine, played a critical role. The Apostles', the Nicene, and the Athanasian creeds embody the core teachings of the fathers on the Trinity. For primary sources on the development of Trinitarian doctrine in the ancient church, see *Ante-Nicene Fathers*, edited by Alexander Robert and James Donaldson, 10 volumes (1885-96; reprint Grand Rapids: Eerdmans, 1951-56), and *Nicene and Post-Nicene Fathers*, edited by Philip Schaff et al., two series of 14 volumes each (1887-94; reprint Grand Rapids: Eerdmans, 1952-56). For secondary studies, see W. S. Bishop, *The Development of Trinitarian doctrine in the Nicene and Athanasian Creeds* (New York: Longmans, Green, 1910); L. Prestige, *God in Patristic Thought*, 2nd ed. (London: SPCK, 1952); J. Quasten, *Patrology*, 3 vols. (1950-86; reprint Westminster, MD: Christian Classics, 1983-86); J. N. D. Kelly, *The Athanasian Creed* (London: A. & C. Black, 1964), *Early Christian Doctrines* (New York: Harper & Row, 1965), and *Early Christian Creeds* (London: Longmans, 1972); Edmund J. Fortman, *The Triune God: A Historical Study of the Doctrine of the Trinity* (Philadelphia: Westminster, 1972); and Thomas F. Torrance, *The Trinitarian Faith: The Evangelical Theology of the Ancient Catholic Church* (Edinburgh: T. and T. Clark, 1988).

Surprisingly, few helpful books are written on the Trinity from a sound Reformed perspective, considering that the Reformers were very concerned to affirm their unity with the ancient church in this doctrine. Standard Reformed dogmatics often have valuable sections on the Trinity; consult especially Calvin's *Institutes*, which is organized around a Trinitarian framework. The best Puritan works on the Trinity are Volume 2 of John Owen's *Works* (reprint Edinburgh: Banner of Truth Trust, 1965) and the last one hundred pages of Volume 2 of John Howe's *Works* (reprint Ligonier, PA: Soli Deo Gloria, 1990). Owen's major work in Volume 2, *Of Communion with God the Father, Son, and Holy Ghost* (365 pages), is unsurpassed in Christian literature in detailing how the believer experimentally communes with each person in the Trinity. Also, consult B. B. Warfield, "The Biblical Doctrine of the Trinity," in *Biblical and Theological Studies*, edited by Samuel G. Craig (Philadelphia: Presbyterian and Reformed, 1968), pp. 22-59.

There are four, recommendable, popular-level works on the Trinity. A nineteenth-century classic, Edward H. Bickersteth, *The Trinity* (reprint Grand Rapids: Kregel, 1965) is the best older work. First published in 1859 under the title, *The Rock of Ages*, this little work promotes a worshipful tone in approaching the doctrine of the Trinity and provides considerable biblical evidence for belief in the eternal Godhead of the Father, Son, and Spirit. The concluding chapter, "Faith, the Scriptures, and the Trinity," is particularly helpful. Also reliable and basic is Loraine Boettner's section on the Trinity in *Studies in Theology* (1947; reprint Grand Rapids: Baker, 1975), pp. 79-138. The most readable, contemporary works on the Trinity are Stuart Olyott, *The Three are One* (Welwyn, Herts: Evangelical Press, 1979), and Alister E. McGrath, *Understanding the Trinity* (Grand Rapids: Zondervan, 1990).

For works of greater depth, consult the following: G.

A. F. Knight, *A Biblical Approach to the Doctrine of the Trinity* (Edinburgh: Oliver and Boyd, 1953) and E. Calvin Beisner, *God in Three Persons* (Wheaton: Tyndale, 1984) provide an account of the biblical foundations of the doctrine of the Trinity. A. W. Wainwright, *The Trinity in the New Testament* (London: SPCK, 1962) argues that the doctrine of the Trinity is essential to the New Testament message. *One God in Trinity* (Westchester, IL: Cornerstone, 1980), edited by Peter Toon and James D. Spiceland, contains lectures of varying merit delivered at the British Tyndale Fellowship, Durham, 1978. Gordon H. Clark, *The Trinity* (Jefferson, MD: Trinity Foundation, 1985) is a clear historical-theological work on the church's understanding of the doctrine of the Trinity during the past two millenia. This book suffers, however, from being overly critical of Bavinck, VanTil, Knudsen, and others. Royce Gordon Gruenler, *The Trinity in the Gospel of John* (Grand Rapids: Baker, 1986) is a careful study of the Trinity as presented in John's gospel. Millard J. Erickson, *God in Three Persons: A Contemporary Interpretation of the Trinity* (Grand Rapids: Baker, 1995) is the latest and best all-around work on the Trinity. It covers the Trinity in the Old Testament, the New Testament, and early church history, as well as defends the ongoing importance of a Trinitarian definition of God. Erickson also effectively addresses contemporary questions about the Trinity. This volume, geared to undergraduate theological courses, will no doubt become a staple work, but there remains a need for a biblical, historical, and theological work on the Trinity from a thoroughly Reformed perspective.

For a starter, try Bickersteth. Move on to Calvin, but do not rest until you digest the sublime, second volume of Owen's *Works*.

Article 10 — The Deity of Jesus Christ

The best seventeenth-century works on Christ's deity and glory are from the prince of Puritans, John Owen (1616-1683). Three moving treatises are collected in Volume 1 of the Goold edition of Owen's *Works*, reprinted by Banner of Truth Trust in 1965 and several times thereafter: *A Declaration of the Glorious Mystery of the Person of Christ* (1679), *Meditations and Discourses on the Glory of Christ* (1684), and *Meditations and Discourses Concerning the Glory of Christ Applied* (1691). With regard to the glory of Christ's divine person, Owen's treatises remain unsurpassed. Thomas M'Crie writes of Owen's works on Christ in Volume 1, "Of all the theological works published by individuals since the Reformation, next to Calvin's *Institutes*, we should have deemed it our highest honour to have produced [these]."

Helpful eighteenth-century works on the Godhead of the Son include August Hermann Francke, *Christus Sacrae Scripturae Nucleus: Or, Christ The Sum and Substance Of all the Holy Scriptures* (London: J. Downing, 1732), which focuses on the divinity of Christ in John 1 in a judicious and heart-warming manner; John Guyse, *Jesus Christ God-Man: or, The Constitution of Christ's Person, with the Evidence and Importance of the Doctrine of His True and Proper Godhead* (Glasgow: David Niven, 1790), which is a series of sermons expounding Romans 9:5; William Laing, *Philemon's Letters to Onesimus: Upon The Subjects of Christ's Atonement and Divinity* (Newry: D. Carpenter, 1791), which is an able, 432-page defense of Christ's divinity in sixteen engaging letters; Robert Hawker, *Sermons on the Divinity of Christ* (1792; reprint London: E. Spettigue, 1847), which includes eight moving sermons by an experiential, Calvinist Anglican that spell out the spiritual and daily ramifications of believing in Christ as the Son of God.

Noteworthy nineteenth-century works on Christ's deity include Ambrose Serle, *Horae Solitariae: Or, Essays Upon some Remarkable Names and Titles of Jesus Christ, Occurring in the Old Testament, and Declarative of His Essential Divinity...*, Volume 1 (Dublin: Thomas Connolly, 1849), which is particularly helpful in proving Christ's divinity from the Old Testament; Henry Parry Liddon, *The Divinity of Our Lord and Saviour Jesus Christ* (1868; reprint Minneapolis: Klock & Klock, 1978), which is a standard, frequently reprinted treatment of Liddon's Bampton lectures; Joseph C. Philpot, *Eternal Sonship of Christ* (1865; reprint Grand Rapids: Sovereign Grace, 1971), which is a scriptural, polemical, and experiential treatment.

Several twentieth-century books uphold an orthodox view of Christ's divinity in an edifying manner. Benjamin B. Warfield, *The Lord of Glory* (London: Hodder and Stoughton, 1907) provides a scholarly examination of the biblical evidence for the deity of Christ. Robert Anderson, *The Lord from Heaven* (1910; reprint Grand Rapids: Kregel, 1978) ably expounds Christ's deity from both testaments, focusing on Him as King of kings. William E. Vine, *The Divine Sonship of Christ*, 2 vols. in 1 (Minneapolis: Klock & Klock, 1984) contains *Christ's Eternal Sonship* and *The First and the Last*, both of which emphasize the benefits that flow to the believer from Christ's divinity. Herbert Lockyer, *All the Divine Names and Titles in the Bible* (Grand Rapids: Zondervan, 1975) devotes two hundred pages to an edifying exposition of scores of Christ's names that shed light on His divinity. Josh McDowell and Bart Larson, *Jesus: A Biblical Defense of His Deity* (San Bernardino, CA: Here's Life, 1983) is designed as an apologetic for college students. Murray J. Harris, *Jesus as God: The New Testament Use of Theos in Reference to God* (Grand Rapids: Baker, 1992) carefully exegetes ten texts in an evangelical, scholarly manner and provides an excellent up-to-date bibliography.

For the historical development of the doctrine of Christ's divinity, see Edward Burton, *Testimonies of Ante-Nicene Fathers to the Divinity of Christ*, 2nd ed. (Oxford, 1829); Izaak August Dorner, *History of the Development of the Doctrine of the Person of Christ*, 5 vols. (Edinburgh, 1861-63); Albert Reville, *History of the Doctrine of the Deity of Jesus Christ* (London, 1870).

Where should you begin? Read the gospel of John again, paying particular regard to the apostle's affirmations of Christ's divinity (see also A. T. Robertson, *The Divinity of Christ in the Gospel of John* [1916; reprint Grand Rapids: Baker, 1976]). Then read some of the creedal statements of the ancient church, such as the Nicene, Chalcedonian, and Athanasian creeds. Follow this up with a reading of John H. Gerstner's helpful, introductory booklet, *A Primer on the Deity of Christ* (Phillipsburg, NJ: Presbyterian and Reformed, 1984).

Article 11 — The Deity of the Holy Spirit

Some scholars say that the Holy Spirit is the forgotten person of the Trinity, but Reformed theologians have produced numerous tomes on the work of the Spirit, including several classics written by such capable Puritans as John Owen and Thomas Goodwin. Much less, however, has been written on the Person of the Spirit, particularly on His deity. Frequently books on the Holy Spirit include a short chapter on the divinity of the Spirit but do not address this important subject in depth. Even John Owen's third chapter in *A Discourse Concerning the Holy Spirit*, titled, "Divine Nature and Personality of the Holy Spirit Proved and Vindicated" (*Works*, Volume 3, reprint Banner of Truth Trust, 1965), while supplying a solid foundation and polemical defense (especially against the Socinians) for the Spirit's deity, lacks the author's characteristic thoroughness. A definitive work on the Spirit's divinity, together with its implications, has yet to be written from a biblical, Reformed perspective.

The most helpful eighteenth-century works devoted to expounding the Godhead of the Spirit include John Guyse, *The Holy Spirit a Divine Person: or, the Doctrine of His Godhead represented as evident and important* (Glasgow: David Niven, 1790), which includes a series of sermons expounding 1 Corinthians 12:11; Robert Hawker, *Sermons on the Deity and Operations of the Holy Spirit* (1792; reprint London: E. Spettigue, 1847), which includes eight sermons that spell out the spiritual and daily ramifications of believing in the Spirit as the third person of the Trinity.

Noteworthy nineteenth-century volumes that address the Spirit's deity include Ambrose Serle, *Horae Solitariae: Or, Essays Upon some Names, Titles, and Attributes of the Holy Spirit, revealed in the Two Testaments...*, Volume 2 (Dublin: Thomas Connolly, 1849), which is a fascinating, 450-page work expounding twenty-eight names and attributes ascribed to the Spirit in the Scriptures, conclusively proving His divinity and bringing that divinity to bear upon daily, Christian living. Edward Bickersteth, *The Spirit of Life* (1850; reprinted as *The Holy Spirit: His Person and Work* [Grand Rapids: Kregel, 1959]) provides a readable, scriptural summary of the eternalness of the Spirit's Godhead. Robert Balmer, "On the Divinity of the Holy Spirit," in *Theological Tracts, Selected and Original*, edited by John Brown (London: A. Fullarton, 1854), pp. 186-203, is a helpful, succinct treatment. Joseph C. Philpot, *Meditations on the Person, Work and Covenant Offices of God the Holy Ghost* (1865; reprint Harpenden, Herts: O. G. Pearce, 1976) devotes three chapters to aspects of the Spirit's deity in a helpful, scriptural, and experiential manner. George Smeaton, *The Doctrine of the Holy Spirit* (1882; reprint Edinburgh: Banner of Truth Trust, 1958) combines theological accuracy with practical teaching in expounding the Spirit's deity in relation to the doctrine of the Trinity.

Several twentieth-century books uphold an orthodox view of the Spirit's divinity but add little to the older works. The first four chapters of R. C. Sproul, *The Mystery of the Holy Spirit* (Wheaton: Tyndale, 1990) is helpful for anyone struggling with the deity of the Spirit and the mystery of the Trinity.

For a listing of more than 2,000 works written on various aspects of the person and work of the Holy Spirit, see Watson E. Mills, *The Holy Spirit: A Bibliography* (Peabody, MA: Hendrickson, 1988).

Begin with George Smeaton. His work on the Spirit is readable, thorough, and edifying.

Article 12 — Creation, Angels, and Devils

Creation

A plethora of books and articles have been written in recent decades on creation and/or science. The best series of articles on creation from a Reformed perspective is "Symposium on Creation," in *The Journal of Christian Reconstruction* 1 (Summer 1974). For an in-depth study of Genesis 1, especially the first three verses and their interrelationship, see Edward J. Young, *Studies in Genesis One* (Philadelphia: Presbyterian and Reformed, 1973; originally published in the *Westminster Theological Journal* as three articles).

Helpful books include Rousas J. Rushdoony, *Mythology of Science* (Nutley, NJ: Craig, 1967), which exposes a number of naive theories long held by secular scientists; Walter E. Lammerts, ed., *Scientific Studies in Special Creation* (Grand Rapids: Baker, 1971), which effectively answers basic questions about special creation; and R. L. Wysong, *The Creation-Evolution Controversy* (East Lansing, MI: Inquiry, 1976), which fully supports Scripture's account of creation on revelatory and reasoned grounds.

For additional books advocating biblical creationism, contact the Institute for Creation Research (ICR), in San Diego, California. Consult the writings of institute scientist Duane T. Gish (such as *Up With Creation* [San Diego: Creation-Life, 1974] and *The Battle for Creation* [San Diego: Creation-Life, 1976]), and especially those of the institute's president, Henry M. Morris (e.g., *Evolution in Turmoil* [San Diego: Creation-Life, 1982]; *The Biblical Basis for Modern Science* [Grand Rapids: Baker, 1984]; *A History of Modern Creationism* [San Diego: Master, 1984]; *The Long War Against God: The History and Impact of the Creation/Evolution Conflict* [Grand Rapids: Baker, 1989]).

Angels

An old, scarce, but valuable work that focuses on the ministry of angels to believers is "The Ministration of, and Communion with Angels," in *The Works of Isaac Ambrose* (London: Tegg, 1810), pp. 473-560. Ambrose (1604-1663) was one of the most meditative of Puritans; he annually took the month of May for solitary retreat. His *magnum opus* is the classic *Looking Unto Jesus* (1658).

Alexander Whyte, *The Nature of Angels* (1930; reprint Grand Rapids: Baker, 1976), though a bit imaginative at times, remains a helpful book of eight, expository sermons addressing different aspects of angelology.

For shorter but enlightening pieces on the biblical doctrine of the angels, see "On the Ministry of Angels," in *The Works of John Newton* (reprint Edinburgh: Nelson, 1839), letter #41, pp. 123-126; Henry Harbaugh, "Angelic Sympathy," in *Heaven* (Philadelphia: Lindsay and Blakiston, 1854), pp. 221-257; *The Works of Jonathan Edwards*, Vol. 2 (1834; reprint Edinburgh: Banner of Truth Trust, 1974), pp. 141-156, 604-617. For Edwards's views on angels, see John H. Gerstner, *The Rational Theology of Jonathan Edwards* (Powhatan, VA: Berea, 1992), 2:203-236.

For a historical-theological approach, consult E. Langton, *The Ministries of the Angelic Powers According to the Old Testament and Later Jewish Literature* (London: Clarke, 1936); G. B. Caird, *Principalities and Powers: A Study in Pauline Theology* (Oxford: Clarendon, 1956); J. Danielou, *The Angels and their Mission According to the Fathers of the Church*, translated by D.

Heimann (Westminster: Newman, 1957); G. Davidson, *A Dictionary of Angels* (New York: Free Press, 1967).

Devils

The best over-all contemporary study of biblical demonology is Frederick S. Leahy, *Satan Cast Out* (Edinburgh: Banner of Truth Trust, 1975). For books on combating Satan's temptations, two classics still stand head-and-shoulders above the rest: Thomas Brooks, *Precious Remedies Against Satan's Devices* (London: Baynes, 1804), which is presently available in Banner of Truth Trust's Puritan paperback reprint series; and Richard Gilpin, *Daemonologia Sacra; or, A Treatise of Satan's Temptations* (Edinburgh: James Nichol, 1867).

Other good titles include A. W. Pink, *Satan and His Gospel* (Swengel, PA: Reiner, n.d.); Edward M. Bounds, *Satan: His Personality, Power and Overthrow* (reprint Grand Rapids: Baker, 1972); C. S. Lewis, *Screwtape Letters* (reprint New York: Macmillan, 1969).

For more scholarly works, consult E. Langton, *Satan, A Portrait: A Study of the Character of Satan Through All the Ages* (London: Skeffington, 1945) and *Essentials of Demonology: A Study of Jewish and Christian Doctrine* (London: Epworth, 1949); S. Eitrem, *Some Notes on the Demonology in the New Testament* (Oslo: Universitetsforlager, 1966); J. B. Russell, *Satan: The Early Christian Tradition* (Ithaca: Cornell, 1981); E. Ferguson, *Demonology of the Early Christian World* (New York: Mellen, 1984).

Where should you turn for a Reformed exposition on the creation of the world and the angels, as well as the reality of devils? Try Benjamin B. Warfield's excellent essay, "Calvin's Doctrine of the Creation" in *Calvin and Calvinism* (New York: Oxford, 1931), pp. 287-351, which addresses Calvin's view of the angels and devils as well as of creation as a whole.

Article 13 — Divine Providence

The best work by a church father on the doctrine of providence is Augustine, *Divine Providence*, translated by R. P. Russell, in *The Fathers of the Church*, Volume 5 (Washington, D.C.: Catholic University of America Press, 1948). See also the writings of John Chrysostom, sometimes dubbed "the great theologian of providence" (e.g., *No One Can Harm the Man Who Does Not Injure Himself*, translated by W. R. Stephens, in *Nicene and Post-Nicene Fathers*, edited by P. Schaff, et al., Series 1, Volume 9 [reprint Grand Rapids: Eerdmans, 1954]).

For a classic, Reformed treatment of providence, consult *Calvin's Calvinism: Treatises on the Eternal Predestination of God & the Secret Providence of God*, translated by Henry Cole (reprint Grand Rapids: Reformed Free, 1991), in which Calvin defends the sovereignty of God in providence (pp. 210-350). For a broader, more concise treatment of providence by Calvin, read *Institutes of the Christian Religion*, Book 1, Chapters 16-18 (pp. 197-237 of Volume 1, edited by John T. McNeill and translated by Ford Lewis Battles [Philadelphia: Westminster Press, 1960]). For an excellent treatment of providence by Calvin's successor, Theodore Beza, try Ian McPhee, "Conserver or Transformer of Calvin's Theology? A Study of the Origins and Development of Theodore Beza's Thought, 1550-1570" (Ph.D. dissertation, Cam-

bridge University, 1979), pp. 226-290. For additional Reformed sources on providence, consult Heinrich Heppe, *Reformed Dogmatics: Set Out and Illustrated From the Sources*, translated by G. T. Thomson (1950; reprint Grand Rapids: Baker, 1978), pp. 251-280, as well as standard systematic theologies, such as those by Louis Berkhof and Charles Hodge.

The Puritans superseded the Reformers in handling the doctrine of providence in an experiential, practical manner. The classic in the field is John Flavel, *Divine Conduct: or, The Mystery of Providence* (reprint London: Banner of Truth Trust, 1963; see also Volume 4 of Flavel's *Works*, pp. 336-497). First published in 1678 and reprinted dozens of times, this classic shows how divine providence affects every aspect of a believer's life. It is an invaluable work for instructing God's children in understanding and bowing under God's purposes for their lives. Flavel knew of what he wrote; often persecuted and narrowly escaping arrest on several occasions, his personal life was full of trials. Three times he was left a widower. He died suddenly at the age of sixty-four, confessing, "I know it shall be well with me."

Second-best among the Puritans on providence is Stephen Charnock, "A Treatise on Divine Providence" in *Complete Works*, Volume 1 (Edinburgh: James Nichol, 1864), pp. 3-120. Two excellent Puritan sermons succinctly summarizing the benefits of providence for the believer are Ezekiel Hopkins, *Works*, Volume 3 (Philadelphia: Leighton, 1867; reprint Morgan, PA: Soli Deo Gloria, 1997), pp. 368-388 (on Matthew 10:29-30); and Thomas Lye, "How Are We to Live by Faith on Divine Providence?" in *Puritan Sermons 1659-1689: Being the Morning Exercises at Cripplegate*, Volume 1 (reprint Wheaton: Richard Owen Roberts, 1981), pp. 369-400 (on Psalm 57:8).

The most readable and recommendable nineteenth-century treatment of providence is William S. Plumer, *Jehovah-jireh: A Treatise on Providence* (1865; reprint Harrisonburg, VA: Sprinkle, 1993). Separate chapters discuss God's providence as mysterious, retributive, kind, and vast. Chapter 16, "God's Providence Towards His Church Renders Unnecessary All Tormenting Fears Respecting Her Safety and Final Triumph," is particularly helpful. Hosea Preslar, *Thoughts on Divine Providence, Or a Sketch of God's Care Over and Dealings with His People* (1867; reprint Streamwood, IL: Primitive Baptist Library, 1977) is doctrinally inferior to Plumer but does afford an edifying treatment of providence from a more biographical perspective. Alexander Carson provides us with two frequently reprinted books that trace the acts of providence throughout Scripture: *The History of Providence as explained in the Bible* (reprint Grand Rapids: Baker, 1977) and *Confidence In God in Times of Danger: God's Providence Unfolded in the Book of Esther* (reprint Swengel, PA: Bible Truth Depot, 1962).

Two twentieth-century monographs on providence are noteworthy: Gerrit C. Berkouwer, *The Providence of God*, translated by Lewis B. Smedes (Grand Rapids: Eerdmans, 1952), asks thought-provoking questions about providence in relation to knowledge, sustenance, government, concurrence, history, miracles, and theodicy. Benjamin B. Farley, *The Providence of God* (Grand Rapids: Baker, 1988) is the best study of the development of the doctrine of providence throughout history from a Reformed perspective.

Where should you begin? Read Flavel, then Plumer.

Article 14 — Our Creation, Fall, and Bound Will

Our Creation

The best twentieth-century works from a Reformed perspective on our creation in God's image are Gerrit C. Berkouwer, *Man: The Image of God,* translated by Dirk W. Jellema (Grand Rapids: Eerdmans, 1962); Anthony A. Hoekema, *Created in God's Image* (Grand Rapids: Eerdmans, 1986); and Philip Edgcumbe Hughes, *The True Image: The Origin and Destiny of Man in Christ* (Grand Rapids: Eerdmans, 1989). Berkouwer provides an in-depth treatment that interacts with numerous (especially Dutch) theologians; Hoekema's volume is a readable, comprehensive study of the biblical doctrine of man. It upholds the traditional Reformed balance between the image of God in a narrower or structural sense (what man is), and in a broader or functional sense (what man does). Hughes presents a wide-ranging biblical, historical, and theological study that profoundly integrates the doctrines of man and Christ.

Two excellent introductions to the Reformed doctrine of man written on a popular level are J. Gresham Machen, *The Christian View of Man* (1935; London: Banner of Truth Trust, 1965) and James I. Packer, *Knowing Man* (Westchester, IL: Cornerstone, 1979).

Other recommendable volumes include Wallie A. Criswell, *Did Man Just Happen?* (Grand Rapids: Zondervan, 1957), which deals on a popular level with the factual material relating to the creation of man, the evidence of biology for special creation, and the mystery of man; Leonard Verduin, *Somewhat Less Than God: The Biblical View of Man* (Grand Rapids: Eerdmans, 1970), which offers a systematic approach to the Christian doctrine of man; Francis Nigel Lee, *The Origin and Destiny of Man* (Nutley, NJ: Presbyterian and Reformed, 1974), which includes five biblical lectures delivered at the inauguration of the Christian Studies Center in Memphis; Paul Brand and Philip Yancey, *Fearfully and Wonderfully Made* (Grand Rapids: Zondervan, 1980), which discusses the marvels of God's handiwork in the human body; Gordon H. Clark, *The Biblical Doctrine of Man* (Jefferson, MD: Trinity Foundation, 1984), which compares Christian and humanist views of man.

For significant historical studies, see J. E. Sullivan, *The Image of God: The Doctrine of St. Augustine and Its Influence* (Dubuque: Priory, 1963); Thomas F. Torrance, *Calvin's Doctrine of Man* (London: Lutterworth Press, 1949).

Our Fall

The best devotional, expository study of Genesis 3 that provides a careful exegesis of the original text is Edward J. Young, *Genesis Three* (London: Banner of Truth Trust, 1966). No Reformed theologian, however, has matched Calvin's superb treatment of the fall, in the opening chapters of Book Two of his *Institutes.*

For fostering personal conviction of our tragic fall and profound sin in Adam, read Thomas Boston, *Human Nature in Its Fourfold State* (1720; London: Banner of Truth Trust, 1964). This classic focuses on our four states of innocence, depravity, grace, and glory, but Boston's section on our imputed and inherited depravity is especially poignant. He details how our sin in Adam tragically and radically broke our relationship with God, as well as each of the Ten Commandments. For a twentieth-century Boston, read Arthur

W. Pink, *Gleanings from the Scriptures: Man's Total Depravity* (Chicago: Moody, 1969).

For historical studies marred by liberal thinking but providing valuable source material, consult F. R. Tennant, *The Sources of the Doctrines of the Fall and Original Sin* (Cambridge: University Press, 1903) and N. P. Williams, *The Ideas of the Fall and of Original Sin* (London: Longmans, Green, 1927).

The Bondage of Man's Will

Augustine laid the groundwork for Reformed treatises on the bondage of our will in *On the Grace of Christ* and *On Original Sin* (two treatises written in 418 A.D.), and *On Grace and Free Will* (written in 426 A.D.). They can be found in English in *Saint Augustin's Anti-Pelagian Works,* translated by Peter Holmes and Robert Wallis and revised by Benjamin B. Warfield, *Nicene and Post-Nicene Fathers,* edited by Philip Schaff (Grand Rapids: Eerdmans, 1991), First Series, Volume 5, pp. 214-257, 436-467.

Three Protestant classics have been written on the bondage of the will: Martin Luther, *The Bondage of the Will,* translated by J. I. Packer and O. R. Johnston (Westwood, NJ: Revell, 1957), is a modern, accurate translation of Luther's reply to the diatribe of Erasmus, *De Servo Arbitrio.* Erasmus realized that Luther's classic ably expounded one of the major themes of the Reformation's gospel message. (For a good translation of both documents in one volume, see *Luther and Erasmus on Free Will,* translated and edited by E. Gordon Rupp and Philip S. Watson [Philadelphia: Westminster Press, 1969].) John Calvin's less famous work on the will has finally been translated into English. It's *The Bondage and Liberation of the Will: A Defence of the Orthodox Doctrine of Human Choice against Pighius,* edited by A.N.S. Lane, translated by G.I. Davies (Grand Rapids: Baker, 1996). While Calvin's work is not as significant as Luther's, it is his fullest treatment of the relation between grace and free will, and it contains important material not found elsewhere in his writings. Jonathan Edwards, *Freedom of the Will,* edited by Paul Ramsey, Volume 1 of *The Works of Jonathan Edwards* (1754; New Haven: Yale, 1957) is a detailed inquiry into the prevailing theory of Edwards's day regarding the freedom of the will and human determinism. Edwards employed the distinction between natural and moral inability. Fallen man's inability to do good is a moral inability, consisting of the opposition or lack of inclination to good. It is not a natural inability.

For further Puritan sources, read the statement on free will in *The Westminster Confession of Faith,* Chapter 9, as well as John Owen, who effectively addresses questions that swirl around free will in *Display of Arminianism,* Volume 10 of *The Works of John Owen* (reprint London: Banner of Truth Trust, 1968), pp. 1-140.

For historical-theological studies, see William Cunningham's essay, "Calvinism, and the Doctrine of Philosophical Necessity," in *The Reformers and the Theology of the Reformation* (1862; reprint London: Banner of Truth Trust, 1967). It's an invaluable guide for understanding the view of the Reformers on the will of man. Harry J. McSorley, *Luther: Right or Wrong? An Ecumenical-Theological Study of Luther's Major Work, The Bondage of the Will* (Minneapolis: Augsburg, 1967) contains valuable, primary-source material reviewing issues involving the bondage of the will in Augustine, Thomas Aquinas, and Luther (notwithstanding the author's erroneous conclusions), as well as a superb bibliography.

For popular treatments, read *God's Will, Man's Will, and Free Will: Four Discussions* by Horatius Bonar, Jonathan Edwards, Charles H. Spurgeon, and Jay Green (Wilmington: Sovereign Grace, 1972); W. E. Best, *Free Grace Versus Free Will* (Grand Rapids: Baker, 1977); John H. Gerstner, *A Primer on Free Will* (Phillipsburg, NJ: Presbyterian and Reformed, 1982).

For additional books on creation, see bibliographical notes on Article 12, and for additional books on our fall, see notes on Article 15.

Article 15 — Original Sin

Augustine's brief treatise, *On Original Sin*, laid the groundwork for later Reformed treatises (see *Saint Augustin's Anti-Pelagian Works*, translated by Peter Holmes and Robert Wallis and revised by Benjamin B. Warfield, *Nicene and Post-Nicene Fathers*, edited by Philip Schaff [Grand Rapids: Eerdmans, 1991], First Series, Volume 5, pp. 237-257).

Jonathan Edwards, *Original Sin*, Volume 3 of *The Works of Jonathan Edwards*, edited by Clyde A. Holbrook (1758; New Haven: Yale, 1970), is *the* Calvinistic classic on the subject. Pastors need to familiarize themselves with this treatment if they are to preach effectively against the moral and theological drift of today. The best secondary source on the Edwardsean view is C. Samuel Storms, *Tragedy in Eden: Original Sin in the Theology of Jonathan Edwards* (Lanham, MD: University Press of America, 1985). Storms concludes that there are weaknesses in Edwards's argument that move toward a "system of constitutional depravity and strict volitional determinism [that] inevitably makes God the author of sin."

For an able nineteenth-century work, see Henry Augustus Boardman's *A Treatise on the Scripture Doctrine of Original Sin* (Philadelphia: Presbyterian Board of Publication, 1839). Boardman was the renowned minister of Philadelphia's Tenth Presbyterian Church. This work established his reputation as an upholder and defender of Old School Presbyterian theology.

For a thorough twentieth-century Reformed treatment of Romans 5:12-19, read John Murray, *The Imputation of Adam's Sin* (Grand Rapids: Eerdmans, 1959). Murray, who prefers the term *imputed sin* rather than *original sin,* definitively refutes Pelagian and Roman Catholic views of original sin. He clarifies the *realistic* approach to original sin as advocated by William Shedd and Augustus Strong, but pleads for the *representative* or *federalist* view. The best, brief article on the imputation of sin is Benjamin B. Warfield, "Imputation," in *Biblical and Theological Studies*, edited by Samuel Craig (Philadelphia: Presbyterian and Reformed, 1968), pp. 262-269.

American theologians have done much of the important theological debate on the doctrine of original sin. For the tensions in American theology on this critical, yet often neglected doctrine, see H. Shelton Smith, *Changing Conceptions of Original Sin: A Study in American Theology Since 1750* (New York: Scribners, 1955); Gary D. Long, "The Doctrine of Original Sin in New England Theology from Jonathan Edwards to Edwards Amasa Park" (Th.D. dissertation, Dallas Theological Seminary, 1972); George P. Hutchinson, *The Problem of Original Sin in American Presbyterian Theology* (Philadelphia: Presbyterian and Reformed, 1972). Hutchinson

is the most helpful. His short, lucid work on original sin is written from a historical and theological perspective, and covers American theologians from Jonathan Edwards through John Murray. This is the best introduction to the issues at stake in the doctrine of original sin.

Other historical studies on original sin worthy of being mentioned (though not written from a Reformed perspective) include Henri Rondet, *Original Sin: The Patristic and Theological Background*, translated by Cajetan Finegan (Staten Island: Alba House, 1972), and G. Vandervelde, *Original Sin: Two Major Trends in Contemporary Roman Catholic Interpretation* (Amsterdam: Rodopi, 1975).

For the dread consequences of original sin, no work is more powerful than Thomas Goodwin, *An Unregenerate Man's Guiltiness Before God in Respect of Sin and Punishment*, Volume 10 of *The Works of Thomas Goodwin* (Edinburgh: James Nichol, 1865; reprint Eureka, CA: Tanski, 1996). See also Gerrit C. Berkouwer's probing 600-page work, *Sin*, translated by Phillip C. Holtrop (Grand Rapids: Eerdmans, 1971). Berkouwer is particularly helpful on the relationship of sin to the law (Chapter 6) and to the gospel (Chapter 7). Also helpful on most issues is Bernard L. Ramm, *Offense to Reason: A Theology of Sin* (New York: Harper & Row, 1985).

For additional books on mankind's fall in Paradise, see notes on Article 14.

Article 16 — Predestination: Election and Reprobation

The best pre-Reformation writing on predestination is Augustine's "On the Predestination of the Saints," in *Nicene and Post-Nicene Fathers of the Christian Church*, First Series, Volume 5, edited by Philip Schaff (reprint Grand Rapids: Eerdmans, 1975), pp. 493-520. For a secondary source on Augustine, consult J. B. Mozley, *A Treatise on the Augustinian Doctrine of Predestination* (New York: E.P. Dutton, 1878). For a secondary source on the views of several of the major theologians of the ancient church (including Augustine, Chapter 7), see George Stanley Faber, *The Primitive Doctrine of Election* (New York: Charles Henley, 1840). Faber also covers the Reformation period on predestination.

The great Reformation theologian on predestination was, of course, John Calvin. For a concise treatment of his views, read *Institutes of the Christian Religion*, edited by John T. McNeill, translated by Ford Lewis Battles (Philadelphia: Westminster Press, 1960), Book 3, Chapters 21-24. For Calvin's most polemical, extended treatment of predestination, see *Concerning the Eternal Predestination of God*, translated by J.K.S. Reid (London: James Clarke, 1961; a lessser translation of this work is also taken up in *Calvin's Calvinism*, translated by Henry Cole [1856; reprint Grand Rapids: Reformed Free, 1991]). Also see *Thirteene Sermons of Maister Iohn Calvine, Entreating of the Free Election of God in Jacob and of Reprobation in Esau* (London, 1579; reprinted as *Sermons on Election and Reprobation* [Audubon, NJ: Old Paths, 1996]). Though predestination is not a dominant theme in Calvin, valuable material on the doctrine can be found in many of his commentaries, sermons, treatises, and letters.

Secondary sources on Calvin's doctrine of predestination are numerous. For a succinct, able treatment, see *Collected Writings of John Murray* (Edinburgh: Banner of Truth Trust, 1982), 4:191-204. The best, most balanced work on Calvinian predestination, however, is Fred H. Klooster, *Calvin's Doctrine of Predestination* (Grand Rapids: Baker, 1977). Klooster successfully argues that for Calvin election is always sovereign and gracious; reprobation, always sovereign and just. Two older, important articles are Theodore F. Herman, "Calvin's Doctrine of Predestination," *Reformed Church Review* 13 (1909):183-208; S. Leigh Hunt, "Predestination in the Institutes of John Calvin," *Evangelical Quarterly* 9 (1937):38-45. Significant, unpublished dissertations include Mcknight Crawford Cowper, "Calvin's Doctrine of Predestination and its Ethical Consequences" (Ph.D., Union Theological Seminary, 1942); George Hupp DeHority, "Calvin's Doctrine of Predestination: Criticisms and Reinterpretations" (Ph.D., Union Theological Seminary, 1948); John Weeks, "A Comparison of Calvin and Edwards on the Doctrine of Election" (Ph.D., University of Chicago, 1963); David F. Wells, "*Decretum dei speciale*: An Analysis of the Content and Significance of Calvin's Doctrine of Soteriological Predestination" (Th.M., Trinity Evangelical Divinity, 1967); David N. Wiley, "Calvin's Doctrine of Predestination: His Principal Soteriological and Polemical Doctrine" (Ph.D., Duke University, 1971). Of these dissertations, Wiley's and Wells's are the most helpful.

Other Reformers also wrote classics on predestination. The most famous work is Hieronymous Zanchius, *Absolute Predestination* (reprint Grand Rapids: Sovereign Grace, 1971). Unfortunately, contemporary reprints use the edition produced by Augustus Toplady, who liberally sprinkled comments throughout the volume without proper footnotes.

The best secondary source defending the position that the Reformers were united on the doctrine of predestination (despite the differences of some from Calvin in methodology) is Richard Muller, *Christ and the Decree: Christology and Predestination in Reformed Theology from Calvin to Perkins* (Grand Rapids: Baker, 1988). This volume is a substantial revision of an excellent dissertation, "Predestination and Christology in Sixteenth Century Reformed Theology" (Ph.D., Duke University, 1976). Other helpful writings on the predestinarian views of Calvin's successor, Theodore Beza, and other Calvinists include Benjamin B. Warfield, "Predestination in the Reformed Confessions," *The Presbyterian and Reformed Review* 12 (1901):49-128 (reprinted in *Studies in Theology*); Harry Buis, *Historic Protestantism and Predestination* (Philadelphia: Presbyterian and Reformed, 1958); John Murray, "Calvin, Dort, and Westminster on Predestination: A Comparative Study," in *Crisis in the Reformed Churches: Essays in Commemoration of the Great Synod of Dort, 1618-1619,* edited by Peter Y. DeJong (Grand Rapids: Reformed Fellowship, 1968; reprinted in *Collected Writings*, 4:205-215); John S. Bray, *Theodore Beza's Doctrine of Predestination* (Nieuwkoop: B. DeGraaf, 1975); Herman Hanko, "Predestination in Calvin, Beza, and Later Reformed Theology," *Protestant Reformed Theological Journal* X, 2 (1977): 1-24; Paul Helm, *Calvin and the Calvinists* (Edinburgh: Banner of Truth, 1982); Donald W. Sinnema, "The Issue of Reprobation at the Synod of Dort (1618-19) in Light of the History of This Doctrine" (Ph.D. dissertation, University of St. Michael's College, 1985).

For the views of the English Reformers, see O. T. Hargrave, "The Doctrine of Predestination in the English Reformation" (Ph.D. dissertation, Vanderbilt University, 1966).

For the English Puritans, see "A Christian and Plain Treatise on the Manner and Order of Predestination, and of the Largeness of God's Grace," in *The Works of William Perkins* (London: John Legate, 1609), 2:687-730; "Reprobation Asserted," in *The Works of John Bunyan*, edited by George Offor (1859; reprinted Edinburgh: Banner of Truth Trust, 1994), 2:335-58; Anthony Burgess, *Spiritual Refining* (1652; reprint Ames, IA: International Outreach, 1990), pp. 643-74. For secondary sources, consult Dewey D. Wallace, Jr., *Puritans and Predestination: Grace in English Protestant Theology, 1525-1695* (Chapel Hill, NC: University of North Carolina, 1982); Iain Murray, "The Puritans and the Doctrine of Election," in *The Wisdom of our Fathers* (Puritan Conference, 1956), pp. 1-13.

For a reliable eighteenth-century book on predestination, see William Cooper, *The Doctrine of Predestination unto Life Explained and Vindicated* (London: Dilly, 1765). One of the best nineteenth-century works is James H. Thornwell, *Election and Reprobation* (1871; reprinted in *The Collected Writings* [Edinburgh: Banner of Truth Trust, 1974], 2:105-203). See also Charles Hodge, *Systematic Theology* (New York: Scribner, Armstrong, & Co., 1877), 2:313-353.

The most basic, reliable, and readable twentieth-century works on predestination are Loraine Boettner, *The Reformed Doctrine of Predestination* (1932; reprinted Philadelphia: Presbyterian and Reformed, 1968); Gordon H. Clark, *Biblical Predestination* (Nutley, NJ: Presbyterian and Reformed, 1969); Arthur W. Pink, *The Doctrines of Election and Justification* (Grand Rapids: Baker, 1974); John H. Gerstner, *A Predestination Primer* (Winona Lake, IN: Alpha, 1979); C. Samuel Storms, *Chosen for Life: An Introductory Guide to the Doctrine of Election* (Grand Rapids: Baker, 1987). Gerrit C. Berkouwer, *Divine Election*, translated by Hugo Bekker (Grand Rapids: Eerdmans, 1960), is imbalanced on election and weak on reprobation, as has been pointed out in Alvin L. Baker, *Berkouwer's Doctrine of Election: Balance or Imbalance?* (Phillipsburg, NJ: Presbyterian and Reformed, 1981). Although unreliable in many of his other writings, Paul K. Jewett is at his best in *Election and Predestination* (Grand Rapids: Eerdmans, 1985). He firmly rejects Karl Barth's interpretation, and sees the appropriate response to the awesomeness of divine sovereignty as worship.

Where should you begin? Read and study John 6:37-44, Romans 9-11, Ephesians 1, and all the texts listed in *Nave's Topical Bible* that affirm predestination. Then read Calvin's *Institutes*, 3.21-24, Chapter 3 of the Westminster Confession of Faith, the first head of the Canons of Dort, and finally, Boettner or Storms.

Article 17 — God Promises Salvation in Christ to Fallen Man

The Promises of God in General

Having already noted sources on the fall and misery of man (see Articles 14 and 15), only works related to the promises of God in Christ Jesus need to be noted here. Concerning the personal application of the promises of God, the most helpful book is by William Spurstowe, *The Wells of Salvation Opened: or A Treatise discovering the nature, preciousness, and usefullness, of the Gospel Promises, and Rules for the Right Application of them* (London: T. R. & E. M. for Ralph Smith, 1655). Unfortunately, this work has not been reprinted since 1821. Its biblical, doctrinal, experiential, and practical substance and balance are consistent with the best of the Puritan tradition. Two additional, valuable writings on receiving the promises of God are Andrew Gray, "Great and Precious Promises," in *The Works of the Reverend and Pious Andrew Gray* (1839; reprint Morgan, PA: Soli Deo Gloria, 1992), pp. 115-168; and Robert Brown, "The Application of the Holy Scriptures," in *Doctrinal and Experimental Theology* (London: William Wileman, 1899), pp. 113-153. Herbert W. Lockyer, *All the Promises of the Bible* (Grand Rapids: Zondervan, 1962) is too brief and simplistic to be of much help, but it could be used for devotional reading.

Messianic Promises in Particular

The best Puritan work in this field is Thomas Taylor, *Christ Revealed: or The Old Testament Explained; A Treatise of the Types and Shadowes of our Savior* (London: M. F. for R. Dawlman and L. Fawne, 1635; reprint Delmar, NY: Scholars' Facsimiles & Reprints, 1979).

Several good, late-nineteenth-century works focus on the messianic promises of the Old Testament. Ernst W. Hengstenberg, *Christology of the Old Testament and a Commentary on the Messianic Predictions,* 4 volumes (1872-1878; reprint Grand Rapids: Kregel, 1956) is a valuable study of Old Testament promises, types, and prophecies of Christ. Also helpful are Alfred Edersheim, *Prophecy and History in Relation to the Messiah* (New York: Randolph, 1885); Caspar Von Orelli, *The Old Testament Prophecy of the Consummation of God's Kingdom* (Edinburgh: T. & T. Clark, 1889); David Baron, *Rays of Messiah's Glory: Christ in the Old Testament* (1895; reprint Winona Lake, IN: Alpha, 1979). Two virtually unobtainable works were reprinted in one volume in 1983 as *The Messianic Prophecies* by Klock & Klock (of Minneapolis): Franz Delitzch, *The Messianic Prophecies in Historical Succession* (Edinburgh: T. & T. Clark, 1891) offers a series of famous lectures designed to reawaken interest in some long-neglected Old Testament passages; Paton J. Gloag, *Messianic Prophecies* (Edinburgh: T. & T. Clark, 1879) offers a series of Baird lectures delivered at the University of Glasgow.

The most exhaustive twentieth-century work is Gerard Van Groningen, *Messianic Revelation in the Old Testament* (Grand Rapids: Baker, 1990), which traces in more than a thousand pages the messianic expectation progressively revealed in the Hebrew Scriptures. Van Groningen has included an extensive bibliography of books and articles for additional study. Herbert W. Lockyer, *All the Messianic Prophecies of the Bible* (Grand Rapids: Zondervan, 1962) is devotional in nature and covers even more prophecies than Van Groningen. But it lacks careful exegesis and depth.

Recent studies that view the entire Old Testament from the perspective of God's covenantal promises in Christ include Walter C. Kaiser, Jr., *Toward an Old Testament Theology* (Grand Rapids: Zondervan, 1978); O. Palmer Robertson, *The Christ of the Covenants* (Nutley, NJ: Presbyterian and Reformed, 1980); Thomas E. McComiskey, *The Covenants of Promise: A Theology of the Old Testament Covenants* (Grand Rapids: Baker, 1985).

For an easy, edifying read, try Edmund P. Clowney, *The Unfolding Mystery: Discovering Christ in the Old Testament* (Colorado Springs: NavPress, 1988).

The Recovery of Fallen Man

Concerning the overall theme of the recovery of fallen man through the Mediator, no work surpasses that of

Thomas Goodwin, *Christ our Mediator* (reprint Grand Rapids: Sovereign Grace, 1971; reprinted as Volume 5 in *The Works of Thomas Goodwin* [Eureka, CA: Tanski, 1996]). It ably expounds primary New Testament texts on the mediatorship of Christ. Goodwin is particularly enlightening on his exposition of several key passages from Hebrews (2:14-17; 4:14-16; 10:3-10, 19-22; 13:20-21). His intelligent piety and experimental depth promotes clarity of thought and warmth of soul.

Article 18 — The Incarnation

The oldest classic on the incarnation is Athanasius, *The Incarnation of the Word of God* (London: A.R. Mowbray and Co., 1963), in which the author, unquestionably the best theologian of his day, uses arguments based on the incarnation to refute Arianism. For representative patristic texts that treat the doctrine of incarnation, see E. R. Hardy, *Christology of the Later Fathers*, Volume 3 (Philadelphia: Westminster, 1954), and R. A. Norris, *The Christological Controversy* (Philadelphia: Fortress, 1980).

For a Reformed treatment, consult Calvin's *Institutes*, Book 2, Chapters 12-14, and Christological writings by Reformed theologians such as Charles Hodge, B. B. Warfield, Louis Berkhof, and John Murray.

Two nineteenth-century works by Edwin H. Gifford and Samuel J. Andrews were reprinted in one volume as *The Incarnation of Christ* (Minneapolis: Klock & Klock, 1981). Gifford discusses Philippians 2:5-11 with theological acumen and Andrews ably discourses on the necessity of Christ's humanity. M. F. Sadler, *Emmanuel, Or, The Incarnation of the Son of God the Foundation of Immutable Truth* (New York: Scribner, Welford, & Co., 1866) shows how the doctrine of incarnation impinges on the whole of Christology. William M. Ramsay, *Was Christ Born at Bethlehem?* (London: Hodder and Stoughton, 1898) concentrates on the enrollment of Quirinius and, in the process, provides a rather formal and dry defense of the accuracy of Luke's gospel on the birth of Jesus. J. J. Van Oosterzee, *The Person and Work of the Redeemer*, translated by Maurice J. Evans (London: Hodder and Stoughton, 1886) contains a helpful chapter on the voluntary character of Christ's incarnation.

For a scholarly defense of the supernatural conception of Christ, see J. Gresham Machen's timely treatment, *The Virgin Birth of Christ* (1930; reprint Grand Rapids: Baker, 1967). Also, consult Howard A. Hanke, *The Validity of the Virgin Birth* (Grand Rapids: Zondervan, 1963) and C. F. D. Moule, *The Origin of Christology* (Cambridge: Cambridge University Press, 1977), both of which complement Machen's work. Leon Morris, *The Story of the Christ Child* (Grand Rapids: Eerdmans, 1960) combines scholarship and devotion in expounding the nativity stories in Matthew and Luke. Charles Lee Feinberg, *Is the Virgin Birth in the Old Testament?* (Whittier, CA: Emeth, 1967) includes helpful studies on Genesis 3:14-15, Isaiah 7:14, and Jeremiah 31:22. Robert G. Gromacki, *The Virgin Birth* (Nashville: Nelson, 1974) dispels popular misinterpretations of Christ's conception and birth.

The best recent books on Christ incarnate are David F. Wells, *The Person of Christ: A Biblical and Historical Analysis of the Incarnation* (1984; reprint Alliance, OH: Bible Scholar Books, 1992), and Millard J. Erickson, *The Word Became*

Flesh: A Contemporary Incarnational Christology (Grand Rapids: Baker, 1991). Wells's book is neatly divided into three sections: biblical foundations, historical development, and modern interpretation. Justice is done to each section. Of Erickson's work, J. I. Packer says, "Erickson shows convincingly that an incarnational Christology of classic Chalcedonian type remains possible and natural today, and fits the biblical data better than any other."

Where should you begin? Read Machen.

Article 19 — Christ's Two Natures in One Person

Read the Chalcedonian Creed, which provided the entire Christian church with a standard of Christological orthodoxy in declaring that Christ's two natures exist "without confusion, without change, without division, without separation" (see *The Seven Ecumenical Councils*, edited by Henry R. Percival, in *Nicene and Post-Nicene Fathers*, edited by Philip Schaff and Henry Wace, 2nd series [1899; reprint Grand Rapids: Eerdmans, 1991], Vol. 14, pp. 243-296; also, R. V. Sellers, *The Council of Chalcedon: A Historical and Doctrinal Survey* [London: SPCK, 1953], and A. Grillmeier, *Christ in Christian Tradition* [Atlanta: John Knox, 1975], pp. 520-557). Read, too, the Chalcedonian-based Athanasian Creed, Articles 29-43.

The best seventeenth-century work on Christ's two natures in one person is John Owen, *A Declaration of the Glorious Mystery of the Person of Christ* (1679), reprinted in Volume 1 of the Goold edition of Owen's *Works* (London: Banner of Truth Trust, 1965).

A. B. Bruce, *The Humiliation of Christ* (1876; reprint New York: George H. Doran, 1898) is a widely used study of Christ's state of humiliation based on Philippians 2:5-8 and other passages. Also helpful is Bruce's historical survey of the interpretation of this doctrine from the Council of Chalcedon to Schleiermacher.

For standard evangelical works on the basic issues involved in the doctrine of Christ's two natures in one person, see Nathan E. Wood, *The Person and Work of Jesus Christ* (Philadelphia: American Baptist Publication Society, 1908); Hugh Ross Mackintosh, *The Doctrine of the Person of Christ* (Edinburgh: T. and T. Clark, 1914); Loraine Boettner, *The Person of Christ* (Grand Rapids: Eerdmans, 1943); Leon Morris, *The Lord from Heaven* (London: InterVarsity Press, 1958). Of those treatments, Boettner's is the simplest and most Reformed guide.

For a deeper discussion, read Benjamin B. Warfield, *The Person and Work of Christ*, edited by Samuel G. Craig (Philadelphia: Presbyterian and Reformed, 1950) and the companion volumes by Gerrit C. Berkouwer, *The Person of Christ* and *The Work of Christ* (Grand Rapids: Eerdmans, 1954, 1965). Warfield's massive volume, second only to Owen's, sets forth the doctrine of Christ exegetically and polemically. Composed in the context of the so-called "quest for the historical Jesus," Warfield stresses that the only Jesus discoverable in the New Testament is a supernatural person. He maintains that it is "the desupernaturalized Jesus which is the mythical Jesus, who never had any existence, the postulation of whose existence explains nothing and leaves the whole historical development hanging in the air."

Berkouwer's volumes discuss the historical pronouncements of the ecumenical councils and the Reformed confessions as well as the nature, unity, and sinlessness of Christ. They provide an in-depth discussion of Christ's work in the states of humiliation and exaltation. While Berkouwer is fully abreast of current theological literature, he is too often influenced by it, and takes a position too moderate or vague on many issues. The value of Berkouwer lies in his grasp of Reformed thinkers and presentation of issues in theology. He asks and begins to answer some of the most difficult questions.

For books that focus on the divinity of Jesus, see Article 10.

Article 20 — Justice and Mercy in Christ

No Reformed confessional statement deals with the justice and mercy of God in Christ unto salvation more biblically, poignantly, and experientially than the Heidelberg Catechism in Questions 9-18. Begin here, then read sermons, commentaries, and works on the Heidelberg Catechism. Though sources for the Heidelberg Catechism are most common in Dutch, adequate works are available in English. Consult the following chronological list:

Olevian, Caspar. *An Exposition of the Symbol of the Apostles, or rather of the articles of faith. In which the chiefe points of the everlasting and free covenant between God and the faithful are briefly and plainly handled. Gathered out of the catechizing sermons of Caspar Olevian.* Translated by Iohn Fielde. London: H. Middleton, 1581.

Bastingius, Jeremias. *An Exposition or Commentarie upon the Catechisme of Christian Religion which is taught in the Schooles and churches both of the Lowe Countryes and of the dominions of the Countie Palatine.* Cambridge: John Legatt, 1589.

Ames, William. *The Substance of Christian Religion; Or a plain and easie Draught of the Christian Catechisme in LII Lectures.* London: T. Mabb for T. Davies, 1659.

Witte, Petrus de. *Catechizing upon the Heidelbergh Catechisme of the Reformed Christian Religion.* Translated for the English Reformed Congregation in Amsterdam. Amsterdam: Gillis Joosten Saeghman, 1662.

Ronde, Lambertus de. *A System Containing the Principles of the Christian Religion, Suitable to the Heidelberg Catechism.* New York, 1763.

Vander Kemp, John. *The Christian Entirely the Property of Christ, in Life and Death. Fifty-three sermons on the Heidelberg Catechism wherein the doctrine of faith, received in the Reformed Church, is defended against the principal opponents, and the practical improvement and direction of it to evangelical piety, enforced.* 2 vols. Translated by John M. Van Harlingen. New Brunswick, NJ: Abraham Blauvelt, 1810.

Fisher, Samuel Reed. *Exercises on the Heidelberg Catechism adapted to the use of Sabbath Schools and Catechetical Classes.* Chambersburg, PA: Publication office of the German Reformed Church, 1844.

Ursinus, Zacharias. *The Commentary of Dr. Zacharias Ursinus on the Heidelberg Catechism.* Translated by George W. Williard. Columbus: Scott & Bascom, 1852.

Bethune, George Washington. *Expository Lectures on the Heidelberg Catechism.* 2 vols. New York: Sheldon & Co., 1864.

Whitmer, Adam Carl. *Notes on the Heidelberg Catechism: for*

Parents, Teachers and Catechumens. Philadelphia: Grant, Faires & Rodgers, 1878.

Thelemann, Otto. *An Aid to the Heidelberg Catechism.* Translated by Rev. M. Peters. Reading, PA: James I. Good, 1896.

Richards, George. *Studies on the Heidelberg Catechism.* Philadelphia: Publication and Sunday School Board of the Reformed Church in the United States, 1913.

Kuiper, Henry J., ed. *Sermons on the Heidelberg Catechism.* 5 vols. Grand Rapids: Zondervan, 1936-1956.

Van Baalen, Jan Karel. *The Heritage of the Fathers, A Commentary on the Heidelberg Catechism.* Grand Rapids: Eerdmans, 1948.

Van Reenen, G. *The Heidelberg Catechism: Explained for the Humble and Sincere in Fifty-two Sermons.* Paterson, NJ: Lont & Overkamp, 1955.

Vis, Jean. *We Are the Lord's.* Grand Rapids: Society for Reformed Publications, 1955.

Bruggink, Donald J., ed. *Guilt, Grace and Gratitude: A Commentary on the Heidelberg Catechism commemorating its 400th Anniversary.* New York: Half Moon Press, 1963.

Kersten, Gerrit Hendrik. *The Heidelberg Catechism in 52 Sermons.* 2 vols. Translated by Gertrude DeBruyn and Cornelius Quist. Grand Rapids: Netherlands Reformed Congregations, 1968.

Josse, James, ed. *Sermons on the Heidelberg Catechism.* Grand Rapids: Board of Publication of the Christian Reformed Church, 1970.

Hoeksema, Herman. *The Triple Knowledge, An Exposition of the Heidelberg Catechism.* 3 vols. Grand Rapids: Reformed Free Publishing Association, 1970-1972.

Jones, Norman L. *Study Helps on the Heidelberg Catechism.* Eureka, SD: Publication Committee of the Eureka Classis, Reformed Church in the United States, 1981.

Praamsma, Louis. *Before the Face of God: A Study of the Heidelberg Catechism.* 2 vols. Jordan Station, Ontario: Paideia Press, 1987.

DeJong, Peter Y., and Kloosterman, Nelson D., eds. *That Christ May Dwell in Your Hearts. Sermons on the Heidelberg Catechism, Lord's Days 1-20.* Orange City, IA: Mid-American Reformed Seminary, 1988.

Klooster, Fred H. *A Mighty Comfort: The Christian Faith According to the Heidelberg Catechism.* Grand Rapids: CRC Publications, 1990.

Stam, Clarence. *Living in the Joy of Faith: The Christian Faith as outlined in the Heidelberg Catechism.* Neerlandia, Alberta: Inheritance, 1991.

Heerschap, M. *Zion's Comfort in Life and Death: Fifty-two Sermons on the Heidelberg Catechism.* 2 vols. Lethbridge, Alberta: Netherlands Reformed Congregation, 1992-94.

Olevianus, Caspar. *A Firm Foundation: An Aid to Interpreting the Heidelberg Catechism.* Translated by Lyle D. Bierma. Grand Rapids: Baker, 1995.

Beeke, Joel R. "Heidelberg Catechism Sermons." 5 vols. Jordan Ontario: Heritage Reformed Church, 1998.

Of those authors, most helpful on the relationship of justice and mercy are Ursinus, Olevianus, Thelemann, Kersten, and Hoeksema.

Article 21 — Salvation in Christ as High Priest

Article 21 of the Belgic Confession merges three Chris-

tological themes: the suffering Christ, the priestly Christ, the atoning Christ.

Christ in His Sufferings

No work on Christ's suffering begs reprinting more than that of James Durham, *Christ Crucified; or, The Marrow of the Gospel in 72 Sermons on Isaiah 53,* 2 vols. (1683; reprint Glasgow: Alex Adam, 1792). Of these sermons, Spurgeon rightly notes: "This is marrow indeed. We need say no more; Durham is a prince among spiritual expositors." John Brown, *The Sufferings and Glories of the Messiah* (New York: Robert Carter, 1853) also offers a solid, exegetical, and practical exposition of Psalm 18 and Isaiah 52:13 through 53:12.

No volume on Christ's sufferings, however, surpasses that of the great German Reformed writer, Friedrich W. Krummacher. *The Suffering Saviour* (1856; reprint Chicago: Moody Press, 1966), which is warmly personal, instructive, and experiential, is worthy of multiple readings. At times Krummacher's exegesis is faulty and his imagination too picturesque, but those weaknesses scarcely tarnish this unparalleled treatise.

The greatest twentieth-century work on Christ's sufferings is the *magnum opus* of Klaas Schilder, *Christ in His Suffering; Christ on Trial; Christ Crucified,* translated by Henry Zylstra, 3 vols. (1938-40; reprint Minneapolis: Klock and Klock, 1978). Schilder's "Lenten trilogy" is often profound and contains much food for meditation. Unfortunately, however, these volumes are marred by speculation and philosophical tendencies not based on exegetical evidence. The best one-volume twentieth-century work is Herman Hoeksema, *When I Survey...: A Lenten Anthology* (Grand Rapids: Reformed Free, 1977). A single, basic theme underlies each of six sections that were originally published as books of radio messages (1943-56) titled *The Amazing Cross, The Royal Sufferer, The Power of the Cross, Rejected of Men, Jesus in the Midst,* and *Man of Sorrows.* Erich H. Kiehl, *The Passion of Our Lord* (Grand Rapids: Baker, 1990) focuses on the last week of Christ's sufferings. It offers copious insights from historical and archaelogical sources.

Christ as High Priest

There are not many good, Reformed books on Christ as High Priest. The best is H. H. Meeter, *The Heavenly High Priesthood of Christ: An Exegetico-Dogmatic Study* (Grand Rapids: Eerdmans-Sevensma, 1916). Note especially Chapters 4-5 on Christ as a priest after the order of Melchizedek. George Stevenson, *Treatise on the Offices of Christ* (Edinburgh: W. P. Kennedy, 1845), a noteworthy Anglican work on the offices of Christ, includes a helpful section on Christ's priestly work. J. C. Philpot is at his best in *Meditations on the Sacred Humanity of the Blessed Redeemer* (1859-60; reprint Harpenden, Herts: O. G. Pearce, 1975), which includes three experimental chapters on Christ as the "great High Priest." The most recent, soundly Reformed work that covers Christ's threefold office with a particular focus on his atoning priestly work is Robert Letham, *The Work of Christ* (Downers Grove, IL: InterVarsity Press, 1993). Letham is particularly helpful in discussing the viewpoints of significant Christian thinkers, from the church fathers to contemporary theologians.

Christ's Atonement

The best and most prolific Reformed treatments on the atonement of Christ were produced in the last half of the nineteenth century. They include Charles Hodge, *The Orthodox Doctrine Regarding the Extent of the Atonement Vindicated* (Edinburgh, 1846); Francis Turretin, *The Atonement of Christ,* translated by James R. Willson (1859; reprint Grand Rapids: Baker, 1978); Robert Smith Candlish, *The Atonement: Its Reality, Completeness, and Extent* (London: T. Nelson, 1861); Archibald Alexander Hodge, *The Atonement* (1867; reprint Grand Rapids: Baker, 1975); George Smeaton, *The Doctrine of the Atonement as Taught by Jesus Christ Himself* (1868; reprint Edinburgh: Banner of Truth, 1992); George Smeaton, *The Doctrine of the Atonement as Taught by the Apostles* (1870; reprint Edinburgh: Banner of Truth, 1992); Thomas Jackson Crawford, *The Doctrine of Holy Scripture Respecting the Atonement* (1871; reprint Grand Rapids: Baker, 1954); Hugh Martin, *The Atonement* (1882; reprint Edinburgh: John Knox Press, 1976); Robert L. Dabney, *Christ Our Penal Substitute* (1898; reprint Harrisonburg, VA: Sprinkle, 1985).

For good, basic, twentieth-century treatments of the atonement from a Reformed perspective, read Louis Berkhof, *Vicarious Atonement Through Christ* (Grand Rapids: Eerdmans, 1936) and Rienk B. Kuiper, *For Whom Did Christ Die?* (1959; reprint Grand Rapids: Baker, 1982). Berkhof and Kuiper offer the best introduction to the doctrine of the atonement.

For historical studies on the atonement, see William Cunningham, *Historical Theology* (1862; reprint London: Banner of Truth, 1960), Vol. 2, pp. 237-370; G. C. Foley, *Anselm's Theory of the Atonement* (London, 1909); H. Rashdall, *The Idea of Atonement in Christian Theology* (London: Macmillan, 1919); Dorus Paul Rudisill, *The Doctrine of the Atonement in Jonathan Edwards and His Successors* (New York: Poseidon, 1971).

For additional material on the above doctrines, consult traditional, Reformed systematic theologies and the bibliographical notes in articles 10, 18, and 19. For an edifying work that summarizes the Christological doctrines covered in Article 21, see Philip Henry, *Christ All in All, or What Christ is Made to Believers* (reprint Swengel, PA: Reiner, 1970). In the three centuries since this book was published by the father of the well-known commentator, Matthew Henry, its forty-one chapters (which expound Colossians 3:11) have lost none of their power to move the heart and motivate the mind.

Article 22 — Salvation by Faith in Christ Alone

To understand the ancient church's teaching on salvation by faith, see Clement of Alexandria, *Miscellanies* (2.1-6, 11-12; 5.1); Ambrose, *On the Faith*; Augustine, *On the Value of Believing* and *On Faith in Things Not Seen.* For a secondary source, consult H. A. Wolfson, *Philosophy of the Church Fathers* (Cambridge: Harvard, 1956), pp. 102-140.

For Reformation writers, consult *Luther's Works,* edited by J. Pelikan, et al., 55 vols. (St. Louis: Concordia, Vols. 1-30; Philadelphia: Fortress Press, vols. 31-55, 1955-79), and Calvin's *Institutes of the Christian Religion* (Philadelphia: Westminster Press, 1960), Book 3, Chapters 2-3. Norman Shepherd provides a succinct summary of one Reformer's view

in "Zanchius on Saving Faith," *Westminster Theological Journal* 36 (1973):31-47.

The Puritans excelled in writing on the doctrine of saving faith in Christ from a scriptural and experiential perspective. Significant titles in print or fairly accessible include Jonathan Edwards, "Justification by Faith Alone," in *Works of Jonathan Edwards*, ed. Edward Hickman, Vol. 1, pp. 620-654 (1834; reprint Edinburgh: Banner of Truth Trust, 1974); Thomas Goodwin, "The Object and Acts of Justifying Faith," in *The Works of Thomas Goodwin, D.D.,* ed. John Miller, Vol. 8 (1865; reprint Edinburgh: Banner of Truth Trust, 1988); Andrew Gray, *The Mystery of Faith Opened Up: Or, some Sermons Concerning Faith* (Edinburgh: Andrew Anderson, 1697 [reprinted in *The Works of the Reverend and Pious Andrew Gray* (1813; Ligonier, PA: Soli Deo Gloria, 1992)]; John Owen, "The Doctrine of Justification by Faith" (1677), in *The Works of John Owen*, ed. William H. Goold, Vol. 5, pp. 1-400 (1851; reprint Edinburgh: Banner of Truth Trust, 1976); John Preston, *The Breast-Plate of Faith and Love*, 5th ed. (1632; reprint Edinburgh: Banner of Truth Trust, 1979); Robert Traill, "A Vindication of the Protestant Doctrine Concerning Justification," in *The Works of the late Reverend Robert Traill*, Vol. 1, pp. 252-96 (1810; reprint Edinburgh: Banner of Truth Trust, 1975).

Listed chronologically, scarce Puritan works on faith include Thomas Wilson, *A Dialogve About Ivstification by Faith* (London: W. Hall for N. Butter, 1610); Miles Mosse, *Ivstifying and Saving Faith Distingvished from the faith of the Deuils* (Cambridge: Cantrell Legse, 1614); John Rogers, *The Doctrine of Faith: wherein are particularly handled twelve Principall Points, which explaine the Nature and Vse of it* (London: for N. Newbery and H. Overton, 1629); Ezekiel Culverwell, *A Treatise of Faith: Wherein is Declared How a Man May Live by Faith, and Find Relief in all His Necessities* (London: I. D. for Hen: Overton, 1633); John Downame, *A Treatise of the True Nature and Definition of Justifying Faith* (Oxford: I. Lichfield for E. Forrest, 1635); John Cotton, *The Way of Faith* (1643; reprint New York: AMS Press, 1983); Samuel Rutherford, *The Trial and Triumph of Faith* (1645; reprint Edinburgh: William Collins, 1845); Matthew Lawrence, *The Use and Practice of Faith: or, Faiths Vniversal Vsefulness, and Quickning Influence into every Kinde and Degree of the Christian Life* (London: A. Maxey for Willian, 1657); Robert Dixon, *The Doctrine of Faith, Justification, and Assurance* (London: William Godbid, 1668); Edward Polhill, *Precious Faith* (London: Thomas Cockerill, 1675); Thomas Cole, *A Discourse of Regeneration, Faith, and Repentance* (London: for Thomas Cockerill, 1689).

The best eighteenth-century works on faith are James Fraser, *A Treatise concerning Justifying and Saving Faith* (Edinburgh: John Mosman and Company, 1722), and the well-known classic by William Romaine, *The Life, Walk and Triumph of Faith* (1765; reprint London: James Clarke, 1970), which stresses the need to trust the divinity of Christ and to walk by faith in subjection to the Word of God.

For historical-theological, twentieth-century studies on faith, see Geoffrey F. Nuttall, *The Holy Spirit in Puritan Faith and Experience* (1946; reprint Chicago: University of Chicago Press, 1992); David Broughton Knox, *The Doctrine of Faith in the Reign of Henry VIII* (London: James Clarke, 1961); Robert Letham, "Saving Faith and Assurance in Reformed Theology: Zwingli to the Synod of Dort," 2 vols. (Ph.D. dissertation, University of Aberdeen, 1979); Victor A. Shepherd, *The Nature and Function of Faith in the Theology of John*

Calvin (Macon, GA: Mercer University Press, 1983); Joel R. Beeke, *Assurance of Faith: Calvin, English Puritanism, and the Dutch Second Reformation* (New York: Peter Lang, 1991).

For a persuasive apologetic that presents biblical Christianity as the only antidote for the modern drift towards skepticism, see J. Gresham Machen, *What is Faith?* (1925; reprint Grand Rapids: Eerdmans, 1962). Also helpful is Gordon Clark, *Faith and Saving Faith* (Jefferson, MD: Trinity, 1983).

Where should you begin? Consult the great Pauline chapters on faith, the classic Reformed doctrinal standards, and the major Reformed dogmatics. Then try Alexander Comrie, *The ABC of Faith*, translated by J. Marcus Banfield (Ossett, W. Yorks: Zoar, 1978). A Scots-turned-Dutch Second Reformation divine, Comrie (1706-1774) wrote extensively on the doctrine of saving faith and its relation to justification. In this work he explains the characteristics of saving faith by presenting twenty-eight scriptural words or phrases that describe the activity of faith (such as *coming, thirsting, believing, taking, committing*), and devoting a short chapter to each word.

Article 23 — Justification

Happily, there is a rich supply of material on the doctrine of justification from a Protestant perspective. The seventeenth-century Reformed and Puritan divines have produced the best books on this critical "article by which the church stands or falls" (Luther). In addition to Reformed commentaries on Pauline epistles, Reformed confessional statements, and major Reformed dogmatics, consult the following:

Sixteenth and Seventeenth Centuries

Baxter, Richard. *A Treatise of Justifying Righteousness*. London: for N. Simmons and J. Robinson, 1676. The only unsound treatment on justification by a Puritan; neonomian in theology.

Brown, John (of Wamphray). *The Life of Justification Opened*. Edited by J. Koelman and M. Leydekker. Utrecht: n. p., 1695. Scarce, insightful.

Burgess, Anthony. *The True Doctrine of Iustification Asserted and Vindicated, From the Errors of Papists, Arminians, Socinians, and more especially Antinomians*. London: Robert White for Thomas Vnderhil, 1648. Thorough work by an able Puritan and Westminster Assembly divine. Soundly exegetical, experimental, and polemical.

Calvin, John. "Acts of the Council of Trent with the Antidote." In *Tracts and Treatises*, Vol. 3. Translated and edited by Henry Beveridge. Edinburgh: Calvin Translation Society, 1851; reprint Grand Rapids: Eerdmans, 1958, pp. 19-162. (Cf. Calvin's *Institutes*.)

Clarkson, David. "Justification by the Righteousness of Christ." In *The Works of David Clarkson*. Vol. 1, pp. 273-331. Edinburgh: Banner of Truth Trust, 1988. Brief Puritan treatment.

Davenant, John. *A Treatise on Justification, or the Disputatio de Justitia Habituali et Actuali*. Translated by Josiah Allport. 2 vols. London: Hamilton, Adams, & Co., 1844-46. Massive; shows strains of moderate Calvinism.

Downame, George. *A Treatise of Justification*. London: Felix Kyngston for Nicolaus Bourne, 1633. Solid and savory Puritan work.

Eaton, John. *The Honey-combe of Free Justification by Christ Alone*. London: R. B. at the charge of R. Lancaster, 1642. Sound on justification, but contains hyper-Calvinistic tendencies.

Foxe, John. "Of Free Justification by Christ." In *Writings of John Fox, Bale, and Coverdale*. London: Religious Tract Society, 1831, pp. 131-286. Reveals that Foxe was more than a martyrologist.

Grew, Obadiah. *A Sinner's Justification, or the Lord Jesvs Christ the Lord our righteousnesse*. London: Printed for Nevil Simmons, 1670. Solid Puritan work.

Hooker, Thomas. *The soules Justification, on 2 Cor. 5:21*. London: Iohn Haviland, for Andrew Crooke, 1638. Experimental.

Traill, Robert. "A Vindication of the Protestant Doctrine Concerning Justification." In *The Works of Robert Traill*. Edinburgh: Banner of Truth Trust, 1986, Vol. 1, pp. 252-96. Defends Protestant doctrine from antinomian charges.

Nineteenth Century

Buchanan, James. *The Doctrine of Justification: An Outline of Its History in the Church and of Its Exposition from Scripture*. Edinburgh: T. & T. Clark, 1867; reprint Grand Rapids: Baker, 1977. Thoroughly grounded in the Scriptures; stresses the imputation of the righteousness of Christ to the believer.

Girardeau, John L. *Calvinism and Evangelical Arminianism: Compared as to Election, Reprobation, Justification, and Related Doctrines*. Columbia, 1890; reprint Harrisonburg, VA: Sprinkle, 1984. Capable work by a Southern Presbyterian theologian.

Halyburton, Thomas. "An Inquiry into the Nature of God's Act of Justification." In *The Works of Thomas Halyburton*. Edited by Robert Burns. Glasgow: Blackie & Son, 1837, pp. 559-67. The most helpful short treatment.

Hodge, Charles. *Justification by Faith Alone*. Reprint Hobbs, NM: Trinity Foundation, 1994. Hodge at his best.

Huntington, William. "The Justification of a Sinner and Satan's Lawsuit with Him." In *The Works of the Reverend William Huntington*, Vol. 4. London: for E. Huntington by T. Bensley, 1833, pp. 3-285. Strikingly helpful in places, but leans in a hyper-Calvinistic direction.

Ritschl, Albrecht. *A Critical History of the Christian Doctrine of Justification and Reconciliation*. Translated by J. S. Black. Edinburgh: Edmonston and Douglas, 1872. Famous work by a German Protestant theologian, but denies the propitiatory character of Christ's death. Liberal and unsound.

Twentieth Century

Beeke, Joel R. *Justification by Faith: Selected Bibliography*. Grand Rapids: Reformation Heritage Books, 1995. Contains 550 bibliographical entries.

Berkouwer, Gerrit C. *Faith and Justification*. Translated by Lewis B. Smedes. Grand Rapids: Eerdmans, 1954. Helpful but ambiguous in places.

Boehl, Edward. *The Reformed Doctrine of Justification*. Translated by C. H. Riedesel. Reprint Grand Rapids: Eerdmans, 1946. Read Berkhof's enlightening introduction.

Carson, D. A., ed. *Right with God: Justification in the Bible and the World*. Grand Rapids: Baker, 1993. A real mix of essays, but overall insightful.

Gerstner, John H. *A Primer on Justification*. Phillipsburg, NJ: Presbyterian and Reformed, 1983. Basic, simple treatment.

MacArthur, John, R. C. Sproul, Joel Beeke, John Gerstner, John Armstrong. *Justification by Faith Alone: Affirming the doctrine by which the church and the individual stands or falls*. Morgan, PA: Soli Deo Gloria, 1995. Authors focus on Reformed understanding of each word in the phrase, "justification by faith alone."

Packer, James I., et al. *Here We Stand: Justification by Faith Today*. London: Hodder and Stoughton, 1986. Essays of mixed value.

Pink, Arthur W. *The Doctrines of Election and Justification*. Grand Rapids: Baker, 1974. Edifying.

Sproul, R.C. *Faith Alone: The Evangelical Doctrine of Justification*. Grand Rapids: Baker, 1995. Helpful; good place to start.

Toon, Peter. *Justification and Sanctification*. Westchester, IL: Crossway, 1983. Helpful treatment.

Historical Studies

Bennett, James. *Justification as Revealed in Scripture, in opposition to the Council of Trent, and Mr. Newman's Lectures*. London: Hamilton, Adams, & Co., 1840.

Cunningham, William. "Justification." *Historical Theology*. Reprint London: Banner of Truth Trust, 1960, 2:1-120.

Duurschmidt, Kurt. "Some Aspects of Justification and Sanctification as seen in the Writings of some of the Magisterial and Radical Reformers." Ph.D. dissertation, Syracuse University, 1971.

Gore, Ralph J. "The Lutheran Ordo Salutis with Special Reference to Justification and Sanctification: A Reformed Analysis." Master's thesis, Faith Theological Seminary, 1983.

Green, Lowell C. *How Melanchthon Helped Luther Discover the Gospel: The Doctrine of Justification in the Reformation*. Fallbrook, CA: Verdict Publications, 1979.

Hagglund, Bengt. *The Background of Luther's Doctrine of Justification in Late Medieval Theology*. Philadelphia: Fortress Press, 1971.

Heinz, Johann. *Justification and Merit: Luther vs. Catholicism*. Berrien Springs, MI: Andrews University Press, 1981.

Leaver, Robin A. *The Doctrine of Justification in the Church of England*. Oxford: Latimer House, 1979.

_____. *Luther on Justification*. St. Louis: Concordia, 1975.

McGrath, Alister E. *Iustitia Dei: A History of the Doctrine of Justification*. 2 vols. Cambridge: Cambridge University Press, 1986.

Plantinga, Jacob. "The Time of Justification." Th.M. thesis, Westminster Theological Seminary, 1977.

Snell, Farley W. "The Place of Augustine in Calvin's Concept of Righteousness." Th.D. dissertation, Union Theological Seminary, 1968.

Article 24 — Sanctification and Holiness

For the classic Reformed view of sanctification, holiness, and good works, one could do no better than read substantial portions of Book 3 of John Calvin's *Institutes of the Christian Religion* (Philadelphia: Westminster Press, 1960).

Whereas the Reformers excelled in the doctrine of justification, the Puritans were best on sanctification. Most frequently reprinted is Walter Marshall (1628-1680), *The Gospel Mystery of Sanctification* (1692; reprint Grand Rapids: Zondervan, 1954). Marshall effectively grounds the doctrine of sanctification in a believer's union with Christ and underscores the necessity of practical holiness in everyday living. By grace, he lived what he wrote. In the preface to his funeral sermon, Samuel Tomlyns says about his friend: "He wooed for Christ in his preaching, and allured you to Christ by his walking." Also stimulating is Thomas Brooks (1608-1680), "The Crown and Glory of Christianity: or Holiness, The only way to Happiness," in *The Works of Thomas Brooks* (1864; reprint Edinburgh: Banner of Truth Trust, 1980). It's a heart-searching, 450-page treatise on holiness which has been mysteriously neglected in contemporary studies. Richard Baxter (1615-1691), "The Spiritual and Carnal Man Compared and Contrasted; or, The Absolute Necessity and Excellency of Holiness," in *The Select Practical Works of Richard Baxter* (Glasgow: Blackie & Son, 1840), pp, 115-291, is similar to the writing of Brooks. But Baxter, though edifying in the area of sanctification, is not a reliable guide on justification.

An excellent eighteenth-century treatise on sanctification is James Fraser, *A Treatise on Sanctification* (1774; reprint Audubon, NJ: Old Paths, 1992).

The three best, nineteenth-century works on sanctification are: George Bethune, *The Fruit of the Spirit* (1839; reprint Swengel, PA: Reiner, 1972), which is based on Galatians 5:22-23; Horatius Bonar, *God's Way of Holiness* (1869; reprint Pensacola, FL: Mt. Zion Publications, 1994), which is plain, packed, poignant, and powerful; J.C. Ryle, *Holiness: Its Nature, Hindrances, Difficulties, and Roots* (1879; reprint Greensboro, NC: Homiletic Press, 1956), which has long been regarded as a readable classic. Of Ryle's work, M. Lloyd-Jones wrote, "Ryle, like his great master, has no easy way to holiness to offer us, and no 'patent' method by which it can be obtained; but he invariably produces that 'hunger and thirst after righteousness' which is the only indispensable condition to being filled."

The last half of the twentieth century has produced a plethora of books on holiness. Noteworthy titles include Gerrit C. Berkouwer, *Faith and Sanctification*, translated by John Vriend (Grand Rapids: Eerdmans, 1952); A. W. Pink, *The Doctrine of Sanctification* (Swengel, PA: Bible Truth Depot, 1955); Stephen C. Neill, *Christian Holiness* (Guildford, England: Lutterworth, 1960); John W. Sanderson, *The Fruit of the Spirit* (Grand Rapids: Zondervan, 1972); Jay Adams, *Godliness Through Discipline* (Grand Rapids: Baker, 1973); Jerry Bridges, *The Pursuit of Holiness* and *The Practice of Holiness* (Colorado Springs: NavPress, 1978, 1983); Hugh D. Morgan, *The Holiness of God and of His People* (Bridgend, Wales: Evangelical Press of Wales, 1979); Kenneth Prior, *The Way of Holiness: A Study in Christian Growth* (Downers Grove, IL: InterVarsity Press, 1982); Peter Toon, *Justification and Sanctification* (Westchester, IL: Crossway, 1983); Roger Roberts, *Holiness: Every Christian's Calling* (Nashville: Broadman Press, 1985); Sinclair Ferguson, "The Reformed View," in *Christian Spirituality: Five Views of Sanctification*, edited by Donald L. Alexander (Downers Grove, IL: InterVarsity Press, 1988); James I. Packer, *Rediscovering Holiness* (Ann Arbor: Servant,

1992); Joel R. Beeke, *Holiness: God's Call to Sanctification* (Edinburgh: Banner of Truth Trust, 1994).

Where should you begin? Read Bonar, Ryle, Packer, Pink, and Marshall in that order.

Article 25 — The Ceremonial Law

Sixteenth Century

The best work on the ceremonial law by a Reformer is *The Decades of Henry Bullinger*, translated by H.I. (1550 in Latin; Cambridge: University Press, 1850), Vol. 3, Sermon 6 ("Of the Ceremonial Law of God, but especially of the Priesthood, Time, and Place, Appointed for the Ceremonies," pp. 125-217) and Sermon 8 ("Of the Use or Effect of the Law of God, and of the Fulfilling and Abrogating of the Same: Of the Likeness and Difference of Both the Testaments and People, the Old and the New," pp. 236-300).

Seventeenth Century

For a balanced treatment on the ceremonial law from a great seventeenth-century theologian, see Francis Turretin, *Institutes of Elenctic Theology*, Vol. 2, translated by George Musgrave Giger, edited by James T. Dennison, Jr. (1683 in Latin; Philipsburg, NJ: P & R, 1994), Chaps. 24-25. Turretin answers these questions: "What was the end and use of the ceremonial law under the Old Testament? Was the ceremonial law abrogated under the New Testament? When and how?"

Eighteenth Century

Helpful eighteenth-century works on the ceremonial law include Wilhelmus à Brakel, *The Christian's Reasonable Service*, translated by Bartel Elshout, Vol. 4 (1700 in Dutch; Morgan, PA: Soli Deo Gloria, 1995), pp. 421-502; Herman Witsius, *The Economy of the Covenants Between God and Man*, translated by William Crookshank, Vol. 2 (1772; reprint Escondido, CA: Den Dulk Foundation, 1990), Chaps. 9-14; John Brown of Haddington, *An Introduction to the Right Understanding of the Oracles of God* (Albany: Barber & Southwick, 1793), Chap. 3 on "Jewish Laws and Types."

Nineteenth Century

There is a plethora of nineteenth-century works on the tabernacle and temple. Among the best are Henry W. Soltau, *The Holy Vessels and Furniture of the Tabernacle* (1851; reprint Grand Rapids: Kregel, 1974) and *The Tabernacle, The Priesthood, and the Offerings* (1857; reprint Grand Rapids: Kregel 1972); Alfred Edersheim, *The Temple: Its Ministry and Services* (1874; reprint Grand Rapids: Eerdmans, 1958); Dirk H. Dolman and Marcus Rainsford, *The Tabernacle*, 2 vols. in 1 (reprint Minneapolis: Klock & Klock, 1982).

Standard conservative works of the past century that contain substantial sections on ceremonial law include Patrick Fairbairn, *The Typology of Scripture*, 2 vols. (1845; reprint Grand Rapids: Baker, 1975) and *The Revelation of Law in Scripture* (1869; reprint Grand Rapids: Zondervan, 1957); J. H. Kurtz, *Sacrificial Worship of the Old Testament*, translated by James Martin (1863; Grand Rapids: Baker, 1980); Ernst W. Hengstenberg, *History of the Kingdom of God Under the Old Testament*, translated by Theodore Meyer and James Martin, 2 vols. (1871-72; reprint Grand Rapids: Kregel, 1975). Gustav Friedrich Oehler, *Theology of the Old Testament*, translated by Ellen D. Smith and Sophia Taylor, revised by George E.

Day (1883; reprint Grand Rapids: Zondervan, n.d.), pp. 246-352, is generally sound but occasionally lapses into rationalism.

Twentieth Century

For this century, the primary conservative works on Old Testament theology that elaborate on the ceremonial law include John Howard Raven, *The History of the Religion of Israel: An Old Testament Theology* (1933; reprint Grand Rapids: Baker, 1979), pp. 42-155; Geerhardus Vos, *Biblical Theology* (1948; reprint Grand Rapids: Eerdmans, 1975), pp. 143-82; J. Barton Payne, *The Theology of the Older Testament* (Grand Rapids: Zondervan, 1962).

See Vern Poythress, *The Shadow of Christ in the Law of Moses* (Brentwood, TN: Wolgemuth & Hyatt, 1991) for some fresh thinking on the ceremonial law and for an excellent bibliography. For a helpful analysis of the state of the field and an extensive bibliography in Old Testament theology, see Gerhard F. Hasel, *Old Testament Theology: Basic Issues in the Current Debate*, rev. ed. (Grand Rapids: Eerdmans, 1991).

Where should you begin? Read Turretin for an introduction to the subject, then turn to à Brakel, Vos, and Poythress. But don't neglect Bullinger, if you can obtain a copy.

Article 26 — Christ's Intercession

Christ's intercession is a comfort for believers and ought to be the endearing subject of many treatises. Surprisingly, few good works have been written from a Reformed perspective on the intercession of our Lord at the Father's right hand.

For pre-eighteenth-century material, consult the various Reformed confessions and Reformed dogmatics (cf. *Reformed Dogmatics Set Out and Illustrated from the Sources*, edited by H. Heppe, translated by G. T. Thomson [Grand Rapids: Zondervan, 1978]).

For an eighteenth-century work that includes a substantial portion on Christ's intercession, see John Hurrion, *The Knowledge of Christ Glorified, Opened and Applied in Twelve Sermons on Christ's Resurrection, Ascension, Sitting at God's Right Hand, Intercession and Judging the World* (London: Clark and Hett, 1729). This scarce book is a gold mine of scriptural, experimental truth displaying the riches of Christ in a series of sermons preached in 1700.

The two best, nineteenth-century treatises on Christ's intercession are William Symington, *On the Atonement and Intercession of Jesus Christ* (New York: Robert Carter, 1863) and William Milligan, *The Ascension and Heavenly Priesthood of Our Lord* (Edinburgh: T. & T. Clark, 1891). In a succinct, 50-page treatment, Symington covers the reality, nature, matter, properties, and results of Christ's intercession. Milligan's book, the Baird lectures for 1891, focuses on Christ's post-resurrection ministry on earth and His present ministry in heaven. Though Milligan is often underrated as a writer, he is full of valuable, scriptural substance.

The best twentieth-century work is Henry H. Meeter, *The Heavenly High Priesthood of Christ: An Exegetico-Dogmatic Study* (Grand Rapids: Eerdmans-Sevensma, 1916). Chapters 12 and 13 masterfully cover the intercession and benediction of our heavenly High Priest. Henry B. Swete, *The Ascended*

Christ: A Study in the Earliest Christian Teaching (London: Macmillan, 1913) stresses Christ's role as intercessor and advocate. Peter Toon, *The Ascension of Our Lord* (Nashville: Thomas Nelson, 1984) explores all aspects of Christ's ascension: its foreshadowing in the Old Testament, accounts of it in the New, and the teaching of the church through the ages.

For helpful works on our Lord's intercession in John 17, read Thomas Manton, "Sermons Upon the Seventeenth Chapter of St. John," in *The Complete Works of Thomas Manton*, (London: Nisbet, 1872), 10:109-490; 11:1-149; Charles Ross, *The Inner Sanctuary* (1888; reprint London: Banner of Truth Trust, 1967), pp. 199-247; H. C. G. Moule, *The High Priestly Prayer: A Devotional Commentary on the Seventeenth Chapter of John* (1907; reprint Grand Rapids: Baker, 1978); Marcus Rainsford, *Our Lord Prays for His Own: Thoughts on John 17* (Chicago: Moody Press, 1950); four volumes of Martyn Lloyd-Jones on John 17, *Studies in Jesus' Prayer for His Own* (Westchester, IL: Crossway, 1988-89).

For a historical-theological study, see W. H. Marravee, *The Ascension of Christ in the Works of St. Augustine* (Ottawa: University of Ottawa Press, 1967).

Article 27 — The Doctrine of the Church

Sixteenth Century

Calvin's *Institutes*, Book 4, Chapter 1, "The True Church with Which as Mother of All the Godly We Must Keep Unity," presents the basics of Reformed ecclesiology (Battles edition, 2:1011-1040). The first four sermons of Volume 5 of Henry Bullinger's *Decades*, translated by H. I. (Cambridge: University Press, 1852), pp, 1-163, are more pervasive and helpful than Calvin, particularly in dealing with the attributes and unity of the church.

Eighteenth Century

Wilhelmus à Brakel, *The Christian's Reasonable Service*, translated by Bartel Elshout (Ligonier, PA: Soli Deo Gloria, 1993), 2:3-187, is an early eighteenth-century work that covers ecclesiology in nearly the same order as the Belgic Confession.

Nineteenth Century

James Bannerman, *The Church of Christ*, 2 vols. (1869; reprint London: Banner of Truth Trust, 1960) is the most extensive (950 pages), standard, Reformed treatment of the doctrine of the church. The Banner edition supplies an able biographical introduction on Cunningham and Bannerman by Iain Murray. Subtitled *A Treatise on The Nature, Powers, Ordinances, Discipline, and Government of the Christian Church*, Bannerman's *magnum opus* remains the classic Reformed work on ecclesiology.

The volumes of James Bannerman are edited and prefaced by Douglas Bannerman, who has also written an able 590-page treatise, *The Scripture Doctrine of the Church Historically and Exegetically Considered* (1887; reprint Grand Rapids: Eerdmans, 1955), covering the development of the church from the time of Abraham through the ministry of Paul.

Charles Hodge, *Church and Its Polity* (London: Nelson and Sons, 1879) is a masterful presentation of Reformed ecclesiology in addition to the treatment of this subject in his systematic theology.

Twentieth Century

R. B. Kuiper, *The Glorious Body of Christ: A Scriptural Appreciation of the One Holy Church* (Grand Rapids: Eerdmans, 1955) is the most basic, poignant Reformed treatment of the doctrine of the church in English. It is a wide-ranging volume, covering more than fifty topics in short, edifying chapters, including the church's unity, marks, offices, responsibilities, privileges, and relationship to the world. Kuiper is vigorous, clear, and comprehensive.

G. C. Berkouwer, *The Church*, translated by James E. Davison (Grand Rapids: Eerdmans, 1976) emphasizes the unity, catholicity, apostolicity, and holiness of the church as it expounds its true ministry. Indecisive and provocative in places, it is enlightening and edifying elsewhere.

Edmund Clowney, former president of Westminster Theological Seminary (Philadelphia), has written cogently and extensively on the Reformed doctrine of the church. For a succinct exposition, see *The Doctrine of the Church* (Philadelphia: Presbyterian and Reformed, 1976); for a more in-depth treatment reflecting the author's mature thought, read *The Church* (Downers Grove, IL: InterVarsity Press, 1996).

Historical-Theological Studies

Thomas M. Lindsay, *The Church and the Ministry in the Early Centuries* (1910; reprint Minneapolis: James Family, 1977) details how the image of the church, its officers, and its ministry changed after the completion of the New Testament. It proficiently covers events from the New Testament to the fourth century.

For a scholarly treatment of the views of the Reformers on ecclesiology, with a special focus on Luther, see Paul D. L. Avis, *The Church in the Theology of the Reformers* (Atlanta: Knox Press, 1981). Unfortunately, Avis's personal development of an ecclesiology based on Luther's views is unscriptural and stained with liberalism. For Calvin's views, see *John Calvin and the Church*, edited by Timothy George (Louisville: Westminster/John Knox Press, 1990), especially Part 3, which shows how Calvin serves as a centering focus of various issues that touch on the life of the church.

For an extensive bibliography on ecclesiology that can provide assistance despite its Roman Catholic orientation, see A. Dulles and P. Granfield, *The Church: A Bibliography* (Wilmington: Glazier, 1985).

Where should you begin reading? Definitely with R.B. Kuiper, then Calvin and à Brakel. Then you will be ready to study James Bannerman.

Article 28 — Church Membership

The best brief treatment on church membership is Wilhelmus à Brakel, "The Duty to Join the Church and to Remain with Her," in *The Christian's Reasonable Service*, translated by Bartel Elshout (Ligonier, PA: Soli Deo Gloria, 1993), 2:55-86. Brakel takes seriously the commitment of church membership and warns earnestly against the dangers of schism.

Books that explain the questions publicly confessed in the Dutch Reformed tradition include Nicholas J. Monsma, *This I Confess: Being a brief Explanation of the Form for the Public Profession of Faith* (Holland, MI: n.p., 1936); John D. Hellinga and Harry VanDyken, *"Do You Heartily Believe...?" A Preparation Manual for Public Confession of Faith* (n.p., n.d.).

Works of varying merit on how to practice the obligations of church membership include the following: John Angell James, *Christian Fellowship, Or the Church Member's Guide*, edited by J. O. Choules (Boston: Lincoln & Edmands, 1829), which includes excellent chapters on the purpose and privileges of church membership, the duties of church members in relationship to themselves, to each other, to their pastor, to other Christian organizations, and to their own unique personalities and callings; William Crowell, *The Church Member's Manual* (Boston: Gould, Kendall, & Lincoln, 1847), subtitled *Ecclesiastical Principles, Doctrine, and Discipline: Presenting a Systematic View of the Structure, Polity, Doctrines, and Practices of Christian Churches, as Taught in the Scriptures*; Jan Karel VanBaalen, *If Thou Shalt Confess* (Grand Rapids: Eerdmans, 1927), which covers believing and confessing, reading, teaching, social life, tithing, temptations, prayer, trials, recreation, the Lord's Day, and serving others; Abraham Kuyper, *The Implications of Public Confession*, translated by Henry Zylstra (Grand Rapids: Zondervan, 1934), which addresses a variety of subjects such as prayer, communion with other believers, practicing good stewardship, and participating in the life of the church; L. H. VanDerMeiden, *God's Yea and Your Amen*, translated by Cornelius Lambregtse (Grand Rapids: Board of Publications of the Old Christian Reformed Church, 1972), which focuses especially on the sacraments in relation to public profession of faith; J. Geertsema, W. Huizinga, A.B. Roukema, G. Van Dooren, W.W.J. VanOene, *Before Many Witnesses* (Winnipeg: Premier, 1974), which explains what public profession means and examines a member's obligation to serve others within and outside of the body of Christ; A. Hoogerland, *Making Confession and Then...?*, translated by Garret J. Moerdyk (Grand Rapids: Eerdmans, 1984), which relates confession of faith to parents, walk of life, dress, the Lord's Supper, the Lord's Day, the covenant of grace, church offices, marriage, reading material, and death.

For a confession-of-faith course, see Joel R. and James W. Beeke, *Bible Doctrine Student Workbook: An Introductory Course* (Grand Rapids: Eerdmans, 1982), which contains 568 questions for confession-of-faith class attendees and covers the basics of Reformed doctrine, including the commitments and implications involved in full, professing church membership. An accompanying *Teacher's Guide*, which provides answers to all the questions, is available upon request.

Article 29 — The True and the False Church Compared

For a condensed treatment, see John Calvin, *Institutes of the Christian Religion* (Philadelphia: Westminster Press, 1960), pp. 1041-1052 (Book 4, Chapter 2). Calvin's focus here is on the false church; he argues that departure from true doctrine and worship invalidates the Roman Catholic Church's claim to be the true church. For a somewhat fuller explanation, read Wilhelmus à Brakel, *The Christian's Reasonable Service*, translated by Bartel Elshout (Ligonier, PA: Soli Deo Gloria, 1993), 2:15-54. Brakel excels in explaining the distinguishing marks of the true church; that the true church is separated from the world and united internally, confesses Christ and His truth, engages in spiritual warfare, and glorifies God. He also makes a formidable case

from Scripture for linking the Antichrist with the papacy (pp. 44-53).

For works exposing the fallacies of the Roman Catholic Church, see Loraine Boettner, *Roman Catholicism* (London: Banner of Truth Trust, 1966), which is a basic yet perceptive evaluation, that exposes the false teachings of the Roman Catholic Church; J. B. Rowell, *Papal Infallibility* (Grand Rapids: Kregel, 1970), which examines the foundations and claims on which the Roman Catholic church is founded. Two of the most helpful contemporary authors who provide considerable assistance in exposing Roman Catholic theology for what it is are William Webster (*Salvation: The Bible and Roman Catholicism* [Edinburgh: Banner of Truth Trust, 1990]; *The Church of Rome at the Bar of History* [Edinburgh: Banner of Truth Trust, 1995]) and John Armstrong (ed., *Roman Catholicism: Evangelical Protestants Analyze What Divides and Unites Us* [Chicago: Moody, 1994] and *A View of Rome* [Chicago: Moody, 1995]). The infamous statement, titled *Evangelicals and Catholics Together (ECT)* released in March 1994, has evoked a number of reactions, including John Ankerberg and John Weldon, *Protestants and Catholics: Do They Now Agree?* (Eugene, OR: Harvest House, 1995); Kevin Reed, *Making Shipwreck of the Faith* (Dallas: Protestant Heritage, 1995). ECT has also prompted a trio of books edited by Don Kistler and published by Soli Deo Gloria, each of which affirms historic Protestant doctrine: *Justification by Faith Alone* (1995); *Sola Scriptura! The Protestant Position on the Bible* (1996); *Trust and Obey* (1997).

For guidance on how to deal with scandal and heresy in the church, read John Calvin, *Concerning Scandals,* translated by John W. Fraser (Grand Rapids: Eerdmans, 1978). It covers intrinsic and extrinsic scandals, as well as "troubles of various kinds." Calvin is profitable, as usual, but no work has superseded that of James Durham, *The Dying Man's Testament to the Church of Scotland or, A Treatise Concerning Scandal,* edited by Christopher Coldwell (Dallas, TX: Naphtali Press, 1990). First published in 1680, this classic has finally been properly edited and freshly printed. After introducing the subject of scandals in general, Durham ably addresses public scandals, doctrinal scandals, and scandalous divisions. His work concludes with how to foster genuine unity in the church. J.C. Ryle, *Warnings to the Churches* (London: Banner of Truth Trust, 1967), first published in 1877 as part of *Knots Untied,* deals with various dangers facing the church and how we ought to respond to them.

Article 30 — Church Government and Offices

Two helpful works advocating Presbyterian church government were written in 1646 while the Westminster Assembly was in session. *Jus Divinum Regiminis Ecclesiastici or The Divine Right of Church Government, originally asserted and evidenced by the Holy Scriptures by the Ministers of Sion College, London, December 1646* (Dallas: Naphtali Press, 1995) contains an able introduction by David Hall on the Westminster Assembly's original intent in church government as clarified by this work. Samuel Rutherford, *The Divine Right of Church Government and Excommunication* (London: Iohn Field for Christopher Meredith), is quite polemical but touches on a number of church-government issues that are still debated today.

Helpful nineteenth-century works on church government include John Brown (of Gartmore), *Vindication of the Presbyterian Form of Church Government* (Edinburgh: H. Inglis, 1805); Samuel Miller, *Presbyteriansim the Truly Primitive and Apostolical Constitution of the Church of Christ* (Philadelphia: Presbyterian Board of Publication, 1835); R. J. Breckinridge, *Presbyterian Government,* edited with helpful introductory essay by Kevin Reed (Dallas: Presbyterian Heritage, 1988) — extracted from Breckinridge's major work, *Presbyterian Government, Not a Hierarchy, But a Commonwealth: and, Presbyterian Ordination, Not a Charm, But an Act of Government,* which was originally published in 1843 as a supplement to *The Spirit of the XIX Century*; William Cunningham, *Discussions on Church Principles: Popish, Erastian, and Presbyterian* (1863; reprint Edmonton: Still Waters Revival Books, 1991), as well as Cunningham's chapter on church government in *Historical Theology* (1862; reprint Edinburgh: Banner of Truth Trust, 1979), 2:514-56.

For a newer, helpful booklet on church government, read Kevin Reed, *Biblical Church Government* (Dallas: Presbyterian Heritage, 1983). For how government ought to be exercised by church office-bearers, a recent volume edited by Mark R. Brown is most helpful. *Order in the Offices: Essays Defining the Roles of Church Officers* (Duncansville, PA: Classic Presbyterians Government Resources, 1993) contains fifteen essays (Charles Hodge, Edmund Clowney, Iain Murray, Leonard Coppes, Robert Rayburn, Charles Dennison, etc.) that help foster "peace and order in the church, as the roles and relationships of ministers, elders, and deacons are clarified." It includes an excellent, annotated bibliography.

Where should you begin? For church government, study Reed; for church offices, read Brown.

Article 31 — Ministers, Elders, and Deacons

Ministers

Solomon's adage, "Of making many books there is no end," certainly applies to the office of the ministry. Some of the best works on homiletics (i.e., preaching) are: William Perkins, *The Art of Prophesying with The Calling of the Ministry* (1605-1606; reprint Edinburgh: Banner of Truth Trust, 1996); Philip Doddridge, *Lectures on Preaching* (London: Richard Edwards, 1804); Gardiner Spring, *The Power of the Pulpit* (1848; reprint Edinburgh: Banner of Truth Trust, 1986); John Claude, *An Essay on the Composition of a Sermon,* edited by Charles Simeon (New York: Carlton & Phillips, 1853); James W. Alexander, *Thoughts on Preaching* (1864; reprint Edinburgh: Banner of Truth Trust, 1975); Robert L. Dabney, *Sacred Rhetoric or A Course of Lectures on Preaching* (1870; reprint Edinburgh: Banner of Truth Trust, 1979); John A. Broadus, *On the Preparation and Delivery of Sermons,* 4th ed. (1870; reprint New York: Harper & Row, 1979); M. Reu, *Homiletics: A Manual of The Theory and Practice of Preaching,* translated by Albert Steinhaeuser (Chicago: Wartburg, 1924); Albert N. Martin, *What's Wrong with Preaching Today?* (London: Banner of Truth Trust, 1967); D. Martyn Lloyd-Jones, *Preaching and Preachers* (Grand Rapids: Zondervan, 1971); Homer C. Hoeksema, "Homiletics" (Grandville, MI: Protestant Reformed Theological Seminary, 1975); Pierre Charles Marcel, *The Relevance of Preaching,* translated by R. R. McGregor (Grand Rapids: Baker, 1977); John R. W. Stott, *Between Two Worlds: The Art of Preaching in the Twentieth Century* (Grand Rapids: Eerdmans, 1982); Samuel T. Logan, Jr., ed., *The*

Preacher and Preaching: Reviving the Art in the Twentieth Century (Philipsburg, NJ: Presbyterian and Reformed, 1986); John MacArthur, Jr., et al., *Rediscovering Expository Preaching* (Dallas: Word, 1992).

Significant works on pastoral theology (i.e., the minister's personal life, pastoral duties, and preaching) include: Richard Baxter, *The Reformed Pastor* (1656; unabridged reprint New York: Robert Carter, 1860); Herman Witsius, *On the Character of a True Theologian,* edited by J. Ligon Duncan III (1675; reprint Greenville, SC: Reformed Academic Press, 1994); Samuel Bownas, *A Description of the Qualifications Necessary to A Gospel Minister* (London: Luke Hinde, 1750); John Mason, *The Student and Pastor* (London: H. D. Symonds, 1807); John Brown, ed., *The Christian Pastor's Manual* (1826; reprint Ligonier: Soli Deo Gloria, 1991); Charles Bridges, *The Christian Ministry* (1830; reprint London: Banner of Truth Trust, 1959); John Angell James, *An Earnest Ministry: The Want of the Times* (1847; reprint Edinburgh: Banner of Truth Trust, 1993); Samuel Miller, *Letters on Clerical Manners and Habits* (Philadelphia: Presbyterian Board of Publication, 1852); A. Vinet, *Pastoral Theology,* translated by Thomas H. Skinner (New York: Ivison & Phinney, 1854); William G.T. Shedd, *Homiletics and Pastoral Theology* (1867; reprint London: Banner of Truth Trust, 1965); Patrick Fairbairn, *Pastoral Theology* (1875; reprint Audubon, NJ: Old Paths, 1992); William M. Taylor, *The Ministry of the Word* (1876; reprint Grand Rapids: Baker, 1975); Thomas Murphy, *Pastoral Theology* (1877; reprint Audubon, NJ: Old Paths, 1996); J. J. VanOosterzee, *Practical Theology: A Manual for Theological Students,* translated by Maurice J. Evans (London: Hodder and Stoughton, 1878); Charles H. Spurgeon, *Lectures to My Students* (1881; reprint Pasadena, TX: Pilgrim, 1990); George Campbell Morgan, *The Ministry of the Word* (1919; reprint Grand Rapids: Baker, 1970); Homer A. Kent, Sr., *The Pastor and His Work* (Chicago: Moody, 1963); Ralph G. Turnbull, ed., *Baker's Dictionary of Practical Theology* (Grand Rapids: Baker, 1967).

For historical studies on preaching, see John Ker, *Lectures on the History of Preaching* (New York: A.C. Armstrong & Son, 1893); Charles Smyth, *The Art of Preaching: A Practical Survey of Preaching in the Church of England, 737-1939* (London: SPCK, 1940); Hugh Thomson Kerr, *Preaching in the Early Church* (New York: Fleming H. Revell, 1942); Edwin Charles Dargan and Ralph G. Turnbull, *A History of Preaching,* 3 vols. (reprint Grand Rapids: Baker, 1974).

Elders

Helpful books on the eldership include: John Glass, "Of the Unity and Distinction of the Elder's Office," in *Works of John Glass,* Vol. 2 (Perth, 1782); Samuel Miller, *An Essay on the Warrant, Nature and Duties of the Ruling Elder* (1832; reprint Dallas: Presbyterian Heritage, 1987); Thomas Smyth, *The Name, Nature, and Functions of Ruling Elders* (1845; reprint Duncansville, PA: Classic Presbyterians Government Resources, 1992) — best read in conjunction with his two later sets of journal articles, "Theories of the Eldership," in *Complete Works of Rev. Thomas Smyth,* 4:167-275, 277-358; Peter Colin Campbell, *The Theory of Ruling Eldership* (1866; reprint Duncansville, PA: Classic Presbyterian Government Resources, 1992); David Dickson, *The Elder and His Work* (1875; reprint Dallas: Presbyterian Heritage, 1990); J. Aspinwall Hodge, *The Ruling Elder at Work* (Philadelphia: Presbyterian Board of Publication, 1901); William Henry Roberts, *Manual for Ruling Elders* (Philadelphia: Presbyterian Board of Publication, 1905); T. Graham Campbell, *The Work of the Eldership* (Glasgow: John Smith & Son, 1915); Cleland Boyd McAfee, *The Ruling Elder* (Philadelphia: Presbyterian Board of Christian Education, 1931); G. D. Henderson, *The Scottish Ruling Elder* (London: James Clark, 1935); Robert W. Henderson, *Profiles of the Eldership: 1974* (Geneva: WARC, 1975); Lawrence R. Eyres, *The Elders of the Church* (Philadelphia: Presbyterian and Reformed, 1975); Gerard Berghoef and Lester DeKoster, *The Elders Handbook: A Practical Guide for Church Leaders* (Grand Rapids: Christian's Library Press, 1979), with a companion study guide published in 1994; Paul S. Wright, *The Presbyterian Elder* (Philadelphia: Westminster, 1986); Elsie Anne McKee, *Elders and the Plural Ministry* (Geneva: Librairie Droz, 1988); Alexander Strauch, *Biblical Eldership: An Urgent Call to Restore Biblical Church Leadership* (Littleton, CO: Lewis and Roth, 1988); John R. Sittema, *With a Shepherd's Heart: Reclaiming the Pastoral Office of Elder* (Grandville, MI: Reformed Fellowship, 1996).

For enlightening articles on the nature and validity of the office of elders, start with Iain Murray's "Ruling Elders — A Sketch of a Controversy," *Banner of Truth* No. 235 (April 1983): 1-9, and "The Problem of the 'Eldership' and Its Wider Implications," *Banner of Truth* No. 395-96 (Aug-Sep 1996):36-56. See also R.E.H. Uprichard, "The Eldership in Martin Bucer and John Calvin," *Evangelical Quarterly* 61:1 (1989):21-37. Uprichard aims to prove that Calvin rediscovered rather than invented the eldership (contra T.F. Torrance, *The Eldership in the Reformed Church* [Edinburgh: Handsel Press, 1984]).

Deacons

Helpful works on the diaconate include William Guthrie, "A Treatise of Ruling Elders and Deacons," in *The Works of William Guthrie* (Glasgow, 1771); Peter Y. DeJong, *The Ministry of Mercy for Today* (Grand Rapids: Baker, 1968); Leonard J. Coppes, *Who Will Lead Us: A Study in the Development of Biblical Offices with Emphasis on the Diaconate* (Philipsburg, NJ: Pilgrim, 1977); Andrew Jumper, *Chosen to Serve: The Deacon* (Atlanta: John Knox Press, 1977); Gerard Berghoef and Lester DeKoster, *The Deacons Handbook: A Manual of Stewardship* (Grand Rapids: Christian's Library Press, 1980), with a companion study guide published in 1994.

Article 32 — Church Order, Worship, and Discipline

Church Order

The best overall work on Reformed church order is edited by David W. Hall and Joseph H. Hall, *Paradigms in Polity: Classic Readings in Reformed and Presbyterian Church Government* (Grand Rapids: Eerdmans, 1994). This work also contains an outstanding bibliographical essay (pp. 603-616). Other generally helpful works include Charles Hodge, *Discussions in Church Polity* (New York: Charles Scribner's Sons, 1878) and J. L. Schaver, *The Polity of the Churches,* 2 vols. (Chicago: Church Polity Press, 1937). Schaver is oriented to the polity of the Christian Reformed Churches.

The famous Church Order of Dort (1619) is expounded most ably by Dutch church order experts such as H. Bouwman, F.L. Rutgers, and J. Janssen. English works rely heavily on those Dutch scholars. The most helpful work in English is Idzerd Van Dellen and Martin Monsma, *The Church Order Commentary* (Grand Rapids: Zondervan, 1941), which expounds the old Christian Reformed version of the Church Order of Dort. After the Christian Reformed Church adopted extensive revisions to their church order in 1965, Martin Monsma revised this useful work and published it under the same authorship as *The Revised Church Order Commentary* (Grand Rapids: Zondervan, 1967). Additional sources on the Church Order of Dort or denominational versions of it include: J. L. Schaver, *Christian Reformed Church Order* (Grand Rapids: Zondervan, 1937); Howard B. Spaan, *Christian Reformed Church Government* (Grand Rapids: Kregel, 1968); Herman Hanko, "Notes on the Church Order" (Grand Rapids: Theological School of the Protestant Reformed Churches, 1973); K. DeGier, *Explanation of the Church Order of Dordt in Questions and Answers,* edited by Joel Beeke (Grand Rapids: Eerdmans, 1980); G. VanRongen and K. Deddens, *Decently and in Good Order: the Church Order of the Canadian and American Reformed Churches* (Winnipeg: Premier, 1986); W.W.J. VanOene, *With Common Consent: A practical guide to the use of the Church Order of the Canadian Reformed Churches* (Winnipeg: Premier, 1990).

Richard DeRidder has produced two helpful manuscripts that, unfortunately, remain unpublished: "A Survey of the Sources of Reformed Church Polity" (Grand Rapids: Calvin Theological Seminary, 1983), and "The Church Orders of the Sixteenth Century Reformed Churches of the Netherlands Together With Their Social, Political, and Ecclesiastical Context" (Grand Rapids: Calvin Theological Seminary, 1987). This latter manuscript is a massive work of 660 pages that contains full translations of all the articles of the major synods held in the Netherlands from 1568 to 1638.

For church polity of the New Testament, Samuel Davidson, *The Ecclesiastical Polity of the New Testament Unfolded* (London: Jackson and Walford, 1848) is more conservative than Eduard Schweizer, *Church Order in the New Testament* (London: SCM, 1961).

Worship and Liturgy

For Reformed worship and liturgy, see William Ames, *A Fresh Suit Against Human Ceremonies in God's Worship* (1633; photocopy format, Edmonton: Still Waters Revival Books, 1996); *The Directory for the Public Worship of God; agreed upon by the Assembly of Divines at Westminster* (1645); Jeremiah Burroughs, *Gospel Worship* (1646; reprint Morgan, PA: Soli Deo Gloria, 1990); Howard Hageman, *Pulpit and Table* (Richmond: Knox, 1962); James Hastings Nichols, *Corporate Worship in the Reformed Tradition* (Philadelphia; Westminster Press, 1968); G. VanDoren, *The Beauty of Reformed Liturgy* (Winnipeg: Premier, 1980); *Liturgy of the Reformed Churches* (1767 version used by the RCA; 1914 version printed with *The Psalter*; 1934 version printed with the *Psalter Hymnal*; 1991 version, which includes entire Dutch Reformed liturgy, printed as *The Doctrinal Standards, Liturgy and Church Order*); David Lachman and Frank J. Smith, eds., *Worship in the Presence of God* (Greenville, SC: Greenville Seminary Press, 1992); Arthur Pontier, "Call to Greatness:

A Theology of Worship" (unpublished, 1994); Kevin Reed, *Biblical Worship* (Dallas: Presbyterian Heritage, 1995).

For historical-theological material on worship and liturgy, see especially Horton Davies, *Worship and Theology in England, 1534-1965,* 5 vols. (Princeton: University Press, 1961-75), as well as, *The Worship of the English Puritans* (Westminster: Dacre Press, 1948) and *The Worship of the American Puritans (1629-1730)* (New York: Peter Lang, 1990). Also see Charles Baird, *A Chapter on Liturgies: Historical Sketches* (London: Knight & Son, 1856); Bard Thompson, *Liturgies of the Western Church* (New York: Collins, 1962); Hughes Oliphant Old, *The Patristic Roots of Reformed Worship* (Zurich: Juris Druck, 1975); James F. White, *Protestant Worship: Traditions in Transition* (Louisville: Westminster/John Knox, 1989); John Harper, *The Forms and Orders of Western Liturgy from the Tenth to the Eighteenth Century* (Oxford: Clarendon Press, 1991); Paul Bradshaw, *The Search for the Origins of Christian Worship: Sources and Methods for the Study of Early Liturgy* (New York: Oxford, 1992); D. A. Carson, ed., *Worship: Adoration and Action* (Grand Rapids: Baker, 1993); James F. White, *A Brief History of Christian Worship* (Nashville: Abingdon, 1993).

Church Discipline

There is little good Reformed material on church discipline. The best work is Jay E. Adams, *Handbook of Church Discipline* (Grand Rapids: Zondervan, 1986). Also see Warham Walker, *Harmony in the Church: Church Discipline* (1844; reprint Rochester, NY: Backus, 1981); John White and Ken Blue, *Church Discipline that Heals* (Downers Grove, IL: InterVarsity Press, 1985); John Calvin, *Calvin's Ecclesiastical Advice,* translated by Mary Beaty and Benjamin W. Farley (Louisville, KY: Westminster/John Knox, 1991).

Article 33 — The Sacraments

Though numerous, sound Reformed treatises expound baptism or the Lord's Supper, few treat both sacraments under one cover. Two of the best, succinct works are Ezekiel Hopkins, "The Doctrine of the Two Sacraments," in *The Works of Ezekiel Hopkins,* Vol. 2 (1867; reprint Morgan, PA: Soli Deo Gloria, 1997), pp. 301-359, and James S. Candlish, *The Christian Sacraments* (Edinburgh: T & T Clark, 1857). Stephen H. Tyng, *Fellowship with Christ: A Guide to the Sacraments* (New York: Protestant Episcopal Society for the Promotion of Evangelical Knowledge, 1854) is instructive and edifying. More detailed but not always as reliable are John S. Stone, *The Christian Sacraments* (New York: Anson D.F. Randolph, 1866), and Gerrit C. Berkouwer, *The Sacraments,* translated by Hugo Bekker (Grand Rapids: Eerdmans, 1969). Berkouwer provides an able critique of the teaching of Romanism and Lutheranism as well as various contemporary views of the sacraments.

Some of the best treatments of both sacraments from a Reformed perspective are buried in systematic theologies or sermon books, such as John Calvin, *Institutes of the Christian Religion* (Philadelphia: Westminster Press, 1960), 2:1276-1484; Henry Bullinger, *The Decades,* translated by H.I. (Cambridge: University Press, 1852), 4:226-351; Wilhelmus à Brakel, *The Christian's Reasonable Service,* translated by Bartel Elshout (Ligonier, PA: Soli Deo Gloria, 1993), 2:469-600. Also consult expositions of Lord's Days 25-30 of the Heidelberg Catechism, such as Herman Hoeksema, *The Triple Knowledge*, Vol. 2 (Grand Rapids: Reformed Free Pub. Assn., 1972).

For historical-theological works on the sacraments, see Ronald S. Wallace, *Calvin's Doctrine of the Word and Sacrament* (London: Oliver and Boyd, 1953); Joseph C. McLelland, *The Visible Words of God: An Exposition of the Sacramental Theology of Peter Martyr Vermigli, 1500-1562* (Grand Rapids: Eerdmans, 1957); Robert S. Paul, *The Atonement and the Sacraments* (London: Hodder and Stoughton, 1960); E.B. Holifield, *The Covenant Sealed: The Development of Puritan Sacramental Theology in Old and New England, 1570-1720* (New Haven: Yale University Press, 1974).

Article 34 — Holy Baptism

Some of the best works on the doctrine of holy baptism include:

Eighteenth Century

William Wall, *The History of Infant Baptism* (London: Joseph Downing, 1707); William Wall, *A Defence of the History of Infant Baptism Against the Reflections of Mr. Gale and Others* (London: R. Bonwicke, et al., 1720); Samuel Clarke, *Three Practical Essays on Baptism, Confirmation and Repentance* (London: John and Paul Knapton, 1740).

Nineteenth Century

John Hubbard, *An Attempt to Explain God's Gracious Covenant with Believers; and Illustrate the Duty of Parents to Embrace This Covenant, Dedicate Their Children in Baptism and Train Them Up in the Fear of God* (Amherst, NH: Joseph Cushing, 1805); John Reed, *An Apology for the Rite of Infant Baptism, and for the Usual Modes of Baptizing* (Providence: Heaton & Williams, 1806); Nathaniel S. Prime, *A Familiar Illustration of Christian Baptism: in Which the Proper Subjects of that Ordinance and the Mode of Administration are Ascertained* (Salem, NY: Dodd & Stevenson, 1818); Charles Jerram, *Conversations on Infant Baptism* (New York: Swords, Stanford, & Co., 1839); Alexander Hay, *A Treatise on Baptism* (New York: J.A. Sparks, 1842); William Goode, *The Doctrine of the Church of England as to the Effects of Baptism in the Case of Infants* (London: J. Hatchard and Son, 1850); Thomas M'Crie, *Lectures on Christian Baptism* (Edinburgh: Johnstone & Hunter, 1850); William Sommerville, *A Dissertation on the Nature and Administration of the Ordinance of Baptism* (Edinburgh: Oliver & Boyd, 1866); E. Greenwald, *The Baptism of Children* (Philadelphia: Sherman, 1872); N. Doane, *Infant Baptism Briefly Considered* (New York: Nelson & Phillips, 1875); J.W. Etter, *The Doctrine of Christian Baptism* (Dayton, OH: United Brethren Press, 1888).

Twentieth Century

Lewis Bevens Schenck, *The Presbyterian Doctrine of Children in the Covenant: An Historical Study of the Significance of Infant Baptism in the Presbyterian Church in America* (New Haven: Yale University Press, 1940); Raymond R. Van Heukelom, "The Meaning of Baptism in Reformed Theology" (Th.M. thesis, Calvin Theological Seminary, 1943); W. H. Flemington, *The New Testament Doctrine of Baptism* (London: S.P.C.K., 1953); Pierre Ch. Marcel, *The Biblical Doctrine of Infant Baptism: Sacrament of the Covenant of Grace*

(London: James Clark, 1953); Geoffrey W. Bromiley, *Baptism and the Anglican Reformers* (London: S.P.C.K., 1953); M. Eugene Osterhaven, *What is Christian Baptism?* (Grand Rapids: Society for Reformed Publications, 1956); Robert G. Rayburn, *What About Baptism?* (St. Louis: Covenant Theological Seminary, 1957); Dwight Hervey Small, *The Biblical Basis for Infant Baptism: Children in God's Covenant Promises* (Westwood, NJ: Revell, 1959); Joachim Jeremias, *Infant Baptism in the First Four Centuries*, translated by David Cairns (Philadelphia: Westminster Press, 1962); J.G. Vos, *Baptism: Its Subjects and Modes* (Pittsburgh, PA: Crown and Covenant Publications, 1969); John A. Schep, *Baptism in the Spirit According to Scripture* (Plainfield, NJ: Logos International, 1972); John Murray, *Christian Baptism* (Grand Rapids: Baker, 1974); Jay E. Adams, *Meaning and Mode of Baptism* (Philipsburg, NJ: Presbyterian and Reformed, 1976); Francis A. Schaeffer, *Baptism* (Wilmington, DE: Trimark, 1976); Wilbert M. Van Dyk, "'Forbid Them Not': A Study in Infant Baptism" (Th.M. thesis, Calvin Theological Seminary, 1976); Robert K. Churchill, *Glorious is the Baptism of the Spirit* (Philipsburg, NJ: Presbyterian and Reformed, 1976); Edmund B. Fairfield, *Letters on Baptism* (Uxbridge, MA: Reformation Seminary Press, 1979); Geoffrey W. Bromiley, *Children of Promise: The Case for Baptizing Infants* (Grand Rapids: Eerdmans, 1979); Willem Balke, *Calvin and the Anabaptist Radicals*, translated by William Heynen (Grand Rapids: Eerdmans, 1981); Samuel Miller, *Baptism and Christian Education* (reprint Dallas, TX: Presbyterian Heritage Publications, 1984); Duane E. Spencer, *Holy Baptism: Word Keys Which Unlock the Covenant* (Tyler, TX: Geneva Ministries, 1984); James W. Dale, *Classic Baptism: An Inquiry into the Meaning of the Word as Determined by the Usage of Classical Greek Writers* (Philipsburg, NJ: Presbyterian and Reformed, 1989); H. Oliphant Old, *The Shaping of the Reformed Baptismal Rite in the Sixteenth Century* (Grand Rapids: Eerdmans, 1990); Jonathan Neil Gerstner, *The Thousand Generation Covenant: Dutch Reformed Covenant Theology and Group Identity in Colonial South Africa, 1652-1854* (Leiden: E.J. Brill, 1991); Rowland S. Ward, *Baptism in Scripture and History* (Brunswick, Australia: Globe Press, 1991); Frederick S. Leahy, *Biblical Baptism* (Belfast: Cameron Press, 1992); Robert R. Booth, *Children of the Promise: The Biblical Case for Infant Baptism* (Philipsburg, NJ: Presbyterian and Reformed, 1995); Robert Grossmann, *The Meaning and Administration of Biblical Baptism* (Garner, IA: Elector, 1995); Gerald Procee, *Holy Baptism: The Scriptural Setting, Significance and Scope of Infant Baptism* (Hamilton, Ontario: Free Reformed Church, 1998).

Article 35 — The Holy Supper

Some of the best works on the Lord's Supper include:

Seventeenth Century

Simon Patrick, *Mensa Mystica, or a Discourse Concerning the Sacrament of the Lord's Supper* (London: Francis Tyton, 1676); Simon Patrick, *The Christian Sacrifice: A Treatise Shewing the Necessity, End and Manner of Receiving the Holy Communion* (London: R. Royston, 1679).

Eighteenth Century

Jabez Earl, *Sacramental Exercises in Two Parts: The Christian's Employment before, at, and after the Lord's Supper; and The Christian's Conduct in his Afterlife* (London: Richard Hett, 1742); W. Fleetwood, *The Reasonable Communicant: Or, An Explanation of the Doctrine of the Sacrament of the Lord's Supper* (London: John, Francis, and Charles Rivington, 1784).

Nineteenth Century

John Warden, *A Practical Essay on the Lord's Supper to which is Added an Assistant in Examining the Heart; or Questions of the Greatest Moment, which Every Christian Ought, with Sincerity, and as in the Sight of God, to Put to his own Heart* (Leith: Archibald Allardice and W. Coke, 1809); Thomas Haweis, *The Communicant's Spiritual Companion; or, An Evangelical Preparation for the Lord's Supper* (New Haven: Oliver Steele, 1810); Henry Grove, *A Discourse Concerning the Nature and Design of the Lord's Supper* (Salem, NY: Joshua Cushing, 1812); John Willison, *A Sacramental Directory; or a Treatise Concerning the Sanctification of a Communion-Sabbath* (Edinburgh: Ogle, Allardice, & Thomson, 1817); Hugh Blair, *A Companion to the Altar; Shewing the Nature and Necessity of a Sacramental Preparation in Order to our Worthy Receiving the Holy Communion* (London: Scatcherd and Letterman, 1820); Edward Bickersteth, *A Treatise on the Lord's Supper: Designed as a Guide and Companion to the Holy Communion* (London: R.B. Seeley and W. Burnside, 1830); Capel Molyneux, *The Lord's Supper* (London: James Nisbet, 1850); James W. Alexander, *Plain Words to a Young Communicant* (New York: Anson D.F. Randolph, 1858); Samuel Luckey, *The Lord's Supper* (New York: Carlton & Porter, 1859); Matthew Henry, *The Communicant's Companion; or, Instructions for the Right Receiving of the Lord's Supper* (Philadelphia: Presbyterian Board of Publication, 1865); Thomas Houston, *The Lord's Supper: its Nature, Ends, and Obligation; and Mode of Administration* (Edinburgh: James Gemmell, 1878); John Glas, *A Treatise on the Lord's Supper* (London: Sampson Low, et al., 1883); Nicholas Ridley, *A Brief Declaration of the Lord's Supper*, ed. H.C.G. Moule (London: Seeley, 1895).

Twentieth Century

W. Mason, *The Christian Communicant; or a Suitable Companion to the Lord's Supper* (London: Chas. J. Thynne, 1904); Robert Bruce, *The Mystery of the Lord's Supper*, edited by Thomas F. Torrance (London: James Clarke, 1958); Ernest F. Kevan, *The Lord's Supper* (London: Evangelical Press, 1966); Joachim Jeremias, *The Eucharistic Words of Jesus*, translated by Norman Perrin (London: SCM, 1966); Gerard Wisse, *May I Partake of the Lord's Supper?* (Wilmington, DE: Trimark, 1979); Richard Bacon, *What Mean ye by This Service? Paedocommunion in Light of the Passover* (Texas: Presbyterian Heritage Publications, 1989); John Willison, *Meditations on the Lord's Supper* (abridged reprint Stornoway: Reformation Press, 1990).

Historical-Theological Studies

Numerous historical-theological studies have been undertaken on the Reformation view of the Lord's Supper. Alexander Barclay, *The Protestant Doctrine of the Lord's Supper* (Glasgow, 1927), shows the affinity between Luther and Calvin but regards Calvin's doctrine as the natural development of Zwingli's later thinking on the Lord's Supper. Cyril C. Richardson, *Zwingli and Cranmer on the Eucharist* (Evanston, IL, 1949) asserts that Cranmer did not move beyond the Zwinglian framework. Joseph C. McLelland, *The Visible Words of God: An Exposition of the Sacramental Theology of Peter Martyr Vermigli* (Grand Rapids: Eerdmans, 1957) establishes the theological harmony between Vermigli, Bucer, and Calvin on the Holy Supper. George B. Burnet, *The Holy Communion in the Reformed Church of Scotland 1560-1960* (London: Oliver & Boyd, 1960) reveals the rich Scottish heritage on Communion. Peter Newman Brooks, *Thomas Cranmer's Doctrine of the Eucharist* (New York: Seabury Press, 1965) argues that Cranmer held much the same doctrine of a "true presence" of Christ in the supper as did Bucer, Bullinger, and Calvin. Leigh Eric Schmidt, *Holy Fair: Scottish Communions and American Revivals in the Early Modern Period* (Princeton: University Press, 1989) explores the historical development of the Scottish communion season from the Reformation to the nineteenth century, documents its extension to colonial America and its important relationship to revivals on both sides of the Atlantic. Brian A. Gerrish, *Grace and Gratitude: The Eucharistic Theology of John Calvin* (Minneapolis: Fortress Press, 1993) puts Calvin's doctrine of the Lord's Supper in the context of his theology as a whole, and compares him with Zwingli and Luther.

Article 36 — Church and State

The most informative research tool on church-state relations is Albert J. Menendez, *Church-State Relations: An Annotated Bibliography* (New York: Garland, 1976). Menendez, however, includes only English language, full-length books that treat the subject in some depth or completeness.

The classic Christian work on church and state is Augustine's *City of God*, translated by Marcus Dods (New York: Random House, 1952). For an able exposition of Augustine's ideas, see John H.S. Burleigh, *The City of God: A Study of St. Augustine's Philosophy* (London: Nisbet, 1949); also, consult James Boice, *Two Cities, Two Loves* (Downers Grove, IL: InterVarsity, 1996). See Claudio Morino, *Church and State in the Teaching of St. Ambrose*, translated by M. Joseph Costelloe (Washington, D.C.: Catholic University of America, 1969), for information on another ancient churchman who dealt with church-state relations.

For medieval thought on church-state relations, see Heinrich A. Rommen, *The State in Catholic Thought* (St. Louis: B. Herder, 1947); Arthur L. Smith, *Church and State in the Middle Ages* (New York: Barnes & Noble, 1964); Brian Tierney, *The Crisis of Church and State, 1050-1300* (Englewood Cliffs, NJ: Prentice-Hall, 1966); Bennett D. Hill, *Church and State in the Middle Ages* (New York: Wiley, 1970); Thomas J. Renna, *Church and State in Medieval Europe, 1050-1314* (Dubuque, IA: Kendall/Hunt, 1974). Also, consult Thomas Aquinas, *Compendium of Theology*, translated by C.O. Vollert (London: Herder, 1948).

For pre-Reformation thinking on church and state, see *The English Works of John Wyclif*, 3 vols., edited by F.D. Matthews (London: Wyclif Society, 1880); John Hus, *The Church*, translated by David Schaff (New York: Scribners, 1915). For Reformation thought, consult H.R. Pearcy, *The Meaning of the Church in the Thought of Calvin* (Chicago: University Press, 1941); William A. Mueller, *Church and State in Luther and Calvin* (Nashville: Broadman, 1954); Thomas F. Torrance, *Kingdom and Church* (Edinburgh: Oliver and Boyd, 1956); Geddes MacGregor, *Corpus Christi: The Nature of the Church According to the Reformed Tradition* (Philadelphia: Westminster, 1958); John Tonkin, *The Church and the Secular Order in Reformation Thought* (New York: Columbia University Press, 1971). For the Anabaptist view, see John Toews, "The Anabaptist Conception of the Church" (Ph.D. dissertation, United College of Winnipeg, 1950); Franklin H. Littell, *The Anabaptist View of the Church* (Boston: Beacon Press, 1952), which was revised and reissued as *The Origins of Sectarian Protestantism* (New York: Macmillan, 1965).

Numerous treatises have been written on church-state relations in the United Kingdom. For Scotland, see the *First Book of Discipline* (1560); the *Second Book of Discipline* (1578); Samuel Rutherford, *Lex Rex, or The Law and the Prince* (1644; reprint Harrisonburg, VA: Sprinkle, 1982), and *A Free Disputation Against Pretended Liberty of Conscience* (London: R.I. for Andrew Crook, 1649); George Gillespie, *Aaron's Rod Blossoming; or, The Divine Ordinance of Church Government Vindicated* (1646; reprint Harrisonburg, VA: Sprinkle, 1985); Thomas Brown, *Church and State in Scotland* (Edinburgh: Macniven and Wallace, 1891); Francis Lyall, *Of Presbyters and Kings: Church and State in the Law of Scotland* (Aberdeen: University Press, 1980). For England, see Gilbert W. Child, *Church and State Under the Tudors* (London: Longmans, 1890); Henry M. Gwatkin, *Church and State in England to the Death of Queen Anne* (London: Longmans, 1917); A.F. Scott Pearson, *Church and State: Political Aspects of Sixteenth Century Puritanism* (Cambridge: University Press, 1928); Adrian Hastings, *Church and State: The English Experience* (Exeter: University Press, 1991); Stuart E. Prull, *Church and State in Tudor and Stuart England* (Arlington Heights, IL: H. Davidson, 1993).

For church-state relations in Europe, consult William Graham, *A Review of Ecclesiastical Establishments in Europe* (Glasgow: D. Niven, 1792); H. Geffcken, *Church and State: Their Relations Historically Considered* (London, 1852); Adolf Keller, *Church and State on the European Continent, 1864-1914* (London: Epworth, 1936); Ernst C. Helmreich, ed., *Church and State in Europe* (St. Louis: Focrum Press, 1979).

For church-state relations in America, the best resource is John F. Wilson, ed., *Church and State in America: A Bibliographical Guide*, 2 vols. (New York: Greenwood Press, 1986-87). Volume 1 covers the colonial and early national periods; Volume 2, from the civil war to the 1980s. Each volume has eleven bibliographic essays, with approximately 250 entries each. For specific works, see Joseph P. Thompson, *Church and State in the United States* (Boston: James R. Osgood, 1873); Philip Schaff, *Church and State in the United States* (New York: G.P. Putnam's Sons, 1888); William A. Brown, *Church and State in Contemporary America* (New York: Scribners, 1936); Anson P. Stokes, *Church and State in the United States*, 3 vols. (New York: Harper, 1950); James E. Wood, Jr., ed., *Religion and the State* (Waco, TX: Baylor University Press, 1985).

For church-state relations in general, see William E. Gladstone, *The State in Its Relations to the Church* (London: J. Murray, 1841); Samuel Taylor Coleridge, *On the Constitution of Church and State*, edited by John Colmer (1852; reprint London: Routledge & Kegan, 1976); Albert Hyma, *Christianity and Politics: A History of the Principles and Struggles of Church and State* (Philadelphia: Lippincott, 1938); Luigi Sturzo, *Church and State*, 2 vols., translated by B.B. Carter (1939; reprint Notre Dame, IN: University Press, 1962); Finley M.

Foster, *Church and State: Their Relations Considered* (New York: Peerless, 1940); G. Elson Rupp, *The Dilemma of Church and State* (Philadelphia: Muhlenberg, 1954); Jacob Marcellus Kik, *Church and State: The Story of Two Kingdoms* (New York: Nelson, 1963); Albert G. Huegli, *Church and State Under God* (St. Louis: Concordia, 1964); Thomas Sanders, *Protestant Concepts of Church and State* (New York: Holt, Rinehart, and Winston, 1964).

Article 37 — The Last Judgment; Hell and Heaven

For helpful material on the last judgment, hell and heaven, and eschatology in general, consult the great Reformed orthodox systematicians as well as Reformed commentators on the book of Revelation, such as James B. Ramsay, *Revelation* (1873; reprint Edinburgh: Banner of Truth Trust, 1977); William Hendriksen, *More Than Conquerors* (Grand Rapids: Baker, 1939); Herman Hoeksema, *Behold He Cometh!* (Grand Rapids: Reformed Free, 1969); Philip E. Hughes, *Revelation* (Grand Rapids: Eerdmans, 1990).

Seventeenth Century

The Puritans wrote extensively on what they called "the four last things": death, judgment, heaven, and hell (e.g., Robert Bolton, *The Four Last Things* [1633; reprint Pittsburgh: Soli Deo Gloria, 1990]; William Bates, "The Four Last Things" [1691] in *Complete Works,* ed. W. Farmer [reprint Harrisonburg, VA: Sprinkle, 1990], 3:237-507, which is probably Bates's greatest work). The greatest and most massive Puritan classic on heaven is Richard Baxter, *The Saints' Everlasting Rest* (1650; reprinted often in abridged versions, e.g. Grand Rapids: Zondervan, 1962). For the doctrine of man's soul in the face of eternity, see John Flavel, "Pneumatologia: A Treatise of the Soul of Man," in *The Works* (reprint London: Banner of Truth Trust, 1968), 2:475-609, 3:1-238.

Eighteenth Century

The greatest eighteenth-century classic on man's eternal abode is Isaac Watts, *The World to Come* (1739; reprint Chicago: Moody, 1954). For moving and searching sermons on "the last things" that no preacher has ever surpassed, see Jonathan Edwards (a variety of sermons in *The Works,* Vol. 2 [reprint Edinburgh: Banner of Truth Trust, 1974]). Some of those sermons have been reprinted in Jonathan Edwards, *The Wrath of Almighty God* (Morgan, PA: Soli Deo Gloria, 1996). For Edwards's views, see John H. Gerstner, *Jonathan Edwards on Heaven and Hell* (Grand Rapids: Baker, 1980).

Nineteenth Century

The best nineteenth-century works are Wilson C. Rider, *A Course of Lectures on Future Punishment* (Ellsworth: Daniel T. Pike, 1836); J. Edmondson, *Scripture Views of the Heavenly World* (New York: Lane & Scott, 1852); W.G.T. Shedd, *The Doctrine of Endless Punishment* (1885; reprint Edinburgh: Banner of Truth Trust, 1986).

Twentieth Century

Helpful twentieth-century theological treatises on various aspects of eschatology include Geerhardus Vos, *The Pauline Eschatology* (1930; reprint Grand Rapids: Baker,

1979); Diedrich H. Kromminga, *The Milennium in the Church: Studies in the History of Christian Chiliasm* (Grand Rapids: Eerdmans, 1945); Klaas Schilder, *Heaven: What Is It?* (Grand Rapids: Eerdmans, 1950); Louis Berkhof, *The Second Coming of Christ* (Grand Rapids: Eerdmans, 1952); Harry Buis, *The Doctrine of Eternal Punishment* (Grand Rapids: Baker, 1957); Loraine Boettner, *Immortality* (Philadelphia: Presbyterian and Reformed, 1958); Leon Morris, *The Biblical Doctrine of Judgment* (London: Tyndale Press, 1960); Herman N. Ridderbos, *The Coming of the Kingdom* (Philadelphia: Presbyterian and Reformed, 1962); Bernard Ramm, *Them He Glorified: A Systematic Study of the Doctrine of Glorification* (Grand Rapids: Eerdmans, 1963); Oswald T. Allis, *Prophecy and the Church* (Philadelphia: Presbyterian and Reformed, 1964); Jay E. Adams, *I Tell You the Mystery* (Lookout Mountain, TX: Prospective Press, 1966); Wilbur M. Smith, *The Biblical Doctrine of Heaven* (Chicago: Moody, 1968); George L. Murray, *Millenial Studies: A Search for Truth* (Grand Rapids: Baker, 1972); Gerrit C. Berkouwer, *The Return of Christ,* translated by James VanOosterom (Grand Rapids: Eerdmans, 1972); Philip E. Hughes, *Interpreting Prophecy: An Essay in Biblical Perspectives* (Grand Rapids: Eerdmans, 1976); Leslie H. Woodson, *What the Bible Says About Hell* (Grand Rapids: Baker, 1976); Anthony A. Hoekema, *The Bible and the Future* (Grand Rapids: Eerdmans, 1979); Stephen Travis, *I Believe in the Second Coming of Jesus* (Grand Rapids: Eerdmans, 1982); Robert A. Morey, *Death and the Afterlife* (Minneapolis: Bethany, 1984); Eryl Davies, *The Wrath of God* (Mid-Glamorgan, Wales: Evangelical Press of Wales, 1984); Peter Toon, *Heaven and Hell: A Biblical and Theological Overview* (Nashville: Nelson, 1986); John Gilmore, *Probing Heaven: Key Questions on the Hereafter* (Grand Rapids: Baker, 1989); Paul Helm, *The Last Things: Death, Judgment, Heaven, Hell* (Edinburgh: Banner of Truth Trust, 1989); John H. Gerstner, *Repent or Perish: With a Special Reference to the Conservative Attack on Hell* (Ligonier, PA: Soli Deo Gloria, 1990); John MacArthur, *The Glory of Heaven* (Wheaton, IL: Crossway, 1996); Herman Bavinck, *The Last Things: Hope for This World and the Next,* edited by John Bolt, translated by John Vriend (Grand Rapids: Baker, 1996).

For twentieth-century historical-theological studies, see Heinrich Quistorp, *Calvin's Doctrine of the Last Things,* translated by Harold Knight (London: Lutterworth Press, 1955); D.P. Walker, *The Decline of Hell: Seventeenth-Century Discussions of Eternal Torment* (Chicago: University Press, 1964); J. A. Mourant, *Augustine on Immortality* (Philadelphia: Villanova University Press, 1969); Peter Toon, *The Puritans, the Millennium, and the Future of Israel* (London: James Clarke, 1970); Iain Murray, *The Puritan Hope: A Study of Renewal and the Interpretation of Prophecy* (London: Banner of Truth Trust, 1971); Timothy P. Weber, *Living in the Shadow of the Second Coming: American Premillennialism, 1879-1925* (New York: Oxford University Press, 1979); Colleen McDannell and Bernhard Long, *Heaven: A History* (New Haven, CT: Yale University Press, 1988); B.E. Daley, *The Hope of the Early Church: Eschatology in the Patristic Age* (Cambridge: University Press, 1991).

Where should you begin? Read the book of Revelation again. While doing so, consult Herman Hoeksema's *Behold He Cometh.* Then read Paul Helm's *The Last Things,* followed by Anthony Hoekema's *The Bible and the Future,* and Herman Bavinck's *The Last Things.*

TEXTUAL INDEX

67:18	181	100:3	28	119:133	185	6:19	165
68:1	179	101:2	234	119:136	137	6:30-33	169
68:18	179	101:5	165	119:137-38	8,106,180	6:32-33	169
68:4	145(2x)	102:14	188	119:140	11	6:32-35	169
68:18	79	102:18	145	122:6	175	6:33	165
69:4	76,100	102:19	12	122:7-9	167	7:5	161
69:5	72(2x)	102:28	189	122:9	233	7:10	161
69:10	165	103:1	179	123:1	179	7:13	161,169
71:8	106,180	103:3	110,230	123:1-2	227	7:14-15	169
71:19	137	103:3-4	100	125:4	175	7:21-22	161
72:17	189	103:10-11	100	127:1-2	44,182	7:24-27	161
73	43	103:13	109(2x)	127:2	157	8:12	22(2x)
73:2-3	139	103:14	122,184	127:3-5	155	8:15	234
73:3	163	103:19	41(2x)	130:3	100,117	8:15-16	233
73:13	225	103:20	38,106,182	130:3-4	183	8:22	22
73:13-15	139	103:20-21	39,181,183	130:4	129	8:33-36	95(2x),209(2x)
73:14-15	147	104:4	38,39,41	130:7	137	8:34	145,211,213
73:15	127,129	104:9,etc	42	132:2	74	10:4	163
73:22	139	104:10	38	132:2-5	149	11:1	162,163
73:22-23	225	104:14-15	38	132:11	76(2x)	11:14	203,235
73:23	127	104:24	37,41(3x)	135:6	41	11:15	163
73:24-28	3	104:27	6,136	138:1-2	145	11:26	163
73:25	137	105:2	145	138:1-3	179	12:18	156,159,232
73:25-28	3	105:5	145	138:2	145	12:22	164
74:18	179	105:25	42	139:1-13	7	13:5	164
74:22-23	179	106:39	143	139:2,etc	42	13:13	139
75:7-8	42	107	145	139:3-4	40	14:5	165(2x)
76:10	43	110	71	139:7	26	14:25	165(2x)
76:11	141,149	110:1	71,79	139:20	147	14:26	109(2x)
77:1	43	110:1-2	71	140:4	179	14:30	159
77:1-10	129	110:2-4	190	140:8	179	15:1	157,159
77:1-12	127,129,225	110:3	71,91	143:1	174	15:3	41
77:10	43	110:4	64,70(2x)	143:2	100,117(2x)	16:4	7,29,37,42(2x)
77:12	43	112:9-10	167	145	179	16:26	157
78:5-7	211	113:4-6	40	145:3	7	16:33	29
78:17	167,169	113:5-6	53	145:7	41	17:9	165
78:22	139	115:1	100,106,180,184	145:8-9	8,106,180	17:15	165
78:32	167,169	115:1-2	189	145:15	44,182	17:22	157
78:34-37	169	115:3	7,40,42	145:17	9,41(3x)	18:9	163
78:56	167,169	115:5	28,140	145:18	174,175	19:5	164,165
81:10-11	137	115:9	189	145:18-19	175	19:9	164
81:11	139	116:12-13	115	147:5	7(2x),9	19:26	155
81:11-12	43,89,185	116:12-14	110,230	147:19-20	90,179,189	20:9	47
82:1	234	118:22	151	148:2	38	20:10	163
82:3-4	233	118:24	151			20:25	169
82:4	157	119:1	183	**PROVERBS**		21:1	42
82:6	234	119:4-5	183	1:10-11	157	21:6	163
83	179(2x)	119:4-6	135	1:15-16	157	21:17	163(2x)
83:18	179	119:5	180,244	1:19	133	21:20	163
85:8	227	119:6	109(2x)	1:20-21	145	21:28	164
86:10-13	179	119:8	183	1:23	55	22:1	165
86:15	179	119:11	211,213	1:24	145	22:2	42
88	127,129(3x),225	119:18	11,211(2x),213	2:1	213	22:19-21	9
89:30-34	135	119:32	129	2:1-5	95(2x),209(2x)	23:5	163
89:31-32	121	119:35-36	183	2:1-6	211	23:10	163
89:31-33	101,119	119:36	181	2:14	169	23:20-21	163(2x)
89:37-38	190	119:59	109(2x)	2:16-20	159	23:22	152,153,155(2x),232
90:2	7(3x)	119:68	9,141	2:17	169,235	23:25	153
92:title	149,151(2x)	119:69	165	3:5	211	23:29	159
92:13-14	151	119:71	171	3:29-30	163	23:30-33	161
94:3	42	119:80	183	4:3-4	155	23:35	169
94:7-9	42	119:97	211	4:18	119,127	24:11-12	157
94:8-11	41	119:101	135	5:7	161	25:9-10	165
94:11	56	119:104	135	5:8	159,161	25:16	157
95:2-3	143	119:105	15	5:8-9	165	25:23	165
95:6	143	119:106	109	5:8-12	169	25:27	157
95:6-7	137	119:112	183	5:16	162	26:24-25	165
97:7	179	119:128	109(2x),135	5:19-20	159	27:22	169
100:2	183	119:129	11	6:1-6	163	27:23-27	163
100:2-3	53	119:130	15	6:16	165	28:13	111,165

Ref	Pages
6:12	50,101,102,110,119,143,175,181,183,184
6:13	122,181,183,184(2x),185(2x)
6:14-15	102,143,175,183,184
6:16	89,114,117,147
6:23	48
6:25	44,163
6:25,etc	182
6:26	40(2x)
6:30	95,109,127
6:31	159,163
6:32	109(2x)
6:33	176
6:34	159,163
7:1	165
7:1,etc	164
7:1-2	244
7:3-5	165
7:6	201,225(2x)
7:7	174
7:8	174
7:9-11	40,178
7:11	175
7:12	137,158,162
7:17	116(2x)
7:17-18	114
7:21	175,189
7:22	89(2x)
7:22-23	127
8:9-10	233
8:10	95,127
8:31	41,42(2x)
8:31-32	42
9:2	94
9:15	145
9:38	181
10:15	48
10:20	12
10:28	6,39(2x),136
10:29	40
10:29-30	42(2x)
10:29-31	41(3x)
10:30	2,118
10:32	64,104,144,196,197,199,243,244,245
10:37	6,136
10:42	116,118
11:8	163
11:21	29,35
11:21-24	169
11:22	244
11:23	29
11:25-26	29,31,35,128
11:27	64,70,72
11:28	30,62,225
11:29	192
12:1-13	149,151
12:1-31	151
12:7	135
12:20	225
12:25	173
12:28	22
12:30	192
12:31-32	169
12:34-35	46
12:36	111,244
12:36-37	243
12:40	77
13	88
13:2	174
13:11	35,128
13:12	43
13:19	143
13:20	124
13:20-21	89(2x)
13:22	193
13:24-30	189
13:25	40
13:26	194
13:29	206
13:40-42	75
13:43	244
13:47	189(2x),194
14:5-6	234
14:8	155
15:3	16
15:4-6	133,135,153,155
15:8-9	16
15:9	114,115,116,141,143,171,204,223,228
15:19	47(2x),49,159,161
16:17	8,94,106,180
16:18	189,190(3x)
16:19	141,198,200(2x),201,205,233
16:24	106,182
17:12	29,57
17:24	234
18:3	205
18:6	169
18:7	169
18:10	183
18:14	30
18:15	202
18:15-17	141,173
18:15-18	193,200,202
18:17	169,200,201,202,204,233
18:17-18	71,198,201,230
18:17-20	203
18:23-26	100
18:24-25	183
18:35	181,183
19:5	161
19:5-6	235
19:6	237
19:8-9	237
19:9	237
19:10-11	161
19:11-12	149
19:14	208,220(2x)
19:17	6,131
20:15	33
20:28	99
21:5	65,69
21:15	165
21:38-39	169
22:5	143
22:14	89(2x),189
22:21	152,155,232
22:24-31	147
22:29	17
22:30	39
22:31	17
22:37	6,136
22:37-39	133
22:37-40	131(2x),133
22:39	137,158,163
23:2	155
23:3	89,117,206
23:4	155
23:8-10	171,191
23:9	139
23:13	143
23:14	147
23:15	169
23:23	114
23:25	163
23:33	244
24	76
24:24	34,120
24:28	192
24:30	80,81,244
24:36	39,243,244,245
24:42	243
24:42-44	245
24:44	243
25	76
25:13	244
25:14	205
25:21	117
25:23	117,197,243
25:29	43
25:31	39,40,81,244
25:33	199,243(2x),245
25:34	80,196,199,244,245
25:34-35	116
25:35-36	157
25:41	29,40,49(3x),76,80,169,196,244
25:41-43	89,117,243
25:42-43	159
25:45	89,117
25:46	49(2x),199,243,244,245
26	75
26:11	68,228
26:26	223,224,225,226(2x)
26:26,etc	228
26:26-27	223
26:26-28	213(2x),215,222(2x),223(4x)
26:27	230
26:27-28	209,211,215
26:28	210,223,225(2x),227,228
26:29	223
26:36	210
26:37-38	75
26:38	74,75(2x),76
26:39	175,181
26:40-41	181
26:41	122,181,184,185(2x)
26:52	156(2x),232(2x)
26:56	77
26:60-61	165
26:69-72	129,185
26:70	121
26:72	121
26:74	121
26:75	101,119
27	75
27:4	49,77,197
27:26-50	77
27:28-29	165
27:46	72,75(2x),77,78
27:50	68
28:2	193
28:18	64,67,70,72,80,205
28:18-20	65,201
28:19	20(2x),21(3x),22(2x),25,26,27,55(2x),96,102,122,141,145,193,200,208,209,210,211,213(2x),215(3x),216(2x),217(5x),218,220(2x)
28:19-20	12,55(2x),79,94,189(3x),211(3x),215,217(2x)
28:20	80(2x),120,141(2x),188

MARK

Ref	Pages
1:4	216,217(2x)
1:15	109
3:28-29	46,112
4:19	185
6:18	161,237
6:22	161
6:24	155
6:26	147,149,226
6:52	121
7:4	217
7:6-7	16
7:7	16
7:21-22	183
8:38	41,147
9:24	129,225
9:43-44	49
9:44	76,197
9:46	49
9:48	49
10:13-16	217
11:24	143,175(2x)
12:17	234
12:33	141
13:33	122,184
13:35-37	245
14:22	224,226
14:22-24	222,223(2x)
14:23	223
14:24	226
14:66ff	43,107,115
15:42	151
15:43	78
15:46	78
16:14	121
16:15	12,53,55,140
16:15-16	189,198,217
16:16	53,89,102,200,216,218(2x),220
16:19	72,75(2x),77,80,118,228

LUKE

Ref	Pages
1:3-4	9
1:6	109(2x)
1:14-15	220
1:20	101,119
1:22	59
1:27	25,67,75(2x)
1:31	25,67,75(3x),76
1:32-33	190
1:33	63,64,69,70
1:34-35	76
1:35	20,22,25(4x),67(4x),74,75(2x)
1:42	75(2x),76

3:21	116	12:10-11	179,181	17:3-4	193	21:4	244
4:8	7(4x)	12:14	189,190	17:6	169,193	21:8	244
4:8-11	181	13:6	191	17:12	141,173	22:9	140
4:11	9,38	13:8	70,85,212	17:14	192,233	22:12	71
5:3	50	13:12	171	17:16	233	22:17	180,227,244
5:12-14	9	13:15-17	233	17:16-17	141,173	22:18	16(2x)
6:11	244	13:16-17	171	18:2	189	22:18-19	10,11,13
6:15-16	244	14:7	244	18:4	192,193	22:20	179,180,181,244(2x),
7:4	194	14:13	143,175,199,241,245	18:12-18	169		245
7:9	189(2x),194	14:14	192	19:10	6,136,139,140,141	22:20-21	183,185
12:4	193	15:3-4	143,145(2x)	19:13	22		
12:6	189,190	15:4	7(2x)	20:12-13	244(3x)		